Cambodia

written and researched by

Beverley Palmer and Steven Martin

ROUGH
GUIDES

NEW YORK · LONDON · DELHI

www.roughguides.com

Contents

Festivals and
ceremonies colour
section following p.112

Temple architecture
colour section
following p.208

3

Introduction to
Cambodia

Though much less visited than neighbouring Thailand or Vietnam, Cambodia has established itself firmly on the Southeast Asian tourist trail. The stunning temples of Angkor are the obvious draw for most visitors, but the country has much else to offer: white-sand beaches, unspoilt forest, a balmy climate, and a relaxed atmosphere that's refreshingly low on hassle.

For a small country, Cambodia encompasses a surprisingly diverse range of terrain and scenery. Rice fields may be the quintessential feature of this predominantly flat and agricultural land, but there are also significant highland areas and 440km of coastline, as well as the massive Tonle Sap, Southeast Asia's largest freshwater lake, which dominates the heart of the country. In the east, the mighty Mekong River forms a natural divide, beyond which rise the jungle-clad mountains of Rattanakiri and Mondulkiri. In the southwest, the heavily forested Cardamom Mountains run down to the sea, while parts of the southeast are regularly inundated, as the Mekong and its sister river the Bassac overflow their banks.

For all its natural beauty and rich heritage, Cambodia is still probably best known in the West for its suffering at the hands of the fanatical Khmer Rouge, who came to power in the 1970s, with a programme of mass execution, which resulted in the death of a fifth of the population. Their three-year terror was followed by a protracted guerrilla war that only ended in 1998 and left much of the country in ruins. Nowadays, however, Cambodia is at peace, and visiting is no longer dangerous.

Supported by Western aid, the infrastructure is at last improving; new roads now connect all but the most remote provincial centres, rendering most air and ferry routes redundant, and enterprise is booming, attested to by the thronging markets and modest middle class that has re-emerged in the capital and major towns – there are even several restored colonial villas,

▲ Monks at an Internet café

Fact file

• Cambodia is about one and a half times the **size** of England – roughly the same area as Oklahoma. Around one twentieth of the country is covered by the waters of the Tonle Sap lake. The highest point is Phnom Aural (1771m) in the Cardamom Mountains.

• Cambodia's population is nearly **14 million**, of which ninety percent is Khmer. The remainder consists of ethnic Chinese and Vietnamese (together around 6.5 percent), the Cham (2.5 percent) and the chunchiet (1 percent).

• **Theravada Buddhism** is practised by 95 percent of the population, alongside some animism and ancestor worship; the Cham are Muslim.

• Cambodia is a **constitutional monarchy**, with an elected government comprising two houses of parliament, the National Assembly and the Senate.

• Average **annual income** is just $480 per capita, putting Cambodia among the world's poorest countries; average life expectancy is only 57 years.

newly opened as boutique hotels. Cambodian food, influenced by the cuisines of both China and Thailand, is delicately flavoured and quite delicious, while the country's long tradition of artisanship is undergoing a revival, with weaving, stone-carving and silversmithing much in evidence. Temple sites, some dating back to the sixth century, dot the countryside, of which several have only recently been made accessible and many are finally being restored. The majority of the country's towns still retain some old-world charm, preserving quaint shophouse terraces and colonial architecture dating back to the period of French rule – though their most tangible colonial legacy is the piles of crusty baguettes heaped up in baskets and hawked around the streets in the early morning.

> The stunning temples of Angkor are the obvious draw for most visitors, but the country has much else to offer

Though much still has to be done before Cambodia is properly back on its feet, and before most of the population see a substantial improvement in their standard of living, the recovery of the country is largely down to the Cambodians themselves, eternally optimistic, tenacious and tirelessly hospitable.

Where to go

Most tourists make for the cosmopolitan capital, **Phnom Penh**, at some point during their visit. A pleasing, low-rise city graced with leafy boulevards, the capital offers the chance to take in the splendour of the Royal Palace and Silver Pagoda, while the cream of ancient Khmer art is housed a stone's throw away at the National Museum. The capital also boasts a vibrant riverside dotted with cafés and bars and is the best place in the country to shop, its colourful markets stocked with shimmering silks and intricate handicrafts.

Sugar palms

Dotting rice paddies with their distinctive mops of spiky leaves, sugar-palm trees are of great importance to the rural Cambodian economy, since every part of the tree can be put to good use. Arguably the most significant product is the **juice**, extracted by climbing a rickety ladder lashed to the trunk, cutting the stalk bearing the flowers and fixing in place a container to collect the juice. This tends to be a dry-season occupation, as high monsoon winds and wet trunks make the climb hazardous at other times of year. The liquid, initially cloudy, is cleared by first smoking the collection tube with burning palm fronds and then adding bark from the *popael* tree (of the honeysuckle family). Both the sweet, fresh juice and its fermented form, alcoholic **palm beer**, are sold by hawkers from containers suspended either from a shoulder pole or from bicycle or moto handlebars. **Palm sugar**, much used by sweet-toothed Cambodians for cooking, is made by thickening the juice in a cauldron and then pouring it into cylindrical cauldrons to set, after which it resembles grainy honey-coloured fudge. Nearly as important as the juice are the **leaves**, which are collected two or three times a year for use in thatch, wall panels, woven matting, baskets, fans and even packaging. Until quite recently, specially treated leaves were used to record religious teachings by **inscribing** them with a metal nib.

Palm **fruits**, slightly larger than a cricket ball, have a tough, fibrous black coating containing juicy, delicately flavoured kernels, which are translucent white and have the consistency of jelly; they're eaten either fresh or with syrup as a dessert. The **root** of the tree is used in traditional medicine as a cure for stomach aches and other ailments. Perhaps because the trees furnish so many other products, they are seldom cut for their **wood**, which is extremely durable. Palm-wood souvenirs are now available in Phnom Penh and Siem Reap, easily identifiable by their distinctive light-and-dark striped grain.

What's a wat – and what's not

Cambodia's **wats** are Buddhist monasteries, often generically referred to as "pagodas", although they bear no resemblance to their Chinese namesakes. Wats are easily identified by the bright orange tiled roof of the principal building, the vihara, and can be vibrant, even wacky, affairs; the wealthier the foundation that runs the pagoda, the more extravagant the decoration, both inside and outside, with buildings painted in the most garish of primary colours, and courtyards featuring abundant and cartoonish statues of mythical beasts.

The term **"temple"**, on the other hand, is usually reserved for ancient Khmer monuments, dating from the sixth to the thirteenth centuries. Temples were generally built by kings, commonly to honour their ancestors or to serve as their state-temple – a place where an image of the devaraja god associated with the king could be housed in a sanctuary tower (see the *Temple architecture* colour section). State-temples were seldom reused by successive kings, though occasionally they gained a new lease of life as monasteries.

▲ Underwater carvings at Kbal Spean, Angkor

The main reason that most people come to Cambodia, however, is to visit the world-famous **temples of Angkor**, just outside the engaging town of **Siem Reap**. Chief is the majestic **Angkor Wat**, but close by are the compact **Banteay Srei**, with enchanting bas-reliefs of demure divinities; **Kbal Spean**, exquisite riverbed carvings in the Kulen Mountains; **Ta Prohm**, clamped in the grip of giant kapok trees; and the intricately designed **Bayon**. The pre-Angkorian temple **Sambor Prei Kuk** lies just to the northeast of the provincial town of Kompong Thom, while more intrepid travellers can escape the crowds and head for remote temples such as **Preah Vihear**, which clings dramatically to an escarpment right on the Thai border in the far north, and **Koh Ker**, a day-trip northeast of Siem Reap.

After seeing the temples of Angkor, many people head down to **Sihanoukville** to spend a few days lazing on pristine white-sand beaches lapped by

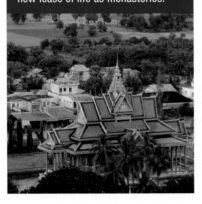

Banlung Market

the waters of the Gulf of Thailand. The coast is peppered with islands and there is a nascent diving industry. Just outside Sihanoukville is the **Ream National Park** where you can putter downstream as monkeys play in the mangroves and fishing eagles soar overhead.

East of Sihanoukville, **Kampot** is a delightful town with mixed French and Chinese influences and the base for a visit to the jungle-clad slopes of the **Bokor National Park**, with its atmospherically deserted hill station. Another side-trip from Kampot brings you to the beguiling seaside resort of **Kep**, with a minuscule beach and atmosphere of faded gentility. Its decrepit buildings are being restored, and the tiny town already hosts some of the country's most stylish accommodation. Inland from here is **Angkor Borei**, third-century capital of Cambodia, accessible only by water for much of the year.

Northeast of the capital, the Mekong at **Kratie** is home to a graceful population of Irrawaddy dolphins. Getting out to the remote northeastern provincial capitals of **Banlung** – where trekking is in its infancy – and **Sen Monorom** takes more time and effort, but the natural beauty of this part of the country is unrivalled, the jungled hillsides brimming with wildlife, dotted with scenic water- falls and home to villages of the minority chunchiet tribes.

The northwestern border crossing from Thailand at **Poipet** is an increasingly popular point of entry to Cambodia, while nearby **Battambang** retains some of the country's most attractive colonial architecture and makes a convenient stopover on the way to Phnom Penh or an interesting side-trip from Siem Reap.

◄ French colonial architecture, Battambang

9

When to go

Dirt roads crisscross rural Cambodia

A tropical country, Cambodia is warm all year round, though there are several distinct seasons. Little rain falls from November to May, the so-called **dry season**, which itself divides into two distinct phases. The **cool season** (Nov–Feb) is the peak time for tourism, when it's cool enough to explore the temples in comfort and yet warm enough to sunbathe by the coast. Temperatures typically hover around 24–28°C, but occasional cold snaps can bring them below 20°C, which feels decidedly chilly in a country where everything is designed to keep you cool. The **hot season** (typically March–May) is when humidity and temperatures soar, with Phnom Penh and Battambang seeing peak daytime temperatures of 33–35°C. At this time, it's best to do as the locals do, rising early to get out and about, returning for a snooze at midday and emerging again late in the afternoon. This is also when the dust thrown up from the country's dirt roads is at its worst, the billowing clouds ensuring that everything and everyone is coated in a fine film of grit. At Angkor, the unrelenting sun, allied to the lack of any breeze, makes for a baking visit, though this is an excellent time to hit the coast.

The **rainy season** lasts roughly from June to October, as the southwest monsoon coming off the Gulf of Thailand deposits rain on the whole of the country. River levels rise dramatically, and in September and October the country's infrastructure is at its most stretched, with dirt roads reduced to deep slurry and a risk of flooding in provincial areas. Thankfully, the rains aren't unrelenting and fall mainly in the afternoon, so provided you don't want to get off the beaten track and don't mind doing most of your sightseeing in the mornings (which are normally dry), this isn't a bad time to visit. It's also the quietest time for tourism (at Angkor, you'll have the temples pretty much to yourself) and the countryside is at its lushest.

Average maximum daily temperatures (°C) and average monthly rainfall (mm)

	Jan	Feb	Mar	Apr	May	June	July	Aug	Sept	Oct	Nov	Dec
Phnom Penh												
°C	31	32	34	35	34	33	32	32	31	30	30	30
rainfall (mm)	10	10	45	80	120	150	165	160	215	240	135	55

21

things not to miss

It's not possible to see everything that Cambodia has to offer in one trip – and we don't suggest you try. What follows is a selective and subjective taste of the country's highlights: colourful festivals, serene beaches and nature reserves, and – of course – the finest of the temples at Angkor and elsewhere. They're all arranged in five colour-coded categories to help you find the very best things to see, do and experience. All entries have a page reference to take you straight into the Guide, where you can find out more.

01 **A sunset trip on the Mekong** Page **97** • Cruise along the river through Phnom Penh enjoying the spectacular views as the sun sinks behind the Royal Palace and Silver Pagoda.

02 **Tonle Sap lake** Page **203** • Akin to an inland sea, this freshwater lake supports hundreds of floating villages and is home to abundant birdlife.

03 **Royal Palace and Silver Pagoda** Page **88** • Situated in the heart of the capital, the extravagant Royal Palace and Silver Pagoda are home to fabulous murals and a treasure-trove of statues, including a famous emerald Buddha.

04 **Sambor Prei Kuk** Page **216** • These mellow, well-preserved brick ruins are among the very earliest Khmer monuments.

05 **Preah Vihear** Page **220** • Superb temple perched on a remote hilltop on the border between Cambodia and Thailand.

06 Ream National Park Page 280 • One of Cambodia's finest national parks, with secluded, palm-fringed bays, a river lined with lush mangroves and lots of wildlife.

07 Irrawaddy dolphins Page 240 • These rare mammals live in small groups along a stretch of the Mekong in the northeast.

08 National Museum, Phnom Penh Page 93 • The country's top museum, home to a stunning collection of Khmer art.

09 Sihanoukville Page 267 • Cambodia's liveliest resort, with tropical beaches, abundant seafood and a busy nightlife.

10 Apsara dance Page **171** • Elegantly stylized form of Khmer classical dance, evoking the apsaras – celestial goddesses of Hindu mythology.

12 Wat Phnom Page **100** • One of Phnom Penh's most important shrines, dedicated to Daun Penh, the legendary lady who gave her name to the capital.

11 Kep Page **294** • Once-deserted villas are being restored to luxurious accommodation in this tiny seaside resort, while its crab market is the place to feast on succulent crustaceans.

13 Bokor National Park Page **291** • Often swathed in cloud, the mysterious upland plateau of Bokor is dotted with waterfalls and the desolate ruins of an old colonial hill station.

14 Bonn Om Tuk Page **96** • Phnom Penh's annual water festival, celebrated with three days of fiercely contested boat races on the Tonle Sap.

15 Yeak Laom lake Page **251** • Sparkling lake, set in an almost perfectly circular volcanic crater.

16 Cambodian cuisine Page **33** • Richly flavoured with herbs and using only the freshest ingredients, the country's fragrant and distinctive cuisine offers plenty of culinary surprises – or learn to prepare it yourself on a cookery course.

17 Psar Toul Tom Poung Page **109** • One of Phnom Penh's most attractive markets, packed with vibrant silks and intriguing curios.

18 Angkor Thom Page **185** • Expansive walled city, entered through a huge gateway decorated with enormous stone faces.

19 Banteay Srei Page **201** • This beautiful rose-pink temple is the most elaborately decorated of all Angkor's monuments.

20 Ta Prohm Page **192** • Nature holds this ruined temple in a vice-like grip, with gigantic tree roots wedged between massive stones.

21 Angkor Wat Page **179** • The zenith of Khmer architecture, this unforgettable temple, crowned with soaring towers and embellished with intricate bas-reliefs, is one of Cambodia's – and Asia's – most memorable sights.

Basics

Basics

Getting there

There are no direct flights to Cambodia from Europe, North America, Australasia or South Africa, so if you plan to fly into the country you'll need to get a connecting flight from elsewhere in Southeast or East Asia. There are regular direct flights to Phnom Penh and Siem Reap from an increasing number of cities in the region; these include Bangkok, Hanoi, Ho Chi Minh City, Kuala Lumpur, Seoul, Singapore, Taipei and Vientiane. Airfares to Cambodia peak during the high season (July, August and the latter half of December) and are cheapest during the low season (roughly from mid-April to the end of May).

Flights from the UK and Ireland

There are plenty of daily flights, many nonstop, from **London Heathrow** to Southeast Asian cities, with some airlines offering connections to Phnom Penh. Flight times vary depending on routing; it takes 11–12 hours to fly nonstop from London to Bangkok, and another hour on to Phnom Penh. Departing from elsewhere in the UK it may be more convenient to fly from a regional airport with a European carrier, such as Air France or KLM, which offer flights to Southeast Asia via their respective hub cities. From **Ireland**, it's a matter of either getting a cheap connection to London Heathrow or flying to Cambodia via a different European hub city.

Thai Airways, Singapore Airlines and Malaysia Airlines offer some of the most competitive **fares** to Cambodia, with flights via **Bangkok**, **Singapore** and **Kuala Lumpur** respectively, from where there are regular connections on to Phnom Penh and Siem Reap (note, though, that these flights sometimes involve an overnight stopover and you'll have to pay for your own accommodation). Return fares to Phnom Penh start at around £600 in low season, rising to £850 or more in high season.

Flights from the US and Canada

Flying from the **east coast** of North America to Cambodia it's quickest to travel via Europe. Conversely, from the **west coast** it may well be cheaper to fly westward via an Asian city such as Seoul or Taipei (the latter has direct connections to Phnom Penh on EVA Airways). There are daily flights from New York and Los Angeles to Bangkok, Hong Kong, Kuala Lumpur and Singapore, all of which have onward connections to Phnom Penh and Siem Reap. Fares from both east and west coast to Phnom Penh in low season are around $1000-1200, rising by $300 and more in high season. From Canada, return fares from Toronto to Phnom Penh start at around CA$1180, and CA$1000 return from Vancouver, in low season.

Flights from Australia, New Zealand and South Africa

There's a wide selection of flights into Southeast Asia from Australia and New Zealand, with onward connections to Phnom Penh and Siem Reap from Bangkok, Kuala Lumpur, Singapore and Ho Chi Minh City. See p.22 for full details. Return **fares** from Australia to Phnom Penh start at around A$850 in low season, rising to as much as A$2000 in high; from Auckland, Christchurch and Wellington expect to pay between NZ$1500 and NZ$2500, subject to seasonal variations.

Travelling to Phnom Penh via an Asian hub city in low season from Cape Town you should expect to pay around R12,000 return, while a return trip from Johannesburg will be about R13,315.

Round-the-World flights

If Cambodia is only one stop on a longer journey, you might want to consider buying a

Round-The-World (RTW) ticket. Cambodia can be added to itineraries offered by the airline consortium Star Alliance (@www .staralliance.com) and to the Great Escapade ticket offered by Virgin, Air New Zealand, Singapore Airlines and Malaysia Airlines. Bangkok or Singapore are more common ports of call for many RTW tickets; from the UK, figure on around £1000 plus taxes for an RTW ticket including either of these destinations.

Getting there from neighbouring countries

If you're travelling overland to Cambodia, you can consider a number of border crossings open to foreigners, currently six from Thailand, five from Vietnam and one from Laos.

Overland trips to Cambodia from Thailand are well publicized in Bangkok, particularly on Khao San Road, where travel agents try to sell their **Bangkok–Siem Reap** trips by alleging that doing the trip independently entails various problems (dealing with Cambodian border officials, sorting out onward transport, and so on). In fact, it's straightforward enough to travel to Cambodia from Bangkok independently by public transport, and the convenience of travelling with one of these private firms is offset by the frustrations of waiting around until the required number of passengers turn up (anything from four to eight hours) and various scams: "we'll get your visa" (for 1200 baht); "the border's closed, so we have to go a different way"; "it's too late, you'll have to stay at this guesthouse." Travelling independently, the trip from Bangkok to Siem Reap costs anything from $8 (train to Aranyaprathet, then a place on a pick-up) to $35 (bus to the border and then a taxi onwards) and takes around ten hours; using Khao San Road packages ($15–25) the journey can be considerably longer – anything up to seventeen hours or more. Though some of the companies which run these packages are reputable, others aren't, and a significant number of travellers are reporting problems like those mentioned above. If you're intent on travelling with one of these outfits, it's worth asking fellow travellers or staff at your guesthouse about companies they would recommend or avoid.

All border crossings between Thailand and Cambodia are open daily (7am–8pm) and visas are issued on arrival at all points; however, **e-visas** (see p.58) are only accepted at Koh Kong. The Aranyaprathet/**Poipet border crossing** is ideal if you want to start your visit to Cambodia in the north at Battambang and Siem Reap. From Bangkok you can reach Aranyaprathet by train (1 daily; 7hr) or a/c bus from Bangkok's northern bus terminal (frequent departures from 4am; 4hr). Onward transport on the Cambodian side of the border is readily available from Poipet to Sisophon, Siem Reap, Battambang and Phnom Penh; see p.25 for details. Contrary to some maps, the railway line to Poipet is derelict, and the nearest train station is at Battambang (but see p.138).

The Trat/**Koh Kong** crossing further south is good for Sihanoukville and Phnom Penh. From Bangkok there are a/c buses from Bangkok's eastern bus terminal to Trat (12 daily; 5hr). On the Cambodian side of the border there is now a road linking Koh Kong through Sre Ambel to National Route 4, giving you the option of continuing your journey by either land or sea, depending on what time you arrive at Koh Kong. An express boat runs in the early morning from Koh Kong to Sihanoukville; see p.27 for details.

The other crossings are in the east at Ban Paakard/**Pailin (Psar Prom)** and Ban Leam/**Daun Lem**, from where you can head to Battambang and in the north at Surin/**O'Smach**, and Chong Sa-Ngam/**Anlong Veng** (actually the border is about 25 km north of Anlong Veng) – both 150km north of Siem Reap. Be aware though that these are not busy crossing points so your transport options on the Cambodian side will be limited.

An increasing number of border crossings are open to foreigners travelling overland from Vietnam. Currently there are five: Moc Bai/**Bavet**, 200km southeast of Phnom Penh; Chau Doc/**K'am Samnar** on the Bassac River; Tinh Bien/**Phnom Den** near Takeo; Hat Tien/**Prek Chak** east of Kep; and the recently opened **Trapeang Phlong** east of Kompong Cham. Cambodian visas are issued on arrival at all points. From **Bavet**, it's easy to get shared taxis to Phnom Penh (around 3hr) on National Route 1. Phnom Penh Sorya Transport Company runs a

Fly less, stay longer! Travel and climate change

Climate change is the single biggest issue facing our planet. It is caused by a build-up in the atmosphere of carbon dioxide and other greenhouse gases, which are emitted by many sources – including planes. Already, flights account for around 3–4 percent of human-induced global warming: that figure may sound small, but it is rising year on year and threatens to counteract the progress made by reducing greenhouse emissions in other areas.

Rough Guides regard travel, overall, as a global benefit, and feel strongly that the advantages to developing economies are important, as are the opportunities for greater contact and awareness among peoples. But we all have a responsibility to limit our personal "carbon footprint". That means giving thought to how often we fly and what we can do to redress the harm that our trips create.

Flying and climate change

Pretty much every form of motorized travel generates CO_2, but planes are particularly bad offenders, releasing large volumes of greenhouse gases at altitudes where their impact is far more harmful. Flying also allows us to travel much further than we would contemplate doing by road or rail, so the emissions attributable to each passenger become truly shocking. For example, one person taking a return flight between Europe and California produces the equivalent impact of 2.5 tonnes of CO_2 – similar to the yearly output of the average UK car.

Less harmful planes may evolve but it will be decades before they replace the current fleet – which could be too late for avoiding climate chaos. In the meantime, there are limited options for concerned travellers: to reduce the amount we travel by air (take fewer trips, stay longer!), to avoid night flights (when plane contrails trap heat from Earth but can't reflect sunlight back to space) and to make the trips we do take "climate neutral" via a carbon-offset scheme.

Carbon offset schemes

Offset schemes run by ⓦ**www.climatecare.org**, ⓦ**www.carbonneutral.com** and others allow you to "neutralize" the greenhouse gases that you are responsible for releasing. Their websites have simple calculators that let you work out the impact of any flight. Once that's done, you can pay to fund projects that will reduce future carbon emissions by an equivalent amount (such as the distribution of low-energy light bulbs and cooking stoves in developing countries). Please take the time to visit our website and make your trip climate-neutral.

ⓦ**www.roughguides.com/climatechange**

twice-daily international bus service between Ho Chi Minh City and Phnom Penh. From **Chau Doc** there's an express boat (1 daily; around 5hr) up the Mekong River direct to Phnom Penh in the morning. *Sinh Café* in Ho Chi Minh City organizes a daily transfer by minibus and boat to Phnom Penh and the *Capitol Hotel* in Phnom Penh does the trip in the other direction. Entering Cambodia at the other border crossings your transport options are at present more limited; taxis run from Phnom Den to Takeo and Phnom Penh, while at Hat Tien you'll most likely have to take a moto to Kep or Kampot.

From **Laos** you enter at **Voen Kham**, which is about 50km from the Cambodian town of **Stung Treng**. Cambodian visas are available on entry. From the border you can either get a bus or taxi to Stung Treng or Phnom Penh; alternatively you could cross by land and then charter a private boat for the two-hour trip from the border down the Mekong, but expect to pay anything up to $50.

Airlines, agents and operators

Online booking

ⓦ**www.expedia.co.uk** (UK), ⓦ**www.expedia .com** (US), ⓦ**www.expedia.ca** (Canada)

Ⓦ www.lastminute.com (UK)
Ⓦ www.opodo.co.uk (UK)
Ⓦ www.orbitz.com (US)
Ⓦ www.travelocity.co.uk (UK), Ⓦ www
.travelocity.com (US), Ⓦ www.travelocity
.ca (Canada)
Ⓦ www.zuji.com.au (Australia), Ⓦ www.zuji
.co.nz (New Zealand)
Ⓦ www.travelonline.co.za (South Africa)

Airlines

Air Canada UK ☎ 0871/220 1111, Republic
of Ireland ☎ 01/679 3958, US 1-888/
247-2262, Australia ☎ 1300/655 767,
New Zealand ☎ 0508/747 767; Ⓦ www
.aircanada.com.
Air France UK ☎ 0870/142 4343, US ☎ 1-800/
237-2747, Canada ☎ 1-800/667-2747, Australia
☎ 1300/390 190, South Africa ☎ 0861/340 340;
Ⓦ www.airfrance.com.
Air New Zealand UK ☎ 0800/028 4149, US
☎ 1800-262/1234, Canada ☎ 1800-663/5494,
Australia ☎ 13 24 76, New Zealand ☎ 0800/737
000; Ⓦ www.airnz.co.nz.
Bangkok Airways UK ☎ 01293/596626, US &
Canada ☎ 1-866-BANGKOK, Australia 02/8248
0050, New Zealand ☎ 09/969 7600; Ⓦ www
.bangkokair.com.
British Airways UK ☎ 0870/850 9850, Republic
of Ireland ☎ 1890/626 747, US & Canada
☎ 1-800/AIRWAYS, Australia ☎ 1300/767 177,
New Zealand ☎ 09/966 9777, South Africa
☎ 114/418 600; Ⓦ www.ba.com.
Cathay Pacific US ☎ 1-800/233-2742, Canada
☎ 1-800/2686-868, Australia ☎ 13 17 47, New
Zealand ☎ 09/379 0861, South Africa ☎ 11/700
8900; Ⓦ www.cathaypacific.com.
EVA Air UK ☎ 020/7380 8300, US & Canada
☎ 1-800/695-1188, Australia ☎ 02/8338 0419,
New Zealand ☎ 09/358 8300; Ⓦ www.evaair.com.
KLM (Royal Dutch Airlines) US and Canada
☎ 1-800/225-2525, UK ☎ 0870/507 4074,
Republic of Ireland ☎ 1850/747 400, Australia
☎ 1300/392 192, New Zealand ☎ 09/921 6040,
South Africa ☎ 11/961 6727; Ⓦ www.klm.com.
Jetstar Ⓦ www.jetstar.com.
Korean Air UK ☎ 0800/413 000, Republic of Ireland
☎ 01/799 7990, US & Canada ☎ 1-800/438-5000,
Australia ☎ 02/9262 6000, New Zealand ☎ 09/914
2000; Ⓦ www.koreanair.com.
Malaysia Airlines UK ☎ 0870/607 9090, Republic
of Ireland ☎ 01/6761 561, US ☎ 1-800/5529-264,
Australia ☎ 13 26 27, New Zealand ☎ 0800/777
747, South Africa ☎ 11/8809 614; Ⓦ www
.malaysia-airlines.com.
Oasis Hong Kong Airlines UK ☎ 0844/482
2323, Canada ☎ 1-888/983 0808; Ⓦ www
.oasishongkong.com.
Northwest/KLM US ☎ 1-800/225-2525,
Ⓦ www.nwa.com.
Singapore Airlines UK ☎ 0844/800 2380,
Republic of Ireland ☎ 01/671 0722, US
☎ 1-800/742-3333, Canada ☎ 1-800/663-3046,
Australia ☎ 13 10 11, New Zealand ☎ 0800/808
909, South Africa ☎ 11/880 8560 or 11/880 8566;
Ⓦ www.singaporeair.com.
South African Airways South Africa ☎ 11/978
1111, Ⓦ www.flysaa.com.
Thai Airways UK ☎ 0870/606 0911, US
☎ 1-212/949-8424, Australia ☎ 1300/651 960,
New Zealand ☎ 09/377 3886, South Africa
☎ 11/455 1018; Ⓦ www.thaiair.com.
Vietnam Airlines UK ☎ 0870/224 0211, US
☎ 1-415/677-0888, Canada ☎ 1-416/599-2888,
Australia ☎ 02/9283 9658; Ⓦ www
.vietnamairlines.com.

Agents and operators

ebookers UK ☎ 0800/082 3000, Ⓦ www.ebookers
.com, Republic of Ireland ☎ 01/488 3507, Ⓦ www
.ebookers.ie. Low fares on an extensive selection of
scheduled flights and package deals.

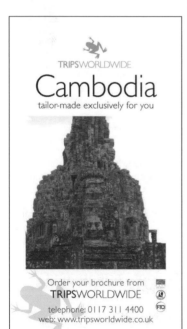

Flight Centre UK ☎0870/499 0040, ⓦwww
.flightcentre.co.uk, US ☎1-866/967 5351,
ⓦwww.flightcentre.us, Canada ☎1-877/967
5303, ⓦwww.flightcentre.ca, Australia ☎133
133, ⓦwww.flightcentre.com.au, New Zealand
☎0800/24 35 44, ⓦwww.flightcentre.co.nz, South
Africa ☎0860/400 727, ⓦwww.flightcentre.co.za.
Competitive choice of worldwide fares.

North South Travel UK ☎01245/608 291,
ⓦwww.northsouthtravel.co.uk. Friendly, competitive
travel agency, offering discounted fares worldwide.
Profits are used to support projects in the developing
world, especially the promotion of sustainable tourism.

Trailfinders UK ☎0845/058 5858, Republic of
Ireland ☎01/677 7888, Australia ☎1300/780 212;
ⓦwww.trailfinders.com. One of the best-informed
and most efficient agents for independent travellers.

STA Travel UK ☎0871/2300 040, US & Canada
☎1-800/781-4040, Australia ☎134 STA, New
Zealand ☎0800/474 400, South Africa ☎0861/781
781; ⓦwww.statravel.com. Worldwide specialists in
independent travel; also student IDs, travel insurance,
car rental, rail passes, and more. Good discounts for
students and under-26s.

Tour operators

If you want to avoid the hassle of making
your own arrangements you might consider
travelling with a **specialist tour operator**.
Plenty of small-group tours are available,
some with the emphasis on contributing to
the local communities. Cambodia is increasingly well covered by tour companies,
although some still include it only as part of a
visit to another Southeast Asian country.

Abercrombie & Kent UK ☎0845/618 2200,
ⓦwww.abercrombiekent.co.uk, US ☎1-800/554
7016, ⓦwww.abercrombiekent.com. Luxury tours
to Asia covering Cambodia in five-day extension trips
to Siem Reap and Phnom Penh.

Absolute Asia US ☎1-800/736-8187, ⓦwww
.absoluteasia.com. Deluxe private trips to Asia and
Cambodia include a 16-day golfing tour of Vietnam
and Cambodia (price on application).

Adventure Center US ☎1-800/228-8747,
ⓦwww.adventurecenter.com. "Soft adventure"
specialist with Cambodia offerings from a selection
of tour operators ranging from a few days to nearly
three weeks.

Audley Travel UK ☎01993/838160, ⓦwww
.audleytravel.com. Offers an interesting choice
of Cambodia tours as well as tailor-made travel.
The 13-day Temple Safari trip includes camping at
Banteay Chhmar and Koh Ker, while the Undiscovered
Cambodia and Laos tour explores Mondulkiri and

Rattanakiri before crossing into Laos. Audley supports
a school at Lolei near Siem Reap and sometimes
there's an opportunity to visit it.

Explore Worldwide UK ☎0844/499 0901,
Republic of Ireland ☎01/677 9479, US
☎1-800/227-8747, Canada ☎1-888/456-3522,
Australia ☎08/913 0700, South Africa ☎028/313
0526, ⓦwww.explore.com. This respected small
group operator offers several Cambodia options
including a comprehensive 16-day Heart of Cambodia
trip travelling from the capital to the coast and up
to Bokor, and taking in Kratie before finishing with
Angkor (from £1599).

Gecko Travel UK ☎023/9225 8859, ⓦwww
.geckotravel.com. Although it mainly offers
Cambodia combined with other Southeast Asian
countries, its Images of Cambodia is a photographic
holiday covering Cambodia only (from £995 ex
Bangkok).

Geographic Expeditions US ☎1-800/777-8183,
ⓦwww.geoex.com. These small-group luxury tours
to Asia don't come cheap: for example the 23 days in
Thailand and Cambodia, Off the Beaten Track, will set
you back $6775.

Intrepid Travel UK ☎01373/826611, US &
Canada ☎1-800/970 7299, Australia ☎1300/364

512, New Zealand ☏0800/600 610; ☻www.intrepidtravel.com. Southeast Asia specialist with an impressive choice of Cambodia offerings, either on its own or combined with neighbouring countries. The emphasis is on cross-cultural contact and low-impact tourism; tours include community projects and cycling options.

Kuoni UK ☏01306/747002 ☻www.kuoni.co.uk. Upmarket city-spa-beach breaks in Cambodia can be combined with trips to Rattanakiri or Mondulkiri and cycling around Angkor. Escorted or tailor-made options.

Noble Caledonian UK ☏020/7752 0000, ☻www.noble-caledonian.co.uk. Cambodia by boat. Boarding at the Vietnamese Delta port of My Tho, you cruise to Phnom Penh and on to Kompong Cham on the Mekong, before exploring the Tonle Sap and disembarking at Siem Reap for the temples of Angkor (from £3395 for 15 nights).

Peregrine UK & Republic of Ireland ☏0844/736 0170, Australia ☏1-300/791 485; ☻www.peregrineadventures.com. Six-day Classic Cambodia tour or the ultra-adventurous Cardamom Mountains Trek, which visits Siem Reap and Phnom Penh before starting the six-day trek through the little-explored jungle of the Cardamom Mountains (latter from £1345).

Responsibletravel.com UK ☏01273/600030, ☻www.responsibletravel.com. This online travel agent has consolidated a range of Cambodia tours from different companies; all tours have an ethical basis and there's an explanation with each one of how it benefits the local community.

Travel Indochina UK ☏01865/268 940, US ☏212/674 2887, Canada ☏416/345 9899, Australia ☏02/9244 2133; ☻www.travelindochina.co.uk. A wide range of Cambodia-specific tours lasting from five to 18 days. The adventurous 18-day Cambodia Encounter tour takes in Phnom Penh, Battambang and Angkor, plus the coast at Kep, Bokor and Kratie.

Getting around

Given the size of the country, there's a remarkable range of transport in Cambodia. Major routes are served by train, boats, planes and air-conditioned buses, while shared taxis, minibuses and beaten-up pick-up trucks ferry people and goods around the rest of the country. Cambodian towns lack any form of public transport, but you'll find tuk-tuks (a motorbike pulling a passenger carriage) and motos (motorbike taxis) readily available, making it quite simple to get around.

That's not to say travelling is easy. **Roads** in Cambodia, in spite of recent upgrading, remain among the worst in Southeast Asia. During the rainy season (June–Oct) sections of highway regularly get washed away, while many minor roads are little more than cart tracks, making travelling a time-consuming and uncomfortable experience. Cambodian drivers are not known for their patience or safety-consciousness either (driving lessons and the need for a driving licence have recently been introduced, but the instructor often has little more clue than the learner). Traffic in Phnom Penh is particularly chaotic and it's common for drivers to weave through impossibly small gaps in the opposite direction to the traffic flow – bad enough if you're closeted in the relative security of a Land Cruiser, but absolutely terrifying if you're perched on the back of a moto. However, there aren't nearly as many as accidents as you might expect, as Cambodian road-users have evolved their own conventions for avoiding collisions.

Recent road improvements have cut hours off some journeys and have opened up new routes to buses (including Phnom Penh to Stung Treng and Banlung). **National Route 1** to the Vietnamese border has been rebuilt, though there are still hold-ups getting out of Phnom Penh across the Monivong Bridge and at Neak Leung's ferry crossing – a bridge is planned over the Mekong but there's no sign of it yet.

Note that travel to the provinces and within Phnom Penh can be difficult over **public holidays**, especially the Khmer New Year (mid-April; see p.51). On New Year's Eve everyone heads for their home village and all available transport heads out of town – even more packed than usual. Phnom Penh in particular becomes very quiet, with hardly a moto available, while those that remain make a killing by doubling their fare.

Planes

Cambodia has no national airline, but does have several privately owned ones, though these change with a disturbing regularity: Angkor Airways, Royal Khmer Airways and PMTair currently all operate **internal flights** linking the capital with Siem Reap. In an attempt to encourage tourists visiting Siem Reap to spend longer in Cambodia, the airport at Sihanoukville was recently re-opened and a few flights between the towns introduced; unfortunately, a plane crashed in June 2007 and services on the route are suspended at the time of writing.

The **Phnom Penh–Siem Reap** route is served by all local carriers, with a dozen flights running from early morning until late evening. Flights to other parts of the country have been a casualty of the improvements in the roads and there are no longer flights to Battambang, Banlung, Koh Kong, Sen Monorom or Stung Treng. It is mooted that the airstrip at Banlung (Rattanakiri) may be extended and surfaced, but at the time of writing there is nothing to substantiate the rumour.

You'll need to **buy your ticket** at least a day before you want to travel, either at one of the airline offices or at a travel agent in Phnom Penh, Siem Reap or Sihanoukville. A single **fare** costs $75, double that for a return.

Buses

Phnom Penh is Cambodia's transport hub and thanks to road improvements its **bus network** is booming. Air-conditioned express buses run by Phnom Penh Sorya Transport Company, and 15–20 seater VIP coaches (*laan destjow*) serve most provincial destinations, while GST and Mekong operate services from Phnom Penh to Sihanoukville

and Siem Reap. However, it's as well to be aware that in general there are few links between provincial centres (see "Travel details" at the end of each guide chapter for details).

Express buses (*laan tom*) run from Phnom Penh to the major towns, including Sihanoukville, Siem Reap, Battambang and Kompong Cham. These timetabled, a/c services offer a clean and pleasant way to travel, giving you a good view of the countryside. Fares are very reasonable at $4 to Sihanoukville and $6 to Siem Reap. To guarantee a place, buy your **ticket** the day before from the bus station; no standing passengers are allowed, and if all the seats have been sold you can't travel (see p.125 for frequencies).

Smaller 20–30 seater coaches run by Phnom Penh Sorya and 12–15 seater VIP Coaches run by their competitors Hua Lian and Ly Heng serve less accessible towns like Kratie, Stung Treng and Banlung. As yet services linking provincial centres are scarce, although a coach does now run between Kompong Cham and Siem Reap and between Sihanoukville and Kampot/Kep.

Small **city buses** (*laan kerong*) run regularly between **Phnom Penh** and the nearby towns of **Kompong Chhnang**, **Kompong Speu**, **Neak Leung** and **Takeo**. Although these vehicles are often packed to capacity, they do more dropping off than taking on, so they get to be less of a squeeze as the journey progresses. Although slower than a shared taxi, and not as comfortable as the express buses, these are still a reasonable way to make local journeys: services run to a timetable and are cheap (10,000 riel to Kompong Cham, for example) and safe.

Buses display their destination in Cambodian and English. At bus stations you'll need to buy your **ticket** from the ticket office; if you get on a bus elsewhere, pay the conductor.

Shared taxis, minibuses and pick-ups

If you want to travel off the beaten track, you'll have no choice but to use the country's plethora of badly maintained minibuses, shared taxis and pick-up trucks. **Shared taxis** – normally Toyota Camrys – operate a speedy if not necessarily comfortable service between provincial centres, while crowded **pick-up trucks** cover some of the same routes and also bump their way across the worst of the country's roads. **Minibuses** are best avoided. Although cheaper than taxis they are cramped, particularly badly maintained and sorely overloaded – accidents are frequent and often fatal. In general, take a taxi if possible, or go in the cab of a pick-up.

All these forms of transport are straight-forward enough to use. Turn up at the local **transport stop** and state your destination, at which point you'll be swamped by touts trying to get you on their vehicle. Transport only leaves when full, so the fuller the vehicle, the sooner it's likely to leave. Once you've chosen a vehicle, agree the fare with the driver – most are honest, but a few have been known to hike their prices up for foreigners, so if in doubt ask other passengers what they are paying and stick to that.

Breakdowns do happen, but Cambodian drivers are adept at roadside repairs and Cambodian passengers remain stoic in the face of delays; needless to say the worse the road the more likely there is to be a problem. You aren't expected to pay until you reach your destination, although occasionally the driver may ask for some money in advance for fuel – let the locals take care of this, and pay what you owe at the end.

Shared taxis

Shared taxis take four passengers in the back, plus two in front, which means that you are not necessarily going to be comfortable. You can improve things by **paying for two places**, and if you want to get away in a hurry you could even buy up any remaining seats or hire the whole vehicle. Shared taxis depart from transport stops in all provincial towns (though not to any schedule) throughout the day – the best time to turn up is between 7am and 8am (earlier if you're going a long way). It's more difficult to get away after lunch, as fewer people travel then. For far-flung destinations such as between Phnom Penh and Sen Monorom, you may not have much choice as there may only be one vehicle leaving per day; it pays to check at the transport stop the day before and to reserve your place.

Shared taxis may not the cheapest way to travel, but they do allow you a degree of flexibility in terms of departure time and are relatively quick; from Phnom Penh, typical fares are 25,000 riel to Battambang, 12,000 riel to Kampot. On some routes the driver shares his seat with a passenger, a practice which is accepted by the Khmers. If this bothers you, you might wish to pay for the place that would have been shared with the driver so it can be kept vacant.

Minibuses

Clapped-out **minibuses** run from Phnom Penh and provincial destinations, typically along routes which are also served by small city buses. Minibuses depart only when absolutely packed, with people, goods and livestock piled inside, on the roof and

Tourist transport

Many guesthouses now operate their own **transport**, either minibuses or large buses, between tourist centres. Costs vary, but are typically a dollar or two more than in a shared taxi or public bus, and you'll also be picked up from your guesthouse or hotel rather than having to traipse out to the nearest transport stop. Such buses are convenient, although not without their own problems – you might wait (literally) hours for the bus to fill up, and also be pressured into staying at a particular guesthouse when you arrive at your destination.

Travelling to Bangkok, Ho Chi Minh City and the Laos border can also be done with the guesthouses, own transport but considerable delays have been reported by travellers particularly on the Bangkok route. Check out services with Phnom Penh Sorya Transport before you book. *Capitol Hotel* in Phnom Penh and *Sinh Café*, its associate organization in Ho Chi Minh City, also run a tourist boat service from Phnom Penh to Chau Doc for around $8 through to Ho Chi Minh City.

hanging out of the back – not only is this the most uncomfortable way to travel, but it is unsafe and best avoided. The only thing going for them is their cheapness, with **fares** just slightly more than on the back of a pick-up truck. Minibuses do not display their destination, so just ask around at the transport stop.

Pick-up trucks

Nissan and Toyota **pick-up trucks** are the workhorses of the Cambodian transport system, conveying people and goods over the roughest roads and tracks, even along river beds or up rocky hillsides.

Seats in the cab – four in the rear, two in the front – cost roughly the same as in a shared taxi; as in taxis, you can pay for an extra seat if you want more comfort. Other than the train, the **back of a pick-up** is the cheapest way to get around, costing around half the price of seats inside, though you'll have to sit on (or fit around) the goods being transported, and you risk being bounced around with nothing much to grab hold of. Take plenty of water and a sense of humour, and dust-proof your face by wrapping it in a scarf or *kramar*. In the wet season on the notorious northeast hike to Sen Monorom (Mondulkiri) you'll have no choice but to take a pick-up as it's the only thing that can take on the mud.

Boats

For years, travelling by boat was the principal means of getting between the capital and **Siem Reap**, but road improvements mean that it's now easier and as quick to travel by bus or taxi. Remarkably, one boat a day still forges up the Tonle Sap to Siem Reap at the thoroughly overpriced foreigners' fare of $25; it's not even a particularly scenic trip across the Tonle Sap lake, which is so vast that it's more like being at sea.

Speedboats, seating either twelve or thirty people, operate between **Battambang** and **Siem Reap**, although in rough weather the Tonle Sap can whip up some fierce waves and travelling on these boats can be uncomfortable and even downright unsafe – even in relatively good weather you and your luggage are likely to get soaked.

An express boat service runs daily south along the Mekong between Phnom Penh and the Vietnamese border at **Chau Doc** ($17 for foreigners); but the easiest way is to book with the *Capitol Hotel* or *Neak Krohorm Travel* in Phnom Penh who can arrange a boat to Chau Doc and onward transport through to Ho Chi Minh City for around $8.

A boat leaves Sihanoukville for **Koh Kong** near the Thai border daily at noon; in the other direction it leaves at 8am, travelling along the coast, though services are occasionally suspended during rough weather, and even during calm weather the trip can be decidedly uncomfortable.

Slow boats operate to no published timetable on the Tonle Sap and Mekong, taking up to three days to travel upstream between Phnom Penh and Siem Reap or Kratie – though it's unlikely you'll ever want or need to travel on one.

Unfortunately, boats up the Mekong from Kompong Cham to **Stung Treng,** the most scenic boat trip in Cambodia, have been suspended for the foreseeable future.

Trains

Completed in 1932, Cambodia's rail network has suffered from both neglect and terrorism (the Khmer Rouge regularly tried to blow up the line and the trains) to such an extent that only one route – the service between Phnom Penh and Battambang – is still running (just). Doing this trip by train is both painfully slow (12–15hr) and uncomfortable, and unless you're a serious train buff or desperately short of cash it really isn't worth the bother. **Tickets** cost just 6,500 riel for the journey from the capital to Battambang, though bizarrely the trip back from Battambang costs three times as much.

The train leaves from Phnom Penh on **odd-numbered dates** in the month at 6.30am, returning to the capital the following day (though there are no services on the 31st of any month or on February 29 in leap years). As **breakdowns** are frequent, it's worth checking at the station the evening before you want to travel to see if the train has arrived; on the day of travel itself, get to the station early to buy your ticket and get a seat. The train has only three passenger **carriages,** all with **hard seats**; the rest of it consists of **freight trucks** and although you can travel in them it isn't recommended. Water and soft drinks are available on the train, and food vendors get on at every stop with snacks, but you may prefer to bring your own provisions with you.

Plans to restore the decrepit rail network were recently announced, including the restoration of a rail link to Poipet with train speeds increased from 20kph to 50kph. Needless to say, the main use will be for freight.

City and town transport

There is no public transport in any Cambodian town, including Phnom Penh (a trial bus service was abandoned a few years ago due to lack of support). Instead the usual mode of transport is the *romorque*, aka tuk-tuk, a passenger carriage pulled by a motorbike; and the motorbike taxi, the **moto**, a small motorbike-cum-moped with a space in front of the driver for baggage. In Phnom Penh you'll also find **cyclos**, Cambodia's version of the pedicab or trishaw. All these forms of transport are hailed from the side of the road and drop you at your destination. **Taxis** are available in Phnom Penh and Siem Reap, but elsewhere you'll only find cars, with driver, for hire by the day (or longer).

Motos

Motorbike taxis, or **motos**, are the staple means of travelling short (and sometimes long) distances in Cambodia, although riding on the back of a moto in the middle of anarchic traffic isn't everybody's idea of fun, and you may feel safer taking a taxi. Motos are easily identified by their drivers' baseball caps (although you'll sometimes get one wearing a soft safari hat or even motorcycle helmet) – other motorcyclists tend not to wear hats to avoid being mistaken for a moto driver. Not that you'll normally need to flag down a moto – just stand by the road and moto drivers will usually come up and offer their services. Moto drivers indicate that they are available for hire by holding up a finger (usually the index one). Drivers come from a variety of backgrounds – you'll often find you are being driven by an off-duty policeman or a moonlighting government official.

If you have **bags**, the driver will squeeze them into the space between his knees and the handlebars – moto drivers are adept at balancing baggage, from rice sacks to backpacks, between their legs while negotiating chaotic traffic. Passengers sit behind the driver on a pillion seat – Cambodians typically squeeze as many passengers as possible onto this (three is common), although it's best not to follow their example and to stick to just one passenger per bike (in Siem Reap the police do not allow motos to take more than one foreigner). Although you'll see Cambodian women sitting side-saddle, it's safer if you sit astride and, if necessary, hang onto the driver.

Moto drivers have an image of foreigners as having bottomless pockets, so avoid misunderstandings by **agreeing the fare** beforehand; a typical journey around town will set you back 2000–4000 riel. If you want to hire a driver for longer periods, count on around 4000 riel per hour, or $6–10 per day (fares increase if there are two passengers, but you shouldn't pay twice the single-person price). Many drivers head home to their villages during public holidays, when Phnom Penh in particular is largely devoid of transport and consequently fares can double at these times. Curiosity and the remote chance of a fare will mean that even if you are already negotiating with someone, other moto drivers gather round. Etiquette dictates that you should go with the one you summoned, though in the unlikely event that someone offers you a cheaper fare you'll probably find "your" driver acquiesces.

Motos can be taken on quite long trips **out of town** – indeed it's the only way to get to some places, although it's not particularly comfortable. You'll probably have to pay for fuel in addition to the day hire. Drivers are sometimes irrationally fearful of bandits and can be reluctant to travel in remote areas late in the afternoon, so bear their concerns in mind when planning your excursions.

Tuk-tuks

The introduction of tuk-tuks to Cambodia came about in 2001, when police in Siem Reap banned foreigners riding three-up on a moto (in spite of the fact that Cambodians are allowed to be three, four or even more up). Tuk-tuks have now caught on in Phnom Penh and are gaining prominence in some provincial towns too. Pulled by a motorbike, these covered passenger cabs seat four people (six at a push) and have the advantage of affording some protection against the sun, and rain – as they have drop down side-curtains. The motorbikes that pull them, however, are the same ones used as motos, and so are woefully underpowered, which makes for a slow trip. However, they are excellent for two or more travelling together and when you have baggage; they're also good for trips up to about 30km out of town.

Cyclos

Found only in Phnom Penh, the **cyclo** (pronounced *see-klo*) is Cambodia's version of the cycle rickshaw (trishaw). Slower and more expensive than a moto, a trip across town by cyclo gives you time to take in the city and street scenes (although traffic fumes can be unpleasant). Cyclos take one passenger (or two at a squash) in a seat at the front, with the driver perched on a seat behind over the rear wheel.

Taxis

Both Phnom Penh and Siem Reap have **city taxis** (as opposed to shared taxis). These don't tout for fares on the streets, but instead congregate outside major hotels. In Phnom Penh you can order one by phone (see p.114). Fares are around $5 per journey.

In other towns you'll need to hire a **car and driver**. These can be hired for both short hops around town and long journeys (expect to pay around $25–30 per day for running around town, $40 plus for an out-of-town trip).

Car rental

Only a couple of companies in Cambodia have **self-drive vehicles** to rent; rates start at $25 per day excluding petrol (there are plenty of filling stations on the outskirts of towns and on some main roads). Driving yourself presents quite a few headaches, however, and really isn't worth the hassle when you can hire car and driver for about the same price. Problems for the self-driver include finding appropriate documentation: a

passport is required by the hire company and (oddly) a Cambodian licence by the police – although an international driving licence may now be accepted, despite the fact that Cambodians are only just getting licences themselves. You'll also have to deal with the state of Cambodia's roads, the lack of designated car parks and haphazard signposting, plus the fact that insurance is at best cursory – any loss or damage to the vehicle is your responsibility. During the day, whenever you park you should get someone to look after the vehicle; in town you'll usually find a parking attendant near markets and restaurants who will keep an eye on the vehicle for 1000 riel. It's normal to park as directed and leave the handbrake disengaged so that the car can be pushed out of the way to let other cars in or out. To prevent theft and damage at day's end you'll need to look for a hotel with parking or find a local with off-road space where they'll let you park for a nominal charge of around 4000 riel. Given all these hassles, it's far more practical to hire a **car and driver** (see under Taxis, above).

Motorbikes and bicycles

Whether you ride a **motorbike** or **bicycle**, it's worth wearing sunglasses, long trousers and a long-sleeved shirt to protect you not only from the sun but also from the grit and gravel thrown up on the dusty roads.

When heading off into the countryside, remember that Cambodia has a huge problem with **land mines**, and no matter how tempting it may be to go cross-country, stick to well-used tracks and paths.

Motorbike rental

Renting a motorbike has become a popular way to see Cambodia. The same **security** issues apply to rented motorbikes as to cars (see above), however, so make sure you leave your motorbike somewhere secure at night – guesthouses will often bring it inside for you.

You can rent an **off-road 250cc bike** for around $6 per day or $40 a week from a number of companies, particularly in Phnom Penh (see the relevant city listings for details), although you'll have to leave your passport as security. Check the condition of the bike before heading off on a long trip – if it breaks down, it's your responsibility to get it repaired or returned to the owner– and take advice on local road conditions, as often even relatively short distances can take a long time if the road has been washed away.

In Siem Reap and Sihanoukville the police have clamped down on motorbikes being ridden by foreigners, citing "safety" as the reason for the "ban". It's unlikely that this is the case; a more probable reason is that it's a protectionist move to keep the moto "mafias" in business. One or two places in these towns are still renting out bikes, but be prepared for hassle from the authorities if you rent one.

In other towns it's easiest to use the **110cc run-arounds** available for rent from guesthouses and hire shops; rates are $4–6 per day.

Wearing a motorbike **helmet** is essential and might save your life on Cambodia's bumpy roads; rental companies will supply them on request. Even with the improvements in the road conditions, poor driving by other motorists make it safer to travel only in daylight hours.

Cycling

Renting **bicycles** in Cambodia is more difficult than you might expect. They are sometimes available at guesthouses in larger towns for $2–3 per day, although what you get varies considerably, from swish mountain bikes to sturdy but gearless affairs. Compared to Thailand or Vietnam, Cambodia's potholed, dusty roads and manic traffic can be a bit of a shock, but cycling here can be a rewarding experience even so: not only will you get a warm reception from Cambodians (who will be puzzled at your reliance on pedal power when a moto would do), but you'll be able to enjoy the countryside at your own pace.

In view of the state of the roads, when planning your trip don't reckon on covering more than 50km a day, and try to get to your destination by late afternoon since many of

the overloaded trucks and lorries on the road don't have lights and so won't see you as darkness falls. There are plenty of refreshment stalls along major roads, so you'll seldom go hungry. If you get stuck between guesthouses you'll need to stop at a village (camping is technically illegal and potentially dangerous because of the risk of land mines), where someone will give you space on their floor for a small consideration. It's essential to note that all motorized traffic takes precedence over bicycles, and you'll have to veer onto the verge if necessary to get out of the way of speeding cars and trucks.

A couple of places are now renting out electric bicycles, which can be a fun – if not necessarily faster – way to get around.

Organized tours

If you're short on time, or simply don't want to do it yourself, then taking an **organized tour** can get you around the country to the major sights with minimum effort. An increasing number of travel agencies and tour operators in Phnom Penh (see p.114) and Siem Reap (see p.174) arrange individual tours, so you don't need to conform to a fixed departure date or worry that a trip won't run if the group isn't large enough. Costs vary according to the type of accommodation you choose, where you go and what you do; allow upwards of $120 per person per day excluding food. Travelling is by a/c vehicle, with guide, and includes accommodation.

A cheaper alternative to such tours are the transport and accommodation deals arranged by some of the established **guesthouses** in Phnom Penh. On these trips, a private bus takes a group of tourists between the capital and Siem Reap or Sihanoukville, with accommodation and day-trips to major sights arranged through partner guesthouses in these towns (expect to pay up to $25–30 per person per day).

Addresses

Most Cambodian towns are laid out on a grid plan; a few main streets have names but the majority are only numbered. Outside of Phnom Penh and a couple of other cities you'll be hard pushed to find a street sign. As most Cambodians have little idea of street numbers, to locate a specific address you're best off heading for a nearby landmark and asking from there.

Accommodation

Finding accommodation is seldom a problem, and even provincial towns have a choice of budget guesthouses and modest hotels. Phnom Penh, Siem Reap and Sihanoukville have plenty of accommodation in all categories, and many other towns too now have some classier hotels. Off the beaten track you'll find a basic guesthouse or two, but probably little else.

Arriving anywhere by road transport, the driver may well drop you at a guesthouse or at least point you in the right direction for one.

In the main tourist centres touts meet incoming transport and will take you free of charge to their establishment; if you don't like it, feel free to go elsewhere. In a similar vein, tuk-tuk and moto drivers get a commission of around 1000–2000 riel in the popular tourist venues for dropping you off at a guesthouse if you don't specify one of your choice; this premium may be added to your room rate.

In general, you can't pre-book budget accommodation, but as internet access increases, a few places in major tourist centres are beginning to take reservations. They will also meet you off a bus, boat or plane if you let them know you're coming.

In basic accommodation, **rooms** are either *moi kreh* (one-bed) or *bpee kreh* (two-bed), meaning they come with one or two double beds respectively; having paid for the room it's up to you how many people share it. Mid-range accommodation tends to comprise conventional singles and doubles, but at the lower end they may feature rooms with anything from one to four double beds. Upmarket hotels typically play by international standards, with rates for single or double rooms. **Breakfast** is increasingly included in mid-range and upmarket establishments; ask when you book in. Off the tourist route, guesthouses probably won't have dining facilities and you'll need to go out for all meals.

Hotels often have **safes** in the rooms for guests' valuables, and in tourist centres guesthouses can usually lock things away for you. Wherever you stay, it's customary **to pay** when you check out, not when you arrive.

Budget

Basic **budget rooms** all over Cambodia cost $4–5 a night. At worst they can be tiny, windowless affairs with paper-thin walls, that come with a double bed, a nylon sheet, a blanket, a towel and an electric fan; in this price range bathrooms are usually shared. While the bottom sheet should be clean, the blanket is not laundered between guests, so you may want to make sure you have a sarong or sheet with you. Outside Phnom Penh and Siem Reap, rooms should come with a mosquito net; if there isn't one when you arrive, make sure to ask for one.

Bathrooms, whether shared or en suite, vary considerably, but these days you'll mainly get Western-style toilets and at least a cold shower, although in out-of-the-way spots you may still come across squat toilets with cold *mandi* – a tub of cold water that you ladle over yourself (don't get into it as others will need to use the water too). In tourist areas and most towns you'll usually get an en-suite bathroom, with a towel, toilet paper and a small bar of soap provided (increasingly you also get a disposable toothbrush and tiny tube of toothpaste).

Even at budget level there's a lot of variation in quality; and for just $5 or a little more it is possible to find rooms with cotton sheets (more comfortable in Cambodia's humid climate), a TV and sometimes a fridge. Pay a few dollars above this and you'll get you a top sheet and, more often than not, a hot shower. Increasingly, guesthouses in the main tourist venues are installing air conditioning, which can usually be turned off if you don't want it, though if you do use it expect to pay $5–10 more per night for the electricity.

Accommodation price codes

Accommodation throughout the guide has been categorized according to the following price codes, based on the cost of the cheapest **double room, with en suite facilities** (but, in lower categories at least, not necessarily hot water) available at each particular establishment. Where **dormitory accommodation** is available, a riel or dollar price for a dorm bed (typically $1–2) is given in the text. Note that other than in Phnom Penh, Siem Reap and Sihanoukville, you'll be hard pressed to find rooms priced above ❹.

❶ $5 and under   ❹ $16–25   ❼ $81–140
❷ $6–10   ❺ $26–50   ❽ $141–200
❸ $11–15   ❻ $51–80   ❾ over $200

Guesthouses are the mainstay of budget accommodation in Cambodia, but vary enormously in style. The least attractive are single-storey establishments reminiscent of stables, with plywood-partitioned rooms in a row; these are typically found around transport stops. Undistinguished concrete blocks abound, particularly in town centres, and though clean, they lack atmosphere. However, from time to time you'll come across guesthouses in traditional wooden stilt-houses, which don't feature air conditioning or en-suite facilities, but compensate for this with masses of mellow wood and attractive balconies. Note that the demarcation between a guesthouse and a cheap hotel can be a bit fuzzy in Cambodia; Siem Reap's "guesthouses", for example, charge rates bordering on those in the cheaper hotels.

Tourism has caught on in a big way in Cambodia with the younger Cambodians taking leisure trips themselves. As a result, new guesthouses are springing up in most towns as everyone tries to get in on the act; these are usually clean, but plain, typically costing $5 (fan) to $10 (a/c) per night, and are gradually replacing the dark, dingy guesthouse of yesteryear. Another sign of the times is that occasional budget places are accepting payment by credit card – but don't rely on being able to do this quite yet.

Mid-range

Mid-range accommodation covers a broad spectrum from around $15 to $80. Most hotels in this bracket have a variety of rooms, so it's worth asking to see a few before you make your choice. At the cheaper end, expect rooms to have a bathroom with hot shower, air conditioning, fridge and TV; going up in price brings coordinated decor and possibly an actual bathtub; breakfast will most likely be included too.

You'll probably be able to pay by credit card in places rated ❺ and above, although there may be a surcharge of around four percent. It's also worth checking whether government tax and service are included in the rack rate, as these can add up to twenty percent onto the bill.

A number of upmarket guesthouses feature in this mid-range price bracket. This is a deliberate choice by the owners, often because they don't provide all the services you'd expect in a hotel – such as 24-hour reception; alternatively it could be that by remaining a guesthouse the government's hotel tax can be avoided.

Luxury

You'll now find **upmarket accommodation** (priced above $80 a night for a double room) in Phnom Penh, Siem Reap, Battambang, Sihanoukville and Kep. It's worth making a reservation if you want to stay in one of these hotels, as the rooms are often booked out by conference or tour groups. Besides opulent, supremely comfortable rooms, hotels in this price range have their own restaurant and bar, and often a swimming pool; your room will probably have either Wi-Fi or an alternative internet facility. Facilities in the establishments at the very top end of the market rival those of the best hotels anywhere, stretching to a range of restaurants, bars and shops, a fitness centre, tennis courts, swimming pool and spa.

Food and drink

Cambodian food isn't particularly spicy, although it's often delicately flavoured with herbs such as lemon grass and coriander. Many dishes are variations on fare from other Asian countries, especially China, on which Khmer cuisine draws heavily.

Food is traditionally cooked in a single pot or wok over a charcoal stove; although gas burners are being introduced in the cities, many people prize the smoky flavour that they claim food acquires when it's cooked over charcoal. A lot of dishes are fried in palm oil and aren't drained before serving, so food can be quite greasy; if you're vegetarian it's worth being aware that the pan is seldom washed out between the meat and vegetable dishes. Few Cambodians have refrigerators, and even if they do, they prefer to buy produce fresh from the markets as needed.

As in many countries where rice is the staple food, the most common way to refer to eating in Cambodia is *nyam bai*, literally "eat rice".

Where to eat

The cheapest food in Cambodia is available from **street hawkers with** handcarts or baskets dangling from a shoulder pole, who sell anything from fried noodles or baguettes, to fresh fruit and ice cream. Another source of cheap food is the country's **markets** – open both by day and by night, though often in separate locations – where stalls sell a variety of dishes and desserts at prices only slightly higher than those charged by street hawkers. Each stall usually has its own speciality, and you can order from any stall in the market irrespective of where you're sitting. When you've finished, you pay the stall closest to you for the whole lot and they'll sort out the money amongst themselves.

Noodle shops and cheap restaurants can be found all over town centres and are especially plentiful around markets and transport stops. **Noodle shops** (*haang geautieuv*) open around 5.30am for the breakfast trade, serving various noodle soups, along with dumplings and rice porridge in the larger establishments. By 9am or 10am they turn into **coffee shops**, serving hot and cold coffee and tea, as well as soft drinks and fresh coconuts, until they close at around 4pm or 5pm.

Cheap restaurants (*haang bai*) are recognizable by a row of pots set out on a table out front, containing the day's fare, not dissimilar to Cambodian home cooking. To find out what's on offer, lift the lids and peer inside; the dishes you have chosen will be served to you in separate bowls along with a plate of rice. These are inexpensive places to fill up as the food is not only pretty decent but invariably good value at around 2000 riel per option – similar in price to eating at a market stall – inclusive of rice and iced tea, a jug of which is kept replenished at the table.

For **international cuisine**, Phnom Penh and Siem Reap have an enormous amount of choice: French, Japanese, pizzas, burgers, Sunday roasts and so on. In Sihanoukville there is also a decent – if slightly less eclectic – selection of international places. At the other end of the scale, eating possibilities in rural areas and very small towns can be quite restricted, and in the evenings you may be hard pushed to find anything more than a bowl of instant noodles. In between, most towns are limited to Khmer food only, although some may have a menu translated into English, and larger towns generally have a few smarter Chinese restaurants with quite extensive menus.

Practically all restaurants are **open daily**, although some Western tourist-oriented places may close one day of the week, in which case this is stated in the reviews in the guide. Khmers eat early by Western standards: breakfast is normally over by 8am, lunch by 12.30pm, while the dinner trade is relatively quiet and short-lived, as people (in the provinces, especially) prefer to take away meals to eat at home. Thus Khmer restaurants are generally open from around 6am until 7pm or 8pm in the provinces, or until around 9pm or 10pm in Phnom Penh, Siem Reap and Sihanoukville. In general, there's no need **to book in advance**, even to eat at expensive restaurants – although we've given telephone numbers in the guide for the few establishments where you might want to reserve for special events or where meals are packaged with a cultural performance (as in a handful of venues in Siem Reap).

How to eat

Most Cambodian meals are based around polished white **rice**, which is usually served either in a large bowl from which you help yourself, or as individual platefuls. The rice is eaten off a shallow bowl, like a soup plate, using a fork and spoon (Cambodians don't use knives), the spoon held in the right hand and used to eat from, the fork serving to break up the food and to push it onto the spoon. **Noodles**, eaten with chopsticks and a Chinese soup spoon, are also common, but tend to be consumed more as a snack than a meal in themselves. In Chinese restaurants you'll be given a small rice bowl and chopsticks, whether you're eating rice or noodles.

Diners typically order two or three dishes – fish or meat, vegetables and perhaps a soup – which are placed in the centre of the table; each person helps themselves from the communal fare in small amounts at a time. If not served with the meal, the soup follows at the end (though in Chinese restaurants it normally comes at the beginning of the meal), and is ladled into individual bowls from a much larger serving bowl.

Before eating, it's common for diners to wipe the bowls, eating implements and glasses with the tissues provided on every table. Although Cambodians typically do not eat with their fingers, it is acceptable to pick up pieces of meat or chicken with your right hand (the left hand is deemed unclean as it's used to clean yourself after going to

the toilet). Toothpicks are provided on every restaurant table; etiquette dictates that you should hold the toothpick in one hand and cover your mouth with the other.

What to eat

Many Cambodian dishes are variations on Chinese equivalents and are stir-fried in a wok to order. Just about any combination of ingredients can be ordered: chicken, pork or frogs' legs might be stir-fried with ginger, spring onions and garlic; prawn or chicken with basil leaves. Rice or noodles can themselves be stir-fried with chopped pork, beef, crab or vegetables, with an egg scrambled in or fried and served on top. Stir-fried **sweet and sour** dishes are also available, usually made with fish or pork – though you can ask for a vegetarian version – and flavoured with a combination of ingredients including pineapple, onion and either green or red tomatoes.

Stews and curries are often available at market stalls and cheap restaurants. Cambodian **stews** are usually based on a light stock (with beef or fish), complemented by bitter gourd or field melon; it's not unusual for them to contain hard-boiled eggs either. **Curries**, usually made with beef, are only mildly spicy and generally quite dry.

Smoky, **charcoal-grilled** chicken and fish are available everywhere from roadside stalls to restaurants, the fish served with a dip of grated green mango, chilli, garlic and fish sauce, while the chicken comes with a salad garnish and a sweet chilli sauce.

Khmer cuisine features two kinds of soup: **sumlar**, freshly prepared to order and cooked quickly, and **sop**, based on a stock which has been simmering for a while. One of the commonest soups on restaurant menus is *sumlar sngouw jerooet*, made from either chicken or fish and cooked with onion, lemon and chives.

Breakfast

For **breakfast**, Cambodians often eat rice with either fried chicken or fried pork, served with a sliced cucumber and pickled vegetables, and a side bowl of clear soup. Also popular in the mornings is **geautieuv sop**, rice noodles in a clear broth with chicken, pork or beef pieces; you might wish to decline the other ingredients, namely sliced-up intestines or gizzard and a chunk of congealed blood, which the Khmers slurp with relish, as it's said to make you strong. A dish of bean sprouts and a slice of lime will be provided on the side, which you can add to taste.

In the tourist centres **Western breakfasts** are available in guesthouses, hotels, cafés and restaurants catering for tourists and expat workers. In the provinces an occasional restaurant will cater for NGO workers and serve fried eggs or omelettes with bread, but otherwise it's difficult to find anything other than Khmer fare first thing in the morning.

Snacks

Cambodian snack foods are legion, the range varying with the time of day. Eaten with breakfast or as an afternoon snack, *noam bpaow* are steamed dumplings, originating from Chinese cuisine, made from white dough filled with a mix of minced pork, turnip, egg and chives. They're readily available from street vendors and at restaurants; there's a second, less common version, smaller and sweeter and filled with a green mung-bean paste.

In the afternoon and evening, crusty **baguettes**, filled with your choice of meat pâté or sardines and pickled vegetables, can be bought from street hawkers for around 2000 riel. At beer stalls in night markets, you'll find **grueng klaim**, fibrous strips of dried beef or pork served with pickles and generally eaten with alcoholic beverages.

Bany chaev are savoury wok-fried pancakes commonly available at market stalls; they're made from rice flour flecked with chives and coloured vivid yellow using turmeric. Filled with fried minced pork, onion, prawns and bean sprouts, they're eaten by wrapping pieces of the pancake in a lettuce leaf and dipping them in a fish sauce mixed with garlic, lemon and crushed peanuts.

Steamed or grilled eggs are incredibly popular as snacks and are available everywhere, most commonly from street vendors, night markets and at transport stops – where you'll often get a choice of eggs, with bite-sized quails' eggs easy to find. The black "thousand-year eggs" that you see at markets and food stalls are duck's eggs that have been stored in jars of salt until the shells turn black; by that time the whites and the yolks have turned into a jelly, not dissimilar in texture to soft-boiled eggs. They are eaten with rice or *borbor*, a soupçon of egg being taken with each spoonful of rice.

Often found at night markets or served up with beer is **pong dteer gowne**, literally ducks' eggs with duckling. Said to give strength and good health, it really does contain an unhatched duckling, boiled and served with some herbs and a sauce of salt, pepper and lemon juice – not too bad if you don't look too closely at what you're eating.

Cooked bananas are also much eaten as snacks, seasoned with salt and grilled over charcoal braziers, or wok-fried in a batter containing sesame seeds; the latter are most delicious when they're piping hot. Both are available in the markets, as are **noam ensaum jayk**, sweet sticky-rice parcels in different shapes, such as pyramids or rolls,

Cambodian delicacies

Cambodians eat just about everything, and nothing escapes a true gourmet, not even **insects**. In the markets you'll see big trays of grasshoppers, beetles and crickets, usually fried and sold by the bag, which are eaten like sweets. **Spiders** are a speciality of Skone, a town between Phnom Penh and Kompong Cham, where big, black, hairy tarantulas are skewered and fried.

Phnom Penh has a number of upmarket Chinese and seafood restaurants where, besides many varieties of shellfish and fish, **snake**, **turtle** and **game** such as deer, wild pig, rabbit and monitor lizard are served up. Some places also offer illegally hunted animals such as pangolin and bear, although a recent clampdown has reduced the practice. More mundanely, tiny sparrows, *jarb jeyan*, and other small birds can be found deep-fried in many Khmer restaurants.

containing a piece of banana and wrapped in banana leaves.

Among the more unusual snacks is the much prized **grolan**, bamboo tubes containing a delicious mix of sticky rice, coconut milk and black beans, cooked over charcoal and sold bundled together by hawkers (usually in the provinces). The woody outer layer of the bamboo is removed after cooking, leaving a thin shell which you peel down to get at the contents. Seasonally available are **chook**, the cone-shaped, green seeds of the lotus flower, sold in bundles of three or five heads; to eat, pop the seeds out from the green rubbery pod, peel off their outer skins and consume the insides, which taste a bit like garden peas.

Accompaniments

No Cambodian meal is complete without a variety of accompaniments. One of the most prized of these is **prohok**, a salted, fermented fish paste which looks like a pinkish pâté and has an incredibly strong anchovy-like taste. A dollop of the paste is served on a plate with raw vegetables, *gee* and edible flowers; it's eaten either by adding a tiny amount to the accompanying vegetables or by taking a morsel with a spoonful of rice. *Prohok* isn't usually found on the menus of classy restaurants but is always available at market stalls and in Cambodian homes.

Though it's less pungent than *prohok*, **fish sauce** is still pretty smelly. Used as a dip with every type of food, it's made from both salt- and fresh-water fish, which are layered with salt in large vats; as the fish ferments the juice is extracted from the bottom and bottled.

Other accompaniments include **dips** of chilli sauce and soya sauce – to which you can add chopped-up chillies and garlic – which are either left in pots on the table or served in individual saucers.

Rice and noodles

Besides boiled rice, Cambodians enjoy rice cooked up as a porridge called **borbor**, usually available at market stalls, night markets and in some cheap restaurants,

either as breakfast or an evening dish. *Borbor* can either be left unseasoned and used as a base to which you add your own ingredients – dried fish, pickles, salted egg or fried vegetables – or cooked in stock, with pieces of chicken, fish or pork and bean sprouts added before serving. Shredded ginger, a squeeze of lime and spicy soya-bean paste from pots at the table can also be added to taste.

White rice-flour noodles, **geautiev** (pronounced "*goy teal*"), are available in different shapes and sizes – in fine threads for noodle soup, or wide and thick for use in *nom bany jowk*. The latter is sold by female street vendors from baskets dangling on shoulder poles and consists of noodles served cold with a lukewarm curry sauce over the top. Yellow egg noodles – **mee** – made from wheat flour are used in soups and stir-fries. Freshly made *mee* – called *mee kilo* because it's sold by weight – are available in the major towns, though elsewhere people make do with instant noodles imported in packets from Thailand and Vietnam. **Loat chat**, a hollow noodle similar to macaroni, is fried up by hawkers using hand-carts equipped with charcoal burners; a plate topped with a fried egg goes for 1000–1500 riel.

Meat

Meat is comparatively expensive and is invariably cut up into small pieces and mixed with plenty of vegetables. **Pork** is commonly available, attested to by the number of pigs wandering around even the smallest village, but **beef** is more difficult to obtain as cows are prized as work animals and not necessarily killed for food. The best beef is available in large towns; elsewhere it's often tough and chewy.

Not so much a soup as a meal in itself, **sop chhnang day** is a bit like a fondue: a clay pot of hot stock and meatballs is brought to the table and placed on a small burner in the middle. Once the soup is boiling you add a selection of ingredients to the pot according to taste, choosing from side plates featuring slices of raw beef (or venison), often mixed with raw egg prior to cooking; sprigs of herbs; various vegetables; yellow and white noodles; tofu; dried sheets of soya bean (which looks a bit like chicken skin); and mushrooms. Both the stock and the dishes are replenished as long as you keep on eating, and at the end of the meal the bill is calculated according to the number of side plates on the table. Restaurants specializing in *sop chhnang day* often display a sign outside depicting a steaming pan over a burner.

Another Cambodian favourite is **sait gow ang**, beef grilled over a small charcoal burner at the table. Nibbled with pickled vegetables and fresh herbs, it tends to be eaten as an evening snack to accompany drinking. Similar in style but more of a meal is **chhnang phnom pleung**, "volcano pot", so named because the burner is said to resemble a volcano in appearance; the beef (venison is also used) comes to the table ready sliced, with a raw egg stirred into the meat before cooking. It's accompanied by side dishes of raw vegetables such as green tomatoes, capsicum and salad greens. Once you've grilled the meat and vegetables to your taste, they're wrapped in a salad leaf and dipped in a sauce before being eaten.

Typically found at cheap restaurants, **kaar** is a stew usually made with pig's trotters and green cabbage (it can also be made with fish or bamboo shoots) and eaten with unseasoned rice porridge (*borbor*). Pork is the usual ingredient in **spring rolls** (though Vietnamese restaurants especially may do a vegetarian version as an appetizer); they're either steamed or fried and then rolled up in a lettuce leaf with sliced cucumber, bean sprouts and herbs and eaten dipped in a sweet chilli sauce.

Chicken and duck

Chicken and duck in Cambodia often have a high bone-to-flesh ratio; except in tourist restaurants, the whole carcass is chopped up, which means you have to pick out the bones from each mouthful.

A refreshing option is **sumlar ngam ngouw,** a clear chicken broth made with pickled limes and herbs. Worth trying if you can find it is **baked chicken**, cooked in a metal pot in a wood-fired oven and really tasty. It's usually prepared to order, so there is quite a wait involved.

Fish

Fish is plentiful and the main source of protein for most Cambodians. Near the Tonle Sap there's a particularly good choice of **freshwater** varieties, and **sea fish** is plentiful along the coast, though inland it's only readily available in the specialist (and inevitably expensive) restaurants of Phnom Penh.

Fish is served up in all manner of ways – grilled, fried, in soups and stews. Increasingly available in tourist areas is **amok**, a mild Cambodian-style fish curry (chicken is also used); the fish is mixed with coconut milk and seasonings and baked wrapped in banana leaves (a variation, offered by several Siem Reap restaurants, is to cook the fish in the shell of a young coconut).

Dried fish is a particular favourite. Much prized for sun-drying are large freshwater fish from the Tonle Sap, which are sliced lengthwise like kippers and grilled over charcoal, to be eaten with rice. When fish is cheap you'll even see people drying their own in baskets outside their houses.

Vegetables

Cambodia's markets offer up a wide range of vegetables, some of which will be unfamiliar, all delivered fresh daily. Regrettably, you won't come across much of this produce on restaurant menus, though one unusual vegetable you will find in restaurants is the *trokooen*, **morning glory**, a water plant with a thick, hollow stem and elongated heart-shaped leaves, which are carefully removed prior to cooking; it's often served stir-fried with garlic and oyster sauce, and tastes a bit like spinach.

Fried mixed vegetables are ubiquitous in Khmer restaurants, the constituents varying according to what's available (in some establishments you may be able to choose from a selection). Green tomatoes, crisp and refreshing, are often added to this and other dishes; red ones are only available in limited quantities for special recipes. For a decent selection of vegetable dishes, though, you'll need to try the Chinese restaurants. At street stalls and in the markets you'll find *noam gachiey*, best described as chive burgers; made from rice flour, chives and herbs, they're steamed or fried, and dished

Vegetarians and vegans

Although strict Buddhists do have a vegetarian meal once every two weeks on offering days, Cambodians in general can't understand why anyone who can afford meat or fish would not want to eat it, and even the monks aren't strictly vegetarian nowadays.

The best way to get a **vegetarian dish** is to ask for your order to be cooked without meat (*ot dak sait*) or fish (*ot dak trei*); in principle, most stir-fries and soups can be done this way. You might be told that the dish is "not delicious" without meat, and the waiter may also come back a couple of times just to check he's got it straight. However, to be sure that prawns, chicken, duck or even intestines aren't substituted, or that a meat stock isn't used, you'll need to specify a whole list of things to avoid, so some flexibility on your part wouldn't go amiss. **Vegans** will need to make sure that no eggs are used (say *ot yoh pong mawn* or *pong dteer*) as these are widely used, but should have few problems avoiding dairy products, which are unlikely to be found outside Western restaurants.

up with either a sweet sauce (note that this is based on fish sauce) or soy sauce. Oddly enough, **French fries**, although not usually eaten by Cambodians, are available in many Cambodian restaurants, served with a variety of condiments and seasonings, including pepper with lemon juice, and bright orange sweet chilli sauce.

Gee is the generic Cambodian term for all manner of herbs, used in cooking, served up by the plateful to be eaten on the side, or taken medicinally. You'll probably only recognize a few, such as mint and coriander; others include various types of water grass, vines, young tree leaves and weeds.

Pickles made with brine are frequently served in Cambodia as an appetizer or a side dish, and as a filling for baguettes. There are many variations, made from combinations of cabbage, cucumber, ginger, turnip, bamboo shoots, onions and bean sprouts, often sculpted into shapes for extra visual appeal. Green papaya salad, made from shredded green papaya, dried shrimp, and fish paste topped with crushed peanut, is served up as a dish in restaurants, to be eaten as a starter or snack.

Desserts and sweetmeats

Specialist stalls, opening around lunchtime in the markets or in the late afternoon and evening along the street, serve Cambodian **desserts** in a vast range of colours and textures. Small custards, jellies and sticky-rice confections are displayed in large flat trays and cut or shaped into bite-sized pieces to be served in bowls, topped with grated ice and a slug of condensed milk; mixes of dried and crystallized fruits, beans and nuts are also on offer, served with ice and syrup. Other desserts include sweet sticky rice mixed with corn kernels, mung beans or lotus seed, poached pumpkin with syrup, and palm fruit with syrup, all of which are served up from large bowls by market stalls.

Khmer restaurants seldom serve desserts other than fresh fruit, though recently a few upmarket places are starting to offer them along with imported ice creams. Large towns have a sprinkling of bakeries producing a variety of **cakes**, many of which are approximations of familiar goodies, including custard-filled éclairs, small sponges and coconut tarts. Market stalls in all towns sell small, freshly baked sponge cakes. In Phnom Penh, Siem Reap and Sihanoukville you'll find Western-style cakes and pastries.

Fruits

Colourful **fruit** stalls can be found everywhere in Cambodia, and the selection is enormous – stallholders will always let you try before you buy if you don't know what you're looking at. Imported apples, pears and grapes are also available, though comparatively expensive.

Even **bananas** come in several varieties, some of which are seldom seen in the West; they're grown just about everywhere, and are sold in huge quantities – cheaply at around 1000 riel a hand – for snacking, cooking and as offerings for the pagoda. Quite easy to find are *jayk oumvong*, which is slender and stays green when ripe; *jayk numvar*, a medium-sized, plump, yellow banana, said to cool the body; and the finger-sized, very sweet *jayk pong mowan*, said to be warming, which is a little pricier than the other varieties. Relatively uncommon are the large, dry and fibrous red or green bananas, generally used for cooking.

The **durian** is a rugby-ball-sized fruit with a hard, spiky exterior. Much sought after by Khmers, it's an acquired taste for most Westerners as it has a rather fetid smell. Inside are several segments, each containing two or three stones surrounded by pale-yellow, creamy-textured flesh, which can be quite addictive once you've got over the odour.

Longans have a long season and are often sold still on the twig. The fruit are cherry-sized and have a hard brown skin; the flesh inside is similar to that of lychees in texture and flavour. Bright green and prickly skinned, **soursops** are pure white inside and have a tart but sweet taste. Hard, round and a bit like a bright green cricket ball, **guavas** have a crunchy, dry texture a bit like a hard pear. The flat brown pods of **tamarind** are simple to eat: split open the pods and discard the fibrous thread inside, then suck off the rich brown tangy flesh, but mind the hard seeds. The most picturesque of Khmer fruits, though, has to be the rosy-pink **dragon fruit**, from a climbing cactus-like vine. Inside its waxy skin, the moist pure white flesh is dotted with black seeds and has quite a subtle taste, verging on bland.

Drinks

Bottled water is found everywhere, as Cambodian **tap water** isn't considered safe to drink. Be aware that the ice that's invariably added to cold drinks (unless you request otherwise) may not be hygienic except in Western restaurants; for more on this, see p.43.

Tea and coffee

Cambodians drink plenty of **green tea**, which is readily available in coffee shops and from market stalls; it's normally served free of charge with food in restaurants. If you like your tea strong, try **dtai grolab**, made by putting water and a mass of tea leaves into a small glass, placing a saucer on top, and turning the whole thing upside down to brew. When it's dark enough, the tea is decanted into another cup and plenty of sugar added, but no milk. **Lemon tea**, made with Chinese red dust tea and lemon juice, is refreshing both hot and iced, and is generally served with a hefty dose of sugar. **Indian tea**, sold locally under the Lipton brand, is only served in hotels and restaurants that cater to foreigners.

Noodle shops, coffee shops and restaurants serve **coffee** from early morning to late afternoon, but in the evenings it can be difficult to find except at restaurants geared up for foreigners. The beans are generally imported from Laos and Vietnam – domestically produced coffee from Rattanakiri and Mondulkiri is seldom used in the country. Each shop generally blends the coffee to its own particular recipe, adding wine, butter or chocolate powder during the roasting process, resulting in a thick, strong brew. White coffee is served with a slug of sweetened condensed milk already at the bottom of the glass, so don't stir it all in if you don't like your drink too sweet. Black coffee will often be served with sugar unless you specify otherwise.

Cambodians often have their coffee or tea **iced**, even for breakfast; if you want yours hot, ask for it to be served *ot dak tuk kork*, without ice. Most of the milk available is either sterilized, canned or sweetened condensed; when not added to coffee or tea, it's sometimes drunk iced, perhaps with a bright red or green cordial added.

Juices and fizzy soft drinks

For a drink on the hoof, iced **sugar-cane juice**, *tuk umpow*, is very refreshing and not actually that sweet. It costs 500–1000 riel a glass and is sold everywhere from yellow carts equipped with a wringer through which the peeled canes are passed, sometimes with a piece of orange added for extra taste. Equally refreshing is the juice of a **green coconut** (1500–2500 riel): the top is cut off and you drink the juice before getting it cut in half so you can eat the soft, jelly-like flesh.

Fruit shakes, *tuk krolok*, are an important part of an evening's entertainment: juice stalls, recognizable by their fruit displays and blenders, set up in towns all over the country from the late afternoon. You can order a mixture of fruits to be juiced or just one or two; coconut milk, sugar syrup, condensed milk and shaved ice are also added, as is a raw egg (unless you specify otherwise – *ot pong mowan*).

Freshly made **soya milk** is sold in the morning by street vendors; the green version is sweetened and thicker than the unsweetened white. Soya milk is also available canned, as is **winter-melon tea**, a juice made from the field melon which has a distinctive sweet, almost earthy taste. **Fizzy soft drinks** such as Coca-Cola, 7-Up and Sprite are widely available either in bottles or increasingly in cans; in many places you'll also be able to get Schweppes tonic and soda water.

Alcohol

Every Cambodian town has its **karaoke bar** where local men hang out of an evening; alcohol is readily available at these and also at the profusion of nightclubs and discos in Phnom Penh, Siem Reap and Sihanoukville.

Besides nightclubs and bars, most restaurants and night-market stalls serve **beer**. Cambodia's national beer is Angkor, brewed by an Australian/Cambodian joint venture in Sihanoukville; it's available in cans, large bottles and sometimes on draught, prices varying from around 4000 riel a can to 6000–8000 riel for a large bottle. Tiger, VB, Beer Lao and ABC Stout are also readily available, and there are many more local brews. Even if already chilled, beer is often drunk iced.

Spirits are generally only found in larger restaurants, nightclubs and Western bars. Imported wines are increasingly available in smarter restaurants and Western-oriented bars, and can be purchased in supermarkets, mini-markets such as those attached some garage (such as Caltex) in larger towns. When not downing beer, Cambodians themselves usually prefer to stick to local, medicinal **rice wines**, which are available at stalls and shops where glasses of the stuff are ladled from large jars containing various plant or animal parts. Though quite sweet, they're strong and barely palatable, but cheap at a few hundred riel for a glass. Another local brew is sugar-palm beer, sold and brewed straight from the bamboo tubes in which the juice is collected (see p.7). It's quite refreshing and readily available in villages, and from vendors in the towns.

Beer girls and taxi girls

Cambodia's **beer girls** will approach you almost before you've sat down in a Cambodian restaurant. Smartly dressed in uniforms colour-coded according to which brand of beer they're promoting, they rely on commissions based on the amount of beer they manage to sell, and will keep opening bottles or cans and topping up your glass, hoping to get you to drink more. You don't pay them for the beer, as the cost is added to your bill at the end by counting up the empties. Beer girls will often drink with Cambodian men to up their consumption, but that's generally as far as it goes, as the beer companies make sure the women get home safely afterwards.

"Decent" Cambodian women neither go to bars nor drink alcohol – indeed it's only in the last few years that they've begun to venture out to restaurants – so, while beer girls are somewhat looked down upon, the **taxi girls** who frequent the karaoke parlours and nightclubs are beyond the pale. Usually from very poor families, they have a role akin to that of hostess, dance partner and sometimes call girl rolled into one. If you invite them to join you at your table or dance with you, the charge will be added to your bill at the end of the evening, as will the cost of their drinks.

Health

Health care in Cambodia is poor. Even the best hospitals have inadequate facilities, low standards of cleanliness and appalling patient care; use them only in the event of dire emergency. For anything serious, get to Bangkok if you are able to travel. Should you have no option but to go to a Cambodian hospital, try to get a friend – ideally, a Khmer-speaker – to accompany you for support.

In Phnom Penh a couple of private Western-oriented **clinics** offer slightly better care at increased cost. If you get ill outside Phnom Penh, self-diagnosis and treatment is often better than visiting a clinic. Wherever you seek medical attention, you will be expected to pay upfront for treatment, medication and food.

Although every town has a number of **pharmacies** (typically open daily 7am–8pm) stocking an extensive range of medications, the staff aren't required to have a dispensing qualification, so you may want to check the product sheets (and even expiry dates) before you buy. The exception is Phnom Penh, which does have a couple of reputable pharmacies (see p.114) employing qualified personnel, who can help with diagnosis and remedies for simple health problems.

Consider getting a pre-trip **dental check-up** if you're travelling for an extended period, as the only place to get dental treatment in Cambodia is in Phnom Penh; elsewhere you'll have to grin and bear it. If you wear **glasses**, it's worth taking along a copy of your prescription (or a spare pair of glasses); you can get replacements made quite cheaply in Phnom Penh.

Medical resources for travellers

UK and Ireland

British Airways Travel Clinics ☎0845/600 2236, ⓦwww.britishairways.com/travel /healthclinintro/public/en.gb. Lists your nearest clinic.
Hospital for Tropical Diseases Travel Clinic ☎0845/155 5000 or ☎020/7387 4411, ⓦwww .thehtd.org.
MASTA (Medical Advisory Service for Travellers Abroad) ☎0870/606 2782, ⓦwww .masta.org or. Lists your nearest clinic.

Travel Medicine Services ☎028/9031 5220.
Tropical Medical Bureau Republic of Ireland ☎1850/487 674, ⓦwww.tmb.ie.

US and Canada

CDC ☎1-877/394-8747, ⓦwww.cdc.gov/travel. Official US government travel health site.
International Society for Travel Medicine ☎1-770/736-7060, ⓦwww.istm.org. Has a full list of travel health clinics.
Canadian Society for International Health ⓦwww.csih.org. Extensive list of travel health centres.

Australia, New Zealand and South Africa

Travellers' Medical and Vaccination Centre ☎1300/658 844. ⓦwww.tmvc.com.au, Lists travel clinics in Australia, New Zealand and South Africa.

Vaccinations and immunizations

It's worth checking that you are up to date with **routine immunizations**, such as tetanus and diphtheria. For Cambodia, you should consider immunizing yourself against hepatitis A, tuberculosis and typhoid; hepatitis B, rabies and Japanese encephalitis are recommended if you are going to be at a particular risk (for example if you're working in a remote area). You'll need to produce proof that you've been vaccinated against yellow fever in the (admittedly unlikely) event of arriving from an infected area (West and Central Africa, or South America).

It is as well to consult your doctor or travel clinic as early as possible – even while you are planning your trip – since it can take anything up to eight weeks to complete a full course of immunizations (you may also

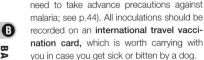

need to take advance precautions against malaria; see p.44). All inoculations should be recorded on an **international travel vaccination card,** which is worth carrying with you in case you get sick or bitten by a dog.

Hepatitis

Hepatitis A, a viral infection of the liver, can be contracted from contaminated food and water – shellfish sold by hawkers and untreated water are particular risks in Cambodia – or by contact with an infected person. Symptoms include dark-coloured urine, aches and pains, nausea, general malaise and tiredness, with jaundice following after a few days. A blood test is needed for diagnosis, and rest, plenty of non-alcoholic fluids and a high carbohydrate diet are recommended for convalescence. A single shot of immunoglobulin offers short-term protection against hepatitis A.

Far more serious is **hepatitis B**, passed via contaminated body fluids; it can be contracted through non-sterile needles (including those used in tattooing and acupuncture), sexual contact or from a blood transfusion that hasn't been properly screened. Symptoms include non-specific abdominal pain, vomiting, loss of appetite, dark-coloured urine and jaundice. Immunization may be recommended if you are staying in Asia for longer than six months. In the event that you think you have contracted hepatitis B, it's especially important to seek medical attention.

A **combined vaccine** has recently become available offering ten years' protection against hepatitis A and five years' against hepatitis B; your doctor will be able to advise on its suitability for you.

Tuberculosis, rabies and tetanus

Tuberculosis, contracted from droplets coughed up by infected persons, is widespread in Cambodia and is a major cause of death in young children. It is quite possible that you will have been inoculated against the disease in childhood, but if you're unsure, consider a skin (Heaf) test, which will determine if you already have immunity.

Rabies is contracted from the bite or saliva of an infected animal. Vaccinations are recommended if you're going to be spending a long time in rural areas. Even if you've been vaccinated, if you are bitten (or licked on an open wound) you will need to get two booster injections as quickly as possible, preferably within 24 to 48 hours.

Tetanus, a bacterial infection which causes muscular cramps and spasms, comes from spores in the earth and can enter the blood circulatory system through wounds and grazes. If left untreated it can cause breathing problems and sometimes death. It's worth checking if you've been vaccinated against tetanus in the last ten years and getting a booster if necessary.

Typhoid and cholera

Bacterial infections that affect the digestive system, typhoid and cholera are spread by contaminated food and water, and outbreaks are thus usually associated with particularly unsanitary conditions.

Symptoms of **typhoid** include tiredness, dull headaches and spasmodic fevers, with spots appearing on the abdomen after about a week. Vaccination is suggested if you plan to stay in rural areas of Cambodia, but it doesn't confer complete immunity, so maintaining good standards of hygiene remains important.

Sudden, watery diarrhoea and rapid dehydration are among the symptoms of **cholera**, and medical advice is essential to treat the infection with antibiotics. Vaccination is no longer recommended for cholera due to its poor efficacy.

General precautions

Cambodia is a hot and humid country, and **dehydration** is a potential problem, its onset indicated by headaches, dizziness, nausea and dark urine. **Cuts** and raw blisters can rapidly become infected and should be promptly treated by cleaning and disinfecting the wound and then applying an air-permeable dressing.

Bites and stings

Insects and **flies** are legion in Cambodia and are at their worst at the start of the dry season. Even during the hot season (March–May) they come out in the evenings, swarming around light bulbs and warm flesh, though they are annoying rather than harmful (with the exception of mosquitos, which can carry dengue fever or malaria – see p.44).

On the coast, **sand flies** appear in the late afternoon and evening, delivering nasty bites which don't erupt until a few hours later, when they become incredibly red and itchy. Once you scratch, the bites become even more inflamed and can take up to a month to recede, leaving behind nasty scars. These little blighters have a limited range and mostly attack victims on the sand; if on or near the beach, it's probably best to use an insect repellent.

Sun and heat

Even when the sky is overcast the Cambodian sun is fierce, and you should take precautions against sunburn and heat stroke wherever you are. Use a high-protection-factor **sunscreen**, wear a hat and drink plenty of fluids throughout the day.

Hygiene and stomach complaints

Though catering facilities at many restaurants and food stalls can appear basic, the **food** you'll be served is usually absolutely fresh; all ingredients are bought daily and are mostly cooked to order. A good rule of thumb when selecting a place to eat is to pick one that is popular with local people, as the Khmers are fussy about their food and seldom give a place a second chance if they've found the food isn't fresh. Food from street hawkers is usually okay if it's cooked in front of you. Bottled water is available everywhere and it's best to stick to drinking that and to be cautious with ice, which is often cut up in the street from large blocks and handled by plenty of people before it gets to your glass (though in Western restaurants it will probably come from an ice-maker).

Stomach complaints

The most common travellers' ailment is **upset tummy**. Travellers' **diarrhoea** often occurs in the early days of a trip as a result of a simple change in diet; it can also be due to food poisoning, indicated by stomach cramps and vomiting. If symptoms persist for more than a couple of days, seek medical help as you may need antibiotics to clear up the problem.

Most diarrhoea is short-lived and can be handled by drinking plenty of fluids and avoiding rich or spicy food. Activated charcoal tablets sold across the counter at pharmacies help by absorbing the bad bugs in your gut and usually speed recovery. It's often a good idea to rest up for a day or two if your schedule allows. In the event of persistent diarrhoea or vomiting, it's worth taking **oral rehydration salts**, available at most pharmacies (or make your own from half a teaspoon of salt and eight teaspoons of sugar per litre of bottled water).

Unless you're going on a long journey, avoid taking Imodium and Lomotil. These bung you up by stopping gut movements and can extend the problem by preventing your body expelling the bugs that gave rise to the diarrhoea in the first place.

Dysentery and giardiasis

If there is blood or mucus in your faeces and you experience severe stomach cramps, you may have dysentery, which requires immediate medical attention. There are two forms of the disease, the more serious of which is **amoebic dysentery**. Even though the symptoms may well recede over a few days, the amoebae will remain in the gut and can go on to attack the liver; treatment with an antibiotic, metronidazole (Flagyl) is thus essential. Equally unpleasant is **bacillary dysentery**, also treated with antibiotics.

Giardiasis is caused by a protozoa usually found in streams and rivers. Symptoms, typically watery diarrhoea and bad-smelling wind, appear around two weeks after the organism has entered the system and can last for up to two weeks. Giardiasis can be diagnosed from microscope analysis of stool samples, and is treated with metronidazole.

Mosquito-borne diseases

Given the prevalence in Cambodia of serious diseases spread by mosquitoes, including drug-resistant malaria, it is important to **avoid being bitten**. In the provinces and high-risk areas – around lakes for example

– most guesthouses provide **mosquito nets**; if there isn't one in your room, make sure to ask. Some guesthouses don't provide nets as they have installed window screens, but these are seldom completely effective as mosquitoes can also get in through ventilators or the gaps under doors. It's also worth asking for your room to be sprayed with insecticide when you go out in the evening; the disgusting stuff will have time to dissipate by the time you return.

Wearing long trousers, socks and a long-sleeved top will reduce the chances of being bitten. **Insect repellents** containing DEET are the most effective, although you may want to consider a natural alternative such as those based on citronella.

Malaria

The primary killer of both children and adults in Cambodia, **malaria** is prevalent year-round, throughout the country – with the exception of Phnom Penh and the area closest to the Tonle Sap. Malaria is still a risk in Siem Reap and at Angkor Wat. It is contracted from the night-biting female *anopheles* mosquito, which injects a parasite into the bloodstream. Chills, fevers and sweating ensue after an incubation period of around twelve days, often along with aching joints, a cough and vomiting, and the symptoms repeat after a couple of days. In Cambodia the dangerous **falciparum** strain of the disease predominates; if untreated, it can be fatal.

Before you travel, it is important to take advice on a suitable **prophylaxis** regime, as a course of antimalarial medication needs to be started in advance of arriving in a risk area. **Mefloquine** (aka Larium) may be recommended, but has much-publicized side effects which should be discussed with your doctor. If you take it, you'll need to start a couple of weeks before you enter the malarial area and continue medication for at least four weeks after leaving, to cover the incubation period of the parasite. In western Cambodia, the malarial parasite is often mefloquine-resistant; alternatives are the antibiotic **doxycycline**, which should be taken a couple of days before you enter the malarial zone and continued for two weeks after you leave, or Malarone, an atovaquone/proguanil combination that has recently been approved. Note that taking antimalarials doesn't guarantee that you won't contract the disease, a fact which reinforces the need to avoid being bitten.

Emergency treatment for falciparum malaria is 600mg of quinine sulphate, taken three times a day for three days, followed by a single dose of three Fansidar tablets once the quinine course is completed. These tablets are available over the counter at pharmacies throughout Cambodia, but if you suspect malaria you should still see a doctor for a diagnostic blood test.

Dengue fever

Cambodia suffered more than 300 deaths (mainly children) as a result of dengue fever in the summer of 2007. Spread by the day-biting female *aedes* mosquito, **dengue fever** is a viral disease which takes about a week to develop following a bite. It resembles a bad case of flu; symptoms include high fever, aches and pains, headache and backache. After a couple of days a red rash appears on the torso, gradually spreading to the limbs. There may also be abnormal bleeding, which requires medical attention.

No vaccine is available at the time of writing, and there is no effective treatment, although paracetamol can be taken to relieve the symptoms (*not* aspirin, which can increase the potential for bleeding); you should also drink plenty of fluids and get lots of rest. Although the symptoms should improve after five or six days, lethargy and depression can last for a month or more – consult a doctor if symptoms persist. Those who have previously suffered from dengue fever are at particular risk if they subsequently contract a different virus strain, which can result in **dengue haemorrhagic fever**. In this condition the usual symptoms of dengue fever are accompanied by abdominal pain and vomiting; immediate medical help should be sought as this condition can be fatal.

Japanese encephalitis

Japanese encephalitis is a serious viral disease carried by night-biting mosquitoes which breed in the rice fields. The risk is highest between May and October. It's worth considering vaccination if you're going to be in rural areas of Cambodia for over a month or intend to visit during the high-risk period. Symptoms, which appear five to fifteen days after being bitten, include headaches, a stiff neck, flu-like aches and chills; there's no specific treatment, but it's wise to seek medical advice and take paracetamol or aspirin to ease the symptoms.

Sexually transmitted diseases

Cambodia is seriously at risk of an **HIV/ AIDS** epidemic, with one percent of the male population aged between 15 and 49 already infected. It isn't known how the virus first arrived in Cambodia, but a steep rise in the number of prostitutes during the UNTAC years certainly didn't help. A high proportion of Khmer men visit prostitutes and have a cultural aversion to the use of condoms, which sex education programmes haven't resolved. This fact, allied to an increase in intravenous drug abuse, means that the virus is now running unchecked through the population.

Syphilis and **gonorrhoea** are rife, but while both are unpleasant and require a medical diagnosis, they can be treated effectively with antibiotics. Using reliable **condoms** – preferably Western brands – will reduce the chances of contracting an infection.

Other hazards

Severe Acute Respiratory Syndrome, or **SARS**, is a highly contagious virus, first identified in 2002, which is spread through close contact with an affected person. Symptoms include a high temperature (over 38°C), a dry cough and severe breathing difficulties (though it's worth noting that most people with breathing difficulties are likely to be suffering from pneumonia). Cases of SARS have been reported in China, Vietnam and Thailand, but at the time of writing, none has ever been reported in Cambodia.

Avian flu (bird flu) was first identified in poultry in Southeast Asia in 2003. Occurring primarily in wild and domesticated birds (amongst which it is highly contagious and deadly), the virus is spread by contact with affected birds. At the time of writing, the WHO advises that there is no threat to health from the consumption of poultry or poultry products, including eggs. Although most reported cases of the virus have been contracted by bird-to-human contact, experts believe that human-to-human transmission is increasing, although currently only the closest family members of infected people have been contaminated. **Symptoms** are similar to influenza, with fever, sore throat and cough. Seven fatalities from the virus have been confirmed in Cambodia to date, the most recent in early 2007. However, the virus is not thought to pose a serious threat to tourists.

Crime and personal safety

Cambodia is now pretty safe to visit with the major danger being from explosives: it remains one of the world's most heavily mined countries and, furthermore, no one knows quite how much ordnance was dropped by the Americans over the country in the 1970s, or how much of it failed to explode. In the countryside, it still pays to observe the simple rule of not leaving well-worn paths.

Crime

On the whole, Cambodians are remarkably honest people (as attested by the money changers who sit unprotected on street corners surrounded by piles of notes), and crime is not a major problem. If you're using public transport, good care will be taken of your bags, and it's unusual to have anything go missing.

That said, **pickpockets** and petty thieves do operate, and it's advisable to take good care of your purse or wallet, especially in markets, on motos or tuk-tuks and on the beach at Sihanoukville. Incidents of **armed mugging** are not unknown either (some committed by robbers masquerading as police), so if you go out after dark, particularly in Phnom Penh, Siem

---

Children at risk

Cambodia has developed an unfortunate reputation as a destination for paedophiles to the extent that the UK National Crime Squad are advising the Cambodian police of possible sex offenders in their territory, the highest-profile case being when Gary Glitter (now in prison in Vietnam) was deported in 2003. Originally a side-product of the boom in prostitution during the UNTAC years, child sex tourism has recently grown in Cambodia as a result of crackdowns on child prostitution in other Southeast Asian countries, and remains a serious problem in spite of the hefty prison sentences which have been handed out to brothel owners and visitors involved in child sex tourism.

The Ministry of the Interior (National Police) ask that anyone witnessing child prostitution in Cambodia immediately report it to the police **on their national hotline** ☏023/997919 (don't try to take matters into your own hands). You could also consider contacting **ECPAT** (End Child Prostitution in Asian Tourism; ⊛www.ecpat.net). In the UK, US and Australia offenders who commit paedophilia abroad can be prosecuted under the relevant national laws, so you can also report them when you get home: in the UK contact Crimestoppers ☏0800/555 111, ⊛www.crimestoppers-uk.org; in the US contact US Customs Immigration Enforcement on ☏703/274 3900, ⊛www.cybertipline.org; in Australia contact the Australian Federal Police ☏1800/333 000, ⊛www.afp.gov.au. Be aware, however, that there are lots of mixed-race couples in Cambodia and, consequently, many sons and daughters (actual and adopted) of these relationships – so make sure of your facts before launching into any accusations.

ChildSafe (186 Street 13 Phnom Penh) has a 24-hour hotline to report children at risk ☏012/311 112, ⊛www.childsafe-cambodia.org). The organization aims to protect Cambodian children from abuse. Their guidelines ask that tourists – tempting though it is to try to help – refrain from buying from children and giving money to children or to parents with young children; this is felt to keep them on the streets and in vulnerable situations. Instead, they ask that you help by supporting social workers or purchase products and services that sport the ChildSafe logo.

Reap and Sihanoukville, it's wise to leave most of your money in the safe at your hotel or guesthouse, taking just enough cash for the evening.

If you are held up by muggers or armed robbers, don't resist and put yourself in danger, but do report the incident to the **police** as soon as possible – you'll need a signed, dated report from them to claim on your travel insurance – and, if you lose your passport, to your embassy as well. In Phnom Penh, Siem Reap and Sihanoukville, English-speaking **tourist police** will help, but in the provinces you'll have to deal with the local police, who are unlikely to have more than a smattering of English, so try to take a Khmer-speaker with you, if possible.

Though the vast majority of Cambodian police will do their best to help in an emergency, a small minority are not averse to trying to elicit money from foreigners. If you're riding a motorbike or driving a motor vehicle, they may well deem that you've committed an offence. You can argue the "fine" down to a few dollars and may as well pay up, although if you can stand the hassle and don't mind wasting a lot more time you may feel it worth reporting such incidents to the police commissioner.

Road accidents usually attract vast crowds of curious onlookers, and if any damage to property or injury to a person or domestic animal has occurred, then you'll have to stay at the scene until the police arrive. It's the driver's responsibility to come to a financial arrangement with the other parties involved. In spite of their general amiability, it's not unknown for locals to try to coerce foreigners into coughing up money, even if they are the innocent party or merely a passenger.

There are occasional instances of **banditry** in the provinces, though such events are rare and aren't targeted at tourists. Incidents involving grenades or bombs going off also occur occasionally, but these are generally the result of local disputes, quite often over protection rackets, and have nothing to do with tourism.

Drugs offences

The possession and use of marijuana (called *ganja* locally), cocaine and heroin

are illegal. Although the penalty for drugs offences does not include the death sentence as in some other Southeast Asian countries, it is likely to entail a lengthy prison sentence which, in the absence of repatriation agreements with other countries, is likely to have to be spent in full in a Cambodian jail.

Land mines and unexploded ordnance

Over ten million **land mines** were laid in Cambodia between 1979 and 1991. The Vietnamese and the government laid them as protection against Khmer Rouge guerrillas, who in turn laid them to intimidate local populations; neither side recorded the locations of the minefields. Though over two thousand minefields have now been identified (usually through members of the local population being blown up), they are thought to represent just a small fraction of the total number. Three NGOs are actively working at demining the countryside, but given the scale of the problem, it may be a couple of generations before the mines are cleared completely (see p.147 for more).

Although the Angkor temple complexes are safe, mines are still a risk in the countryside around Siem Reap and in many other areas of the country; the border with Thailand, from Koh Kong to Preah Vihear, is particularly hazardous. In rural areas, take care not to leave well-trodden paths and don't take short cuts across rice fields without a local guide. Badly contaminated areas are signed with a red skull and the words "Beware Mines".

As if this problem weren't enough, in the 1970s the United States dropped over half a million tonnes of bombs on Cambodia. This began as part of a secret and illicit plan to expose the Ho Chi Minh Trail used by communist North Vietnamese troops, and ended up in a massive countrywide bombing campaign to support the pro-American Lon Nol government fighting the Khmer Rouge. **Unexploded ordnance** (UXO) remains a risk in rural areas, with the southeast, centre and northeast of the country particularly affected; in the countryside it's sensible not to pick up or kick any unidentified metal objects.

Money

Alongside the local currency, the riel, Cambodia has assimilated the US dollar into its economy, a situation that began with UNTAC in the early 1990s, when high-earning troops stationed in the country began spending their dollar salaries. Today you can use the dollar and riel interchangeably in all but a few cases.

Currency

Riel notes (there are no riel coins, nor is US coinage used in Cambodia) are available in denominations of 100, 500, 1000, 2000, 5000, 10,000, 50,000 and 100,000 (a new style of smaller-sized notes was introduced in 2002, these now circulate alongside older notes and can be used interchangeably; you may also be passed an old 200 riel note, which is valid although no new notes of this denomination are being issued). The **exchange rate** is stable at around 4000 riel to the dollar; the best rates can be had in Phnom Penh, usually around Psar Thmei.

You can **pay** for most things purely in dollars, or purely in riel, or using a mixture of the two currencies; the larger the amount the more likely it is that the price will be quoted in dollars – note that the exchange rate when paying for dollar services in riel is around two to three percent inferior to the rate at the money changer. Generally, you'll be charged in dollars for accommodation, when shopping in supermarkets or eating in Western restaurants, and when paying for air tickets and some boat fares. In markets, at noodle shops and food stalls, and when using local transport (such as motos, tuk-tuks, buses and pick-ups) prices are in riel (unless you wish to hire transport for the day, in which case you're likely to be quoted a dollar price). Things get a bit more confused near the Thai border, where people prefer to deal in the Thai currency, baht, or at Bavet, the Vietnamese border crossing where you may be quoted in dong. If you don't have baht you can generally pay in US dollars or riel, though you might end up paying fractionally more – you can change riel and dollars into baht at local money changers. Throughout the guide, prices are given in the currency in which you're most likely to be charged.

In the provinces, any dollars you carry should ideally be in small denominations, as these can be used to pay for local services or changed easily at the markets. When paying in dollars, **change** will be usually be given back in dollars for larger amounts, while for small sums you'll be given riel.

Bargaining

Prices at deluxe hotels, shops, and all food stalls, noodle shops and restaurants are fixed, as are fares for flights, bus journeys and boat trips. However, when shopping in markets, taking motos, tuk-tuks or cyclos and hiring a car, bargaining is pretty much expected. Mid-range hotel prices can often be negotiated, although at the budget end, guesthouse owners will seldom budge on price, preferring to leave the room empty.

Carrying your money

The safest way to carry your money is as US-dollar **traveller's cheques** from either American Express or Thomas Cook, both of which brands are well known in Cambodia; cheques from other providers aren't widely accepted.

The usual fee for traveller's cheque sales is one or two percent, though this may be waived if you buy the cheques through a bank where you have an account. It pays to get a selection of denominations. Make sure to keep the purchase agreement and a record of cheque serial numbers safe and separate from the cheques themselves. In the event that cheques are lost or stolen, the issuing company will expect you to report the loss forthwith. None of the issuing companies is represented in Cambodia, though Thomas Cook will replace lost cheques by transferring funds using Moneygram or Western Union.

Arriving in Cambodia there are ATMs at Phnom Penh international airport and at Siem Reap airport so you can get $US cash as soon as you arrive; you'll only be able to change traveller's cheques at Phnom Penh and Siem Reap airports at one of the banks. If you arrive by road you'll need to get to one of the main towns to change cheques. Note also that unless you have obtained a **Cambodian visa** in advance, you'll need $20 in cash to buy one on arrival.

Credit cards, banks and ATMs

An increasing number of places now accept **credit cards**, typically mid- and upper-range hotels and Western-oriented restaurants and shops in Phnom Penh, Siem Reap and Sihanoukville. Use of credit cards is increasing but is still not as prevalent as in the West; card payment may also attract a four-percent surcharge.

You can get a **cash advance** on Visa or MasterCard at banks in Phnom Penh, Battambang, Siem Reap and Sihanoukville, and at branches of the Canadia Bank, and some Acleda (pronounced *A-See-Lay-Dah*) banks, in most major towns. There are ATMs in Phnom Penh, Siem Reap, Sihanoukville and Battambang; note, though, that your money will be dispensed in US dollars. It's worth remembering that all cash advances are treated as loans, with interest accruing daily from the date of withdrawal; there may be a transaction fee on top of this.

Banking hours throughout Cambodia are generally Monday to Friday 8.30am to 3.30pm (often also Sat 8.30–11.30am).

Changing money

Banks (other than Acleda Bank) do not change foreign currency into riel, so to **change dollars to riel**, you'll need to go to a **money changer** (apart from Thai baht, pounds sterling and euros, it's difficult to exchange other currencies, although you'll possibly be able to do so at Psar Thmei in Phnom Penh and around the market in Siem Reap). Money changers are plentiful in all towns and are always found around markets, typically within goldsmiths' or

jewellers' kiosks – look for the cabinets stacked with notes. When changing money, the dealer will do the sums on a calculator for you to agree, before counting out the notes in front of you; it is accepted practice that you then recount the money, as any discrepancy will not be considered once you've left the desk. Feel free to reject any notes in particularly dire condition. While riel are accepted regardless of condition, a dollar bill with even a minuscule blemish will be returned as unacceptable.

When changing money, it's better to opt for mid-value notes – 5000 or 10,000 riel for instance – which can be changed more readily at stalls. Outside of market hours, you can still change dollars at shops, especially those selling phone cards; you'll need to ask around, and the rates will be worse to the tune of a few riel per dollar. If you are given brand-new notes check the rate, as artful money changers will sometimes give you less than the advertised rate (new notes being perceived as somehow carrying slightly more value); if so, ask for the difference or say you'll accept old notes.

You can change riel back into dollars at most money changers when **leaving the country**, or into baht at money changers in Poipet. It's impossible to exchange riel once you've left the country.

Cashing traveller's cheques

Most major banks will cash dollar traveller's cheques (into dollars only) for a two-percent commission. Traveller's cheques in other currencies are sometimes viewed with suspicion and may be rejected. Don't rely on using traveller's cheques as payment for services or on cashing them other than at the banks, as they are accepted at very few outlets.

In Phnom Penh, the Foreign Trade Bank of Cambodia (Mon–Fri 8am–4pm) charges just a one-percent commission for cashing traveller's cheques, but is rather bureaucratic: take both your passport and your purchase receipts with you.

Wiring money

Having money **wired from home** using Western Union or Moneygram is never convenient or cheap, and should be considered as a last resort. It's also possible to have money wired directly from a bank in your home country to a bank account in Cambodia. If you choose this route, your home bank will need the name and address of the Cambodian bank, their bank code and your account name and number; money wired this way normally takes three to five working days to arrive

and costs around £25/$35 per transaction (you'll also have to pay a handling fee in Cambodia). Both the Acleda Bank and the Cambodia Asia Bank handle Western Union transfers, while the Canadia Bank is the agent for Moneygram;

Western Union UK ☎ 0800/833 833, Ireland ☎ 1800/395395, US & Canada ☎ 1-800/325-6000, Australia & New Zealand ☎ 0800/005253; ⓦ www .westernunion.com.

The media

Much of Cambodia's media is sponsored by the country's political parties, and though the prime minister has declared his support for press freedom, the media continues to be subject to the government's whims. There's a reasonable selection of English-language media, with two newspapers, a selection of magazines, plus satellite/cable TV and radio stations.

Newspapers and magazines

Cambodia has a surprisingly wide choice of **Khmer-language publications**, including around seven daily newspapers and a selection of monthly magazines, though they're only available in the capital and a few provincial towns. All the newspapers are pretty sensationalist, splashing graphic pictures of accidents and murders over their front pages; you're most likely to come across *Reaksmei Kampuchea* and *Kaoh Santepheap*, both pro-government.

Cambodia's **English-language newspapers**, the *Cambodia Daily* (published daily except Sunday) and the *Phnom Penh Post* (alternate Fridays) can be found at newsstands around Phnom Penh, Battambang, Siem Reap and Sihanoukville. The *Cambodia Daily* carries a selection of foreign and domestic news, while the *Phnom Penh Post* contains Cambodian news and features. Newsstands also sell the weekly French-language paper, *Cambodge Soir*, covering both international and local news.

It's also worth looking out for the several English-language magazines. *Cambodia*

Scene is a glossy magazine (bi-monthly, $2) which runs Cambodia-based features on people, crafts and places, and which you can buy at a few newsstands and craft shops in Phnom Penh. *Bayon Pearnik* is a free satirical monthly, usually containing a travel feature on an unusual Cambodian destination and advertising bar and club launches; it's available in Internet shops and Western restaurants in Phnom Penh and (sometimes) in Siem Reap. *Asia Life* (free from cafés and restaurants) is the *Time Out* of Phnom Penh with a host of articles related to new things happening in the city. *Globe* ($4) is available in Western bars and restaurants, and although focused on Cambodia, it takes a broader look at current affairs and economic events in the region, and includes items of consumer interest.

Radio

Among the many **Khmer radio stations**, just a couple carry English programmes. The principal local station listened to by foreigners is **97.5 FM**, featuring a mix of Western pop and news stories; Love FM 99 plays Western music and conducts phone-ins about the local entertainment scene. You'll only be able to pick up these programmes in the capital, however.

English-language broadcasts can be heard throughout the country on short wave on the BBC World Service (visit ⓦwww .bbc.co.uk/worldservice for frequencies and schedules), Voice of America (ⓦwww .voa.gov), Radio Canada International (ⓦwww.rcinet.ca) and ABC Radio Australia (ⓦwww.abc.net.au/ra). The BBC World Service is available 24 hours a day in the capital on 100 MHz FM; ABC Radio Australia also broadcasts 24 hours a day on 101.5 MHz FM in Phnom Penh and Siem Reap.

Television

The Cambodians are TV addicts and even in the remotest villages you'll find people ensconced around someone's battery-powered TV. The country's six **Khmer TV stations** broadcast a mix of political coverage, game shows, concerts, cartoons, sport – kick-boxing is a huge favourite – and Thai soaps dubbed into Khmer. The state broadcaster TVK, on Channel 7, is owned by the ruling CPP, who also have influence with most of the other channels, apart from Channel 9, which is loyal to FUNCINPEC.

Guesthouses and hotels usually offer **cable TV** (a few may even offer satellite stations), enabling you to watch a vast selection of foreign channels, typically including BBC World, CNN, CNBC, HBO, National Geographic and Star Sport.

Festivals

Cambodians are always celebrating a festival of some sort, heading out to a popular pagoda with family and friends or taking off for the provinces; unsurprisingly, festivals are the busiest times for shopping and travelling.

The major celebrations of the year are **Bonn Chaul Chhnam** (Khmer New Year; mid-April) and **Bonn Pchum Ben** (Festival of the Ancestors; mid-Sept to early Oct). These are festive occasions with everyone gathering at the family home and always involve lots of food and trips to the pagoda. The other big public holiday is Bonn Om Tuk (Water Festival; mid-Oct to late-Nov), which occurs when the waters of the Tonle Sap reverse; activity is mainly centred on Phnom Penh with dragon boat crews from around the country congregating to show off their prowess and massive crowds of supporters thronging the riverfront to cheer them on.

Buddhist **offering days** (exact dates vary from month to month according to the lunar calendar) are also colourful occasions: stalls do a roaring trade in bunches of flowers which are taken to pagodas and used to decorate shrines at home; lotus buds – the traditional offering flower to the Buddha – are artistically folded to expose their pale-pink inner petals, while jasmine buds are threaded onto sticks and strings as fragrant tokens.

For more on festivals, see the *Festivals and ceremonies* colour section; for details of public holidays see box on p.61.

Culture and etiquette

The traditional Cambodian form of greeting is the *sompeyar*, a gesture of extreme politeness as well as a sign of respect. Typically, the *sompeyar* is performed with hands placed palms together, fingers pointing up, in front of the body at chest level, and the head is inclined slightly forward as if about to bow. When greeting monks, however, the hands should be placed in front of the face, and when paying respects to Buddha (or the king), the hands are put in front of the forehead. The *sompeyar* is always used towards those older than yourself, and is taught to children at an early age. The handshake has become common quite recently, and is used between Cambodian men or when Cambodian men greet foreigners; women greeting foreigners, though, still use the *sompeyar*.

Cambodians are reserved people and find **public displays of affection** offensive; people in the provinces are particularly conservative, the chunchiet, Cambodia's minority hilltribe people, even more so. Holding hands or linking arms in public, though quite a common sign of friendship between two men or two women, is considered unacceptable if it involves a member of the opposite sex; even married couples won't touch each other in public. Cambodian women who value their reputation do not go out drinking and dancing and many will not want to be seen out with a man unless he is her fiancé (and even then she will be chaperoned). Things are, of course, different for Cambodian men, who are seen out and about drinking, eating and partying everywhere. However, times are changing, and a more cosmopolitan attitude is gaining ground, particularly in Phnom Penh (and larger towns), where you'll see groups of girls and boys out together, and women eating in restaurants and going out with a group of friends.

Everywhere in Cambodia, travellers will gain more respect if they are **well dressed**. Cambodians themselves dress modestly, men usually wearing long trousers and a shirt. Women wear blouses rather than T-shirts, and sarongs or skirts to below the knee, though in Phnom Penh women often wear trousers or jeans and the younger ones skimpier tops. At formal events men will wear jacket and tie, women a traditional *sampot* – an ankle-length tube of material that you step into and then fold and tuck around the waist. For the tourist, all this means it's best to avoid skimpy clothes and shorts unless you're at the beach, and even there you will be stared at as Cambodians wouldn't dream of exposing any flesh and even now usually go swimming in all their clothes. At Angkor Wat, where things are fairly relaxed due to the level of tourism, smart shorts are acceptable, although shoulders should be covered.

When **visiting pagodas** it's all the more important to wear clothes that keep your shoulders and legs covered. Hats should be removed when passing through the pagoda gate and shoes taken off before you go into any of the buildings (shoes are also removed before entering a Cambodian home). If you sit down on the floor inside the pagoda, do so with your feet to one side, not cross-legged, and don't point your finger or the soles of your feet towards the image of the Buddha (in fact, you should observe the same rule towards people generally, in any location). **Monks** are not allowed to touch women, so women should take care when walking near monks, and should avoid sitting next to monks on public transport.

Displaying anger won't get you far, as the Khmers find this embarrassing and will laugh, not to be provocative, but to hide their confusion. Being rational and calmly assertive will get you much further than getting annoyed. In fact, Cambodians can laugh at apparently inopportune moments, such as after an accident or if they can't understand you – again this is to cover their embarrassment.

Cambodians are intrigued at the **appearance of foreigners**, and it is not considered rude to stare quite intently at visitors. Local people will also giggle at men with earrings – in Cambodia boys are given an earring in the belief it will help an undescended testicle. It's hard to preserve your **personal space** in Cambodia, as Cambodians don't understand why anyone might want to be on their own; as a foreigner, you may find yourself being stared at, or notice that Cambodians deliberately sit near you. You needn't feel disconcerted by this, as it's just a friendly way of showing attention, and people will soon move on.

If you want to **beckon someone**, such as a waiter, don't wave your finger about, as this is considered rude. Instead hold your hand out with the palm facing down, and pull the fingers in towards the palm a few times, as if gripping something.

Shopping

Cambodia has a wide range of souvenirs and handicrafts: colourful textiles ranging from traditionally patterned silks to coarser chunchiet cloth; antiques and curios, such as wooden boxes for betel nut; and religious texts written on prepared palm leaves. Local handicrafts have been given a boost by various training schemes set up to help Cambodia's large disabled population, and there's now a phenomenal variety of quality products available. If you're shopping for items sold by length or weight, Cambodia uses the metric system.

Most shopping takes place in the **markets**, with those in Phnom Penh and Siem Reap offering a good selection of items, and in the capital there are some **specialist markets**, notably Psar Toul Tom Poung (Russian Market), which is the acknowledged place to buy souvenirs – and also motorcycle spares. Local children at the Angkor temples sell bangles, hair slides made from coconut shell, handmade bamboo flutes in colourful woven straw sleeves – all of them costing just a couple of thousand riel. Phnom Penh is proud of its recently opened shopping malls; though more akin to department stores both Sorya Mall and Paragon Mall offer a vast range of consumer goods at fixed prices. In Phnom Penh and Siem Reap you'll also find specialist shops, galleries and hotel boutiques which are much more expensive, though the quality should be significantly better.

As a general rule, buy it when you see it: something unusual you chance upon in the

Bargaining

Prices are fixed in shops, but you're expected to bargain in markets and when buying from hawkers. Bargaining is seen as something of an amicable game, in which both parties aim to win. The seller usually starts at a moderately inflated price: for cheapish items, priced below $10 or so to start with, expect to be able to knock around a third off the starting price, whereas with pricey antiques and curios you'll be lucky to get a reduction of five percent. To keep a sense of perspective while bargaining, it's worth remembering that on items like a T-shirt or *kramar*, the vendor's margin is often just 500–1000 riel.

provinces may not be available in Phnom Penh or Siem Reap. Skor dae traditional drums, for instance, are produced by artisans in Kompong Thom and sold only there.

Concerns from NGOs about the sustainability of harvesting rattan from the wild have yet to be addressed, but if de-forestation continues at its current pace there will be scant forest left in Cambodia to worry about.

Textiles

The ubiquitous chequered scarf, the **kramar**, worn by Cambodian adults and children both male and female, is arguably the country's most popular tourist souvenir, and there are plenty to buy in markets everywhere. **Silk cloth** is also widely available, woven in a variety of traditional designs and colours; in the last few years modern patterns have begun to creep in and can be found in the markets of Phnom Penh. In Rattanakiri, you'll be able to find cloth produced by the **chunchiet**, normally cotton with some synthetic thread mixed in; it's coarser in texture than silk or pure cotton.

Kramars

Many *kramar*s offered to tourists are woven from mixed synthetic threads; although the cloth feels soft, a *kramar* of this sort is hot to wear and doesn't dry very well if you want to use it as a towel. The very best *kramar*s are made from cotton (*umbok*) and are usually to be had from women pedlars in the markets. A large *kramar* costs around 5000–7000 riel.

Though cotton *kramar*s feel stiff and thin at first, a few good scrubs in cold water will soften them up and increase the density of texture. They last for years and actually improve with wear, making a cool, dust-proof and absorbent fabric.

Silk

The weaving of **silk** in Cambodia can be traced back to the Angkor era, when the Khmer started to imitate imported cloth from India. Weaving skills learnt over generations were lost with the Khmer Rouge, but the 1990s saw a resurgence of silk-weaving in many Cambodian villages (the thread is usually imported from Vietnam, though a few Cambodian villages have again started

to keep their own silkworms). Most of the cloth is produced to order for the dealers and silk-sellers of Phnom Penh, so if you visit a village where silk is woven, don't be surprised if they haven't any fabric for sale. Unpatterned silk is sometimes available by the metre in dark and pastel colours.

Silk is produced in fixed widths – nearly always 800mm – and sold in two lengths: a **kabun** (3.6m), sufficient for a long straight skirt and short-sleeved top; and a **sampot** (half a *kabun*), which is enough for a long skirt. A *sampot* starts at around $15, but you can easily pay double this depending on quality and design. Sometimes the silk will have been washed, which makes it softer in both texture and hue – and slightly more expensive. **Silk scarves** are inexpensive ($4–5) and readily available. They come in a range of colours and are usually pre-washed, with the ends finished in hand-tied knots.

There are several different styles of fabric, with villages specializing in particular types of weaving. **Hol** is a time-honoured cloth decorated with small patterns symbolizing flowers, butterflies and diamonds, and traditionally produced with threads of five basic colours – yellow, red, black, green and blue (modern variations use pastel shades). The vibrant, shimmering hues change depending on the direction from which they are viewed. **Parmoong** is a lustrous ceremonial fabric, made by weaving a motif or border of gold or silver thread onto plain silk. Some *parmoong* is woven exclusively for men in checks or stripes of cream, green or red, to be worn in sarongs. Traditional wall-hangings, **pedan**, come in classical designs often featuring stylized temples and animals such as elephants and lions; they're inexpensive ($5–10) and easily carried.

Chunchiet cloth

The **chunchiet** weave a range of cloth, employing generally simple designs based on a range of stripes woven with a motif, which could be a bird and animal or perhaps a helicopter. Traditionally the colours would have been from natural dyes in muted black, dark blue, red or cream; the weave was quite loose, giving a fairly coarse but quite durable fabric. Increasingly though, textiles are made from mixed-fibre thread; this gives a wider range of colours, although some can be startlingly bright, with the advantage that the dyes are colourfast.

Wood and marble carvings

Wood carvings are available in a wide range of sizes, from small heads of Jayavarman VII, modelled on the bust in the National Museum and costing just a couple of dollars, to almost life-sized dancing apsaras at $50 or more. In Phnom Penh you'll find a good selection along Street 178 near the National Museum, or in Psar Toul Tom Poung, though the fact that they're mass-produced means that they lack certain finesse; to find something really fine you're better off at the workshop of the Chantiers École in Siem Reap.

Marble carvings, varnished to a glossy finish, can be bought in the capital or Siem Reap, or directly from workshops in Pursat, where they are produced. Although some pieces – the Angkor Wat towers are one obvious example – are rather tacky, there are plenty of other items to choose from, including Buddha and animal statues.

Antiques and curios

Phnom Penh is the only place to find antiques and curios, with plenty of specialist stalls in and around Psar Toul Tom Poung. Look out for the partitioned **wooden boxes** used to store betel-chewing equipment (see *Festivals and ceremonies* colour section); you'll also find elegant silver boxes for the nuts, phials for the leaves and paste, and cutters – a bit like shears – for slicing the betel nuts. There are plenty of **religious artefacts** available too, ranging from wooden Buddha images and other carvings, to brass bowls and offering plates.

You may occasionally find antiquated traditional **musical instruments**, such as the *chapei*, a stringed instrument with a long neck and a round sound box; and the *chhing*, two small brass plates similar to castanets in appearance, played by brushing them against each other.

Compasses used in the ancient Chinese art of feng shui can be bought for just a few dollars; they indicate compass directions related to the five elements – wood, fire,

earth, metal and water. You might also be able to search out **opium weights**, used to weigh out the drug and often formed in the shape of small human figures or animals.

Be aware that Cambodians are expert at artificially ageing their wares, so if you intend to pay a lot for an item, be sure that you want it for its own sake rather than because it's verifiably authentic. Cambodia's ancient temples have suffered massively from looting, and although it's unlikely that you'll be offered ancient figurines in Phnom Penh (most of the trade goes to Bangkok or Singapore), many other stolen artefacts – such as chunchiet funerary statues from Rattanakiri – are finding their way to the capital, so rather than encouraging the looters, avoid buying anything purporting to be an antique.

Woven baskets, rattan and bamboo

A versatile fibre, **rattan** is used to produce furniture – sold in Phnom Penh and popular with Cambodia's expats – and household items such as baskets, bowls and place-mats, which are sold in the markets of Phnom Penh and Siem Reap. Difficult to track down are the small, fine baskets produced around Oudong, which are made by weaving the *kunung* vine; the best place to buy them is the hill at the site itself, where there's a good selection of pieces for a few thousand riel each.

In Rattanakiri you can find **khapa**, deep, conical rattan-and-bamboo baskets fitted with shoulder straps so that they can be worn on the back; they cost $6–10 and are still used by the chunchiet to carry produce to market. Everyday items made from rattan and bamboo and available in the markets can also make interesting souvenirs, including noodle ladles and nested baskets; the latter are used to measure out portions of rice but are also useful for storing fruit and vegetables.

Silver and gold

Most of the **silverware** in Cambodia is sold in Phnom Penh and produced in villages nearby, particularly at Kompong Luong, which can easily be visited as part of a trip to Oudong. The price will give you an indication of whether an item is solid silver or silver-plated copper – a few dollars for the silver-plated items; more than double that for a comparable item in solid silver.

Small silver or silver-plated boxes in the shape of fruits or animals are delightful and make terrific, inexpensive gifts. Considerably more expensive are ceremonial plates and offering bowls, usually made of solid silver and intricately decorated with leaf motifs. Silver necklaces, bracelets and earrings, mostly imported from Indonesia, are sold only for the tourist market (Khmers don't rate the metal for jewellery) and go for just a few dollars in the markets; modern silver designer jewellery is also available, in the NGO-run shops and hotel boutiques of Phnom Penh and Siem Reap.

There's nothing sentimental or romantic about the Khmer obsession with **gold jewellery** – which Cambodians see as a means of investment. This in part explains the hundreds of gold dealers in and around the markets all over the country, where it's not unusual to see local people negotiating to trade in their jewellery for more expensive pieces. Gold is good value and items can be made up quickly and quite cheaply to your own design, and even set with gems from the mines of Pailin and Rattanakiri.

Travelling with children

With the population of Cambodia spiralling it's easy to feel that the country is full of children; but travelling through Cambodia with your children is not for the nervous parent. Not only is health care poor, but the protectiveness of the West is non-existent and there are no special facilities or particular concessions made for them. That said Cambodians adore children, although they do have a habit of greeting them with an affectionate pinch, which can be a little painful; foreign children are not exempt. On public transport, children travel free if they share your seat; otherwise expect to pay around a third less than the adult fare. If you need an extra bed in your room for your child, hotels will charge a third less than the rate for an extra adult to share.

In the tourist centres of Phnom Penh, Siem Reap and Sihanoukville you'll be able to buy disposable nappies, formula milk and tins or jars of baby food. Outside these cities you need to take your own supplies.

There are no real activities designed for children, but with a little ingenuity resourceful parents should get by. In Phnom Penh, Monument Books sells children's books and a limited supply of Western games and toys; a ride around Wat Phnom on Sambo should pass an hour or so. At Sihanoukville, the gently shelving beaches of Ochheuteal or Sokha are pretty safe, with parental supervision; while at Siem Reap clambering over ancient monuments should tire even quite long legs.

Travel essentials

Costs

On the whole, Cambodia is an inexpensive place to visit and prices at the lower end of the market have scarcely changed in the last fifteen years. Outside the upmarket hotels tipping is not expected, but a few hundred riel extra for a meal or a moto ride is appreciated.

Budget **rooms** are available for $5 across the country, and eating is also cheap – you'll pay around $1–2 for a breakfast of noodles and a coffee at a cheap restaurant or noodle shop, and around the same for a lunch or dinner of two dishes with rice (although a meal in a Western-oriented restaurant will set you back around $4–5). The cheapest bottled water costs a fairly constant 600 riel per litre pretty much everywhere, while a can of Coke is 2000 riel and Angkor beer is $1 per can, $2.5 for a large bottle.

The most economical form of **transport** is in the back of a pick-up truck, the price of a trip varying according to the distance involved and the state of the road – during the rainy season (June–Oct) fares can rise by around twenty percent. Fares also rise a bit over holidays, particularly the Khmer New Year. That said, even the most arduous trip in the country, the eight-hour drive from Phnom Penh to Sen Monorom in Mondulkiri, costs no more than 30,000 riel in the back of a truck (or 50,000 riel inside). Speed and comfort come at a price: Phnom Penh–Siem Reap by plane is $75 ($6 by bus), but these options don't exist on many routes. Train travel is also incredibly cheap (6500 riel from Phnom Penh to Battambang, for example).

Staying in guesthouses, eating at noodle shops and cheap restaurants and travelling on public transport can be done on just $10–15 a day. If you want to stay in mid-range hotels, eat three Western-oriented meals per day and get around by hiring a car with a driver you'll need around $75 per day. And if you want to sample the best in luxury accommodation and top-notch food that Phnom Penh and Siem Reap have to offer, you could spend two or three hundred dollars a day.

Although it doesn't happen as blatantly as in Vietnam, foreigners in Cambodia are charged a **premium** in a number of situations. For example, a Cambodian pays $10 less than a foreigner to use the express boat between Phnom Penh and Siem Reap, and sights targeted at foreign tourists also have a dual-pricing policy, most notably Angkor, which is free for Cambodians but costs foreigners $20 for a day pass.

A **sales tax** (comprising a ten percent government tax and ten percent service) is often charged in mid-range hotels. Where this applies, it should be advertised on an English sign at reception.

Customs

You will need to fill out a **customs declaration** on arrival in Cambodia, although customs requirements are fairly loose and baggage checks are rare. On entry, you're allowed four hundred cigarettes (or the equivalent in cigars or tobacco), one bottle of spirits and a "reasonable" amount of perfume. You cannot bring in more than US$10,000 in cash, or take out more than 100,000 riel.

Transport costs

As we go to print, fuel prices in Cambodia have suddenly doubled (to 7000 riel per litre). Naturally this will be passed on in the fares charged for transport; it has not been taken account of in the costs given in this Guide. At the time of writing the exchange rate remains at around 4000 riel to the dollar.

Electricity

The electrical supply is 220 volts AC, 50Hz. Cambodian sockets take two-pin flat-pronged plugs. In the towns the supply is pretty reliable, although during the night some hotels do switch to generators which can be noisy. In some towns there may be power cuts from time to time, while in smaller towns there may only be power until 9pm or 10pm; in rural areas most villages survive on a generator and batteries. If you buy electrical goods in Cambodia, note that you might need a transformer or to adjust their voltage setting before use abroad.

Entry and Exit requirements

Visas for Cambodia are required by everyone other than nationals of Laos, Malaysia, the Philippines and Singapore. These are issued on arrival at Phnom Penh and Siem Reap international airports, and at all overland crossings from Thailand and Vietnam and at Voen Kham from Laos. Arriving overland, make sure that the officials at the border put an entry stamp in your passport, as not having one is likely to cause hassle when you eventually leave the country. Single-entry tourist **e-visas** are available on line, but they are only supported if you enter through the airports at Phnom Penh or Siem Reap, or overland at Cham Yeam (Koh Kong). They are valid for three months from the date of issue and there's a $5 processing charge.

A single-entry **tourist visa** obtained on arrival ($20; one passport photograph required) is valid for thirty days, including the day of issue, and can be extended once only, for one month. (Note that at the Thai border you may well be charged 1000 baht or more (around $25-30) by Cambodian officials, though if you ask for a receipt this does usually gets reduced to $20), see p.284 for more on this. You can also buy a **business visa** ($25; one passport photo) on arrival. Like the tourist visa this is valid for thirty days, but can be extended in a variety of ways (ranging from one-month single-entry extension, three months' single-entry, six months' multiple-entry and twelve months' multiple-entry; costs range from $50 to $180). Multiple entries are only available on a business visa.

Both tourist and business visas can only be **extended** in Phnom Penh at the inconveniently located Department for Immigration (Mon–Fri 8–11am & 2–4pm; ☏012/854874), 8km out of town opposite Pochentong airport. A tourist visa extension ($35) takes 28 days to process and takes effect from the date you submit your passport – an absurd situation which means you'll only get a few extra days' use out of the extension. As few people can afford to be without their passport for that length of time, they are forced into taking the **three-day service** at $40 for a one-month extension. Even then, applying for the extension is a time-consuming exercise involving at least two trips out to the airport. A far easier option is to use the **visa-extension services** offered by travel agents and guesthouses in town, who will do all the running around for just a few dollars' commission. If you **overstay** your visa you'll be charged $5 per day. From Phnom Penh and Siem Reap the departure tax is $25 for international flights and $6 for domestic departures (at Phnom Penh you can pay by credit card). There is no departure tax when leaving by land.

Embassies and consulates

Australia 5 Canterbury Crescent, Deakin, ACT 2600 ☏02/6273 1259, ✉cambodia@embassy.net.au, ⊕www.embassyofcambodia.org.nz/au.
France 4 Rue Adolphe Yvon, 75116 Paris ☏01/45 03 47 20, ⊜45 03 47 40, ✉ambcambodgeparis@mangoosta.fr.
Germany Benjamin-Vogelsdorf Str. 2, 13187 Berlin ☏30/4863 7901, ✉Rec-berlin@t-online.de.
Hong Kong Room 3606, Singga CC 144, 151 Connaught Rd West ☏2546 0718, ⊜2803 0570,✉cacghk@netvigator.com.
Laos Thadeua Rd, KM2 Vientiane, BP 34 ☏02/131 4950, ⊜02/314 951, ✉recamlao@laotel.com.
Malaysia 83/JKR 2809 Lingkungan U-Thant, 55000 Kuala Lumpur ☏03/4257 1150, ✉reck@tm.net.my.
Singapore 152 Beach Rd, #11-05 Gateway East, Singapore 189721 ☏299 3028, ✉cambodiaembassy@pacific.net.sg.

Rough Guides travel insurance

Rough Guides has teamed up with Columbus Direct to offer you **travel insurance** that can be tailored to suit your needs. Products include a low-cost **backpacker** option for long stays; a **short break** option for city getaways; a typical **holiday package** option; and others. There are also annual **multi-trip** policies for those who travel regularly. Different sports and activities (trekking, skiing, etc) can be usually be covered if required.

See our website (⊛ ww.roughguides.com/website/shop) for eligibility and purchasing options. Alternatively, UK residents should call ☏0870/033 9988; Australians should call ☏1300/669 999 and New Zealanders should call ☏0800/55 9911. All other nationalities should call ☏+44 870/890 2843.

Thailand 185 Rajdamri Rd, Lumphini Patumwan, Bangkok 10330 ☏02/254 6630, ℮RECBKK @hotmail.com.
UK 64 Brondesbury Park, Willesden Green, London NW6 7AT ☏0208/451 7850, ⊛www.cambodiaembassy.org.uk; also covers Ireland.
US 4500 16th St, Washington DC 20011 ☏202/726-8042, ⊛www.embassy.org/cambodia; Suite G, No. 422 Ord St, Los Angeles, CA 90012 ☏213/625-7777, ℮cambodiaconsulate@usa.net.
Vietnam 71A Tran Hung Dao St, Hanoi ☏04/942 4788, ℮arch@fpt.vn; 41 Phung Khac Khoan, Ho Chi Minh City ☏08/829 2751, ℮cambocg@hcm.unn.vn.

Gay and lesbian Cambodia

Gay and lesbian travellers shouldn't experience any problems when travelling in Cambodia – homosexuality is not illegal, although neither is it recognized and talked about. It's acceptable for two men or two women to link hands or arms in public, which would be unacceptable for straight couples; however, as any overt display of affection is embarrassing to Cambodians, it's as well to be discreet. There is no gay scene or support network

Insurance

Before travelling to Cambodia you'd do well to take out an insurance policy to cover against theft, loss of personal items and documentation, illness and injury. However, before you pay for a new policy, it's worth checking whether you are already covered: some all-risks home insurance policies may cover your possessions when overseas, and many private medical schemes include cover

when abroad. In Canada, provincial health plans usually provide partial cover for medical mishaps overseas, while holders of official student/teacher/youth cards in Canada and the US are entitled to (albeit meagre) accident coverage and hospital in-patient benefits. Students will often find that their student health coverage extends during the vacations and for one term beyond the date of last enrolment.

A typical **travel insurance policy** usually provides cover for the loss of baggage, tickets and – up to a certain limit – cash or cheques, as well as cancellation or curtailment of your journey. Most of them exclude so-called "dangerous" activities unless an extra premium is paid: in Cambodia this can mean scuba diving, riding a motorbike and trekking.

Internet access

Getting online in Cambodia is no longer the problem it once was, and you'll now find a host of Internet shops and cafés in Phnom Penh, Siem Reap, Battambang, Sihanoukville and Kampot – even the remote outpost of Banlung now has the Internet (albeit with slow connections and at twice the price of other towns). Access is typically under $2 per hour and connections are generally fairly reliable, though they may not be as fast as you are used to at home. Although their equipment may not be up-to-the-minute, you'll be able to use your memory stick and email photographs from CDs at most places in the tourist centres. Outside the towns, you'll be lucky to find any Internet access at all. Staying in smart, up-to-date hotels you may find Wi-Fi available, although more commonly you'll get an Internet socket in your room.

Laundry

You can get laundry done practically everywhere, at both hotels and guesthouses or at private laundries in all towns – look for the signs in English. Prices are pretty uniform, at 500–1000 riel per item.

Living in Cambodia

It's hard to find paid work in Cambodia, and even finding a post teaching English is pretty difficult. If you want to do voluntary work in Cambodia, the UK charity Voluntary Service Overseas (ⓦwww.vso .org.uk) and the Australian Volunteers International (ⓦwww.ozvol.org.au) both recruit volunteers to work on projects in Cambodia, paid at local rates. Outreach International (ⓦwww.outreachinternational.co.uk) offers three- to six-month placements aimed at gap-year students; projects in Cambodia include working with children (in orphanages, plus working with disabled children and street children) and conservation projects.

Mail

All Cambodia's **mail** is consolidated in Phnom Penh. Sending mail from provincial cities is as reliable as posting from the capital, though it costs a little more. Within the capital itself, only the main post office is geared up to accept mail bound for abroad.

Mail to Europe, Australasia and North America takes between five and ten days, leaving Phnom Penh for major international destinations around twice a week – the specific days can be checked at the main post office. Stamps for **postcards** sent from the capital cost 1800–2200 riel (add 300 riel if posting from the provinces).

Parcels can only be posted in Phnom Penh, though at a whopping $17 for a one-kilogram parcel going abroad, it is worth deferring the task if you're heading to Thailand, where postage is cheaper. You'll be charged 3000 riel for the obligatory customs form, detailing the contents and their value, but it isn't necessary to leave the package open for checking. Post offices sell mailing boxes if you need them.

Poste restante mail can be received at the main post offices in Phnom Penh, Sihanoukville and Siem Reap, at a cost of 500 riel per item. When collecting mail, bring your passport as proof of identity and ask them to check under both your first name and your family name.

Post office staff, in Phnom Penh especially, sometimes try to make a bit of money on the side by overcharging. **Postage rates** are displayed on a notice board inside Phnom Penh's main post office, so you can make your own calculations and query the charge if it seems excessive – it often reduces dramatically upon recalculation.

Maps

Understandably, Cambodia was poorly surveyed for many years and, thus, some older maps show roads and villages inaccurately. Many maps have now been updated, but it's worth bearing in mind that just because a road is marked as major on a map it doesn't mean it will be in decent condition. (In any case, Cambodia remains heavily contaminated with land mines, so it pays to stick to well-defined roads and tracks; see p.47 for more on this.)

Above and beyond the maps given in this guide, you might consider one of the Cambodia-only maps from Periplus, Nelles and Globetrotter. Although they all have minor shortcomings, they should get most travellers around with minimal problems. If you're only travelling between the main cities and tourist sites, the Rough Guide map of Vietnam, Laos and Cambodia should suffice.

Within Cambodia, bookstalls at Psar Thmei and Psar Toul Tom Poung in Phnom Penh sell a selection of maps. American military survey maps are among the most detailed available, but you may have to check out a lot of stalls to find the map for the sector of the country you want, as nobody stocks the whole range; expect to pay around $5 for one of these maps. These bookstalls also sell the country maps published by the Ministry of Tourism; these show the country in detail on one side and city plans of Phnom Penh, Siem Reap and Sihanoukville on the reverse, and they cost a couple of dollars each.

Public holidays

Dates for religious holidays are variable, changing each year with the Buddhist lunar calendar.

January 1 International New Year's Day.

January 7 Victory Day over the Genocide Regime. Celebrates the liberation of Phnom Penh in 1979 from the Khmer Rouge.

February (variable) Meak Bochea Day. Buddhist festival commemorating and worshipping the Dhamma.

March 8 International Women's Day.

April 13–15 Bonn Chaul Chhnam – Khmer New Year.

May 1 International Labour Day.

May 13–15 Birthday of King Norodom Sihamoni.

May (variable) Visakha Bochea. Commemorates the birth of Buddha.

May (variable) Bonn Chroat Preah Nongkoal, the Royal Ploughing Ceremony. Celebrated just before the rains begin, this marks the start of the rice-planting season, and a ceremonial furrow is ploughed on the grounds in front of the National Museum in Phnom Penh.

June 18 Birthday of King-Mother Norodom Monineath Sihanouk'.

September 24 Constitution Day.

September/October (2–3 days, variable) Bonn Pchum Ben, the Feast of the Ancestors. Celebrated on the day of the new moon, when families head out to the pagoda to make offerings to the dead.

October 29 Coronation Day of King Norodom Shiamoni.

October 31 Birthday of King-Father Norodom Sihanouk.

October/November (variable) Bonn Om Tuk, the Water Festival. Held at a variable time from late October to mid-November, it marks the end of the rains and the time when the water again starts to flow out of the Tonle Sap. A busy and colourful three-day event ensues, with boat races on the river near the Royal Palace in Phnom Penh and on the moat around Angkor Wat.

November 9 Independence Day. Marks independence from the French in 1953.

December 10 International Human Rights' Day.

Any public holidays that fall on a Saturday or Sunday are taken the following Monday.

Opening hours and public holidays

In theory, government offices work Monday to Friday between 7.30am and 11.30am, and between 2pm and 5pm. In practice, though, you'll be lucky to find anyone at their desks before 9am and they'll probably be gone by 10.30am, returning – or not – for an hour or two in the afternoon. Positions in the public service aren't well paid (if they're paid at all), but carry quite a bit of prestige, so officials ensure they show their faces in the office a few times each week, while moonlighting to earn a living wage.

Post offices are open daily, excluding a few public holidays such as the Khmer New Year and Bonn Pchum Ben. The main office in Phnom Penh is open daily from 7am to 6pm; in the provinces, post office hours are 8am to 5.30pm, though they may close early on Saturday and Sunday if they're not busy or if the staff have other commitments. **Banks** are open Monday to Friday from 8.30am to 3.30pm, and sometimes on Saturday as well between 8.30am and 11.30am. **Markets** open daily from around 6am until 5pm, **shops** between 7am and 7pm.

Key **tourist sights**, such as the National Museum, the Royal Palace Silver Pagoda

Calling home from Cambodia

There is no international directory enquiries service in Cambodia.

To the UK: ☏001 + 44 + area code without initial zero

To the Republic of Ireland: ☏001 + 353 + city code

To the US and Canada: ☏001 + 1 + city code

To Australia: ☏001 + 61+ city code

To New Zealand: ☏001 + 64 + city code

Note that the international access code becomes ☏007 with a Tele.2 phone card.

and Toul Sleng Genocide Museum in Phnom Penh, are open every day including most public holidays. In the provinces museums open on an *ad hoc* basis; the best bet is on a weekday morning between 9am and 10am (indeed they'll probably shut once you've left). The temples at Angkor, Tonle Bati and Sambor Prei Kuk and the country's national parks are open daily from dawn to dusk.

Phones

Most of Cambodia's phone lines were destroyed during the Khmer Rouge era and have yet to be replaced. The advent of mobile phones dramatically improved communications around the country, with most people getting by with a mobile phone only.

The major mobile phone service providers in Cambodia are Samart (code ☏015 & 016), Mobitel (☏012 & 092) and Camshin (☏011). **Mobitel** is the most widely used network and has transmitters in all major towns and at staging posts in between, so reception now is pretty universal. It is virtually impossible for non-residents to acquire a Cambodian mobile phone, or a SIM card for a Cambodian network.

You can make **domestic** and **international phone calls** at the post offices and telecom offices in most towns. These services are invariably run by the government telecommunications network, **Camintel** (☏www.camintel.com), which along with the Australian firm Telstra also runs **public call boxes** in Phnom Penh and Siem Reap; to use these, you'll need a phone card, available in denominations ranging from $2 to $50; look for shops displaying the phone company logos. Camintel and Telstra phone cards can't be used in each other's facilities,

but buying a Tele.2 phone card, you can make international calls from any call box by dialling ☏007 (instead of the usual ☏001 international access code), then the country code and number as usual. It's worth checking out options with your own telecommunications service provider before you travel to see if they have any arrangement for calling home from Cambodia. Whichever option you use, making international calls is expensive – at least $3 per minute – so it's worth looking out for deals offered by Internet shops, guesthouses and travel agents, which can halve the cost.

If you know you will be wanting to make lots of calls home, it's well worth signing up for an account with **Skype** before you go, which allows you to make free computer to computer calls and very cheap computer to telephone calls. Some Internet cafes in Phnom Penh and Siem Reap have sets of headphones with a microphone so that you can use Skype with some privacy. All you pay is the posted fee for use of the Internet.

For **domestic calls** only, the cut-price **glass-sided booths**, found in all major towns are by far the cheapest option at around 600 riel per minute, payable to the attendant. The booths vary in their coverage of Cambodia's various networks: accessible numbers will be written on the side of the booths (the usual numbers covered are ☏012 and ☏092 Mobitel, ☏011 Camshin, ☏015 and 016 Samart).

Faxing is extortionate in Cambodia, at $7–8 per page. If you really must send a fax, the hotel business centres and Internet shops are the most reliable places to do so.

To call Cambodia from abroad, dial your international access code, followed by

855, then the local area code (minus the initial 0), then the number. Note that phone companies may charge slightly more to call Cambodian mobile numbers.

If you want to use a mobile phone that you bought at home, you'll need to check with your phone service provider whether it will work abroad, and what the call charges are to use it in Cambodia. It's unlikely that a mobile bought for use inside North America will work outside the US and Canada, unless it's a tri-band phone. However, most mobiles in the UK, Australia and New Zealand use GSM, which works well in Southeast Asia.

Photography

Cambodians (other than the chunchiet) generally love being photographed – although it is common courtesy to ask first; they also take a lot of photos themselves and may well ask you to stand in their photo. It's best to avoid taking photographs of anything with a military connotation, just in case.

Whilst most people now have digital cameras film can still be obtained (more easily than at home), with a 36-exposure roll of print film costing around $2.50 and slide file around $5–6. Developing and printing cost around $4 per roll of 36 photos, though quality is variable.

You can get your digital shots transferred to CD or printed at most photographic shops in Phnom Penh and Siem Reap, although, as for film, the quality of the prints may not be as good as you'd get at home.

Time

Cambodia is 7hr ahead of GMT; 12hr ahead of New York and Montréal; 15hr ahead of Los Angeles and Vancouver; 1hr behind Perth; 4hr behind Sydney and 5hr behind Auckland; 5hr ahead of South Africa.

Toilets

Apart from places used to catering for foreigners, squat toilets are the rule. There are practically no public toilets, although at some tourist sights and transport stops, enterprising individuals may have set up private facilities which you can use for a few hundred riel. It is fine to ask to use the loo at restaurants, even if you're not eating there, although you may sometimes wish you hadn't as they are often unsavoury. Toilet paper is sold in the markets and it's probably worth carrying some with you. In the country you will have to do as the locals do and take to the bushes – but remember there is a risk of mines, so don't stray off well-trodden paths.

Tourist information

There is a wealth of information readily available on the temples of Angkor, which you can access both in Cambodia and outside the country; information on the rest of Cambodia is obtainable via the Internet and the increasingly documented experiences of other travellers; supplementary information to that given in the guide can also be obtained from local guesthouse owners.

Tourist offices

Most provincial towns now have a **tourist office** (*destjow montepiak*), although they can be difficult to find, often being hidden away in the local government compound. Their opening hours are generally quite loose (typically Mon–Fri 8–11am & 2–4pm), and it can take quite a few visits to catch anyone in. Generally, someone at the office will speak a little English or French, but they seldom have much information or literature to impart beyond a street plan and the chance to look at some photographs of local attractions.

There are no Cambodian tourist offices abroad, and Cambodian embassies aren't equipped to handle tourist enquiries.

Travellers with disabilities

Cambodia has the unhappy distinction of having the highest proportion of disabled people per capita in the world (1 in 236 people) – due to land mines and the incidence of polio and other wasting diseases. There is no special provision for the disabled, so travellers with disabilities will need to be especially self-reliant, though Cambodians will be only too pleased to help out where they can.

Before travelling to Cambodia, disabled visitors should check out the airline facilities

Cambodia online

Online representation of Cambodia has improved greatly, with an increasing amount of information from government departments, private companies (particularly tour operators) and individuals.

Travel advisory services

Australian Department of Foreign Affairs and Trade ⓦ www.smartraveller.gov.au. Provides up-to-date advice and reports by country and region.

British Foreign and Commonwealth Office ⓦ www.fco.gov.uk/travel. Country profiles and constantly updated advice for travellers on circumstances affecting safety and security, health and general issues.

Canada Department of Foreign Affairs and International Trade ⓦ www.voyage .gc.ca. Country information, covering warnings with recent updates, health, safety and general travel information.

Ireland Department of Foreign Affairs ⓦ foreign affairs.gov.ie. General travel information by country.

New Zealand Ministry of Foreign Affairs and Trade ⓦ safetravel.govt.nz. Country-specific advice and regional reports on safety and security, plus consular information.

US Department of State ⓦ www.state.gov/travelandbusinesss. Provides country-specific information for travellers, including warnings and risks.

General Cambodia information

Beauty and Darkness ⓦ www.mekong.net/cambodia. Documents the dark side of Cambodia's recent history, and contains a photo gallery and biographies of some of those who survived the Khmer Rouge atrocities; also some travelogues.

Cambodia Daily ⓦ www.cambodiadaily.com. Carries selected features and supplements from recent editions of the newspaper.

Cambodian Embassy in Washington DC ⓦ www.embassyofcambodia.org. Government reports and some tourist information.

Cambodian Information Centre ⓦ www.cambodia.org. Varied site offering information on everything from clubs and organizations to the legal system and even e-cards.

Cambodia Tribunal Monitor ⓦ www.cambodiatribunal.org. Offers the latest information on the Genocide Tribunal.

for both long-haul and domestic services. Stock up on any medication and get any essential equipment checked out. It's also worth checking that your travel insurance covers you for most eventualities, such as the loss of a wheelchair. Check out hotel facilities as well, as lifts are still not as common in Cambodia as you might hope.

Getting around pagodas and temples can be a problem, as everything seems to involve steps; even at relatively lowly pagodas there are flights of steps and entrance kerbs to negotiate. The temples at Angkor are particularly difficult, with steps up most entrance pavilions and the central sanctuaries. However, you can hire a helper cheaply at $15–20 a day, and in any case you don't need to reach every nook and cranny to find visiting a temple hugely rewarding.

Go Cambodia ⓦ www.gocambodia.com. Easy to navigate, general-purpose site featuring articles on all aspects of Cambodian life – from sport to music to women's rights – with links to other sites.

His Majesty King Norodom Sihamoni ⓦ www.norodomsihamoni.org. The king's official website.

Library of Congress ⓦ www.loc.gov. Cambodia country study dating from the 1980s, but containing much historical, economic and political information that's still of relevance.

King-Father Norodom Sihanouk ⓦ www.norodomsihanouk.info. Website of the king-father (and queen-mother) featuring biographies and the daily documents issued by this prolific scribe (mostly in French).

Phnom Penh Post ⓦ www.phnompenhpost.com. Key articles from the fortnightly English-language newspaper.

Royal Government of Cambodia ⓦ www.cambodia.gov.kh. Official website of the Cambodian government, with profiles of the king, premier and information about the senate and constitution.

Travel and tourism

Andy Brouwer ⓦ www.andybrouwer.co.uk. This Cambodiaphile's site is full of travelogues, interviews with eminent Cambodian experts and plenty of links to associated sites.

Bayon Pearnik ⓦ www.bayonpearnik.com. Online version of the free magazine, with travel features on Cambodia, particularly related to biking excursions to remote areas.

Cambodian Ministry of Tourism ⓦ www.mot.gov.kh. Features the country's highlights, province by province, plus information on accommodation, history and Khmer culture.

Canby Publications ⓦ www.canbypublications.com. Convenient online extracts from their Cambodian city guides.

City of Phnom Penh ⓦ www.phnompenh.gov.kh. Covers points of interest around Cambodia's capital and also features a detailed city history.

Tales of Asia ⓦ www.talesofasia.com. In-depth look at Cambodia by Siem Reap resident, Gordon Sharpless, with plenty of tales and practical information on the vagaries of the country.

Women travellers

The Cambodians are respectful to and protective of women, so travelling around the country shouldn't pose any problems for foreign women. All the same, it's as well to dress modestly and to avoid over-familiarity, which can be misconstrued, particularly after men have had a few beers. If someone does overstep the mark, a firm "no" will normally suffice to ward them off. A good ruse used by Khmer women is to subtly put yourself in a position of superiority, by referring to yourself as the older sister (*bpong serey*) or aunt (*ming*) or by addressing the man as nephew (*kmaoy bprohs*). If this doesn't work, then kick up a huge fuss so that everyone in the vicinity knows that you're being harassed, which should shame the man into backing off.

Guide

Guide

1

Phnom Penh
and around

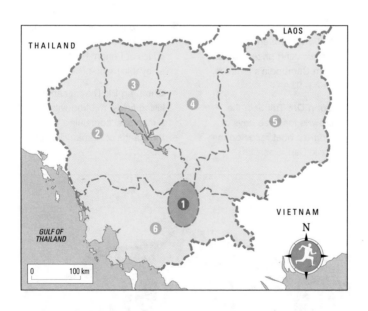

CHAPTER 1 # Highlights

* **Cyclo rides** Enjoy an unhurried spin through the old French quarter. See p.82

* **Royal Palace** The soaring golden spires of the ceremonial Throne Room are Phnom Penh's most memorable sight. See p.88

* **Silver Pagoda** Home to a sacred emerald Buddha and a vast *Ramayana* mural. See p.91

* **National Museum** Showcasing prized statuary from Cambodia's temples. See p.93

* **Bonn Om Tuk** Join the crowds for three days of long-tail boat races on the Tonle Sap. See p.96

* **Mekong boat trips** Cruise the river as the sun sinks behind the spires of the Royal Palace. See p.97

* **Toul Sleng** Former torture chamber, now a sobering museum to Khmer Rouge atrocities. See p.99

* **Wat Phnom** On a leafy hill, Wat Phnom affords a view that has changed little in half a century. See p.100

* **Psar Toul Tom Poung** Bargain for fine silks, antiques and curios at Phnom Penh's most enjoyable market. See p.109

* **Choeung Ek** The macabre killing fields, marked with a memorial containing thousands of human skulls. See p.120

▲ The Royal Palace

Phnom Penh
and around

The capital of Cambodia and the heart of government, **PHNOM PENH** retains much of its original charm, crisscrossed by broad tree-lined boulevards and dotted with old colonial villas. Situated in a virtually flat area at the confluence of the Tonle Sap, Bassac and Mekong rivers, the compact city hasn't yet been overwhelmed by towering high-rise developments, and imparts a sense of openness and light. The city throbs with enterprise and energy, which makes it difficult to comprehend that a generation ago it was forcibly evacuated and left to run to ruin by the Khmer Rouge. Inevitably, and in spite of many improvements, some of the scars are still evident: side roads are pot-holed and strewn with rubble, some of the elegant villas are ruined beyond repair, and when it rains the antiquated drainage system backs up, flooding the roads.

It's a testimony to the unflappable good nature and stoicism of the city's inhabitants that, despite past adversity, they remain upbeat and determined to improve their lot. Many people do two jobs to get by, keeping government offices ticking over for a few hours each day and then moonlighting as moto drivers or tutors; furthermore, the Cambodian belief in **education** is particularly strong here, and anyone who can afford to sends their children to supplementary classes outside school hours. This dynamism constantly attracts Cambodians from the provinces, who find it impossible to believe that Phnom Penh's streets aren't paved with metaphorical gold. Newcomers soon discover that it's tougher being poor in the city than in the country, and are forced to rent tiny rooms for themselves and their families in one of the many shanties on the city's outskirts, ripped off for the privilege by affluent landlords.

For tourists and locals alike, the lively **riverfront** – a wide grassy promenade that runs beside the Tonle Sap for nearly 2km – is the city's focal point. In the evenings, Phnom Penh residents come here to take the air, snack on hawker food and enjoy the impromptu waterside entertainment; the strip also shows the city at its most cosmopolitan, lined with Western restaurants, cafés and bars. Three key tourist sights lie close by. Arguably the most impressive of the city's attractions is the elegant complex housing the **Royal Palace** and **Silver Pagoda**. The palace's distinctive four-faced spire towers above the pitched golden roofs of its Throne Hall, and the adjacent Silver Pagoda is home to a stunning collection of Buddha statues. A block north of the palace is the **National Museum**, a dark-red building set in leafy surroundings housing a fabulous collection of ancient Cambodian statuary dating back to as early as the sixth century. Also near the river are a number of lesser attractions, including two pagodas: **Wat Ounalom**, one of five founded during Phnom Penh's first spell as the capital, and the bustling hilltop **Wat Phnom**, one of the city's prime pleasure spots, whose foundation is said to actually predate that of the city. The old French administrative area surrounds the hill on which Wat Phnom sits, and you can admire many fine **colonial buildings**, some restored, on a jaunt around the area. Also on many tourist itineraries, though for completely

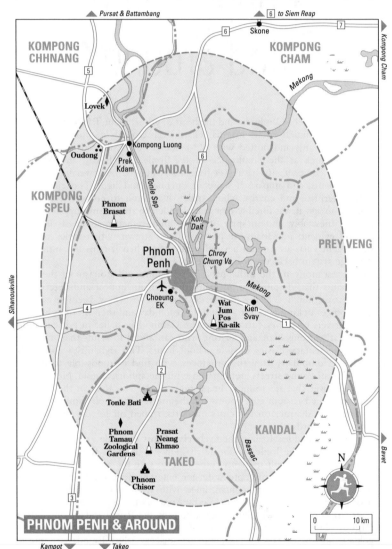

different reasons, is the **Toul Sleng Genocide Museum** south of the centre; this erstwhile school became a centre for the torture of cadres who fell foul of the Pol Pot regime.

Many visitors spend just a couple of days in Phnom Penh before hopping on to Siem Reap and Angkor, but there are plenty of reasons to linger longer. The capital boasts the best **shopping** in the country, with a vast selection of souvenirs and crafts, plus an excellent range of **cuisines** in its many restaurants. In addition, Phnom Penh offers a rare opportunity to get a glimpse of the **traditional culture** which the Khmer Rouge tried to wipe out, including classical dance and shadow puppetry.

If you do linger, there are also several rewarding **day-trips** from the capital out into the surrounding countryside. The most obvious trip is a combined excursion to the Angkor-era temples of **Tonle Bati**, featuring well-preserved wall-carvings, and **Phnom Chisor**, which boasts a stunning hilltop site. Especially poignant if you've visited the Genocide Museum is a trip to the killing fields at **Choeung Ek**, where a memorial stupa contains the remains of some of those murdered here. Among other possible day-trips are the old capitals of **Oudong** and **Lovek**, though for a genuine contrast to the historical treasures and bustle of Phnom Penh, there are a smattering of **rural villages** and **riverside pleasure spots** to explore quite close at hand.

Some history

Cambodian legend – passed down through so many generations that the Khmers regard it as fact – has it that in 1372 a wealthy widow, **Daun Penh** (Grandmother Penh), was strolling along the Chrap Chheam River (now the Tonle Sap), when she came across the hollow trunk of a *koki* tree washed up on the banks. Inside it she discovered five Buddha statues, four cast in bronze and one carved in stone. As a mark of respect, close to her house she created a sanctuary for the statues on the top of a low mound, which became known as **Phnom Penh**, literally the hill of Penh; in due course, the hill gave its name to the city that grew up around it.

Phnom Penh began its first stint as a **capital** in 1432, when King **Ponhea Yat** fled south from Angkor and the invading Siamese. He set up a royal palace, increased the height of Daun Penh's hill and founded a number of **monasteries** – Wat Botum, Wat Koh, Wat Lanka, Wat Ounalom and Wat Phnom – all of which survive today. When Ponhea Yat died, his sons variously took succession, but for reasons that remain unclear (sibling rivalry and political infighting are possibilities), the court had moved out to Lovek by 1505 (it didn't last long, though, as Lovek was destroyed by the Thais in 1594 and the capital relocated once again, to Oudong), and Phnom Penh reverted to being nothing more than a fishing village.

Little is known of the subsequent three hundred years of Phnom Penh's history, though records left by missionaries indicate that by the seventeenth century a multicultural community of Chinese, Indian, Portuguese and Spanish traders had grown up along the banks of the Tonle Sap, and that Phnom Penh, with its easy access to the ocean via the Mekong, had developed into a prosperous **port**, trading in gold, silk cloth and incense, and in hides, bones, ivory and horn from elephants, rhinoceros and buffalo. Phnom Penh's prosperity had declined in the later part of the century, though, as a direct result of the Vietnamese invasion of the Mekong delta, which cut off Phnom Penh's access to the sea.

The eighteenth century was a period of **dynastic squabbles** between pro-Thai and pro-Vietnamese factions of the royal family; in 1770, Phnom Penh was actually burnt down by the Siamese, who proceeded to install a new king and take control of the country.

Late in the eighteenth century, the Vietnamese assumed suzerainty over Cambodia, and from 1808 all visits to Phnom Penh had to be approved by them. Phnom Penh became the capital once again when King Chan moved here from Oudong in 1812, though the court would return to Oudong twice during the next fifty years amid continuing tussles between the Thais and Vietnamese for influence in Cambodia.

In 1863, King Norodom (great-great-grandfather of the current king, Norodom Sihamoni), fearing another Vietnamese invasion, signed a treaty for Cambodia to become a **French protectorate**. At the behest of the French, over the next few years he uprooted the court from Oudong and the role of capital returned decisively to Phnom Penh, a place which the recently arrived French described as "an unsophisticated settlement made up of a string of thatched huts clustered along a single muddy track, the river banks crowded with the houseboats of fisher-folk". In fact, an estimate of its population at the time put it at around 25,000. Despite Phnom Penh regaining its access to the sea (the Mekong delta was also under French control) it remained very much an outpost, as the French effort to develop Saigon was absorbing most of their attention and Indochina budget.

In 1889, a new Senior Resident, **Hyun de Verneville**, was appointed to the protectorate. Wanting to make Phnom Penh a place fit to be the French administrative centre in Cambodia, he created a chic colonial town. By 1900, roads had been laid out on a grid plan, a law court, public works and telegraph offices set up, and banks and schools built. A French quarter grew up in the area north of Wat Phnom, where imposing villas were built for the city's French administrators and traders; Wat Phnom itself gained landscaped gardens and a zoo.

In the 1920s and 1930s, Phnom Penh grew prosperous. The road network was extended, facilitated by the infilling of drainage canals; the Mekong was dredged, making the city accessible to seagoing vessels; parks were created and communications improved. In 1932, the city's **train station** was built and the railway line linking the capital to Battambang was completed. Foreign travellers were lured to Cambodia by exotic tales of hidden cities in the jungle. In 1929, Robert Casey, an American visitor, described Phnom Penh as "a city of white buildings, where spires of gold and stupas of stone rocket out of the greenery into the vivid blue sky", noting also the shady, wide streets and pretty parks. His account bears a remarkable resemblance to the Phnom Penh of today, and life then seems to have been much as it is now, the open-fronted shops and shophouses bustling with haggling traders, and roadsides teeming with food vendors and colourful busy markets.

The country's first **secondary school**, Lycée Sisowath, opened in Phnom Penh in 1936, and slowly an educated elite developed, laying the foundations for later political changes. During **World War II**, the occupying Japanese allowed the French to continue running things and their impact on the city was relatively benign; in October 1941, after the Japanese had arrived, the coronation of Norodom Sihanouk went ahead pretty much as normal in Phnom Penh.

With **independence** from the French in 1954, Phnom Penh at last became a true seat of government and an educated middle class began to gain prominence; café society began to blossom, cinemas and theatres thrived, and motorbikes and cars took to the boulevards. In the mid-1960s a national sports venue, the Olympic Stadium, was built and world celebrities began to visit – Le Royal, the city's premier hotel, played host to Jacqueline Kennedy.

This period of optimism was not destined to last, however. Phnom Penh started to feel the effects of the Vietnam War in the late 1960s, when refugees began to flee the border areas for the capital. The **civil war** of the early 1970s turned this exodus into a flood. **Lon Nol**'s forces (see p.316) fought a losing battle against the **Khmer Rouge** and, as the city came under siege, food became scarce despite US efforts to fly in supplies.

On **April 17, 1975** the Khmer Rouge entered Phnom Penh. At first they were welcomed as harbingers of peace, but within hours the soldiers had ordered the population out of the capital. Reassurances that it was "just for a few days" were soon discredited, and as the people – the elderly, infirm and the dying among them – left carrying such possessions as they were able, the Khmer Rouge set about destroying the city. Buildings were ransacked, roofs blown off, even the National Bank was blown up in the Khmer Rouge's contempt for money. For three years, eight months and twenty days Phnom Penh was a ghost town.

With the **Vietnamese entry** into Phnom Penh on January 7, 1979, both returnees and new settlers began to arrive – although many former inhabitants either could not or would not return, having lost everything and everyone. Those arriving in the city took up residence in the vacant buildings, and to this day many still live in these same properties. During the Vietnamese era, the capital remained impoverished and decrepit, with much of the incoming aid from the Soviet Union and India finding its way into the pockets of senior officials. By 1987, Vietnamese interest was waning, and by 1989 they had withdrawn from Cambodia.

The UN subsequently took charge of Cambodia, and by 1992 the country was flooded with highly paid **UNTAC** forces. The atmosphere in Phnom Penh became surreal: its infrastructure was still in tatters, electricity and water were spasmodic, telecommunications nonexistent and evening curfews were put in force, but the city boomed as hotels, restaurants and bars sprang up to keep the troops entertained. Many Phnom Penh residents got rich quick on the back of this – supplying prostitutes and drugs played a part – and the capital gained a reputation for being a free-rolling, lawless city, one which it is still trying to lay to rest.

The city of today is slowly **repairing** the dereliction caused nearly three decades ago: roads are being repaired, the electricity mostly works and many of the charming colonial buildings are being restored. With tourism not far from its sights, the municipal government has set out elaborate plans to continue smartening up the city, ranging from dictating the colour in which buildings will be painted – creamy yellow – to evicting squatters from areas designated for development. Aspirations of car-ownership are attested to by the increase in traffic, while a building frenzy is trying to satisfy the desire for new apartments; not so long ago the Cambodians abhorred banks, preferring instead to buy gold, but now even monks can be seen queuing for the ATM. However, corruption remains rife, but with its middle class firmly re-established, the city is facing the future with renewed optimism.

Arrival

The city of Phnom Penh roughly extends from the **Chroy Chung Va Bridge** in the north to **Mao Tse Toung Boulevard** in the south, with the area around the yellow-domed **Psar Thmei** (literally New Market, although it's known locally as the Central Market) loosely regarded as the **centre**.

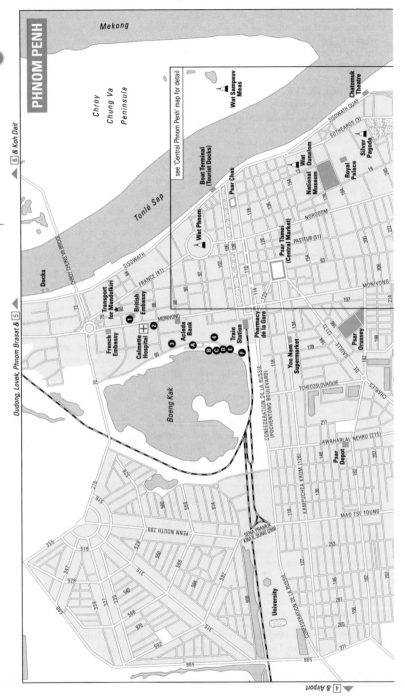

PHNOM PENH

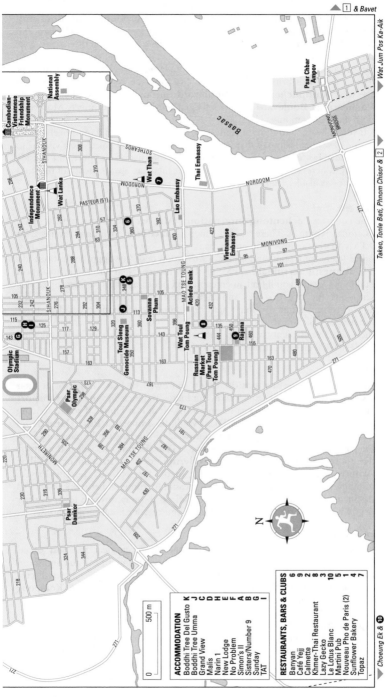

PHNOM PENH AND AROUND

▲ 1 & Bavet

▶ Wat Jum Pos Ka-Aik

▶ Takeo, Tonle Bati, Phnom Chisor & 2

Pear Chbar Ampov

MONIVONG BRIDGE

National Assembly

Cambodian-Vietnamese Friendship Monument

Independence Monument

Wat Lanka

Bassac

SIHANOUK

308

310

Wat Than 7

SOTHEAROS

NORODOM

Thai Embassy

PASTEUR (51)

282

57

6

360

334

310

63

392

Lao Embassy

294

400

422

288

Vietnamese Embassy

MONIVONG

95

240

97

101

242

256

242

Acleda Bank

105

348 K

432

232

278

5

Sovanna Phum

MAO TSE TOUNG

488

520

115

282

304

105

125

117

129

320

J

362

420

143

Wat Toul Tom Poung

396

8

135

650

Rajana

9

460

143

135

155

444

163

480

Toul Sleng Genocide Museum

113

Russian Market (Psar Toul Tom Poung)

163

167

470

271

G H I

157

163

173

Olympic Stadium

Psar Olympic

123

173

181

290

328

358

181

182

MONIREATH

220

298

384

402

271

230

316

336

182

193

430

Psar Damkor

592

324

344

271

218

N

500 m

0

▶ Choeung Ek & 10

172

77

There are two major north–south routes, **Norodom** and **Monivong** boulevards, both intersected by the two great arcs of **Sihanouk/Nehru** and **Mao Tse Toung** boulevards, which act as ring roads; together, these four thoroughfares cut the city into segments and can be useful points of reference for specifying locations to taxi, tuk-tuk and moto (see Basics p.28) drivers. Two major roads bring traffic into the city from the coast and the airport to the west: **Kampuchea Krom Boulevard** runs directly to Psar Thmei, while **Pochentong Boulevard** (aka Confédération de la Russie) meets Monivong near the train station.

If you're heading to Phnom Penh by road, rail or boat, you'll most likely arrive at one of several terminals that lie within 1.5km of Psar Thmei. Most visitors to Cambodia, however, arrive at Phnom Penh's international airport, just outside the city. Wherever and whenever you arrive, there are always plenty of tuk-tuks or motos available.

By air

The compact **Pochentong International Airport** is 8km west of the city on National Route 4. There's a full range of **facilities**, including several 24hr ATMs in the arrivals hall, and a bank (daily 7.30am–7.30pm), phones, post office (daily 8am–6pm) and tourist information desk (see opposite) just outside. The **domestic terminal** has recently been incorporated into the main airport building. Outside you'll find an efficient **taxi** booth operating a fixed-price ($7) service to the city. Tuk-tuks and motos are not allowed to hang around the airport terminal, but you may catch one dropping someone off at departures; otherwise, walk out to the main road, about 200m across the car park, where there are always plenty waiting. The fare into town is $4 for a tuk-tuk, and 7000–10,000 riel for a moto.

By road

Buses arrive at the **bus station**, 200m southwest of Psar Thmei (or at their respective depot). Most shared taxis, minibuses and pick-ups use the **transport stop** (and the streets around it) 100m northwest of Psar Thmei. If you're arriving from Kampot, Sihanoukville or Takeo you'll be dropped at **Psar Damkor** on Mao Tse Toung Boulevard in the southwest of the city, while transport from Sre Ambel stops a bit nearer the centre, at **Psar Depot** on Nehru Boulevard. Transport from Bavet arrives at **Psar Olympic** near the stadium, or at **Chbar Ampov**, east of the Monivong Bridge in the far south of the city. Private minibuses (see Listings p.113) are increasingly running between provincial destinations, on request they'll drop you off on the way through town to their depot; it's also worth asking if they'll take you to your hotel or guesthouse.

By boat

Boats arrive at the **tourist docks** on the riverfront near the post office. Guesthouse touts meet the boats, though there are plenty of tuk-tuk and moto drivers on hand to take you elsewhere; a moto ride into the centre will cost you about 2000 riel. Note that there is no longer a boat service from Kompong Cham and Kratie.

By train

The train that comes every other day from Battambang is scheduled to arrive in the early evening at the **train station**, close to the intersection of Monivong and Pochentong boulevards in the north of the city. There is always some transport on hand no matter what time the train actually gets in.

Information and city transport

The **tourist information desk** at the airport's international arrivals hall (Mon–Fri 8am–4pm) has a free booklet on Cambodia that contains useful general information. It's also worth trying to track down the *Phnom Penh Visitors Guide*, a free quarterly English-language booklet that contains details of places to stay, restaurants and sights, a map and a bit of history. Guesthouses, restaurants and the like stock copies, but supplies tend to dry up as the next issue's publication approaches; extracts of the guide are available online at ⓦ www.canbypublications.com. *Asia Life* (ⓦ www.asialifecambodia.com), a free "What's On" guide to Phnom Penh, is published monthly – can be picked up in Western cafés and restaurants; it has features and useful accounts of new openings and exhibitions. **Online** ⓦ www.talesofasia.com takes a refreshingly opinionated look at the local tourist scene. For **listings** of film screenings, theatre performances and other entertainment, the *Cambodia Daily* has a "What's On" section on Fridays, with classified ads for restaurants and bars on Tuesdays and Thursdays; the fortnightly *Phnom Penh Post* is another useful source of information on what's happening in town.

City transport

Although it's possible see many of the sights on foot, Cambodia's heat and humidity, allied with the city's traffic and dust, don't make walking a particularly pleasant experience. **Motos**, **cyclos** and **tuk-tuks**, are the workhorses of local transport, readily available all over town, picking you up from the kerb and dropping you right outside your destination. Phnom Penh has no public transport system – some years ago an experimental bus service ran on two central routes in the city for a couple of months and was greeted with much scepticism, Cambodians being too used to the convenience of door-to-door transport.

▲ Tuk-tuk ferrying passengers around the capital

Most towns and cities in Cambodia can be reached directly from Phnom Penh. Siem Reap is particularly easy to get to, served by regular flights, by a daily boat up the Tonle Sap and by road transport along National Route 6; for Sihanoukville, there are efficient air-conditioned coaches which run from early morning to early afternoon.

By bus

All buses out of Phnom Penh operate scheduled departures from the bus station (or their depots). Several companies, including Phnom Penh Sorya Transport Company, Mekong Express and GST, operate air-conditioned express coaches on the popular **Siem Reap** (24,000 riel) and **Sihanoukville** (12,000 riel) routes. Phnom Penh Sorya covers practically every other provincial town (at the time of writing Sen Monorom was the only exception), using smaller twenty-to-thirty seat coaches, for the less popular, more distant destinations. Places closer to the city, including Kompong Chhnang, Kompong Cham, Kompong Speu, Neak Leung, Oudong, Tonle Bati and Takeo, are served by small city buses also run by Phnom Penh Sorya.

Though not necessarily the quickest or cheapest option, the **Capitol Hotel, Neak Krorhorm Travel** and several other guesthouses and travel companies, operate their own tourist buses to Siem Reap, Sihanoukville and Bangkok, and to the Laos and Vietnam borders. Although through tickets are available to both **Bangkok** and **Ho Chi Minh City** (HCMC), you'll have to walk across the borders, complete the necessary formalities and change to transport from the guesthouse's Thai or Vietnamese associates. Guesthouse bus prices vary a bit, so it's worth comparing before you buy. For Laos, check if your ticket is to the border or through to Don Det, 4,000 Islands, in Laos. A comfortable alternative is Phnom Penh Sorya's air-conditioned coaches, which run daily to Bangkok, the border with Laos and to HCMC for $12–15.

By shared taxi, minibus and pick-up

From the transport stop at the northwest corner of Psar Thmei, plenty of shared taxis, minibuses and pick-up trucks head throughout the day for destinations north of Phnom Penh: **Kompong Thom**, **Siem Reap**, **Kompong Cham**, **Battambang**, **Sisophon** and **Poipet**. If you're going a long way, it's worth getting there by 6am or 7am. Later in the day when fewer people travel, you can have a long wait while the drivers gather up enough customers to make the trip worthwhile. For destinations closer to town you'll easily be able to get a shared taxi until mid-afternoon, after which departures become less frequent. Dramatic improvements in the roads mean that taxis and minibuses now run to Kratie, Stung Treng, Rattanakiri and Mondulkiri. However, some sections of road on the arduous Rattanakiri and Mondulkiri (30,000 to 50,000 riel) routes are still not paved and in the wet season the taxis and minibuses stop, leaving it to pick-up trucks with specially raised suspension to make the run; at this time of year on these routes it's worth checking the day before you want to travel that transport will be running. Pick-ups for Rattanakiri leave from the transport stop at Psar Thmei, while those for Mondulkiri leave from the roadside on Street 80, opposite Wat Preah Put Khowsarjar, in the north of the city.

Taxis can be hired at any of the major hotels, or by calling one of the firms recommended in **Listings** p.114; expect to pay $3–5 for a single daytime journey within the city, or $5–7 at night. Taxis for hire by the day can be found lined up on the east side of Monivong Boulevard, near the intersection with Kampuchea Krom; the going rate is $25–30 per day around the city, $40 (plus) per day out of town. Taxis don't cruise for fares, although a few enterprising drivers meet incoming boats. There are proposals for a metered taxi service, which may be up and running by 2008.

Key provincial destinations are also served by several private companies who run VIP express minibuses, seating 12–15 people (see Listings p.113); these are a good way to travel, quicker than the large buses and safer than taxis.

For the southern provinces of **Takeo**, **Sihanoukville** and **Kampot**, shared transport leaves from Psar Damkor; fares to the coast are 10,000 to 16,000 riel. Shared taxis for **Sre Ambel** and Koh Kong for the Thai border leave from Psar Depot and cost 50,000 riel. Destinations southeast of Phnom Penh, **Neak Leung** (for **Prey Veng** and the boat to **Chau Doc** in Vietnam), **Svay Rieng** and the border town of **Bavet** (commonly called Moc Bai after the town on the Vietnamese side of the border) are served by transport leaving from both Psar Olympic and Psar Chbar Ampov, the latter across the single-lane (and thus almost inevitably traffic-jammed) Monivong Bridge. Dramatic improvements to National Route 1 may mean that the journey to Bavet is now quicker, but until another bridge is thrown across the Bassac River you could experience delays in leaving the city. Expect the trip to the border to take approximately three hours. The taxi fare to Bavet is around 15,000 riel.

By train

There's usually one train every other day at 6am heading north to **Battambang** via **Pursat**. The only way to find out if it's running is by going along to the station the evening before to check that it's arrived; in theory it departs from Phnom Penh on odd-numbered days of the month, but if it breaks down on the inbound journey (which is not unknown) the schedule gets thrown out. You can only buy your **ticket** on the day of travel (6500 riel); the ticket booth opens at around 5am. The trip to Battambang takes 12–15 hours on average and is not in the least bit comfortable – take a cushion. The train service to **Sihanoukville** via Kampot, was suspended a few years ago, but may start up again in the future. Rail network improvements were recently announced, but it is not known when these will commence, or be completed.

By boat

Boats for Siem Reap and Chau Doc (foreigners' fare $25 and $17 respectively) leave from the passenger boat terminal (also known as the tourist docks) on the river near the main post office. **Express boats** take around five hours to power up the Tonle Sap to Siem Reap, subject to variations in the river's flow; they leave at 7am and have reserved seating; you can buy your ticket the day before or at the docks on the morning of departure.

By plane

The airport can be reached in under half an hour by moto or tuk-tuk ($3 and $6) or taxi ($7–8). All domestic carriers operate flights on the profitable route to Siem Reap; however, carriers in Cambodia come and go with alarming frequency and schedules change regularly, so it's best to check with a travel agent for the latest timetable. Flights to Rattanakiri and Stung Treng are currently suspended; it's not known if, or when, they will be reinstated.

Due to the chaotic driving, the shameless speed traps and the police checks, the vast majority of visitors to Phnom Penh find hiring a ride better than driving. If you do intend to **drive yourself** or rent a motorcycle you should be aware that, even compared to the impatient standards of Cambodian driving, the people of Phnom Penh take the biscuit. Cambodian drivers can also be rather hot-headed, so if you are driving, it's best not to insist on claiming your right of way or to be too heavy on the horn – incidents of road rage here can be violent. More an annoyance than a danger are the policemen who stop foreigners and blatantly demand a $5 "fine" (ie bribe), usually with the phrase "beer money". Even if you're not in the wrong, it's unlikely you'll get away without paying, so it's easier to simply pay up rather than going through the hassle of an argument; you can usually bargain them down to a dollar or two.

Pedestrians *never* have the right of way in Cambodia, and Phnom Penh is a place to exercise 360-degree vision, even at traffic lights and the striped, so-called pedestrian crossings.

Motos, tuk-tuks and cyclos

Fares around the city are creeping up: expect to pay around $1–2 per trip for a moto, but note that you will have to pay more if you are going out of the central area, or travelling in the rain or after dark, when prices go up to around $3–5 per trip. Some moto drivers speak a little English, especially the ones who hang around outside the FCC, Psar Toul Tom Poung and other places where foreigners congregate. Away from these places you'll find English-speaking drivers few and far between. Although you shouldn't have too much of a problem getting around, few people in Phnom Penh have any idea of street numbers so it's worth carrying a map.

Exercise a bit of caution when riding motos **at night**. While Phnom Penh is no longer the Wild West town it once was, robberies are not unknown, and moto passengers have recently been the target of bag-snatchers. It's certainly not worth being paranoid, but taking a tuk-tuk at night may be a safer option, keeping your bag on the inside and out of sight from passing motorbikes.

A recent introduction to the capital, tuk-tuks are more comfortable than motos, especially when two or more people are travelling together, or in the rain – as they have roll-down side-curtains; journeys around town cost $2–4. Don't expect a speedy trip though; tuk-tuks are powered by titchy motorbikes and progress can be painfully slow, particularly if there are a few people and their bags aboard.

Unique to the capital, **cyclos** (see Basics p.29) remain popular and offer a leisurely way to get around, although they do cost slightly more than motos. The Cyclo Centre Phnom Penh is a NGO set up help cyclo drivers. They offer showers, medical care and education, and can be found at 9 Street 158, not far from Sorya Mall (☎023/991178; Mon–Fri 8–11am & 1–5pm, Sat 1–5pm). You can't book for a trip, but if you turn up here there are usually cyclos around and starting your ride from here is a good way to support the drivers, who rank among the poorest people in the capital. Alternatively you could contact

---

Phnom Penh addresses

Thanks to the French, who laid out the city on a **grid system**, Phnom Penh is remarkably easy to navigate. The **major streets** all have little-used official names, which have been changed periodically to honour particular regimes or sponsoring countries; the current names have been around since the mid-1990s. The rest of the streets are **numbered** and generally pretty easy to find. North–south streets have the odd numbers, with the low numbers nearest the river; even-numbered streets run east-west, with the low numbers in the north of the city. Signage is improving though, and areas of town are even acquiring district names that are posted above the road.

Individual **buildings** are numbered, but are almost without exception difficult to locate, as the numbering doesn't run consecutively – for example, the Ministry of Tourism, 3 Monivong Boulevard, is actually situated around the street's midpoint. Often the only way to find the place you want is simply to cruise the street until you spot it.

Khmer Architecture Tours who organize a cyclo trip around the key post-1953 architectural sights on the second Sunday of each month (@ www.ka-tours.org); tours cost $10 and last two to three hours.

Accommodation

There's no shortage of accommodation in Phnom Penh, with an increasing number of guesthouses and hotels across the city catering for all pockets and tastes, from basic rooms to opulent colonial-era suites. No matter when you arrive, you should have no difficulty **finding a room**, although the very cheapest rooms fill up quickly. Arriving in the **morning** means you stand a better chance of getting really inexpensive accommodation, as many people check out early to catch onward transport. If you intend to stay for more than a couple of nights, it's worth asking for a discount at guesthouse and mid-range places. With deluxe accommodation you'll often get a better deal by booking through a travel agent or taking a two-to-three-night package. As yet, you will find few of Phnom Penh's hotels on accommodation broker websites.

Budget accommodation clusters along the edge of Boeng Kak, a large lake choked with water hyacinth in the northern part of the city, and south of Psar Orussey in the centre of town. There are also several cheap places scattered around town, including a few establishments with coveted locations close to the riverside. Recent years have seen increased competition in the **mid-range** bracket, with plenty of centrally located hotels along Monivong Boulevard. Boeng Keng Kang, broadly around Street 278, near the NGO residential area, is an up-and-coming area where you'll find both mid-range and budget accommodation. **Deluxe** hotels in Phnom Penh rival those of any country, with the pride of place going to *Raffles Hotel Le Royal*; even if you're not staying there, it's worth a visit to admire the stunning colonial building or to enjoy a cocktail in its famous *Elephant Bar*.

If you are staying for a month or more, you could consider one of the serviced **apartments** offered by several hotels around town. Comprising bedroom, sitting room, bathroom and kitchenette, these go for around $600–1000 per month.

Psar Thmei (Central Market) and east to the riverfront

The following places are shown on the map on p.84.

Holiday International 89 Monivong Blvd ☎ 016/817333, @ www.holidayhotelcambodia.com. Relaxing city-centre hotel with convivial staff and over a hundred spacious rooms and suites equipped to international standards. Rooms have hot-water shower and bath, hair dryer, tea- and coffee-making equipment and satellite TV; breakfast is included. Swimming pool, with poolside bar, spa and 24hr restaurant (with Malaysian, Chinese and Western cuisine). Booking online the rate drops by $20 per night. ❻

🏃 **Last Home** 21 Street 172 ☎ 012/831702, @ www.lasthomecambodia.com. Recently relocated to this central spot in a converted three-storey family house, this friendly family-run guesthouse takes some beating. It has tidy rooms with plenty of space for hanging out on the airy balconies or in its cheerful and cheap restaurant. All travellers' services including ticketing, money exchange, information and transport. ❷–❸

Pacific 234 Monivong Blvd ☎ 023/218592, @ www .pacifichotel.com.kh. The fifty or so rooms here are large, bright and nicely furnished, with sturdy Cambodian wood furniture. Breakfast included. ❺

🏃 **Royal** 91 Street 154 ☎ 023/218026 or 012/854806, ℮ hou_leng@yahoo.com. Enduring family-run guesthouse, with a good selection of clean, comfortable accommodation and a café-bar serving good, inexpensive Western and Asian fare. They can also arrange onward transport, tickets and exchange. The lack of space here has been solved by building up; the new rooms at the top have tiny balconies and great views of the city. ❷–❸

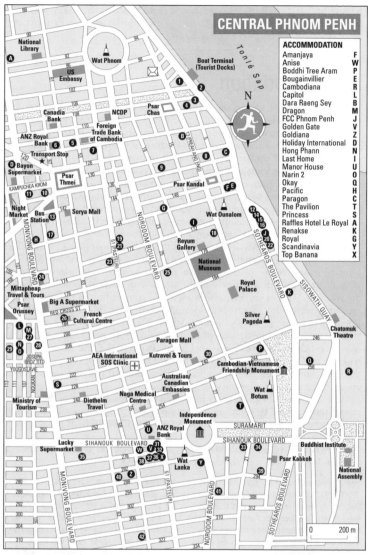

CENTRAL PHNOM PENH

ACCOMMODATION

Amanjaya	F
Anise	W
Boddhi Tree Aram	P
Bougainvillier	E
Cambodiana	R
Capitol	L
Dara Raeng Sey	B
Dragon	M
FCC Phnom Penh	J
Golden Gate	V
Goldiana	Z
Holiday International	D
Hong Phann	N
Last Home	I
Manor House	U
Narin 2	O
Okay	Q
Pacific	H
Paragon	C
The Pavilion	T
Princess	S
Raffles Hotel Le Royal	A
Renakse	K
Royal	G
Scandinavia	Y
Top Banana	X

RESTAURANTS, BARS & CLUBS

Al Ameen	31	East India Curry	5	Herb Café	32	Romdeng	35
Aman Indian Restaurant	17	Elephant Bar	A	Howies	21	Royal India	29
Beef Soup Restaurant	28	FCC Phnom Penh	J	Java	34	Sam Doo	11
Bites	27	Fizz	25	Khmer Borane	22	Sharky's	9
Boat Noodle 1	40	Friends	18	Khmer Restaurant	37	Shiva Shakti	33
Broken Bricks	8	Frizz	14	Malis	41	Sorya	13
Café 151	3	Garden Centre Café	42	Mamak's	6	Talkin' to a Stranger	39
Le Café du Centre	26	Garden Centre 2	38	Mountain Village	36	The Shop	30
Café Fresco	J	Gold Fish River	2	Nouveau Pho de Paris	24	Walkabout	23
Cantina	15	Green Vespa	1	Peking Canteen	10		
Cathouse Tavern	7	Happy Herbs Pizza	16	Ponlok	12		
Chi Cha	4	Heart of Darkness	19	Pop Café da Giorgio	20		

The riverfront

The following places are shown on the map on p.84.

Amanjaya 1 Street 154 and Sisowath Quay ⓣ023/219579, ⓦwww.amanjaya.com. In a prime location opposite Wat Ounalom, this appealing, classy hotel has an abundance of polished wooden floors and stylish, modern wooden furniture, all enhanced by the imaginative use of Cambodian textiles in its soft furnishings Many of the rooms have a river view and all of them have bright, modern bathrooms. The downside is that there's no garden or pool, but that aside, the street-side terrace is a great place to sip an early evening cocktail. In the retro booths of the *K-West* restaurant you can dine on succulent steaks, or Western and Asian alternatives. ❼–❾

Boddhi Tree Aram 70 Street 244 ⓣ011/854430, ⓦwww.boddhitree.com. The most recent of the Boddhi Tree "group", this charming boutique hotel is just a few minutes' walk from the Royal Palace and riverfront. Booking is essential though to secure one of the eight individual rooms with their crisp white linen and marble tiles. Pot plants abound and the atmosphere is serene with a hint of the luxurious. The terrace restaurant is open for breakfast, lunch and dinner. ❻

Bougainvillier 272G Sisowath Quay ⓣ023/220528, ⓦwww.bougainvillierhotel.com. Well-appointed, spacious hotel rooms gain an ethnic touch through the use of Cambodian textiles and furnishings. It has a terrific location and great rooms, so it's a shame that given the price bracket it's a bit stingy – breakfast and Internet access are extra, and there's no lift. Oddly, you also have to weave your way between the white-tablecloth-clad tables of its French restaurant to reach reception. ❻

Cambodiana 313 Sisowath Quay ⓣ023/426288, ⓦwww.hotelcambodiana.com. Set on the river, the *Cambodiana* hasn't quite accepted that its days as the city's premier hotel have long gone. Still, the rooms are large and comfy enough, the views are great and the casino gives the hotel just the slightest air of the illicit. Amenities include a choice of Asian and Western restaurants, a selection of bars, bakery, spa, gym, tennis courts, swimming pool and grounds running down to the river. ❽

Dara Raeng Sey Street 118. ⓣ023/428181. Functional rooms in rambling corner building, conveniently located for both the riverfront and the old French quarter, come with either fan or a/c, as well as TV. The staff are very friendly and helpful, and as a result the hotel gets a lot of repeat custom. ❷–❸

FCC Phnom Penh (was Foreign Correspondents Club of Cambodia) 363 Sisowath Quay ⓣ023/724014, ⓦwww.fcccambodia.com. Booking

is essential to secure one of the seven individual rooms (all named after Angkorian temples) at this legendary restaurant and bar. Comfortable, modern accommodation is equipped to satisfy the needs of the visiting journo crowd, with writing desk, high-speed Internet, cable TV and up-to-date bathrooms. Breakfast included. ❻

Okay 38 Street 258 ⓣ023/986534 or 012/300804, ⓔhello0325@hotmail.com. This guesthouse, just off the riverfront, has the cheapest beds in town – a spot in its immaculate dorm can be had for just $1 per night. It's a sprawling place – the owners keep adding to the accommodation – with a good range of rooms. The tree growing through the roof of the travellers' restaurant and bar adds a quirky twist; other services include TV, DVDs, visa extensions, onward travel and laundry. ❶–❸

Paragon 219B Sisowath Quay ⓣ023/222607, ⓔinfo_paragonhotel@yahoo.com. This is a no-frills place and you need to be fit to make the steep climb up narrow stairs to the accommodation, but for the price and location it's a real bargain. Rooms are plain, but spotless and those with a river view and private balcony can be had for $25. ❹

Renakse 40 Sothearos Blvd ⓣ023/215701, ⓔrenakse-htl@camnet.com.kh. Set in a traditional Khmer building with colourfully tiled pitched roofs, this charming, if decrepit, colonial-era hotel has arguably the best location in all of Cambodia, opposite the Royal Palace and Silver Pagoda. The rooms come with TV, fridge and en-suite hot-water bathroom, though most are smallish and dark; some also have a small verandah. Service can be a bit haphazard and double-booking not unknown, but taking breakfast on the balcony, surrounded by frangipani trees and looking across to the palace, makes it all worthwhile. ❺

The Pavilion 227 Street 19, behind the Wat Botum ⓣ023/222280, ⓔthepavillion@online.com.kh, ⓦwww.pavillion-cambodia.com. This stunning eighteen-room, French-owned guesthouse has been created by the impeccable conversion of two colonial mansions. From the understated decor of the rooms to the most up-to-date mosquito attractant equipment in the gardens no expense has been spared to present the very best of accommodation with an eco-friendly ethos. The swishest rooms have their own plunge pools and private terrace; others have balconies, and there's one vast suite. With a swimming pool (guests and members only), sunbeds, verdant gardens, Jacuzzi, Wi-Fi and a restaurant and bar, it's almost too hard to leave. Advance reservations required by email only. ❻

Around Wat Phnom

The following is shown on the map on p.84.

Raffles Hotel Le Royal Street 92, off Monivong Blvd ☏023/981888, ⓦwww.phnompenhraffles.com. Dating from 1929, this impressive Art Deco hotel, set in lush gardens, was completely renovated in 1997 and restored to its original understated elegance, with the bonus of every modern convenience. Engravings of old Cambodia grace the corridors, and the luxurious guest rooms are individually decorated with specially commissioned prints and Cambodian artefacts. Amenities include a choice of restaurants and bars plus a patisserie, shop, spa and swimming pool. Happy-hour (daily 5–7pm) cocktails in the *Elephant Bar* are one of the capital's must-dos (although sadly a pool table has been installed). ❾

Boeung Kak

The alleyways around Boeung Kak bristle with cheap **guesthouses** (shown on the map on p.76), many built on stilts out over the lake. There's practically a contest between guesthouse owners here to see who can get their terrace furthest out over the water, and although it's choked by invasive water hyacinth, the lakeside is still a great place to sip a beer while you watch the sun go down. The area is popular with backpackers and long-stay travellers, and there's a vast selection of small **restaurants, bars, Internet cafés** and a **shop** or two, which is just as well as it's a bit of a stretch into town. Mosquitoes can be a problem in the area – ask for a mosquito net.

Grand View 4 Street 93 ☏023/430766 or 012/666547. The main draw here is the rooftop restaurant and its fine views of the lake. Rooms are smallish but clean and have a choice of fan or a/c; Visa and MasterCard accepted. ❶
Malis 19 Street 93 ☏016/868545, ⓔmalis .guesthouse@yahoo.com. Big rooms in a brick guesthouse just off the lake. Restaurant and bar with pool table and TV. ❶
New Lodge 18 Street 93 ☏012/916441, ⓔnewlodge@hotmail.com. This lakeside guesthouse has hammocks strung out on the balcony for a lazy sunset view. Rooms are either in the wooden block over the lake or in brick bungalows on land. ❶
No Problem Off Street 93 ☏012/689589, ⓔnoproblem-gh@yahoo.com. Stretched out over the lake at the end of the street this wooden guesthouse is a quiet place to relax. All rooms come with mosquito nets. Restaurant and bar with Western and Asian food. ❶
Simons' II 10 Street 93 ☏012/608892. On the main drag, this friendly, immaculately kept guesthouse has palatial, a/c rooms with heavy wooden furniture; the restaurant serves a range of Western and Asian food. ❸
Sisters/Number 9 9 Street 93 ☏012/424240, ⓔnumber9–guesthouse@hotmail.com. These twin guesthouses offer a choice of rooms, the nicest of which are in smart wooden bungalows off an orchid-lined walkway. Restaurant, bar and sunset views of the lake. ❶–❷

Around Psar Orussey and the Olympic Stadium

The following places are shown on either the map on p.76 or that on p.84.

Capitol 14 Street 182 ☏023/217627 or 724104, ⓔcapitol@online.com.kh. Easy to spot from the hordes of moto drivers outside, this is the original Phnom Penh backpackers' guesthouse. As well as tours and tickets, they run their own buses to most popular destinations including Bangkok and Ho Chi Minh; traveller's cheques accepted and changed, and an in-house ATM has recently been installed. Rooms have no frills, though some have a/c and hot-water bathrooms. The restaurant serves inexpensive food, mostly stir-fries. ❷
Dragon 238 Street 107 ☏012/239066, ⓔvireakcambodian@yahoo.com. This tidy, first-floor guesthouse offers a welcome respite from the bustle at street level with unpretentious, clean rooms; its balcony restaurant is great for a quiet drink and a snack. ❶
Hong Phann 12B Street 107 ☏023/986672, ⓔhong_phann@yahoo.com. Modern airy guesthouse owned by the *Capitol*, with a range of rooms, including some with a/c. It's clean and friendly, and a lot quieter than the *Capitol* itself as it doesn't suffer from hordes of moto drivers hanging around waiting to pick up a fare. ❶
Narin 1 50 Street 125 ☏023/991955 or 012/852426. Another of Phnom Penh's early guest-

houses, this old wooden house is now a sprawling place with basic rooms with shared bathrooms spread over several annexes. It has cheap food and a range of services for travellers, including tours around Phnom Penh and its own bus service to popular destinations. At the time of writing a new guesthouse was being planned just across the road. ❷

Narin 2 20 Street 111 ☎ 023/986131 or 012/555568, ⓔ touchnarrin@hotmail.com Subsidiary guesthouse of the original *Narin* with basic rooms in a modern purpose-built block. Large, airy restaurant; all the usual travellers' services offered. ❷

🏃 **Sunday** 97 Street 141 ☎ 023/211623, ⓔ sundayguesthouse@hotmail.com. Welcoming guesthouse on a quiet street with comfortable rooms, a small restaurant and a friendly atmosphere. Internet access. ❷

🏃 **TAT** 52 Street 125 ☎ 023/986620, ⓔ tatguesthouse@hotmail.com. This cheerful family-run guesthouse is an old favourite with bright, decent-sized rooms (mostly with private bathrooms), Internet access, a communal TV and video and a rooftop restaurant serving decent Cambodian and Chinese food. ❷

Boeng Keng Kang and around the Independence Monument

The following places are shown on the map on p.76.

Anise 2 Street 278 off Street 57 ☎ 023/222522, ⓦ www.anisehotel.com.kh. A sparkling addition to the city's mid-range hotels, *Anise* has twenty stylishly decorated rooms, all with air conditioning, minibar, tea- and coffee-making equipment, flat-screen TV and safety box. The best rooms have balconies and DVD players. Its bakery produces fresh croissants, while the indoor restaurant serves smallish, but delicious portions of Southeast Asian cuisine; the *Terrace Café* is a relaxed place for a coffee or cocktail. ❺

Golden Gate Street 278 ☎ 023/721161 or 721005, ⓦ www.goldengatehotels.com. Old stalwart with deluxe rooms and suites in the main building, and cheaper rooms in an annexe across the road (which is actually lighter and airier than the main building). All rooms come with TV, fridge, hot water and a/c. Deluxe rooms are larger and better appointed; rooms in the suites are quite small. Rates include laundry service. ❹

Goldiana 10–12 Street 282 ☎ & ⓕ 023/219558, ⓦ www.goldiana.com. Popular with NGOs, this hotel may have rather dated decor, but the rooms are comfy and come with private bathroom, satellite TV, minibar, a/c, and spare phone lines for Internet access. There's also a fitness centre, a rooftop swimming pool and a restaurant serving Khmer, Chinese and Western food. ❺–❻

Manor House 21 Street 262 ☎ 023/992566, ⓦ www.manorhousecambodia.com. The Australian-Khmer owner has created a relaxed villa-style guesthouse, with a leafy garden and swimming pool. Once the home of a Japanese diplomat, the house's spacious rooms have capacious bathrooms and still have some of the original owner's furniture. Breakfast is included, as is Wi-Fi. ❺

Princess 302 Monivong Blvd ☎ 023/801089, ⓔ princess@camnet.com.kh. A stylish and efficient modern hotel. The fifty or so rooms are large, light and well equipped. It sometimes has special deals when the room rates drop significantly. Breakfast included. ❺

Scandinavia 4 Street 282 ☎ 023/214498, ⓔ scandinaviahotel@yahoo.com. Good-value small hotel with swimming pool, restaurant, bar and helpful staff. The rooms are smartly decorated, with TV and a/c. It's off the tourist trail and has a relaxed and laid-back atmosphere. ❹

Top Banana Corner Streets 51 & 278 ☎ 012/885572, ⓦ www.topbanana.biz. Two floors of simple budget rooms with a/c or fan in a popular location. Services include a balcony restaurant and bar; free collection from bus, port and airport; communal TV and DVDs; laundry; onward transport and tours. ❶–❸

South of the centre

The following places are shown on the map on p.84.

Boddhi Tree del Gusto 43 Street 98 ☎ 011/854430, ⓦ www.boddhitree.com. Tranquil guesthouse with accommodation in one of several adjoining 1930s colonial houses. The cream-coloured walls, shuttered windows and billowing white muslin create a colonial atmosphere,

while outside you can relax in one of the shady courtyards. Restaurant and bar. ❹

🏃 **Boddhi Tree Umma** Across from the Toul Sleng Museum, on Street 113 ☎ 011/854430, ⓦ www.boddhitree.com. Set in a luxuriant, secluded courtyard garden this intimate guesthouse has recently been extended and refurbished. Its twelve rooms are individually decorated using traditional Cambodian materials.

The restaurant makes creative use of local produce in its excellent continental menu. ❷–❹

The City

Most of the sights are located between the Tonle Sap and Monivong Boulevard, in an area bordered by Sihanouk Boulevard in the south and Wat Phnom in the north. The fabulous **Royal Palace** and **Silver Pagoda** dominate the southern riverfront, the gleaming golden roofs and towering spires soaring from behind its crenellated wall. A block to the north is the dramatic, hybrid building of the **National Museum**, housing a rich collection of Cambodia's ancient heritage, including the very best of Khmer sculpture. **Wat Ounalom**, one of Cambodia's principal pagodas, stands on the riverfront a few hundred metres to the north of the museum, its austere grey stupa housing the ashes of many prominent Khmers. The **riverside** is a sight in itself, a pleasant walkway along the Tonle Sap with a host of places to eat and drink.

Set back from the riverfront, at the northern end of Norodom Boulevard, the distinctive tall white chedi of **Wat Phnom** sits atop the hill that gave the city its name. The area around contains several delightful French colonial buildings, including the main post office, the National Library, *Raffles Hotel Le Royal* and the rather grand train station.

South of the centre, the area around **Independence Monument** is a plush residential district and contains several more monuments and a restful park. Two disparate attractions lie in the far south of the city: a short moto ride from the centre is the disturbing **Toul Sleng Genocide Museum**, with its sobering evidence of the paranoia and inhumanity of Pol Pot and his followers; fifteen minutes' walk further south, **Psar Toul Tom Poung** has the best souvenir-shopping in the country.

Royal Palace and Silver Pagoda

Phnom Penh's most illustrious sight is the complex containing the **Royal Palace** and **Silver Pagoda**, surrounded by over a kilometre of crenellated walls behind which graceful pagodas gleam in the tropical glare. The complex is built in traditional Khmer style, with religious symbolism playing an important part; the surrounding wall is painted pale yellow and white, the two colours representing respectively the Buddhist and Hindu faiths. Little is visible from outside the walls, other than the vividly coloured, multi-tiered roofs edged with soaring golden nagas and spires that glint enticingly against the sky.

The **entrance** to the complex (daily 7.30–11am & 2.30–5pm; $6.25 or 22,000 riel, inclusive of camera fee) is located opposite the *Renakse Hotel*. English-speaking **guides** can be hired by the ticket office (payment is discretionary, but a few dollars will be appreciated); they can provide a wealth of information on not just the palace and pagoda, but also Buddhist and Khmer culture. You must dress appropriately to be admitted: no shorts, singlets, short skirts or skimpy tops (including cap sleeves); neither are you allowed to wear hats or carry a backpack. To do the complex justice you'll need at least two hours, but note that the staff start to close up a full half-hour before the actual closing time. **Photography** isn't permitted inside the Throne Hall or the Silver Pagoda; on occasions the Throne Hall is closed for royal receptions and when the king has a meeting with his ministers. The royal residence itself, northwest

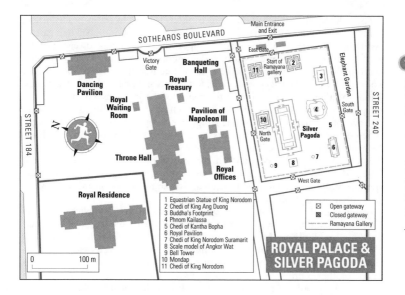

Map legend:

SOTHEAROS BOULEVARD
Main Entrance and Exit
East Gate
Victory Gate
Banqueting Hall
Royal Treasury
Dancing Pavilion
Royal Waiting Room
Pavilion of Napoleon III
Throne Hall
Royal Offices
Royal Residence
Start of Ramayana gallery
South Gate
North Gate
Silver Pagoda
West Gate
Elephant Garden
STREET 240
STREET 184
N

1 Equestrian Statue of King Norodom
2 Chedi of King Ang Duong
3 Buddha's Footprint
4 Phnom Kailassa
5 Chedi of Kantha Bopha
6 Royal Pavilion
7 Chedi of King Norodom Suramarit
8 Scale model of Angkor Wat
9 Bell Tower
10 Mondap
11 Chedi of King Norodom

⊠ Open gateway
⊠ Closed gateway
∙∙∙∙∙ Ramayana Gallery

ROYAL PALACE & SILVER PAGODA

0   100 m

of the Throne Hall, is always closed to the public. Unfortunately, with the short opening hours, the steep entrance fee and the fact that many of the most impressive articles are no longer on display, although it's still worth a visit, there's a definite sense of exploitation.

A **shop** on the site sells expensive silk, postcards and silver pieces, and there are a couple of pricey refreshment stalls.

Royal Palace

The current palace is less than 100 years old, most of the buildings having been reconstructed in concrete in the early part of the twentieth century. The site was once that of the palace of King Norodom – the great-great-grandfather of the current king – who moved his capital here from Oudong in 1863; originally, it was also the site of the palace of King Ponhea Yat in 1434, of which nothing now remains.

Entering the pristine gardens dotted with topiaried trees you'll be close to the **Victory Gate**, which opens onto Sothearos Boulevard and faces the entrance steps to the distinctive, gleaming Throne Hall. This was traditionally only used by the king and queen, though it's now used to admit visiting dignitaries. Just to the north of the gate, the **Dancing Pavilion** (Preah Tineang Chan Chhaya) was built for moonlit performances of classical Cambodian dance.

The Throne Hall

The present **Throne Hall** (Preah Tineang Tevea Vinicchay) was built by King Bat Sisowath in 1919 as a faithful reproduction of Norodom's wooden palace. As befits a building used for coronations and royal ceremonies, it's the most impressive building in the royal compound, topped by a much-photographed four-faced, five-tiered tower. The roof has seven tiers (counted from the lowest level up to the base of the spire) tiled in orange, sapphire and green, representing, respectively, prosperity, nature and freedom. Golden nagas are placed at the corners of each level as protection against evil spirits.

The hall's broad entrance staircase, its banisters formed by seven-headed nagas, leads up to a colonnaded verandah, each column of which is topped by a garuda with wings outstretched, appearing to support the overhanging lower tier of the roof. Entering the **Throne Room** by the east door, you'll find a ceiling painted with finely detailed scenes from the *Reamker* (see *Ramayana* box p.92) in muted colours, and walls stencilled with pastel leaf motifs and images of celestial beings, hands together in *sompeyar*. Down the centre of the hall runs a 35-metre-long, deep-pile carpet, its pattern and colours matching the surrounding tiles flanked by rows of gilt standard **lamps**, the lampshades supported by ceremonial nagas. The north and south entrance doors are protected by large mirrors, which are believed to deflect bad spirits.

Two elaborate golden **coronation thrones** sit on a dais in the centre of the hall, above which a nine-tiered white and gold parasol, symbolizing peacefulness, heaven and ambition, is suspended; two large garudas guard the thrones from their position on the ceiling.

At the rear of the hall is an area (sometimes closed to the public) where the king holds audiences with visiting VIPs and where the busts of six royal ancestors are displayed. **Anterooms** off the hall are used for different purposes: there are separate bedrooms for the king and the queen, to be used during the seven nights after the coronation, during which the royal couple have to sleep apart; another room serves as the king's prayer room; the last room is used to store the king's ashes after his death, while his chedi is being built.

Around the Throne Hall

On either side of the Throne Hall are two small but elaborate buildings. To the north, the **Royal Waiting Room** (Hor Samranphirum) is used on coronation day, when the king and queen rest upstairs before mounting ceremonial elephants from the platform attached to the east side of the building for the coronation procession. A room at ground level serves to store the royal musical instruments and coronation paraphernalia. The pavilion is now a museum for the king-father (the former King Sihanouk). To the south is the **Royal Treasury** (Hor Samritvimean), housing regalia vital to the coronation ceremony, including the Great Crown of Victory, the Sacred Sword and the Victory Spear.

The incongruous grey cast-iron building with a domed clock tower and observation gallery is the **Pavilion of Napoleon III**, used by Empress Eugénie during the inauguration of the Suez Canal in 1869. Presented to King Norodom by Napoleon III in 1876, the pavilion was re-erected here and now serves as a museum of **royal memorabilia**. Downstairs, glass cases line the hallway, containing a collection of royal silver and china tableware. There's also an anteroom housing a motley collection of paintings on subjects ranging from Venetian canals to Chinese landscapes, and room glinting with gleaming medals resting on blue velvet cushions. At the top of the stairs, the austerity of the building is relieved by a collection of stunning silk costumes elaborately embroidered in gold thread; these were made by Queen Kossomak, the present king's grandmother, for the Royal Ballet. A collection of royal portraits on display upstairs includes various pictures of the former King Sihanouk as a dashing young man.

Back outside, the building west of the pavilion houses the **Royal Offices** (Preah Reach Damnakchan). Dating from the 1950s, this is now part museum (housing a collection of gifts to the royal family) and part office for the Ministry of the Royal Palace. The rather plain building just to the east is **Preah Tineang Phochani**, the Banqueting Hall; it is used to host banquets and royal orations, as well as performances of classical dance and music.

Leaving the royal complex by the south gate, you cross the alleyway to enter the courtyard of the Silver Pagoda by its north gate.

Silver Pagoda

Constructed in 1962 by former King Sihanouk to replace the wooden pagoda built by his grandfather in 1902, the **Silver Pagoda** is so named because of its 5329 silver floor tiles, each around 20cm square and weighing more than a kilogram. It's also known as **Wat Preah Keo Morokot**, the Pagoda of the Emerald Buddha, after the green baccarat crystal Buddha within. The pagoda itself is clearly influenced by Bangkok's Wat Phra Kaeo, also home to a precious crystal Buddha to which the one in Phnom Penh bears an uncanny resemblance. Although more than half its contents were stolen during the Khmer Rouge years, the pagoda itself survived pretty much unscathed, and was used to demonstrate to the few international visitors that the regime continued to care for Cambodia's cultural history. A rich collection of artefacts and Buddha images remains, though, and the pagoda is more a museum than place of worship.

The vihara is approached by a stairway of specially imported Italian grey marble. On the verandah you'll need to leave your **shoes** in the racks and check in your **camera** with the security guards. Upon entering the pagoda, the fabulous floor tiles are immediately evident, some delicately engraved with leaf motifs. Atop a five-tiered dais in the centre of the pagoda is the **Emerald Buddha**, seated in meditation. Some sources say this is a modern reproduction, though others date it from the seventeenth century; whatever the case, at just 50cm in height it's put in the shade by the magnificence of the images surrounding it. One of the most dazzling is the life-sized **solid gold Buddha** at ground level, in the centre of the dais; produced in Phnom Penh in 1907 for King Sisowath, it weighs ninety kilograms and is encrusted with 2086 diamonds and precious stones taken from royal jewellery. To its left, a silver seated Buddha is perched on top of a display case, while to the right is a case containing some delightful gold **statuettes** depicting key events from the life of Buddha. The tiny, highly detailed representations show him taking his first steps as a child on seven lotus pads, meditating under a bodhi tree and reclining on reaching nirvana.

Tucked away behind the dais is a serene life-sized standing Buddha from Burma, the elegance of its aged, cream marble not diminished by the brash red of the wooden pedestal. A haphazard, though nonetheless interesting, collection of Buddhas and other artefacts lines the back wall. The weighty gilded-wood **ceremonial litter**, over two metres long, and complete with throne, was used to transport the king on coronation day and required twelve men to carry it.

Display cases containing a diverse collection of objects line the pagoda walls, which include daggers, cigarette cases, some small Buddha images and headdresses and masks used for performances of the *Reamker* by the Royal Ballet. Recently, many of the most impressive and precious exhibits have been replaced by a motley selection of frankly not very exciting items. It's not known if they are away for restoration or have been removed permanently. Before leaving, check out the unusual **stained-glass windows**, one shows Hanuman (see p.92) astride a winged tiger.

The courtyard

Quiet and verdant, the pagoda courtyard is full of monuments, though the most appealing feature is the fabulous 642-metre-long **mural** which runs around the full perimeter of the compound. Telling the epic tale of the *Ramayana* in minute detail, the mythical scenes were painted in vibrant colours by forty artisans working in 1903–04. Although protected by a covered gallery, many of the panels have been damaged by water, and despite a partial restoration in 1985, more work will be needed to preserve what remains. Running **clockwise**, the depiction begins with the **birth of Rama**, to the south of the east entrance gate, and covers his marriage to **Sita** and her abduction and rescue by the **monkey army**. Two of the most delightful scenes, both in good condition, show the monkey army setting out for Lanka (south gallery) and crossing to the island (north gallery).

Of the monuments in the compound, the most eye-catching is the **horseman** directly in front of the Silver Pagoda. Now bearing a head of Norodom, it began life as an equestrian statue of Napoleon III, a typically megalomanic gift from the French emperor to the king.

To either side of the statue are heavily embellished twin **chedi** – Norodom's to the north, Ang Duong's to the south (the latter also has a chedi at Oudong). In the east corner of the compound, a small plain pavilion contains a **footprint of the Buddha** (Buddhapada), a representation of the Buddha dating from the time before images were permitted to be made. There are also ancient manuscripts written on palm leaves, rare survivors of Cambodia's humid climate. Another stylized Buddha's footprint, this one a gift from Sri Lanka, can be found nearby in the pavilion atop the artificial hill, Phnom Kailassa.

The Ramayana

The famous Hindu epic poem the **Ramayana** addresses the moral themes of good versus evil, duty, suffering and karma through the story of **Rama**, the seventh avatar of **Vishnu** (see p.325). A popular theme in Cambodian art and culture, its many episodes are depicted in temple carvings, pagoda art, classical dance and shadow puppetry. A simplified Cambodian version, the **Reamker**, also exists, more often portrayed in dance than in visual art.

At the outset of the story, ten-headed, twenty-armed **Ravana**, king of the **rakasa** demons, is terrorizing the world. As only a human can kill him, Vishnu agrees to appear on earth in human form to re-establish peace, and is duly born as Rama, one of the sons of Emperor Dasaratha. In due course, a sage teaches Rama mystical skills which come in handy in defeating the demons which crop up in the tale and in stringing Shiva's bow, by which feat Rama wins the hand of a princess, **Sita**.

The emperor plans to name Rama as his heir, but the mother of one of Rama's half-brothers tricks her husband into **banishing** Rama to the forest; he is accompanied there by Sita and another of his half-brothers, the loyal **Lakshmana**. After Rama cuts off the ears and nose of a witch who attacks Sita, Ravana gets his revenge by luring Rama away using a demon disguised as a golden deer; Lakshmana is despatched to find Rama, whereupon Ravana abducts Sita and takes her to his island kingdom of **Lanka**. While Rama enlists the help of Sugriva, the monkey king, Sita's whereabouts are discovered by **Hanuman**, son of the wind god. Rama and the monkey army rush to Lanka, where a mighty battle ensues; ultimately Rama looses the golden arrow of Brahma at Ravana who, pierced in the heart, dies ignominiously.

Although the tale as told in Cambodia often ends here, there are two standard denouements. In one, Sita steps into fire and emerges unscathed, proving she has not been defiled by Ravana, after which the couple return home to a joyous welcome and Rama is crowned king. In the alternative, sad, ending, Sita is exiled back to the forest, where she gives birth to twins. When they are 12, the twins are taken to court and Rama is persuaded that he is really their father. He begs forgiveness from Sita and she calls on Mother Earth to bear witness to her good faith. In a moment she is swallowed up by the earth, leaving Rama to mourn on earth for 11,000 years, until he is recalled by death to Brahma.

King Sihamoni

Dancer, teacher, artistic director and United Nations representative, **Norodom Sihamoni** was elected to be Cambodia's next king by the Throne Council in October 2004 on the surprise abdication of his father. The son of **Norodom Sihanouk** and his seventh wife Monineath, Sihamoni's name is made up from the first four letters of Sihanouk and the first four letters of Monineath. Born on May 14, 1953, most of his life was spent out of Cambodia: from the age of 9 he was educated in Prague where he learnt dance, music and theatre; he later studied cinematography in Korea.

In fact, other than his early childhood, the three years he spent **imprisoned** with his family in Phnom Penh during the Khmer Rouge years was the longest he spent in the country until becoming king in October 2004. On the arrival of the Vietnamese, the royal family went into **exile** and for a year Sihamoni acted as private secretary to his father, but from 1980 he was in France (where he spent the next twenty years) as a professor of classical dance in Paris.

From 1992, Sihamoni was Cambodia's permanent representative at the United Nations, and in 1993 he became its **UNESCO ambassador** – resigning both positions on becoming king. Sharing his father's love of cinema, Sihamoni was also director general of Khemara Pictures and has a couple of ballet films to his credit (**Dream** and **4 Elements**).

King Sihamoni keeps a lower profile than his father and as yet hasn't done anything to excite the media, though he is seen around the country and seems well regarded by his subjects. He holds regular meetings with the government and apparently isn't averse to bawling out his ministers, to keep them on their toes.

To the southwest of Phnom Kailassa lies the open-sided chedi of the daughter of King Norodom Sihanouk, Kantha Bopha, who died as an infant in 1952 of leukemia and whose name has been given to children's hospitals in both Phnom Penh and Siem Reap. Behind the Silver Pagoda is a **scale model** of Angkor Wat – incongruous amid the religious and funerary relics. In the west corner of the compound is a **bell tower**, the pealing of whose bell used to signal the opening and closing of the gates to the compound. By the north gate is the **Mondap**, once housing palm-leaf texts, though now it houses a statue of Nandin, the bull ridden by Shiva.

Leaving the courtyard by the south gate, there is a jumble of buildings and a small garden where elephants were tied up when not at work: look out for the display of elephant-shaped boxes and a pavilion of howdahs and cow carts. Another building houses an exhibition related to the coronation of King Sihamoni.

National Museum

The impressive dark-red sandstone building of the **National Museum of Cambodia** houses a rich collection of sculpture, relics and artefacts, dating from prehistoric times to the present. The collection had to be abandoned in 1975 when the city was emptied by the Khmer Rouge; it was subsequently looted and the museum's director murdered. By 1979, when the population returned, the roof had collapsed and the galleries and courtyard had succumbed to the advances of nature – for a time the museum had to battle constantly to protect its exhibits from the guano produced by the millions of **bats** which had colonized the roof; these were finally driven out in 2002.

The museum opened in 1918, and, designed by the French archeologist, George Groslier, comprises four linked **galleries** that form a rectangle around a leafy courtyard, its roof topped with protective nagas.

The **entrance** to the museum (daily 8am – 5pm; $3, photography – courtyard only – $1) is via the central flight of steps leading to the East Gallery. The massive wooden doors here, dating from 1918, and each weighing over a tonne, are worth checking out, their carvings reminiscent of those at Banteay Srei. Inside, there's a place to leave your bags (free) and a stall with a good range of books, including the useful guidebook *Khmer Art in Stone* ($2), or the more comprehensive *New Guide to the National Museum Phnom Penh* ($10), as well as postcards and reproductions of some of the exhibits. English-speaking guides can be hired here ($5); they'll give you information on the archeological styles in the collection and an insight into life during the different periods of Cambodian history. The collection is arranged broadly chronologically, going clockwise from the southeast corner. If you visit the museum after you've seen Cambodia's temples, you'll be able to visualize how the museum's sculptures would have looked in their original surroundings.

East Gallery

The most striking piece in the East Gallery is a massive **Garuda** – over two metres tall and carved from grey sandstone – which dates from the tenth-century Koh Ker period and stands with wings outstretched. The rest of the gallery contains a collection of bronze artefacts, some dating back to the Funan period. To the left, the displays comprise mainly statuary, including many Buddha images, some plain, others more elaborate; some from the fifteenth to seventeenth centuries are of gilded copper and lacquer. The case closest to the entrance houses a fine statuette of Shiva and Uma on Nandin, while another case contains a fine head of an **ascetic** in the style of Banteay Srei; just beyond is a miscellaneous collection of hands and feet from long-disintegrated statues, varying in size from tiny to downright enormous.

Display cases to the right (north) of the gallery contain an assortment of elaborate candleholders, heavy elephant bells, religious water vessels and the paraphernalia for **betel–nut** preparation – including betel-nut containers in the shape of peacocks. The corner chamber hosts the museum's collection of **wooden Buddha statues**, all post-Angkor and showing signs of the red and gilt paints they were once decorated in, although they are in various states of decay, wood not being a durable medium in the Cambodian climate.

South Gallery

Cambodia's **prehistoric period** is skimmed over in a limited exhibition in the southeast corner of the museum. Many of the items on display are drawn from caves around Laang Spean, southwest of Battambang, known to have been inhabited by hunter-gatherers back in 6800 BC, and from excavations of the circular earthworks of ancient rice-farming villages in many parts of the country. You'll see a collection of beads and decorated ceramics, not dissimilar to those in use today. Bronze-working was well advanced by the fourth to second centuries BC, as illustrated by the huge ceremonial drums and bells on display. In the corner is a cast of the skull of Som Ron Sen man; the original was excavated by the French in the early twentieth century and the cast was donated to the museum in 2000.

Pre-Angkor

The South Gallery focuses on the pre-Angkor period, with slim, shapely sixth-century Buddha in relaxed postures, their hair piled on top of their heads in tight ringlets. These early sculptors, though dextrous – the carved garments cleverly give an impression of the contours of the bodies underneath – had yet to master carving in the round, so these statues are carved in **high relief**, with stone remaining between the legs and arms.

Occupying pride of place is a massive, three-metre-tall, eight-armed image of **Vishnu** dating from the Phnom Da era (sixth century). The figure wears a simple, short, pleated loincloth low at the front and pulled up between the legs; the hands variously hold a flame, a conch and a staff, all symbols of Vishnu. A stone arc supports the figure, but in a step towards carving in the round, the stone has been chipped away between the arc and the limbs. Close by, on the south wall, is a sixth-century high relief of **Krishna**, standing left arm aloft, holding up Mount Govardhara.

Images of **Harihara**, a united divinity of Shiva and Vishnu, were popular in pre-Angkorian art, and there are a couple of examples tucked in the corner by the doorway to the courtyard. Nearby, a fine Vishnu from the ninth century (in Kulen style) unusually for Khmer sculpture displays good muscle definition. A series of female statues of Durga and female divinities, all with voluptuous bodies and wearing elegantly draped *sampot*s, line the wall by the courtyard; the statue near the centre of the gallery is particularly elegant, the lady's ear lobes elongated as though from wearing heavy jewellery, symbolizing wealth.

Angkor

A ninth-century, Kulen-style **Vishnu** in the portico of the South Gallery marks the shift to the more formal Angkor period – notice how the sculptors stabilized the statue's bulk, carving the right leg slightly forward of the body and supporting the arms with a staff and sword. The late-ninth-century **Preah Ko period** is characterized by comely figures, epitomized by the shapely statue of Queen Rajendradevi in the west corner of the central section of the South Gallery. Also here is a contemporaneous image of a stocky Shiva.

Passing between a pair of delicately carved sandstone columns you enter the west section of the South Gallery and move into the **Bakheng period** (late ninth to early tenth century). This period is exemplified by a two-metre-tall Shiva from Phnom Krom, whose head was stolen from the Angkor Conservation Department in 1993 and illicitly traded. Through the *Missing Objects: Looting in Angkor* list it was discovered in the Metropolitan Museum of Art in New York, from where it was returned and is now reunited with its body. During the **Koh Ker period** (early to mid-tenth century) sculpture became more dynamic, as illustrated by the athletic torsos of two wrestlers entwined in a throw (near the courtyard). It's worth stepping outside here to see some of the original heads from the divinities of the causeway to Angkor Thom, and also an unusual ablutions bowl made from polished schist, the spout in the shape of a buffalo head.

This section also contains some particularly fine statues from the tenth-century temple of **Banteay Srei**, regarded by many scholars as one of the high points of Khmer art. By the wall a seated image of a smiling **Shiva** has a flat spot on his knee where his wife, Uma, would have sat. He is unadorned save for a carved necklace, but in situ they would both have been draped with precious jewellery. It's impossible to miss the impressive red sandstone statues of the temple guardians, Yasha and Simha; the squatting Simha has bulging eyes and displays a fine set of pointed teeth. On the wall a pediment from Banteay Srei illustrates a scene from the *Mahabharata*, the epic Hindu epic of two warring families, showing two cousins, Bhima and Duryodhana in mortal combat.

West Gallery

Dating from the late tenth century on, the statuary here is more formal than in earlier periods. An elegant example of a graceful female statue of the eleventh-century **Baphuon period** is the slender, small-breasted Lakshmi, consort of Vishnu; her *sampot* dips at the front to reveal her navel and rises above the waist at the back. The museum's pre-Angkor Wat collection contains only a few Buddha images as the kings of the time were mostly adherents of Hinduism, but by the eleventh century, Buddhism was gaining in influence, illustrated here by the Baphuon-era seated Buddhas, some showing a faint smile and sheltered by the seven-headed naga.

The **Angkor Wat period** is lightly represented, freestanding sculptures having been largely replaced by the mighty bas-reliefs carved in situ at the temples. One of the few noteworthy examples, by the west wall, is a pediment from the west entrance of Angkor Wat, depicting part of the *Jataka*, the stories describing the previous incarnations of the Buddha, extracts of which are translated on the wall.

Towards the far end of the gallery is the museum's most famous statue, the image, possibly of **Jayavarman VII,** from the **Bayon period** (late twelfth century). Sitting cross-legged in meditation, the king is portrayed as a clean-shaven, slightly rotund middle-aged man, the expression peaceful. The head of Jayavarman VII is much reproduced as a tourist souvenir. The Buddhist theme resumes in the Bayon-period exhibits at the north end of the gallery, where a thirteenth-century pediment from Prah Palilay shows a seated Buddha in the earth-witnessing *mudra*. The tale of Vishnu riding Garuda is commemorated by a statue from Banteay Chhmar, and retold in English on the wall.

North Gallery

Leaving the stone statuary behind, you skip forward a few centuries to the miscellany of the North Gallery. By far the most impressive exhibit here is the cabin of a nineteenth-century **royal boat**, made of elaborately carved *koki* wood. Inside, the floorboards are smooth and polished, while leaves, flowers and dragons decorate the exterior; the cabin would have been lavishly furnished, ensuring that the king could travel in relative comfort.

The massive funerary **urn** in the centre of the gallery, nearly three metres tall and made of wood, silver and copper overlaid with gilt, was used for the ashes of King Sisowath in 1927 and again for those of King Norodom Suramarit, the grandfather of the present king in 1960.

Not to be missed, just outside under the eaves, is a magnificent **wall panel**, one of a pair looted from Banteay Chhmar temple in 1998 by the military personnel who were supposed to be guarding it. The blocks were cut out from the enclosing wall using machinery, loaded onto lorries and smuggled across the Thai border en route for sale in Bangkok, but were seized by Thai police on the way. Both were returned to Cambodia in 2000. A panel reassembled here depicts a larger-than-life, multi-armed image of Lokesvara.

The riverfront

Sisowath Quay, hugging the river for nearly 4km from the Chroy Chung Va Bridge to Chatomuk Theatre, is the heart of the tourist scene in Phnom Penh, with a plethora of Western bars and restaurants. From Street 106, midway along, the quay forms a broad promenade extending almost 2km south, and there are plans to extend this walkway by a further 4km, all the way to the bridge at Chbar Ampov. Every autumn, the river thrums with crowds flocking to the boat races and festivities of Bonn Om Tuk, the water festival (see *Festivals and*

▲ Restaurant on the riverfront

ceremonies colour section). For the rest of the year, the riverfront is fairly quiet by day, when it's a pleasant place to walk, and gets busier in the late afternoon when the inhabitants of Phnom Penh come out to *dah'leng*, a term that means anything from a short stroll to an all-day trip out of town. At about 5pm, the pavements around the public garden by the Royal Palace turn into a huge picnic ground as mats are spread out, food and drink vendors appear and impromptu entertainment springs up; locals come here to rent a mat and enjoy an alfresco meal. Many will also head across the road to the shrine with the statue of a four-armed Buddha. The story goes that many years ago a crocodile-shaped flag appeared in the river and on Buddhist holidays it would miraculously appear on a flag pole. Now, the spirit of the flag, Preah Ang Dong Kar, has a permanent home here and people make offerings asking for wealth and happiness – at the same time helping the flower, fruit and incense vendors to make a living. Motorized boats with boatman can be hired for a late-afternoon **cruise** on the Mekong ($8 per hour; look out for the signs at the north end of the promenade), where you can sup a beer (bring your own) and watch the sun set behind the Royal Palace.

Between 4pm and 5pm, **Sam Bo**, the Wat Phnom **elephant**, strolls home through the rush-hour traffic along Sisowath Quay; if you have some bananas, he's happy to stop for a snack and a snapshot. The best place to catch up with him is around the *FCC*.

Wat Ounalom

The rather sombre concrete chedi that fronts Sisowath Quay belies the fact that **Wat Ounalom** is one of Phnom Penh's oldest and most important pagodas, dating all the way back to the reign of Ponhea Yat in the fifteenth century – though there's little evidence now of its age. In the early 1970s, over five hundred monks lived at the pagoda, which also housed the library of the *Institut Bouddhique*, subsequently destroyed, along with many of the buildings, by the Khmer Rouge.

The pagoda gets its name from its role as repository for an *ounalom*, a hair from the **Buddha's eyebrow**, contained in the large chedi behind the vihara; you can gain access if you ask at the small bookshop near the entrance. Within the chedi are four sanctuaries, the most revered being the one facing east, where there's a fine bronze Buddha. The **vihara**, which dates from 1952, is only open for the monks' use in the early morning; unusually, it's built on three floors, and houses a commemorative statue of Samdech Huot Tat, the venerable fourth patriarch of Cambodian Buddhism, who was murdered by the Khmer Rouge. Despite its unappealing exterior, the dark-grey chedi is worth a quick look for its **crypt**, in which hundreds of small cubicles hold the funerary urns of Cambodian notables, most of which are adorned with bright plastic flowers and a photograph of the deceased.

The Independence Monument and around

The riverfront south of the Royal Palace is home to the Chatomuk Theatre; while beyond the *Cambodiana* hotel is Hun Sen Park, an area under development. The **Buddhist Institute** is here and just around the corner is the enormous, new **National Assembly** building. This stretch of road is popular with the city's rich boys who come here to road-race their powerful SUVs in full sight of the police on guard at the Assembly building.

Alternatively, cut **inland** through a peaceful park to the Independence Monument, at the intersection of Sihanouk and Norodom boulevards. A golden stupa in the park commemorates the sixteen people killed outside the old National Assembly (corner of St 240 and Sothearos Blvd) on March 30, 1997, when grenades were thrown into a rally led by Sam Rainsy. Beyond it is the **Cambodian–Vietnamese Friendship Monument**, commemorating the Vietnamese liberation of Phnom Penh from the Khmer Rouge in January 1979; it features massive sandstone figures of a Khmer woman holding a baby, flanked by two armed Vietnamese liberation soldiers.

Across the park, **Wat Botum** is another of the five original pagodas founded by Ponhea Yat in 1442. The present structure was built by King Sisowath Monivong and dates from 1937; fortunately, it escaped damage by the Khmer Rouge. The grounds are crammed with elaborate and picturesque chedis, many of which hold the ashes of rich politicians and important monks; enormous, gaudy statues of giants, lions and tigers pepper the grounds.

From here, there's a good view west past the fountains to the recently refurbished **Independence Monument** (aka Victory Monument), commemorating independence from the French in 1953, and now also serving as a cenotaph to the country's war dead. The distinctive, dark-red sandstone tower, completed in 1958, is reminiscent of an Angkorian sanctuary tower, its multi-tiered roofs embellished with over a hundred nagas. At night it makes a dramatic sight when the fountains are floodlit in red, blue and white, the primary colours of the national flag.

Like Wat Botum, sprawling **Wat Lanka**, across from the monument, was also founded in 1442 and gets its name from its historic ties with monks in Sri Lanka. The pagoda vies with Wat Ounalom for importance, and many of the monks here are highly regarded teachers. Within the vihara there are scenes from the Buddha's life featuring an idiosyncratic local touch – one shows Angkor Wat, while another depicts tourists climbing Wat Phnom. Meditation classes for the public are held in the vihara twice a week (see "Listings" p.114).

The alleys around Wat Prayuvong, a couple of hundred metres south on Norodom Boulevard, are the city's centre for the manufacture of **spirit houses** (see p.329) and religious statuary in the capital – you can't miss the brightly painted displays on the roadside. Although everything is now made in concrete, the artistry remains elaborate and the variety of statues and statuettes fascinating; a number of artists here also do religious paintings, some on an impressive scale.

Southwest of the centre

The main reason to venture out towards the southern districts of the city is to visit the **Toul Sleng Genocide Museum**, an inevitably harrowing and heart-rending experience, but one which puts into context the suffering of the Cambodian people and country. More history from 1975 crops up 1500m east, at the site of the **former US Embassy** (now belonging to the Ministry of Fisheries and bearing no outward clues to its past), on the northeast corner of the intersection of Norodom and Mao Tse Toung boulevards. Under threat from advancing Khmer Rouge troops, US marines airlifted 276 Americans, other foreigners and Cambodians to safety – the last to leave, with the "Stars and Stripes" clutched under his arm, was the ambassador, John Gunter Dean. The evacuation was completed just five days before the Khmer Rouge entered Phnom Penh, and the Khmer Rouge subsequently used the premises as a place of execution, slaughtering senior officers of Lon Nol's army in the grounds.

Toul Sleng Genocide Museum

Originally the Toul Svay High School, from 1975 to 1979 the **Toul Sleng Genocide Museum** (daily 7.30–5.30am; $2; entrance off Street 113) was the notorious Khmer Rouge prison known as **S-21**, through whose gates more than thirteen thousand people (up to twenty thousand according to some estimates) passed to their death. S-21 was an interrogation centre designed for the educated and elite: here doctors, teachers, military personnel and government officials all passed through Khmer Rouge hands. The regime was indiscriminate in its choice of victims; even children, some of them just babies, were among those detained here and subsequently slaughtered.

Although the compound is surrounded by high walls and ringed by barbed wire, it's still difficult to comprehend, as you admire the peaceful grounds fragrant with frangipani blossom, that this was once a detention, interrogation and torture centre. Up to 1500 prisoners were housed here at any one time, either confined in tiny cells or chained to the floor or each other in the former classrooms. The **balconies** on the upper floors are still enclosed with the wire mesh that prevented the prisoners jumping to a premature death. Some cells still contain **iron bedsteads** to which inmates were shackled; others are so small that there is hardly room for someone to lie down. When the Vietnamese army entered the prison in January 1979, they found just seven prisoners alive; the corpses of some prisoners who had died shortly before were discovered in the cells and buried in graves in the courtyard. On the ground floor there is a display of thousands of black and white **photographs** of the victims, their eyes expressing a variety of emotions, from fear through defiance to emptiness. Each one of them holds a number – the Khmer Rouge were meticulous in documenting their prisoners. Although the majority murdered here were Cambodian, foreigners, both Western and Asian, were also interrogated and tortured.

Things get no easier emotionally after the photographic display, as you progress to a display detailing the methods of **torture** practised here, some of which are unflinchingly depicted in paintings by the artist Van Nath, one of the survivors. Prominent is a **water chamber** where prisoners were systematically drowned until they confessed. Worth reading are the sombre extracts in the exhibition area from forced "confessions", and the exchanges of letters between the cadres, who sadistically continued to victimize prisoners until their declarations conformed to the guards' own version of the truth.

Every day at 10am and 3pm a made-for-television docu-drama, *Bophana* by Rithy Panh, traces the tangled, tragic romance between two Cambodians caught up with the Khmer Rouge. It's shown upstairs in the Documentation Centre of Cambodia building on the same site.

Although the most notorious exhibit, a map of Cambodia made up of the **skulls** of victims tortured here, is no longer on display, one room houses a shrine surrounded by skulls, a rather morbid memorial to those murdered.

Wat Phnom

In the northeast of the city, just a few hundred metres from the riverfront, **Wat Phnom** (daily dawn–dusk; foreigners $1), where the hilltop sanctuary from which the capital got its name once stood, is one of the principal pleasure spots for the inhabitants of Phnom Penh, drawing the crowds especially at weekends and on public holidays. Before climbing the hill (which, even at a mere 27m high, is sufficient to dwarf anything else in the capital), you'll be directed to one of the payment booths to buy your **ticket**. The nicest way up the hill is by the **naga staircase** on the east side, passing some bronze friezes (depicting scenes of battle) and dancing apsaras (reproductions of bas-reliefs at Angkor Wat) on the way. The sanctuary on the summit has been rebuilt many times, most recently in 1926, and nothing remains of the original structures; the surrounding gardens were originally landscaped in the late nineteenth century by the French, who also installed a zoo (of which nothing remains) and the clock on the south side of the hill, restored for the Millennium, now sports a dial that glows in fluorescent colours as night draws in.

As with other Buddhist sites, you must take off your shoes (it's best to take them in with you, as Western shoes are popular amongst the petty thieves who operate on the hill) to enter the **vihara**, always hazy from burning incense. Over the years, the smoke has darkened the wall-paintings, making it hard to make out the depictions of the *Jataka* stories. A constant stream of Khmer pass through the pagoda, paying their respects and trying to discover their fortunes by holding a palm-leaf book above their heads and, without looking, inserting a small pointer between the pages; the page thus picked out contains the prediction, although sometimes it takes three attempts to get an acceptable fortune.

Behind the vihara is a shrine to **Daun Penh**, the woman credited with founding the sanctuary here see p.73); the shrine contains her genial image, much revered. The large white chedi contains the ashes of King Ponhea Yat (*d.* 1467). On the north side of the hill just below the summit is a busy shrine to **Preah Chao**, a Taoist goddess whom people come to ask for good luck, health or success with their business; her helpers, Thien Ly Than (who can see for 1000 miles) and Thuan Phong Nhi (who can hear sounds 1000 miles away), stand close by Judging by the elaborate **offerings** on the altar, requests are obviously granted – it's not unusual to see whole cooked chickens, surrounded by their cooked innards and unlaid eggs offered on plates. Resident **monkeys** are very good at stealing the offerings, and feeding them is said to be a good way of acquiring merit for the next life, as is releasing the tiny birds which hawkers sell from cages all around the hill – you might well spot a Cambodian buying up the entire cage. There is some local debate about the worthiness of the exercise, though, as it's said that the birds just fly back to their cages again.

Before leaving, it's worth paying a call on **Sam Bo**, the 40-something elephant who gives rides around the base of the hill for $5. He's very appreciative if you want to feed him some bananas or sugar cane, and it's OK to take photos without going for the ride.

Around Wat Phnom

During the colonial era, Wat Phnom was at the heart of the **French quarter**, its leafy boulevards graced by public buildings, offices and villas for the administrators. Many of these structures survive today and the immediate area is worth exploring to get a taste of their historic grandeur.

Phnom Penh's **main post office** is housed in a fine colonial building to the east of Wat Phnom, on Street 13. Dating from the early twentieth century, it occupies one side of a colonial square just off the river which in pre-Khmer Rouge years bustled with cafés and restaurants; an attempt is being made to resurrect the area, but there's a little way to go yet. The post office itself was restored in 2001; an old photograph of the interior hangs on the wall inside, the counters shown still recognizable today, though in other respects the building has had numerous makeovers.

West along Street 92 from Wat Phnom, the **National Library** (daily 8–11am & 2–5pm) is another fine colonial building, dating from 1924. During Pol Pot's regime, books from the library's collection were either destroyed or tossed out onto the pavement, and the building was turned into a stable. In the 1980s, the Vietnamese filled up the shelves with their own books, though barely a decade later these were being bound with string and sold by the kilo. It's now the French who are helping to re-stock the library (though again with titles in their own language). The vast majority of the residents of Phnom Penh still have no idea that their city even has a public library, however, making it a good place to go if you're looking for a little solitude. A room off the main reading room contains a collection of rare palm-leaf manuscripts, the colour of parchment, and the walls are decorated with some nice etchings and photos of the country

Hello, what-is-your-name?

Though you may be approached by older people who learnt French in their school-days, they represent the fortunate few who survived the murder of the educated during the Pol Pot era, when the number of French-speakers in Cambodia was drastically reduced. In the aftermath, the emphasis began to switch to English, as the arrival of UNTAC and the NGOs gave rise to a demand for English-speaking interpreters. Nowadays computers, tourism and Cambodia's membership of the Association of Southeast Asian Nations (ASEAN), whose working language is English, are driving the rush to learn the language.

English is now taught in **state schools**, though cursorily at best, so parents who can afford it send their children to supplementary English-language classes at private institutions immediately after school hours, with adults piling in to take courses after the children leave at 5pm. At 500–1000 riel an hour, these lessons are an expensive business for many, but the outlay is regarded as an investment well made, comprehension of English being perceived as essential to getting a decent job. Thanks to massive demand, any establishment with a few desks and chairs can set itself up as a language school, and the shortage of qualified teachers means that the instructor is often only a couple of study books ahead of their students. Classes are advertised on signs and banners in Phnom Penh and all major towns; the place to glimpse them being conducted in the capital is **Street 164**, parallel to and just north of Charles de Gaulle Boulevard, near Psar Orussey.

Although learning **by rote** is the norm in Cambodia, many students in the cities now have a reasonable understanding of English; elsewhere though, teaching is at best rudimentary and it is still possible that you'll encounter giggling children rattling off the well-worn phrase "Hello, what is your name?" before running off. without any expectation of a reply.

from the early twentieth century. The Archive Centre, in a separate building behind the library, sometimes has exhibitions of newly restored material. A few minutes' walk further along, at the western end of Street 92, the **Raffles Hotel Le Royal** is a fabulous blend of colonial, Khmer and Art Deco styles, set in lush tropical gardens; its conservatory is a delightful spot to take morning coffee or afternoon tea.

The **train station**, a little way to the southwest, occupies a commanding position facing the boulevard which runs between streets 106 and 108 all the way to the river. Built in the early 1930s, it has an impressive Art Deco facade, but there's little activity here except when the train to Battambang arrives or leaves. The unmistakable blue chedi in front of the station, **Preah Sakyamoni**, contains a sliver of a bone of Buddha, while behind the station, an old 1929 steam train has been restored and put on permanent display. The train was used until the early 1990s when diesel locomotives were introduced.

Traditional healers can be seen at work in front of the station, treating patients either by "coining", scraping the flesh of arms, back or chest with a copper disc to cause raised blood vessels; or "cupping", the alternative therapy championed in the West by Gwyneth Paltrow, where a heated glass jar is applied to the back, chest or forehead, causing raised red circles of flesh. Headaches, cold and flu symptoms, general aches and pains – indeed, just about any ailment – are claimed to be treatable by these methods.

Around Chroy Chung Va Bridge

Despite a smattering of colonial buildings, the area north of **Wat Phnom** is not an especially attractive part of the city, but it's worth a short detour for historical reasons. Spanning the Tonle Sap, the **Chroy Chung Va Bridge** carries National Route 6, the major trunk road to Kompong Cham and Siem Reap. The original bridge was blown up in 1973 either by (depending on who you believe) Lon Nol forces attempting to prevent the Khmer Rouge entering the city or by the Khmer Rouge forces advancing on the capital. For years the bridge was known as *spean bak*, "broken bridge", though many locals now refer to it as *chuowa chuoul hauwy*, "not broken anymore". Expats often call it the "Japanese Bridge", as it was rebuilt with funds from Japan in 1993. North of the bridge are Phnom Penh's **docks**.

The traffic island at the northern end of Monivong Boulevard, just before the bridge, contains the city's most bizarre monument. In 1999, the government, concerned about the proliferation of firearms, seized all the guns it could lay its hands on and, amid great political fanfare, had them crushed. Pointedly, the remains were melted down and a nameless sculpture of a **revolver** with a knot tied in its barrel was cast; however, cynics say that only the broken guns were smashed and that the good ones were handed out to the police and military. Recently its twin was installed in Kompong Thom, with plans for a third in Battambang.

High white walls screen the **French Embassy** on the western side of Monivong, just south of the traffic circle. The embassy is noteworthy only because of the events of April 1975, when eight hundred foreigners and six hundred Cambodians took refuge here from the Khmer Rouge. The Khmer Rouge then held everyone here captive, denying them any diplomatic privileges. Eventually foreigners and Cambodian women married to foreign men were released, escorted to the airport and allowed to leave the country; Cambodian men married to foreign women had to remain, subsequently disappeared and were never seen again.

Prices

Eating **inexpensively** is not difficult in Phnom Penh if you stick to market stalls, simple Cambodian restaurants and some of the Indian and Chinese places listed in this guide. Using these you can fill up for $2.5 to $5. In backpacker guesthouses you'll be able to eat for about $3-4, but once you venture into tourist-centred and Western-oriented establishments prices rise and you'll be looking at around $4–6 for a simple main course. In slightly plusher places, and those with a prestigious location expect to pay upwards of $6–10 for a main course, maybe slightly more depending on what you choose. The **most expensive** places to eat are in the restaurants of the premier hotels and in a few French restaurants around town, where you should expect to pay $15 and above for a main course, with extra for vegetables and accompaniments.

Eating

Although Cambodia still ranks among the world's poorest countries, Phnom Penh has a vast range of places to eat to suit all pockets and tastes, from noodle shops and market stalls, where you can eat for a few thousand riel, to sophisticated Western places where prices for a main course rise to $15–$20. Many guesthouses have small restaurants serving economical, if unexciting, fare for a couple of dollars or so a dish.

Restaurants

On the whole, the food in Phnom Penh is of a reasonable standard, so you're unlikely to go far wrong if you pick somewhere to eat at random. The **riverfront** is a good place to start looking, with a gamut of cafés, restaurants and bars serving both Khmer and international dishes. Although the attractive location means you need to pick carefully if you're on a budget, it's possible to get a decent single-course meal for $2–3. Newly popular, is **Boeng Keng Kang**, broadly Street 278 from streets 51 to 63; the area is packed with cafés, restaurants and bars, and the atmosphere is more laid-back than the riverfront (where the myriad of vendors and beggars can get a little wearing). For fine-dining on imported meat and wine, one of the French restaurants should fit the bill; even though they're expensive in Cambodian terms they cost a fraction of what you would pay in the West.

In the heart of town, a great place to fill up and try a selection of **traditional Khmer dishes** is at the bustling **night market**, on Street 107 just west of the bus station, where the stalls set up for business in the late afternoon. There aren't many tables as most Cambodians come here to buy takeaway meals, but stallholders will usually try to find you a spot to sit and eat. For *sop chhnang day*, a fondue-like dish where you cook meat and vegetables in a pot of stock at your table, there are plenty of establishments to try on Monivong and Sihanouk boulevards. When the Cambodians want to **splash out** they head across the Chroy Chung Va Bridge to **Prek Leap**; about 1km east of the bridge, the road is flanked by vast, gaudy, brightly lit restaurants built above the flood plain on enormous stilts. It's not really the place for solitary diners, but for a group, a traditional Khmer meal comprising soup, a couple of fish and meat dishes with accompanying plate of vegetables and rice you'll pay around $8-10 per person. The restaurants are packed out by noon for lunch, 7pm for dinner, their planked car parks groaning under the weight of four-wheel drives. It's not certain how much longer these places will survive, as the floodplains are being filled in for the development of apartment blocks.

Phnom Penh has lots of good **Chinese** restaurants. **Street 136**, west of Psar Thmei, is home to a cluster of inexpensive – and roaringly popular – Chinese places. For a slap-up meal, several of the deluxe hotels have excellent Chinese restaurants. There are plenty of **Indian**, **Pakistani** and **Bangladeshi** places to eat in town, which are especially popular with the expat community. The city boasts a staggering variety of **Western restaurants**, and it's easy to eat something different every night, from pizza and pasta to grilled steaks and crunchy salads. Unsurprisingly, French food is particularly good. **Sisowath Quay** features a concentration of Western-oriented restaurants and bars, as well plenty of **cafés** where you can linger over a glass of wine, a coffee or a meal; given the location, prices here are a little higher, though by no means prohibitive.

In addition to sit-down meals, stalls and roadside vendors sell grilled chicken and fish to take away, while fresh baguettes and rolls are sold in the markets in the morning and are available all day around the city from hawkers with handcarts. Fresh fruit can be bought from markets and at the specialist stalls on Monivong Boulevard south of Sihanouk, and on Sihanouk Boulevard itself southwest of the Olympic Stadium. To **self-cater**, it's easy enough to buy fresh produce and tinned goods from the markets; to buy Western provisions such as cheese, yoghurt, chocolate, and even brown bread, you'll have to go to one of the supermarkets listed on p.112.

Eating with a conscience

There are several cafés and restaurants around town that either train the under-privileged in the hospitality trade or donate profits to helping those in need. These establishments are moderately priced, so expect to pay around $10 for a starter and main course. All places listed here are shown on the maps on p.76 or p.84.

Café 151 151 Sisowath Quay. You'll have to look hard so as not to miss this tiny coffee shop which also serves juices and shakes; street children are the beneficiaries of its profits.

Café Yejj 170 Street 450, across the road from Psar Toul Tom Poung, Serving Siem Reap coffee, with free refills, and Western bistro-style food, paninis and wraps, the café helps women at risk by providing them with training and support. Daily 7am–6pm.

Friends (Mith Samlanh) 215 Street 13 near the National Museum. Trains street youths in the restaurant and catering trade; tapas, Western and Cambodian snacks, shakes, iced coffees and great cocktails. Daily 11am–11pm.

Le Café du Centre Street 184, in the grounds of the French Cultural Centre. Serving sandwiches, daily specials, cakes and ice creams, this is another project of the street children's NGO Mith Samlanh. Daily 8am–9pm.

Le Lotus Blanc at Stung Meanchey (7min from the **Inter-Continental Hotel**), call ☏012/508537 for directions. This vocational training restaurant serves 3-course set French and Asian menus for $6. Profits support the children from Stung Meanchey rubbish dump. Open Mon–Fri, October–July.

Romdeng 21 Street 278, near Monivong Blvd. This non-profit training school for former street youths serves up Cambodian fare in a colonial villa. Lunch and dinner Monday–Saturday.

Around Psar Thmei

Aman Indian 46 Street 84, near the GST bus station. Cheap, authentic Indian food, including mouth-watering chicken tikka roasts on the outdoor barbecue at lunchtime, with *palak paneer*, a spicy spinach and Indian cheese dish, as a good alternative for veggies. Closed 2.30–5.30pm & all day Sun.

East India Curry 9 Street 114. Extensive range of moderately priced dishes, all enticingly presented on banana leaves; excellent vegetarian options too, including a generous vegetarian *thali*.

Mamak's 18 Street 114. Since opening in 1992, this inexpensive halal Malaysian restaurant has become something of a Phnom Penh institution. *Roti chanai*, a paper-thin bread cooked on a griddle and eaten with curry sauce, is a popular breakfast dish, washed down with *teh tarek*, a sweet, milky-red tea, or *teh thomada*, the same but without the sweet milk. At midday they lay out an array of dishes to choose from, including spicy fish steaks, crispy fried chicken and plenty of vegetable dishes.

Peking Canteen 93 Street 136. The modest setting is more than made up for by the food, with divine steamed spring rolls and excellent beef with green peppers. Veggies should try their noodles with "special sauce" – a tasty soy and peanut dressing. Portions are plentiful and cheap.

Sam Doo 56–58 Kampuchea Krom Blvd. The basic surroundings belie the delicious fare, including juicy Szechuan prawns with a spicy dressing, Peking duck and renowned dim sum. Depending on your choice of food, and hunger level, it's an inexpensive to moderately priced establishment.

Sorya Street 142. Once an old cinema, (hence the vast interior with palatial staircases), this inexpensive to moderately priced place does a roaring breakfast trade and cooks up a particularly delicious *geautieuv sop*, breakfast noodle soup. It also specializes in sweetmeats – the lurid green *ktohi*, like a cloudy Turkish delight subtly flavoured with sweetly fragrant pandanus leaves, is unforgettable.

The riverfront

Chi Cha 27 Street 110, near Psar Chas. Excellent budget Indian restaurant: for $2.50 you get a meat curry and a vegetable dish, roti, rice, dhal and salad, plus free second helpings of roti or rice.

FCC Phnom Penh 363 Sisowath Quay ☎023/210142. Set upstairs in a fabulous colonial-era building, this renowned place is a favourite meeting place for expats and travellers and has a great menu with everything from Khmer dishes to Mexican fare. Perch on a stool overlooking the Tonle Sap, laze in the comfy lounge chairs with a glass of wine or sit out on the terrace and enjoy the view

of the National Museum. Expect to pay around $8 for lunch, $12 for dinner, excluding drinks.

Frizz 335 Sisowath Quay. The menu at this small but excellent, moderately priced restaurant helpfully includes an accurate English translation of Cambodian dishes. The *chhnang phnom pleung*, "volcano pot", a table-top charcoal brazier, on which you can cook your own meat and vegetables is worth trying. Also does cookery courses (see p.113 for details).

Gold Fish River Sisowath Quay, on the river bank at the junction with Street 106. This place has a lovely location out over the Tonle Sap and a menu that's consistently good, including tasty squid and frog dishes and good French fries. Dishes are around $2–4 each, depending on what you pick.

Happy Herbs Pizza 345 Sisowath Quay ☎023/362349. This place has been running for years and still serves up the best pizzas in town (and good vegetarian choices). Also does tasty pasta dishes, plus omelettes, pork chops and steak for a moderate price. Call for free delivery.

Khmer Borane 389 Sisowath Quay, near the corner with Street 184. In a prime river-front spot this unpretentious restaurant serves up great Khmer food. The staff are attentive, the food well prepared and the prices economical.

Ponlok 319 Sisowath Quay. Khmer food with some concessions to the Western palette, and a picture menu to help you choose a moderately priced meal. The stir-fried pork with ginger and sweet-and-sour fish are firm favourites.

Pop Café da Giorgio 371 Sisowath Quay, near the *FCC*. This tiny Italian restaurant is where the expats come to eat authentic pasta and other Italian dishes. What it lacks in size, it more than makes up for in atmosphere and the quality of its moderately priced food. Open 11am–2.30pm, 6–11pm.

Around Boeung Kak and Wat Phnom

Calmette Monivong Blvd, near the hospital. Popular local restaurant serving a tangy *sumlar ngam ngouw*, lemon chicken soup, and spicy *bok lehong*, papaya salad at about $2 per dish.

Lazy Gecko 23 Street 93, near Boeung Kak lake. Friendly, with a responsible ethos, this inexpensive travellers' café features all the old favourites, from banana pancakes to French fries and burgers, along with some Khmer dishes.

Around Psar Orussey and the Olympic Stadium

Beef Soup Restaurant *Favour Hotel*, Monivong Blvd. Locals reckon this is the best place for *sop chhnang day* in town; the beef version – as the restaurant's name suggests – is the house speciality and will set you back around $6 per person for one plate each of all the accompaniments, which include thinly sliced meat, several plates of vegetables – including mushrooms, noodles, tofu and a bubbling pot of stock. The waitresses will help you with the protocol, or just copy what the locals do.

Bites 240B Street 107. Serving tasty Mamak – Indian Muslim – food from Malaysia, this welcoming restaurant is a great addition to the eating options in this part of town. Try the melt-in-the-mouth *roti-chani*, but the cheeseburgers aren't bad either.

Nouveau Pho de Paris 258 Monivong Blvd. An enduring favourite, this popular Chinese, Cambodian and Vietnamese restaurant serves up huge steaming bowls of tasty *pho*, spring rolls with a dipping sauce of chilli and ground peanuts, and succulent crispy duck, to name but a few for around $3–4 each. There's a picture menu, and the waiters also speak English. Branch on Monivong Blvd, near the French Embassy.

Royal India 21 Street 111. This simple, friendly restaurant dishes up consistently good and reasonably priced Indian food. The comprehensive menu includes chicken and mutton curries, freshly made samosas and good sweet lassis.

Around the Independence Monument

Al Ameen Indian & Malaysian 5 Street 51, near the corner with Street 278. Popular with Indian expats, the *thalis* are great value at $3 for a vegetarian version or $3.5 for the chicken one, and there are extra free chapatis for the hungry.

Boat Noodle 1 184 Street 63. Serves up a decent Thai green curry, and other economical Thai and Khmer food. Service can be a bit slow.

Khmer Restaurant Street 278, near the *Golden Gate Hotel*. Excellent Western food (and a reasonable selection of Khmer dishes) including a mouth-watering vegetarian lasagne, decent baked potatoes, fish and chips and sandwiches with fries. Portions are generous and inexpensive.

Garden Centre 2 4 Street 57. Soothing water fountains relax the mind while plates of moderately priced salads, tasty toasted paninis and the like satisfy the stomach. Closed Tues.

Malis 136 Norodom Blvd ☎023/221022. This trendy, upmarket Cambodian restaurant is unique in Phnom Penh, with its stylish

modern building and tables around a raised pond in the courtyard. Popular with wealthier Khmers and the city's expat business and NGO workers, it serves traditional and modern Khmer food from 7am–11pm. It's not cheap though; a breakfast of *geautieuv sop* and coffee will set you back around $4, while dinner dishes range from moderate to expensive.

Mountain Village 5 Street 278. Hidden behind potted palms this little café-cum-crafts-shop serves up a selection of inexpensive Western and Asian fare from beans on toast to curried pumpkin soup. As befits its name, the coffee comes from Rattanakiri, and when you've tasted it you can take home a packet, or, if you prefer, a bottle of palm wine.

Shiva Shakti 70 Sihanouk Blvd, near the Independence Monument. Classical Indian–Mogul cuisine in an upmarket setting, with specialities including tender kebabs and tandoori dishes. Expect to pay upwards of $8 for a single dish with rice and chapati or nan bread. Closed Mon.

South of the centre

Banyan 245 Street 51, next to Tabitha (see p.111). The $2 Thai buffet at lunchtime in a garden setting takes some beating; at night you can dine on more expensive, though still moderately priced Thai food under the stars. (This used to be the *Baan Thai* and has a loyal following among NGO workers.)

Garden Centre Café 23 Street 57 ☎023/363002. As befits the name, the potted plants amidst the tables in the shady courtyard really are for sale, and there's also an extensive daytime menu of moderately priced Western and Asian food, and some excellent vegetarian dishes including appetizing quiches and freshly made salads. Closed Mon.

Khmer-Thai Restaurant 26 Street 135, near Wat Toul Tom Poung. Out on a limb in terms of location, this classy restaurant doesn't advertise, but is still packed out every night by locals in the know. Its inexpensive Khmer and Thai food ($2–$3 per dish) is served efficiently and in good-sized portions; the fish cakes with chilli dip are enough for two as a starter.

Topaz 182 Norodom Blvd, next to Wat Than. Arguably the best French food in Phnom Penh, served in a startlingly modern building, with fine wines and succulent steaks that are exceptional. Expensive, but worth it.

Cafés and coffee shops

Phnom Penh's busy **café** society of the 1950s and 1960s vanished during the war years, but there has now been a massive revival and wherever you are in town you're pretty sure to find a place to have a break. Many are attached to galleries, shops or Internet centres and new ones are opening every week, so this is just a selection of what's on offer.

Café Fresco 361 Sisowath Quay, under the *FCC*. Whether you want breakfast pastries, a mid-morning coffee, a smoothie or to create your own lunchtime sandwich (including a choice of breads) you'll be satisfied here. Not the cheapest place in town but given the quality and the location you're unlikely to be disappointed. Daily 7am – 8pm.

Fizz Street 178. Trendy juice bar serving smoothies, juices and fizzes (fruit juices with soda). The watermelon fizz is fabulously refreshing.

Java Sihanouk Blvd, east of Independence Monument. As well as full breakfasts with a choice of coffees, this café-gallery does light meals and a delightful range of home-made bagels, muffins and desserts. Changing exhibitions in the gallery feature works by local and foreign artists. The bakery at the back has delicious pastries to take away. *Java* also runs the coffee shop in Monument Books.

The Shop 39 Street 240. More London than Phnom Penh, you'll be hard-pressed to remember where you are. Not only does *The Shop* offer a fantastic café atmosphere, but it has great deli sandwiches and pastries and coffee too. Open 7am–7pm Mon–Sat, 7am–3pm Sun.

Sunflower Bakery Street 93. A huge slab of freshly baked carrot or banana cake, and a cafetière of coffee will set you back just 4000 riel – a real bargain.

Drinking, entertainment and nightlife

There are plenty of Western-oriented **bars** in Phnom Penh, although not much else in the way of entertainment – for the most part nightlife in the city comes down to drinking, drinking and more drinking. Fortunately the range of venues is varied, ranging from stylish cocktails on the breezy verandah of a colonial-era mansion to a sleazy beer in a dark bar with loud music, smoky air and pushy hostesses.

The rest of Phnom Penh's **nightlife** – that which doesn't specifically target foreign visitors and expats – is geared to men only and revolves around girlie bars, karaoke, dance halls and local discos. Under the strobe lights, you'll hear a deafening mix of Thai and Filipino pop, a selection of Western numbers, as well as traditional Khmer music and songs – such as those by Cambodia's pop idol, Sin Sisamouth. After a few drinks, you'll probably want to have a go at the elegantly flowing **rhom vong**, in which the men and women dance side by side, couples one behind the other, a bit like a double conga; the chain slowly progresses around the floor, hands gracefully weaving in and out. These venues are at their best after 10pm; entrance is usually free. Beer girls (see box, p.40) will be on hand to pour the drinks and for pay-as-you-go dances. These places are usually OK for foreigners, as long as you don't get too drunk or obnoxious. Bear in mind too that there is sometimes a thuggish element in places frequented by the rich, bored sons of the Cambodian nouveaux riches. Step on their feet while dancing or stare at their female companions and you may have a real incident on your hands.

Bars and clubs

In addition to the bars on and around the riverfront, the serious bar-fly should visit Street 51. Starting at the *Cathouse Tavern*, in the north, there's enough to keep you moving south until the early hours, when you could seek out some early-morning food stalls before heading back to your guesthouse for bed. Many of the bars open in the late afternoon, closing when the last person leaves.

Broken Bricks Corner of streets 130 and 5. Check out the run-down look and graffitied walls at this snug, street-corner bar; eclectic music and laid-back atmosphere.

Cantina Sisowath Quay. Run by well-known Phnom Penh expat Hurley Scroggins, this no-frills bar and eatery on the riverfront stands out from its immediate neighbours thanks to its cheerful staff, while the crowds sitting outside on the pavement at weekends give the place a party atmosphere.

Cathouse Tavern Corner of streets 51 and 118. This Filipino bar retains much of the sleazy atmosphere of its UNTAC days, though it now boasts a pool table and TV. Daily from 4pm.

Elephant Bar *Raffles Hotel Le Royal,* Street 92. Splash out on a cocktail and soak up the 1930s elegance, with ambience and service to match, plus live music from the resident pianist. Happy hour 5–7pm.

FCC Phnom Penh Sisowath Quay ☎023/210142. Possibly the most atmospheric bar-cum-restaurant in the region (imagine a Southeast Asian version of the bar in *Casablanca*). The balmy air, whirring ceiling fans and spacious armchairs invite one to spend a hot afternoon getting slowly smashed. Relatively pricey, but worth it.

Green Vespa 95 Sisowath Quay (opposite the Tourist Dock). Popular Irish-owned bar has a huge drinks menu, with icy cold beer in high demand; it runs regular promotions and has a limited choice of food.

Heart of Darkness 26 Street 51. This overrated bar has been here for ages and is one of those places everybody has to visit once. The gothic decor and eclectic music made it the hipster hangout of Phnom Penh a decade ago, but the belligerent sons of the city's wealthy elite who frequent it now have taken the shine off the place. Buy a T-shirt, but wait until you get home to wear it. Nightly from 7pm.

Herb Café Corner of streets 51 and 278. Laid-back bar/restaurant with a good atmosphere. Even reticent single travellers will be at ease here whiling away a few hours in their comfy chairs while sipping a draught beer or cocktail.

Howie's 32 Street 51. A good bar to move on to if you've visited the nearby *Heart of Darkness* and found it disappointing, although it's worth arriving early to stake out a table on the pavement outside.

Martini Pub 48 Street 95. The advertising says it all – "Lonely, bored, hungry? We have everything you need". This Cambodian institution has a reputation across Asia for girls and drinking that keeps the punters flocking in. It's worth a visit for the chance to people-watch and dance to an eclectic range of music, while its 120-inch video screen shows the latest movies. Nightly from 7pm.

Sharky's 126 Street 130 ⊛www .sharkysofcambodia.com. Cambodia's longest-running rock-and-roll bar serves decent Mexican, Thai and American food, has a big-screen TV and also serves as a low-key pick-up spot. Daily drink specials from 5pm.

Talkin' to a Stranger 21B Street 29. Beer garden, with a great selection of wines and imported beer. Regular live music events. Closed Mon.

Walkabout 109 Street 51. Australian-run hotel with a 24hr bar, a pool table and satellite sports.

Arts and culture

After being virtually obliterated by the Khmer Rouge, Cambodia's artistic and cultural traditions have seen a revival in recent years, thanks largely to the few performers and instructors who survived the regime. **Cultural shows** in Phnom Penh are still irregular; you're most likely to find something happening at **Sovanna Phum** (☎023/987564), a performing arts society at the corner of streets 360 and 105, just south of Toul Sleng Museum; on Fridays or Saturdays they stage performances of classical and folk dance, and shadow puppetry (see p.172) at 7.30pm ($5). From time to time there are performances of classical dance and shadow puppetry at the **Chatomuk Theatre**, on the riverfront near the *Cambodiana*. See the *Phnom Penh Post* and Friday's *Cambodia Daily* for details of what's on.

The former King Norodom Sihanouk was once an avid film-maker, and Phnom Penh used to boast dozens of **cinemas** – a handful have been restored, showing Cambodian movies (the current trend is for fearsome horror flicks) or films dubbed into Khmer. One cinema to survive the Khmer Rouge years is the Vimean Tep on Monivong Boulevard, showing films daily in Khmer (subtitled in Thai, French or Chinese). Two screens on the 6th floor of Sorya Mall, Street 63, near Psar Thmei, have screenings throughout the day, from 9am to 6.30pm.

Regular free screenings of French films, usually subtitled in English, take place at the **French Cultural Centre** at 214 Street 184.

Galleries, hosting changing exhibitions of art and sculpture, proliferate, and the magazine *Asia Life* is a good place to find out what is coming up. **Meta House** at 6 Street 264 (Ⓦwww.meta-house.com) is unique as a night gallery and is open Friday and Saturday night (from 6pm until late) with exhibitions of contemporary Asian fine arts, multi-media and light installations. **Reyum** at 47 Street 178, near the National Museum (Ⓦwww.reyum.org), in conjunction with the **Institute of Fine Arts and Culture**, puts on exhibitions of work by Cambodian students; these could be art or a display based on someone's research project.

Shopping

Phnom Penh is the best place to shop in Cambodia, with numerous **traditional markets**. There are also a growing number number of fixed-price shops and boutiques selling clothes to affluent Cambodians, and crafts or antiques to tourists and expats. Newly opened are the **Sorya Mall** and **Paragon Mall**, which are actually more like huge department stores than malls, selling a vast range of consumer goods from clothes to sports equipment and from CDs to electrical gizmos. The dome-roofed **Sorya Mall**, corner of streets 63 and 140, is the swankiest thing to hit town: Cambodians come to gawp at the goods, and to ride the elevators to the top floor – from where there's a superb bird's-eye view of the city. **Lucky** supermarket has a branch on the ground floor; there are shakes and burgers at the fast food stalls and a roller-skating rink on the top floor.

Psar Thmei is good for books, stationery, gold jewellery, watches (look out for the one with a picture of the king on the face), T-shirts and textiles; the east side is largely devoted to plants and flowers. Until the mid-1990s, the only place to buy luxury goods in Cambodia was **Psar Toul Tom Poung**, the Russian Market – so named because all its goods used to come courtesy of Russia, one of the few countries to provide aid to the country during the Vietnamese occupation. The collapse of the USSR put paid to cheap imports, but the market retains its reputation as *the* place to buy textiles, antiques and silver – not to mention motorbike parts of every sort.

▲ Psar Thmei

Vendors from all over Cambodia, selling just about anything from dried fish to televisions, trade at the newly constructed **Psar Orussey** on Street 182, a sprawling place on two floors and a mezzanine. The stalls are crammed together and it can be confusing to find your way around, but the merchandise here is a good bit cheaper than at other markets. The adjacent Street 166 is big on traditional Khmer **medicine shops**, where leaves, tree bark and various animal parts are sold as tonics, the commodities usually boiled in water or soaked in wine. There are plenty of local markets around Phnom Penh where you can buy basics, fruit and vegetables and get a cheap meal; the most easily accessible are **Psar Chas**, on the corner of Street 13 and Ang Duong, and **Psar Kandal**, near Wat Ounalom. **Psar Olympic**, off Street 199 southwest of the Olympic Stadium, is visited by people from all over the country who make wholesale purchases here for resale elsewhere.

Antiques and curios

Psar Toul Tom Poung is a tremendous place to rummage for artefacts, curios and antiques; old wooden pagoda statues (watch out for damage from wood-boring beetles), brass bowls and bells, palm-leaf manuscripts and old Khmer Rouge banknotes can all be found here, and now and then a real curiosity turns up. If you're in the market for antique-looking decorative items, the market abounds in reproductions, as well as Chinese-style furniture, signs with Chinese characters and a huge assortment of decorative boxes and trunks. These are not antiques; they are all mass-produced in Vietnam, but don't expect them to be cheap. Bargaining is essential, and it's worth looking around to compare prices, since many of the stalls sell identical items.

Books

The best places for books are Monument Books, 111 Norodom Blvd (near Street 240) and the airport departure lounge. Monument has a superb selection of English-language books on Cambodia and Southeast Asia, plus a good selection on most other subjects; it also sells a range of arty greetings cards and postcards. For **secondhand** books, head to D's Books, with branches at 79 Street 240, 12 Street 178 (near the *FCC*) and on Street 93 (Boeung Kak). Though they're a bit pricey, all branches stock an extensive collection of books on many subjects and in many languages. **Bookstalls** at Psar Thmei and Psar Toul Tom Poung are good sources of Cambodia-related titles, although most of these are bound photocopies, the enforcement of copyright laws being nonexistent in Cambodia.

Clothing

With Western firms using Cambodia as a base to manufacture garments, it's no surprise that the country is one of the cheapest in Southeast Asia for clothes shopping, including **surplus designer-label** items. **Psar Toul Tom Poung** is the best place to look for them – take $10 and bargain away till your bag is stuffed. For something traditional, a popular purchase is the lovely Khmer top (*aow*) worn by men and women, in every conceivable fabric from bright cottons to subdued slub silks; at Psar Toul Tom Poung you can also pick up a *kabun*, the traditional Khmer top and skirt, or *sampot* – just the skirt. For something unique, buy some silk at one of the stalls and get it made up to your own design; there are plenty of clever seamstresses around the market who are used to working from sketches.

If you can't bear the hassle of the market, try Lacoste on Monivong Boulevard or one of the fashion **boutiques** on Sihanouk Boulevard, near Lucky Supermarket. Alternatively, head to Sorya or Paragon malls, where you can find everything from underwear to sportswear.

Bliss, 29 Street 240, is a boutique specializing in fashionable women's wear. Tabitha, 26 Street 294, produces Western-styled clothes from Cambodian textiles – it particularly prides itself on the range of scarves and shawls. Elsewhere, Street 51 (near Street 254), specializes in clothing in natural fibres for "women-of-a-certain-age" (35–45) who work and live in the capital.

Crafts

Despite losing most of its artisans to the Khmer Rouge, Cambodia's arts and crafts movement is now flourishing once again, thanks to NGOs that have set up **workshops** to give some of the thousands of disabled people a trade. Prices

Shopping with a conscience

Numerous NGOs, other organizations and some private individuals have shops and outlets that directly help street children, women at risk and/or the disabled and other disadvantaged groups.

Cambodian Craft (aka **Chamber of Professional and Micro-Enterprises of Cambodia**) Wat Phnom (just off Norodom Boulevard). With poverty widespread throughout the country, this co-operative provides training and support to rural villagers. Their Phnom Penh premises, housed in a beautiful 70-year-old traditional building on the south side of Wat Phnom traffic circle, host regular exhibitions and occasional demonstrations by artisans. The outlet has recently been given a face-lift and is well stocked with quality silverware, baskets, ceramics and textiles.

Colours of Cambodia 373 Sisowath Quay (near the *FCC*). The ethos here is to promote natural materials and eco-awareness, with original jewellery, textiles, clothing, ceramics and leather among the goods for sale. Many of the items are made by ReHab, for the disabled craft co-operative, but the owners also commission bespoke crafts directly from villagers in the country. The shop supports disadvantaged individuals, providing training or just giving a one-off donation so that they can help themselves; you can ask about specific artists/individuals at the shop.

NCDP (National Centre of Disabled Persons) Compound of the Ministry for Women's Affairs, Norodom Boulevard, just south of junction with Kramuon Sar. A retail outlet for quality products made by disabled (primarily land-mine-disabled) people throughout the country. Especially worth visiting for the silk bags, purses and hanging mobiles.

Nyemo Stall 14, Psar Toul Tom Poung (south side). Unique designs of soft furnishings, accessories, bags and toys, with profits helping to train and support vulnerable women.

Peace Handicrafts 39C Street 155, near Psar Toul Tom Poung. Land-mine- and polio-disabled people produce carefully crafted silk items for sale in their co-operative shop.

Rajana Street 450, near Psar Toul Tom Poung. Sales of silk and bamboo crafts and jewellery help to support the NGOs' Fair Trade training programmes.

Tabitha-Cambodia Corner of Street 51 and 360. This not-for-profit NGO-run outlet sells super silks made into garments and soft furnishings, cards, packed coffee and more. It operates by training disadvantaged women to sew. They then work from home and Tabitha purchases their output.

Tooït Tooït Stall 312, Psar Toul Tom Poung (main aisle, west side of the market). Supporting parents so that their children can go to school, the items on sale include shopping bags, beads and toys made from recycled materials such as newspapers, plastic bags and rice sacks.

Watthan Artisans Cambodia (WAC) Wat Than, 180 Norodom Blvd. A co-operative of disabled artisans who produce a range of handicrafts: silk scarves, home furnishings, woodcarvings and basketwork are just some of the items available for purchase.

at these outlets are fixed and higher than in the markets, but it's worth spending some of your money here to support vital training programmes.

For something distinctive, head to one of the city's many privately owned shops and galleries: *Northeast Cambodia Souvenir Shop*, 52 Street 240, sells goods made with textiles from Rattanakiri, while across the road at 87 Street 240, *Art Steel* has rather cute, hand-painted pressed-steel geckos, for mounting on the wall (or ceiling).

Jewellery

Many stalls at Psar Toul Tom Poung specialize in **silver** items, from tiny boxes in the shape of animals, to necklaces, pendants and bangles. Shops on Sothearos Boulevard, south of Wat Ounalom, sell similar items, although at higher prices. When bargaining, bear in mind that the silver is almost always **low grade**. Nearby, Rajana, on Street 450, sells a selection of quality contemporary **jewellery** crafted in Cambodia. Items of jewellery can be made up cheaply and quite quickly (3–5 days, typically) to your own design at stalls in Psar Thmei and Psar Toul Tom Poung. Go along with a sketch of what you want and get a quote before committing yourself.

Silk fabric

The best silk in the country at the keenest prices is available from Psar Toul Tom Poung, Psar Thmei and Psar Orussey; a *sampot*-length of traditional patterned *hol* costs between $15 and $30. You can also find wall-hangings and plain silk in Psar Toul Tom Poung from around $3 per metre. **Antique silks**, either *hols* or *sampots*, can also be found here, although prices run into hundreds of dollars. Antique silks were usually coloured with natural dyes, and so the hues are pleasingly muted.

Woodcarvings and marble statuary

Contemporary woodcarvings and marble statues make bulky souvenirs, but are so evocative of Cambodia that it's hard not to pick up one or two; you can buy them along Street 178, near the National Museum, and in Psar Toul Tom Poung. Although most carvings have an Angkorian theme, there are plenty of options, ranging from intricate **apsaras** to various divinities and the much-copied head of **Jayavarman VII**, based on the one in the National Museum. Most places seem to think tourists want a marble image of a Bayon-style *prang*, but with a little searching you can find some appealing sculptures of animals, such as water buffalo, plus simple bowls and Buddhas. The price should reflect the quality and colour of the marble – green is particularly prized – or the grade of wood used.

Supermarkets

Phnom Penh has a decent range of supermarkets, which – in addition to local produce – sell a wide selection of imported goods. The original, and still best-known, supermarket in Cambodia is Lucky, on Sihanouk Boulevard near the corner of Monivong (daily 8am–9pm). It also has a branch on the ground floor of Sorya Mall, which is especially good for **toiletries** and **delicatessen** food. A similar range of merchandise is available at slightly lower prices at You Nam (daily 8am–8pm), 400m southwest of the train station on Kampuchea Krom Boulevard, where there's a good choice of **wines and spirits**, and at Big A Supermarket, on Monivong Boulevard between streets 178 and 184 (daily 8am–9pm). Bayon Supermarket, 133–35 Monivong Blvd, near the intersection with Kampuchea Krom (daily 7am–8pm), does a good selection of **cheeses** and other chilled products. Some petrol stations around town have mini-markets

Festivals and ceremonies

You are unlikely to be in Cambodia for long before coming across a vibrant festival or noisy religious ceremony. Most Cambodians like nothing more than to don their glad-rags, pack up a picnic and head off to a pagoda, where after lighting some incense sticks and making an offering of flowers or food to the Buddha, they throw an impromptu party. As Theravada Buddhism follows the lunar calendar, the dates of most festivals and ceremonies vary with the phases of the moon.

Bonn Chaul Chhnam

Bonn Chaul Chhnam (Khmer New Year) is celebrated in April. The festivities usually continue for a week, providing an opportunity for young people to get together and play various games – all of them barely disguised excuses for eyeing up a potential marriage partner – including a version of skittles using the disc-like seed of the *angkunh*, a forest vine. The winner gets to smack two *angkunh* seeds against the loser's knee, holding them in one hand like castanets; if they fail to produce the required clacking sound, the "loser" gets to do it back at them. In the provinces, it's common to throw talcum powder and water at passers-by as part of the festivities, so watch out.

Bonn Chaul Chhnam ▲

Pagoda offerings ▼

Bonn Pchum Ben

Bonn Pchum Ben (Festival of the Hungry Ghosts) takes place between mid-September and early October. Families are supposed to visit seven different pagodas to pay their respects to their ancestors, risking a year of bad luck if they do not. Cambodians believe that at this time the doors to hell are opened and the "hungry ghosts" – those who have no families to make offerings for them – come out to feed, so rice is cast for them into dark corners of the pagoda.

Bonn Om Tuk

Bonn Om Tuk ▼

During the rainy season (June–Oct), so much water pours down the Mekong that the water flows back up the Tonle Sap river forming the massive Tonle Sap lake. Come October or November, the flow returns to its usual direction, an event marked by **Bonn Om Tuk**, the **Water Festival**. There are three days of boat races, manned

by teams from all over the country, on the river at Phnom Penh, and people from the provinces pour in to support their local boat crews as they race from the Chroy Chungvar Bridge to the Royal Palace.

Bonn Chroat Preah Nongkoal

Marking the start of the planting season in May, the ceremony of **Bonn Chroat Preah Nongkoal (Royal Ploughing Ceremony)**, held at Lean Preah Sre park in Phnom Penh, combines animism, Buddhism and plenty of pomp. It begins with chanting monks asking the earth spirits for permission to plough. Then ceremonial furrows are drawn, rice is scattered and offerings are made to the divinities. The most important part of the ceremony, however, is what the Royal Bull chooses when it is offered rice, grain, grass, water and wine. Rice or grain augur well; water signifies rain; grass is a sign that crops will be devastated by insects, and wine, that there will be drought.

▲ Ploughing ceremony, Phnom Penh

Weddings

Most marriages in Cambodia are arranged, with the couple given the chance to get to know each other on several occasions before the union is finalized. Then a propitious day for the wedding is decided, usually with the help of a fortune-teller. The day begins with the bridegroom and his party processing through the streets to the bride's house, bearing presents and trays of food, including an obligatory pig's head.

Most brides have at least six changes of costume for the day, ranging from ceremonial silk *sampots* to an often garishly coloured Western-style wedding

▲ Wedding guests

▼ Traditional wedding ceremony

Nun with red-stained lips, Angkor Wat ▲

Offering day flowers in a Cambodian market ▼

gown. Receptions often take over the whole road, as each family member will have invited practically everyone they know. This began as an opportunity to find partners for unmarried sons and daughters, but these days the aim is to make a profit, and guests are required to give cash, not presents.

Observance days

Buddhism is an intrinsic part of Khmer life, and Buddhist observance days occur on the days of the full, new and both quarter moons. On such days, old ladies make early morning visits to the pagoda, and everyone else tries at least to make an offering of flowers or fruit at home, so market stalls do a roaring trade in bunches of bananas and flowers. Lotus buds, the traditional offering flower to the Buddha, are folded artistically to expose their pale-pink inner petals, jasmine buds are threaded onto sticks and strings, and other flowers are bunched into vivid posies, to be taken to pagodas or used to decorate domestic shrines.

which stock a good range of products – Caltex Star Mart has a convenient outlet at the corner of Sihanouk and Monivong, and Total La Boutique is on Monivong, north of Sihanouk.

Listings

Airlines Angkor Airways, 32 Norodom Blvd ☏ 023/222056, ⊛ www.angkorairways.com; Bangkok Airways, 61 Street 214 ☏ 023/722545, ⊛ www.bangkokair.com; China Southern Airlines, A3 Regency Square, 168 Monireth Blvd ☏ 023/424588, ⊛ www.cs-air.com; Dragon Air, A4–A5 Regency Square, 168 Monireth Blvd ☏ 023/424300, ⊛ www.dragonair.com; EVA Air, Suite 11, 14B Street 205 ☏ 023/219911, ⊛ www .evaair.com; Jet Star Asia Airlines, 333B Monivong Blvd ☏ 023/220909, ⊛ www.jetstaraisa.com; Lao Airlines, 58C Sihanouk Blvd ☏ 023/222956, ⊛ www.laoairlines.com; Malaysia Airlines, 1st Floor, *Diamond Hotel*, 172–84 Monivong Blvd ☏ 023/218923, ⊛ www.malaysiaairlines.com; PMTair, Suite 9B, 294 Mao Tse Toung Blvd ☏ 023/224714, ⊛ www.pmtair.com; Royal Khmer Airlines 36B, 245 Mao Tse Toung Blvd ☏ 023994502, ⊛ www.royalkhmerairlines.com; SilkAir, *Himawari Hotel*, 219B Monivong Blvd, ☏ 023/426808, ⊛ www.silkair.net; Thai Airways, 294 Mao Tse Toung Blvd ☏ 023/214359, ⊛ www .thaiair.com; Vietnam Airlines, 41 Street 214 ☏ 023/363396, ⊛ www.vietnamair.com.

Banks and exchange Acleda Bank, 61 Monivong Blvd and 28 Mao Tse Toung Blvd; ANZ Royal, corner Street 114 (Kramoun Sar) with branches around town; Canadia Bank, 265–269 Street 114 (Ang Duong St); Foreign Trade Bank of Cambodia, 3 Street 114 (Kramoun Sar) (no advances on Visa or MasterCard). There are 24hr ATMs at the Acleda (though some only accept cards issued by the bank), ANZ, Canadia and Cambodian Asia (branches around town) banks; note that these dispense US dollars and there may be a minimal handling charge. In addition to the banks, Western Union has branches all over town where you can exchange traveller's cheques, receive/make money transfers and get money on Visa and MasterCard. You can change US dollars to riel at any of the exchange booths around town, most of which display their rates; some of the best rates are to be had at Psar Thmei.

Bus companies A couple of reliable private companies operate 12–15 seater VIP express buses to destinations around the country including Sihanoukville, Poipet (via Siem Reap) and Rattana-kiri. Contact Hua Lian on Charles de Gaulle Blvd, just north of the Olympic Stadium (☏ 023/880761 or 012/376807), or Ly Heng Express (and Mekong Tours) corner of Street 106 and Sisowath Quay (☏ 023/991726).

Car rental The Car Rental Co., 49 Street 592 (☏ 012/950950), has a selection of vehicles available with or without driver.

Cookery Courses Learn to prepare traditional Khmer food with a choice of courses at Cambodia Cooking Class, 14 Street 285 (☏ 023/882314) or book through *Frizz* restaurant, 335 Sisowath Quay (☏ 023/220953).

Dentists International SOS Medical & Dental Clinic, 161 Street 51 (☏ 023/216911), has English-speaking staff. European Dental Clinic 160A Norodom Blvd (☏ 023/211363, emergency 012/854408), Mon–Sat 8am–noon, 2–7pm, has French, Thai and Khmer dentists.

Doctors English is spoken at International SOS Medical & Dental Clinic, 161 Street 51 (☏ 023/216911, ⊛ www.Internationalsos.com), 8am–5.30pm Mon–Fri, 8am–noon Sat; Naga Medical Centre, 11 Street 254 (☏ 023/211360 or 011/8111175, ⊛ www.nagaclinic.com; 24hr); Tropical and Travellers Medical Clinic, near Wat Phnom at 88 Street 108 ☏ 023/366802.

Embassies and consulates Australia, 11 Street 254 ☏ 023/213470, ⊛ www.cambodia .embassy.gov.au; Canada,11 Street 254 ☏ 023/213470, ⊛ www.phnompenh.gc.ca; Great Britain, 29 Street 75 ☏ 023/427124, ⊛ www .britishembassy.gov.uk/cambodia; Laos, 15–17 Mao Tse Toung Blvd ☏ 023/982632; Thailand, 196 Norodom Blvd ☏ 023/726306, ⊛ www.mfa .go.th/embassy/phnompenh; US, corner of streets 96 and 51, ☏ 023/728000, ⊛ www.phnompenh .usembassy.gov; Vietnam, 426 Monivong Blvd ☏ 023/362531.

Emergencies Ambulance ☏ 119 (from an 023 phone) or 023/724891; fire ☏ 118 (from an 023 phone) or 023/786693; police ☏ 117 (from an 023 phone) or 023/724793; hotline for the police to report child exploitation (national and in Phnom Penh) ☏ 023/997919 – English is spoken on all these numbers.

Hospitals American Medical, 7 Street 282 ☏ 012/891613; Calmette, north end of Monivong Blvd ☏ 023/426948.

Internet access There are Internet cafés all over town. Rates are typically around $1–1.50 per hour.

Kick boxing Reproduced on the bas-reliefs of Angkor Wat, the ancient tradition of kick boxing is now enjoying a revival. Bouts start with loud music and much posturing by the contestants – though watching the animated antics of the crowd, for whom betting on the fight is the main attraction, can be as fascinating as the fights. Ask at your hotel or guesthouse for details of forthcoming bouts, which are advertised in the Khmer press.

Mail and courier services The main post office, on Street 13, between streets 98 and 102 (Mon–Sat 7am–6pm), provides the full range of services, including parcel post, fax, telephones and *poste restante*. There's a booth inside where you can buy aerogrammes, postcards, envelopes, writing paper and stamps. You can courier material abroad using EMS, Ministry of Posts and Telecommunications, corner of streets 13 and 102 (T023/427428), which offers an efficient and cost effective service. Alternatively, try TNT (T023/430923), DHL (T023/427726), UPS (T023/427511) or Fedex (T023/216712).

Massage Many massage parlours double as brothels, but there are now a number of reputable private spas where you can get a massage, aroma-therapy, body scrubs and other treatments. Amret Spa, 3 Street 57 (T023/99794), and Aziadée, 16A Street 282 (T023/996921), both have Jacuzzis and offer a range of treatments. Seeing Hands, set up with the help of an NGO which works with the blind in Cambodia, offer Anma, Thai and Shiatsu massage and reflexology; they're at 6 Street 178, just around the corner from the *FCC* (T012/234519; daily 8am–10pm; $5 per hour), and at 12 Street 13, opposite the post office (T012/680934; same times and price).

Meditation One-hour meditation sessions are held at Wat Lanka (Mon & Thurs at 6pm), supervised by English-speaking monks.

Motorbike rental Adventure Moto, 16 Street 136 (T012/1896729, W www.Adventure-moto.com), Western-run outfit with smart new bikes, from $8 per day for a city runabout to $50 per day for a powerful off-roader; 24/7 support; tours organized. Lucky! Lucky!, 413 Monivong Blvd (T012/939601), charges $5 per day for a 110cc moped and $9 per day for a 250cc off-road bike, with discounts on rentals of a week or longer. Helmets are provided, but no insurance.

Opticians Opticians cluster along Sihanouk Boulevard near Lucky Supermarket, and in general offer a speedy and proficient service. Modern Optics, corner of Sihanouk Blvd and Street 63, has a good reputation, or try I Care Optical, 166 Norodom Blvd T023/215778.

Pharmacies Arguably the best pharmacy in Cambodia, Pharmacie de la Gare, corner of Monivong and Pochentong boulevards (daily 8.30am–6pm), has English-speaking pharmacists and a good selection of Western drugs; they even accept credit cards. U-Care (new to Phnom Penh) has two branches with English-speaking pharma-cists: corner Sothearos Blvd and Street 178 and corner of Sihanouk Blvd and Street 55.

Photography and film There are outlets all over town, with some of the better ones on Monivong Blvd, near Psar Thmei.

Police for foreigners and tourists T012/942484.

Running The Hash House Harriers meet on Sundays at 2.45pm outside the train station (W www.p2h3.com).

Swimming The *Inter-Continental*, *Cambodiana*, *Goldiana* and *Phnom Penh* hotels have pools open to non-residents for around $5 per visit. The Phnom Penh Water Park on the airport road has water slides and swimming pools.

Taxis Expect to pay $3–$5 for a daytime single fare, $5–7 at night, plus waiting time if you ask them to hang around for you. Bailey's (T012/890000) offers reliable 24 hr service; Taxi Vantha (T023/993433 and 012/855000, W www.taxivantha.com) has been operating since 1996; it has an on-call service 24/7 and is also available for long-distance trips; check its website for prices.

Travel agents The following well-established firms employ English-speaking staff and act as both travel agents and domestic tour operators: KU Travel & Tours, 77 Street 240 T023/723456, W www.kucambodia.com; Mittapheap, 262 Monivong Blvd T023/222801, W www.mittapheap.com; Neak Krorhom Travel & Tours, 127 Street 108, T023/219496, E nkhtours@hotmail.com.

Visa extensions At the Department for Immigra-tion near the airport; see p.58 for more.

Around Phnom Penh

If you tire of Phnom Penh, a short journey will get you out of town and into a landscape of rice paddies and sugar palms, scattered with small villages and isolated pagodas. The **Chroy Chung Va peninsula**, the tip of land facing the city centre at the confluence of the Tonle Sap and Mekong rivers, is home to a collection of villages and feels very removed from the bustle of central Phnom Penh; its western side, facing the Royal Palace, is being transformed into a riverside park. A short way further northeast, reached by a short ferry trip from Phnom Penh, lies **Koh Dait**, a lush green island in the Mekong, whose inhabitants weave silk and grow a wide variety of produce on the fertile alluvial soil. **Wat Jum Pos Ka-aik**, east of town off National Route 1, has a remarkable collection of ten thousand Buddhas and can be tied in with a trip to **Kien Svay**, a popular riverside village about 12km from the city.

Phnom Brasat, some 25km northwest of town off National Route 5, is home to a kitsch collection of pagodas which are more reminiscent of the work of Salvador Dalí than of classical Khmer architecture – the experience is definitely more theme park than religious. Further north rise the distinctive hills of the old capital **Oudong**, dotted with the chedi of various kings; Khmerophiles might want to combine a trip here with a visit to the scant remains of nearby **Lovek**, its predecessor as capital.

A short moto ride southwest of the city, the killing fields and memorial at **Choeung Ek** make a logical, if macabre, progression from a visit to the Toul Sleng Genocide Museum. Also south of the city, off National Route 2, the compact Angkorian temple of **Tonle Bati** enjoys a riverside location, and is a good place for a picnic and a swim. Further south, there are spectacular views from the ancient hilltop temple of **Phnom Chisor**. Both sites could be combined as a day-trip, although this means missing out on the tigers and bears at **Phnom Tamau**, Cambodia's only state-run zoo and wildlife rescue centre.

Chroy Chung Va peninsula

The three-kilometre spit of land that makes up the **Chroy Chung Va peninsula** used to be a farming area, though the Phnom Penh municipality has now controversially cleared out the villagers from the western side of the peninsula and turned it into a riverside park, facing the promenade on the city side. It's worth a visit to sip a coconut at one of the refreshment stalls while watching the sunset over the city, along with young lovers who come to spend some illicit time together out of sight of ever-watchful family eyes. If you make your way northeast along the banks of the Mekong you'll pass through several friendly villages inhabited by the **Cham**, Cambodia's Muslim minority.

The peninsula can easily be **reached** by moto; once across the Chroy Chung Va Bridge, take the first right, which heads right around the headland.

Koh Dait

Set in the middle of the Mekong 15km from Phnom Penh, **Koh Dait** is an oasis of calm and tranquillity. Primarily an agricultural community (peanuts are an important cash crop), the ten-kilometre-long island is home to a number of stilt-house villages, and you'll get to see a good cross-section of rural life as you meander along its leafy tracks. The island is noted for its **weaving** of *sampot*s, and in the dry season looms clack away beneath the houses. As the river level falls after the rainy season, a wide sandy **beach** (entry 1000 riel) is exposed at the northern end of the island, where food stalls and picnic huts serve tasty fried chicken.

The island is easily reached from Phnom Penh by catching a moto, followed by any one of the several **ferries** whose jetties are signposted off National Route 6, about 14km from the city. The ferries run regularly throughout the day, departing when full; motorbikes and bicycles all go aboard with no problem (moto and driver 1000 riel, foot passengers 500 riel).

Wat Jum Pos Ka-aik and Kien Svay Beach

The ten thousand Buddha statues at **Wat Jum Pos Ka-aik**, fashioned in just about every possible shape, size and material, were donated by wealthy patrons, from whose gifts the pagoda derives its conspicuous affluence. Indeed, the monks of Wat Jum Pos Ka-aik are much respected and well connected – it's not unusual to find them performing elaborate ceremonies for the dignitaries and well-heeled Cambodians who wish to gain merit in the next life or to receive blessings in this one.

The pagoda is entered through an avenue lined with *deva*s (gods) on one side and *asura*s (demons) on the other; the modern-looking **hall** across the compound is where the Buddhas are arrayed in air-conditioned splendour, ranged in tiers from floor to ceiling, and illustrating every one of the forty *mudra*s along the way. One of the most sublime images – a life-size standing bronze Buddha – is at the centre of the display towards the front; it wears a benign smile, while its lifelike eyes seem to follow you around the hall. The hands are held out in front of the body, palms facing out with fingers pointed up in *abhaya mudra*, the position of giving protection; a diamond is embedded in the centre of each palm.

If the **vihara** is open, it's worth putting your head inside to see the unusually decorated walls – by Cambodian standards these are stark, painted pale yellow and stencilled with golden Buddha images. A small white stupa nearby, in front of the bathing pool, contains bones found in the pagoda grounds of people murdered by the Khmer Rouge.

Kien Svay

Optimistically hailed by some locals as "the new Kep", **Kien Svay** (or Koki Beach, as it's also known) is really more of a muddy river bank. That said, it positively throngs at weekends with people venturing out from Phnom Penh to picnic at the rows of stilt-huts on the banks of the Mekong. The village is particularly noted for its crispy **fried bugs** – different sorts of beetle, cricket, silkworm and a variety of pupas. Hawkers and food stalls here also sell all sorts of other edibles, the idea being to buy your food and then laze around at the huts (it costs just a few thousand riel to rent one for a few hours or the day). To top it all, small boats ply the river with fish and lobsters for sale, cooking your choice of food on the spot using their on-board braziers.

The villages around Kien Svay are well known for their **weaving**, traditionally done by the women, though it's a family business these days and more men are joining in; silk and mixed-thread scarves and *kramar*s are produced here for the markets in Phnom Penh.

Practicalities

Both Wat Jum Pos Ka-aik and Kien Svay are reached off **National Route 1**, across the Monivong Bridge. For the Wat Jum Pos Ka-aik, take the first right after the bridge (Street 369) along the Bassac River. At first the road is narrow and bumpy, but it widens out as it passes through longan orchards. The pagoda is on the left after 7km, its entrance flanked by statues of *niek* and *yeak*, gods and giants, a favourite Cambodian theme. To reach **Kien Svay**, stay on National Route 1 until, 8km from the bridge, you pass the *L'Imprevu* resort; the turning for the beach is 1km beyond, to the left (north), through an ornate portico which looks like a pagoda gateway. The beach can also be reached by taking a bus to Psar Koki, the town market, then a moto for the half-kilometre ride to the beach.

Just before the Kien Svay turn-off, and opposite the Cambodia Brewery hoarding, there's a good lunchtime Khmer **restaurant**, 777, overlooking paddy fields and a fishing lake. The speciality here is huge, succulent freshwater crayfish, *bong kong*, priced by weight – expect to pay around $10 for a dish to feed two.

Phnom Brasat

The complex of pagodas at **Phnom Brasat**, 27 km northwest of Phnom Penh, originally comprised just two hilltop sites, but now sprawls over four locations. The monks and nuns here have a vision of developing the site to Angkorian proportions, and the programme of construction seems never-ending, with the latest being a futuristic glass-domed edifice. As the building of new sanctuaries is seen as gaining particular merit, it's not unusual for wealthy patrons to make sizeable financial contributions. Supplemented with roadside collections from the public along with volunteered labour, construction on the site has really taken off.

Phnom Brasat is readily accessible by **moto** ($6–10 return) and tuk-tuk ($10–15); you'll probably want some transport to get around the sites anyway, as they're spread over a distance of about 5km.

The site

The most popular of the sites is **Wat Phnom Reap,** reached through a Bayon-style gateway of enormous faces flanked by elephants, with plenty of refreshment stalls and souvenir-sellers. Dominating the compound is the amazing carmine-red concrete reproduction of Angkor Wat, **Prasat Mahar Nokor Vitmean Sooer**; it was completed in 1998, after just two years' work. A colonnaded gallery runs around the outside, sheltering elaborately decorated walls; apsaras nestle in niches, while bas-reliefs illustrate scenes from the life of Buddha and commemorate the construction of the temple by depicting the people who donated either money or labour, with a nearly life-size brass statue of the principal benefactor, Rohs Sarouen.

In the same complex, the entrance to **Prasat Pik Vongkot Boreay Brom Mlop** is guarded by two imposing statues of Hanuman, each standing on one leg with sword raised. Inside, an enormous seated Buddha dominates the hall; behind it and curling around it, a cheerful mural of the bodhi tree is dotted with birds and animals, rather like a child's pop-up book.

Preah Vessandaa

A popular theme at Cambodian pagodas is the tale of Preah Vessandaa – one of the previous **incarnations of the Buddha** – which is often told in tableaux, the figures usually life-sized and garishly coloured. According to the story, an old man, Chuchuk, was given a young woman, Amita, to be his wife in repayment of a debt. The couple were unable to have children, and Amita was snubbed by the other women. Knowing of King Vessandaa's generosity, Amita persuaded her husband to go to ask Vessandaa for two of his children. When depicted in temples, the story, usually told in a series of ten or so scenes, tells of Chuchuk's adventures on the way to the palace. One scene at Phnom Brasat shows Chuchuk dangling in a tree where he has been chased by the hunter Chetabut and his dogs; to escape, the old man lies that he is one of the king's messengers. As Chuchuk approaches the palace, the king's children run off, only to be discovered hiding under lily pads by the king, who grants them to the old man. After getting lost on his way home, Chuchuk ends up in the kingdom of the children's grandfather, who pays a ransom to buy them back. As told in Cambodia, the story ends when Chuchuk spends the money on a feast at which he gorges himself to death – a graphic injunction against the vice of gluttony.

A few kilometres up the road, on the first hill you come to, is a much-restored, fifteen-metre-long reclining Buddha, carved out of the hillside. It's reputedly quite ancient – to quote one of the *achar*s, "here 1400 years already" – and may conceivably be the only surviving part of the sixth-century pre-Angkorian ruins known to have been here. Steps lead up to the summit and vihara, where a series of **tableaux** illustrate scenes from the story of Preah Vessandaa. Bizarrely, Cambodia's gun culture pervades even here; in a painting of Angkor Wat, a man – presumably the benefactor – proudly displays his pistol holster.

Oudong and around

Oudong was the capital of Cambodia for 248 years, playing host to the crowning of several monarchs, including Ang Duong and his son, Norodom, great-great-grandfather of the current king, Norodom Sihamoni. However, in 1866, King Norodom was persuaded by the French to relocate the capital from here to the more strategically positioned Phnom Penh; the court, totalling more than ten thousand people, moved en masse and Oudong was abandoned. The old wooden city has long since rotted away, but the site, scattered with shrines and chedi, remains an important site for pilgrimage.

Oudong is 37km from the capital and can be reached by the Kompong Chhnang **bus**; get off at the billboard with the picture of the hill, then hop on a moto for the final 3km. You can also get to Oudong on a guesthouse-run bus – the *Capitol*, for instance, runs a trip there daily. With your own transport – a tuk-tuk for instance would cost around $15 – you could also take in several villages en route to get a glimpse of the traditional Cambodian rural lifestyle, and combine Oudong with visits to Phnom Brasat or Lovek.

En route to the site

Heading north out of the capital, **National Route 5** follows the Tonle Sap most of the way to Oudong, passing Cham villages and newly built mosques (most mosques having been destroyed – and Cham religious leaders murdered – by the Khmer Rouge). This area is important for the production of *prohok*, fermented fish paste, in January and February, when the air is pungent with the odour of drying fish. The only village of any size on the way is **PREAK G'DAM** (literally, Crab Creek), where a busy ferry still crosses the Tonle Sap (this was the only crossing point for twenty years until the Chroy Chung Va Bridge was repaired in 1993). Good Khmer food is served up at the **restaurants** opposite the ferry entrance, with the bonus of terrific views across the rice fields to Oudong from their terraces at the back. Along the road, two more Khmer delicacies are on offer: **steamed turtle**, a village speciality proudly displayed on trays by the roadside, and *chook*, the seed pods of the lotus flower which Khmers eat as a snack.

A few kilometres beyond Preak G'dam, just off the highway on the right, is the village of **KOMPONG LUONG**. Once the royal port for Oudong, the village has for centuries been famous for its **silverwork**, and several generations of silversmiths still work together here to craft cups, bowls and all manner of small boxes in animal and fruit designs, shaping and decorating them by hand. Visitors are welcome to watch and purchase, though there's not much difference in price from the markets of Phnom Penh. Back on the road, it's just a few kilometres further to the two hills of Oudong, reached by turning left at the billboard for Angkor Beer, which also shows the chedi.

Oudong

Visible from afar, the multiple chedi on the larger of the two hills at **OUDONG** are something of a landmark, heralding your imminent arrival in the capital if you're arriving from the north. Designated for development as a local tourism site, at weekends and holidays Oudong can get unbearably busy, but during the week it's pretty quiet, with just a few tourist buses and the occasional local outing.

Approaching from National Route 5, you'll arrive at the foot of the larger hill, sometimes called **Phnom Preah Reach Troap**, the Hill of Royal Fortune, as the royal treasure was hidden here during the war with the Siamese in the sixteenth century. As you approach the hill you'll pass a small building on the left which contains human remains collected from nearby fields, another site of execution used by the Khmer Rouge. It makes no difference whether you start with the first set of steps you see or at the far end, since to explore the site you'll need to make a circuit around the hills; the following account follows the route using the furthest set of steps.

An air of mystery pervades the ruined columns and rotten roof beams of **Preah Atharas** (*athara*s being an ancient unit of measure equal to eighteen cubits), the vihara at the top. It was built by the Chinese in the thirteenth century to seal the cave – so legend has it – of a mythical sea monster, which had to be contained to stop the Chinese losing their dominance over the Khmer. The vihara was heavily damaged during fighting between Lon Nol and Khmer Rouge forces in 1973–74, and more destruction was wrought upon it by the Khmer Rouge post-1975, and for many years only a shoulder and part of the right side of the thirteenth-century eleven-metre-high seated Buddha remained; now it's being rebuilt and when complete it'll certainly be impressive, though not as evocative as the damaged one.

The ridge has an increasing number of shrines and several of the older ones are worth seeking out as you walk north. One of the first you'll come to is **Preah Ko**, featuring a particularly appealing statue of Nandin, the sacred mount of Shiva. Worshippers pour water over the bull's head, rendering the water holy – it's then collected and taken home. Further north, **Neak Ta Dambang Dek** contains a Buddha seated on a coiled naga, its multiple heads curved over to afford him protection. Easily recognized by the four faces that cap its spire, the pale-yellow chedi of **Chet Dey Mak Prohm** contains the ashes of King Sisowath Monivong (reigned 1927–41). Higher up the hill is the crumbling chedi **Tray Troeng**, built in 1891 by King Norodom for the ashes of his father, King Ang Duong (though there's some dispute as to whether the ashes are really here or in the Silver Pagoda in Phnom Penh). Some of the glazed ceramic flowers that once covered the chedi can still be seen, but the local children used to sell them to tourists when they "fell off", and now they are being replaced with modern alternatives.

The oldest chedi on the hill is **Damrei Sam Poan**, built in 1623 by Preah Bat Chey Cheta for the ashes of his uncle and predecessor, King Soriyopor. Surrounded by charmingly decayed elephant statues, the chedi is badly overgrown and the inner brick is starting to crumble. Nevertheless, until recently it boasted the tallest spire on the hill; today the chedi is dwarfed by the spire of the adjacent new pagoda, which boasts an impressive terrace with stunning views over the countryside to the Tonle Sap. From here, a staircase of 509 steps leads to the foot of the hill.

The smaller hill can be reached by a separate stairway, at the top of which is a small, damaged mosque, **Vihara Ta Sann**. Close by are the ruins of a large reclining Buddha and, dating from 1567, a chedi built by King Bat Boromintho Reachea – for whom, no one seems to know.

①

The legend of Lovek

When Lovek was capital, it was said to house two statues of Preah Ko and Preah Kaew which contained **sacred texts**, written in gold, recording "all the knowledge and wisdom in the world". During one of the periodic conflicts between the Thai and Khmer, the Thai army was encamped outside Lovek, which it had repeatedly failed to capture, and it was about to make its seasonal retreat in advance of the rains. The story goes that the Thai fired a cannon loaded with silver coins into the bamboo thickets that afforded the city some natural protection. During the rainy season, the Khmer gradually cleared the bamboo in their search for the coins, such that the Thai were easily able to capture the city in the following dry season. Removing the statues to Ayutthaya, the Thai were able to read the sacred texts and so became more knowledgeable than the Khmer. The legend has it that the statues are still hidden in Bangkok and that when they are returned to Cambodia the country will once again have ascendancy over Thailand.

Lovek

Little is known about **LOVEK**, the capital of Cambodia during the reign of King An Chan in the sixteenth century. It was captured by the Siamese in the latter part of the century, and the name has been passed down through a well-known local legend (see box above) as much as anything else. Today a tiny village occupies the site, consisting of a few houses, a school and two **shrines**: Wat Preah Ko (Pagoda of the Sacred Cow) and Wat Preah Kaew (Pagoda of the Emerald Buddha). Wat Preah Ko is distinguished by its laterite foundations; inside, the walls are decorated with murals of scenes from the legend.

Finding Lovek is a bit of a challenge, so unless you're a devoted Khmer-culture buff, it's probably not worth the effort. To reach the village, head north from Oudong on National Route 5 in the direction of Kompong Chhnang; after 12km you'll come to a low, broken stone wall on the left, opposite which is a dirt track towards the Tonle Sap; the village lies a couple of kilometres down. Rather than use a moto, you could get here on the Phnom Penh–Kompong Chhnang bus, which passes the turning, but if the driver doesn't understand a request for Lovek, you'll have to work out where to alight – although the chances are that the bus driver will guess where you want to get off.

Choeung Ek

Just 12km southwest of Phnom Penh is the notorious site of **CHOEUNG EK** (daily 7am–5pm; $2), where prisoners from Toul Sleng were brought for execution. As graphically portrayed in the film *The Killing Fields*, certain sites around the country – Choeung Ek is the best known – became places of **mass murder**, where the genocidal Khmer Rouge disposed of its enemies: men, women and children who had allegedly betrayed the state. Early on, the regime's victims were shot; later, to save on valuable bullets, they were bludgeoned or stabbed to death. As fuel became scarce, victims were dragged out of the city and killed en route, their bodies dumped in the rice paddies closer to town.

Set amid peaceful fields and pleasant countryside, in what was once a longan orchard, the **Choeung Ek Memorial** now contains the remains of 8985 bodies exhumed here in 1980, when 86 of the burial pits were excavated. Anecdotal estimates suggest that over 17,000 people may have been slaughtered here, and a further 43 mass graves at the site remain untouched; there are no plans as yet for these to be investigated. Inside the memorial, a gleaming modern chedi of glass panels, set in a white framework and topped by a classical Khmer golden roof, skulls and bones are piled on shelves, arranged by age and gender, their tattered clothes below. Around the stupa, a pavilion houses a small exhibition describing the history of the site, while an emotional (if ungrammatical) declaration close by states, "We are absolutely determined no to let this genocidal regime to reoccur in Kampuchea". Grassy mounds and excavated **pits** can be found scattered around, small wooden markers at each indicating how many bodies were found there.

The site is easily accessible by moto and tuk-tuk or on excursions run by various Phnom Penh guesthouses (some of which also include side-trips to Tonle Bati); you could even cycle there if you're prepared to brave the traffic. To drive here, find Monireth Boulevard and follow it south, forking left at the large petrol station, from where it's about 5km to Choeung Ek.

Tonle Bati and Phnom Chisor

Some 35km south of the capital down National Route 2 are the two small but appealing temples at **Tonle Bati**, while another compact and peaceful temple lies some 30km further south off the same road at **Phnom Chisor**. Tonle Bati can be easily reached on the bus for Takeo: get off by the Sokimex petrol station – where there's a large hoarding showing the temple – and take a moto the final 2.5km to the temple; alternatively, you can do the whole journey from the capital by moto and tuk-tuk ($6–10 return). To see Phnom Chisor, you'll need to either hire some transport in Phnom Penh for the day (there are no motos at the turn-off for the hill on National Route 2) or take an excursion operated by one of the capital's travel agents or guesthouses.

Tonle Bati

The peaceful site of **Tonle Bati** (daily 7am–6pm; $3, including a soft drink) is set on the banks of the Bati River in a well-tended grove of coconut and mango trees, where you can swim and picnic as well as seeing the two temples. The first temple you come to on entering the site is the larger of the two, **Ta Prohm**. Constructed by Jayavarman VII – creator of the magnificent Angkor Thom – on the site of a sixth-century shrine, it's dedicated to the Hindu

▲ Tonle Bati

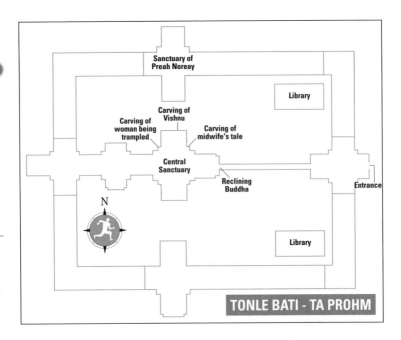

Sanctuary of
Preah Noreay

Library

Carving of
Vishnu

Carving of
woman being
trampled

Carving of
midwife's tale

Central
Sanctuary

Reclining
Buddha

Entrance

N

Library

TONLE BATI - TA PROHM

god Shiva (though Jayavarman eventually adopted Theravada Buddhism). The main entrance is from the east along a laterite causeway, edged by flowers and shrubs; piled up to the side here are broken chunks of masonry, some elaborately carved with scenes from the Churning of the Ocean of Milk (see p.183) or the *Ramayana* (see box, p.92).

At the centre of the inner enclosure are the temple's five **sanctuaries**, its antechambers built in a cruciform shape, with shrines to the cardinal directions. Above the entrance, a carved stone image of a reclining Buddha has been colourfully coated in paint. The **main sanctuary**, of sandstone, contains an upright Buddha image, while the antechambers house damaged stone linga. Another image of Buddha, over the north arm of the cruciform, has been superimposed with a carving of a six-armed Vishnu, a change probably made when the Angkorian kingdom reverted to Hinduism after the death of Jayavarman VII.

Well-preserved **carvings** decorate the outside of the sanctuary and several tell unusual tales. High up on the northeast corner is a scene of two women and a kneeling man: one woman carries a basket on her head, containing the after-birth from her recent confinement; the midwife, shown standing, was not given sufficient respect during the birth and has condemned the new mother to carry the basket for the rest of her life; her husband is shown begging for forgiveness. The corresponding spot on the northwest corner shows a king sitting next to his wife, who is said to have been unfaithful; below she is put to death by being trampled by a horse.

The north gopura used to contain a statue of **Preah Noreay**, a Hindu deity who is said to bestow fertility upon childless women; although the statue is still undergoing restoration at the National Museum, women continue to arrive here to seek his help.

Yeah Peau

Some 100m north of Ta Prohm in the grounds of the modern Wat Tonle Bati, lies the small, twelfth-century temple of **Yeah Peau**. Various legends surround the temple. One tale tells how King Preah Ket Mealea fell in love with a young girl named Peau, who gave birth to his son, whom she named Prohm. The king returned to his court but left behind a ring and sacred dagger so that in years to come Prohm would be able to prove his regal descent. Prohm duly went to his father's court and stayed many years, presumably forgetting his mother, for when he finally returned home he fell in love with her, refusing to believe her when she said he was her son. To resolve the matter, it was agreed that Peau and Prohm would each build a temple; if he finished first she would marry him, and if she finished first he would acknowledge her as his mother. The contest took place at night with the women helping Peau and the men assisting Prohm. In the middle of the night, the women raised a lighted candle into the sky. The men, thinking this was the morning star, settled down to sleep in the belief that they could not be beaten, leaving the women to carry on working and complete their temple first. (This rivalry between women and men is a common theme in Cambodian pagodas, cropping up many times in different guises.)

Wat Tonle Bati was badly damaged by the Khmer Rouge and some pieces of gnarled metal behind the main Buddha are all that is left of the original statue. Beside the Buddha is a statue of Peau, while outside in the courtyard are five large seated Buddhas, each with their hands in a different *mudra*.

There are plenty of **picnic huts** built on stilts over the river (5000 riel day rental), 300m northwest of the temples. The owners vie to get you to stop at their huts; once you've made your choice, they provide floor mats and cushions, plus a tray of drinks and snacks, and even inflated inner tubes for swimming. You pay for anything you use or consume, although as prices are higher than in restaurants, you might want to bring your own provisions. Even if you only want to picnic, you'll have to pay the $3 entry fee.

Phnom Chisor and around

Originally known as Suryadri ("Sun Mountain"), **Phnom Chisor** (daily; $2 for foreigners) was built early in the eleventh century by Suryavarman I and was once a site of some significance, housing one of four sacred linga installed by the king in temples at the boundaries of his kingdom. A hot and tiring flight of 412 steps ascends the hill from the south, though there are a couple of shady pavilions along the way in which to rest, and refreshment-sellers are on hand. A modern pagoda is established at the summit and there are a burgeoning number of sanctuaries scattered about. One of the more interesting, to the right from the top of the steps, is **Prasat Preah Ko Preah Kaew**, containing images of the cow and small boy from which it gets its name: according to one far-fetched legend, these were the children of a pregnant woman who fell from a mango tree she had climbed, whereupon she gave birth to them in her shock.

At the far, northern, end of the hill, the ancient temple of **Prasat Boran** still retains some well-preserved carved sandstone lintels. The temple was built opening to the east, from which side you get a good view across the plains. From the eastern doorway, the old entrance road leads straight to the foot of the hill and still retains its two gatehouses. In the entrance, two stone **basins** are filled with water, which is ladled out for blessings using a couple of large seashells. The *achars* say the basins used to fill naturally – presumably from a spring – but after a US bomb came through the roof of the central sanctuary in the 1970s (thankfully it didn't explode) this stopped; to this day the roof remains covered with corrugated iron. The internal doors to the central sanctuary are very fine and decorated with images of Shiva standing on the back of a pig – although no one knows why. To the east a path leads around the hill to a small **cave shrine**, really more a collection of rocks, but containing enough room for two or three people to squeeze inside the crevice. An *achar* here dispenses blessings for a consideration, and will sell you one of his handkerchiefs decorated with holy symbols for protection and prosperity.

Around Phnom Chisor

Prasat Neang Khmao, 5km to the west of Phnom Chisor, is much visited by local people and features on guesthouse tours, but after the delights of Tonle Bati and Phnom Chisor there's relatively little to see. Just two ruined towers remain on a low mound, surrounded by a modern pagoda, during whose construction three other towers were removed.

The villages east of Phnom Chisor weave very fine traditional *hol* patterned **silk**. It's worth buying a piece if you can find someone with a finished length, although this isn't easy as most is produced to order. UNESCO is helping the weavers here re-learn the use of natural dyes, a skill that was lost during the Pol Pot years.

Phnom Tamau

The **Phnom Tamau Zoological Gardens and Wildlife Rescue Centre** is set in an area of regenerating scrub forest between Tonle Bati and Phnom Chisor. Most animals in the zoo here were rescued from desperate situations:

▲ The Killing Fields at Choeung Ek

many were confiscated as they were being smuggled out of the country to satisfy demand for exotic foods and medicine in China and Thailand; others were found for sale in the markets, kept as pets in tiny cages or destined for the restaurant tables of Phnom Penh. Although many of the animals still have far from adequate facilities, the team of dedicated keepers do their best with limited finances. With an annual feeding bill alone of over $100,000, the centre relies on private donations and sponsorship for funding.

The star attractions are undoubtedly the **tigers**, which by day prowl around a purpose-built deluxe enclosure, endowed with natural boulders to soak up the sun and scrub cover for shade. At night they are secured indoors and protected by armed keepers – poachers are still a cause for concern and a dead tiger can net thousands of dollars. Close to the tiger enclosure a spacious compound is home to a collection of **sun bears** and **black bears**, while further enclosures contain other indigenous species – elephants, crocodiles, pangolins, various wild cats, deer, monkeys and snakes. A two-year old baby elephant who lost a foot in a snare is a recent addition; he'll be in the zoo for life and goes by the name Lucky. The **cranes** and other birds are by now quite tame and you can wander around inside their enclosure, getting quite close to them.

Practicalities

The zoo is 50km south of Phnom Penh off National Route 2. Look out for the **billboard** of animals 10km beyond Tonle Bati, from where it's a further 5km up the side road to the zoo entrance (daily 8.30am–4.30pm; foreigners $5, car 2000 riel, motorbike 1000 riel). The **Takeo bus** passes the turning, but given that there are seldom motos available at the main road, and that the site is more of a safari park than a zoo, it is best visited with your own transport. On the way from the main road you'll have to run the gamut of beggars that line the road; many are elderly, who, having no one to care of them, walk daily from their villages to ask for alms, so it's an idea to take a bundle of small notes that you can dispense as you feel appropriate. The layout plan at the entrance is worth studying as the zoo's set-up budget was largely squandered on a grandiose scheme of roads meant to emulate Singapore Zoo, as a result of which there are now a lot of overgrown tracks going nowhere.

Travel details

Trains

Phnom Penh to: Battambang (1 every other day; at least 12hr); Pursat (1 every other day; 6–7hr).

Buses

Phnom Penh to: Bangkok, Thailand (daily; 10–12hr); Banlung (daily; 10–12hr); Battambang (5 daily; 5hr); Ho Chi Minh City, Vietnam (twice daily; around 6hr); Kampot (twice daily; 4–5hr); Kep (twice daily; 4–5 hr); Kompong Cham (10 daily; 2hr); Kompong Chhnang (10 daily; 2hr); Kompong Speu (9 daily; 1hr 30min); Kratie (daily; 7hr); Neak Leung (10 daily; 2hr); Oudong (10 daily; 1hr); Poipet (5 daily; 8hr); Pursat (5 daily; 3hr); Siem Reap (6 daily; 8hr); Sihanoukville (6 daily; 3hr 30min); Sisophon (4 daily; 7hr); Stung Treng (daily; 8hr); Takeo (4 daily; 2hr); Voen Kham, Laos border (daily; 8–10hr).

Shared taxis, minibuses and pick-up trucks

Phnom Penh to: Banlung (several daily; at least 10hr); Battambang (12 daily; 6hr); Bavet (20 daily; 3hr); Kampot (12 daily; 3hr); Koh Kong (several daily; 6hr); Kompong Cham (20 daily; 2hr 30min);

Kompong Chhnang (4 daily; 2hr 30min); Kompong Thom (12 daily; 3hr); Neak Leung (20 daily; 1hr 30min); Pailin (10 daily; 6hr); Poipet (10 daily; 8hr); Pursat (10 daily; 4hr); Sen Monorom (several daily; at least 8hr); Siem Reap (hourly; 6–8hr); Sihanoukville (20 daily; 3hr 30min); Sisophon (10 daily; 7hr); Svay Rieng (6 daily; 3hr 30min); Takeo (12 daily; 2hr).

Boats

Phnom Penh to: Siem Reap (daily; 5hr); Chau Doc, Vietnam (daily; 5hr).

Flights

Phnom Penh to: Siem Reap (at least 6 daily; 45min).

Battambang and the northwest

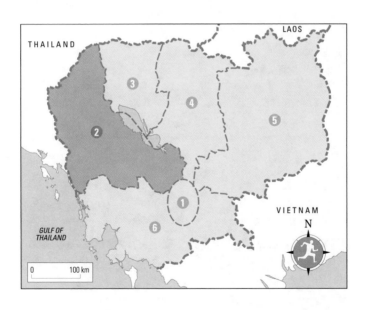

CHAPTER 2 # Highlights

* **Floating villages** Take a boat out to explore the floating villages on the Tonle Sap near Kompong Chhnang. See p.133

* **Battambang** Laid-back town with characterful colonial architecture, a lazy riverside and a fledgling Western bar scene. See p.136

* **Wat Banan** Well-preserved ancient hilltop pagoda near Battambang, with superb views from summit. See p.144

* **Banteay Chhmar** Remote, ruined, fabulously carved temple. See p.151

* **Choob** Small village famous for its intricate sandstone statues. See p.152

▲ Banteay Chhmar

Battambang and the northwest

S trike north from Phnom Penh, keeping west of the Tonle Sap, and you'll be following the route along which the Khmer Rouge retreated from Phnom Penh in 1979, ahead of the liberating Vietnamese forces. This is also the route that the invading Thai armies used in the opposite direction, as they headed south repeatedly from the sixteenth to the nineteenth centuries to sack and pillage whichever settlement happened to be Cambodia's capital at the time. Much of the northwest still shows clear Thai influence, especially in the style of the houses – not surprising given that the area came under Thai control at the end of the eighteenth century, and was only finally returned to Cambodia in 1946. These days the route is a busy transit corridor linking the capital to the Thai border and bringing rice from the sparsely populated but fertile plains to the more populous south. Communications here are steadily improving, and though the train from Phnom Penh takes around twelve hours to get to Battambang, National Route 5 has been sealed all the way and is in good condition, meaning that the journey now takes only about six hours.

The first two towns of any size along National Route 5 out of Phnom Penh are Kompong Chhnang and Pursat. A busy river fishing port, **Kompong Chhnang** takes its name from the terracotta pots (*chhnang*) which are produced here and used all over Cambodia, while quiet **Pursat** is home to marble workshops where you might see craftsmen at work. From both towns you can get out to visit the **floating villages** on the Tonle Sap.

North of Pursat is laid-back **Battambang**, one of Cambodia's largest towns with a lazy riverside ambience and handful of colonial-era villas, shophouses and an Art Deco market. The surrounding province once had more temples than Siem Reap, although none was on the scale of Angkor Wat and most have long disappeared. The couple that remain are worth a visit, however, especially the hilltop site of **Wat Banan**, which you can see in a day-trip from Battambang.

On the Thai border in the far northwest, **Poipet** is increasingly used as a place to make a quick stop and change vehicles on the way between Bangkok and the temples at Siem Reap. If you're travelling along this route it's well worth breaking your journey at **Sisophon**, the crossroads town at the junction of national routes 5 and 6, to visit the little-touristed **Banteay Chhmar**, a ruined Angkorian temple which is still completely unrestored and overgrown by jungle.

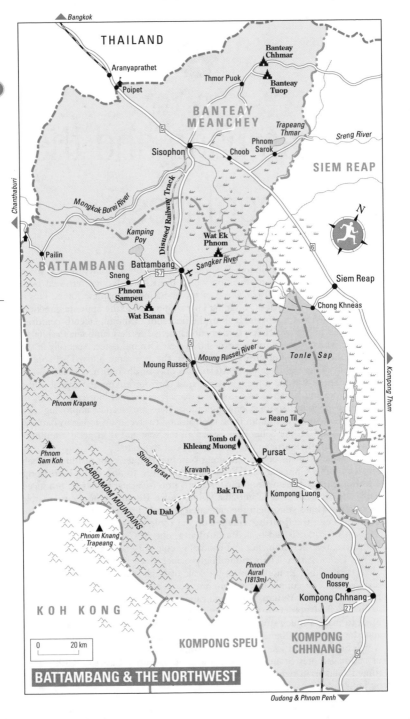

BATTAMBANG & THE NORTHWEST

It was to the mountainous border that the Khmer Rouge fled after their defeat, and from here that they waged a disruptive guerrilla war until 1996; in the far north, the remote Dangkrek Escarpment was their last foothold until the death of Pol Pot in 1998. The war was vicious and both the government and the Khmer Rouge laid **land mines**; the border is the most heavily mined area of the country and under no circumstances should you wander from defined tracks.

Kompong Chhnang and around

The old colonial town of **KOMPONG CHHNANG**, 83km north of Phnom Penh on National Route 5, is a quiet place to stop over for a day or to take a weekend break from Phnom Penh. The town gets its name from the *chhnang* (terracotta pots), produced hereabouts, which are distributed all over Cambodia by boat or ox cart (the slow pace of transport reducing the risk of damage to the fragile cargo). Ox carts laden with pots trudge along the highway, and several villages where the **pottery** is made can be visited nearby. Relaxing atmosphere apart, the chief attraction here is a trip to the **floating villages** on the Tonle Sap, where you'll get a flavour of life on the water.

Arrival and information

All road transport to and from Phnom Penh uses the **bus station**, north of the Independence Monument in the old part of town. Transport from Battambang and the north arrives at (and leaves from) the road just north of Psar Leu. There are plenty of **motos** around town during the day, but they can be hard to find at night; if you're staying far from the centre ask your guesthouse to arrange for you to be picked up after dinner.

The **post** and **telephone offices** are 100m west of the bus station. For **Internet access**, head to one of the cafes around Psar Leu or the Independence Monument. To **change money**, go to Acleda Bank (Mon–Fri 7.30am–4pm), 100m southeast of the monument. The **hospital** is nearby, just east of the monument.

Accommodation

On the riverfront, the town's oldest **hotel**, the *Rathisen* (T026/988634; **❷**), is decrepit but conveniently placed on the waterfront; some rooms have

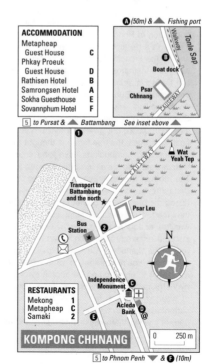

ACCOMMODATION

Metapheap Guest House	C
Phkay Proeuk Guest House	D
Rathisen Hotel	B
Samrongsen Hotel	A
Sokha Guesthouse	E
Sovannphum Hotel	F

⑤ to Pursat & ▲ Battambang   See inset above ▲

Ⓐ (50m) & ▲ Fishing port

Tonle Sap

Ⓑ

Boat dock

Psar Chhnang

CAUSEWAY

Walkway

⑤ to Pursat & ▲ Battambang

Wat Yeah Tep

Transport to Battambang and the north ★

Psar Leu

Bus Station Ⓑ ❷

N

Independence Monument

RESTAURANTS

Mekong	1
Metapheap	C
Samaki	2

Acleda Bank Ⓓ

KOMPONG CHHNANG

0   250 m

⑤ to Phnom Penh ▼ & Ⓕ (10m)

views of the river or across the rice paddies, though others are windowless and dingy. A much newer option is the *Somrongsen Hotel* (☎026/989011; ❷) about half a kilometre north of Psar Leu. Rooms are spacious and clean and have all the expected amenities, but being away from the bustle of the waterfront makes it a little dull. A much better bet is the charming *Sokha Guesthouse* (☎012/762988; ❷), with a range of rooms set around a lovely courtyard garden on a leafy back-street near the Independence Monument; breakfast and dinner are available for guests if ordered in advance. Right next to the monument, the *Metapheap Guest House* (☎012/949297; ❷) has some bright, clean rooms above its restaurant, while the *Sovannphum Hotel* (☎012/812459; ❸), on National Route 5 touts itself a business hotel and has Internet access.

The Town

From the town centre around the Psar Leu market, it's a short walk southwest to the old **French quarter** (roughly the area around the *Sokha Guesthouse*), where shady tree-lined streets and overgrown parks surround faded colonial villas. Northeast of the centre, a broad causeway crosses a marshy flood plain and connects the town to its port, 2km away on the Tonle Sap. The houses which line the causeway balance precariously on high stilts, though even these are scarcely tall enough to prevent river water lapping at the doors

The ethnic Vietnamese

The first Vietnamese settlers in Cambodia were **rice farmers**, many of whose ancestors migrated across disputed borders as long ago as the late seventeenth century; over generations they moved north along the Mekong and today mostly farm in the southeast provinces. The educated, predominantly Christian, Vietnamese population of Phnom Penh has its origins in the **civil servants** brought over during Vietnam's suzerainty over Cambodia during the first half of the nineteenth century, and by the French protectorate. Indeed, records of the time suggest Phnom Penh was more Vietnamese than Khmer. These days the majority of Cambodia's commercial fishing is accounted for by impoverished ethnic Vietnamese **fishing families**; predominantly Buddhist, they live in floating villages on the Tonle Sap and Mekong River, moving around at will or with the annual inundation in their houseboats. Government estimates put the number of ethnic Vietnamese living in Cambodia at around 100,000, but given the difficulty of monitoring the large number who live in floating villages, the true figure is thought to be much higher.

Historically, Cambodians have long entertained feelings of hostility towards the Vietnamese, who are all too often referred to using the derogatory Khmer term, **yuan**. The roots of this resentment go back to the Vietnamese annexation of the Mekong Delta in the seventeenth century. The following century, tensions were exacerbated during the brief period of Vietnamese rule over the whole country, during which time they tried to impose their language, names and mores on the Khmer. The situation was further aggravated during the French protectorate, when Vietnamese clerks were installed in the administration in Cambodia, nor were matters helped when the French redrew the Cambodia–Vietnam border in favour of the Vietnamese after World War II.

Although you're unlikely to witness any racism against the Vietnamese today, it's as well to note that no Cambodian would be seen dead in the pointed hats worn by Vietnamese rice farmers, and that no provincial Cambodian woman would dream of wearing trousers, for fear of being mistaken for a Vietnamese. The country's current leader, Hun Sen, is often accused by his opponents of being a "Vietnamese puppet", while Vietnamese town-dwellers and rice farmers are accused of taking Cambodian jobs.

during the rains. At the far end of the causeway, at **Wat Yeah Tep**, the monks have created small gardens around their quarters and there's a good view across the river.

Kompong Chhnang is the principal fishing port for Phnom Penh, and throughout the year supplies of fresh fish are packed with ice and loaded daily onto a fleet of trucks to drip their way towards the city. The fishing families, primarily ethnic Vietnamese, live on the river in **floating villages**, their houses built on pontoons which bob on the waters of the Tonle Sap. The villages are served by floating markets and coffee shops, and though facilities can be basic (their water, for example, comes from the river itself), most homes have TV and many have small floating gardens, while pens between the pontoons house farmed fish.

If you want to get out on the river and around the floating villages, **boats** can be hired from the riverfront near the boat dock (around 20,000 riel per hour). Taking to the water offers an interesting insight into the daily life of these unusual communities and is a more relaxing experience than visiting the commercialized floating villages on the Tonle Sap at Siem Reap (see p.203).

A statue near the boat dock depicts two figures of local legend, **Pothy Sen** and his wife **Neing Kong Ray**; the former is shown on a flying horse, his hand outstretched to fend off his weeping wife. The tale begins with twelve sisters who are wed en masse to a king. Things go wrong when the king takes a thirteenth wife, Santema, an evil giantess in disguise. Santema blinds the sisters and plots to kill Pothy Sen, the son of one of them, to stop him becoming king. Pothy Sen then falls in love with and marries Santema's own daughter, Neing Kong Ray. When he subsequently discovers his mother-in-law's treachery, in his disgust he uses a magical potion to escape from his wife, creating a river between them. **Phnom Neing Kong Ray**, the long low hill with two distinctive peaks across the river, is said by locals to be the lady's corpse, her hair flowing across the ground to the southeast, her feet to the northwest.

Eating

Restaurants in Kompong Chhnang are most often very basic and serve little more than the Vietnamese noodle soup known as *pho*. If you tire of noodles, there are guesthouse eateries. Most of the *pho* stalls close early – some by 7pm if they have no customers. A decent place is the *Metapheap Restaurant*, by the Independence Monument, which has an English menu and serves good Khmer soups and fish dishes, plus excellent fried noodles; it's open from early in the morning until about 7pm, although things get quiet after lunch. The *Mekong Restaurant*, on the Battambang road, has a reasonable choice of dishes. Just across from the bus station, the *Samaki Restaurant* does decent enough food, though unless you speak Khmer, you'll need to choose what you want in the kitchen, as there's no printed menu. During the daytime, noodle stalls and coffee shops open up around both Psar Leu and Psar Chhnang markets, but at night all you'll find are stalls selling fresh fruit and fruit shakes.

Around Kompong Chhnang

The roads in Kompong Chhnang are lined with stalls selling unglazed terracotta pots and dishes, from plates indented with round dimples (used to bake tiny coconut cakes over charcoal fires) to capacious lidded pots for cooling and purifying water. Most of these pots are crafted in villages around Kompong Chhnang, and you can ride into the country to see the potters at work.

One potting village is **ONDOUNG ROSSEY**, about 7km northwest of town, where you'll see locals busy preparing clay and working at the wheel in the shade of their houses; a small **Cambodian Crafts Federation shop** here sells a range of pottery. To get to Ondoung Rossey, either hire a moto (about $5 round trip) or, if you have your own transport, follow the Battambang road about 5km north from Kompong Chhnang and look for a small sign for the village on the left. Turn left here through a gateway onto a sealed road, then right through another gateway after about 1km onto a dirt road that leads to the village.

Pursat

Named after a tree that used to grow along its river banks, **PURSAT** is a pleasant rural town, 174km from Phnom Penh and 106km from Battambang. Pursat is little visited by tourists, and most of the foreigners who do come are NGO workers. Apart from some **floating villages** 35km away, there's not a lot to see hereabouts, but it's a pleasant place to overnight or rest up for a day.

Arrival and information

Arriving by road, ask to be dropped by the **main bridge** (*spean thmor*), from where it's a couple of hundred metres to the hotels and guesthouse. Pursat's **train station** is 2km northwest from town on National Route 5. Trains arrive from Phnom Penh between noon and early afternoon, while those from Battambang should arrive a little earlier; a moto into town from the station is about 1000 riel. All road transport leaves from the **transport stop** a few hundred metres west of the bridge on National Route 5.

You'll find most facilities in Pursat along the west bank of the river, including the **post office**, a handful of **Internet** outlets; and the **hospital**. There's also a branch of the Acleda Bank – on the north side of the main road in the second block west of the main bridge – where you can **change money**. You can also convert dollars to riel at the market, near which you'll find cheap-rate **phone** booths for domestic calls and a couple of shops where international calls can be made.

Accommodation

New Thansour Hotel One block west of the river, 100m north of the main road ☎052/951506. A bit run-down. The cheapest rooms, in the old block, are a good deal, while those in the new concrete extension are a little more expensive but come with a/c and hot water; there's also a small restaurant. ❶

Phasokakpheap Guest House One block north of the main road between the second and third streets west of the river ☎012/915932. Friendly, family-run place with a mix of cheap fan and a/c rooms. ❶

Phnom Pich Hotel 200m north of the main bridge on the west bank of the river ☎052/951515. This hotel offers the best-value accommodation in town, with large, bright and airy en-suite rooms with either fan or a/c. Unfortunately rooms facing the river are very noisy. ❷

Vimean Tip On the third street west of the bridge ☎012/836052. New hotel with a range of smart and spacious rooms. ❷

The Town

Pursat town straddles the **Stung Pursat**, which flows northeast into the Tonle Sap. The **market**, west of the river and north of the main road (National Route 5), is centrally located and a useful landmark; the other helpful landmark is the **bridge** that carries the National Route 5 across the Stung Pursat. Sights in town are decidedly low-key, the main attraction being the island in the river overlooking the weir, 500m or so north of the market. A pedestrian bridge crosses the river close by and you can take a pleasant stroll along a shady track that runs downstream along the river bank – though you'll need to return the same way as there are no bridges further along.

Pursat is the main centre in Cambodia for **marble carving**, the marble coming from the rocky outcrops of the nearby Cardamom Mountains. Popular subjects include Buddhas and dancing apsaras, as well as bangles and animal statues, and the quality is high, though so are the prices. You might see craftsmen working either marble or wood at a simple workshop behind the now-defunct museum west of the bridge on the main road, and marble statues are sold on the roadside around the *Lam Siv Eng* restaurant a bit further west along the main road.

Eating

Don't leave it too late **to eat** in the evening, as places near the centre tend to close quite early. For a really inexpensive meal, there's the usual assortment of noodle shops by the market and cheap restaurants on National Route 5 near the bridge.

Chenai Stung On the east side of the river, about 1km southeast from the main bridge. This easy-to-find riverside establishment is lit up with twinkling fairy lights from late afternoon. The food is excellent and you can pick the size of serving you want – *jain toight* is a small plate, enough for one or for two people to share, while *jain tom* is a large helping.

Community Villa Restaurant In town, just south of the *Vimean Tip Hotel*. Khmer and Western dishes

on a pleasant shady patio; some of its profits go to needy people.

Lam Siv Eng Restaurant On National Route 5, 200m west of the main bridge. Decent Khmer food, though the setting isn't as pleasant as at other places along the river.

Tepmachha Restaurant Standing alone in a yellow building on the west bank of the river, 500m north of the market. Inexpensive Khmer and Chinese food, and a great setting for a late-afternoon drink.

Around Pursat

Easily reached by moto from Pursat, the small, well-tended tomb of **Khleang Muong** is popular with locals who come here to pay their respects to one of Cambodia's national heroes, though it's only really worth dropping by if you're completely at a loose end. The tomb is located at the village of **BANTEAY CHEI**, several kilometres west of Pursat off National Route 5, surrounded by rice fields. In 1605, the Khmer were losing the war against the Thais; legend has it that Khleang Muong ordered his soldiers to dig a pit and to cast their weapons into it, then he threw himself into the pit, killing himself. Seven days later the Thai army was defeated by the Khmer army with help from the ghosts of Khleang Muong and his army of soldiers. The victory over the Thais is marked by an offering ceremony here in April or May each year, just before the rains and the planting season. The pavilion at the tomb contains a life-size bronze statue of Khleang Muong, and a matching one of his wife, who, according to legend, also killed herself.

The Cardamom Mountains and Ou Dah

Mostly inaccessible and unexplored, the **Cardamom Mountains** are an area of outstanding natural beauty, the primary jungle rich in flora and fauna. A biodiversity study in 2000 established the presence of nearly 400 different species of animals, including tiger, Asian elephant, gaur and a population of critically endangered Siamese crocodiles, previously considered extinct in the wild.

Ou Dah, 56km from Pursat, is an attractive spot in the jungle-clad hills and, for the time being, pretty much the only place where you can easily get into the Cardamom Mountains. Having said that, the trip there (when not scuppered by collapsed bridges and the poor state of the road) is more interesting than the place itself: the road winds slowly through scrub at first before climbing steeply through the forest, crossing tiny gorges and streams. At Ou Dah there are some rapids and a small waterfall, and opportunities for a swim, though there's also a high risk of malaria in the mountains, so take precautions against mosquito bites.

Kompong Luong floating village

KOMPONG LUONG is the closest of the Tonle Sap's floating villages to Pursat, though its precise distance from town varies, ranging from around 35km in the dry season to 40km in the rainy. Populated by a mixed community of Cham and Vietnamese families, the village has its own shops, restaurants and even petrol stations.

Kompong Luong can be reached by **moto** from Pursat (around $5 return), or by **car** (about $20); both can be arranged through hotels in Pursat. To drive to Kompong Luong, head east out of Pursat on National Route 5 for 30km, where there's a turning north at Krakor to the Tonle Sap. Once you arrive at the lake, boatmen will offer to take you out to look around the village for around $5–10, depending on how long you want to stay out on the water.

Battambang and around

Just 280km by road from the capital, **BATTAMBANG** is the only major town on National Route 5 to the Thai border. It is a rather somnolent place – much of its allure deriving from the rows of endangered colonial-era shophouses around the centre of town and a handful of French-style villas in the leafy streets to the south. The town itself has enough minor attractions to fill a gentle half-day, including a couple of tranquil **pagodas**, Wat Phephittam and Wat Dhum Rey Sor, and a **museum**, overlooking the meandering Sangker River, which houses a small collection of statuary from some of the province's temples.

Around town, **Wat Banan** has well-preserved Angkor Wat-style sanctuary towers built on a low hill overlooking the river, while **Phnom Sampeu** features hilltop pagodas and cave shrines with a fine view over the rice fields from the summit. The two sites can be combined into an enjoyable day-trip.

Some history

The history of Battambang is quite separate from the rest of Cambodia, because for much of its existence it fell under **Thai**, rather than Khmer jurisdiction. Founded in the eleventh century, Battambang first came under Thai influence after the fall of Angkor to the Thais in the fifteenth century. Thanks to the town's location on the primary route between Thailand and Cambodia's capitals (variously Lovek, Oudong and Phnom Penh), the Thai army was perpetually passing through in order to intervene in squabbles within the Cambodian royal family.

In 1795, a Cambodian named **Baen** became lord governor of **Battambang province** (which at the time incorporated territory as far away as Siem Reap) in return for his help in returning the pro-Thai King Ang Eng to the Cambodian throne. Baen showed his loyalty to Thailand by paying tribute to the king in Bangkok, which effectively moved Battambang from Cambodian rule into Thai dominion.

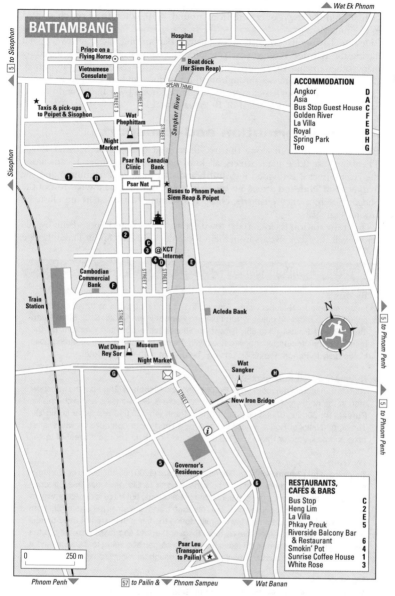

BATTAMBANG

to Sisophon

Hospital

Prince on a
Flying Horse

Vietnamese
Consulate

Boat dock
(for Siem Reap)

SPEAN THMEI

Taxis & pick-ups
to Poipet & Sisophon

STREET 3

STREET 2

Wat
Phephittam

STREET 1

Sangker River

Sisophon

Night
Market

Psar Nat
Clinic

Canadia
Bank

❶ ❷

Psar Nat

Buses to Phnom Penh,
Siem Reap & Poipet

❷

Ⓒ
❸
@ KCT
Internet

Ⓔ

Cambodian
Commercial
Bank Ⓕ

Ⓓ
❹

STREET 2

STREET 1

Train
Station

STREET 3

Acleda Bank

N

Wat Dhum
Rey Sor

Museum

Night Market

Ⓖ

STREET 1

Wat
Sangker

Ⓗ

New Iron Bridge

✉

ⓘ

Governor's
Residence

❺

❻

ACCOMMODATION	
Angkor	D
Asia	A
Bus Stop Guest House	C
Golden River	F
La Villa	E
Royal	B
Spring Park	H
Teo	G

RESTAURANTS, CAFÉS & BARS	
Bus Stop	C
Heng Lim	2
La Villa	E
Phkay Preuk	5
Riverside Balcony Bar & Restaurant	6
Smokin' Pot	4
Sunrise Coffee House	1
White Rose	3

to Phnom Penh

to Phnom Penh

to Phnom Penh

0   250 m

Phnom Penh ▼

to Pailin & ▼ *Phnom Sampeu*

Psar Leu
(Transport
to Pailin)

Wat Banan ▼

Wat Ek Phnom ▲

Throughout the **nineteenth century** the province, although nominally under Thai jurisdiction, was largely left to its own affairs under a succession of all-powerful governors from the Baen family – a self-sufficient fiefdom, isolated from both Thailand and Cambodia. The province was returned to Cambodia in 1907, at which time Battambang town was little more than a collection of wooden houses on stilts. Despite their seeming great age, the colonial buildings seen around the town only date from around 1910, when the **French** moved in to modernize it.

Despite having its population evacuated, Battambang fared relatively well during the **Khmer Rouge** years, escaping the damage which was suffered by many other towns. After the Khmer Rouge were driven west to Pailin, they launched repeated attacks throughout the province, and in 1994 even briefly captured Battambang; ferocious battles occurred around Wat Banan and Phnom Sampeu until the amnesty deal of 1996 was struck.

Arrival, information and transport

Battambang is laid out along the tree-lined west bank of the Sangker River. There are just three main streets, all known by number. Street 1 runs along the river, Street 2 is divided into north and south by Wat Phephittam and the market, **Psar Nat**, and Street 3 is the main route through the town. Most of the budget hotels, money changers, cheap restaurants and fruit stalls are clustered around Psar Nat.

The **train station** is close to the town centre. Trains from Phnom Penh usually arrive well after dark. **Boats** from Siem Reap dock close by Spean Thmei bridge,

---

Moving on from Battambang

By bus

Improvements to National Route 5 mean that it's now possible to travel in relative speed and comfort on privately run buses to **Phnom Penh** (4–5hr; $10), **Siem Reap** (3hr; $5) and **Poipet** (3hr; $5). Private minibuses leave from the riverfront by the market or from your hotel once a day early in the morning (there are also three public buses daily to Phnom Penh). Tickets can be bought at the **Royal Hotel**.

By shared taxi and pick-up

There's transport in the morning to **Poipet** (3hr) and **Sisophon** (2hr) from the transport stop in the northwest of town near National Route 5. Shared taxis and pick-ups for **Pursat** (1hr 30min; 10,000 riel) and **Phnom Penh** (4hr; 30,000 riel) leave from Psar Thmei, on National Route 5 near the airport, a short moto ride out of town; shared taxis and pick-ups for **Pailin** (20,000 riel; 4hr) go from Psar Leu, southwest of town.

By train

Trains leave for **Phnom Penh** (25,000 riel) and **Pursat** (6000 riel) at 6.30am on Sundays only (see p.154 for more details). The service north to Sisophon has been discontinued. The train is very slow and subject to breakdowns, but there is no better way to observe the countryside. The so-called "bamboo trains" are small rail cars made from bamboo and wood scrap that ply the rails during the times they are not used by real trains. A motorcycle engine makes them fly over the rails and one's proximity to the ground only makes them seem faster. Fares are charged according to distance, and a ride of a kilometre or two (and back) is usually enough for most visitors.

By boat

The boat trip down the Sangker River to **Siem Reap** remains very popular, even though improvements to the Sisophon road mean that it's now quicker and cheaper to get there by road. Two operators run boats to Siem Reap from Spean Thmei bridge (northeast of town opposite the hospital) at 7am daily; foreigners pay $15 and the journey takes 3–7hr depending on water levels. The speedboats that used to ply the route have been withdrawn, and the journey is now done in slower but more comfortable 35-seater boats.

just under 1km north of the centre. They generally get in at around 1pm and are met by hotel touts and moto drivers, many of whom speak decent English – this is a good place to find potential guides.

Visitors arriving via **National Route 5** from Phnom Penh, Poipet, Siem Reap and Sisophon are generally dropped at the **transport stop** in the north of town, although shared taxis will often drop you at a hotel of your choice or at Psar Nat in the town centre; transport from **Pailin** arrives at Psar Leu, 1km southwest of town. There's an **airport** just outside town, but thanks to the improved condition of the road, flights have been suspended, though they may resume in future depending on demand.

The **tourist office** (hours are variable, but officially Mon–Fri 7–11am & 2–5pm) is south of the centre in a lovely colonial house near the area of government offices. The staff are friendly but have little information. **Moto** fares around the town are around 1000 riel, a bit more if you're going across the river.

Accommodation

Angkor Street 1 ☏053/952310. Overlooking the river (the rooms at the front have good river views), this hotel has one of the nicest locations in Battambang, so it's a shame the rooms don't quite match up – though clean and en suite, with a/c, TV and fridge, they're run-down, and hot water costs a bit extra. ❸

Asia North of the market, towards the transport stop ☏016/944955. A good budget option, this modern hotel has small en-suite rooms with TV and fan or a/c. ❷

Bus Stop Guest House Street 2 ☏053/730544. A new budget option, this place is clean and efficiently run. The cheapest rooms have a shared hot-water bathroom, but for $2 more you get your own. All rooms have wide-screen TV with cable and a choice of fan or a/c. Wi-Fi Internet access can be included in the package for a fee. The guesthouse bar is a welcoming place. ❸

Golden River 234 Street 3 ☏053/730165 or 016/913138. Spacious but dilapidated en-suite rooms with TV; a/c is available in some rooms. ❷

La Villa 185 Pom Romchek ☏012/991801, ⓦwww.lavilla-battambang.com. On the river opposite and overlooking tiny downtown Battambang, *La Villa* is easily the town's most atmospheric place to stay. Situated in a renovated 70-year-old mansion, rooms have high ceilings and a stylish colonial ambience. All rooms come with TV, a/c, and hot shower. There is also an excellent restaurant serving French and Khmer food. ❻

Royal 100m west of Psar Nat ☏016/912034. One of the best-value hotels in town, with clean, decent-sized en-suite rooms and helpful staff, who can organize local trips and transport. A/c rooms with TV and hot water are available for a small premium. ❷

Spring Park 100m east of the new iron bridge on the east side of the river ☏015/789999. From the outside this looks like one of those modern Chinese-inspired monstrosities with a mirrored glass facade, but inside there are good-value rooms with hot showers, a/c, TV and fridge. The only downside is the location, a brisk 20min walk from the downtown area. ❸

Teo Street 3 ☏012/857048. A little way south of the centre, but nonetheless very popular with expat NGO workers, this hotel has spacious rooms with hot showers, a/c, TV and fridge. There's also a pleasant roof terrace and a restaurant serving Asian and Western food. ❸

The Town

Sleepy Battambang lacks both the traffic of Phnom Penh and the tourists of Siem Reap, making it a pleasant, if sprawling, town to stroll around. At the centre of town is the modern **Psar Nat**, a stylish, angular, pale yellow building, with white clock towers at both ends and a certain Art Deco charm. The streets just south of the market are lined with colonial **shophouses**, more and more of which are being "restored" with bathroom tile facades, mirrored glass and garish plastic advertising signs. Much more charming are the faded, shabby buildings still awaiting restoration, most of which retain their original wrought-iron balustrades on overhanging balconies.

Colonial architecture

An enduring legacy of the French protectorate is the European colonial architecture which still graces Phnom Penh and many of Cambodia's provincial towns. Particularly evocative of the period are the colonial **shophouses**, open-fronted shops at ground level set back under a wide colonnaded walkway created by an overhanging upper storey – often with balconies. Also characteristic of the period are the country's colonial **villas**, typically adorned with shuttered windows, balconies and turrets. Some of the best examples of shophouses can be found in Battambang, clustered along the main street leading to the market and, close by, on the riverfront. There are also good examples of colonial architecture around the river and old market area in Kampot, and around the main post office in Phnom Penh. Sadly, many of these old gems – especially the shophouses – are being renovated in a style popularized in modern China: glazed tiles more fitting for bathrooms are fixed to the facades (to save having to whitewash) and old shuttered windows are being sealed with mirrored glass to keep in the air conditioning. Sadly the trend seems irreversible, as very few Cambodians see any reason to preserve their colonial past.

The **riverfront** is picturesque, with wide grassy banks, but the riverside road is dull, lined with print shops and mobile-phone outlets. Originally the Sangker River was just 5m wide here, but when the Dambang River, south of town, was dammed by sinking a boat filled with earth across it, the Sangker gradually widened. Nowadays its banks lie at least 30m apart.

One treasure to be found along the riverfront is a small sixteenth- or seventeenth-century **Chinese temple**, a one-storey structure restored in 1921 whose dark-red doors and heavily ridged roof tiles edged with ceremonial dragons look quite incongruous amid the area's colonial architecture. Inside the temple, a rather ferocious-looking god is worshipped at a small altar.

Further south on Street 1 is the town's **museum** (Mon–Fri 8–11am & 2–5pm; $1; no photography), with a small but interesting collection of statues and temple carvings from the surrounding area. There are some wonderfully detailed sandstone lintels outside the building, and shiny linga and impressive carvings inside. Two particularly interesting pieces are a thirteenth-century statue of a Bodhisattva "tattooed" with a thousand Buddhas, and a well-worn depiction of Yama on a buffalo. The museum is often closed despite the posted operating hours. If you want to visit you may have to ask the guard out front to contact the curator who can open the museum – that is if the curator doesn't have more pressing matters at hand. Next door to the museum is a good **photographic display**, annotated in English, comprehensively covering sights in Battambang and the surrounding area and providing information on local agricultural and fishing practices, legends and folk tales.

The two oldest **pagodas** in Battambang, Wat Dhum Rey Sor and Wat Phephittam, have both been restored several times since their construction in 1848. Behind the museum lies **Wat Dhum Rey Sor** (Pagoda of the White Elephant) – unsurprisingly, a statue of a white elephant adorns the western steps up to the vihara. Outside the vihara are fine murals depicting scenes from the *Ramayana*; look out for Hanuman riding a steam engine on the east wall. The pagoda's stained-glass windows are delightful when the sun catches their brightly coloured panes. While you're here, look out for a section of high stone wall on the road running down to Psar Leu; this is all that remains of the **Kamphaeng**, the town's fort, demolished by the French.

Back at Psar Nat, the most interesting approach to **Wat Phephittam** is from the south, where the gates are guarded by two *yeak*s (giants); the monks claim that these used to sport threatening expressions, though now they wear a benign look – a strange example of the Khmer belief in metamorphosis. Many of the monks here speak English and are happy to give you a tour of the vihara, which features some elaborate modern murals illustrating the life of Buddha.

While you're in town you may see two distinctive **statues** relating to a bizarre legend surrounding Battambang, a name which literally translates as "lost stick". According to the tale, a man named Dambang Krognuing turned black after eating rice stirred with a black stick; he then deposed the king and assumed the throne. The erstwhile king's son subsequently defeated Dambang Krognuing with the aid of a magical flying horse, despite a vain attempt by the interloper to hurl his black stick at the prince's steed. A massive statue of Dambang Krognuing decorates the traffic circle on the way out of town towards the airport, while a statue of the prince on his flying horse sits at the north end of Street 3.

Eating

There are some good, cheap **restaurants** within walking distance of the centre that serve decent Khmer and Chinese food and have English-language menus. There are also a couple of places geared to Westerners. For an authentic Khmer eating experience, check out the inexpensive **food stalls** in and around Psar Nat. Also, in the late afternoon, a busy night market sets up on the street south of Wat Phephittam, which is an excellent place to try out a wide range of Cambodian home cooking – tasty pork with green beans and chilli and beef in a dry curry are standard, but it's very much a case of what the cook feels like making on the day, so the way to choose is to lift the lids on the pots and see what's on offer. More stalls set up at about 4pm on the riverfront near the post office; this is the place to come for savoury chicken *borbor*, baguettes, Khmer desserts or fruit shakes.

Restaurants

Heng Lim Street 3. Inexpensive restaurant serving good-sized portions of Khmer and Chinese food from an extensive menu. Besides fried rice and fried noodles, they do a delicious "sour fish deep fried" – sweet-and-sour fish with plenty of crunchy vegetables and pineapple chunks.

La Villa 185 Pom Romchek ☏012/991801, ⊛www.lavilla-battambang.com. In the hotel of the same name, *La Villa* is by far Battambang's classiest restaurant. Located in a renovated colonial-era mansion, *La Villa* does a wide range of dishes with style and flair. This is also the place to come for that atmospheric cocktail.

Phkay Preuk South of *Teo Hotel* about 1km from the centre. Popular with locals, this restaurant serves Khmer, Thai and Western dishes, and ice-cream sundaes at tables set under thatched pavilions around a pleasant courtyard. English-language menu.

Riverside Balcony Bar & Restaurant On a quiet bend of the river just 300m south of the old stone bridge. An old wooden house is the venue for this excellent bar and eatery. Good burgers, French fries and pasta can be had here, although it is the beer and the euphoria-inducing views that the place is really known for.

Smokin' Pot Just west of the *Angkor Hotel*. This attractive café-restaurant features Battambang's best-value food. The emphasis is on Thai cuisine but there are Khmer and Western dishes on the menu as well. Cookery classes are sometimes available.

Sunrise Coffee House Just west of the *Royal* Hotel. The first stop in town for caffeine addicts, it also has a good range of filling breakfasts and teas. If you can't stomach rice or noodles for breakfast, this is your place.

White Rose Street 2. Long-running, friendly restaurant with a lengthy menu of economically priced Khmer and Chinese dishes, including excellent spring rolls, and shrimp and vegetable dishes. They also do fried chicken and French fries, baguettes, fruit shakes and simple breakfasts.

Drinking and nightlife

Nightlife for locals in Battambang mainly revolves around the abundant, often seedy karaoke restaurants and bars near the train station. For tourists, the pick of Battambang's nightlife is the *Riverside Balcony Bar* (Tues–Sun 4–11pm) in an old wooden house off Street 1 on the curve of the river near Psar Chas, with soft lighting, good music and a range of cocktails. The bar of *La Villa* (daily 5–9.30pm) is very easily the most evocative space in the whole province, needing only a little imagination and a cocktail or two to transport you to the days of old French Indochina. The only downside is the early closing hour.

Listings

Banks and exchange Both the Cambodian Comercial Bank, near the train station, and the Canadia Bank, north of the market, change traveller's cheques at the usual two-percent commission. The Canadia Bank gives commission-free cash advances on MasterCard, while the Cambodian Commercial gives cash advances on Visa and MasterCard, but charges commission. For Western Union money transfers, go to the Acleda Bank across the river east of the train station.

Consulate Vietnam, north of Psar Nat on Street 2 (Mon–Fri 8–11am & 2–5pm).

Hospital and clinics Avoid the provincial hospital near the river, where facilities are basic and conditions none too clean. You'll be better off at a private clinic; try the Psar Nat Clinic, north of the market.

Internet access There are many Internet cafés all over town; the ones geared towards serving foreigners are on the stretch of Street 1 near the

Angkor Hotel. KCT Internet ($1.50 per hour) is one of the best.

Pharmacies There are plenty of pharmacies near Psar Nat, though staff speak only limited English.

Phones There are cheap-rate phone booths near the market for domestic calls, and a couple of Camintel booths on the south side of the market for international calls, though they usually don't work. Alternatively, it's possible to make international calls from some hotels but it's of course much, much cheaper to place Internet webcalls through Skype at one of the many Internet cafés in town.

Post office The post office (Mon–Fri 7–11am & 2–5pm) is on the riverfront in the south of town.

Supermarkets The nearest that Battambang gets to a supermarket is Chea Neing, west of Psar Nat, which has a pretty good selection of imported luxuries.

Around Battambang

Phnom Sampeu, the main tourist sight close to town, has several active pagodas, a number of atmospheric caves (for which you'll need a torch) and a fine view of the surrounding countryside. Combining a visit to Phnom Sampeu with **Wat Banan**, its Angkor-style towers sitting atop a small hill, makes for an excellent day out. Other places of interest near town are **Kamping Poy**, a vast reservoir created using forced labour during the Pol Pot era, and **Wat Ek Phnom**, an eleventh-century Hindu temple to the north of town. All these sites are covered by a single-entry **ticket** ($2), valid for one day and available at each of the sites – although it's not really practical to see all four places in a day. The best way to get to these sites is by hiring a **moto** in Battambang; the round trip to Phnom Sampeu and Wat Banan should cost around $5.

Phnom Sampeu

The elongated rocky outcrop of **Phnom Sampeu** (Boat Mountain), about 15km southwest of Battambang on National Route 10, consists of two peaks connected by a narrow pathway. Local legend says that the outcrop is the broken hull of a ship, sunk by a crocodile whose love for a girl was unrequited; when she and her fiancé took to sea, they were attacked by the crocodile and drowned. Some distance away to the northwest, another quite separate small hill, **Phnom Kropeu** (Crocodile Mountain), continues the tale: the local population, scared of the crocodile, drained all the water from the area so that he couldn't swim away; eventually the poor croc died and turned into a hill.

On arrival, you'll be dropped at the foot of the **steps** leading steeply up the larger hill, near a cluster of refreshment stalls. You'll first need to buy a ticket ($2) at a small kiosk by the steps. At the foot of the steps is a gateway topped by a sculpture of a boat, and a large red chedi nearby, which holds the ashes of people who die with no next of kin.

If you have your own transport it's possible to drive to the top by following the track along the foot of the hill for a few hundred metres, then taking the cemented road on the right where the road forks (you could also walk up this route, and walk back down the main path). If you don't have a **guide**, there are plenty of local children who will accompany you up the hill and show you how to find the caves. They'll expect a small tip, but it's a good idea to let them tag along as there are unmarked forks in the paths, and they'll probably have a torch as well. Don't stray from the defined paths here as most of the hills hereabouts are thought to be mined.

The **main path** up the hill is a steep and tiring walk of around thirty to forty-five minutes. A right fork about halfway up makes a detour to the so-called **wind cave** (*leahng kshal*). The cave is approached through a pagoda-style gateway, beyond which steps lead down to a shady, rocky platform where a number of shrines have been placed. The cave itself is open at two ends, and a light, cool breeze usually blows through it (hence its name). The mouth of the cave is marked by a square wooden doorframe set into the cliff face. You can walk through the cave to the other side of the hill in about fifteen minutes – the cave floor is dry but uneven – though without your own torch you'll have to buy a candle from the guardian here, as the locals do, and hope it doesn't go out in the breeze.

Retrace your steps from the cave and then, just after the pagoda-style gateway, take the small path straight ahead which leads back to the main track up the hill. Turn right and walk for a few minutes to the **Chinese pagoda**, from where the path carries on climbing for another couple of hundred metres to reach a **Buddhist pagoda**. In 1994–95 Phnom Sampeu was at the front line of fighting between government forces and the Pailin faction of the Khmer Rouge. Remnants of the conflict can be seen in two abandoned Russian-built **anti-aircraft guns** by the Buddhist pagoda; signs warn against approaching the guns as the area around may be mined.

Beyond the pagoda it's just a hundred metres to the summit of the hill and the **Preah Jan** vihara. From here, there are panoramic views over the surrounding rice fields and countryside to Battambang. During the Khmer Rouge era, the pagoda buildings were used as a prison and **interrogation centre** – victims were pushed through a hole in the roof of a cave to fall to their deaths. A narrow rocky path behind the pagoda leads to the **Theatre Cave** (*leahng lacaun*). Although theatrical productions were once staged here, it's hard to imagine that this sinister cave was ever a place of enjoyment: a host of bats chirp in the roof crannies, and in the dim light it's easy to think you see the outlines of haunted faces on the cave walls. A reclining Buddha keeps watch, while a small metal cage contains the skulls and bones of bodies which were found all over the cave floor. A second cave, further down the hill, was the theatrical dressing room, and a cage here also contains human bones.

From here, the easiest way down is to follow the cemented road back down to the foot of the hill and the refreshment stands. Alternatively, you could take the narrow path off to the left just below the steps and cross to the other peak, then make your way down from there.

▲ Wat Banan

Wat Banan

The best preserved of the temples around Battambang, **Wat Banan** can be reached from Battambang by following Street 1 south out of town for 20km until you see some distinctive Angkor Wat-like towers; the temple lies immediately at the top of a steep laterite stairway which ascends a seventy-metre-high hill. Alternatively, you can get here directly from Phnom Sampeu via a narrow dirt road which passes through some delightful countryside. If you don't have a driver who knows the way, local kids will offer to guide you if you give them the moto fare back (about $1).

It's known that Wat Banan was consecrated as a Buddhist temple, but scholars are uncertain who built the temple or exactly when it was completed – estimates put this between the tenth and thirteenth centuries. Five corn-on-the-cob towers remain, all in a somewhat collapsed state, and several of the carvings have lost their heads to vandals, though there are a few still in reasonable condition. You will likely be accompanied on the climb by young kids who hope for a tip by telling you a bit about the temple. It's certainly worth the steep clamber up to see the detailed lintels, beheaded apsaras and views out over endless paddies, with Phnom Sampeu clearly visible to the north.

Kamping Poy

The prettiness of the lake at **Kamping Poy** belies the fact that it was created by the Pol Pot regime using slave labour – over ten thousand people died during the construction of the eight-kilometre **dam** which bounds the lake. The dam lay at the heart of an extensive irrigation system, now sadly silted up and collapsed, which transported water to the surrounding fields, allowing dry-season rice cultivation and hence boosting foreign income for the regime. From the lakeside there are fabulous views across the plains and lake to the distant hills; **boats** can be hired (around 3000 riel per hour) to go out onto the lake, which is packed at weekends and holidays with Cambodians frolicking in the water. The rim of the dam is navigable by moto or on foot for several kilometres, which means that even at busy times you can get away for a quiet swim. Kamping Poy is reached on a rough track running northwest off National Route 10 and to the south of Phnom Sampeu; the lake is around 15km from the turn-off.

Wat Ek Phnom

The ruined eleventh-century Hindu temple at **Wat Ek Phnom**, 12km north of Battambang on the river road, now sits in the grounds of a modern pagoda, surrounded by lotus ponds, small streams and rivers, giving the feeling of being on an island. The temple itself is enclosed by a crumbling laterite wall, and the sandstone buildings of the main sanctuary are lined up in a row, joined by an enclosed walkway. The temple would originally have been reached via a couple of two-metre-high terraces, though these have collapsed, and you'll now have to scramble up a small hill. To enter the sanctuary itself, you'll have to climb through a window or a broken section of wall, or walk round to the slightly better-preserved south side, where a crumbling doorway survives, along with some carvings.

Pailin and around

Ringed by hills on the border with Thailand, the gem-mining centre of **PAILIN** revels in its isolation. After being ousted from power in 1979, the Khmer Rouge were easily able to hole up here, supporting their campaigns against the government by tapping into the area's rich natural resources – gemstones and untouched forests; it's said that gem-mining alone earned them a monthly revenue of $10 million. They held out until August 1996 when, in a move that marked the beginning of the end for the Khmer Rouge, Ieng Sary, the local commander, struck a deal with the Cambodian government, gaining immunity from prosecution for himself and taking three thousand defectors over to the government side. Even now though, older Pailin residents still reminisce about the Khmer Rouge years, when education and health care were available and food was given to the old and needy – these days, reliance on the free market means there are few public services.

It's 80km from Battambang to Pailin along National Route 57. This road can be in poor condition during the monsoon season, with flooding, collapsed bridges and trucks getting bogged down in the mud frequently causing long delays. The road passes a couple of sites of interest including, after 15km, Phnom Sampeu (see p.142) and then, about 10km further on in the village of **SNENG**, the remains of a tenth-century temple, **Prasat Yeah Ten**. Three of the temple's entrances retain beautifully carved lintels, while behind the modern temple are three extremely old brick sanctuaries, perhaps also dating back to the tenth century.

The main reason for coming here, however, is to **cross the border** into Thailand. At the border there are a couple of casinos popular with Thais, but no other attractions as such, so Pailin is only worth the ride from Battambang if you have a couple of days to spare and want to see a little-visited part of the country; you'll need to overnight in the town if you're not crossing the border as the journey from Battambang takes anywhere between three and seven hours.

The town and around

Pailin is a sprawling and haphazard frontier town; only the few government buildings and the bank give it any feeling of permanence. In the south of town, on the road in from Battambang, is a small but unmistakable hill, **Phnom Yat**, the summit dominated by mobile-telephone transmitters and a stupa, built with funds from an overseas Khmer in 2000. A peaceful vantage point from which to watch the sunset, the hill was named after a Buddhist pilgrim couple who arrived in Pailin at the end of the nineteenth century. Hunting and gem-mining had already begun to destroy the countryside, and Yeah Yat and her husband set up a meditation centre on the hill where they could be close to nature and the mountain spirits. Yat began to receive messages from the spirits that there would continue to be a plentiful supply of gems in the soil as long as the miners respected the land, built pagodas and made appropriate offerings. As word of this prediction spread, superstitious miners did as they were told and continued to find gems; today, however, their luck is growing thin (although you might see visitors vainly scratching about in the soil around the temple). Locals say that to prevent bad luck, before you leave Pailin you should make a small offering here and thank the spirits for letting you use their water and air. Gory **tableaux** at the pagoda illustrate the fate that befalls those destined for hell, including a man having his tongue pulled out, someone being boiled in oil and another man being poked with a sharp fork to make him climb a pole of thorns. Tucked away behind the modern vihara is all that's left of the previous pagoda – wall-paintings, floor tiles and a cracked stupa – after it was destroyed by the Khmer Rouge.

Close by, on the bend of the road, is **Wat Ratanasaoporn**, its enclosing wall covered in a bas-relief depicting the Churning of the Ocean of Milk (see p.183). The pagoda hit the headlines in 2000 when it emerged that the monks had been entertaining "ladies of the night" and eighty monks were defrocked following the scandal.

From here, the road runs down a ridge into town. Go straight at the roundabout and, just before the road makes a sharp left, you'll see a **gem-cutting school** on the left, and during the week you may be able to see gems mined locally being cut. Following the sharp turn to the left, the road runs downhill to the **market** on the right, where there are a few **gem dealers** hawking their wares alongside vendors of vegetables and household goods.

The gem mines

Pailin is surrounded by excavated plots of land, the red mounds of earth marking the sites of **gem mines**, though most are abandoned, and those prospectors who are still at work are rather secretive about their diggings. Moto drivers may offer to take you to see them, though there's little to see apart from a hole in the ground and a pile of earth. Pailin has been a gem-mining centre for nearly a hundred years, and it's said that sapphires, rubies and garnets once lay everywhere on the surface. Now much of the land is mined out, and fortune-seekers have to dig deep into the rocky ground in search of the stones, which in their raw state resemble fragments of broken glass. Typical finds today are small **garnets** and **topazes**, and occasional **rubies**; sapphires are now rare. It's hard toil for the prospectors, and for most, hope turns to wistfulness as they sift painstakingly through mounds of red dirt, sorting earth from rocks; piles of spoil scar the landscape, creating an almost lunar scene. The soil is taken to be washed in the local river, which daily runs red with the run-off from panning, silting up the river bed and destroying the fishing for many kilometres. Plastic tarpaulins provide shade at midday and a rough shelter at night, when most sleep in or near their claims, both to save the expense of a bed and to deter robbers from stealing their hard-earned sacks of dirt.

The Phnom Ching Chok Reservoir and O Chrah Waterfall

If you fancy a day out in the countryside, you could pick up a lunch box from your hotel or one of the local restaurants and head to **Phnom Ching Chok Reservoir** (5 baht), about 5km southwest of town. The reservoir is popular at weekends among locals, who come to splash about in the water and relax under

Cambodia's land-mine legacy

Land mines are supposed to maim rather than kill, but over a quarter of Cambodians injured by mines die of shock and blood loss before reaching hospital. For those who survive – over forty thousand Cambodians have become **amputees** as a direct result of land-mine injuries – the impact of an injury on their families is financially devastating, emotional consequences aside. To meet the costs of treatment, their families usually have to sell what few possessions they have, reducing them to an extreme poverty from which they seldom recover. For **young women** mine victims, the stigma is often unbearable: being disabled means that they are frequently unable to find a husband and have to remain with their families, where they may be reduced to the status of slaves. The more fortunate amputees have access to a **prosthetics** workshop where, once their injury has healed sufficiently, they can receive a false limb. However, even if they are subsequently able to get a place at a skills or crafts training centre, there's no guarantee of employment once they've completed their training, and without the capital to set up on their own, land-mine victims all too often find their prospects little improved.

In Cambodia, international **NGOs** are undertaking the delicate, painstaking task of mine clearance. Besides training local crews (many of whom are the widows of land-mine victims), they work hard to inform rural communities in heavily contaminated areas of the **dangers** of mines, which are more subtle than might appear: during the rainy season, mines which are buried too deep to go off can move towards the surface as the land floods, rendering previously "safe" territory risky.

The actual process of mine clearance is slow and expensive. As yet no mechanical system is available that is reliable enough to allow land to be declared as cleared. So, once a minefield has been identified, the site is sealed off and divided into lanes for trained **personnel**, lying on their stomachs, to **probe** systematically every centimetre of ground for buried objects, using a thin blade. The mines thus detected are carefully uncovered and destroyed, usually by blowing them up where they lie.

thatched huts at the water's edge. There are usually vendors selling snacks here, and inflated inner tubes to rent for aquatic fun. If you fancy a hike, continue 400m past the entrance to the reservoir until you reach a fork in the road, then go straight on for another 3.5km, crossing a couple of streams, to **O Chrah Waterfall** on the left; there is a **risk of land mines**, so don't stray from the path. A moto should charge about 80-100 baht to take you out there and pick you up later.

To the border

The **Thai border** (open daily 7am–8pm), 20km from Pailin, can be reached in about half an hour by shared taxi (50 baht) or moto (100 baht). At the border itself there's a small market and two rather incongruous **casinos**, which go by the names of Caesar's and Flamengo an entertain an almost exclusively Thai clientele. Lately there have been some hassles here, with Thai border guards insisting that you have a ticket out of Thailand before being admitted to the country. Some travellers have been sent back to Cambodia after going through departure formalities. It's a good idea to ask around in Battambang before crossing here to assess the situation. If your crossing is successful you can take a minibus to Chanthaburi (100 baht), then another bus to Bangkok, or Trat for Koh Chang.

Practicalities

Pailin is reached by taxi or pick-up from Battambang, an eighty-kilometre trip on National Route 57, a bouncy dust bath in the dry season and often unpassable in the wet. From time to time the road is regraded, but it's soon churned up again by the trucks that grind their way along it. As you near town, the road climbs steadily to Phnom Yat, where it executes a ninety-degree turn. A kilometre along the ridge is a roundabout; go straight ahead and follow the sharp turn downhill to the left to reach the **market** on your right. Around here you'll find the town's **transport stop**, food stalls and money changers.

Although dollars and riel are both accepted in town, the Thai **baht** is the currency of choice; change dollars here and you'll be given baht unless you specifically ask for riel. There are branches of the Canadia and Acleda banks on the ridge road towards the pagoda.

The **post office** is near the roundabout on the ridge road behind the **hospital** and near the government offices. There's a small **tourist office** near the *Phkay Proek Restaurant* at the top of the ridge road. **Phone** calls can be made from a couple of shops opposite the market; there's currently no Internet access in town.

Accommodation

The best **hotel** in town is the *Hang Meas* (☎012/787546; ❸), a little west of the centre, towards the border. Rooms here are clean and pleasant, with chunky wood furniture, hot water, en-suite bathrooms, a/c and TV. The *Kim Young Heng Guest House* (☎016/939841; ❶), located a few steps up the hill from the market behind the restaurant of the same name, has a range of fan and a/c rooms, some bright and appealing (although others are windowless cells). Opposite the market, the *Punleu Pich Guest House* (☎016/958611; ❶) offers basic facilities and the cheapest rates in town.

Eating and drinking

Eating in Pailin is no gastronomic delight, but there are plenty of stalls in the market and cheap restaurants nearby. The best **restaurants** in town are at the *Hang Meas Hotel*, which has an English-language menu and does a selection

Illegal logging

During the period between 2000 and 2005, Cambodia lost nearly 30 percent of its tropical hardwood forest cover. If you travel to **Pailin** or in the provinces of **Kompong Thom**, **Kratie**, **Rattanakiri**, **Mondulkiri** and **Koh Kong**, it's almost impossible not to spot evidence of logging – piles of felled trees at the roadside and logging tracks that are often much better than the official roads. After 1995, logging accelerated when concessions throughout the country were awarded, mainly to multinational conglomerates, who used earth-moving equipment to extract massive hardwood trees from deep in the jungle, frequently destroying everything else in their path. The timber was generally shipped on to Thailand or Vietnam, where much of it was turned into garden furniture and sold to Europe. In theory, the government should have received a healthy revenue from the logging operations, but in practice very little reached the treasury coffers; instead, high-ranking officials, military personnel in particular, suddenly became very rich.

Environmentalists began lobbying the government to reduce logging, though the Cambodian government lacked the resources or the will to enforce the terms of the logging licences. It wasn't until 1999, when the Asian Development Bank insisted on independent monitoring of logging as a condition of its aid provision, that the government allowed a watchdog group, London-based Global Witness, to investigate the situation. Their most recent report is sobering. Global Witness charges Cambodia's "shadow state" with subverting the very forest protection laws that it is supposed to be enforcing. Citing the Prey Long forest in Kompong Thom province – Southeast Asia'a largest tract of lowland tropical hardwood forest – the latest report by Global Witness recounts how relatives and close friends of prime minister Hun Sen are enriching themselves through illegal logging while the Prime Minister's personal bodyguard unit serves as a timber-trafficking service. For their part, the Cambodian government denies the charges, citing a dubious survey which claims that Cambodia has actually increased its forest cover over the last few years. Ty Sokun, director-general of the Forestry Administration was quoted in an article in the *International Herald Tribune* denouncing Global Witness staffers as "insane, unprofessional people" with no knowledge of forestry, and charged that their findings were deceptive. Global Witness countered by pointing out that any increased forest area is simply fast-growing bamboo planted to replace the centuries-old hardwoods that are being felled at a frenzied pace. Whatever the case, there is little chance that anything will change as long as the demand for tropical hardwoods is high.

of Khmer, Thai and Western dishes, as well as eggs and bread for breakfast, and the *Kim Young Heng Guest House*, just up from the market, which turns out tasty Khmer food and also has an English menu – try the sweet-and-sour fish and morning glory with garlic. Near the top of the ridge road, the *Phkay Proek*, run by the same people as the *Phkay Proek* in Battambang, is another reliable choice. **Nightlife** in Pailin revolves around numerous karaoke/dining places: the brightly lit *Phnom Kieu* on the ridge road is the best of the lot, though few foreigners venture inside.

Sisophon and around

SISOPHON, called *Svay* (mango) by the locals in these parts (no one seems to know why), is the jumping-off point for a day-trip to the massive Angkorian temple ruins of **Banteay Chhmar** and **Banteay Tuop**. Though there's nothing much to do in the town itself, which is particularly dusty, dirty and

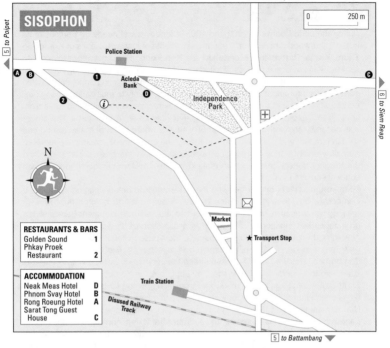

scruffy, it's something of a diamond in the rough, being one of the friendliest towns in Cambodia.

Banteay Chhmar apart, you can also use the town as the base to visit a few minor attractions close to each other on the border with Siem Reap province: the stone-carving village of **Choob**; **Phnom Sarok**, a traditional weaving village where they produce their own silkworms; and **Trapeang Thmar**, a reservoir built under the Khmer Rouge and now designated a reserve for rare Sarus cranes.

Practicalities

Arriving by road, you'll be dropped at the busy **transport stop** just east of the market, where moto drivers are readily available; this is also where you'll need to come to get onward transport when leaving Sisophon. The **tourist office** is helpful and enthusiastic, and a good source of information; look for the newish concrete building north of the market. You can **change money** at the Acleda Bank (on the same road as the *Neak Meas Hotel*, opposite Independence Park) and at the market (dollars, riel and baht are all accepted). **Phone calls** can be made at the cheap-rate booths around town or, for international calls, at the *Phnom Svay Hotel*. The provincial **hospital** is just east of Independence Park, and there are some pharmacies near the market.

Accommodation

One of the most convenient places to stay is the *Phnom Svay Hotel* (☎012 /656565; ❷), an ornate affair on the northwest side of the town centre, opposite the government offices – head for the transmitter tower on the hill. The rooms here have hot showers, a/c and TV, and the helpful staff can help arrange transport to sights around Sisophon. Another centrally located place is the *Neak Meas Hotel* (☎012/971287; ❸); rooms here have a/c, hot water, TV and fridge, but they're rather characterless, and the place also functions as an "entertainment centre", with girls hovering outside the VIP karaoke rooms at the hotel entrance in the evening. A cheaper alternative is the *Rong Roeung Hotel* (☎054/958823; ❷), which has a choice of a/c or fan rooms but no hot water. The cheapest place in town is the *Sarat Tong Guest House* (no phone; ❶) on the north side of the main road heading east out of town (look out for the "Quest House" sign). Some of the small rooms have attached bathrooms, while others share.

Eating and drinking

The tastiest **food** in town is at the *Phkay Proek Restaurant*, 100m downhill from the *Phnom Svay*. The menu, in English, includes Khmer, Thai and Western food and has a good choice of Western breakfast dishes, including enormous pancakes with lemon and honey. Apart from this, the only place with an English-language menu is the restaurant at the *Neak Meas Hotel*, which serves up Khmer, Chinese and Thai dishes. In the late afternoon and early evening, stalls selling basic Khmer food, desserts and fruit juices open on the south side of Independence Park.

Other than the seedy bar-brothels by the train station, and karaoke clubs such as the one at the *Neak Meas Hotel*, Sisophon has little to offer in the way of nightlife.

Banteay Chhmar and Banteay Tuop

Some 60km north of Sisophon, the huge temple of **Banteay Chhmar**, covering an area of around three square kilometres, was built by Jayavarman VII as a memorial to soldiers killed while defending his son in a battle against the Chams. Approaching the site you'll catch a glimpse of the temple's lotus-choked moat and laterite enclosing wall before entering via the entrance causeway to the east, once edged by rows of gods and demons. Generally, everyone reaches the central complex through the multiple collapsed doorways of the eastern entrance. Some of the **carvings** hereabouts are in great condition, but require a little searching to find; look out for a lintel carved with bearded musicians, one playing a harp, and another carved with dancing cranes.

The inner enclosure is surrounded by a **gallery**, mostly filled in by accumulated dust, dirt and rubble; you'll have to scale huge piles of masonry and climb through what's left of the enclosing wall to approach the centre, so make sure you wear sturdy shoes. Tiny Buddha images remain perched in some of the niches along the gallery roof, but many more have been crudely hacked out, either when the state religion switched from Buddhism back to Hinduism in the thirteenth century or as a result of looting. The **faces** of the Bodhisattva Srindradeva look down from the remaining towers, while part of an eight-armed relief of Vishnu remains on the west face of the central tower, though sadly, like so many carvings here, it's missing its head – probably removed and sold for just a few dollars to a middleman, to be sold on for big money internationally.

Some of the magnificently carved **bas-reliefs** that once rivalled those at the Bayon can still be seen on the western exterior of the enclosing wall; one of the most spectacular features a 32-armed god with his hands in two different *mudra*s. Close by, you can see a fresh breach in the wall, the stone unweathered; this is where two massive panels were stripped out by the military in 1998 and trucked across the border en route for sale in Bangkok. Confiscated by the Thai police and returned to Cambodia, the panels are now in the National Museum in Phnom Penh (see p.96). To the north, another section of wall illustrates tales from the *Ramayana* and bears a good image of a *yeak* swallowing a horse.

The paths around the outer walls are kept reasonably clear, and you can return to the entrance either by walking around the outside of the enclosing wall or by scrambling over more rubble, heading back roughly the way you came in. Just across from the southwest corner of the moat is a French-run **silk-weaving project**, *Les Soieries du Mekong*, where you can watch local women weaving silk and buy a colourful scarf.

Practicalities

It's possible to visit Banteay Chhmar by moto from Sisophon, but it's an all-day expedition. National Route 56 heads directly north from Sisophon to **THMOR PUOK**, where there are a couple of unnamed restaurants. From here it's a further 17km to Banteay Chhmar. There are some food stalls near the entrance and although there's no formal **accommodation**, someone will probably offer you a room for the night for a fee if you get stuck – ask at the entrance. There's no **entrance fee**, though the soldiers posted here to protect the site from looting will ask for a tip, as they seldom receive their meagre salary; what you offer is up to you. Their children will help you find your way around the site, but will also hope for a tip for their efforts.

Banteay Tuop

Nine kilometres before reaching Banteay Chhmar (look for a stone sign with gold lettering beside the turn) a minor road branches off to the right from National Route 56. Following this road for about 10km brings you to **Banteay Tuop** (Army Fortress). The site was probably constructed at the same time as Banteay Chhmar, possibly in honour of the army of Jayavarman VII, who defeated the Chams, and though there are fewer carvings here than at Banteay Chhmar, the towers are much taller. The ride there takes you through some classic rural scenery – when the road goes up onto the rim of a reservoir, look for a turning on the right that leads towards the towers.

Choob, Phnom Sarok and Trapeang Thmar

Heading east from Sisophon, there are a few places worth a look along the way to Siem Reap. The easiest to get to – and perhaps most interesting – is the village of **CHOOB**, about 20km along National Route 6 from Sisophon. You'll know when you've arrived as the roadside is lined with sandstone carvings of Buddhas and apsaras, and ranging in size from the tiny to the enormous. The village has a high reputation throughout the country, and even if you don't plan to buy, it's worth stopping to admire the intricacy of the statues and watch the carvers at work: some of the larger pieces take months to complete, and many are commissioned by temples or government offices. If you are prepared to lug a statue home, prices can be very reasonable if you bargain. The most prized types of sandstone have delicate veined markings and command a higher price. A **moto** to Choob from Sisophon costs around $5 return; there's no public transport.

Though silkworms are bred by a couple of NGO projects, **PHNOM SAROK** is one of few villages in the country where **sericulture** has been revived after the Khmer Rouge. Comprising just four streets and a crossroads, the place is also reputed throughout Cambodia for its thick cotton *kramars*, seldom sold outside Sisophon, which are much sought after and command a premium price. Weaving looms clack away under the stilt-houses along the village's north street, and you'll see tree branches flecked with furry silkworm cocoons, looking like yellow balls. The families will be only too pleased to give you a little tour.

The village is 60km from Sisophon, close to the boundary between the provinces of Banteay Meanchey and Siem Reap. From Sisophon, you can get a **moto** all the way to the village (about $10); from Siem Reap you'll need to get a pick-up to the turning on National Route 6 – marked by a statue 34km from Sisophon showing a woman spinning – and a moto the rest of the way; allow a full day to get there and back from either town. The only place to get **food** is a stall by the village crossroads which sells noodles and *borbor*, so it's worth bringing your own provisions.

Easily reached by moto, a few kilometres west of Phnom Sarok is the reservoir of **Trapeang Thmar**, used by over two hundred **Sarus cranes** (*kriel*), as a dry-season refuge. In 2000, some seven hundred families were relocated away from here to create the **Sarus Crane Conservation Area**, which it's hoped will provide a vital refuge for these globally threatened birds – only 1200 remain in Southeast Asia. In the early morning and late afternoon you may also see great and little egrets, purple herons pond herons, and spotted and milky storks when they come out to feed along the banks of the reservoir.

Poipet

POIPET is not a good advertisement for Cambodia, lacking either charm or friendliness. The pushy transport touts who ply the border do it no favours, while the clouds of dust kicked up by trucks and garbage strewn along the roadside add little to its attractions. Unless you need refreshments, have missed the **border opening times** (daily 7am–8pm) or have a yen to gamble at the casinos, there's really no reason to pause. Buses to Siem Reap and Phnom Penh and shared taxis for Sisophon and Battambang depart regularly throughout the day, and pick-up trucks run until the early afternoon through to Siem Reap.

Arriving here from Thailand, it's supposed to be straightforward to obtain a **visa**. In actual fact you will have to run a gauntlet of touts who will officiously take your passport and then try to charge you for simply handing it through the window to an immigration official. Don't expect the Cambodian officials to interfere on your behalf either. You might also be encouraged to change dollars into riel at poor rates, but this isn't necessary, as dollars and baht are accepted everywhere. The best way around all this if you are Cambodia-bound is to arrive with an e-visa (Ⓦ evisa.mfaic.gov.kh) which can be used at this land crossing. After border formalities, most travellers are shepherded into waiting minivans by their tour guides; if you're alone, motos wait to ferry you to the transport stop near the market in **Poipet**, less than a kilometre to the east (20 baht), while pick-ups and taxis for other destinations are usually found on the street immediately beyond the barrier at the border. In actuality the transport touts

---

Crossing into Thailand at Poipet

The border crossing at Poipet is popular with travellers going overland in both directions between Siem Reap and Bangkok. Once across the border and into Thailand you'll need to make for **Aranyaprathet** – a four-kilometre journey by tuk-tuk – to head on to Bangkok by **train** (departure at 1.30pm; 7hr) or **bus** (4 daily; 4hr 30min). If you're on private transport to Bangkok organized by a local travel agent, you'll be dropped on the Cambodian side of the border to make your own way across and meet sister transport on the Thai side for the onward journey. Keep in mind that these packages are fraught with scams – a last-minute switch to an inferior vehicle is the most common one – and many travellers find that it is actually cheaper and much faster to do the trip on their own.

will find you before you even see the onward transport options. Don't expect this to be a civilized experience. Touts and drivers can be a vicious lot. Their aim is to fleece you for everything they can, and intimidation is not uncommon. It's best to arrive as early as possible to sort out the inevitable problems.

Even if you cross over from Thailand late in the afternoon you can usually still get onward transport to Sisophon. If you choose to stay, the new *Orkiday Angkor Hotel* (℡054/967502; ❸), on the left as you emerge from the immigration office, has well-appointed rooms with all facilities and tasteful decor. Just east of the Canadia Bank on the main road, the *Ngy Heng Hotel* (℡054/967101; ❷) has clean rooms with a choice of fan or a/c. Behind the market, the *Hang Meas Thmey* (℡054/967040; ❷) has small but smart rooms, while the best of the cheap options is the *Bayon Guest House* (℡011/866065; ❷), just east of the market. As for **eating**, the *Hope and Health Restaurant*, next to the *Bayon Guest House*, offers Western dishes like spaghetti and hamburgers and gives its profits to the needy. There are also several indistinguishable places along the main road that serve up Khmer staples.

A number of travel companies operate **onward transport** from Poipet. Many of these firms are linked with Bangkok agencies and with guesthouses in Siem Reap, and there have been numerous reports of scams and hassles, the most common being the use of inferior vehicles.

Travel details

A **train** departs weekly from Phnom Penh to Battambang – see p.138 for details of the schedule. **Shared taxis** and **pick-up trucks** leave to no set schedule from early morning until early afternoon (roughly 6am–2pm); you may have to wait for them to fill up before they leave. Note that the frequencies given below are only approximate, and the earlier in the day you get to the transport stop, the easier it is to find transport.

Trains

Battambang to: Phnom Penh (1 every other day; at least 12hr); Pursat (1 every other day; 6–7hr).
Pursat to: Battambang (1 every other day; 6–7hr); Phnom Penh (1 every other day; 6–7hr).

Buses

Battambang to: Phnom Penh (4 daily; 6hr); Poipet (1 daily; 3hr); Siem Reap (1 daily; 3hr).
Kompong Chhnang to: Phnom Penh (6 daily; 2hr 30min).
Poipet to: Battambang (1 daily; 3hr); Phnom Penh (2 daily; 8hr); Siem Reap (3 daily; 2hr 30min).

Shared taxis and pick-up trucks

Battambang to: Kompong Chhnang (4 daily; 4hr); Pailin (6 daily; 4–5hr); Phnom Penh (12 daily; 6hr); Poipet (12 daily; 3hr); Pursat (6 daily; 1hr 30min); Sisophon (6 daily; 2hr).
Kompong Chhnang to: Battambang (4 daily; 4hr); Phnom Penh (4 daily; 2hr 30min); Pursat (4 daily; 2hr).
Pailin to: Battambang (6 daily; 4–5hr).
Poipet to: Battambang (12 daily; 3hr); Phnom Penh (10 daily; 8hr); Siem Reap (20 daily; 4hr); Sisophon (20 daily; 1hr).
Pursat to: Battambang (6 daily; 1hr 30min); Kompong Chhnang (4 daily; 2hr); Phnom Penh (10 daily; 4hr).
Sisophon to: Battambang (6 daily; 2hr); Phnom Penh (10 daily; 7hr); Poipet (20 daily; 1hr); Siem Reap (20 daily; 2hr).

Boats

Battambang to: Siem Reap (2 daily; 3hr 30min).

3

Siem Reap and the temples of Angkor

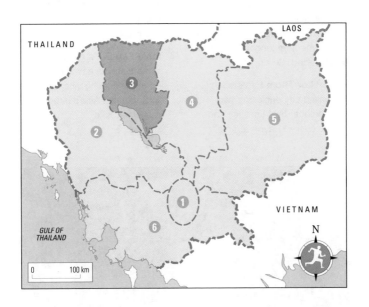

CHAPTER 3 # Highlights

* **Siem Reap** One of Cambodia's most tourist-friendly towns, full of restful pavement cafés, elegant restaurants and buzzing bars. See p.159

* **Apsara dance** Catch a performance of Cambodia's ancient dance form, once performed exclusively for the king. See p.171

* **Angkor Wat** Cambodia's most iconic building, whose soaring towers stay etched in the memory long after you've departed. See p.179

* **Angkor Thom** Expansive walled city enclosing two fabulous royal terraces and the sacred Bayon temple. See p.185

* **Ta Prohm** Atmospheric temple that is gradually being swallowed up by the encroaching jungle. See p.192

* **Banteay Srei** Rosy-red sandstone temple with beautiful carvings of female divinities. See p.201

* **Kbal Spean** Crystal-clear water washes over sacred linga carved into the bedrock at this tranquil riverside spot. See p.203

* **Tonle Sap** Get a glimpse of the distinctive way of life led in the floating villages on Southeast Asia's largest freshwater lake. See p.203

▲ Café life in Siem Reap

Siem Reap and the temples of Angkor

The area around the present-day provincial town of Siem Reap, 310km northwest of Phnom Penh, was once the heart of the Khmer Empire, which began in 802 with Jayavarman II's move to Phnom Kulen and ended when the Thais sacked Angkor Thom in 1431. A ready supply of water and the fertility of the land meant that the area could support large populations, and successive Angkorian kings constructed their royal cities and state-temples here. The empire reached its apogee under the leadership of Jayavarman VII – the greatest temple-builder of all – when it stretched from the coast of Vietnam south to the Malay peninsula, west to Pagan in Burma and north to Laos. However, once abandoned by the court in the fifteenth century, this part of Cambodia sank into obscurity until the end of the eighteenth century when, as part of Battambang province, it came under Thai rule, a state of affairs that lasted until 1907, when the French negotiated its return.

For most visitors, **Angkor Wat**, an unforgettable temple of soaring towers and intricate carvings just a short drive from Siem Reap, is the chief reason to visit Cambodia. The first glimpse of its breathtaking sanctuaries lingers in the memory forever, while its gallery of bas-reliefs – exceptional in both detail and quality of execution – is a delight for novices and experts alike. Running it a close second is the nearby walled city of **Angkor Thom**, its gateways famously topped with four huge stone faces. The motif is continued at the very centre of Angkor Thom in the **Bayon**, Jayavarman VII's state-temple, which has two galleries of bas-reliefs.

There's much more to Angkor than just these main sights, however. The site is both vast and diverse, with buildings ranging in scale from early, tiny brick towers like **Prasat Kravan** to the massive and stark sandstone edifice of **Ta Keo**. You could easily spend two full weeks on a visit and still have more to see, but most people find three days is enough to take in the principal sites, albeit in a bit of a rush; if you have the time and the money, four to five days would be better. Many of the most important temple sites are within a few minutes' drive of **Siem Reap**, but a few are scattered much further afield; transport is easily hired in Siem Reap and access roads are in decent condition.

Political stability and improved safety, together with the active promotion of Angkor Wat as a tourist destination, has resulted in rapidly rising visitor

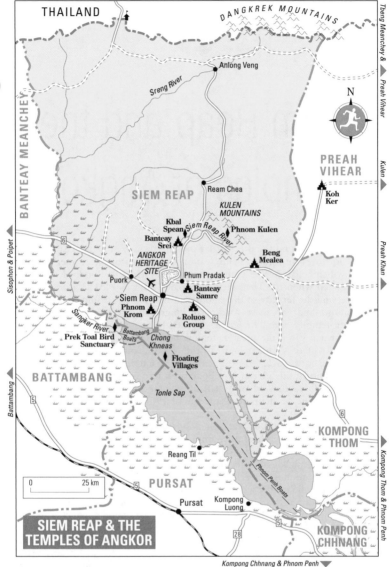

THAILAND

DANGKREK MOUNTAINS

Anlong Veng

Sreng River

N

PREAH VIHEAR

SIEM REAP

Ream Chea

KULEN MOUNTAINS

Koh Ker

Kbal Spean

Siem Reap River

Phnom Kulen

Banteay Srei

Beng Mealea

ANGKOR HERITAGE SITE

Puork

Phum Pradak

Banteay Samre

Siem Reap

Phnom Krom

Roluos Group

Prek Toal Bird Sanctuary

Sangker River

Battambang Boats

Chong Khneas

Floating Villages

BATTAMBANG

Tonle Sap

Phnom Penh Boats

KOMPONG THOM

Reang Til

0   25 km

PURSAT

Pursat

Kompong Luong

KOMPONG CHHNANG

SIEM REAP & THE TEMPLES OF ANGKOR

figures, turning sleepy **Siem Reap** into a Cambodian tourist hot spot. The local airport is linked with several Asian capitals as well as Phnom Penh, while National Route 6 south to the capital and north to Thailand has been improved, and the express boats from Phnom Penh and boats from Battambang are efficient and popular. With tourism, the town is developing apace, and there has been an explosion of new hotels, restaurants and bars, though surprisingly, a small-town atmosphere still pervades, at least in the city centre.

If you tire of temples, the floating villages of **Tonle Sap**, the massive fresh-water lake that dominates central Cambodia, are worth exploring. The land south of Siem Reap is part of the lake's flood plain, and is inundated from June to November; rice is planted as the waters recede, and the fishing is plentiful. North of town, the rice fields stretch out to the natural boundary formed by the Kulen Mountains which divide the lush lowland from the province's more barren north; here, at **Phnom Kulen** is Cambodia's largest reclining Buddha, carved out of a massive rock, while at two spots on the Siem Reap River (which rises in these mountains and flows south to drain into the great lake) the river bed itself has been carved with intricate linga and religious scenes. The far north of the province is only worth visiting if you're curious about **Anlong Veng**, whose morbid claim to fame is that it was the site of Pol Pot's death.

Siem Reap

SIEM REAP (pronounced See-um Ree-up) 310km northwest of Phnom Penh, manages to be simultaneously both a somnolent town and tourist honey-pot. By day, despite a new hotel seemingly under construction on every corner, the town is still about as quiet as it always was, with the tourists mostly at the temples; the busiest it gets is at dusk, when the coaches return from Angkor, though they mostly head straight out again to the hotels along Airport Road. From late afternoon, weary travellers descend on the restaurants and bars in the colonial area around Psar Chas, and by mid-evening a party atmosphere pervades.

You're unlikely to want for anything in Siem Reap, and plenty of visitors hang around much longer than they originally intended. The town offers the best selection of **accommodation** outside the capital, as well as an abundance of restaurants specializing in all manner of cuisine, including exceptional **Cambodian food**; at a handful of places you can also watch a fascinating Khmer **cultural performance** while you dine. There are plenty of opportunities to **shop**, as the town has plenty of quality galleries, craft shops and souvenir stalls. Car and moto hire is straightforward, and if you don't feel like arranging it yourself, one of any number of tour companies will do it for you, collecting you at your door for sunrise and returning you after sunset.

Temples aside, a visit to Siem Reap isn't complete without a boat trip out on the massive Tonle Sap lake (see p.204), where communities live on the water in floating villages. Tours of the area can be arranged with specialist companies in town, although they don't come cheap.

Arrival

Registered taxis ($5) for the six-kilometre ride from the **airport** into town can be hired at a booth just outside the exit from the arrival lounge. Motos ($2) and unregistered taxis ($5) sometimes wait for fares on the main road outside the airport. Minibuses from certain hotels meet planes, so look out for them if you've prebooked or intend to stay at one of them. A road from the airport runs directly to the temples and makes a day-trip from Bangkok to Angkor Wat viable if you arrive early in the morning; you can hire a car and driver at the airport. Prices vary according to how much you want to see.

Boats arrive around noon from Phnom Penh and mid-morning from Battam-bang, docking south of town at the **port** on the Tonle Sap. The port's location varies with the level of the lake: in the rainy season, the port is at the foot of

Leaving Siem Reap by road, boat or plane is straightforward, with good transport connections to other parts of the country, as well as Thailand.

By bus

A number of companies run long-distance buses to **Phnom Penh** and **Bangkok**; these can be booked through the town's travel agents (see p.174). Note that on buses to **Bangkok** via Poipet you must change vehicles at the border. From the border to Aranyaprathet it is about 4km, and a motorcycle taxi costs between 50 and 100 baht. These buses arrive at Poipet – in walking distance of the border – at around 1pm, convenient if you're hooking up with onward road transport, but leaving little time to catch the train from Aranyaprathet; if you want to do the latter, it's best to get an early ride on shared transport out to the border. Guesthouses in town operate their own minibuses to **Phnom Penh** and via Poipet – where they link up with onward transport operated by their Thai associates – but there have been countless scams associated with minibuses going in both directions, so it's best to stick with shared taxis.

By shared taxi and pick-up truck

Shared taxis and pick-up trucks run from Psar Leu to **Phnom Penh** and **Kompong Thom**, **Sisophon** (for **Battambang**), **Poipet** and **Anlong Veng**. When going from Siem Reap to Poipet on the Thai border, a shared taxi is your best bet. If the road to the Thai border is in good condition, you'll be able to get transport in that direction until early afternoon. To hire a shared taxi outright costs $40–50, or about $10 per seat.

By boat

Boats leave from the **port** daily at 7am for **Phnom Penh** ($25) and for **Battambang** ($15). When the water level is really low (Feb–May) the **express boats for Phnom Penh** moor some way out, and you'll be taken out to them on smaller craft; **Battambang** boats are scarcely larger than speedboats and so are usually able to get into port. You'll need to book your ticket at least a day ahead – two days ahead between March and November, when often just one boat runs on each route. If you get your ticket at a travel agent or from the boat company offices (they have several premises around the centre, each displaying a large sign of a boat), you'll need to find your own transport to the port ($6 by car, $2 by moto; allow at least 30min on the truly dreadful road), but if you buy from a guesthouse or hotel, a minibus will collect you, which may mean setting out as early as 5.30am, as the vehicle will pick up passengers from various locations before heading down to the port.

By plane

Besides flights to Phnom Penh, there is an increasing number of **international departures** to **Bangkok**, Chiang Mai, **Ho Chi Minh City** and **Vientiane**, and further afield to **Kuala Lumpur**, **Singapore** and **Hong Kong**. You can buy plane tickets from the airline offices or from travel agents in town. If you're staying at a hotel they'll generally drive you to the airport free of charge. The domestic departure tax is $6; the international departure tax is $25.

Phnom Krom, about 12km south of town, but in the driest months (Nov–May) it's at Chong Khneas, 5km further from town. Hotels will arrange for you to be collected from the port if you're staying with them; otherwise there's no shortage of motos to take you into town ($2), not to mention guesthouse touts.

It's now straightforward to do the trip here **by pick-up from Poipet** on the Thai border (see p.153), a route that is becoming increasingly popular with budget travellers. When the road isn't flooded and if there aren't any breakdowns, the journey all the way from **Bangkok** can be done in a single day. If you're on a through ticket bought from one of the many travel agents on Thanon Khao San in Bangkok, you'll be dropped at one of their affiliated guesthouses in Siem Reap. Buses, pick-ups and shared taxis from Phnom Penh arrive at the **transport stop** 2km east of town at Psar Leu, and can drop you off along the way into town on National Route 6.

Information

The **tourist office** is near the *Grand Hotel d'Angkor*. You'll be given short shrift if you merely want to ask about the town and other places to visit, however, as their main preoccupation is to sell you a tour of the ruins, through the Khmer Angkor Tour Guide Association (KATGA; ☎063/964347), which shares the premises.

It is however, well worth considering **hiring a guide** for the temples ($20–25 per day per group). All guides are KATGA-licensed and have to pass an examination on the history of the temples. They generally speak at least one foreign language and are genuinely knowledgeable about the temples, ensuring that you don't miss any key features on the ground. Licensed guides can be identified by their uniform: brown trousers, beige shirt and name badge. You can hire a guide through KATGA or hotels and guesthouses; the latter are also good sources of information on Siem Reap and the general area. Given how easy it is to meet other travellers in Siem Reap, it shouldn't be hard to get together to share the cost of guide hire, transport or both.

The useful free quarterly *Siem Reap Angkor Visitors Guide*, put out by Canby Publications, is available around town at hotels, guesthouses and restaurants. Besides the usual temple information, it contains up-to-the-minute news of places to stay, eat and drink; extracts of the guide are available online at Ⓦ www .canbypublications.com.

Town transport

Laid out on a grid spreading a couple of kilometres north and south of National Route 6, and east and west of the Siem Reap River, the town is a bit spread out but the centre is easily negotiable on foot. Tourists are not allowed to rent motorcycles or cars, although it is possible to hire a car with driver.

For visitors, the most popular way to get around town and out to the temples is the motorbike-drawn carriage, called a moto-romauk or sometimes tuk-tuk, though they're not the same as those in Thailand. These are without a doubt the most pleasant and comfortable way to get around, seating two passengers in comfort (though you could squeeze in three). They can be hailed on the street or hired from outside the *Grand Hotel d'Angkor* or the *Foreign Correspondents*

Siem Reap addresses

Although many of the roads in town have names, these are not commonly used by the locals, so when travelling around it's better to choose a **landmark**, such as a market or a hotel, as a reference point for giving directions or negotiating a fare with a moto driver. Along National Route 6, we refer to places west of the junction with Sivatha Street as being on the "Airport Road", a commonly used local name. The road north past the *Grand Hotel d' Angkor*, officially Tosamut Boulevard, is more commonly called "Angkor Wat Street", while the road south past the hospital is known as "Hospital Street". Predictably, perhaps, the road through the Psar Chas area, where you'll find most of Siem Reap's nightlife venues, is known as "Pub Street" or "Bar Street".

Club (*FCC*); count on $1–2 for a journey across town. To the temples they can be rented by the day for $13–15.

Less common now are motorcycle taxis or **motos** that cost 2000–4000 riel for a short hop or $1 for a trip across town. The provincial government has decreed that motos are only permitted to take one passenger, a sensible safety measure that, however, doesn't apply to Cambodians.

Transport to the temples

As there's no public transport to Angkor Wat and the temples are spread out over a vast area, it's best to hire your own transport to make the most of your time and entrance ticket. **Hiring a moto or tuk-tuk** is easy; many guesthouses have a selection of drivers who look after their guests, and there are many more around town, plenty of whom speak good English. A moto costs $6–9 from sunrise to sunset, while a tuk-tuk will run you $13–15. The fact that tuk-tuks are covered and provide protection from the sun and rain, as well as having a soft seat to lean back into, makes them well worth the extra expense when touring the temples. Cycling is a wonderful way to see the temples, though you won't be able to get to very many in a day this way as they're so scattered; a few shops around Psar Chas and most guesthouses have bicycles to rent for $2–4 per day. You'll cover even more ground if you opt for an electric bicycle from one of the guesthouses. These eco-friendly bikes have a battery that lasts for about 30km or one hour but there are recharging stations located throughout the main temple complex. Expect to pay about $4-5 per day to rent one.

Accommodation

There's no shortage of accommodation in any category, and to make a visit to Angkor even more memorable, Siem Reap offers some characterful **hotels**, with individually appointed rooms, sometimes making artistic use of local materials. If you want to stay at the town's five-star hotels during the peak season (Nov–Feb), it's best to make a reservation.

The town's **guesthouses** are mainly located east of the river along Wat Bo Street, though there are plenty more elsewhere. In general they offer a range of rooms – some rivalling those in the cheapest hotels – and a budget restaurant. Of late, a large number of rather gaudy Chinese-run **hotels** have sprouted up along Airport Road. For the most part these look impressive from a distance but up close the cracks in the facades are quite evident. Westerners usually find them a disappointment.

Around Psar Chas (Old Market)

Blessed with plenty of restaurants, bars and cafés, the area around **Psar Chas** (also known as the **Old Market**) is an ideal place to stay if you want to be close to the town's nightlife and don't mind a bit of noise.

Angkor Voyage Villa Psar Chas ℡063/965529. A short walk from Psar Chas proper, this place is very good value and pretty quiet. Clean rooms come with a/c and hot water, and bathrooms have bathtubs. The restaurant downstairs has a good selection of both Asian and Western food. ❷

Chao Say Psar Chas ℡063/964032 or 012/884107. This colonial-era shophouse fronting the market has reasonable, if slightly cramped rooms, and there's a popular restaurant downstairs (see p.169). ❷

Mandalay Inn Psar Chas ℡063/761662. Recently moved to new premises, this is an excellent-value and friendly budget-range place. The rooms come with fan or a/c, hot water, TV and fridge, and the restaurant does a number of Burmese dishes. ❷

Prince Mekong Villa Psar Chas ℡063/437972. Good choice if you are on a budget. Not only are the fan-cooled rooms equipped with an en-suite bathroom (cold water only), but there is a communal

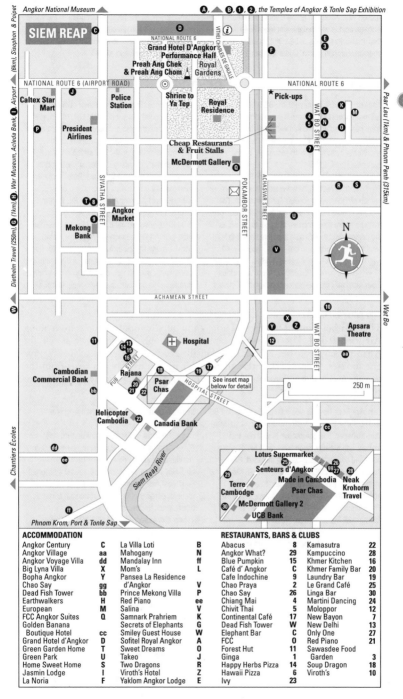

Angkor National Museum ▲ | Ⓐ, ▲ Ⓑ, ❶, ❷, the Temples of Angkor & Tonle Sap Exhibition

Angkor (6km), Sisophon & Poipet | (8km), Airport | Diethelm Travel (250m), ⓦ War Museum, ⓖ (1km), ⓗ Acleda Bank, ❶ Airport

SIEM REAP Ⓒ

National Route 6

Ⓓ

ⓘ

Ⓔ ❸

Ⓕ

Grand Hotel D'Angkor
Performance Hall

Preah Ang Chek
& Preah Ang Chom

Royal
Gardens

NATIONAL ROUTE 6 (AIRPORT ROAD)

NATIONAL ROUTE 6

Psar Leu (1km) & Phnom Penh (315km)

Ⓙ
Caltex Star
Mart

Police
Station

Shrine to
Ya Tep

Royal
Residence

★ Pick-ups

Ⓛ
Ⓝ

Ⓚ
Ⓜ
Ⓞ

WAT BO STREET

Ⓟ

President
Airlines

❹
❺
❻
❼

Cheap Restaurants
& Fruit Stalls

McDermott Gallery

Ⓠ

ⓇⓈ

SIVATHA STREET

ACHASVIAR STREET

POKAMBOR STREET

Ⓣ❽

Angkor
Market

✉

Ⓤ

N

❾

Mekong
Bank

Ⓥ

ACHAMEAN STREET

❿

Wat Bo

ⓦ

Ⓧ
Ⓨ Ⓩ

WAT BO STREET

Apsara
Theatre

⓫

✚ Hospital

⓬

aa

⓮⓭
⓯
⓰

Cambodian
Commercial Bank

PUB STREET

Rajana

⓲

⓳

See inset map
below for detail

0   250 m

⓴
㉑ ㉒

Psar
Chas

HOSPITAL STREET

bb

Helicopter
Cambodia ㉓

Canadia Bank

㉔

cc

Chantiers Écoles

dd

ee

Siem Reap River

Lotus Supermarket

㉕

Senteurs d'Angkor

Terre
Cambodge

㉙

Made in Cambodia

㉖
gg㉗

Neak
Krohorm
Travel

㉘

ff

McDermott Gallery 2

㉚

Psar Chas

UCB Bank

Phnom Krom, Port & Tonle Sap ▼

ACCOMMODATION

Angkor Century	C	La Villa Loti	B
Angkor Village	aa	Mahogany	N
Angkor Voyage Villa	dd	Mandalay Inn	ff
Big Lyna Villa	X	Mom's	L
Bopha Angkor	Y	Pansea La Residence	
Chao Say	gg	d'Angkor	V
Dead Fish Tower	bb	Prince Mekong Villa	P
Earthwalkers	H	Red Piano	ee
European	M	Salina	V
FCC Angkor Suites	Q	Samnark Prahriem	K
Golden Banana		Secrets of Elephants	G
Boutique Hotel	cc	Smiley Guest House	W
Grand Hotel d'Angkor	D	Sofitel Royal Angkor	A
Green Garden Home	T	Sweet Dreams	O
Green Park	U	Takeo	J
Home Sweet Home	S	Two Dragons	R
Jasmin Lodge	I	Viroth's Hotel	Z
La Noria	F	Yaklom Angkor Lodge	E

RESTAURANTS, BARS & CLUBS

Abacus	8	Kamasutra	22
Angkor What?	29	Kampuccino	28
Blue Pumpkin	15	Khmer Kitchen	16
Café d' Angkor	C	Khmer Family Bar	20
Cafe Indochine	9	Laundry Bar	19
Chao Praya	2	Le Grand Café	25
Chao Say	26	Linga Bar	30
Chiang Mai	4	Martini Dancing	24
Chivit Thai	5	Moloppor	12
Continental Café	17	New Bayon	7
Dead Fish Tower	W	New Delhi	13
Elephant Bar	C	Only One	27
FCC	O	Red Piano	21
Forest Hut	11	Sawasdee Food	
Ginga	1	Garden	3
Happy Herbs Pizza	14	Soup Dragon	18
Hawaii Pizza	6	Viroth's	10
Ivy	23		

kitchen where you can prepare your own meals. The management is very helpful and friendly. ❷
Red Piano Psar Chas ☎ 063/963240, ⊛ www .redpianocambodia.com. Under the same management as the nearby restaurant of the same name, this well-run guesthouse is tastefully decorated and comfortable, and all rooms have en-suite bathrooms and a/c. ❹

The Royal Gardens and beyond

Angkor Century Komay Rd ☎ 063/963777, ⊛ www.angkorcentury.com. This modern, luxury hotel has sumptuous rooms with their own lounge areas and safes. There's a choice of restaurants and bars – including a café-restaurant by the swimming pool. ❾

FCC Angkor Suites Pokambor St ☎ 063/760280, ⊛ www.fcccambodia.com. A branch of the famous *Foreign Correspondents Club* (*FCC*) in Phnom Penh, the rooms (as well as adjacent restaurant) are more modern but just as stylish as the original, and there's also a picturesque riverfront location and an adjoining gallery for shopping. ❻

Grand Hotel d'Angkor 1 Vithei Charles de Gaulle ☎ 063/963888, ⊛ siemreap.raffles .com. Opulent colonial-era elegance, with a choice of rooms (including villas with their own pantry and wine cellar) along with plenty of restaurants and bars. There's also a conservatory for tea and drinks, a swanky boutique, a business centre and two swimming pools. The exhibition area has a regularly changing display of photographs or paintings of the Angkor region. Rates include breakfast. ❾

Sofitel Royal Angkor Angkor Wat Rd, 1500m north of the Royal Gardens ☎ 63/964600, ⑤ 964610, ⊛ www.sofitel.com. Modern, low-rise affair with Art Deco touches. The rooms, set in blocks around the colourful gardens, feel like home from home with their own lounges and satellite TV; a swimming pool, fitness centre, shop and a range of restaurants and bars complete the picture. ❾

Airport Road

There's a burgeoning number of hotels and guesthouses to choose from along **Airport Road**. The most noticeable are big, ugly Chinese-style hotels for Asian package tourists, but set back off the road are a handful of inexpensive guesthouses. A drawback is that there aren't many eating places apart from the guesthouse and hotel restaurants – although, that said, it's only a short moto ride to the town centre.

Earthwalkers Down a side road south off Airport Rd ☎ 012/967901, ⊛ www.earthwalkers.no. Scandina-vian-managed, this guesthouse is well run and friendly, and the rooms (en suite, with fan or a/c) are quiet and comfortable. Breakfast included. ❷
Jasmin Lodge 258 Airport Rd ☎ 012/784980. One of the better budget guesthouses. Rooms with attached bath, choice of a/c or fan and cable TV. The rooftop restaurant is a definite plus. ❷
Salina 125 Taphul Village ☎ 063/380221, ⊛ www.salinahotel.net. A well-established hotel that earns plenty of repeat custom. Rooms are pleasant and en suite, with a/c, minibar and TV, and there's a restaurant, bar and swimming pool. Breakfast included. ❻

Secrets of Elephants Airport Rd ☎ 063/964328, ⊛ www.angkor-travel.com. Traditional wooden house where each room is elegantly and creatively themed around a different Southeast Asian country. After a day at the temples the lush gardens offer plenty of tranquil corners where you can unwind. ❺
Takeo 258 Airport Rd ☎ 012/922674. Usually packed with Japanese budget travellers, this friendly, guesthouse offers some of the cheapest rooms in town, though they're correspondingly basic. ❷

Sivatha Street and around

Dead Fish Tower Sivatha St ☎ 063/963060, ⊛ www.talesofasia.com. Lower mid-range place with comfortable rooms and an excellent restaurant and bar attached. ❸
Green Garden Home Off Sivatha St ☎ 012/890363 ⊛ www.greengardenhome.com. Quiet and good-value guesthouse in a picturesque old house with a verdant garden and an outdoor breakfast area. The cheapest rooms have cold showers and fan, with hot water and a/c available for a supplement. ❹
Smiley Guest House Off Sivatha St ☎ 012/852955. One of the cheapest places to stay in town. Rooms are very basic but clean, some

much smaller than others but all with attached bath. Despite the name, the staff can be rather surly – then again backpackers who pinch their pennies till they scream can be a tad trying. 2

East of the river

The backpacker area on **Wat Bo Street** is a good bit quieter than staying on a major thoroughfare such as the Airport Road or Sivatha. Apart from guesthouses, it also boasts a sprinkling of mid-range hotels, a decent range of restaurants and a few bars.

North of National Route 6

Golden Banana Boutique Hotel Phum Wat Damnak ⓣ012/654638. ⓦwww.goldenbanana.info. This newly opened and gay-friendly place has a number of two-storey bungalows around an inviting pool. The bungalows come with a/c, TV and DVD player, and there is Wi-Fi access throughout. Breakfast included. 4

La Noria Achasvar St ⓣ063/964242, ⓦwww.lanoria-angkor.com. Housed in bungalows around a lush garden with a swimming pool, rooms, furnished with traditional Khmer materials, are cool and tranquil, and have their own bathrooms, as well as individual terraces and sitting areas. There's a French restaurant too, hosting regular shadow-puppet shows (see p.171). 5

La Villa Loti Near the Angkor Conservatory ⓣ063/964242, ⓦwww.lavillaloti.com. Just north of the town centre, this traditional Khmer wooden house is nicely furnished, and surrounded by trees. Rooms all have attached bath with a/c or fan. A stylish junior suite has its own courtyard. A great place if you want lots of peace and quiet. 3

Yaklom Angkor Lodge 100m off National Route 6 ⓣ012/983510, ⓦwww.yaklom.com. Clean, spacious bungalows tastefully decorated with chunchiet fabrics, water gourds and *khapas*, set in a lush garden. All have en-suite bathrooms, TV and a/c. Breakfast included. 5

Between National Route 6 and Achamean Street

Bopha Angkor Achasvar St ⓣ063/964406, ⓦwww.bopha-angkor.com. In a garden on the riverfront, this low-rise hotel has been thoughtfully refurbished to a good standard. All rooms are en suite, with bathtubs. There is a well-maintained swimming pool as well. 5

European Up a dead-end street parallel to Wat Bo St ⓣ012/846803. Quiet and friendly guesthouse with its own garden and large rooms, all with en-suite bathrooms; a/c available. 2

Green Park 182 Wat Bo Village, between Wat Bo and Achasvar sts ⓣ063/380352 or 012/890358, ⓔgreenparkgh@hotmail.com. The cheapest rooms at this excellent guesthouse are in the original wooden house, with better-appointed ones in the new block, where a/c is available. There's a restaurant and a booking service for bus tickets, plus a communal TV. 1

Home Sweet Home Off Wat Bo St ⓣ063/693393, ⓦwww.catgen.com/sweethome/EN/. Owned by the same family who runs the *Sweet Dreams* guesthouse across the street, this is a newer property whose rooms feature attached bathrooms, cable TV and a/c. 2

Mahogany 593 Wat Bo St ⓣ063/963417, ⓕ380 025. The hospitable "Mr Prune" still runs this guesthouse, one of Siem Reap's oldest. It hasn't changed much since it first opened in the early 1990s, offering basic rooms in a traditional wooden building, and though it may not be as flashy as newer establishments, the friendly atmosphere is hard to beat. 1

Mom's Wat Bo St ⓣ063/964037, ⓦwww.momguesthouse.com. Another one of Siem Reap's old faithfuls. The wooden house has been replaced with a rather gaudy concrete one, but the same friendly family runs the place. Rooms have TV, a/c and attached bathrooms. 2

Pansea La Residence d'Angkor Achasvar St ⓣ063/963390, ⓦwww.pansea.com/eng/angkor_infor.html. Top-notch establishment, part of a chain specializing in sympathetically designed accommodation in heritage sites worldwide. All rooms are luxuriously appointed with teak furniture, Khmer cotton and silk furnishings, and bamboo screens to mask the massive free-form bathtubs. Facilities include restaurant, bar, souvenir shop and, strategically placed in the heart of the complex, a swimming pool fed with water bubbling from a lion and a linga. 9

Samnark Prahriem Off Wat Bo St, behind *Mom's* ⓣ015/630039, ⓔprahriem@camnet.com.kh. Tranquil guesthouse in a leafy courtyard at the end of a cul-de-sac, with a choice of rooms, some en suite. You can take breakfast in the pavilion in the leafy courtyard and, at the end of the day, put your feet up and listen to the cicadas buzz in the trees. 2

Sweet Dreams Off Wat Bo St ⓣ063/963245, ⓔsweethome@camintel.com. A quiet, family-run guesthouse, some of whose rooms feature attached bathrooms, cable TV and a/c. There's also a good restaurant with a reasonably priced Khmer menu. ❷

Two Dragons Wat Bo St ☎063/965107, ⓦwww.talesofasia.com/cambodia-twodragons.htm. A new, well-run guesthouse with lots of great information for the asking. Rooms are situated in a two-storey house and there is a Thai restaurant on the ground floor. Rooms feature attached bathrooms, cable TV and a/c; there's also Wi-Fi access throughout. Reliable transport can also be arranged from here. ❸

🏃 **Viroth's Hotel** Off Wat Bo St ☎063/761720, ⓦwww.viroth-hotel.com. A stylish boutique hotel with attention paid to every detail. The elegant rooms have all the mod cons, and the tranquil grounds include a cosy swimming pool and even a Jacuzzi. Recommended. ❻

South of Achamean Street

Angkor Village Off Wat Bo St ☎063/963561, ⓦwww.angkorvillage.com. Accommodation in individually furnished wooden bungalows surrounded by leafy gardens, and boasting en-suite bathrooms, TV, a/c and fridge. A pavilion in the grounds houses a French-Asian restaurant, and the swimming pool is picturesquely edged with banana trees. ❺

Big Lyna Villa 659 Wat Bo Village, off Achasvar St ☎063/964807, ⓦwww.catgen.com/biglynavilla /EN. Traditional wooden house in a peaceful spot, with a choice of rooms (the nicest are the large wood-panelled ones upstairs), while the wide, relaxing balcony has plenty of rattan seating and is dotted with massive potted palms. ❹

The Town

Said to mean "Siam defeated" in commemoration of a battle that possibly never happened, little is known about the **history** of Siem Reap, which sprawls to east and west of the river of the same name. Largely overshadowed by the Angkor temples, the town has only recently grown large enough to acquire its own identity. A traveller who visited in 1935, Geoffrey Gorer, described Siem Reap as "a charming little village, hardly touched by European influence, built along a winding river; the native houses are insignificant little structures

▲ Central Siem Reap

in wood, hidden behind the vegetation that grows so lushly… along the river banks." He just missed the opening of the *Grand Hotel des Ruines* in 1937, now the *Grand Hotel d'Angkor*, which was "a mile out of town" according to Norman Lewis, who stayed there sixteen years later, though the hotel has now been swallowed up by the ever-expanding town. Siem Reap remained relatively undeveloped during the first tourist rush of the 1950s and 1960s, and much of what was built was destroyed when the town was emptied under the Khmer Rouge, although the *Grand*, the shophouses of the old market, Psar Chas and the occasional colonial villa escaped unscathed.

Despite a pending government decree to boost recognition (and tourist revenue) by renaming the town "Krong Angkor" (Angkor City), Siem Reap has so far managed to cash in on Angkor's renewed popularity without losing too many of its rustic charms, and though there's not a great deal of specific interest, a stroll around the town centre reveals a number of colourful shrines and a few minor attractions. As good a way to do this as any is to use the smart paved **walkway** that has been laid along the riverside between National Route 6 and Psar Chas.

At the northern end of the walkway, opposite the *Grand Hotel d'Angkor*, are the formal Royal Gardens, one of the most restful spots in town. On the south side of the gardens, a **shrine** to the sister deities Preah Ang Chek and Preah Ang Chom houses figurines of the two – thought to have been Angkorian princesses – in brass and bronze, originally situated in the Gallery of a Thousand Buddhas at Angkor Wat. The statues have had a chequered history, having been hidden from the eyes of invaders and treasure hunters by successive generations of monks, who moved them repeatedly to stop their whereabouts becoming known. Moved to the current shrine in 1990, the statues are heaped daily with offerings; the taller, more slender of the two figures is Ang Chek, whose palm faces outward to show an Sanskrit inscription of protection in Sanskrit. A third statue, of Preah Ang Chom, was found in 1995, though this is not on public view. Just to the west, surrounded by a traffic circle and marked by a huge tree in the middle of the road, is a shrine to **Ya Tep**, a local spirit said to bring protection and luck to the Siem Reap area. The offerings left at the shrine are sometimes quite extravagant – it's common to find whole cooked chickens or other fowl left here.

A one-kilometre stroll south down the riverside walkway brings you to bustling **Psar Chas**, also known as the Old Market; souvenir stalls pack the section of the market facing the river, while further back a fresh-produce area takes over. Many of the surrounding colonial-era shophouses have been converted into vibrant restaurants and bars, the tables spilling out from shaded balconies onto the pavement.

Around 200m east of the river, at the end of Achamean Street, **Wat Bo** is the oldest and most appealing of Siem Reap's Buddhist monasteries, dating back to the eighteenth century. The interior walls of the vihara, still in good condition, were decorated in the nineteenth century with scenes from the life of Buddha. Unusually, the paintings incorporate scenes of everyday life, including a Chinese man smoking opium and French soldiers watching a traditional dance performance.

Out from the centre

Siem Reap's new **Angkor National Museum** (daily 9am–6pm; $12; Wwww .angkornationalmuseum.com) is being filled with choice pieces of ancient Khmer sculpture that were once kept under lock and key at the Angkor Conservatory and off limits to all but VIPs. Despite the name, the museum is actually a private venture with a Thai company, and as of late 2007 there were still many empty plinths and almost no labelling. Once completed, however, it will use modern interactive displays, and there will also be an adjacent "Culture Mall" with souvenirs on offer. The museum is located on the road from Siem Reap to Angkor.

The government-run **War Museum** (daily 7am–5pm; $3) lies west of town on National Route 6, just before the airport turn-off. Its collection of rusting tanks and anti-aircraft guns is no doubt stimulating if you get turned on by model designations and numbers. Better is a bizarre, private **museum** on a plot of land near Banteay Srei temple, crammed full of rusting war scrap and **land mines** (daily 8am–5pm; $1). The owner, Mr Akira, is a self-taught de-miner who was once forced to lay mines as a Vietnamese conscript. Over the years, he's amassed a vast collection of mines, bomb casings, fuses and the like, all displayed on shelves and laid out around the garden complete with trip wires. The city government has tried repeatedly to close Mr Akira down, at one point tearing down his signs, and then forcing him to relocate outside the city limits. Mr Akira's passion for his collection has kept him from giving in.

Closer to town, and off the Angkor Wat road, is the engaging **Tonle Sap Exhibition** (daily 8am–6pm; free), covering all aspects of life on the lake. Put together by Krousar Thmei, a foundation which looks after deprived children (and helps revive Cambodia's lost traditions, such as shadow puppetry – see p.172), the exhibits include photographic displays of traditional fishing practices and maps of the lake's seasonal variation. On the way there, dominated by a massive likeness of the head of Jayavarman VII, is one of Cambodia's unsung wonders, the Kantha Bopha **children's hospital**, where all treatment is free and charitable donations allow staff to be paid a living wage. Adverts outside try to persuade you to part with a few dollars or an armful of blood; see Ⓦ www.beatocello.com for more background on the place and its counterpart in Phnom Penh.

An exhilarating way to see the whole area is to go up in the gondola of a tethered **helium balloon**, located on the road between the airport and Angkor Wat; $11 buys you fifteen minutes at 200m to admire the breathtaking panorama (weather permitting). Call ☏012/520810 for more information.

Near the airport is the oft-overlooked **Cambodian Cultural Village**, one of those "see the whole country in an hour" theme parks that every country in Southeast Asia seems to have. Besides miniatures of many of Cambodia's temples and monuments, there are tableaux of wax figures portraying events from history. One of the more amusing features an UNTAC soldier with his arm around a prostitute. Very few foreign visitors bother, however, as the price of admission is a whopping $12 (Cambodians get in for $1).

Eating

Siem Reap isn't just a great opportunity to satisfy cravings for Western fare, it's also one of the best places in the country to sample **Cambodian cuisine**, with many restaurants serving a good range of skilfully prepared local specialities and offering menus in English. The pick of the Cambodian restaurants is east of the river on Achasvar and Wat Bo streets. Cuisines from elsewhere in Asia are also well represented, in particular Thai, Indian and Japanese.

Inexpensive wholesome dishes with helpings of rice are served up from early morning until late at night at the **food stalls** on west side of Psar Chas (Old Market), and on Achasvar Street just south of National Route 6. Fruit-shake and dessert stalls set up in the evenings on the stretch of Sivatha Street immediately north of the Cambodian Commercial Bank.

Around Psar Chas (Old Market)

Abacus Oum Khun St. Lively restaurant in the garden of a Khmer house. Excellent Cambodian and French country cuisine.

Blue Pumpkin Near the hospital. A great little restaurant and bakery with a pavement café atmosphere and a wide selection of sandwiches, pasta and beverages.

Chao Say North side of Psar Chas, below the guesthouse of the same name. Shaded by a cheerful striped awning, with tables spilling out onto the pavement and a long menu of well-prepared American and European favourites – sandwiches, pasta, fish and chips and the like.

Continental Café By Psar Chas. Tucked away behind potted palms and shaded by the shophouse balcony, this is an excellent riverfront spot to sip a glass of chilled wine while you browse the European-influenced menu and daily specials board, where you'll find things like French salads, pasta with pesto and pizzas.

Happy Herbs Pizza Hospital Rd, opposite the hospital ☏012/838134. The best pizza in town, along with consistently good pasta. Takeaways and deliveries can be ordered by phone.

Kamasutra By Psar Chas. A new and delicious Indian restaurant on "Pub Street" with exposed brick walls, a cool atmosphere and hot curries.

Kampuccino By Psar Chas. Wonderful riverside location. Brunch breakfasts until 11am, then a wide range of pastas, pizzas, grills and salads.

Khmer Kitchen Off Hospital Rd. This outstanding family-run restaurant does great Khmer home cooking with the occasional modern twist.

Le Grand Café By Psar Chas. Restored French colonial building with red velvet booths in a two-storey atrium. Great place for lunch, afternoon coffee or dinner. Mixed menu of French, Italian, Cambodian and international cuisine.

New Delhi Hospital Rd, opposite the hospital. Set in a converted shophouse, this place does some of the best Indian food in town, both vegetarian and carnivorous.

Only One By Psar Chas. Once the only restaurant in Siem Reap, this French place gets honourable mention for longevity but is no longer anywhere near the best in town.

Soup Dragon Hospital Rd. Spread over three floors of a street-corner building, this Vietnamese place has traditional dishes as well as modern touches.

The Royal Gardens and beyond

Café d'Angkor Grand Hotel d'Angkor. Just one of the classy restaurants in this famous hotel, with a fine à la carte menu of Continental dishes, as well as a buffet breakfast and dinner, all of which feature both Western and Asian fare.

Chao Praya Angkor Wat Rd ☏063/964666. You can eat your fill at their buffet lunches and dinners, featuring Western and Asian dishes (mostly Thai, plus some Khmer). Booking recommended in the evening, when they stage open-air cultural performances.

FCC Pokambor St ☏063/760280, ✉www .fcccambodia.com. Serves many of the same Western dishes as the *Foreign Correspondents Club* (*FCC*) in Phnom Penh, in a relaxed seating that will ensure that you linger long after your meal is finished. Count on around $15 for dinner without drinks.

Ginga 291 Angkor Wat Rd ☏063/963366. Top-notch a/c Japanese restaurant 500m north of the *Grand Hotel d'Angkor*, with set menus from $9.

Sivatha Street

Café Indochine Sivatha St. French-run restaurant in a traditional wooden house with excellent Khmer dishes and good daily specials.

Forest Hut Sivatha St. Both Khmer and Western food – though the Khmer is better – and delicious daily specials.

East of the river

The cheaper rents east of the river have resulted in a blossoming of reasonably priced restaurants catering to visitors.

North of National Route 6

Sawasdee Food Garden Second left (north) off National Route 6 as you head east of the river. A moderately priced Thai restaurant with dining under a pavilion and a menu of all the usual favourites, including tasty *phat thai*, *satay* and *som tam*.

Between National Route 6 and Achamean Street

Chiang Mai Wat Bo St. Humble Thai joint with an extensive menu serving generous portions of classics like red curries and *phat thai*.

Chivit Thai Wat Bo St. Thai-style dining in a traditional wooden house where you eat at low tables, seated on cushions. Besides excellent *tom yam* soup, they do a range of delicious stir-fries and soup, and *yam wun sen*, a salad of rice noodles with shrimps. There's another branch on Airport Rd – more upmarket, though much less atmospheric.

Hawaii Pizza Wat Bo St. Fill up on inexpensive sandwiches, salads or pizzas and round your meal off with an enormous icy fruit shake. By late evening it turns into a popular travellers' bar.

New Bayon Wat Bo St, 250m south of National Route 6. A great big bright room full of tables, popular with tour groups, if somewhat lacking in

atmosphere. Good stir-fries, including huge prawns cooked with garlic or ginger, and tasty chicken with basil leaves.

Viroth's Wat Bo St. Excellent Khmer food in an elegant, minimalist open-air restaurant.

South of Achamean Street

Moloppor Wat Bo Village, Sala Kamroeuk Commune. Every dish is a dollar at this hugely popular eatery. Japanese tempura, Chinese stir-fry, *dim sum* and some excellent noodle dishes.

Drinking, nightlife and entertainment

There's no shortage of watering holes where you can meet up with other travellers: **bars** abound around Psar Chas (Old Market) and along Sivatha Street, and there are new places opening up all the time, and plenty which stay open until the wee hours.

Angkor What? A block west of Psar Chas. Long-running pub with pool table and satellite TV.

Dead Fish Tower Sivatha St. The wacky decor here – meandering stairways to the various different levels as well as a crocodile pit with real crocs – makes this place a world-class challenge to navigate while drunk. Live music (days vary) and excellent food.

Elephant Bar At the *Grand Hotel d'Angkor*. Luxurious (and pricey) cellar bar in this venerable hotel, reached by a wide marble staircase and decorated with old photos of Angkor. Their happy-hour cocktails (daily 4–7pm) will help you start the evening off in style.

FCC Pokambor St ☎063/760280, ⓦwww .fcccambodia.com. Fans of the *Foreign Correspondents Club (FCC)* in Phnom Penh will find this branch more modern but with just as much character, with comfortable, low-slung chairs and high ceilings. *The* place for drinks after a day at the ruins.

Ivy By Psar Chas. Very much a foreigners' hangout, with free use of a pool table. Kitchen

closes at 10pm but the bar stays open until the last punter leaves.

Khmer Family Bar Northwest of Psar Chas. Formerly the *Temple* bar, this is one of Siem Reap's more popular watering holes, in part due to the $2 cocktails and $1 beers. There's a DJ, and a sports bar upstairs. Stays open very late.

Laundry Bar Northwest of Psar Chas. Very laid-back and with a cosmopolitan vibe. Stays open very late.

Linga Bar North of Psar Chas. As you might have guessed, this is touted as a gay bar, or at least a gay-friendly bar (although lesbians may wonder why they didn't name it the Yoni Bar). Actually, it's all very low key and anyone would feel welcome here.

Martini Dancing Across the river opposite Psar Chas. Cambodian disco with lecherous boozers and the usual beer girls making sure they're all well soused.

Red Piano 50m northwest of Psar Chas. Attractive bar-restaurant and a great spot to chat over a beer or one of their "Tomb Raider" cocktails.

Entertainment

Outside Phnom Penh, Siem Reap is the only place in Cambodia where you can watch **traditional dance** being performed. Indeed, it's actually easier to catch a performance here than in the capital, as several Siem Reap hotels and restaurants package a **cultural show**, featuring several dance styles, with a meal. Although touristy, these performances are professionally staged, have been going on at Angkor since the 1920s and are well worth booking to see. Shows usually open with the elegant apsara dance, often followed by a light-hearted item or two depicting popular folk tales, such as the fisherman's dance, which takes a comic look at rural courtship. The finale is a vibrant dance retelling part of the *Reamker*, the Khmer version of the Hindu epic *Ramayana* (see box, p.92), involving four

Apsara dance

No visit to Cambodia is complete without at least a quick glimpse of women performing the ancient art of apsara dance, as depicted on the walls of Angkor's temples. Wearing glittering silk tunics, sequinned tops (into which they are sewn before each performance to achieve the requisite tight fit) and elaborate golden headdresses, they execute their movements with great deftness and deliberation, knees bent in plié, heels touching the floor first at each step, coy smiles on their faces. Every position has its own particular **symbolism** – a finger pointing to the sky, for instance, indicates "today", while standing sideways to the audience with the sole of the foot facing upwards represents flying.

In the reign of Jayavarman VII there were over three thousand apsara dancers at court – the dances were performed exclusively for the king – and so prized was their skill that when the Thais sacked Angkor in the fifteenth century, they took a troupe of dancers back home with them. Historically, the art form was taught only at the **royal court**, but so few exponents survived the ravages of the Khmer Rouge that the genre was very nearly extinguished. Subsequently, when Princess Boppha Devi – who had been a principal dancer with the royal troupe – wished to revive it, she found it helpful to study temple panels to establish the movements. It was not until 1995, a full sixteen years after the fall of the Khmer Rouge, that Cambodians once again witnessed a public performance of apsara dance, at Angkor Wat.

These days, the **School of Fine Arts** in Phnom Penh takes responsibility for training a new generation of dancers, who are chosen not only for aptitude and youth (they start as young as 7), but for the flexibility and elegance of their hands. It takes six years for students to learn the intricate positions the dances entail – numbering more than 1500 – and a further three to six years for them to attain the required level of artistic maturity. Also taught here is the other principal Cambodian dance genre, **tontay**, in which the emphasis is on depicting folk tales and episodes from the **Reamker**.

The School of Fine Arts mounts **performances** of apsara dance on special occasions (such as the Khmer New Year or the king's birthday) in front of Angkor Wat and sometimes in Phnom Penh. More commonly, you'll be able to watch both styles of Cambodian dance in the cultural performances put on by hotels and restaurants in Phnom Penh and Siem Reap.

roles – male, female, giant and monkey – with the dancers wearing intricate masks associated with their character. If the costumes for apsara dance are lavish, then those for the *Reamker* dances are positively opulent, heavily embroidered and embellished with tails, epaulettes and wings.

The most popular venue for these cultural shows is the outdoor performance hall of the *Grand Hotel d'Angkor*, on the riverside near the hotel (℡063/963888). Similar in quality are the shows at the *Sofitel Royal Angkor* (℡63/964600), and the *Angkor Village*, which stages performances at its Apsara Theatre opposite (℡063/963561). Performance times, frequency and price of admission change with the seasons; call in advance for show times and reservations. A buffet meal is normally served an hour before the performance commences.

A Cambodian folk art going all the way back to Angkorian times, shadow puppetry was all but lost during the Khmer Rouge era, but is now undergoing a revival, with performances both in Siem Reap and the capital. Entertaining shadow-puppet shows by street children looked after by Krousar Thmei are staged at *La Noria* (℡063/964242; Wed at 7.30pm; $6, or $12 with dinner). Only a few puppets are used at each performance, changes of character being effected by dressing them in different *kramars*. For more on the puppets themselves, see box on p.172.

Shopping

Shopping in Siem Reap is second only to the capital for variety and quality, and in some ways it's much easier to shop here since the various outlets are much closer together. **Psar Chas**, usually referred to by its English name, "Old Market", abounds in inexpensive souvenir stalls selling all manner of goods, including items specific to the Siem Reap area. Besides the usual souvenir T-shirts, stalls along the front of the market sell a good range of silk tops, skirts and trousers, and traditional Khmer **sampots** in Western sizes. Many of the textiles here, such as the fabric used to make the cotton **sarongs** with elephant motifs, are imported from Indonesia, but the tempting, large, chequered **throws** in bright colours are made in Siem Reap and not available elsewhere. Also facing the river are several stalls selling English-language books, including some prominently displayed publications on Angkor. There are **rubbings** of bas-reliefs (in fact, they're taken from wooden reproductions, but are no less attractive for that) at stalls inside or to the south. Look out also for a speciality of Siem Reap, woven **rattan**, used to make baskets, place mats and plates – the ones with holes in are for serving dried fish.

Supermarkets are new to Siem Reap, but a couple of places sell Western goodies like wines, cheeses and the like. The largest selection is at Lotus Supermarket, near Psar Chas. Also good, with a variety of meats, wines and cheeses, is the Angkor Market on Sivatha Street. If you're staying on the Airport Road, the Caltex Star Mart stocks a limited selection of wines, ice creams, chocolate and tampons.

Craft shops and galleries

Until recently the quality of souvenirs in Siem Reap was something of a let-down, but a handful of **international artists** have now set up shop in Siem Reap and are offering their Asia-inspired works to visitors.

To see skills that were lost with the Khmer Rouge being relearnt, consider visiting the **Chantiers Ecoles** off the southern end of Sivatha Street (Mon–Sat 8am–noon & 2–4pm; free). At this crafts training school, English-speaking guides meet visitors for a tour of the workshops, where you can see students – selected from deprived local families – following an extensive curriculum in wood-carving, stone-carving and lacquerwork. The school also operates the **Angkor Silk Farm** at Puok, 16km west of Siem Reap off National Route 6 (daily 7–11.30am & 2–5.30pm; free), where guides are on hand to explain the intricacies of silk manufacture.

Shadow puppets

Shadow puppets are made of stretched, dried **cowhide**, the required outline drawn freehand onto the leather and pared out, after which holes are carefully punched in designated areas to allow back light (traditionally from a burning coconut shell) to shine through onto a plain screen. Once cut and punched, the figures are painstakingly **painted** using natural black and red dyes under the strict supervision of the puppet master. Two different sorts of puppets are produced, *sbaek thom* and *sbaek toich* (literally "large skin" and "small skin"). The *sbaek thom*, used to tell stories from the *Reamker*, are the larger of the two, around 1–2m tall and lack moving parts. By contrast, *sbaek toich* puppets have moveable arms and legs, and are commonly used to tell folk tales and stories of everyday life, usually humorous and with a moral ending. Both types of puppet are manipulated from below using sticks attached to strategic points.

House of Peace 3km from town towards the airport on Airport Rd. This workshop trains artisans to produce traditional Khmer shadow puppets; visitors can watch the process and buy the results.
Les Artisans d'Angkor Chantiers Ecole, off Sivatha St. The school's retail outlet sells an outstanding collection of premium-quality goods, including glossy lacquerwork, exquisite carvings, stunning fabrics and garments from their silk workshops at Puok.
Made in Cambodia Immediately north of Psar Chas. Sells well-made cushion covers, place mats and the like, produced by the disabled.
McDermott Gallery 1 Next to the *FCC Angkor Suites*, Pokambor St ⓦwww.mcdermottgallery .com. Upscale gallery showing fine art photography of Angkor by two internationally acclaimed photographers, John McDermott and Kenro Izu.
McDermott Gallery 2 Next to Psar Chas ⓦwww .mcdermottgallery.com. International gallery showing fine art photography of Asia by

photographers from Cambodia and around the world. Housed in a 1930s Khmer shophouse, renovated by French-Khmer architects. Rotating exhibitions change every two months.
Rajana Just northeast of the *Red Piano* bar, east of Psar Chas. Branch of the Phnom Penh crafts outlet. Simple contemporary silver jewellery and individually produced paintings on silk, which can be made up into greetings cards or wall-hangings.
Red Gallery FCC Pokambor St ⓣ063/760280, ⓦwww.fcccambodia.com. Boutique gallery showing an exclusive selection of sculpture, oil paintings and mixed media works by artists based in Cambodia.
Senteurs d'Angkor Opposite Psar Chas and next to the Lotus Supermarket. French chic is combined here with the imaginative use of traditional Khmer materials to produce tasteful, original silk wall-hangings and clothes. Also bronze reproductions of statues from the National Museum, plus spices and flavoured teas.

Listings

Airlines Angkor Airways, Samdech Tepavong St ⓣ063/964878; Bangkok Airways, 571 Airport Rd ⓣ063/380191; Malaysia Airlines, Siem Reap Airport ⓣ063/964135; Siem Reap Airways, 571 Airport Rd ⓣ063/965427; Vietnam Airlines, 342 Airport Rd ⓣ063/964488.
Banks and exchange Acleda Bank, Airport Rd; Cambodian Commercial Bank, Sivatha St; Canadia Bank, west of Psar Chas; Mekong Bank, Sivatha St (with an exchange booth operating outside the bank Mon–Fri 6.30–8.30am & 4–6pm, Sat 6.30–8.30am); UCB, west of Psar Chas.
Books and newspapers The best place for secondhand English-language books is Blue Apsara next to the Old Market. A decent selection of new books on Cambodia and Angkor-related subjects can be found at the Monument Books shop in the *FCC Angkor Suites*. The shop at the *Sofitel Royal Angkor* has a selection of foreign-language newspapers, and there's a similar kiosk at the *Grand Hotel d'Angkor*. The stalls at the Old Market have a good range of temple guides and books on Khmer history. The *Cambodia Daily* and the *Phnom Penh Post* can be purchased at the Lotus Supermarket and at hotel newsstands.
Car hire A car and driver can be hired from most hotels, travel agents or from KATGA (see p.161); a day-trip will cost $20–30 to Angkor, $40 to Banteay Srei and $50 to Phnom Kulen or Beng Mealea.
Emergencies Fire service, Sivatha St ⓣ063/784464. For police, see p.174.

Hospitals and clinics The Royal Angkor International Hospital, Airport Rd (ⓣ063/761888) has high-standard medical services. 24hour emergency care, ambulance, translation and evacuation to Bangkok. The Naga Medical Centre, 593 Airport Rd (ⓣ016/964500) has English- and French-speaking staff. The government-run Siem Reap Provincial Hospital is 500m north of Psar Chas (ⓣ063/963111), though it's very basic and should be used only as a last resort.
Internet access Expect to pay around $1–2 per hour at any of the many Internet cafés around town.
Laundry There are laundries all over town, charging 500 riel per item.
Massage A number of places around town offer massage. Stress-relieving massages are available at Body Tune Spa, near *Red Piano* (ⓣ012/444066), while traditional Khmer massage is offered at Islands Traditional Massage, near Psar Chas (ⓣ012/982062). The newly opened Bodia Spa, near Psar Chas (ⓣ063/761593) is the most stylish of Siem Reap's rapidly increasing number of spas.
Motorbike rental Foreign tourists – as distinct from expatriates – are banned from riding motorbikes around Siem Reap and the temples, ostensibly to safeguard them from having their bikes stolen by agents of the rental companies in order to elicit a replacement fee (it's also been claimed that tourists can't safely negotiate the chaotic traffic).
Pharmacies There are plenty of pharmacies around Psar Chas and east of the river on National Route 6.

Travel agents and tour operators

Siem Reap tour operators can rustle up a car and guide for tours of the Angkor temples, and can customize tours to many parts of the country. A few specialist operators can organize trips to outlying areas of the countryside, including remote parts of the Tonle Sap, and even a bird's-eye view of the temples from the air.

Diethelm Travel 4 Airport Rd ☎063/963524, ⒻDouble063/963694. Travel agent and tour operator; standard tours take in the temples and the Siem Reap locality, but these can be extended to include other destinations in the country.

Exotissimo Travel Cambodia Airport Rd ☎063/964322, ⓌDoublewww.exotissimo.com. Tours of Angkor and elsewhere in the country.

Helicopter Cambodia South of Psar Chas ☎012/814500, Ⓦwww .helicopterscambodia.com. This reputable, Kiwi-run operation offers helicopter trips ($75 per person for an eight-minute flight) in the vicinity of Angkor Wat (overflying isn't allowed), as well as charters to other parts of Cambodia.

Neak Krorhorm Travel & Tours 3 Psar Chas ☎063/964924. Low-cost transport to Bangkok and elsewhere in Cambodia, and tickets for domestic boat and air services.

Osmose Nature Tours ☎012/832812, Ⓦwww.osmosetonlesap.net. Specialists in Tonle Sap excursions, including trips to the flooded reaches of the lake's flood plain and the bird sanctuary at Prek Toal.

Terre Cambodge Psar Chas ☎012/843401, Ⓦwww.terrecambodge.com. Off-the-beaten-track tours, using four-wheel drives to reach remote temples and villages out of Siem Reap. Also Tonle Sap explorations in converted sampans.

Phones You can make domestic and international calls at the main post office on Pokambor St (daily 7am–5.30pm). Cheap international webcalls via the Internet can be made at many of Siem Reap's Internet cafés.

Photography You'll find a handful of portrait studios that stock batteries, etc. along National Route 6, east of the river.

Police The tourist police office is opposite the main entrance to the Angkor Archaeological Park (☎012/402424).

Post The main post office is on Pokambor St (daily 7am–5.30pm); there is a poste restante service, and you can also make domestic and international calls here.

The temples of Angkor

Designated a UNESCO World Heritage Site in 1992, the **TEMPLES OF ANGKOR** are scattered over some three hundred square kilometres of countryside between the Tonle Sap lake and the Kulen Mountains, although the most famous are clustered close to Siem Reap. Atmospherically surrounded by patches of dense forest and standing proudly above rice paddies, the temples do not feel like sterile museum pieces, but seem still to be part of everyday life – aspects of which continue much as depicted in temple bas-reliefs.

Angkor's sites are as diverse as the kings who built them, and each temple has its own distinct appeal. Steeped in myth and mystery, **Angkor Wat** is unmistakable with its five magnificent towers and vast complex of galleries. Also on everyone's itinerary is the walled city of **Angkor Thom**, whose much-photographed south gate is topped by massive faces looking out to the four cardinal directions and reached by a stunning causeway flanked by huge statues of gods and demons. The faces are repeated in their hundreds at the **Bayon**, which lies at the heart of Angkor Thom and was the very last Angkorian temple to be built; figuring large among its claims to fame are its two galleries of bas-reliefs. Two more must-sees are **Ta Prohm**, sometimes called the "jungle temple", whose appeal has actually been enhanced by the ravages of nature, and **Banteay Srei**, a unique micro-temple of intricately carved reddish stone. The earliest temples, those of **Roluos**, east of Siem Reap, are more for the specialist, but a visit here gives a glimpse of how the architecture evolved, with brick used almost throughout, in contrast with the later, more sophisticated temples where increasing use was made of sandstone, which could be carved and decorated. Roluos aside, there are some forty other sites accessible to the public.

Some history

For all their dramatic architecture, the ancient Khmer did not produce durable **written texts** – regardless of whether the inscriptions stored at temple libraries were made on specially treated palm leaves or animal skins, they have not survived. Consequently the history of Angkor (discussed in detail on p.307) has had to be painstakingly pieced together by scholars from over a thousand inscribed steles recovered across the empire, the inscriptions mostly written in Sanskrit, and from a thorough study of the evolution of temple construction. Even now, the accepted understanding of Angkorian history remains hypothetical to some degree, with the origins of many temples, the dates of their construction and even the names of kings uncertain.

Angkor's **earliest monuments** date from 802, when Jayavarman II came north from Kompong Cham to set up court at Phnom Kulen. No further stone temples were built after the reign of **Jayavarman VII**, the greatest temple-builder of them all, came to an end in 1219; scholars theorize that either the area's resources were exhausted or the change to Theravada Buddhism may have precluded their construction. After Jayavarman VII, the temples and palaces remained in use until they were sacked by the Thais in 1431; the following year, Ponhea Yat took his court south to Phnom Penh and left Angkor to the jungle.

The cult of the god kings

The frenzy of building in the Angkor region was principally a result of the Khmer kings' desire to create **state-temples** to serve the **devaraja cult** (see p.325), which existed alongside the prevailing Hinduism. The Hindu cosmos is symbolized in the **layout** of the majority of state-temples. A central **sanctuary tower** (or group of towers), housing the sacred image of the **devaraja**, would be raised on a platform, often in the form of a multi-level **pyramid** representing the mythical Mount Meru; surrounding this would be a series of concentric rectangular enclosures, created by walls and/or moats; in all but one instance (Angkor Wat), the temples were designed to be approached from the east.

As successive kings sought to outdo their predecessors, and as construction techniques improved, so the temples grew in complexity, making use of multiple sanctuaries, antechambers, galleries and elaborate **gopuras**, or entrance towers. Although practically all the temples were extensively carved with decorative motifs or detailed mythological scenes, the most magnificent carvings of all are undoubtedly the **bas-relief** panels at Angkor Wat and the Bayon. **Statuary** was a key feature also, and the alcoves, antechambers and sanctuaries would have housed images in wood, stone, bronze and even gold, though don't expect to see many of them in situ these days; of those that survived the years of abandonment and avoided being stolen or destroyed, most have been removed for safekeeping, mainly to Angkor Conservation (see box, p.178), though some prize specimens ended up in the National Museum in Phnom Penh. **For more on temple architecture and art**, see the Temple architecture colour section.

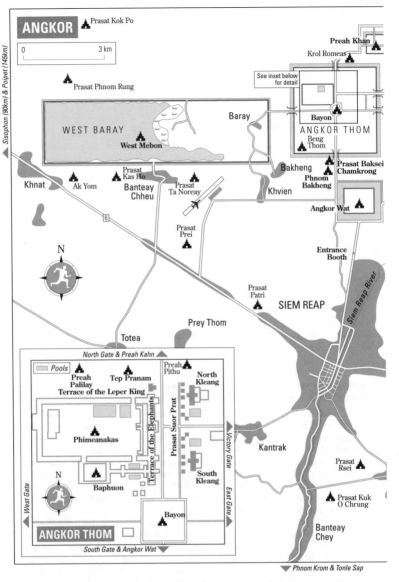

Though Angkor was never completely deserted, the local populace which continued to worship at the temples was unable to maintain them.

Around 1570, **King Satha** was so enchanted when he rediscovered Angkor Thom deep in the jungle that he had the undergrowth cleared and brought his court there, though by 1594 he was back at Lovek for reasons that remain unclear. Another short-lived period of royal interest occurred in the middle of the seventeenth century when, according to a letter penned by a Dutch

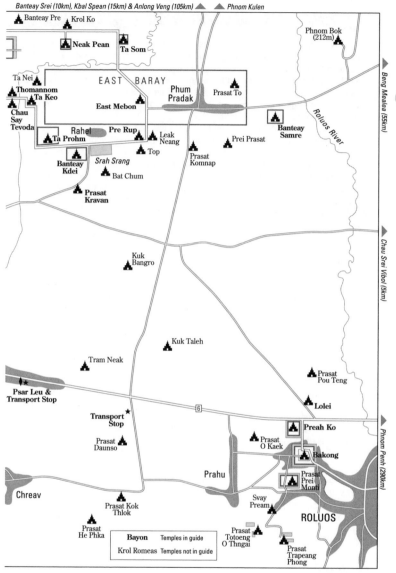

Banteay Srei (10km), Kbal Spean (15km) & Anlong Veng (105km) ▲ ▲ Phnom Kulen

▲ Banteay Pre ▲ Krol Ko

▲ Neak Pean ▲ Ta Som

Phnom Bok
(212m) ▲

Ta Nei ▲ EAST BARAY

▲ Thomannom
▲ Ta Keo

East Mebon

Phum
Pradak

▲ Prasat To

Beng Mealea (55km) ▲

Roluos River

Chau
Say
Tevoda

Rahel

▲ Ta Prohm

Pre Rup ▲ ▲ Leak
Neang

▲ Banteay
Samre

▲ Top

▲ Prei Prasat

Srah Srang

Prasat
Komnap

Banteay
Kdei

▲ Bat Chum

Chau Srei Vibol (5km) ▲

▲ Prasat
Kravan

▲ Kuk
Bangro

▲ Kuk Taleh

▲ Tram Neak

▲ Prasat
Pou Teng

Psar Leu &
Transport Stop

6

▲ Lolei

Transport
Stop

Prasat
Daunso ▲

Preah Ko

Prasat
O Kaek ▲

▲ Bakong

Phnom Penh (290km) ▲

Prahu

Chreav

Prasat Kok
Thlok ▲

Prasat
Prei
Monti

Svay
Pream ▲

ROLUOS

Prasat
He Phka ▲

Bayon   Temples in guide

Krol Romeas Temples not in guide

Prasat
Totoeng
O Thngai

Prasat
Trapeang
Phong

merchant to the governor-general of the Dutch East Indies, "the king [Barom
Rachea VI] paid a visit to a lovely pleasant place known as Anckoor". Subsequently, despite tales of a lost city in the Cambodian jungle filtering back to
the West via missionaries and traders, it wasn't until the nineteenth century
that Cambodia opened up to European explorers. The first proper account of
Angkor Wat, published by the French missionary Charles-Emile Bouillevaux
in 1858, failed to arouse wide interest, but in 1864, the diaries of botanist and

177

By the late nineteenth century, travellers and researchers from many countries, notably France, were arriving in Cambodia in search of its "lost" temples. The first major step towards a proper study of Angkor's legacy was the foundation in Vietnam in 1898 of the **École Française d'Extrême-Orient** (⊛www.efeo.fr); their scholars would subsequently map the temples for the first time, and they created the body now known as **Angkor Conservation**, based 2km north of Siem Reap, which works on the restoration of temples.

Work at Angkor was carried out throughout the first half of the twentieth century, with only a brief pause during World War II. Particularly noteworthy among the researchers of the time were Henri Marchal and Maurice Glaize, the former remembered for his restoration in the early 1930s of Banteay Srei, the latter for restoring Banteay Samre, Bakong, Neak Pean and part of Preah Khan. It was during work on Banteay Srei that the restoration technique of **anastylosis** began to be employed in Cambodia, involving the temporary dismantling and analysis of intact parts of structures so that ruined sections could be reassembled faithfully. In 1960, Bernard-Philippe Groslier assumed control of Angkor Conservation, taking after his father George, who had previously held the post. He was able to commence work on the Baphuon before the monuments were again abandoned during the civil war and the Khmer Rouge years.

Contrary to common belief, the temples suffered little war damage, but looting undoubtedly occurred and the fabric of the temples continued to be at risk from encroaching vegetation. Things improved little during Vietnamese occupation in the 1980s, when only Indian conservators were allowed to work here; their work at Angkor Wat, where they used chemicals to clean the stone and cement to fill gaps, has been much criticized. By 1993, however, UNESCO had declared Angkor a **World Heritage Site**, and conservation projects to the tune of millions of dollars were put in place, sponsored primarily by Japan.

These days, the conservation of the temples is coordinated by **APSARA**, an NGO set up in the 1990s to oversee the preservation of the cultural heritage of Siem Reap province. They face a formidable task: improved access to the temples has given rise not only to growing visitor numbers, which APSARA plans to deal with by restricting access to the temples, but also to a rise in **looting**; the pilfering to order of artefacts has been aided by the jungle cover and the fact that just one or two guards are employed at each site.

explorer Henri Mouhot, who had stumbled on Angkor by accident a few years earlier, were published posthumously, and the temples gripped the world. The Briton J. Thompson published the first photographs of Angkor in 1867, and was the first to suggest a link between temple architecture and the mythical Mount Meru. Close behind him came Doudart Lagrée, who discovered Beng Mealea and Preah Khan (Kompong Thom).

Practicalities

The temples are officially **open** daily from 5am till 6pm, except for Banteay Srei (closes 5pm) and Kbal Spean (closes 3pm). **Entry passes** are required to enter the Angkor area, and must also be shown at several of the temples. Although passes are not required to visit Phnom Kulen, Kor Ker or Beng Mealea, entrance fees of $20, $10 and $5 respectively are collected at these temples. At the **main entrance**, on the Siem Reap–Angkor Wat road, three categories of pass are available, valid for one day ($20), three days ($40) or seven days ($60); additionally, one-day passes only can be bought at Angkor Wat and at Bakong (Roluos). Most people find the three-day pass adequate, giving enough time to see all the temples in the central area and to visit the outlying temples at Roluos, Banteay Srei and Banteay Samre. If you're short of time, you can just about cover Angkor Wat, the Bayon, Ta Prohm and Banteay Srei in one full day. For three- and seven-day tickets you'll need to provide a **passport photograph** of yourself to be laminated into your ticket. Photos can be taken for free at the main entrance but the long queue means you'll waste precious time if you don't come with one. **Children** under 12 are admitted free, but you must take their passport with you as proof of age. Bear in mind that entry passes must be used on consecutive days. For example, a three-day pass that is first used on a Monday will only be valid for the following Tuesday and Wednesday.

Almost all visitors head first to Angkor Wat and Angkor Thom, after which there are various possible routes around the rest of the temples. From Angkor Thom, the so-called **Small Circuit** continues east via the temples located along the road to the bathing pool, Srah Srang, then curves past Prasat Kravan on the final leg back to Angkor Wat; the **Grand Circuit** covers the temples along the semicircular arc of road connecting Srah Srang back to Angkor Thom's northern gate. Some visitors find it useful to see the temples in **chronological order** to understand better how they grew in complexity as new construction methods were tried, though inevitably this involves considerable backtracking: starting at Roluos, you'd have to head out to Bakheng and on to Prasat Kravan before doing Angkor Wat and then shooting out to Banteay Samre.

Refreshment **stalls** can be found at several of the temples, including Angkor Wat, the Bayon, Ta Prohm and Pre Rup. At Angkor Wat, small **restaurants** behind the souvenir stalls serve Khmer and Chinese food at prices only slightly higher than similar establishments in Siem Reap. Opposite the main entrance, the *Angkor Café* was closed at the time of research due to a dispute; next door, Les Artisans d'Angkor (see p.173) has an outlet selling products from their workshops. Cheaper **souvenirs**, from bamboo trinkets to *kramars* are sold at stalls outside the most popular temples, while children at most temples hawk film, postcards, T-shirts and simple handicrafts made from rattan and bamboo.

If you plan to visit outlying temples we've not covered, you should seek advice from registered guides regarding the safety situation, as some of the sites have not been fully de-mined.

Angkor Wat

Nothing prepares you for the majesty of **Angkor Wat**. The temple's five majestic, corncob-shaped towers hold the eye captive, while the mind marvels at the vision of the architects who created this masterpiece of Khmer architecture, consecrated around 1150 to the Hindu god Vishnu; scholars have calculated that it would have taken thirty years to complete. As you approach, the intricacy of the layout becomes apparent, and close up, every nook and cranny reveals itself to be filled with fine detail; around every corner a new feature surpasses the last. If time allows, it's worth visiting at different times of day to see how the colours of the stone change, the spires golden in the dying light at dusk.

Experts have long debated whether Angkor Wat was built for worship or for funerary purposes; much of the confusion has arisen because the site is approached from the west and the gallery of bas-reliefs is designed to be viewed anti-clockwise, the direction associated with death. Nowadays, it's generally accepted that it was used by the king for the worship of the devaraja during his lifetime, and became his mausoleum upon his death.

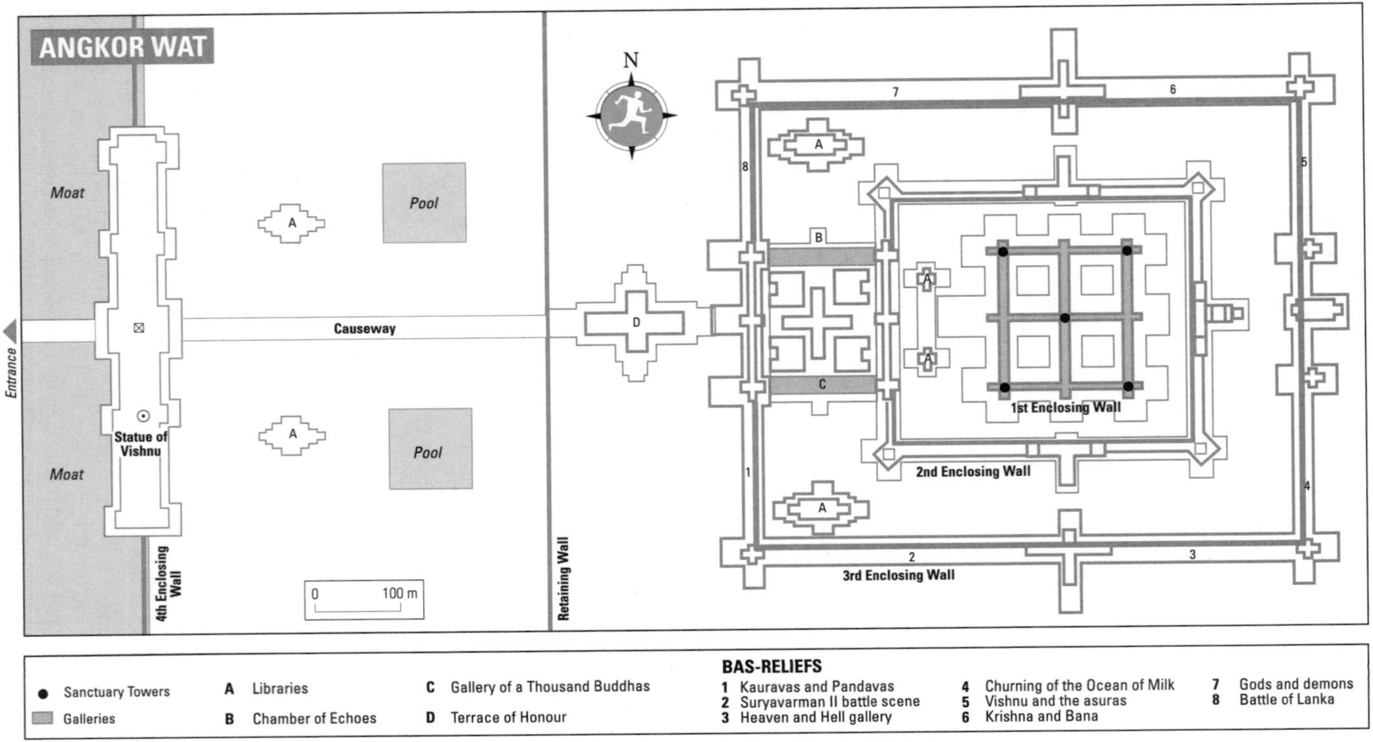
ANGKOR WAT
N
Moat
Moat
Entrance
Statue of Vishnu
4th Enclosing Wall
A
A
Pool
Pool
Causeway
0 100 m
Retaining Wall
D
B
C
A
A
A
A
1st Enclosing Wall
2nd Enclosing Wall
3rd Enclosing Wall
1
2
3
4
5
6
7
8
Sanctuary Towers
Galleries
A Libraries
B Chamber of Echoes
C Gallery of a Thousand Buddhas
D Terrace of Honour
BAS-RELIEFS
1 Kauravas and Pandavas
2 Suryavarman II battle scene
3 Heaven and Hell gallery
4 Churning of the Ocean of Milk
5 Vishnu and the asuras
6 Krishna and Bana
7 Gods and demons
8 Battle of Lanka

Moat and fourth enclosure

Unusually, entry to the complex is from the west, via an impressive, and recently restored, laterite causeway, from which you can look down into the excavations to see the massive blocks used in the causeway's construction. Paved with sandstone and edged by a crumbling naga balustrade with terraces guarded by lions, it crosses the 200-metre-wide **moat** to the west gopura of the **fourth enclosing wall**.

The **west gopura** stretches for nearly 230m and boasts three towers, plus entrances large enough to allow elephants to pass through. Inside the southern section of the gopura, inevitably garlanded with offerings of flowers, is an eight-armed statue of **Vishnu**, over 3m tall. Looking out from the gopura, there's a panoramic view of the temple. The first of Angkor Wat's fabulous **apsaras**, born from the Churning of the Ocean of Milk (see p.183), are delicately carved into the sandstone on the eastern exterior of the gopura, their feet foreshortened and skewed to the side, possibly because of lack of space.

From the gopura, a second **causeway** leads to the temple, 350m long and even more impressive than the one across the moat. The buildings partway along are libraries, the one to the north already restored, the southern one still undergoing work.

In front of the temple is the cruciform-shaped **Terrace of Honour**, framed by the naga balustrade; apsara dances (see p.171) were once performed here and ceremonial processions received by the king. Beyond the terrace, a short flight of steps leads up to the third enclosing wall, whose western gopura is linked to a cruciform cloister and two galleries.

The third enclosure

Portraying events associated primarily with Vishnu, the famous Angkor Wat bas-reliefs, some 2m high on average, are carved into the wall of the magnificently colonnaded **gallery**, which runs around the perimeter of the temple, forming the **third enclosure**. This was as far into the complex as the citizenry of Angkor were allowed to get, and the scenes depicted were meant to impress them with their king's prowess as well as contributing to their religious education.

The early sections of the bas-reliefs are delicately carved with minute attention to detail (in marked contrast to the poorly executed scenes added in the sixteenth century). In some areas you can still see evidence of the red and gold paint that once covered the reliefs, while other areas are black; one theory is that the pigments have been eroded and the stone polished by thousands of hands caressing the carvings over the years (nowadays signs ask you not to touch the reliefs).

Extending over 700m, the bas-reliefs are broken into sections by porches midway along each side, along with corner chambers. The account that follows assumes you progress around the gallery in an **anti-clockwise** direction, in keeping with funerary practices.

West gallery: south section

The battle between the cousins, the **Kauravas** (marching from the left) and the **Pandavas** (from the right), described in the *Mahabharata* is in full swing in the first section of the gallery. Fighting to the death at Mount Kurukshetra, the two families are respectively backed by the supernatural powers of Kama, son of the sun god Surya, and Arjuna. Along the bottom of the panel, the foot soldiers march towards the fray in the centre of the gallery; above them, the generals ride in horse-drawn chariots or on elephants. Amid thrilling hand-to-hand combat, the Kaurava general, Bhisma, is shown shot through with arrows, while Arjuna can be seen on his chariot with Krishna serving as his charioteer.

Southwest corner
Despite erosion, some tales from the *Ramayana* (see box, p.92) and other Hindu legends can still be made out here. One panel shows Krishna protecting shepherds who have decided to worship him rather than Indra; against the storms sent by Indra, he holds up Mount Govardhana in one hand as a shelter. Another depicts the duel between the monkey gods Valin and Sugriva, in which Valin dies in the arms of his wife after he is pierced by an arrow from Rama; monkeys mourn Valin on the surrounding panels.

South gallery: west section
This gallery depicts a **battle scene** that runs west to east on two levels, beginning with a royal audience (upper level) and the palace ladies in procession (below). Further along, the Khmer commanders, mounted on elephants and shaded by parasols, are seen mustering the troops and marching through the jungle. At the centre of the panel they surround Suryavarman II, who is of larger stature and has fifteen parasols around him. Beyond, the army – accompanied by musicians, standard-bearers and jesters – is joined by Cham mercenaries, identified by their moustaches and plumed headdresses. It is thought that the small niches along the wall were used as hiding places for golden artefacts, though some say the chunks of stone were removed by devotees who believed they possessed magical properties.

South gallery: east section
Called the **Heaven and Hell gallery**, this panel, carved on three levels and nearly 60m long, shows the many-armed god Yama mounted on a buffalo and judging the dead. At the start of this section, a path is shown on the top level along which people ascend to heaven, while a corresponding route at the bottom leads to hell, the two paths being separated by a frieze of garudas. The people in heaven can be seen living a life of leisure in palaces, whereas those who have sinned are pushed through a trapdoor into the underworld to have terrible punishments inflicted on them – gluttons are cut in two, vandals have their bones broken and rice stealers have red-hot irons thrust through their abdomens.

East gallery: south section
This gallery contains the most famous of Angkor Wat's bas-reliefs, depicting the **Churning of the Ocean of Milk** (see box opposite). The story picks up when the churning is just about to yield results; in the central band of the panel, 92 bulbous-eyed *asura*s with crested headdresses are shown holding the head of Vasuki and pulling from the left, while on the right, 88 *deva*s, with almond eyes and conical headdresses, hold the tail. To the top, thousands of divine apsaras dance along the wall, and at the bottom, the ocean teems with finely detailed marine creatures.

The chedi just outside the east gopura was placed here in the early eighteenth century when the temple was a Buddhist monastery; its history is recorded on a wall inscription within the gopura itself.

East gallery: north section
The relief here was carved in the sixteenth century and the workmanship is rough and superficial. The scene records the *asura*s being defeated by Vishnu, who is shown with four heads and mounted on Garuda in the centre of the

The Churning of the Ocean of Milk

A popular theme in Khmer art is the Churning of the Ocean of Milk, a **creation myth** from the Hindu epic, the *Bhagavata-Purana*, which is a description of the various incarnations of Vishnu. At the outset of this episode, the *devas* (gods) and *asuras* (demons) are lined up on opposite sides, trying to use Mount Mandara to churn the ocean in order to produce *amrita*, the elixir of immortality. They tug on the serpent Vasuki, who is coiled around the mountain, but to no effect. Vishnu arrives and instructs them to pull rhythmically, but the mountain begins to sink. Things get worse when Vasuki vomits a deadly venom, which threatens to destroy the *devas* and *asuras*; Brahma asks Shiva to drink up the venom, which he does, but it burns his throat, which is blue thereafter. Vishnu meanwhile, in his incarnation as a tortoise, supports Mount Mandara, allowing the churning to continue for another thousand years, when the *amrita* is finally produced. Unfortunately, the elixir is seized by the *asuras*, but Vishnu again comes to the rescue as the apparition Maya and regains the cup of elixir. The churning also results in the manifestation of mythical beings, including the three-headed elephant, Airavana; the goddess of beauty, Lakshmi, who becomes Vishnu's wife; and the celestial dancers, the **apsaras**.

panel. The *asuras* approach from the south, their leaders riding chariots drawn by monsters; from the north, a group of warriors ride peacocks.

North gallery: east section
Also sixteenth-century, and just as poorly rendered, the scenes here show the battle between **Krishna and Bana**, a ruler who had earned Shiva's protection. Krishna, easily spotted with his eight arms and multiple heads, rides Garuda towards Bana, but is forced to halt by a fire surrounding a city wall, which Garuda quells with water from the Ganges. On the far west of the panel, a victorious Krishna is depicted on Mount Kailasa, where Shiva entreats him to spare Bana's life. Also along this stretch of wall can be found an image of the elephant-headed Ganesh, this god's only appearance in the entire temple.

North gallery: west section
Better executed than the previous two sections, the panel here shows 21 gods from the **Hindu pantheon** in a terrific melee between gods and demons. Some of the easier ones to spot are, from left to right, the multi-headed and -armed Skanda, god of war, riding a peacock; Indra standing on the elephant Airavana; Vishnu mounted on Garuda and fighting with all four arms; Yama in a chariot pulled by oxen; and Shiva pulling his bow, while Brahma rides the sacred goose, Hamsa.

Northwest corner
More scenes from the *Ramayana* are to be found here, notably a depiction of Vishnu reclining on the serpent, Anata; a bevy of apsaras float above him, while his wife, Lakshmi, sits near his feet; below, a procession of gods come to ask Vishnu to return to earth.

West gallery: north section
Turning the corner, you come to the superbly carved **Battle of Lanka**. In this action-packed sequence from the *Ramayana*, Rama is shown fighting the ten-headed, twenty-armed Ravana to free his wife, Sita, from captivity; bodies of the soldiers from the monkey army, Rama's allies, fall in all directions. The two adversaries are seen in the centre of the panel, Ravana in a chariot drawn by lions, Rama standing on the monkey king, Sugriva.

First level

Arriving back at the western gopura, you can head east up into the **third enclosure** (which is also the first level of the temple pyramid), bare save for two libraries in the northwest and southwest corners. Within the cloister, if you look up, you'll spot a frieze of apsaras, while below are seated ascetics carved at the bases of the columns; many of the columns also bear Sanskrit and Khmer inscriptions. The **Gallery of a Thousand Buddhas**, to the south, once housed a vast collection of Buddhas, collected here over recent centuries when Angkor Wat was a Buddhist monastery; those that weren't moved to Angkor Conservation in 1970 were eventually destroyed by the Khmer Rouge, though today a few modern images have taken their place. The chamber in the wall of the north gallery is the **Hall of Echoes**, where the sound reverberates if you stand with your back to the wall and thump your chest with your fist – as Cambodians do, thrice, to bring good fortune.

Second and third levels

The **second level** of the pyramid is enclosed by a gallery with windows to the courtyard within, into whose walls are carved a remarkable collection of over 1500 **apsaras**, each one unique. Elegantly dressed, these beautiful creatures display exotic hairstyles and enigmatic expressions; even their jewellery is lovingly carved. These are the earliest depictions in Angkorian art of apsaras in groups, some posed in twos or threes, arms linked and hands touching.

During the time of Suryavarman II, only the high priest and the king were allowed to visit the **third level**, though until recently visitors were allowed to make the ascent. Sadly, though perhaps not surprisingly, this level has now been closed to visitors following a number of injuries and fatalities suffered by tourists losing their footing on the steep steps.

Phnom Bakheng and Prasat Baksei Chamkrong

The first monument to be built in the Angkor area, the temple-mountain of **Phnom Bakheng** was built by Yasovarman I in 889 at the heart of the first kingdom of Cambodia. The summit commands a magnificent view over the West Baray, Angkor Wat and, further afield, south to the Tonle Sap lake and northeast to Phnom Kulen. In the late afternoon, hundreds of tourists make the trek up the steep, badly eroded steps, hewn out of the rock, to watch the sun set over Angkor Wat. At the foot of the hill, **elephants** are sometimes on hand to ferry weary visitors up the hill via a roundabout track ($15 up, $10 down). The best time to see Phnom Bakheng itself is in the early morning, when you'll practically have the temple to yourself, with just a couple of grazing elephants for company.

It was no simple task to convert the natural 67-metre-high hill into a symbolic representation of **Mount Meru**. Steps and terraces were hewn into the rock of the hill and then clad in sandstone, while a moat (originally 4km square) was dug around the hill in line with Hindu cosmology – part of it is still visible on the road in from Siem Reap, 600m before Angkor Wat. The temple pyramid, comprising five levels, has a total of 109 sanctuary towers: 44 around its base, twelve on each level, plus five principal towers at the top arranged, for the first time in Khmer architecture, in a quincunx, supposed to symbolized the five peaks of Mount Meru. The temple was consecrated to Shiva and the central tower would have contained a linga.

A few hundred metres north of Phnom Bakheng is the small, often ignored **Prasat Baksei Chamkrong**, the sole monument built by Harshavarman I. Consecrated to Shiva and his consort, the temple wasn't finished in the king's lifetime, and was re-consecrated by Rajendravarman I in 947. The simple temple comprises four square tiers of decreasing size, rising to a single brick sanctuary tower with decorated sandstone lintels and columns. A Sanskrit inscription on the doorframe here records that the sanctuary contained a golden image of Paramenshavara, as Jayavarman II was known posthumously. If you want to head up to the top of the temple, the northern staircase is the best of a badly worn bunch.

Angkor Thom

"The wall of the city is some five miles in circumference. It has five gates each with double portals... Outside the wall stretches a great moat, across which access to the city is given by massive causeways. Flanking the causeways on each side are fifty-four divinities resembling war-lords in stone, huge and terrifying..."

Still recognizable from this description by the Chinese envoy Chou Ta-Kuan, who visited the Khmer court at the end of the thirteenth century, the great city of **Angkor Thom** (see inset map on p.176) covers an area of three square kilometres, enclosed by a wide moat and an eight-metre-high wall reinforced by a wide earth embankment (constructed by Jayavarman VII after the city had been sacked by the Cham in 1177). Numerous monuments are contained within the city. At the centre is the state-temple, the **Bayon**, one of the great sights of Angkor, dominated by huge faces looking out from its many towers, and boasting two enclosures of bas-reliefs.

North of the Bayon, Jayavarman VII had to squeeze his royal palace (which was built largely of wood, and thus has not survived) into a space between the **Baphuon** – the state-temple of Udayadityavarman II – and **Phimeanakas** – the tiny state-temple of Suryavarman I. In front of the palace he had two huge, gloriously carved **terraces** constructed, to be used as viewing platforms over the royal square and parade grounds.

The entry gates

A laterite wall 8m high, reinforced by a wide earth embankment, runs around the full perimeter of Angkor Thom's moat. The wall has a sanctuary tower at each corner and **five entry gates** – one per cardinal direction, plus an additional eastern portal, the Victory Gate. Actually elaborate gopuras, the gates each feature a tower topped by four huge faces of the benevolent Bodhisattva, Lokesvara, who looks out to each cardinal direction; these were in fact added at a later date.

The site is invariably approached from Angkor Wat through the 23-metre-high **south gate** and along a hundred-metre-long **stone causeway** flanked by 54 almond-eyed gods on one side, and 54 round-eyed demons on the other (though most of the heads are actually replicas, the originals having been either stolen or removed to Angkor Conservation for safety). Both gods and demons hold nine-headed nagas, which are said to protect the city's wealth. The base of the gateway itself is decorated with sculptures of **Indra** on a three-headed elephant; the elephant's trunks hold lotus blossoms which droop to the ground, cleverly forming columns that help support the rest of the sculpture.

The Bayon

From the south gate, the road runs 1.5km through the forest straight to the **Bayon**. You can take an elephant ride to the Bayon from the stand by the south causeway ($10-15). Arriving by car or moto, you'll be dropped at the main approach, from the east, and the driver will go around to the north side to wait for you. Most people visit in the morning, when the light is at its best.

Built in the late twelfth or early thirteenth century, the Bayon was intended to embrace all the religions of the kingdom, including the Islamic beliefs of the newly conquered Cham, but was consecrated as a Buddhist temple; when the state religion reverted to Hinduism, the Buddha in the central sanctuary was torn down and cast into the well beneath. As you approach from the south, all you can initially see down the avenue is a mass of ill-defined stone, dark and imposing. It's only after crossing the stone causeway that the intricacy of the Bayon's design – whether achieved by happy accident or by Jayavarman VII's design isn't known – becomes apparent, and you begin to make out the 54 towers with their massive faces of Lokesvara, more than two hundred in all; exactly why they are repeated so many times remains unclear.

Across the causeway, a few steps lead up to the **third enclosing wall**, a colon-naded gallery whose roof has long since collapsed. Its outer walls bear the first of the temple's **bas-reliefs**, deeper and less fine than those at Angkor Wat (and some are unfinished). Having viewed these, most people follow the passage from the middle of the south gallery to reach the bas-reliefs of the **second enclosing wall**, raised up about 1.5m above the level of the third enclosure. These carvings aren't in great condition, however, so if you're tired of studying yet more multi-armed gods you might as well look out just for those specimens we point out.

Both sets of bas-reliefs were intended to be viewed **clockwise**, starting from the **midpoint of the eastern wall**; this is how they are described below.

▲ The Bayon

Third enclosing wall bas-reliefs: southern half

Heading south along the gallery from the east approach, you'll see a **military procession** depicted on three levels; bareheaded soldiers with short hair march across the uppermost level, while the level just below depicts troops with goatee beards and elaborate hairstyles. Musicians and bareback cavalry accompany them, the commanders (with parasols) seated on elephants. Close to the next door to the courtyard are the army's camp followers, their covered carts just like those in use today. At the lowest level are some fascinating depictions of everyday domestic and rural scenes, many of them still as true to life now as when they were first carved.

The **southeast corner tower** is unfinished, but its carving of a boat is remarkable for continuing around a right-angle. Turning the corner, you come to the finest of the Bayon bas-reliefs, depicting the 1177 **naval battle** between the Khmer and the Cham on the Tonle Sap lake. The victorious Khmer, led by Jayavarman VII, are shown with bare heads, whereas the Cham wear vaguely floral-looking hats. At the start, the king is seen seated in the palace directing preparations for battle, as fish swim through the trees – as in a rainy-season flood. Along the bottom are more carvings drawn from everyday life on the banks of the **Tonle Sap**: fishing baskets – just like those used now – hang from the ceiling, skewers of food are cooked over a charcoal fire and women are seen picking lice out of one another's hair.

A bit further along, the princesses are shown amusing themselves at the palace, while around them wrestlers spar and a boar-fight takes place. Subsequently battle commences, and the Cham disembark from their boats to carry on the fight on land; the Khmers – with short hair and rope tied around their bodies – are given the appearance of giants, and are, of course, victorious. Back at the palace, **Jayavarman VII** himself looks on as the celebratory feast is prepared.

Only the lower level has been carved on the western side of the south wall, including a panel showing the **armaments** of the day, such as a crossbow deployed from the back of an elephant and a catapult on wheels. The first portion of the western wall is unfinished; look out here for an **ascetic climbing a tree** to escape from a hungry tiger, near the centre of the panel. Towards the centre of the panel, before the gopura, a **street fight** is in progress: people shake their arms in anger, while above, two severed heads are shown to the crowd.

Third enclosing wall bas-reliefs: northern half

In the western gallery, it's worth looking out for a scene showing men with sticks chasing other men with round shields, passing a pond where a large fish is shown swallowing a small deer. Around the corner in the north gallery you'll find a light-hearted **circus** scene, featuring not just the usual jugglers, acrobats and wrestlers but also an animal parade, including rhinoceroses, rabbits and deer. The section beyond the north gopura is badly eroded, though with a bit of effort you can just about make out the **fighting** between the Khmer and Cham resuming, with the Khmer running away towards the mountains. By the time you've turned the corner into the east gallery, the battle is in full swing, and even the elephants are taking part, with one shown trying to rip out the tusk of another.

Second enclosing wall bas-reliefs: southern half

The bas-reliefs of the second enclosing wall are more difficult to follow as they are broken up by towers and antechambers into small panels. Most are of religious and mythological significance, and it's likely these were only seen by

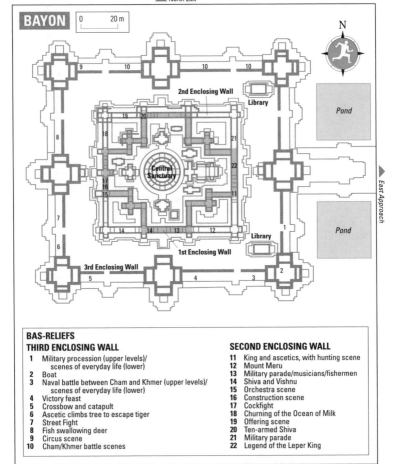

BAYON 0   20 m

2nd Enclosing Wall

Library

Pond

Central Sanctuary

East Approach

1st Enclosing Wall

Library

Pond

3rd Enclosing Wall

N

BAS-RELIEFS

THIRD ENCLOSING WALL

1 Military procession (upper levels)/
   scenes of everyday life (lower)
2 Boat
3 Naval battle between Cham and Khmer (upper levels)/
   scenes of everyday life (lower)
4 Victory feast
5 Crossbow and catapult
6 Ascetic climbs tree to escape tiger
7 Street Fight
8 Fish swallowing deer
9 Circus scene
10 Cham/Khmer battle scenes

SECOND ENCLOSING WALL

11 King and ascetics, with hunting scene
12 Mount Meru
13 Military parade/musicians/fishermen
14 Shiva and Vishnu
15 Orchestra scene
16 Construction scene
17 Cockfight
18 Churning of the Ocean of Milk
19 Offering scene
20 Ten-armed Shiva
21 Military parade
22 Legend of the Leper King

the king and his priests, unlike the scenes in the third gallery, which would have been accessible to the hoi polloi. Interestingly, although the Bayon was dedicated as a Buddhist temple, there are plenty of depictions here of **Hindu gods**.

In the vestibule south of the east gopura, a **hunt** is shown in progress, below which the king is shown tarrying in the palace and surrounded by ascetics. The wall is a bit crumbled as you turn the corner into the south gallery, but it's possible to make out **Mount Meru** rising out of the ocean – here denoted by the fish. Moving on, beyond the tower, warriors **parade** from left to right, while a band of musicians leaves the palace. Below, a dead child is being placed in a coffin; close by, a fisherman casts his net from his boat, while apsaras hover above. **Shiva and Vishnu** appear in numerous, mostly worn, scenes in the section west of the south gopura; towards the end of this section you'll see Shiva standing in a pool while ascetics and animals look on from the bank; in the same area people prostrate themselves around Vishnu, while a funeral is in progress.

In the west gallery, pop into the tower before the gopura and you'll find an **orchestra** playing celestial music while the apsaras dance. Labourers hauling stones over rollers and lifting them into place can be seen in a curious **construction scene**, which oddly enough has had a depiction of Vishnu superimposed on it; you'll find this on the tiny section of gallery between the tower and the gopura. Just before the gopura is a harbour scene, where chess players get on with a game on board one of the boats, and a **cockfight** takes place on another.

Second enclosing wall bas-reliefs: northern half

The first few sections of carvings after the west gopura are in poor condition, so head straight to the section of gallery north of the tower, where there's yet another depiction of the story of the **Churning of the Ocean of Milk** (see p.183). In the centre of the panel, Vishnu, as the tortoise Kurma, holds up the mountain, while gods and demons can be made out hard at work churning. The reliefs around the corner in the north gallery are in better nick; in the first section servants are shown carrying **offerings** to a mountain sanctuary, while boats ferry in worshippers; look out for elephants and other wildlife in the mountains. Beyond the western tower, it's worth pausing to check out the pantheon of gods: a fine ten-armed **Shiva** is flanked by Vishnu on his right and Brahma on his left, and surrounded by apsaras.

Turning the corner, you're back in the east gallery, where there's a **military parade** featuring musicians accompanying cavalry, and a six-wheeled chariot drawn by Hamsa, the sacred goose and mount of Brahma. The final panel of note, in the gallery just before the gopura, pertains to the legend of the **Leper King**, in which the king contracts leprosy after being spattered with the venom of a serpent he fights; as women minister to the king, a cure is sought from ascetics.

The first enclosure and central sanctuary

Besides corner towers, the second enclosing wall appears to have a further three towers per side; these are actually part of the **first enclosing wall**, which takes the form of a toothed cross, the points of which merge into the second enclosing wall. The complexity of the construction is compounded in the first enclosure, where towers bearing four faces stand closely packed, at each angle of the cross and on the small sanctuaries.

Whichever route you take into the first enclosure, you'll be presented with a veritable forest of towers, their massive multiple heads all wearing an enigmatic expression and the glimmer of a smile. Unusually in Khmer architecture, the low platform of the central sanctuary is more or less circular, with eight linked **meditation chambers** spaced around it.

Baphuon

The eleventh-century **Baphuon**, the state-temple of Udayadityavarman II, is currently undergoing restoration and is closed to the public until the work is completed (restoration originally commenced in 1959 but had to be abandoned in 1971 because of war and didn't restart until 1995). It's worth at least taking in the approach from the east, via an impressive sandstone causeway (restored) 200m long and raised on three sets of stone posts, although the remains of the soaring temple-mountain bear little resemblance to the "tower of bronze" described by Chou Ta-Kuan. A cruciform gopura, topped by a lotus-petal motif, contains engaging square carvings depicting the animals of Chinese astrology. A path around the outside leads to a small display detailing the restoration work in progress.

Once comprising five tiers, the pyramid had galleries running round the full circumference on its first, second and third levels. The full length of the west side of the fourth level is taken up with a gigantic **reclining Buddha**.

Phimeanakas

Suryavarman I constructed his small state-temple, **Phimeanakas**, which Chou Ta-Kuan described as a "tower of gold", within the grounds of his royal palace, which preceded that of Jayavarman VII and was the first palace to be built within fortifying walls. Subsequently it was absorbed into Angkor Thom, which was built around two hundred years later. These days, Phimeanakas is usually reached by a short northward trek from the Baphuon through the jungle.

This three-tier laterite temple is relatively simple, rectangular in shape, with damaged elephants at the corners of each level and lions flanking the stairs. The temple is designed to be approached from the east; the stairs up to the top are steep and narrow and don't allow you to step off onto the first two levels. Once at the top, you can walk around the surrounding gallery, at whose centre a single cross-shaped sanctuary tower is raised on a platform. Chou Ta-Kuan records that the sanctuary was said to be home to a **spirit** that took the form of a serpent by day and a beautiful lady after dark. The king was meant to visit her every night before seeing his wife or else disaster would follow. To the north of the temple are two paved bathing ponds, the smaller for women, the larger for men.

Terrace of the Elephants

East of Phimeanakas lies the **Terrace of the Elephants**, a fabulous bas-relief frieze of near-life-sized elephants stretching some 300m. The elephants and their mahouts are shown in profile, mostly hunting, though some are depicted fighting with tigers. Having scrutinized the elephants, it's worth going up onto the terrace behind to get a view over the grounds and, while you're there, to check out the parade of waddling **geese** carved into a low wall atop the terrace at the northern end.

The palace of Jayavarman VII would have stood on the terrace, the edge of its grounds marked by a laterite wall, of which only a ruined gopura remains. The southern steps down from the terrace to the parade ground continue the theme of the frieze, decorated with three-headed elephants, their trunks delicately entwined around lotus buds; in a separate frieze around the terrace, **garudas** stand with wings outstretched as though they alone are supporting the walkway.

Terrace of the Leper King

Adjoining the Terrace of the Elephants, the **Terrace of the Leper King** is believed by scholars to have been the site of royal cremations; appropriately, the headless statue on the terrace is that of Yama, god of the underworld, although the vandalized statue is in fact a reproduction. For many years, the statue was assumed to depict the Leper King, Jayavarman VII himself, who several legends say contracted the disease – although there is nothing to verify this.

The real thing to see here, though, are the two walls – one behind the other with a narrow gap between them – which have been fully restored and boast elaborately bejewelled gods, goddesses and multi-headed nagas, up to seven tiers high. The inner wall is the original – it's assumed that the outer wall was built to allow the terrace above to be extended.

Tep Pranam and Preah Palilay

Tep Pranam, 100m north of the Terrace of the Leper King, dates from the ninth-century reign of Yasovarman I, but was added to over several centuries. Today, it's only worth visiting to see the six-metre-high seated Buddha, dating perhaps from the sixteenth century and reconstructed from the pieces found at the site. At **Preah Palilay**, set in a quiet wooded patch west of Tep Pranam, only the central sandstone sanctuary – dating from the first half of the twelfth century – remains in reasonable condition. It too has a large seated Buddha, of modern provenance.

Prasat Suor Prat and the Kleangs

Opposite the royal terraces, twelve two-storey laterite-and-sandstone towers, each with doors on two sides and windows on three, are currently being restored; they're known collectively as **Prasat Suor Prat**, "Towers of the Tightrope Walkers", though their original purpose isn't known. One legend has it that they were places for resolving disputes – the parties and their families had to sit facing each other until one or other party became ill and so was deemed liable to pay reparations.

Behind Prasat Suor Prat are the **Kleangs** which, as befits their name (meaning "storeroom"), comprise two enormous warehouse-like buildings, with 1.5m thick wall, and open at both ends. The North Kleang is the older of the two and was erected towards the end of the tenth century, possibly by Jayavarman V or Jayaviravarman. The unfinished South Kleang is thought to have been constructed by Suryavarman I to balance the view from the royal palace.

You can leave Angkor Thom by taking the road between the Kleangs, which leads east to the **Victory Gate**, or return to the Terrace of the Leper King and head north.

Thomannon and Chau Say Tevoda

From the Victory Gate, it's only 500m to the tiny temples of **Thomannon** and **Chau Say Tevoda**, nestled in the jungle either side of the road, and another 200m further to a **bridge** built using carved sandstone from nearby temples. Once spanning the Siem Reap River, the bridge is now rather stranded, the river having shifted its course. If you step off the road you'll be able to spot the mismatched carvings visible on some of the stones, which were probably recycled from elsewhere when the bridge was rebuilt in the sixteenth century.

Thomannon

Consecrated to Vishnu, **Thomannon** was built by Suryavarman II in the early twelfth century, towards the end of his reign. Originally surrounded by a high laterite wall and moat, and approached from the east, the temple is nowadays approached from the road to the south, and you'll need to traverse the dry moat and clamber over a collapsed wall en route.

The sanctuary and gopuras were restored in 1935 and are in a good state. There are some decent **carvings** too. Vishnu is shown holding a foe by the hair on the north pediment of the elaborate eastern gopura, and elegant female divinities and fine leaf designs decorate the central sanctuary, reached via a reception hall to the east. The attractive western gopura is smaller than its eastern counterpart, with some tiny human figures decorating the door columns and a depiction of Vishnu on Garuda fighting demons above the door.

Chau Say Tevoda

The sister temple to Thomannon, **Chau Say Tevoda** also dates from the reign of Suryavarman II, but it's unlikely that either temple was completed before his death in 1150. More elaborate than its sibling across the road, but badly eroded, the temple was recently restored by Chinese conservators. The site was surrounded by a laterite wall – now mostly disappeared – with gopuras to the four directions, and designed to be approached from the east across a raised causeway. Much of the site is cordoned off, but it's worth looking at the octagonal columns of the raised causeway, and there are some stylish floral decorations on the long hall which connects the eastern gopura and the central sanctuary.

Ta Keo

At the western end of the East Baray reservoir, **Ta Keo**, the imposing state-temple of Jayavarman V, was begun around 975 but never finished; legend has it that construction was abandoned after the temple was struck by lightning, deemed an unlucky omen. Entirely constructed of sandstone, Ta Keo is practically undecorated; some sources say that the particular sandstone used is exceptionally hard and too difficult to carve, although fine carving around the base of the pyramid seems to contradict that view. Particularly stark in appearance, it is best visited in the early morning when the light is less harsh.

Almost the whole eastern side of the outer enclosure is taken up with two long halls to the north and south, their windows looking inward. In an innovative departure from earlier convention, a **gallery** runs the full perimeter of the inner enclosure, though oddly enough it has no entrance and thus seems to have been constructed for appearances only. The gallery's windows are decorated with balusters, but you'll only be able to look through those on the interior – those on the outside are blocked by a stone wall behind, though they're remarkably convincing from a distance.

From here, you can climb one of the steep stairways up the pyramid, which is nearly 14m high. The five sanctuary towers are arranged in the usual quincunx pattern and are dedicated to Shiva. To the east, the view from the top is of rice fields and scrub, the East Baray now being dry.

Ta Prohm

Thanks to the decision to leave the jungle in place, **Ta Prohm** has become one of the most iconic, evocative and photographed of all the ruins. Enormous kapok trees grow from its terraces and walls, their massive roots clinging to the walls, framing doorways and prising apart giant stones. None of the 39 towers is intact and the partly collapsed, maze-like state of the temple makes it difficult to plan a route or work out its layout, which is in fact on a single level, with three closely spaced galleried enclosures in the central area. It doesn't matter if you get a bit disoriented, though, since part of the charm of a visit here is in leaving the well-trodden paths to clamber over collapsed masonry and duck through caved-in galleries. The temple attracts plenty of visitors, but it's usually quiet in the early morning, as mist rises off the algae-covered stones, or in the late afternoon, as the shadows lengthen.

Constructed by Jayavarman VII around 1186, Ta Prohm was a **Buddhist monastery** dedicated to Prajnaparamita, and would once have housed a statue of this deity in the image of the king's mother (inscriptions say that a further 260 holy images were installed in surrounding chambers and niches). As a working monastery it accommodated twelve thousand people, who lived and worked within its grounds, while a further eighty thousand people were employed locally to service and maintain the complex. Additionally, the monastery supplied provisions and medicines to the 102 hospitals that Jayavarman instituted around the kingdom.

The site

The majority of visitors arrive **from Ta Keo** while on the Small Circuit (see p.179), approaching from the west, but if you use the track off the road northwest of Banteay Kdei, you can enter from the east as was originally intended. From Ta Keo, the path meanders off the road and under towering trees for around 300m until it reaches a collapsed causeway which leads across the moat to the ruined western gopura, topped by the four massive faces of a Bodhisattva. Once through the gopura, you reach the three central enclosures, which take the form of **galleries**, by a paved causeway littered with broken statues and the remains of a naga balustrade. Moving quickly through the site, at the third enclosing wall, you can pause briefly to study the reasonably well-preserved gopura and roof of its colonnaded gallery.

Some of the most photographed **trees** in the country lie further in, scattered inside the second and first enclosures, particularly to the north and east. Few people can resist posing against the tree which crawls over the north side of the second enclosure's gallery – watch your step if you do climb up, as the stones are slippery from the wear caused by the tread of hundreds of tourists each day. It's easy to get so caught up in investigating the galleries and searching out new views of the trees that you actually miss seeing the central sanctuary, with collapsed towers at the corners. Remarkably, the carvings on the buildings are well preserved, almost as if nature has compensated for the overall destruction by preserving the details. The interior of the sanctuary is bare, but small holes in the walls indicate that it was once clad in wood or metal panels.

Banteay Kdei

Banteay Kdei (Citadel of the Cells), believed to have been constructed originally by Rajendravarman in the mid-tenth century, could be omitted in favour of the broadly similar Ta Prohm if you're short on time. Having been turned into a monastery by Jayavarman VII, the site remained in fairly continual use as one until the 1960s, and so has been relatively unravaged by nature. That said, the complex has seen some pretty major masonry collapses, which experts believe is due to a combination of the use of low-quality stone and poor building techniques.

You enter Banteay Kdei from the east, opposite Srah Srang, through a cruciform gopura topped with Lokesvara faces. The site was once linked to Srah Srang by a pavement lined with rest houses for pilgrims, the remains of whose paving stones can be seen by the pool. A 300-metre stroll through the forest leads to the remains of a laterite causeway across the moat, by which you reach the **Hall of the Dancing Girls**, named after its reliefs of apsaras on the columns.

Built of sandstone throughout, the central complex lacks a pyramid, as this was never a state-temple. The walls are intricately carved with elaborate leaf motifs, and niches below still contain delightful statues of female divinities; the Buddha images in the niches at the upper level were less fortunate, and have mostly been scratched out. The two galleries around the main sanctuary tower, linked to each other by corridors, are in fact the first and second enclosing walls.

Srah Srang and Prasat Kravan

East of Banteay Kdei lies the royal bathing pool, **Srah Srang**; this was probably the work of Kavindramantha, an army general-cum-architect, who was also responsible for the building of the temples of East Mebon and Pre Rup. Excavated for Rajendravarman I, the pool once had simple earth embankments, and rules had to be issued to stop people allowing elephants to clamber over them to be bathed in the waters. Two hundred years later, Jayavarman VII had the banks lined with sandstone and built a regal terrace offering views over the water. The remains of a paved causeway edged with naga balustrades, which once linked the pools with Banteay Kdei to the west, can also be seen here.

South of Banteay Kdei is the often ignored **Prasat Kravan**, the Cardamom Sanctuary, comprising a row of five brick-and-sandstone towers sitting on a low platform in a field. The structure has a delightful simplicity and a handful of remarkable reliefs, and remains in good condition thanks to restoration which largely made use of the original bricks. The sanctuary is known to have been consecrated around 921, during the reign of Harshavarman I, though who commissioned it is a mystery.

The central tower, dedicated to Vishnu, is decorated with male guardians in niches on its exterior, but the main interest is in the brick reliefs of Vishnu inside. Here the god is depicted in several different guises: one shows him mounted on Garuda; another shows his dwarf incarnation – taking three steps to span the universe. A rather worn rendering of Vishnu with eight arms was probably once covered in stucco and painted. The northernmost tower is dedicated to Lakshmi, wife of Vishnu and goddess of good fortune; inside you'll find a skilfully carved relief of her, bare-breasted and wearing a pleated *sampot*, flanked by two kneeling worshippers and surrounded by swags of leaves and dangling pendant motifs.

Pre Rup

Back at Srah Srang, you can join the Grand Circuit by following the road east through paddy fields and scrub forest until you see the towers of **Pre Rup**, its name literally meaning "turning the body", a reference to a cremation ritual. Consecrated to Shiva around 962, this state-temple of Rajendravarman II was built primarily of laterite and brick, the materials giving it a warmth lacking in many sandstone monuments.

An archetypal temple-mountain, Pre Rup is seen in its full majesty from the west, when it stands out against the rice fields. The ruined eastern gopura gives access to the second enclosure, its eastern side mostly taken up with two groups of **tall brick towers** – the pair to the north have space for a third tower which was never built. Long halls, now mostly ruined, line the first enclosure, giving it the appearance of having had a gallery, though in fact Pre Rup was the last

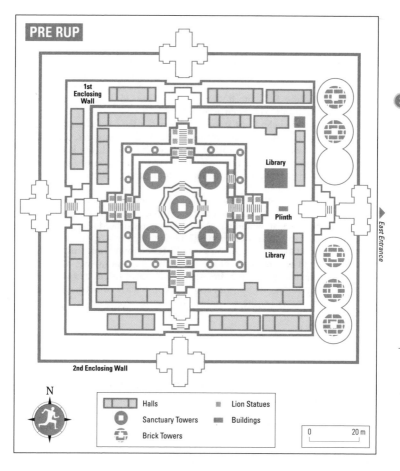

PRE RUP

1st Enclosing Wall

Library

Plinth

Library

2nd Enclosing Wall

East Entrance

N

Halls

Sanctuary Towers

Brick Towers

Lion Statues

Buildings

0   20 m

temple to be built without one. Right in front of you as you enter this enclosure is a small stone cistern, which was for some time assumed to be associated with cremations, though more recently it's been suggested that it might have been a pedestal for a statue. The three levels of holes you'll spot in the brick libraries which flank the pathway leading to the enclosure were in fact for ventilation. An unusual feature in the northeast corner of the enclosure is a small, square, laterite building – open on all sides – which may once have housed a stele.

Stairways guarded by lions lead up all four sides of the **pyramid**, around whose lowest level stand twelve symmetrically placed small shrines. Two extra sets of stairs on the eastern side lead up to the top from the middle level, but these are impossible to get to as they're positioned right behind the small sanctuaries. **Female divinities** are featured in the carved reliefs on the western sanctuary towers, including a female aspect of Brahma on the southwest tower (here you'll spot remnants of the gritty white stucco that once coated the towers); **male carvings** adorn the central and eastern towers. From the summit, you'll get a fine view across the forest canopy to the towers of Angkor Wat on the western horizon.

East Mebon

Erected in 953 for Rajendravarman, the **East Mebon** superficially has the appearance of a state-temple, but was actually built for the king's parents and consecrated to Shiva. The temple stands marooned in rice fields, though the spot was once an island surrounded by the East Baray, now dry; the broad steps which give onto the wide laterite terrace were originally landing stages, since the temple would only have been accessible by boat.

The almost life-sized **elephant statues** positioned at the corners of the temple's two levels were placed there as guardians, and so face outwards. The **outer enclosure**, lined with a series of ruined meditation halls which would have been roofed with wood, features a reasonably preserved carving on the lintel of its western gopura; here you'll find Vishnu in his incarnation as a man-lion, ripping apart the king of the demons.

Pairs of brick-and-sandstone towers flank the steps on each side of the first enclosure, and feature fine decorations of leaf patterns on their false doors. You'll also spot five rectangular, windowless laterite buildings arrayed here, open to the west; their function remains unknown. The five brick sanctuary towers were originally covered in stucco, and you can still see the round holes made to help the coating key. The **carvings** on the sandstone lintels are worth a look: the central tower features Indra on a three-headed elephant (on its east side), Shiva on Nandin (south), Skanda on a peacock (west), while Ganesh has hitched a ride on his own trunk on the east side of the northwest tower.

Ta Som

Once a Khmer Rouge hideout, **Ta Som** was built by Jayavarman VII in the twelfth century and dedicated to his father. Though this tiny Buddhist temple is badly dilapidated as a whole, many of the decorations are still in reasonable condition, and the site retains its charm, feeling like a miniature Ta Prohm without the hordes of visitors. Visitors approach from the road which runs west past the temple, where Bodhisattvas look down from the four cardinal directions. Inside the broad moat, a **gallery** surrounds the main sanctuary, its outer surface embellished with fetching apsaras in niches. Some of these figures are quite unusual – one is wringing out her hair and another has a bird nestling in her tiny hand. The **sanctuary** itself is a single, crumbling cruciform tower and is best approached from the north to minimize the amount of rubble you'll need to climb over. Before you leave the site, it's worth walking out to the **eastern gopura** to see the huge Bodhisattva heads enclosed by the roots of a great kapok tree.

Neak Pean

Originally standing on an island in the northern baray, **Neak Pean** (literally "entwined serpents") uniquely consists of a number of pools joined by walkways, with a single tower sitting in the centre of the largest pool. Scholars dispute the symbolism behind all this, with the most popular theory being that Neak Pean was built to represent Anavatapa, a mythical Himalayan lake whose waters had miraculous curative powers; the temple may even have been a spa, with pilgrims coming to take the waters.

Besides a small island where the sanctuary tower is situated, the **main pool**, 70m square, contains a large statue of a horse with people clinging to its sides; legend has it that Lokesvara turned himself into a horse, Balaha, to rescue merchants who were being attacked by ogresses on an island off Sri Lanka. It's a lazy spot where you may well be able to listen to classical Khmer (*pinpeat*) musicians who play gongs and drums here for visitors. The pool sometimes fills with water in the rainy season, and for much of the rest of the time it's boggy, which means the tower, open to the east and topped by a lotus flower, isn't easy to reach. Even if you can't get over to the island, you'll be able to spot the steps formed from coiled stone serpents, which curl round the base of the tower (hence the temple's unusual name). When the site was a working temple, the main pool would have fed water to smaller peripheral pools; at each cardinal direction, water was directed through ceremonial spouts where pilgrims doused themselves. Each spout takes the form of a head – human to the east, a horse's to the west, a lion's to the south and an elephant's to the north.

Preah Khan

Preah Khan was built by Jayavarman VII on the site of an earlier royal city, Jayasri, and the king came to live here while he was restoring Angkor Thom after it was sacked by the Cham in 1177. The **sacred sword**, as the temple's name translates, is said to have been a weapon ceremonially passed by Jayavarman II to his heir, and Cambodians still believe that whoever possesses this sword has the right to the country's throne – a replica of the sword is still believed to be kept under lock and key at the Royal Palace in Phnom Penh.

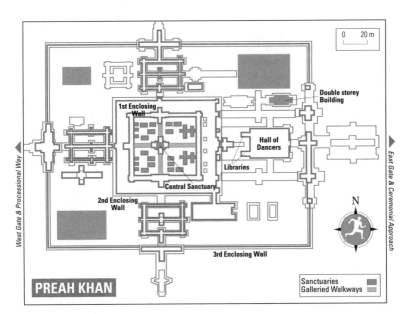

3

The site functioned as both a **monastery** and a **university** for a considerable time; as the latter, it employed over a thousand teachers and 97,840 ancillary staff – inscriptions found here reveal that a daily delivery of ten tonnes of rice was made, enough to feed ten to fifteen thousand people. However, in 1191 Preah Khan was consecrated as an inter-denominational temple, catering to worshippers of Buddha, Shiva and Vishnu, plus a further 282 gods, some made in the image of local dignitaries and national heroes, though the main deity was Lokesvara, made in the image of the king's father, and placed in the central – Buddhist – sanctuary.

Today, despite the temple's semi-collapsed state, the algae- and lichen-encrusted sandstone, surrounded by majestic jungle, lends it an almost enchanted appearance. Some experts attribute the ruinous state to faulty construction – the central area, closely packed with sanctuaries and passages, was extended on numerous occasions. Restoration is ongoing, by the World Monuments Fund, and the main passages are largely cleared of rubble, but some side passages and courtyards are cordoned off; one way to explore the jumble of ruins is to walk right through the centre at first, then dive off in different directions on the way back.

The site

Surrounded by four enclosing walls and a moat, with gopuras and causeways in each cardinal direction, Preah Khan is these days normally approached from the road to the west, along the Grand Circuit just north of Angkor Thom. Extending out here is the outermost enclosing wall, made of laterite and decorated with massive garudas spaced at fifty-metre intervals. From the road, it's a 500-metre stroll to the temple down the processional approach, lined with ceremonial lanterns; niches here once contained Buddha images, which were crudely cut out when the state religion reverted to Hinduism. A display pavilion on the way gives a picture of ongoing restoration work.

Entering the tranquil **third enclosure** you'll see a series of temple buildings which have been encroached upon by towering **kapok** trees. Even more appealing are the gorgeous **carvings** that grace the walls of the main temple buildings within the **first enclosure**, while floral motifs and bands of carved ornamentation enliven the pillars. Also dotted around here are more than twenty tiny sanctuaries which once contained the temple's holy images (Shiva or Vishnu) – more would have been housed in the alcoves of the surrounding gallery. To the south lie the sanctuaries of previous kings – when the temple was consecrated, the deity of Yasovarman II was given the central place, but it was later moved to make way for the deity of Jayavarman VII.

There should be no problems spotting the **central sanctuary**, which contains a dome-shaped **stupa**, added in the sixteenth century. More tricky to find in a collapsed section to the north are two sublime carvings of the sisters **Indradevi** and **Jayadevi**, who were both wives of Jayavarman – you'll need to ask your guide or the temple guards how to find them.

Further on, the eastern side of the second enclosure contains a number of structures, most notably a terrace, surrounded by columns and carved with dancing apsaras; and a two-storey building to the northeast, which it's thought may have housed the sacred sword.

West Baray and West Mebon

Accessible only via the airport road from Siem Reap, Angkor's huge **West Baray**, 8km long and 2.2km wide, was excavated by Suryavarman I; experts calculate that six thousand men would have needed over three years to dig out this reservoir. It was restored in 1957 and, unlike the East Baray, contains water throughout the year, making it a popular local spot for picnics and swimming. Rest huts line the embankment at the leisure area to the south, which is also where you can hire a boat ($5) out to the island-temple, the **West Mebon**. This mid-eleventh-century temple, attributed to Udayadityavarman II, has practically disappeared; only the eastern towers, bearing small decorations of animals in square motifs, are in reasonable condition. The island on which it stands was once linked to the shore by a causeway, and surrounded by a rectangular wall with three pavilions per side and windows overlooking the baray. The huge bronze sculpture of a reclining **Vishnu** was recovered from here, and would have been the main image in the central sanctuary.

Roluos Group

Off National Route 6, 12km east of Siem Reap, the group of temples now referred to as **Roluos** – after the nearby village of that name – is spread out over the former site of the royal city of **Hariharalaya**, and encompasses some of the earliest monuments of the Angkor period. Among those most easily visited are three brick-and-sandstone temples built by Indravarman I and his son, Yasovarman I, in the late ninth century, all featuring finely decorated columns and lintels. These are the **Bakong**, the first state-temple of the Angkor period; **Lolei**, which boasts particularly fine Sanskrit inscriptions; and **Preah Ko**, which preserves some elegant carvings despite its being one of the oldest of Angkor's temples.

Preah Ko

Preah Ko was built by Indravarman I in 879 to honour the spirits of his ancestors, as well as one of his predecessors, Jayavarman II. Nearly square in plan, the temple is entered from the east through the second enclosing wall (the third and outermost wall has pretty much disappeared) via a ruined laterite gopura with sandstone columns and over a crumbling terrace. Within the second enclosure, the most interesting of a number of buildings is the square brick structure with holes in the walls, which may have been a library or crematorium; look out for the **frieze of ascetics** seated in niches above the holes.

At the centre of the temple, on a low platform, stand two groups of brick-and-sandstone sanctuary **towers**. Sacred bulls – sadly now vandalized – guard each of the front three towers, which were dedicated to the king's paternal ancestors and bear carvings of male guardians; correspondingly, the three smaller rear towers, slightly offset on the platform, were dedicated to the maternal ancestors and have female guardians. Among the false doors, the west one of the centre rear tower is an oddity, being of plain brick, while all the others are of beautifully carved sandstone. While you're here, check out the leaf, floral and geometrical designs of the carvings on the octagonal door columns, which rank among the finest in Khmer art. The lintels are also splendidly decorated with garlands and several representations of *kala*, and, remarkably, patches of stucco can still be seen.

Bakong

The **Bakong** is regarded as the first of the state-temples of the Angkor period, having been constructed by Indravarman I and consecrated to Shiva in 881.

The central sanctuary is a sympathetic addition built some 250 years later, and remains in particularly good condition, having been restored in 1940 from original materials.

The temple has four enclosures but only three enclosing walls – the outermost enclosure, where you'll find the remains of 22 brick towers amid jungle and rice fields, is contained within a moat. Close to the parking area and refreshment stalls are the remains of a causeway and naga balustrade, all that's left within the third enclosure.

There's nothing of significance within the second enclosure, so head on to the ruined buildings of the **first enclosure**, where you'll find some sizeable square brick towers, the survivors of a set of eight. Their sandstone false doors display some fine carvings; on the northeast tower one door even has false carved handles. Also here are two square buildings with ventilation holes in their walls, probably crematoria.

The **pyramid** at the centre of the enclosure has five tiers, topped by a single sanctuary tower. Spaced out around the fourth tier are twelve small sandstone sanctuary towers, now empty, though they would once have housed linga.

Lolei

Now within the grounds of a modern pagoda, **Lolei** originally stood on an artificial island in the centre of the **Indratataka Baray**, though the reservoir is now drained and the temple looks out over paddy fields. The temple was dedicated to the parents and maternal grandparents of Yasovarman I and consecrated to Shiva, and originally consisted of four brick towers, though one has now collapsed and the others are crumbling. Lolei is worth a visit even so to see the well-preserved Sanskrit inscriptions in the doorways of the rear towers, detailing the work rotas of temple servants.

Banteay Samre

Remote from the popular sites, **Banteay Samre** lies east of **Phum Pradak**, a village 12km northeast of Siem Reap. You'll have to brave an atrocious road to reach the site, which consequently doesn't attract many visitors despite having been superbly restored. No inscriptions have been found to date the temple, which was named after the Samres, a tribe who lived in the vicinity of Phnom Kulen. However, its style of architecture places its construction in the middle of the twelfth century, around the same time as Angkor Wat.

Banteay Samre is unique among the Angkor temples in having **two moats** within the complex itself. The temple, enclosed by a high laterite wall with cruciform gopuras to each direction, is approached via a 200-metre-long paved causeway which was originally edged by a naga balustrade. Entering through the east gopura, you arrive in an open gallery whose rows of sandstone columns were once part of a roofed walkway which would have run the full perimeter of the enclosure. The paved sunken area ahead was once the first of the moats, forming the second enclosure. Tales from the *Ramayana* are depicted on various **carvings** here – the siege of Lanka is shown on the gopura pediments, the fight between Rama and Ravana on the east tower, and Rama carried by Hanuman on the north tower.

Crossing the moat, you're immediately within another cruciform gopura, with double vestibules to the north and south, the passages of which connect to a raised walkway that separates the two moats. Rising out of the inner moat like islands are the **central sanctuary**, connected to the walkway via a gopura to the east, and two **libraries**, which would only have been reachable by boat when the moats were filled.

Banteay Srei and Kbal Spean

Even if you're feeling pretty templed-out, you'll probably be captivated by **Banteay Srei**, 30km northeast of Siem Reap. Built of fine-grained rose-pink sandstone, it's the most elaborately decorated of all Angkor's monuments, its walls, false doors, lintels and exotic soaring pediments all richly embellished with floral motifs and *Ramayana* scenes. Comprising just a single level, it's positively diminutive compared with the region's state-temples. A little way further out from Siem Reap, at **Kbal Spean**, you can trek along the river to see fabulous scenes of Hindu gods and sacred linga carved into the river bed.

Banteay Srei is easily **reached** from Siem Reap on a good road; you'll need an Angkor Wat pass to visit. To get to Kbal Spean, head 5km on from the temple until you see the parking area on the left. You don't need an Angkor pass to come here. For **refreshments**, you'll find several reasonable restaurants just before the entrance to Banteay Srei.

Banteay Srei

Banteay Srei was built not by a king, but by two local **dignitaries**, Yajnavaraha, who was a trusted guru to the king, and his brother. It was Rajendravarman I who granted them the land and permission for a temple to be built, but although the sanctuary was consecrated in 967 to Shiva, it was not actually completed until the reign of Jayavarman V.

The temple **layout** is relatively simple, with three enclosing walls, an inner moat and a row of three sanctuary towers at the very centre. If the eastern gopura by which you enter the temple seems oddly stranded, that's because there was never an enclosing wall here – although the buildings just beyond the gopura are deemed to be in the "fourth" enclosure. The volume of tourists trooping past

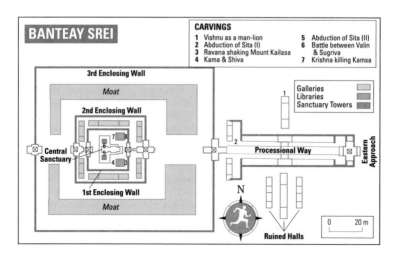

BANTEAY SREI

CARVINGS
1. Vishnu as a man-lion
2. Abduction of Sita (I)
3. Ravana shaking Mount Kailasa
4. Kama & Shiva
5. Abduction of Sita (II)
6. Battle between Valin & Sugriva
7. Krishna killing Kamsa

3rd Enclosing Wall
Moat
2nd Enclosing Wall
Central Sanctuary
1st Enclosing Wall
Moat
Galleries
Libraries
Sanctuary Towers
Processional Way
Eastern Approach
Ruined Halls
N
0   20 m

isn't conducive to lingering here, but it's worth taking a moment to scrutinize the very fine carving above the exterior of the east door, which depicts **Indra** – the sky god, ruling the easterly cardinal direction – squatting on the three-headed elephant Airavana.

From the gopura, a paved **processional way** leads 75m west to the main temple complex. Around the midway point, a pavilion to the north boasts a particularly detailed engraved pediment showing Vishnu in his incarnation as a man-lion. Just before you reach the gopura in the third enclosing wall, you'll find a carved pediment you can admire without craning your neck, as it's lying upright on the ground to the right of the doorway; it shows Sita swooning as she is abducted by Ravana. The gopura itself is one of the most dramatic at the site, with soaring finials and the carved scrolls of fine leaf decorations and floral motifs.

In the rainy season, you'll be treated to marvellous reflections of the temple when the moat within the third enclosure fills. The narrow second enclosure is jammed with six long galleries, each subdivided into rooms which might have been meditation halls.

First enclosure

Virtually no surface within the first enclosure remains unadorned, and all seems perfect in every detail, the site having been **restored** in the 1930s. It's impossible to take in the sheer wealth of decoration here at first glance, so it's a good idea to wander around to get a general feel for the layout before returning to study the details methodically. Unfortunately, due to the large number of visitors and the minuscule size of the chambers, you're no longer allowed inside the sanctuary towers, and the platform on which they stand is roped off to protect the carvings.

The carvings on the **sanctuary towers** are almost fussy in their profusion; the niches around the central sanctuary shelter male **guardians**, while those on the other towers house serene female **divinities**, complete with elegant *sampots* and elaborate jewellery. Crouched near the temple steps are more guardians, mythical figures with animal heads and human bodies; not surprisingly, these are reproductions, the originals having been removed, like many of the best sculptures here, during the French colonial period (they remain at the Guimet museum of Asian art in Paris, despite attempts to have them returned to Cambodia). The *Ramayana* scenes carved on the lintels of the central tower are particularly fine, featuring another depiction of Sita being carried off by Ravana, to the west; and the fight between the monkey gods Valin and Sugriva, to the north. The multi-tiered roofs of the towers are decorated with tiny replicas of the temple towers – meant to be homes for the temple gods.

There are more fine carvings on the east pediment of the **south library**, where Ravana is shown shaking Mount Kailasa; Shiva sits on the mountain's summit with his wife Parvati, while the forest animals run away in fear. On the west pediment, Parvati can be seen asking for the aid of Kama, the god of love, after Shiva ignores her offering of a rosary; she finally wins Shiva's attention and his hand in marriage after Kama obligingly shoots him with an arrow. The **north library** is dedicated to Vishnu, and accordingly the carvings focus on him. The close parallel streaks on the east pediment represent rain pouring down on the forest, through which Krishna – Vishnu's human incarnation – and his brother make their way, surrounded by wild animals. Krishna is seen taking revenge on his cruel uncle, King Kamsa, on the west pediment – note how the palace is in uproar as Krishna seizes him by the hair and prepares to kill him.

Kbal Spean

In a magical area of jungle in the western section of the Kulen Mountains, **Kbal Spean** was used by the Khmer as a hill retreat in the mid-eleventh century, when they carved sacred linga and Hindu gods into the bedrock of the river; the water flowing down the river would thus be blessed by the carvings before coursing on to Angkor. The scenes depicting Vishnu are of marvellous ingenuity, not only for their skilful execution but also for the way they are tailored to the contours of the river bed. Although looters have crudely hacked out some sections of bedrock, the scenes are almost as amazing today as they were when first carved.

The narrow, clearly defined path up from the military camp climbs fairly gently, with a couple of steep stretches; you'll come to the first carvings after about forty minutes' walking. At the top of the hill you can rest awhile on a riverside rock before rolling up your trousers and wading downstream beneath overhanging trees. Further along, as the river deepens, you can either change for a proper swim or do as the Cambodians do and take a clothed shower under the waterfall, before rejoining the track to head back to the bottom.

The Tonle Sap lake

Temples aside, Siem Reap has another unique attraction in the fascinating **Tonle Sap**, the massive freshwater lake that dominates the map of Cambodia. The lake is at once a reservoir, flood-relief system, communications route, home and larder to the people who live on and around it; even Cambodians who live nowhere near depend on it as a rich food source.

At its lowest, in May, just before the rains, the lake covers an area of around 2500 square kilometres. Himalayan **meltwater** flows down the Mekong just as the monsoon rains arrive, causing the level of the river to rise so quickly that at Phnom Penh the pressure is sufficient to reverse the flow of the Tonle Sap River, which would normally drain the lake. As a result of this inflow, each year the lake inundates an area of over ten thousand square kilometres, making it the largest freshwater lake in Southeast Asia. The flow of water reverts to its usual direction in late October or early November, the receding waters leaving behind fertile mud for the planting of rice, and nutrients for the fry which have spawned amid the flooded trees. February sees a bumper fish catch, much of it going to satisfy the insatiable Cambodian appetite for *prohok*.

Fishing is big business on the Tonle Sap, and the government has awarded large concessions to wealthy businessmen at the expense of local fishermen, who have to either practise their trade illegally or rent a share from a concessionaire. The majority of these fishermen are part of the lake's huge itinerant population, mostly stateless ethnic Vietnamese, living in mobile **floating villages** on the lakeshore. The houses – which are utterly basic, with (unscreened) holes in the floor as toilets – are built on bamboo rafts and lashed together to keep them from drifting apart. Despite these Vietnamese villagers having been here for decades, they have not assimilated well into Khmer society and are generally hated by the Khmer.

The lake was designated a UNESCO Biosphere Reserve in 1997 – a status which reconciles sustainable use with conservation. One core area of the reserve, **Prek Toal**, is a sanctuary for a wide range of water birds, including three endangered species – spot-billed pelicans, greater adjutant storks, and white-winged ducks. Prek Toal lies on the northwest edge of the lake in the

▲ A boat heads out onto Tonle Sap

dry season and is easily reached from Siem Reap, though you'll have to take an organized tour (see p.174).

It's easy enough to get out on the lake by hiring a **boat with driver** at the lakeshore ($10–15 for 2hr; each boat takes eight people). In the rainy season, you should head for **Phnom Krom**, 12km southwest of Siem Reap, where the lake laps at the base of the hill at this time of year; in the dry season you'll have to go on to **Chong Khneas**, 5km further along the road from town.

Also moving to and fro with the seasons is the floating office of **GECKO** (Greater Environment Chong Khneas Office; daily 8.30am–5pm), an NGO whose main role is to improve the environmental awareness of the local fishing population. Their exhibition centre (free) houses displays about the local flora and fauna, and an aquarium containing some fish species found in the lake. (If you plan on visiting, it's also worth having a look at Krousar Thmei's exhibition about life on the lake; see p.168.) Alternatively, both Osmose and Terre Cambodge (see p.174) offer a range of pricey **tours** of the lake area using their own boats.

Phnom Krom

If you're hiring a boat at **Phnom Krom**, it's worth heading up the 137-metre hill to the grounds of a modern pagoda on the summit, where there's a ruined tenth-century **temple** built by Yasovarman I. There are commanding **views** over the Tonle Sap from the top, particularly scenic at sunset. The three crumbling sandstone sanctuary towers, dedicated to Vishnu, Shiva and Brahma, stand in a row on a low platform; a few carvings can still be made out, with an apsara evident on the north face of the north tower. To reach the site, take the steep stairway that leads up from behind the petrol station in the village at the foot of the hill.

Floating villages near Siem Riep

A visit to the **floating villages** near Siem Reap isn't quite the authentic ethnic experience that guides in town would have you believe, and it's now all become rather touristy, with all the Siem Reap tour agents offering some sort of trip to the villages and dozens of boats ferrying visitors along the river. The villagers have, naturally enough, capitalized on the interest too by opening a café where many of the boats put in. If you do want to get out to the villages, the most interesting time is during the dry season, when you'll see people fishing in the backwaters and children punting themselves to school as your boat heads down narrow creeks and along the river to reach the lake itself. In the rainy season, you can practically walk from Phnom Krom out to one of the floating villages as they move right up by the hill. Keep in mind that unannounced visits to any village without a local guide may seem like a way of 'seeing the real Cambodia' but more often turns into an exercise of mutual gawking. If despite this, you do decide to visit a village alone, make sure that you make some sort of payment to the village headman, or to those who offer you food or hospitality. Villagers who have made agreements with tour guides will be much happier to receive foreign guests, as visiting times and boundaries will have been worked out, as, most importantly, will some sort of remuneration.

Phnom Kulen

It was at **Phnom Kulen**, then known as Mahendrapura, that Jayavarman II had himself consecrated supreme ruler in 802 (a date that is regarded as marking the start of the Angkorian period), thereby instigating the cult of the devaraja (see p.325). Although ancient temples are scattered here and elsewhere in the Kulen Mountains, none of these can be visited due to the lack of roads and the danger of land mines. Instead, the main reason to visit Phnom Kulen, 50km north of Siem Reap, is to gawp at the massive **reclining Buddha** carved out of a huge rock in the sixteenth century, though once you're here you may find yourself more taken with the piety of the Buddhist devotees who come to worship at a chain of shrines.

You don't need an entry pass to visit Phnom Kulen, but visitors are charged a hefty $20 to visit the site. This, coupled with the cost of hiring a vehicle ($20–50, depending what kind of vehicle and who you hire it from), will keep all but the most dedicated explorers from visiting. However, the scenery along the way is engaging, and there is a small, and very picturesque waterfall nearby.

As the area was heavily mined by the Khmer Rouge and has yet to be cleared, you shouldn't wander off to locations other than those described below unless you have an experienced local guide.

The hill

From the booth at the foot of the hill where you pay the entrance fee, the road climbs steadily through jungle to a sandstone plateau. The first turning you come to, a track on the left, leads to a parking area from where you can walk down to the river and a pleasant little waterfall. You may be able to make out some of the **linga** for which the river is famed, but as they're only 25cm square, they're hard to spot on the riverbed if the waters are high or turbid. A slippery path leads down to the base of the falls, but it's not the most attractive of spots for a swim, with picnic litter everywhere.

Back at the road, it's just 500m on to a small bridge over the river. More linga are carved in the river bed hereabouts, but you'll need a guide to find the spot for you. The road terminates 1km or so further on in a busy parking area surrounded by stalls selling food, refreshments and Khmer medicine. A short climb brings you to a busy pagoda which features a much-revered and rather impressive **reclining Buddha**, carved into a massive boulder – look out for the wonky shack over the top of the rock and the queue of people climbing the steps to it. You'll need to remove your shoes at the bottom of the steps, and once at the top you'll have to squeeze in between Cambodians making offerings and having their photographs taken; from the rock there are good views over the surrounding Kulen Mountains. Around the base of the rock, a simple but impressive frieze of Buddha heads has been carved.

If you've come without a guide, the local children will take you to see the forest **shrines** behind the pagoda – in the hope that you'll come to buy food and refreshments from them before you leave. Alternatively, follow the locals, who come armed with huge bundles of incense to ensure they have enough to make offerings at all the shrines on the circuit. Nearly every boulder has a legend attached to it – one with holes that look like claw marks is said to be where Hanuman crash-landed. At the end of the track, Cambodians come to wash their faces in water from a **holy spring** which gushes from a boulder, believing this will give energy, good health and luck; old bottles are produced and filled to take home.

Beng Mealea

It isn't known exactly when or why the temple of **Beng Mealea**, 60km east of Siem Reap, was built, though experts, making deductions from its stylistic features, have placed its construction in the late eleventh or early twelfth century, possibly by Suryavarman II. The temple, known to have been Hindu, is built on a single level and of impressive size; it has yet to be restored, giving a good idea of what the French archaeologists found when they first arrived at Angkor. Beng Mealea has recently been connected to Angkor and Koh Ker by a graded road, making the site easily accessible as a day-trip from Siem Reap. The site (entry $5) is wonderfully unexplored, and should cost about the same as a trip to Banteay Srei as long as you don't want to make any other stops. If you do, be prepared to add to the basic fare accordingly. The site itself has been de-mined, but you should take care not to stray far beyond the perimeter.

The locals claim that the temple, mostly hidden in scrub, was quite well preserved until the Khmer Rouge looted and destroyed much of it, though Glaize (see p.334) reported it being collapsed in 1944. Just over a kilometre square, with a formidable 45-metre-wide moat, the site was clearly of some consequence, and it has been posited that the temple was built as a precursor to Angkor Wat. All on a single level, the temple once featured three concentric galleries and a central sanctuary tower, though the main attraction of wandering the ruins is to glimpse apsaras peering out of niches amid the jumbled stones. Today, your journey passes through rice paddies and scrub, but it wasn't so long ago that Glaize advocated combining a trip with a hunting party, noting that the area was rich in jungle wildlife, including "tigers, panthers and elephants, herds of oxen and wild buffalo".

Anlong Veng

Some 140km north of Siem Reap near the Thai border, the hot and dusty town of **ANLONG VENG** is of interest solely as the former home and death place of Pol Pot. Fans of places with an edge-of-the-world feel might like this place but most will find it unbearably boring. Accommodation is basic, food is bad, and there are no sights apart from the spot where Pol Pot's body was cremated. Pol Pot actually only lived here for a short time – arriving in 1993 or 1996 depending on whom you believe – before his death, and in fact he didn't stay in the village itself but in a **hideout** up in the Dangkrek Mountains which takes about an hour to reach by moto from the village. Some say he died from a heart attack, but more recently someone has claimed to have witnessed him being murdered by his Khmer Rouge comrades; all we know for sure is that Pol Pot was cremated on a pile of furniture and old tyres close to his house before anyone could verify the details. The sites on which the hut was located and the spot where the hasty cremation took place are signed courtesy of the Deputy Minister of Tourism, and the latter site is maintained by the locals as something of a shrine, though there are only a few blackened rocks to see. The locals are loyal to the memory of Pol Pot, as the Khmer Rouge were benevolent to the people they lived among after their fall in 1979. Bizarrely, Khmers come here in the belief that Pol Pot will reveal winning lottery numbers, heal the sick or provide auspicious luck in some other fashion from the grave.

Back in the village itself, the late Ta Mok, one of the most notorious Khmer Rouge cadres for having been implicated in the murders of three Western backpackers, left behind a house when he died in 2006 (signed "Ta Mok House") – turn left at the traffic circle and then right after the derelict army tanks. He is well regarded locally for creating fishing ponds and endowing a local school, but better known in the world at large as "The Butcher" for having ordered the abduction of three Western backpackers from the Phnom Penh-Sihanoukville train in 1994. They were held for ransom but eventually killed when negotiations fell through. For years there were efforts to have Ta Mok stand trial for the murders, but like so many Khmer Rouge-era killers he died a natural death while Cambodia stalled and quibbled.

Though it's unlikely that you would choose to stay over, there are three **guesthouses** in town – the basic *Reaksmey Angkor* (❶) is the longest-running operation. Rooms are spartan and grubby but this is a legitimate guesthouse and not a brothel, and you will get a better night's sleep here than at the town's other options. There are **restaurants** at each of the guesthouses, and other places serving noodles by the traffic circle. **Pick-ups** to Anlong Veng ($6) leave from the Siem Reap market, and a couple of Siem Reap guesthouses run vans here. It's also possible to get to Anlong Veng from Thailand via the border crossing north of **O'SMACH**. From Thailand the approach is best made via Surin to Sa-Ngam (see p.20), the Thai name for this border crossing. If you're going via Surin, it's a good idea to ask Khun Pirom of *Pirom's Guest House* in Surin what the cheapest or most direct method of transport is. Once you cross into Cambodia, pick-ups at the border market leave for Anlong Veng (5000 riel) throughout the day. From Anlong Veng, pick-ups leave for the border market early in the morning starting at around 5am, and take an hour to make the twenty-kilometre trip. Cambodian and Thai visas are both available on arrival at the border.

Travel details

Buses

Siem Reap to: Battambang (daily; 3hr); Phnom Penh (3–6 daily; 7–11hr); Poipet (3 daily; 2hr 30min).

Shared taxis, minibuses and pick-up trucks

Siem Reap to: Anlong Veng (daily; 3hr); Kompong Thom (12 daily; 3hr); Phnom Penh (hourly; 6–8hr); Poipet (20 daily; 4hr); Sisophon (20 daily; 2hr).

Boats

Siem Reap to: Battambang (twice daily; 3hr 30min); Phnom Penh (1–2 daily; 5hr).

Flights

Siem Reap to: Phnom Penh (6 daily; 45min).

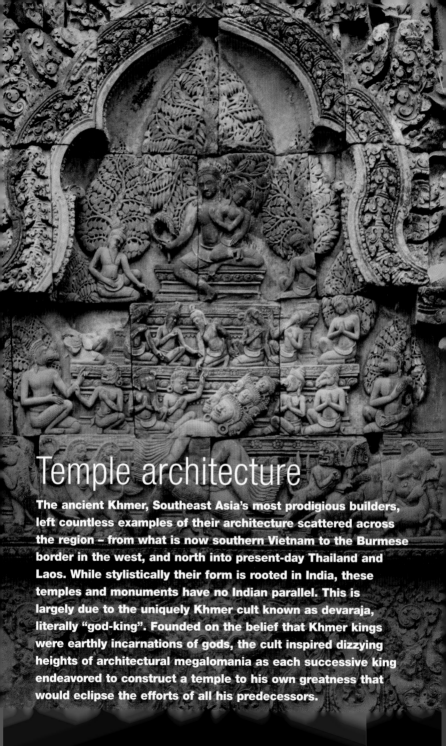

Temple architecture

The ancient Khmer, Southeast Asia's most prodigious builders, left countless examples of their architecture scattered across the region – from what is now southern Vietnam to the Burmese border in the west, and north into present-day Thailand and Laos. While stylistically their form is rooted in India, these temples and monuments have no Indian parallel. This is largely due to the uniquely Khmer cult known as devaraja, literally "god-king". Founded on the belief that Khmer kings were earthly incarnations of gods, the cult inspired dizzying heights of architectural megalomania as each successive king endeavored to construct a temple to his own greatness that would eclipse the efforts of all his predecessors.

Angkor Wat and surrounding Wat ▲

Sunrise, Angkor Wat ▼

Ramayana bas-relief, Angkor Wat ▼

Better by design

While the mathematical equations that dictated the dimensions of Khmer temples are no longer understood, it is known that the ancient Khmer placed great stock in the auspiciousness of **precise measurements**. This can be discerned in the temple layout – most possess a severe symmetry.

A matter of life and death

The majority face **east** to catch the rays of the rising sun, symbolizing life. Angkor Wat, however, faces **west**, the direction of the setting sun – and death.

Religious reflections

Many Khmer temples are actually scale models of the **Hindu-Buddhist universe**, with moats and walls symbolizing the oceans and mountain ranges that encircled five-peaked Mount Meru, the home of the gods, portrayed in Khmer architecture by the central, spiked quincunx formation.

Khmer comics

Equally impressive are the "story telling bas-reliefs" used to striking effect by the ancient Khmer. Illustrating historical events, mythology (such as the *Ramayana* and *Mahabharata*) and exploits of the kings who had them commissioned, the **bas-reliefs** in sandstone cover over a thousand square metres of gallery walls in Angkor Wat alone. Depending on how they were executed, the bas-reliefs could be "read" from panel to panel like pages from a giant comic book. The importance of an image was illustrated by its size in relation to the images around it: a technique also employed in Egyptian art. The bas-reliefs at Angkor Wat depict grand images of the Hindu god Vishnu, his vehicle Garuda, and Vishnu's incarnations as Krishna, Rama and Kurma – evidence that Suryavarman II, the *devaraja* who had Angkor Wat commissioned, believed that he himself was an incarnation of Vishnu.

▲ Apsaras, Angkor Wat

Bring on the dancing girls

To many modern visitors, the most easily admired images on Angkorian temples are the **apsaras**, celestial nymphs that seem to emerge, dancing, from the smooth sandstone walls. Angkor Wat has by far the most sensitively rendered collection of apsaras in the country, and it is readily apparent that the artisans who sculpted them spent much time ensuring that no two were alike.

▲ Angelina Jolie in *Tomb Raider*

▼ South Gate, Angkor Thom

Inspiring Hollywood

Suryavarman II built Angkor Wat, ancient Cambodia's greatest architectural masterpiece, the silhouette of which graces the national flag. Yet it was ancient Cambodia's most prolific builder, Jayavarman VII who produced its most enduring artistic motif: the four colossal stone faces that gaze with blissful detachment from the towers of the Bayon and the gates of Angkor Thom. Not surprisingly, this powerful visual theme – stone visages smiling enigmatically as the roots of mammoth banyan trees threaten to topple them into jumbled heaps – has been used extensively by modern artists, including several **Hollywood film makers**, to symbolize ancient civilizations lost to the ravages of time.

Sculpture at Angkor Thom ▲

Traditional Cambodian dance costume ▼

Tamarind and termites

The building materials used by the ancient Khmer changed over time. Early Angkor-period temples were constructed of **brick**. The most impressive example of brick architecture to be found at Angkor is Prasat Kravan, the interior of which has bas-reliefs carved right into the brick. A type of **stucco** made from such esoteric ingredients as pounded tamarind and the soft earth of termite mounds was used as a medium to sculpt ornamentation for the brick structures. **Laterite**, a porous stone that resembles lava rock, was used for foundations and walls. It was the use of **sandstone**, however, that set Khmer temples apart from those of the ancient Cham, Thai and Burmese, all of whom worked almost exclusively in brick and stucco. As a medium for decoration, soft, and thus easily carveable sandstone allowed the wondrous talent of Khmer sculptors to shine through.

An earthly paradise

While the architecture of the ancient Khmer inspires even in its ruined state, it is important to remember that only the parts of temples built of more resilient materials, such as stone, brick and stucco, have survived. What we do not see are the ornately carved pavilions of **golden teak** that housed troupes of court dancers, minstrels, high priests and the god-kings themselves. Gone, too, are the **sheets of gilded copper** that covered unadorned stone walls and towers; the parasols, banners and tapestries of **delicate silk** that gave colour to dimly-lit galleries and antechambers; and the scent of the finely woven **mats of aromatic grasses** that covered rough stone causeways.

Central Cambodia

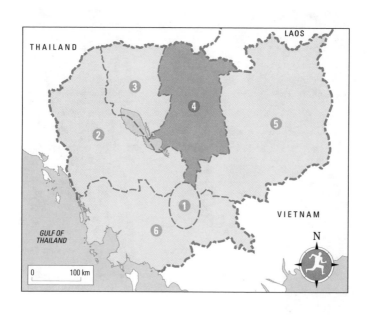

THAILAND

LAOS

③

④

②

⑤

①

VIETNAM

⑥

GULF OF
THAILAND

N

0   100 km

CHAPTER 4

Highlights

✷ **Phnom Suntuk** This bizarre hilltop pagoda is home to a massive rock-carved reclining Buddha. See p.213

✷ **Sambor Prei Kuk** Pre-Angkorian temples uniquely decorated with miniature flying palaces, believed to house the sacred spirits who protect the site. See p.216

✷ **Preah Khan** Once the largest temple in Cambodia, this complex still contains numerous ruined monuments hidden in the undergrowth. See p.219

✷ **Preah Vihear** Imposing temple poised in a spectacular position on a ridge above the Thai border. See p.220

▲ Phnom Suntuk

Central Cambodia

The centre of Cambodia is a forgotten territory stretching north from Phnom Penh through sparsely populated countryside right up to the Thai border. Most of the soil is sandy and barren, and there's practically no way for people to eke out even a basic living, so it's amazing that communities do somehow get by, farming tiny plots and a few scattered rice paddies, and foraging in what remains of the forest. The only really dense vegetation in the region is in the **Boeng Peae Wildlife Reserve**, through which National Route 64 passes on its way north.

The region is hardly a popular tourist destination: all that most visitors see of it are the rice paddies that stretch either side of National Route 6, the major trunk road between the capital and Siem Reap, which cuts across the southern part of the area. But for those prepared to venture into obscure backwaters, central Cambodia has a few ancient temple sites worth visiting, although you'll have to brave the area's largely atrocious roads to reach most of them. The starting point is invariably **Kompong Thom**, the only town of any size hereabouts, and thus also your last taste of comfort for a few days if you're planning a trip north. Thankfully, it's no major expedition if you want to see either **Phnom Suntuk**, a revered though rather kitsch pagoda, or the country's most significant pre-Angkorian site, **Sambor Prei Kuk**, comprising three groups of well-preserved brick-built temples. Beyond here, however, travelling gets much harder, even to reach the massive ruined temple of **Preah Khan**, just 50km further northwest as the crow flies. You'll need to get right to the border to reach the area's jewel, **Preah Vihear**, perched magnificently high on a cliff in the Dangkrek Mountains. Built in the ninth century and added to by a succession of kings, it boasts superb soaring pediments unlike anything else you'll see in Cambodia, and is well worth the effort of getting to (though access is much easier from Thailand). If you're in expedition mode, it's worth considering a side-trip to **Koh Ker**, the only Angkorian capital that wasn't actually near Angkor, being roughly midway between Preah Khan and Preah Vihear.

Given the state of the roads, venturing up the middle of Cambodia is really only feasible in the **dry season** (Nov–May); when the rains come, every path and track turns to a mud slurry, and deep fast-flowing rivers appear as if by magic, cutting off the main tracks and isolating such villages as there are. National Route 6 is the **only sealed road** in this part of the country, and to travel north of Kompong Thom requires plenty of patience and a strong constitution, as National Route 64 takes it out of vehicles and passengers alike on the way to **Tbeng Meanchey**. Away from national routes 6 and 64, most of north central Cambodia is inaccessible; travel here

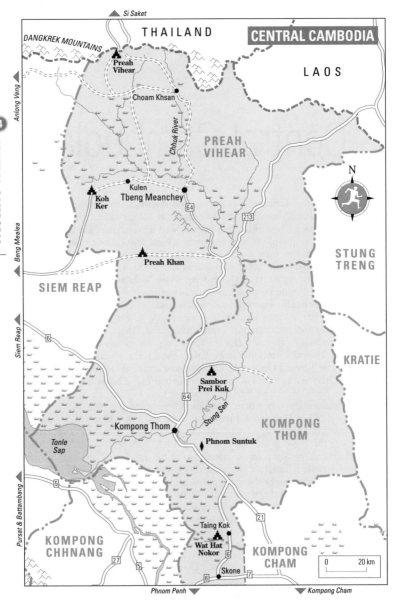

is along rough forest tracks which are frequently blocked by obstacles such as broken bridges and streams. The only way to reach Preah Vihear is by working your way north in stages from Kompong Thom, a journey that takes two long and tiring days, including a gruelling final moto ride from Tbeng Meanchey.

Phnom Penh to Kompong Thom

Leaving the capital, National Route 6 is in reasonable shape, and the journey to Kompong Thom is relatively swift and painless. The scenery along the way is quintessentially Cambodian rice paddies and sugar palms punctuated with occasional diversions, such as blocks of laterite for use in construction for sale along the road.

The busy transit town of **Skone** is also a stopping point for Cambodians to buy the local delicacy, *ah pieng* – hairy **tarantulas**, 5cm or more across. Hawkers swarm around vehicles, their trays piled high with the eight-legged monsters, which are caught in the jungles of Kompong Thom province by poking a stick in their burrows and hooking them out. Sold dry roasted for a few hundred riel apiece here and in Stung Treng, they taste a bit like crunchy fried prawns and are best tackled as though eating a crab: pull off the legs and you can suck the flesh which comes away with them, though be wary of the body, as it can be unappetizingly slushy and bitter. The critters also crop up around the country pickled in wine, a tonic especially favoured by pregnant women. Also much sought after hereabouts, sold in bundles of five or ten for a few thousand riel, are **grolan**, bamboo tubes stuffed with sweet sticky rice cooked with black beans and coconut.

Wat Hat Nokor and Phnom Suntuk

If you've time to spare, you could check out two minor attractions off the road between Skone and Kompong Thom: **Wat Hat Nokor**, a small but enchanting eleventh-century temple around 20km north of Skone, and, close to Kompong Thom, **Phnom Suntuk**, a sacred hill with multiple pagodas and rock-face carvings. Travelling between the capital and Kompong Thom on public transport you could, at a pinch, visit both sites on the way if you're travelling light and not pressed for time, as plenty of vehicles ply the route.

Wat Hat Nokor

Wat Hat Nokor is a small rural pagoda with tranquil, well-tended grounds in which stands a simple, charming laterite-and-sandstone eleventh-century **temple** built by Suryavarman I. The temple was never finished, and it's been surmised that either the architect died or war intervened during its construction. A single gopura on the eastern side of the temple gives access to the courtyard enclosing a cruciform sanctuary, **Prasat Kuk Nokor**, which once contained a linga and niches housing statues of Shiva and his wives. The central section of the south wall has collapsed, but you can still see a chamber, built into the wall, where the sick came to be cured using holy water which had been blessed by flowing over the linga in the central sanctuary. The library in the southeast corner of the courtyard was formerly used as a prison by the Khmer Rouge. The *achar* has a visitors' book which he'll no doubt get you to sign, and it's polite to leave a donation.

The wat is about 2km west of the village of **TAING KOK**. Public transport will drop you either in the village or at the turning for the pagoda; motos are readily available at the turning for the journey to the temple (5000 riel including waiting time). To head on to Kompong Thom, you'll need to flag down a taxi or minibus, best done from Taing Kok's market.

Phnom Suntuk

Something akin to a Buddhist theme park, **Phnom Suntuk** is most easily visited as a half-day trip by moto from Kompong Thom (20,000 riel including waiting time), though you could also stop off using long-distance transport along National Route 6 on the journey between Phnom Penh and Kompong Thom. Conspicuous in the flat countryside, the hill is accessed by a wide road, which is just as well as it gets packed out by locals on Sundays. A steep staircase of 809 steps wends its way up the scrub-covered (and badly littered) hill, squeezing past massive boulders, with occasional rest stops and gaudy shrines at which to pause for breath. Traditional **medicine vendors** line the steps to display their wares, mainly tree bark and twigs to be boiled up in water to produce multipurpose tonics and cure-alls.

At the summit, the pagoda is a hotchpotch of statues and pavilions, mostly contemporary. The mix of garishly painted concrete animals and human figures is decidedly kitsch, but Cambodians love it; probably most alluring are the older Buddha images, many carved into the rock face around the hill, although no one can tell you when they were carved. Near the vihara, a large overhanging rock creates a natural shrine with several small Buddha carvings, and there are more small shrines tucked away in crevices behind the rocky hillside. To the west, a narrow rocky path leads part of the way down the hill to a collection of rock carvings, including an impressive reclining Buddha, though to get back to the main road you'll need to return the way you came up. Once back at the foot of the hill, you might want to pause to sink a glass of sugar-cane juice or fill up on Khmer fare at the veritable village of **food and drink stalls** here.

Kompong Thom

KOMPONG THOM, 177km from Phnom Penh (and slightly closer to Siem Reap), straggles along National Route 6 and the Stung Sen river. The town used to be known as *kompong pos thom*, "place of the big snake", apparently because the locals used to take offerings to a large snake which lived in a cave on the river, though this may be yet another Cambodian myth as no one now has a clue where the cave is. Most visitors to the town stop over just long enough to get to the temples at **Sambor Prei Kuk**, 30km northeast; a couple of hours is quite enough to have a look around the town itself. Kompong Thom is also a possible jumping-off point for the remote **Preah Vihear**, two days' journey to the north, though access is much easier from the Thai side of the border.

The town's main landmarks are the tall *Arunras Hotel*, on the main road just south of the market, and the bridges across the Stung Sen, a concrete one for vehicles alongside an old metal one for pedestrians (though things don't necessarily work like that). The **market** is fairly ordinary, but it's worth taking a look at the **traditional medicine stalls** on its western fringes, which sell not only herbal products but also the shrivelled gall bladders of bears and dried snakes curled up like skeins of rope. Just south of here, you can check out the original lion statues from Sambor Prei Kuk, which were removed from there for safekeeping and now reside in the compound of the province's **Department of Arts and Culture** (Mon–Fri 8–10.30am & 2.30–5pm; $1), on the east side of the main dual carriageway through town. This dingy building also houses other historic artefacts from the province, including statues, lintels and musical instruments, but nothing is labelled and the air of neglect makes it feel more like a junkyard than a museum.

Pleasant enough, especially if you've half an hour to kill, is the gaudy **Wat Kompong Thom**, on the main road about 500m north of the bridge. The wat is hard to miss, as the entrance is flanked by huge, brightly coloured statues of animals, including rhinos, lions, leopards and a bear, while the pagoda buildings and stupas are equally exuberant.

There's a rare opportunity to see **traditional drums** being produced at a workshop 7km south of town. After crossing three bridges on National Route 6, look out for a small sign on the left about 100m before a market. The small-waisted, vase-shaped *skor dae*, about 50cm tall, are carved here by hand from the heart of a jackfruit tree – the yellowish wood is valued for its resonant properties – and embellished with carved decorations; a dried snake skin is stretched across the head. The drums form part of the traditional *pinpeat* ensemble, a gamelan-style orchestra which plays at weddings and classical dance performances. Also made here are *skor sang na*, a kind of cylindrical drum, twice the height of *skor dae*, which are played slung over the shoulder during funeral processions. The welcoming family who own the workshop will encourage you to try your hand at drumming, and might give you an impromptu demonstration even if you don't buy anything.

Wat Kompong Thom ▲ (200m), Siem Reap & Sambor Prei Kuk

KOMPONG THOM

N

Stung Sen

Market

Night Market

DEKCHAUMEAS

Department of Arts & Culture

★ Transport Stop ⓘ

PRACHEATHEPATAY

Phnom Suntuk, Skone & Phnom Penh ▼

RESTAURANTS & CLUBS		ACCOMMODATION	
Arunras Hotel Restaurant	C	Arunras Hotel	C
Arunras Restaurant	2	Sambor Prey Kuh	A
Sambor Prey Kuh	A	Santepheap Guesthouse	D
Stung Sen Restaurant	1	Stung Sen Royal Garden Hotel	B

Practicalities

The town is centred around a stretch of dual carriageway on National Route 6 and the adjacent market. The **transport stop** is in the square behind the Department of Arts and Culture, east of the main road, Pracheathepatay. You won't have to walk more than 500m from here to reach a hotel or guesthouse, but there are always plenty of moto drivers around if you need one. Taxis and minibuses to Phnom Penh go from the south side of the square; transport for Siem Reap and pick-ups to Tbeng Meanchey from the north. For the first stop on the long journey to Preah Vihear, **Tbeng Meanchey** (pronounced "t-behng me-an-chay", though confusingly everyone refers to it as Preah Vihear, after the province of which it is capital), it's best to get to the transport stop early, as the journey by shared taxi (20,000 riel) or pick-up (20,000 riel for an inside seat, or 10,000 riel outside) can take up to seven hours. Riding in the back of a pick-up on this long trip isn't advised, as it's possible to get thrown off on the bumpy road.

Kompong Thom's friendly **tourist office**, upstairs in a wooden building southeast of the transport stop, is a useful source of advice if you happen to find anyone there. For international **phone** calls, the Camintel office is inside the **post**

office on the corner opposite the *Arunras Hotel*; for domestic calls, try the booths near the market. The **hospital** is on Pracheathepatay. The town has nowhere to cash traveller's cheques, but you can **change money** in the market.

Accommodation

The cleanest place to stay is the *Stung Sen Royal Garden Hotel* (☎062/961228; ❹), overlooking the river, where rooms have TV, a/c and en-suite bathrooms with hot water. The biggest place in town is the seven-storey *Arunras Hotel* (☎012/563091; ❷), which has a range of very good-value fan and a/c rooms. The best budget option is the *Santepheap Guesthouse* (☎011/882527; ❶), a traditional wooden house secluded from the noise and dust of the main road; it's on Pracheathepatay east of the transport stop. Rooms (some with shared bathrooms) have fans and simple furnishings, and there's a wide and peaceful balcony. North of the river, the friendly *Sambor Prey Kuh* hotel (☎012/967300; ❷) has en-suite rooms with TV and one of the best restaurants in town.

Eating and drinking

All Kompong Thom's **restaurants** serve Khmer and Chinese food. The restaurant in the *Arunras Hotel* is one of the most popular, but the bland food and lacklustre service may make you wonder why. Its sister restaurant next door, also called *Arunras*, serves up excellent rice and noodle soups for breakfast. Just south of the *Stung Sen Royal Garden Hotel*, the huge *Stung Sen Restaurant* dishes up succulent sweet-and-sour fish and generous portions of stir-fried pork with vegetables, but it's really set up for groups and you can feel a bit lost here when you're alone. Across the river, the restaurant at the *Sambor Prey Kuh* makes a delicious *sumlar mjew vietnam* (and can also easily rustle up a fishless version for vegetarians), though it's not listed on the menu, which features a wide range of soups and stir-fries. Inexpensive **food stalls** at the market open from early morning to mid-afternoon, and you can enjoy your fill of fruit shakes and desserts at the **night market**, which sets up outside the east entrance to the market from late afternoon. If you're pining for cookies or cakes, there's a small **bakery** on the main road just north of the market.

There's no **nightlife** to speak of in Kompong Thom, unless you enjoy listening to locals croaking through Cambodian tunes in seedy karaoke bars.

Sambor Prei Kuk and Preah Khan

Two major temple sites each lie within a day-trip of Kompong Thom, off National Route 64. **Sambor Prei Kuk** is the site of a Chenla-era capital that once boasted hundreds of temples, although many of them have now been lost, perhaps smothered by the encroaching forest. Several temple groups have been cleared, and particularly fine brick carvings and decorated sandstone lintels and columns can be seen. Much further north, the temple enclosure of **Preah Khan** is the largest in Cambodia, its central sanctuary featuring the earliest example of four huge faces looking to the cardinal directions, a motif which later became a standard feature of Cambodian temples.

Beginning at the road fork 5km north of Kompong Thom, **National Route 64** strikes off north, a wide dirt road which can make the going very slow in the rainy season. About 10km north of the fork, the fifteen-kilometre side road to Sambor Prei Kuk is decent enough.

Unfortunately, there's no such thing as an easy trip to Preah Khan, which lies about 30km along a side road that runs west from National Route 64 about 60km past the turn for Sambor Prei Kuk. The side road is in very bad condition and offers plenty of opportunities to take the wrong track. It is also usually impassable in the rainy season. Given the poor condition of the road to Preah Khan, it's impractical to try to visit both sites in one day.

Sambor Prei Kuk

The history of **Sambor Prei Kuk** goes back to the late sixth century, when Cambodia consisted of numerous small states; one of these was a kingdom on the Mekong ruled over by **Mahendravarman**, who extended his domain as far north as Khon Kaen in present-day Thailand. His brother **Bhavavarman** created his own kingdom by conquering lands in central Cambodia and territory as far north as Battambang, setting up his capital in the area of Sambor Prei Kuk. When Bhavavarman died in 598, the two kingdoms were merged under Mahendravarman, who retained Sambor Prei Kuk as his capital. From 610 to 628 the area was known as **Ishanapura** and was ruled by Mahendravarman's son **Ishanavarman**, who built the towers of the temple's south group, the earliest at the site. With his death, the kingdom gradually declined and split into smaller states, though Sambor Prei Kuk remained inhabited; it was from here that Rajendravarman I came to take the throne at Angkor in 944, after which references to it disappear from the records. The site was cleared in 1962, but restoration and research were suspended at the outbreak of civil war in 1970, and post-Khmer Rouge the threat of guerrilla attack meant that it remained inaccessible up until 1998. Today, it is looting rather than insurgency that the guards stationed on site are supposed to be trying to forestall.

The site is easily visited by **moto** from the transport stop in Kompong Thom (about $5 round trip), the journey taking about an hour from Kompong Thom. The site is seldom busy, and as tour groups arriving on day-trips from Phnom Penh are usually on a tight schedule, you'll have the place pretty much to yourself again if you can wait awhile. The admission charge is 5000 riel. There are **food stalls** by the entrance booth.

The site

The temple divides into three main sections: the north and south groups, which date from the seventh century, and the centre group, a ninth-century addition. Separated from these by the access road are the ruined sanctuary tower of **Ashram Issey** and the single-towered **Prasat Bos Ram**, which has a lion's-head channel through which holy water flowed; it is now at ground level, but would originally have been more than a metre up the wall of the tower. The whole site is covered with the remains of towers, and carvings can be seen poking out from piles of earth or partly covered by undergrowth – exploring at random can throw up some real gems. If you've come with a driver, he may well know of new temples that have recently been uncovered.

North group

The north group, sometimes called **Prasat Sambor Prei Kuk** after its central sanctuary tower, was extended and restored during the Angkorian era. Although the main approach is from the east, many people prefer to climb through the wall in the northeast corner, passing the bathing pool. The sanctuary towers are arranged in a quincunx. Carved into the brick on the southern side of the central tower is a **flying palace**, believed to be home to

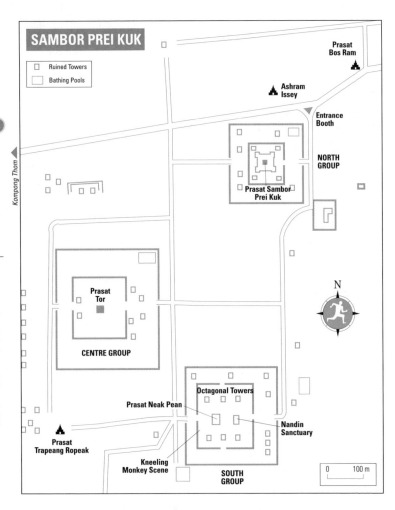

the local spirits who look after the temples (you can make out divinities on three levels of the palace), and several more examples of these palaces can be found in the south group.

The sanctuary is now overgrown and shored up to prevent bits of masonry falling on visitors. Around the entrances you'll be able to make out the remains of decorated sandstone lintels and columns. The carvings on some of the other towers are in reasonably good condition – look out for cute winged horses and tiny human faces. Though there were once numerous other towers here, about all you'll be able to spot amid the ruins is the row of four on the west side. You'll also see a number of carved sandstone **pedestals** lying around the site, each about 1.5m square and designed to carry a linga; these were meant to be portable, allowing worship to take place away from the temples.

Centre group

Although only the main sanctuary tower, **Prasat Tor**, survives here, it's a particularly photogenic structure, its entrance steps flanked by reproduction lions. The lintels to the south are well preserved, and you can still spot the intricate foliage designs for which the Chenla period (see p.306) is famed. Around 200m southwest of here, the crumbling **Prasat Trapeang Ropeak** retains elegant brick arches, and, at ground level, carved decorations, including flowers.

South group

Built as the state-temple of Ishanapura, the south group is also called **Prasat Neak Pean** after its central sanctuary tower. The main towers are located within two concentric enclosures; the ruined outer enclosing wall is of laterite, while the relatively intact inner wall is built of brick. The central section of the west side of the inner wall still bears elaborate **reliefs**, among them a lion fighting and a monkey kneeling as if making an offering. Also worth a look are the reasonably preserved carved **lintels** of the central sanctuary, originally linked to a nearby building which once housed a statue of Nandin. The image is long gone, however, and all that can be seen of the raised causeway that connected the two structures are a few pillars, though the building itself and some of the carvings around its central pedestal are well preserved. The **prasat** contains a damaged linga base which still shows the remains of delicate decoration. A number of unusual octagonal towers are located in the enclosure, their walls decorated with large circular medallion-like carvings and more flying palaces.

Preah Khan

Little is known about the history of **Preah Khan**. To distinguish it from the temple of the same name at Angkor, it is sometimes suffixed with the province name "Kompong Thom" or the district name "Kompong Svay", while just to add to the confusion, locals call it Prasat Bakan. The earliest buildings are attributed to Suryavarman I, and it's believed that Jayavarman VII spent time here before moving to Angkor – the famous carved stone head of the king displayed in the National Museum in Phnom Penh was found on the site. In the 1870s Louis Delaporte carried off the temple's prize sculptures (they're now in the Guimet Museum in Paris), while looters have also pillaged the temple in recent years, using pneumatic drills to remove statues – resulting in collapsed towers, crushed apsaras and the broken images which lie scattered on the ground.

The sprawling site – the largest temple compound of the Angkor period in the country – has a lot to offer, even so, with four different temple groups and numerous prasats and buildings to be explored. A little confusingly, the three-kilometre-long **baray** to the east is partly contained within the outermost enclosing wall. East of the baray, a small ninth-century temple, **Prasat Preah Damrei**, is enclosed by its own laterite wall and guarded by stone elephants. The most noteworthy thing about the baray itself is what remains of **Prasat Preah Thkol**, a cruciform sanctuary on an (inaccessible) island in the centre. At the west end of the baray, 600m inside the enclosing wall, the elaborate eleventh-century **Prasat Preah Stung** boasts galleries, carvings of apsaras and a central sanctuary topped with four massive faces, the latter the hallmark of Jayavarman VII and seldom found outside Angkor. Its terrace, well preserved and not dissimilar to those at Angkor Thom, is decorated with a frieze of swans.

West of here, at the heart of Preah Khan, the **main temple group** dates from the twelfth century and was most likely built by Suryavarman II. Making your way through the complex, via the elaborate east gopura and two sandstone galleries, you'll come to the central sanctuary, where the Bayon-style, four-faced tower seems to be so far untouched by looters.

Preah Vihear and Koh Ker

Overlooking both Cambodia and Thailand, the magnificent **Preah Vihear** takes maximum advantage of the Dangkrek escarpment to which it clings, successive temple enclosures taking you higher up until you reach the summit. Unfortunately, reaching the temple is both difficult and expensive, involving a stopover in **Tbeng Meanchey** before another long haul to the temple itself, although the construction of a new road (dry season only) from Tbeng Meanchey has speeded up the journey somewhat; another road (again, dry season only) leads there from Anlong Veng (see p.207) – both are tough journeys. It is far less arduous to visit **from Thailand** (where the temple complex is known as Khao Phra Wihan), using Si Saket or Ubon Ratchathani as your jumping-off point; see the *Rough Guide to Thailand* for details. In the rainy season, Preah Vihear is usually completely inaccessible, as is Koh Ker.

Tbeng Meanchey is the starting point for visits to another fairly isolated temple, **Koh Ker**, the only Angkorian capital not in the vicinity of Siem Reap. Now practically engulfed by jungle, it's been heavily looted and badly neglected, but plenty of monuments remain for the intrepid explorer, and its grandeur and majesty are still apparent.

Tbeng Meanchey

From Kompong Thom, it's a long, slow haul of over 150km on National Route 64 to **TBENG MEANCHEY**, though the journey is not without interest. Several small settlements line the road, which also passes alongside the **Boeng Peae Wildlife Reserve**, an area that is protected in theory, and which gives some idea of the dense forest cover which used to blanket the country. The road is passable year-round, but can take anywhere between five and eight hours to cover, depending on the season. Try to avoid travelling in the back of a loaded pick-up truck, as it's easy to get thrown off when the vehicle pitches from side to side.

While in Tbeng Meanchey, it's worth visiting the **Joom Noon silk-weaving co-operative** (open Mon–Sat; ☎012/610719; ⊛www.joomnoon.org), run by the Vietnam Veterans of America Foundation. Originally a rehabilitation centre for local disabled people, the enterprise is now a prosperous concern, producing high-quality silk which is sold in the luxury hotels of Phnom Penh and Siem Reap. Visitors are welcome to tour the sericulture chambers and the spinning and weaving workshops, and there is a small selection of silk scarves to buy. There's also a busy prosthetics workshop on site, a distressing reminder that this part of the country is still heavily mined. To get to the co-operative, go north about 200m from the traffic circle at the beginning of town, then turn right at the small sign for the co-operative and keep going about another kilometre – it's on the right.

Practicalities

From the traffic circle at the south end of town, Tbeng Meanchey sprawls northwards over 2km, with wide, straight dirt roads laid out on a simple grid. The main road leads in from the traffic circle, while a second north–south road runs parallel to the west. These two roads are linked by a few east–west roads; the **transport stop** is located on the third of these, about 1km north of the traffic circle. You'll find the town's guesthouses and restaurants in the area around the **market**, 200m west of the transport stop.

All pick-ups and shared taxis arrive at and depart from the transport stop; transport to **Kompong Thom** leaves throughout the day. **Motos** congregate around the transport stop, and this is the best place to find someone who can

▲ Preah Vihear

speak a little English, or to hire a moto for the trip to Koh Ker, Preah Khan or Preah Vihear. Be prepared for some hard bargaining, however, as they ask some outrageous prices.

You can **change money** at the market, but there's nowhere to make international phone calls and no Internet access. The tourist office on the main road, 100m from the traffic circle on the left, is never open.

Accommodation and eating

All **accommodation** in town is pretty basic, and nowhere particularly stands out. Before taking a room, find out what hours the electricity is on, as in some places it is limited to the evening. Perhaps the most convenient place to stay is the *27 May Guesthouse* (℡011/905472; ❶), which has clean en-suite rooms, some with a/c; it's located on the crossroads west of the transport stop, near the market. East of the transport stop on the other side of the road, the *Phnom Meas* (℡012/632017; ❷) has a mix of rooms: some smallish, with TV and bath, others larger but windowless. Heading north from the market and then east at the next block brings you to *Promtep Guest House* (℡011/747177; ❷), which has bright, decent-sized rooms with fan or a/c.

The town's only **restaurant** with an English-language menu is the *Dara Reas*, which may sound like a stomach complaint but actually serves up pretty good soups and stir-fries. It's rather inconveniently situated beside the Vishnu Circle about 200m west of the traffic circle and a kilometre south of the market. Across from the transport stop, a couple of restaurants do fried noodle and rice dishes, plus coffee. There are also some **food stalls** on the west side of the market.

Koh Ker

Located in rocky, scrub-covered terrain, **Koh Ker** was briefly capital of the Khmer Empire in the tenth century, when Jayavarman IV – who was already ruler of his own state here when he ascended the imperial throne – decided not to relocate to Angkor, but decreed instead that the court should come to him. Koh Ker is particularly renowned for its massive **statues**, which were the first in Khmer art to depict movement.

It's a three-hour moto ride of around 70km to Koh Ker, best tackled in the dry season (Nov–May). There are few places to buy food or drink here, and don't stray from the defined paths around the site, as the area is still **mined**.

An alternative approach to Koh Ker is on the recently **upgraded road from Siem Reap**. This road dates right back to the time of Jayavarman IV, when Koh Ker was linked to Angkor, and the temples of Beng Mealea and Banteay Samre – see p.206 and p.200 – were built along it. The road has been reopened by a private company, making it possible to visit Koh Ker as a relatively easy day-trip from Siem Reap, perhaps stopping off at Beng Mealea and Banteay Samre en route; expect it to take around three hours in a Camray and to pay a road toll of $5 in addition to car hire charges of $50–60.

Entrance is supposed to be $5 for foreigners, though it seems the people in charge of collecting the fee aren't always at their posts. Although the site is now officially open, only limited **mine clearance** has been carried out, so stick to trodden paths and resist the temptation to dive off into undergrowth to explore on your own.

The site

The earliest structures here, Prasat Thom and Prasat Kraham, had already been built by the time Jayavarman IV ascended the throne. Entered from the east, **Prasat Thom** features three enclosures arrayed in a line, with the sanctuary at the centre of the final courtyard. The distinctive red-sandstone **Prasat Kraham** is part of the main gopura to the third enclosure, and has a full tower in its own right. A massive fragmented statue of Shiva was found here, with five heads and eight arms (the hands are displayed in the National Museum in Phnom Penh). Through the gopura is a wide moat, crossed by a causeway with naga balustrades, giving onto a narrow second enclosure, where long narrow buildings almost form a gallery. A final gopura through a sandstone wall leads into the first enclosure, where a terrace supports nine small sanctuaries in two rows, five in the front row and four behind; there are also the remains of twelve minor towers spread around the courtyard in various states of disrepair.

To the west, beyond Prasat Thom though unusually sharing a common wall, is the **Prang**, a 35-metre-high, seven-tiered sandstone pyramid; there's a stairway up on its eastern side. The Prang was meant to be Jayavarman IV's state-temple but was never completed; instead of a sanctuary tower, there's just a pedestal at the top, which would have supported a statue of Nandin. Just as high as the Prang is the man-made **hill** beyond, oddly known as **Pnoh Damrei Saw**, the Tomb of the White Elephant. More sanctuaries can be found east of the **Rohal**, a baray over 1km long hewn out of the rock, also at Jayavarman IV's instigation.

PREAH VIHEAR

1st Enclosure

2nd Enclosure

3RD AVENUE

2ND AVENUE

3rd Enclosure

PROCESSIONAL AVENUE

4th Enclosure

Army Camp

Grand Stairway

N

1 Central Sanctuary
2 Galleries
3 Pilgrims Halls
4 Tale from the Mahabarata
5 Churning the Ocean of Milk
6 Bathing Pool
7 Naga Courtyard

0   100 m

Ticket Booth & ▼ Entrance from Thailand

Preah Vihear

Constructed entirely of sandstone, Preah Vihear has an unusual layout for a Khmer temple, with four enclosures laid out in a row (rather than concentrically) linked by avenues and increasingly complex cruciform gopuras with elaborately carved pediments. It's worth looking behind you as you exit each gopura heading up (south), as some of the finest of the temple's decorated lintels are to be found on the south sides. From the summit, there are spectacular views along the jagged line of the Dangkrek Mountains and, stretching as far as you can see, over the jungles of Cambodia, crisscrossed with tiny red tracks. Across in Thailand you can see the border marker posts in the scrub of no-man's-land and the massive road to the temple.

Completely inaccessible for over two decades due to war and the presence of the Khmer Rouge, Preah Vihear was the scene of fighting as recently as 1995. Government troops were withdrawn due to concerns over damage to the complex, leaving the Khmer Rouge in control, but nevertheless bullet holes can still be seen on the outer walls of the temple's uppermost enclosure. The temple reopened to the public in 1998, but the hillside remains heavily **mined**, so don't stray from the well-trodden tracks.

Hugging the boundary between Cambodia and Thailand, Preah Vihear has been the subject of many **border disputes**, culminating in 1962, when the site was awarded to Cambodia by the International Court of Justice in The Hague. The site is now jointly administered by the Cambodians and Thais, but tensions remain, a fact reinforced by a powerful anti-tank gun pointing towards Thai territory from near the summit. In July 2001, Hun Sen sacked a senior tourism official for signing an agreement allowing the Thais to develop the site, and in December 2001 the Thais closed access from their side, citing Cambodian lack of co-operation on cross-border issues. The border was reopened in 2003, since when visitors from Thailand have had to pay a $5 fee to the authorities of both countries to enter the complex.

Practicalities

Getting to Preah Vihear from Tbeng Meanchey doesn't come cheap. Moto drivers charge around $60 for the round trip, but they often open negotiations by asking for $100. It's a three-hour, 100-kilometre journey from town to the army camp at the foot of the escarpment, then a scary ride up the steep mountain. The temple's set opening times (daily from 8am; last entry 3.30pm)

▲ Koh Ker Temple

and entry fee don't apply to those arriving from Cambodia, though note that you can't leave via the ticket booth at the foot of the steps, since this would mean entering Thai territory. A road is currently being constructed to link up with the recently reopened road from Koh Ker to Beng Mealea and Siem Reap, and also with the road between Anlong Veng and Preah Vihear; no timescale has been given for completion, however.

It's as well to bring your own **food and water** from Tbeng Meanchey, though during the day, drinks and some simple fare can be bought at the site.

The temple

Preah Vihear was built over several dynasties from the ninth to the twelfth centuries, but most of the work is attributed to Suryavarman I. He enlarged an old religious centre founded here by a son of Jayavarman II, and installed one of three boundary linga defining the extent of his territory (the others were installed at Phnom Chisor and at the hitherto unidentified site of Ishanatirtha). Later, both Suryavarman II and Jayavarman VII made additions to the temple, which was dedicated to Shiva, and the temple was also referred to as Shikhareshavara, "a place of god under Shiva".

The long grand entrance **stairway** gives onto a courtyard – a little way downhill from your arrival point – decorated with naga balustrades. The **first gopura**, in a ruinous state, is raised on a platform ahead; from here you get a terrific view along the **first avenue**, almost 100m long and boasting a paved area of monumental proportions, lined with pillars that would have supported lanterns; the large **bathing pool** to the east, Srah Srang, is guarded by stone lions. At the end of the avenue, due to the angle of approach and the steepness of the steps, the only thing that can be seen of the well-preserved **second gopura** is the entrance door and the impressive triangular pediment, outlined against the sky. Above the exterior of the south door are two intricate and well-preserved carvings: the lintel shows **Vishnu reclining**, while the pediment shows a scene from the **Churning of the Ocean of Milk** (see p.183). Here Vishnu in the guise of a tortoise supports the mountain – the churning stick – on his back; the serpent Vasuki is coiled around the stick acting as the rope, while gods and demons pull together. On the stick, Vishnu appears again as Krishna, keeping an eye on their progress.

Further uphill, beyond the **second avenue**, the double vestibules of the cruciform **third gopura** form an imposing entrance to the **third avenue**. It was at this level that royal rooms were located for use by the king when he visited the temple; two large buildings nearby were resting houses for pilgrims. The scene above the north door of the gopura is taken from the Hindu epic the *Mahabharata*, and depicts Shiva fighting with Arjuna, a member of the Pandavas family, one of two warring clans in the tale. The final avenue, leading to the **fourth gopura**, feels more like a courtyard as it's flanked by ruined buildings. The ground here is thick with collapsed masonry, some well-preserved carvings lurking in the undergrowth.

Through the gopura is the **main sanctuary**, much of which has collapsed leaving a jumbled heap of massive stones. Dark and austere, the enclosure has none of the vibrancy of the lower levels, but the air here is fragrant with burning incense. In its day, the temple was a pioneering project, and the vaulted galleries which surround the enclosure are some of the earliest examples in Angkorian architecture. Only the north gallery has windows facing out; the windows of the other galleries look in on the enclosure. You can climb through a hole in the western wall to get out onto the mountainside and enjoy the well-earned view.

Travel details

Shared taxis and **pick-up trucks** leave to no set schedule from early morning until early afternoon (roughly 6am–2pm); you may have to wait for them to fill up before they leave, which can take hours. Note that the frequencies given below are only approximate, and the earlier in the day you get to the transport stop, the easier it is to find transport.

Shared taxis and pick-up trucks

Kompong Thom to: Kompong Cham (6 daily; 2hr 30min); Phnom Penh (12 daily; 3hr); Siem Reap (12 daily; 3hr); Skone (12 daily; 1hr 30min); Tbeng Meanchey (3 daily; 3hr).

Tbeng Meanchey to: Kompong Thom (3 daily; 3hr).

5

The northeast

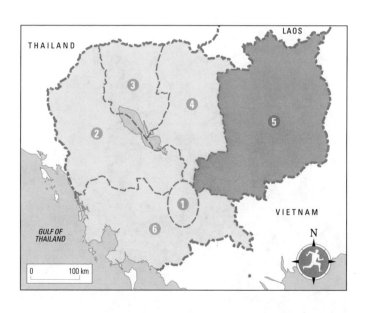

CHAPTER 5 # Highlights

※ **Irrawaddy dolphins** Spot the silver crowns of these rare creatures as they flit through the rapids at Kampie. See p.240

※ **Banlung** A relaxed town emerging as a popular centre for exploring the natural attractions of Rattanakiri, with a bustling chunchiet market and excellent crafts. See p.247

※ **Yeak Laom** Magical lake set in the crater of an extinct volcano surrounded by jungle. See p.251

※ **Bou Sraa waterfall** Falls plunging over 30m into a forested gorge deep in unspoilt jungle. See p.256

▲ Banlung market

The northeast

Flowing south from Laos, the Mekong River forges its way down through the rugged provinces of northern Cambodia, splitting to skirt islands and forming foaming rapids as it cascades over boulders. Further south the scrubby, wooded banks become softer, lined with the tiny vegetable plots of small farms. To the east lie the remote and forested highlands of the sparsely populated Rattanakiri and Mondulkiri provinces. Although the lower slopes of the highlands have been heavily logged, some jungle cover survives, providing a haven for wildlife. The highlands are also home to the country's chunchiet population (see box, p.232) who until recently were virtually unaffected by the modern world. A substantial number of them still eke out a subsistence living, cultivating crops and foraging in the jungle as they have for centuries.

The gateway to the highlands is **Kompong Cham**, a quiet provincial capital that retains an air of faded gentility, easily reached by road from Phnom Penh; the province itself is home to several of Cambodia's Muslim Cham communities. To the north, the rubber plantations of Chhup, originally planted in the 1920s, are now productive again, and more land has been cleared for rubber trees. The big draw at **Kratie**, another old colonial town on the Mekong, is the chance to see the rare Irrawaddy dolphins that inhabit the nearby rapids at Kampie. The most northerly town on Cambodia's stretch of the Mekong, **Stung Treng**, is a quiet backwater which sees hardly any tourists now that a new road and bridge bypasses the town. Though there's nothing by way of sights, it's close to other spots where you can see dolphins, and you might want to make a stopover on the way to or from the border crossing into Laos at Voen Kham.

For jungle scenery, misty mountains, a stunning volcanic lake and scattered chunchiet villages, an increasing number of travellers head to **Rattanakiri** province; far fewer make it to the truly remote **Mondulkiri** province, the journey itself enough of a challenge to put most people off. In both these provinces, you have no choice but to slow down to the pace of life of rural Cambodia. The roads here are some of the worst in the country, billowing with red dust in the dry season (Nov–May) and turning to sticky mud soup in the wet. Outside the provincial capitals, **Banlung** (for Rattanakiri) and **Sen Monorom** (for Mondulkiri), the lack of decent roads, transport, and any other creature comforts means that most tourists restrict themselves to

Note that Cambodians habitually refer to Banlung as Rattanakiri and Sen Monorom as Mondulkiri, as most provinces in Cambodia take their name from their provincial capital.

making day-trips. Rattanakiri is gearing itself more up to travellers now, with an eco-lodge, and a fledgling trekking industry offering overnight treks into the Virachey National Park. From Sen Monorom you can make forays out to a number of spectacular waterfalls or make an expedition by elephant into the jungle.

Kompong Cham and around

Situated on the west bank of the Mekong, the mellow town of **Kompong Cham** has little of the bustle that you'd expect of the biggest city in the northeast. Its small commercial port doesn't exactly hum with activity, and is even quieter since a colossal new bridge over the Mekong was built with Japanese government funding, rendering the cross-river ferry services obsolete. Improved road conditions in the region also mean that the boat services have ceased and most travellers now pass straight through, which is a shame as the place has a distinct charm.

There are several attractions in and around town. A few hours can be happily passed exploring the streets of the **colonial centre** and visiting **Wat Nokor**, just outside the town, a modern pagoda built within an eleventh-century temple. Pleasant **boat trips** can also be made to villages up and down the Mekong, while a day-trip will get you to the pre-Angkorian site of **Banteay Prei Nokor**, surrounded by a massive earth embankment, within which a few ruined towers still stand.

Arrival, transport and information

Buses from Phnom Penh, run by Phnom Penh Sorya Transport Company, arrive at the **bus depot** on Preah Bat Monivong Street, the boulevard northwest of the market. Shared taxis and pick-ups to and from Kratie and Sen Monorom stop on the northeast corner of the roundabout just before the bridge, while those from Kompong Thom and Siem Reap arrive two blocks north of the post office. Other transport pulls up on the northeast side of the market. If you want to hire a **car with driver**, the *Mekong* hotel may be able to sort something out for about $30 per day.

Northwest of the market, the **tourist office** is located behind a swimming pool covered in vegetation, but there's rarely anyone there. East of here across the road is the **Camintel** office, where you can make domestic and international phone calls; the **post office** is a block southeast. **Internet** access ($1/hr) is available at The World Centre, just southwest of the market; access is also

---

Moving on from Kompong Cham

The staging-post for travel to the far northeast of the country, Kompong Cham lies on National Route 7, 144km from Phnom Penh; onward travel beyond Kompong Cham to the northeast is easy, if time-consuming, with a superb new road looping north, via Snoul, to Kratie, Stung Treng and on to the Laos border. But, if you're heading to Rattanakiri, National Route 78 is still graded dirt for all of its 133km to Banlung. Although this may change when Vietnam improves the road from the border to Banlung (for the export of rubber), there's no time scale on it as yet. To get to Mondulkiri it's an even harder slog beyond Snoul, where the road has deteriorated to such an extent that it's worse than a cart track and there's no option but to go by pick-up (or off-road bike). Thanks to road improvements, transport now runs regularly to Kompong Thom, and through to Siem Reap and Poipet.

By bus

Regular buses ply the excellent National Route 7 to **Phnom Penh** throughout the day. It's not normally a problem to get a seat if you just show up, though tickets can be bought in advance at the office on the boulevard west of the market (10,000 riel). Buses now also run on the improved road to Kratie (17,000 riel) and Stung Treng (34,000 riel), while small coaches cover the more difficult route to Banlung, but be prepared for a bumpy trip. Buses for Siem Reap leave the depot twice a day (20,000 riel).

By shared taxi, minibus and pick-up

Transport for Phnom Penh (10,000 riel) leaves from the northeast side of the market throughout the day. For Kompong Thom (8000 riel) and **Siem Reap** (28,000 riel), head for the transport stop at Psar Bung Kok, north of the post office. To head to Sen Monorom, go to the transport stop on the northwest side of the roundabout near the bridge. If nothing is going as far as Sen Monorom, take a pick-up or minibus to Snoul and find a connection there. The fare right through shouldn't be more than $10.

The chunchiet

There are ethnic minority groups throughout Cambodia, Burma, Thailand, Laos, Vietnam and parts of southeastern China. In Cambodia they live primarily in remote highland villages and are usually known as the **chunchiet** (literally "nationality") or the **Khmer Loeu** ("upland Khmer"). It is estimated that the chunchiet make up just one percent of Cambodia's population, but in the provinces of Rattanakiri and Mondulkiri the chunchiet have always been the majority, though the balance is gradually changing with the influx of Khmers from the rest of the country. Small communities of chunchiet also inhabit parts of Stung Treng and Kratie provinces, and a few live in the mountains of southwest Cambodia, near Koh Kong.

Darker-skinned than the Khmer and particularly small in stature, the chunchiet, along with the Khmer, are regarded as **indigenous** inhabitants of the country. There are more than thirty distinct chunchiet tribes, ranging from comparatively large groups like the Tampoun, Kreung-Brou, Jarai, Stieng and Phnong, all of which number in the thousands, to much smaller tribes, such as the Kavat, Lun, Peahr and Meul, which are believed to number fewer than a hundred each. Every group has its own distinct **language**, each with several dialects, which has historically made it hard for them to communicate with Khmers or even among themselves; additionally, none of the chunchiet tongues has a written form. Particular tribes can't usually be distinguished by their clothing, as traditional garments are now used only on ceremonial occasions (the rest of the time the women wear blouses and sarongs, the men T-shirts and trousers), though for the observant they do have subtly different features.

Traditional chunchiet **villages** vary in layout and design from tribe to tribe. The Kreung build their houses on the ground in a circle, leaving a communal open area in the centre, while the Tampoun build stilt houses in a row, and the Phnong, who form the major tribe in Mondulkiri, have houses with roofs that slope to within a metre of the ground. Unique to Tampoun villages are the tiny houses built for people of **marriageable age** to allow them to entertain and choose a partner away from public view; perched precariously on high stilts close to the family home, the houses for young men are taller and have both windows and balconies, while the young women's houses only have doors. There are several Tampoun villages in Rattanakiri.

Animism and **ancestor worship** are central to the chunchiet belief system, with rivers, lakes, rocks and trees regarded as sacred; the Jarai, for instance, place carved images near graves to protect the deceased and to keep them company. In general, however, little is known about chunchiet rituals and ceremonies, as strangers are normally excluded.

Crops are traditionally produced through **swidden agriculture**, in which plots, called **chamkar**s, are created by cutting down and burning patches of jungle near villages; new **chamkar**s are cleared each year as others are left fallow for seven to ten years to regenerate. Generally, each **chamkar** only produces sufficient food to feed the family tending it, but if there is any surplus it is either bartered or sold at market; diet is supplemented by foraging in the forest, which also yields medicinal plants.

available at a couple of nameless places just northeast of the roundabout before the bridge, and on the road between the market and the river. The **police station** is a block back from the riverfront, near the market. Both the Cambodia Asia Bank, near the market, and the Canadia Bank, west of the central boulevard, cash **traveller's cheques** for the usual commission, and will advance cash on Visa and MasterCard. You can change money at the Acleda Bank, just north of the tourist office, or with the money-changers in the market. There are plenty of **pharmacies** on the streets near the market; for medical emergencies the **hospital,** in the northwest of town, is the only place to go.

The chunchiet are some of the poorest people in Cambodia: **money** has not played a major role, being used only to trade with outsiders, and any wealth they did hold was traditionally in the form of animals such as water buffalo or elephants. **Schooling** has only been introduced in the past decade, and life expectancy is low as a result of poverty, malnourishment, poor hygiene and limited access to **health care**.

Repeated attempts have been made to bring the chunchiet round to the Khmer way of life. The French recruited them to work in the rubber plantations and on road-building projects, while the Sihanouk government tried to restrict them to farming fixed plots. In the mid-1960s, government troops seeking the guerrilla **Khmer Rouge** – who had fled to the jungles of Rattanakiri – burnt down chunchiet villages. Bombed by the US in the early 1970s and continually harassed by Lon Nol soldiers, the chunchiet were ripe for recruitment by the Khmer Rouge, although experts now believe that those who did join the Khmer Rouge were siding with them against a common enemy rather than sharing their ideology.

The traditional way of chunchiet life is under threat. In theory, chunchiet lands are state-owned and cannot be sold to private Cambodians, but in 2001 tribal lands were sold by some village headmen to savvy Khmer who cleared the land for farms. Much was made of this in the press who accused the Khmer of duping the chunchiet. More recently, the government has allowed economic land concessions (ELCs), which permit ground to be cleared for plantations. According to Cambodian law, ELCs can only be used to clear non-forested land, but regardless of this, vast swathes of forest have now been **cleared** to make way for plantations of rubber and cashew; according to a report by Global Witness (see p.265) this is a way of flouting the rules regarding illegal logging. The consequence for the chunchiet is that the forest on which they rely for their livelihood is being destroyed, making it virtually impossible for them to continue traditional ways of farming or foraging; in consequence the chunchiet are now publicly appealing for the return of their land.

Education too has brought changes; learning Khmer in school has increased the number of chunchiet able to communicate outside their own communities, while more contact with the outside world has increased the desire for televisions, motor-bikes and a more "Khmer" way of life. Encouraged by the government to stay in one place, and thus benefit from schools and some improvement in health care, even the style of housing is changing and in Mondulkiri many Phnong villages have adopted the stilted, Khmer-style of dwelling. In the long term it's hard to see how they can survive as individual tribes.

That said, although many chunchiet villagers have become somewhat accustomed to foreign visitors, they still remain shy and modest – some may even see your presence as voyeuristic, so it's always better to visit in the company of a local guide who knows some of the villagers and their customs. It's also worth noting that the chunchiet do not like having their pictures taken and are highly embarrassed by shows of public affection and by exposed flesh (bare legs, arms and so on).

Accommodation

Kompong Cham has plenty of guesthouses and inexpensive hotels, and there's never a problem getting a room. The town's hotels are excellent value on the whole, offering spacious, bright accommodation at the same price as a small dingy room in some of the guesthouses.

Angkor Chum 200m west of the bus depot ⊤012/900446. This friendly family-run guesthouse is one of the pleasantest in town: rooms have TV and en-suite showers, and a/c is available. ➊

Mekong On the riverfront ⊤042/941536. The town's premier hotel: comfy enough, and with some great views over the massive Mekong, though the decor is uninspiring. All rooms have TV

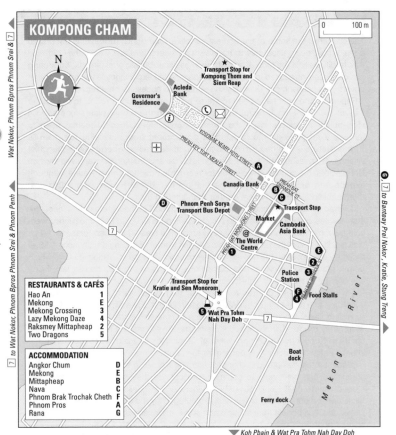

KOMPONG CHAM

0   100 m

N

Transport Stop for
Kompong Thom and
Siem Reap

Acleda
Bank

Governor's
Residence

KOSOMAK NEARY ROTH STREET

PREAH KEY TORT MEALEA STREET

PREAH BAT SIHANOUK ST

Canadia Bank

A

B
C

Phnom Penh Sorya
Transport Bus Depot

Transport Stop

Market

Cambodia
Asia Bank

PREAH BAT KOMKONG STREET

@
The World
Centre

1

E

Police
Station

2

3

PREAH BALAT STREET

Transport Stop for
Kratie and Sen Monorom

Food Stalls

F

4

5 Wat Pra Tohm
Nah Day Doh

7

D

River

Mekong

Boat
dock

Ferry dock

RESTAURANTS & CAFÉS	
Hao An	1
Mekong	E
Mekong Crossing	3
Lazy Mekong Daze	4
Raksmey Mittapheap	2
Two Dragons	5

ACCOMMODATION	
Angkor Chum	D
Mekong	E
Mittapheap	B
Nava	C
Phnom Brak Trochak Cheth	F
Phnom Pros	A
Rana	G

▼ Koh Pbain & Wat Pra Tohm Nah Day Doh

and minibar; the more expensive ones, at the front, come with hot-water showers and a/c. ❷

Mittapheap North of the market ☎042/941565. This immaculate modern hotel has rooms with TV and fridge; a/c available for a small premium. ❷

Nava 457 Preah Bat Sihanouk St ☎012/205615. This family-run guesthouse has smallish but comfortable rooms with TV and is easily identified by the external spiral staircase and plant-laden balcony. ❶

Phnom Brak Trochak Cheth On the riverfront ☎042/941507. Welcoming guesthouse with a nice view over the river. Rooms are clean and basic, with fans, though mostly windowless; some also have TV. ❶

Phnom Pros Kosomak Neary Roth St ☎042/941444. Set around a capacious landing, rooms here are all en suite with TV and fridge. Better room have windows, hot water and a/c; the cheapest are just closed boxes. ❷

Rana 7km towards Kratie on National Route 7 ☎012 686240, ℮roksrey@yahoo.com. Booking by email is essential for stays in this Cambodian home. Coffee, tea and Western breakfast are included in the price but guest numbers are limited to five at a time. The aim is to give visitors a real insight into rural life in Cambodia with trips to local villages and a glimpse of life as it is for most Cambodians. ❸

The town and around

In the 1930s and 1940s, Kompong Cham was a prosperous trading centre for the rubber and tobacco trade, and the most cosmopolitan town in Cambodia.

Evidence of the town's affluent past is still evident in its wide, tree-lined streets flanked by shophouses, although nowadays it's all rather somnolent, and even the centre is pretty quiet. Meandering through the unhurried streets taking in the colonial architecture, particularly around the market, is a good way to pass a couple of hours, and the riverside, though functional, is also good for a late-afternoon stroll and a stop for *tuk krolok* (fruit shake) as you marvel at the towering bridge – known as *Spean Kizuna* after the company that built it – the first in Cambodia to span the Mekong.

Walking south from the bridge along the riverside for about a kilometre brings you to the departure point for rainy season ferries to the river island of Koh Pbain. Just across the road, **Wat Pra Tohm Nah Day Doh** is well worth a wander, even though it's less than a hundred years old. In front of the complex is a huge standing Buddha, while the grounds are scattered with intriguing statues of people and animals, and a forest of miniature stupas.

The town's **market**, a reasonably smart single-level yellow building, doesn't get especially busy, which is just as well as the stalls are jammed so tight together inside, there's hardly a walkway between them. This is a good spot to pick up one of the cotton **kramars** made in Kompong Cham province, which are of good quality and thus in demand all over Cambodia; it's often possible to find colours or patterns that you won't get elsewhere in the country. You'll also be able to get a cheap coffee or economical meal at the food stalls here.

Wat Nokor

Two kilometres west of town on National Route 7, **Wat Nokor** is the most interesting of Kompong Cham's sights, located in the grounds of a modern temple, just off the main road through an arched gateway signed to Nokor Bachey Temple. The eleventh-century temple, surrounded by laterite walls (painted black during the Khmer Rouge occupation), is fairly well preserved, comprising a central sanctuary, over which a modern vihara has been built. Although purists may object to the gaudy modern walls and pillars of the new vihara, these quirky 1990s additions are a hit with Cambodians and ethnic Chinese. The latter closely identify with the temple's **legend**, which tells of a baby boy from Kompong Cham who was gobbled up by a large fish; the fish swam down the Mekong and on to the coast of China, where it was eventually caught and the child, still alive, discovered. The boy subsequently made his way back to Cambodia, bringing with him a retinue of Chinese, who all settled at Kompong Cham, which the locals say explains why so many Chinese live in the area.

River trips around Kompong Cham

There are several interesting places within the vicinity of Kompong Cham that can be reached by boat and make for a rewarding day out. There's the **Maha Leap Temple**, an old wooden building with gilt-adorned teak columns that was somehow spared by the Khmer Rouge; **Prei Chung Kran**, a village where silk is woven on traditional hand looms, located just upstream from Maha Leap Temple on the Tonle Tuok, about 20km south of Kompong Cham; and **Wat Han Chay**, about 20km north of Kompong Cham, where there are fantastic river views from Chenla-era ruins and a modern temple. You can approach local boatmen directly to arrange these trips (expect to pay about $20–30 for a day's boat hire), or ask at **Lazy Mekong Daze** or **Mekong Crossing** (see p.237). If you're travelling alone, most of these sites can also be reached (more cheaply) by moto.

Another modern building, just to the south of the temple complex, contains a **reclining Buddha**, decapitated during the Khmer Rouge era. The head was missing for years until a workman dreamt that it was buried close by; sure enough, the dream came true, and the head was soon dug up in the grounds and reunited with the body. Newlyweds use the temple as a backdrop for their photographs, and it's not unusual to find a group of women in the gopura helping a bride into each of her several wedding outfits.

Koh Pbain

Koh Pbain, a ten-kilometre-long island just southeast of town in the middle of the Mekong, is perfect for an out-of-town jaunt, especially by bicycle. Tiny tracks cross the island, fording small creeks and meandering through fields, and during the dry season the island is fringed with sandy beaches. Though you'll also see sesame and peanuts, the primary crop here is tobacco – the tall, thin, mud-walled buildings are drying-houses where the leaves are hung for several days before being packed into bamboo crates. The island has a number of **Cham villages**. The men work mainly as fishermen, while in the dry season the women weave *hol* silk and cotton *kramars*, using looms set up under the stilt-houses.

Outside the rainy season you can get to Koh Pbain across the sandbank just south of town, via a bamboo toll bridge (600 riel); come the rains, you'll need to take the small ferry, just big enough for a couple of motos and a few passengers, which leaves from about a kilometre south of the new bridge.

The Cham

Originating from **Champa**, a kingdom which extended from Hue to Phan Thiet on the coast of present-day Vietnam, the Cham are the largest minority ethnic group in Cambodia, numbering around 700,000, and thus accounting for about a third of the non-Khmer population. They also represent the largest minority religion, being Sunni Muslims who converted from Hinduism some time after the fourteenth century.

Historically, the Cham were frequently at war both with the Khmer, who bordered their kingdom to the west and south, and the Vietnamese, who occupied the territory to the north. In 1177, the Cham successfully raided Angkor, only to be defeated by the intervention of Jayavarman VII in a ferocious battle on the Tonle Sap – an event depicted in the bas-reliefs at the Bayon temple (see p.186). By the end of the seventeenth century, however, Champa had effectively ceased to exist, due to the gradual whittling away of their territory by the Vietnamese, and many Cham fled to Cambodia. The *traditional* Cham – who retain many of the old beliefs and rituals, but acknowledge non-Islamic gods – make up about two-thirds of Cambodia's Cham population. They settled around the Tonle Sap, along the central rivers, and in what is now Kompong Cham province. The *orthodox* Cham, who are more similar to Muslims in other Islamic countries, settled around Oudong, Kampot and Takeo. Establishing their own villages, they took up fishing, breeding water buffalo, silversmithing and weaving, activities that the vast majority still practise today. Their villages can easily be identified by the presence of a mosque and Islamic school, and by the lack of pigs.

The Cham were not spared by the Khmer Rouge: easily picked out because of their Islamic forms of dress and their distinctive features (they seldom married outsiders) they were either massacred or persecuted – often by being forced to eat pork – and their mosques were destroyed. However, this has been the only ill-treatment they have experienced in Cambodia, where in spite of speaking their own language (Cham) and maintaining separate traditions, there are no racial tensions – even after a raid in 2003 on an Islamic school to the north of Phnom Penh resulted in three foreign teachers being expelled from the country for their links to the Saudi-backed terrorist group Jemah Islamiyah.

Phnom Bpros Phnom Srei

A popular outing amongst locals, **Phnom Bpros Phnom Srei** ("Man and Woman Hills"), as the two hills 8km west of town off National Route 7 are collectively known, can be tacked onto a visit to Wat Nokor. The lower hill, **Phnom Bpros**, is topped by a collection of modern pagodas, the newest a grey cement structure with touches of ersatz Angkor Wat- and Banteay Srei-decoration. It's possible to drive to the top of this hill, which is home to a colony of wild monkeys who hang around in the hope of being fed bananas, conveniently on sale at the refreshment stall.

At the foot of the hill, on the way to the second hill, is a collection of **stupas**, built by relatives of the thousands of victims murdered by the Khmer Rouge in the surrounding fields. Their remains were stored in a building near the huge bodhi tree until 2000, when a large proportion were removed to Phnom Penh. Wealthy Khmer had been buying plots on which to build their own stupas, though in an effort to protect the countryside all building in the vicinity has now been banned.

Past the stupas and reached by the track leading across the fields, **Phnom Srei** is the higher of the two hills, leafy and undeveloped. From the base, a steep stairway goes straight to the top where, in addition to the view, you can take in the vihara's collection of Buddhas, the older ones dating from the colonial period. The statue of Nandin in front of the altar is much revered, and just asks to be stroked, which is what you'll see most visitors doing.

Eating

The town's **restaurants** provide a reasonable choice, though they tend to close early, so don't expect to find much to eat after 9pm. For Western breakfasts, the *Mekong* can rustle up eggs and bread, while *Lazy Mekong Daze* makes breakfast a feast with pancakes and a cake of the day; it also serves food throughout the day. *Mekong Crossing* has a reasonably priced menu of Khmer and Western dishes for lunch and dinner. Also on the riverfront, the welcoming *Raksmey Mittapheap* serves Khmer fare from early morning until early evening. The centrally located *Hao An* has a picture menu of tasty Khmer and Chinese fare, including good fish dishes, and even has a selection of wines. Near the traffic circle for the bridge, the *Two Dragons* is a homely kind of place with a varied menu; the fried fish with coconut is good.

Across the bridge a cluster of open-terraced restaurants have Khmer and Western food; some have live music and in the evenings you'll usually find them packed with local men. There are **noodle shops** and **food stalls** around the transport stop and market, while late in the afternoon stalls selling desserts and fruit shakes set up near the *Mekong* hotel along the riverfront. There's no real **nightlife** in Kompong Cham, though *Lazy Mekong Daze* and *Mekong Crossing*, the only Western-oriented **bars** in town, are good places to catch up with any other tourists.

Kratie and around

Seventy kilometres north of Kompong Cham on the east bank of the Mekong, **KRATIE** (pronounced Kra-cheh) is especially lovely when the river is low and the town seems to be perched on a hill, from the top of which you can look out over the sandy beaches of **Koh Troung**, the large island across from the town. In the rainy season, it's another story, as the surrounding country is engulfed by water and the town turns into a virtual island.

Thanks to the **dolphins** upstream at nearby **Kampie**, Kratie has become a popular stopover on the backpacking circuit. The town itself is a pleasant enough spot to stay overnight, which is about all the majority of visitors do, generally arriving on the boat around midday and spending the afternoon dolphin-spotting before making an escape the next day. A couple of pagodas to the north can easily be visited by moto if you allow yourself a little more time: en route to Kampie you'll pass the appealing hilltop pagoda at **Phnom Sambok**, while further north, about 30km from Kratie, **Sambor** is a quaint little village featuring an outsized pagoda.

▲ Colonial buildings in Kratie

Kratie escaped damage despite being occupied by the Khmer Rouge early in their campaign, and the town still has a distinctly French feel, the riverfront retaining some tatty but attractive colonial terraces. To the south of the town centre are a series of large colonial buildings (now housing government departments) and the gracious provincial governor's residence, where tame deer graze in the garden. Life in Kratie revolves around the river, and the riverfront is a good place to watch the comings and goings while you settle down with some sugar-cane juice at one of the stalls.

Practicalities

Getting to Kratie **by road** has never been easier. National Route 7 from Kompong Cham has been upgraded, and although it remains a roundabout journey via Snoul (2hr 30min; $5 in a shared taxi) it's a pleasant enough trip, passing through rubber plantations and skirting rolling fields of cash-crop cassava. **Shared taxis** and **pick-ups** arrive at and depart from the **transport stop** two blocks north of the market. **Buses** operated by Phnom Penh Sorya Transport and Hua Lian pull up outside the offices of their respective companies, which are both located just south of the boat dock on the riverfront. These companies run daily buses to and from Phnom Penh (25,000 riel), leaving through the morning and taking five to six hours. Heading north to Stung Treng, National Route 7 is in great shape, and the 140-kilometre journey (25,000 riel in a shared taxi) takes two to three hours.

The town is easily negotiated on foot and all accommodation lies within 500m of the bus and the transport stops. There's a **tourist office** just off the riverfront 500m south of the town, but it's usually unstaffed, and even if you do catch someone there all they have to offer is a big smile. You can **change dollars** at the Acleda Bank and the market, but there's nowhere to change traveller's cheques. **Internet** access is limited; try at the *You Hong* guesthouse or Ly Kheang, near the market; prices are around 6000 riel per hour, but don't expect a quick or consistent connection.

Accommodation

There are plenty of reasonable **places to stay** in Kratie.

Heng Oudom Street 10, near the market ☎072/971629. Clean, spacious and competitively priced hotel with a variety of fan and a/c rooms. ❶

Oudom Sambath On the riverfront ☎012/965944. The plushest place in town, this hotel has a choice of rooms: the more expensive ones are large, with fancy furnishings, a/c, hot water, TV and fridge, and there are also cheaper and good-value fan rooms. ❶–❸

Santepheap On the riverfront ☎012/971537. Well-appointed hotel rooms with TV; some also have hot water and a/c. ❷

Star ☎012/753401, ✉Kratiestar@hotmail .com. Highly organized guesthouse which has smart, stylish rooms with cable TV; some have a/c. The restaurant serves Western food, with a range of vegetarian and organic options including home-made yoghurt, and can prepare packed lunches. Bicycles and motorbikes for rent. ❶

You Hong On the north side of the market ☎012/957003, ✉youhong_Kratie@yahoo.com. Great budget guesthouse, with a range of clean and cheap rooms, restaurant, Internet, book shop, bicycle and motorbike hire and all traveller services. ❶

Eating

The first **restaurant** likely to catch your eye is the *Red Sun Falling*, a Western-run place on the riverfront that opens from 6.30am for breakfast; it has a short menu of cheap dishes, a range of beers and cocktails and a cosy atmosphere. Around the corner, the *Mekong* has an English-language menu and offers acceptable Khmer dishes. For a wider choice of food, head for the *Heng Heng*

KRATIE

0   100 m

STREET 1
STREET 2
STREET 3
STREET 4
STREET 5
STREET 6
STREET 7
STREET 8
STREET 9
STREET 10
STREET 11
STREET 12
STREET 13

RIVER ROAD
SHANOUK ST

RESTAURANTS
Heng Heng Hotel **3**
Mekong **2**
Red Sun Falling **1**

ACCOMMODATION
Heng Oudom **E**
Oudom Sambath **A**
Santepheap **B**
Star **D**
You Hong **C**

★ Transport Stop

Boat Dock
Buses

Market

@

N

Acleda Bank

RIVER ROAD
MAHAKSAT TRANEI KOSOMAK

Mekong

ⓘ

Governor's Residence

7 to Kampie, Sambor & Stung Treng

to Kompong Cham, Stung Treng, Rattankiri & Mondulkiri

Hotel, open from early morning to mid-evening. It does a good range of fish and Khmer and Chinese dishes, including pretty good sweet-and-sour vegetables. Of the guesthouses, the *Star* serves a good Western breakfast, great shakes and traveller staples like pancakes, while *You Hong* has similar Asian and Western dishes from around $2.

There's not much **nightlife** in Kratie. Mix with other travellers at the *Red Sun Falling*, *You Hong* or *Star*; sup on a fruit shake at a riverfront stall; or join the louche Cambodian crooners in the dingy, back-street karaoke bars.

Around Kratie

You can see the dolphins at **Kampie** in half a day and still have time to visit the meditation centre of **Phnom Sambok** on the way back. With more time, it's possible to make the lovely journey along the river to **Sambor**, 40km north, a site of importance in pre-Angkor times – though nothing remains of the ancient buildings, and the attraction nowadays is the rural market and pagoda.

You'll have no trouble getting a **moto** for the trip to see the dolphins; count on around $5 return including waiting time. Alternatively you can hire a motorbike ($6 per day) or bicycle ($2 per day) from *You Hong* or 🖈 *Star* guesthouses and go exploring on your own. The fifteen-kilometre trip from Kratie to Kampie takes about forty minutes by moto on a reasonable road along a raised causeway – in the rainy season it looks like a never-ending bridge – and is particularly enjoyable. In Kratie the road is lined with towering tropical dipterocarp trees, all labelled with their botanical names (*Hopea odorata dipterocarpacea*), while a couple of kilometres out of town the highway runs between magnificent teak trees, some of them around a century old (and also tagged with their Latin name, *Tectona grandis*) – these are some of the biggest such trees you're likely to see in your travels, now that mature teak has almost completely disappeared from Asia due to illegal logging. The *kompong* houses in this area are particularly handsome, built from the local teak (identifiable by its silvery-grey patina) and raised on tall stilts, with elaborate red-tiled roofs. Their front doors are level with the road, and you can't help but get glimpses of domestic life – people preparing food, washing clothes, and so on – as you pass by.

Kampie

Cambodians traditionally believe that the **Irrawaddy dolphins** (*psout*) that live around the Mekong rapids at **Kampie** are part human and part fish, and

5

THE NORTHEAST | Kratie and around

consequently they do their best to look after them. However, the dolphins' numbers have declined sharply due to the use of explosives and electric rods for fishing, and in 2004 the Irawaddy dolphin was added to the IUCN Red List of critically endangered species. They can be spotted throughout the year, but you'll get the clearest view in the dry season (Nov–May), when you can take advantage of the low water level to see their backs breaking the surface of the river. They are most active early morning and late afternoon, as this is when they tend to feed, although you'll still need to scan the water carefully to see their snouts or backs emerging a few inches above the murky waters of the Mekong, and photographing them is almost impossible. Environmentalists believe that tourist activity is disturbing them, and the World Wildlife Fund asks that visitors do not go out on the motorized-boat rides offered by some locals, and that boatmen be discouraged from pursuing the dolphins. Nevertheless, this is how most people go, paying around $5–7 per person to stalk the rare creatures for an hour. It's not, however, necessary to go out on a boat to see the dolphins. Just continue about a kilometre upstream, where from dry land, with a little patience, you will almost certainly see them playing near the river bank.

Phnom Sambok

Located in farmland roughly midway between Kratie and Kampie, the tranquil pagoda at **Phnom Sambok** is perfectly suited to its role as a meditation centre. The wooded slopes are dotted with small huts, which act as meditation cells for monks, while at the top the wat is fragrant with frangipani blossom. Murals inside the vihara depict moral fables: as far as these images are concerned, gossips are threatened with having their tongues pulled out; adulterers with being impaled on a spiky tree; and those who cook live animals with being boiled live in a cauldron. Some of the murals show Chinese and Japanese figures sporting bushy eyebrows and moustaches and wearing red shorts and turbans or bandannas, a quirky and unusual touch which is probably a hangover from the brief Japanese occupation during World War II. From the vihara balcony there are great views over the surrounding countryside to the river.

Irrawaddy dolphins

Freshwater rivers, such as the **Irrawaddy** and **Mekong** in Southeast Asia, and the shallow tropical zones of the **Indian and Pacific Oceans** constitute the habitat of the Irrawaddy dolphin (**orcælla brevirostris**). In the Mekong they now inhabit just a 190km stretch in the north of Cambodia, and can be spotted most easily at Kampie and north of Stung Treng near the Laos border, with occasional sightings elsewhere; in 2001, a pair were found just a few kilometres north of Phnom Penh.

Irrawaddy dolphins look more like porpoises than marine dolphins. The head is rounded, and the forehead protrudes slightly over a straight mouth; noticeably, unlike their seagoing cousins, they have no beak. Their dorsal fins are small and basically triangular, though slightly rounded. Colourwise, they vary from a dark blue-grey to slate grey and pale grey, and are darker on the back than the belly.

Irrawaddy dolphins reach maturity at around 5 years of age, when they can measure up to 2.75m in length and weigh up to 200kg. More low-key in behaviour than the marine dolphin, they seldom leap out of the water, instead arching gracefully to expose their heads and backs for a moment before diving again. Family groups, or pods, usually consist of around six individuals, but larger groups are not unknown. In spite of good breeding rates, there is a high rate of calf mortality, which as yet remains unexplained.

Rural development

Based in Kratie, the Cambodian Rural Development Team (CRDT) works in several local subsistence communities, helping them to generate a sustainable income. Twice a month a maximum of five people can join the team on location in the countryside; projects include fishing, animal husbandry and farming. You need to book at least a week in advance and the tour costs $55 for a two-and-a-half day visit; some of the money covers your direct costs – food, transport and guide, while the rest is divvied up between CRDT (for funding its projects) and the host family who provide your meals. CRDT can be contacted at ☏099/834353, ⊛www.crdt.org.kh.

Sambor

Head north from Kampie and you come to the bridge where the Prek Patang joins the Mekong. As the water level drops in the Mekong every dry season, sandy islets are exposed and an impromptu resort (entry 500 riel) springs up, complete with a wooden walkway linking the shore to the islands and picnic huts. The rapids between the islands are fierce, but there are sheltered places where you can swim.

About 8km north of the bridge, the road forks. The right branch is the continuation of the old National Route 7 to Stung Treng (it joins the new National Route 7 after about 10km), while the left follows the river to **SAMBOR**, a sprawling village with a couple of food stalls and a tiny market. Sambor is most notable for a modern pagoda, **Wat Tasar Moi Roi**, the Pagoda of One Hundred Columns, which was built in 1986 with the express intention of beating the number of columns at any other wat in the country. Other pagodas have now surpassed the figure of a hundred, but the locals point out that there are actually 116 columns, if you count both the round *and* the square ones. One of the columns originally belonged to a thatched temple that stood on the site and is believed to be 400 years old, and you may well be dragged along by a local to have a look. The vihara is also unusual in that it was built facing north rather than the normal east. The old white stupa in the grounds is said to have some obscure connection with a king; clearer is the tale associated with the pagoda, depicted in a series of paintings in the pavilion near the vihara. The story tells how a lady once turned herself into a crocodile for fun, while giving a monk a ride on her back – unfortunately an evil fellow-crocodile tipped the monk off and gobbled him up. The woman was eventually caught, in her crocodile form, at Banlung and brought back to the pagoda as a trophy, or perhaps to warn other monks against cavorting with crocodiles.

About 500m behind Wat Tasar Moi Roi is **Wat Preah Gouk**, an old timber-framed pagoda with an air of decaying grandeur and a magnificent tree in the courtyard, said by locals to be 700 years old, its trunk nearly 10m in circumference. The temple's roof was formerly decorated with golden finials and statues inlaid with precious stones, but the temple was looted by the Khmer Rouge and has lapsed into obscurity since the new pagoda was built.

Stung Treng and around

Situated on the Sekong River, 140km north of Kratie and about 200km west of Banlung, the welcoming town of **STUNG TRENG** is a bit of a backwater. Hopes that it was going to attract tourists heading to Laos have been somewhat dashed as the town is now largely skipped by traffic heading for the border on the now excellent National Route 7 which flies across the swanky new bridge a kilometre east of town. The town's only true sight is a rather mediocre temple, **Prasat Preah Ko**, but there are various attractions in the countryside around, and guesthouse owners can arrange visits to a silk-weaving centre, fruit orchards, lakes, waterfalls and boat trips to remote villages. One of the best outings is a **Mekong trip** to the Lao border, with the chance to do some dolphin-spotting and have a look at the waterfalls that make the river impassable here.

The Town

Smack in the centre of town, Stung Treng's **market** features various products from Laos not available elsewhere in Cambodia, including textiles in plain colours with geometric borders, and wicker rice-steamers. A hardware stall along the main north–south alleyway stocks hand-rolled beeswax candles used for various religious ceremonies; resembling tapers, they're sold by length. Sizes include "finger-tip to armpit", "chin to belly button" and "circumference of the head". As well as the usual gold, a couple of jewellery stands sell silver, some produced in Laos. In the morning the streets around the market are busy with women, many of them chunchiet, selling produce and whatever herbs or roots they've foraged from the forest.

A **statue** of a *pasay* fish can be found in the patch of gardens on the riverfront, celebrating a prized local delicacy which is caught locally in June and July near Stung Treng; although the statue is about the size of a whale, the real fish is quite modest, weighing 1–1.5 kilograms. Strolling west along the river road brings you to some of the town's oldest buildings, notably a bow-fronted Art Deco mansion next to the single-storey Ministry of Public Works and Transport (itself over 100 years old). Further on, petite **Wat Pre Ang Tom** is the most attractive of the town's pagodas, reconstructed in 1992 after being destroyed by the Khmer Rouge. The entrance is guarded by animal statues, among them white elephants, horses and tigers, and a huge bodhi tree in the corner of the courtyard shelters some local shrines. Beyond the wat, the road runs past village houses and gardens until it turns south to the dry-season dock on the Mekong, from where you can cut inland to return to town on the back road. Heading east an agreeable improvement to riverfront is the construction of a new promenade with its backdrop of the new bridge and a good view up-river. Keep going along here and you'll end up at the town's disused airport, where the local guys go to cruise on their motorbikes.

Practicalities

The **transport stop** is in the north of town on the riverfront near the old boat dock. Buses run by Phnom Penh Sorya Transport and Hua Lian arrive at their respective depots both on the main street and near the market. The **airport** 7km east of town is currently inoperative and express boats no longer run to Kratie or Kompong Cham.

Stung Treng is easily negotiated on foot; **motos** are (as ever) available but you'll have to flag one down as, unusually, the drivers here don't stop as soon as they see a potential customer. All guesthouse owners can help arrange local **tours** and onward transport; you can rent **bicycles** at the *Riverside Guest House* ($2 for half a day).

There are **pharmacies**, **money changers** and **phone** booths around the market, while **Internet** access ($4/hr) is available at a couple of shops opposite

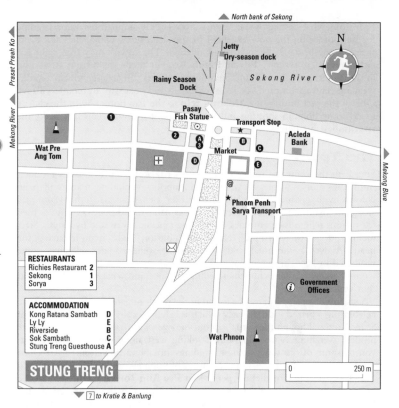

North bank of Sekong

Jetty
Dry-season dock

Rainy Season
Dock

Sekong River

N

Prasat Preah Ko

Mekong River

Pasay
Fish Statue

Transport Stop
★

Acleda
Bank

Wat Pre
Ang Tom

Market

Mekong Blue

@

★ Phnom Penh
Sarya Transport

RESTAURANTS
Richies Restaurant 2
Sekong 1
Sorya 3

ACCOMMODATION
Kong Ratana Sambath D
Ly Ly E
Riverside B
Sok Sambath C
Stung Treng Guesthouse A

Government
Offices

Wat Phnom

STUNG TRENG

0   250 m

7 to Kratie & Banlung

the market's south side. The **hospital** is two blocks west of the market. The Acleda Bank, east of the market will change traveller's cheques, but doesn't yet advance money on cards. The post office is in the south of town on the main road. The **tourist office** has nothing to offer and isn't easy to find either, being located in a collection of ex-UNTAC prefabricated cabins that make up the *salakat,* the local town hall, to the south of town near Wat Phnom. At the time of writing a new market is due to be built opposite the post office, but whether the vendors will move there when it's finished remains to be seen.

Accommodation and eating

The smartest accommodation in town, where any visiting big-wigs stay, is the *Stung Treng Guesthouse* (☎016/888177 or 012/430033; ❷–❸), on the main road opposite the market; the large bright rooms come with heavy polished wooden furniture, TV and fan, or a/c and hot water if you pay more. Nearby, *Kong Ratana Sambath* (☎012/964483, ❷–❸) is a well-appointed guesthouse – again featuring lots of wood (something of a thing around town due to the logging trade). Just by the market (don't be put off by the scruffy ground-floor entrance that makes it look closed), the *Sok Sambath* (☎012/327677; ❷), has a range of comfortable en-suite rooms with TV and a/c on the first and second floors. The cheapest **guesthouse** in town is the *Riverside* (☎012/439454; ❶), conveniently situated next to the transport stop, which has a few small but adequate rooms, though they're often full. Facing the east side of the market, the *Ly Ly* (☎012/1707049; ❷–❸) has en-suite fan rooms, though some are windowless. At the time of writing, the old colonial *Sekong Hotel* is closed for refurbishment.

The **food stalls** on the west side of the market do an excellent selection of cheap dishes and stay open into the evening, by which time the fruit-shake and dessert stalls have set up as well. Along the riverfront, the *Riverside Guest House*, has a restaurant and bar and does Western breakfasts, spaghetti and pancakes; it also has a book exchange and can arrange most services including bicycle hire. Good English is spoken at *Richies Restaurant*, near the *pasay* fish statue, where Chinese and Khmer dishes can be had for a couple of dollars each; their terrace is a nice place to hang out with a beer in the evening. The small restaurant at the *Sekong* serves up reasonable Khmer food and a few Western dishes, while the *Sorya* on the main road turns out some tasty Khmer food, although it's a bit pricey.

Around Stung Treng

There are several places worth visiting around town, some of which can be reached by bicycle or moto, others by boat. One easy-to-reach destination is the Mekong Blue **silk-weaving centre** (🌐www.mekongblue.com; closed Sun), run by the Stung Treng Women's Development Centre, 5km east of town along the river. You can walk round the gallery, training centre and showroom, watch the weavers at work and support them by buying a stylish scarf or bag.

Guesthouses can arrange **boat trips**, either up the Mekong to the Lao border and back (about \$20-30 including lunch) or along the narrower Sekong (about \$15 for a half-day trip). Heading up the **Mekong towards Laos** during the rainy season (June–Oct), you'll float past the treetops of drowned islands – an otherworldly sight. Passing the border post a couple of kilometres south of Voen Kham, but staying near the west bank of the river (which is still Cambodian territory), you can pause to watch Irrawaddy dolphins playing close to the river bank and then go on to look at the thundering Khone Phrapheng falls that block the route on into Laos; created by a huge geological fault they're nearly 6km across. The scenery along the **Sekong** is also enticing, and the wide sand

Moving on from Stung Treng

Shared taxis and pick-ups leave for Banlung from 7am and take about three hours (25,000 riel, or 20,000 riel in the back of a pick-up); VIP buses with 12–15 seats leave at around the same time and take around four hours to complete the trip (25,000 riel if you book direct, \$7 if booked through a guesthouse). For Kratie (25,000 riel by shared taxi, 34,000 riel by bus) allow two to three hours; for Phnom Penh there are just two buses a day (\$9) leaving in the early morning. Alternatively you could leave slightly later (and arrive slightly earlier) by taking a shared taxi (50,000 riel). Heading to the Lao border, you can book a minibus seat through your guesthouse (\$5) or take a spot in a shared taxi from the transport stop (around 15,000 riel). Alternatively, local boatmen will run you up to the border, but even if you're in a group you'll have to negotiate hard as rates are spiralling and people are being charged as much as \$50 per boat.

An adventurous option is to hire a boat for the two-day trip up the Sekong and Srepok rivers to **Voen Sai** (see p.252) or **Lumphat** (see p.254) in Rattanakiri province, though this can cost in excess of \$100, as you'll have to pay for the boatman's return trip; take food and water and be prepared to spend a night on the river bank en route.

bars that emerge in the dry season are great places to stop for a secluded swim. For more information on these trips and others, ask at *Richies Restaurant* or at the *Riverside Guest House*.

Prasat Preah Ko

Across the Mekong from Stung Treng, the riverside settlement of **THALA-BARIWAT** is home to the ruined brick towers of **Prasat Preah Ko**, reachable by local ferry (1000 riel one way) or by private boat (about 10,000 riel round trip); the temple is 500m uphill from the village's market. Inscriptions found at Wat Tasar Moi Roi at Sambor (see p.242) indicate that the area was probably under the jurisdiction of a local ruler, and Prasat Preah Ko may have been built here to control river traffic. Close by, in a small hut, is a stone statue of the sacred bull, Nandin, once inlaid with gems, though these were stolen by Thai raiders; even stripped of its decoration, it's still splendid, with a fine patina and a gentle expression. The statue is flanked by two shrines to an old man, Dah Jouh Juet. A unique annual **festival** is held here in late March or early April by the Jarai (see p.232), involving much loud drumming, men parading with fishing baskets over their heads and great quantities of wine being sprayed around.

Rattanakiri province

Bordering Laos and Vietnam in the far northeast corner of Cambodia, the province of **Rattanakiri** abounds in lush jungle, misty rivers and gushing waterfalls. The provincial town, **Banlung**, located pretty much in the centre of the province, is the only base for exploring the area, and with recent improvements in infrastructure has become a popular tourist destination. There are organized treks into the Virachey National Park, but for visiting sights close to Banlung such as Yeak Laom lake and local waterfalls, it's easy to rent a motorbike or hire a moto. Three or four days are enough to explore the area, though bear in mind if you're travelling from Phnom Penh or Siem Reap it'll take a day to get there and a day to get back, and many find the laid-back atmosphere so attractive that they end up hanging around for a week or more. As befits a province whose name means "gemstone mountain", traditional gem-mining still persists here, a difficult and dangerous activity; miners drag soil to

---

Crossing to and from Laos

Provided you have a valid visa for Laos (called "Lao" in Khmer), you can cross the border (daily 7am–5pm) 57km north of Stung Treng at the Mekong island of **Voen Kham**. The border crossing is straightforward apart from the fact that the immigration officers of both countries have a habit of demanding a **fee** of $2–3 to stamp your passport. This isn't legal and if you ask for a receipt and the officer's name, they will usually back down.

The road to the border **from Stung Treng** is now in excellent condition, with a new bridge spanning the Sekong, so there's really no reason to take an expensive boat. Mini buses can be booked through your guesthouse ($5) or you can take a shared taxi from the transport stop.

Entering Cambodia, visas are issued on arrival ($20). Onward transport on this side of the border is now straightforward with one or two buses a day and plenty of shared taxis (for Stung Treng, Kompong Cham and Phnom Penh). Crossing first thing in the morning should mean you get away speedily and without hassle.

The sites where gems are mined in Rattanakiri province change regularly, so it's best to check in Banlung before setting out to look for them. At present, most activity centres around **Chum Rum Bai Srok**, in Bokeo district. There's not much to see – once you've seen one mining pit, you've seen them all – but the 35-kilometre trip from Banlung is interesting for the scenery, the awfulness of the track and for the sheer exhilaration of having made it. The gem-mining camp is difficult to find without a guide (ask in your guesthouse or hotel; rates are around $15 per day) or a good command of Khmer. South of Ka Chhang, the road soon turns into a narrow churned-up track that winds up and down valleys and forks off left and right through encroaching jungle, until it deteriorates into an even narrower rutted path. If it starts to rain, the track can become impassable and it's not unknown for visitors to have to spend the night in the site's blue-tarpaulin-covered shacks.

Miners dig a circular hole about a metre in diameter and as deep as 10m, without any internal supports or reinforcement, and with only candles for light. As the miner goes deeper, the earth is hauled to the surface in a wicker basket using a variety of low-tech winches made of bamboo and rope. A series of small steps are dug in the wall so that the miner can climb out. The main gemstone found in the area is the semi-precious **zircon**, which looks like brown glass in its raw state but turns pale blue when heated. Also found in Rattanakiri, though not necessarily here, are yellowish-green **peridot**, pale purple **amethyst**, clear **quartz** and shiny black **onyx**.

the surface from deep holes where it is painstakingly sifted for the gems you see in every Cambodian market.

One of the attractions closest to Banlung is **Yeak Laom**, a magical lake set in the crater of an extinct volcano, fringed with bamboo thickets and jungle. The northern part of the province is covered by the largest protected area in Cambodia, **Virachey National Park**, within which many endangered species are thought to shelter. Access to the park is difficult unless you go with an organized tour (see p.251), though you can see some genuine jungle on a day-trip from Banlung to **Voen Sai**, a small town within the park itself, which has Chinese, Lao and chunchiet villages nearby. The journey from Banlung south to **Lumphat** is very different, the countryside consisting of rice fields, tiny streams and scrubby forest. Around here traditional gem-mining still persists.

Banlung

The small town of **BANLUNG** sprang to prominence in 1979, when it was chosen as the new provincial capital, replacing Voen Sai. Set out along wide red-dirt roads, it's reminiscent of a Wild West town in both looks and atmosphere, and although there are no particular sights of interest in town, you could enjoyably base yourself here for a few days while exploring the area.

Arrival and information

The easiest way to reach Banlung used to be **by air**, but flights have recently ceased and although it's claimed that the airstrip is going to be improved and reopened, no further information was available at the time of writing; check with a travel agent for the latest news.

The 150-kilometre stretch of **National Route 78** from Stung Treng is passable year-round but gets choked with dust in the dry season and badly rutted in the rains. The **transport stop** is next to the market, just south of the

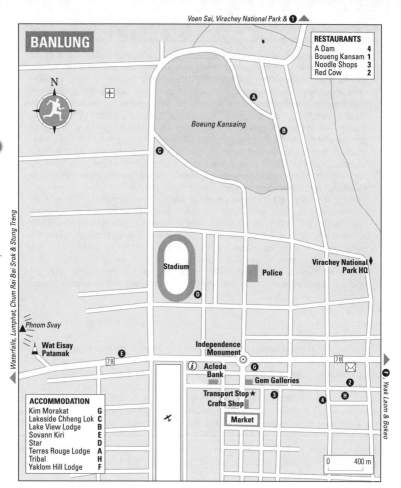

Independence Monument, in the centre of the traffic circle on the main road. The area between the market and the Independence Monument is the nearest the town gets to a centre and is home to an assortment of gem dealers, pharmacies, photo shops and other amenities.

Staff at the town's **tourist office** (Mon–Fri 8–11am & 2–5pm), located behind the "Welcome to Rattanakiri Province" billboard near the airstrip, do their best to be helpful, and though they do have some leaflets, they are strangely reluctant to part with them. Your best bet for local advice remains the hotels and guesthouses; the *Star* and *Tribal* are particularly helpful.

Accommodation

Accommodation in Banlung is improving all the time and there's now a good range of well-equipped hotels and guesthouses. Most now seem to have 24-hour electricity, but it doesn't hurt to check before deciding on where to stay.

Kim Morakat ☏075/974121. This peach-coloured hotel on the main road near the Independence Monument has good-value clean, tidy rooms; bargain hard and you may get hot water thrown in. ❷

Lake View Lodge ☏092/785259, ⓦwww .lakeviewlodge-rattanakiri.com. On the outskirts of town near the lake, this friendly guesthouse used to be the governor's residence. Rooms are simple, but large and airy; with a restaurant, Internet access and free lifts to town. A great place to chill. ❷–❸

Lakeside Chheng Lok ☏075/390063, ⓔlakeside-chhengIokhotel@yahoo.com. Set in its own grounds overlooking the lake, this hotel has a block of budget rooms and more comfortable (and expensive) bungalows dotted around the garden with a view of the lake. ❷–❹

Sovann Kiri ☏075/974001, ⓦwww .sovannkiri_hotel.com. This vast, new palace of a place, set back from the road in pleasant gardens on the way into town, isn't as expensive as its looks, and great rooms can be had at a budget price. Rooms are bright and airy with plenty of polished wood, hot water, a/c and fridges; the cheaper rooms are in the motel-style annex. On-site restaurant serving Khmer food. ❷–❸

Star ☏012/958322, ⓔviraktravel@yahoo.com. Ostentatious, green-tiled hotel down a quiet street off the main road with vast wood-panelled rooms and all mod cons. Run by the inimitable Mr Leng, the hotel has a balcony lounge area, courtyard seating, a great restaurant with Chinese, Khmer and Western food, a hugely popular bar, tours and transport. These well-regarded proprietors tend to move around a bit, so it's worth checking they're still there when you arrive. ❷–❸

Terres Rouge Lodge Boeung Kansaing ☏075/974051, ⓔterresrouges@camnet .com.kh. Stylish wooden guesthouse run by a French expat, overlooking the lake and surrounded by well-tended gardens. The rooms here, which now include a number of bungalow suites, are the most stylish in the province, individually decorated with traditional Khmer fabrics and artefacts. It's a bit of a stretch into town, but with superb surroundings and a terrific French restaurant, you may feel rather disinclined to move. Booking essential. Breakfast included. ❺–❻

Tribal ☏075/974074, ⓔtribal_hotel@yahoo .com. In an attractive compound 1km east of the town centre, this hotel has rooms to suit all budgets. The cheapest accommodation is in the barracks (dormitory) where a bed costs $3; the economy rooms are acceptable, but the most expensive are big and bright and come with a/c, hot water, TV, fridge and balcony. There is a decent restaurant, and tours and transport can be arranged. ❶–❹

Yaklom Hill Lodge 6km east of town, beyond the Hill Tribe Monument ☏012/644240, ⓦwww .yaklom.com. To really get away from it all you can't beat this eco-resort of fifteen sturdy wooden bungalows dotted across the hillside just an arm's-stretch from the jungle. Perched on stilts with ample verandahs, the en-suite rooms are simple but stylish with mosquito nets and candles (electricity is limited). There are hot showers every evening in a separate block from 6–9pm. Tours and guides can be arranged. The main drawback is that a moto to town costs 10,000 riel. Breakfast included, served in the verandah restaurant. ❷–❸

The Town

The town's **market** is a modern concrete building on a rubbish-strewn patch of land south of the Independence Monument. It is most colourful in the early morning, when the chunchiet women walk many kilometres to town, *khapa*s laden with produce, to set up shop on the surrounding land. Chatting among themselves while customers gather round, the women puff on bamboo pipes or large cigars made from tobacco rolled up in leaves. The fruit and vegetables they display neatly on the ground are cheap (strangely, you'll be charged substantially more to buy the same items in chunchiet villages) and often include varieties you don't find in the lowlands, such as big red bananas. Here you can also check out the forest food that they collect: strange-looking flowers and roots are sold for a few hundred riel.

North of the centre, the lake of **Boeung Kansaing** feels quite rural, and although there's nowhere to sit, and no access to the lake edge, late afternoon is particularly nice, when the colours of the sunset are reflected in the water. There are also good views, especially at the day's end, from **Phnom Svay**, where you'll get panoramic vistas over the rolling, wooded countryside. The hill lies about 1km west of the airport crossroads off the Stung Treng road, from where

There's a good shop for **chunchiet crafts**, secured at a fair price by the proprietor, Sok Oeun, in the town centre near the market. Among the interesting buys here are **khapas**, the chunchiet's all-purpose, basketwork backpacks, woven from bamboo strips with plaited rattan shoulder straps. The chunchiet produce them in the evenings after the day's work in the **chamkar**, and the finest take over a week to produce. Styles vary with the tribe: the Jarai put a strip of bamboo around the base, while the Tampoun weave intricate patterns and incorporate red-dyed rattan; the plain ones edged with black are Kreung. A large good-quality **khapa** will cost around $5 and can be put to decorative or even practical use, especially if your backpack is falling apart. While you're at it, you could go totally native and pick up a decent crossbow and set of arrows here for $5.

The chunchiet also produce **textiles** of varying quality and style. Jarai cloth is loosely woven, generally in black with yellow and blue stripes, while the Kreung and Tampoun produce narrow, tightly woven lengths about 2m long for loincloths. Longer, wider lengths suitable for a wrap-around **sampot** are produced by the Tampoun; now that synthetic thread is used the colours are becoming quite vivid – though you can still find cloths in the traditional colours of black, cream and red. You may also come across dried **gourds (kloks)** which are used by the chunchiet for cooling water; carved with geometric patterns on the outside, they're remarkably tough and, being light, are easy to carry home. There are also photographs of the various chunchiet ethnic groups on sale.

Plenty of dealers in the centre sell cut and polished **gemstones**, which you can get made up into jewellery for $10–20 in the markets of Phnom Penh; there are also rings and pendants for sale. For uncut stones and large crystals, check out the gem galleries on the road to the market. The gemstones here are hardly world-class, but there's no evidence of fakes being passed off as genuine. Even so, it's not wise to pay a lot of money for a stone that you like unless you have a trained eye (see p.247).

a track runs behind Wat Eisay Patamak up to the hilltop. The wat's impressive **reclining Buddha** replaces one destroyed by the Khmer Rouge and faces north towards the misty hills of Voen Sai.

Eating, drinking and nightlife

Apart from the restaurants in the hotels and guesthouses, there are a few places to eat. Both the *Star* and *Tribal* hotels have good restaurants, while out of town and best combined with a visit to the nearby lake, *Yak Lom Hill Lodge* turns out a range of Khmer and Western dishes in an attractive setting. For something a bit special, make a reservation for dinner at the *Terres Rouge Lodge* out at Boeung Kansaing, which serves both French and Khmer dishes. Just across the road from the *Tribal* hotel, the *Red Cow* serves Khmer food and specializes in soups, while around the corner the *A Dam* is the local NGO hangout, and serves a great selection of Asian, Western and vegetarian food. For a change head out to Boueng Kansam, Banlung's lesser-known lake, just 5km north of town, where you can have lunch in the restaurant of the same name, and then relax in a hammock until it's time for sundowners. There are a couple of **noodle shops** just 100m east of the transport stop. The best one (furthest east, with the heavy wooden tables and chairs) also does fried eggs and bread for breakfast.

As you might expect, there's not much in the way of **nightlife** in Banlung, though the bar at the *Star* hotel is a good place to swap a few travellers' tales over a beer.

Listings

Boats From Voen Sai or Lumphat it's possible to charter a boat for the two-day trip all the way to Stung Treng – expect to pay upwards of $100.

Elephant rides Ask at your hotel or guesthouse to arrange an elephant ride. These are available in several out-of-town locations, typically Katieng: $15–25 should get you an hour or two on a pachyderm's back.

Exchange Dollars can be changed at the market. Acleda Bank, a block northwest of the market cashes traveller's cheques, but doesn't advance cash on cards.

Hospital Medical services are limited to the basic hospital, north of town by the lake.

Internet Internet access is available at the post office (Camintel) or ask at the guesthouses (*Lake View Lodge* had access at the time of writing) for around $3–4 per hour. There are often connection problems for days at a time.

Motorbike rental 100cc motorbikes can be rented from guesthouses for $5 a day; off-road bikes cost $10 a day. Rates are cheaper for long-term rentals.

Pharmacies There are pharmacies on the street running between Independence Monument and the market.

Phones The post office has facilities for international phone calls; domestic calls can be made at the cheap-rate booths near the market.

Police ☎012/308988. The police station is just north of the Independence Monument.

Post office On the main road east of the Independence Monument (Mon–Fri 8–11am & 2–5pm).

Around Banlung

Road conditions vary dramatically in Rattanakiri, and even the better roads, west to Stung Treng and north to Voen Sai, have bad patches. If you're heading out alone it's worth telling someone at your hotel or guesthouse about your route, as punctures and breakdowns do happen. **Hiring a moto** in Banlung, though a little pricier than usual, at $15 per day, is worthwhile as the drivers not only know their way around the province, but are adept at negotiating the rough roads; many also speak some English and can give you a bit of local background too. **Jeeps** and **pick-ups** with driver can be hired via the *Star* and *Tribal* hotels or *Lake View Lodge* (around $40–50 per day), where you can also ask about hiring a local guide. The only scheduled local transport is the bone-shaker of a **bus** that leaves Banlung market in the early morning for Voen Sai.

Trekking is increasingly popular in Rattanakiri, and guesthouses are keen to sell you a trek or an elephant ride. Treks usually involve a bamboo-raft ride down the river, a bit of a walk and an overnight in a hammock; inclusive rates are around $25 per person per day for two people, or $15 per person for four. But on these you'll scarcely get into the forest. Far better are the **organized treks** arranged by the Eco-tourism Information Office of the Virachey National Park Headquarters (office hours Mon–Fri; ☎075/974176, ⊛www.bpamp.org.kh), located in the Ministry of Forest compound three blocks north of the post office, 2km from the centre. On offer are range of treks from two to eight days, costs are inclusive of transport, food, indigenous guide and contributions to a community project. Their most popular trip is the O'Lapeung River Valley (two day/three night) trek, which includes walking on the Ho Chi Minh trail, kayaking down the river and a home stay. Transport costs mean that treks can be very expensive for solo travellers (up to $144), so try to get a group together (maximum of eight) to share the costs. This can reduce the trek to around $60–70 for three days.

Yeak Laom lake

Surrounded by unspoilt forest, the clear turquoise waters of **Yeak Laom lake** (daily dawn–dusk; 4000 riel) 800m across and up to 50m deep, are warm and inviting. There are wooden platforms for bathing, and the three-kilometre track around the lake perimeter makes for a tranquil little hike. The setting is mesmerizing: stands of bamboo rim the lake, lush ferns sprout from fallen trees, the reflections of clouds skim across the lake's surface, and in the late afternoon an ethereal mist can be seen rising off the water. It's no wonder that visitors often make several return trips.

The area is regarded as sacred by the Tampoun, who manage it for the benefit of their community, and chunchiet culture is showcased at the **Cultural and Environment Centre**, 300m anticlockwise round the lake from the entrance steps, which has different styles of *khapa*, textiles, ceramics and other everyday paraphernalia (although unfortunately the room is dimly lit). The small craft stall next door sells locally produced textiles; the money from sales goes directly to the community.

To reach Yeak Laom, head east out of Banlung. After 3.5km or so turn south-east at the Hill Tribe Monument; dropping down the hill you pass through a Tampoun village and reach the lake after another 1.5km. The round trip by **moto** costs around $5, including waiting time.

North to Voen Sai

On the pretty San River, **VOEN SAI**, 35km from Banlung, is the largest village in Virachey National Park; tourists come here to visit the nearby Chinese, Lao and Kreung villages, and it's easily reached by moto from Banlung.

As you head north out of Banlung past Boeung Kansaing, the road climbs steadily to the O Chum crossroads, about 10km from Banlung and signposted in English. The road east here goes to **Veal Rum Plan**, 4km away, an ancient **lava field** of huge flat stones that could put many a Phnom Penh pavement to shame. To the west, at the crossroads, is Cambodia's first hydroelectric power station, driven by a tiny tributary of the San. The surrounding area is quite pretty, and it's interesting to wander along the flume (water channel) to overlook the river 10m below.

Back on the main road, the jungle has been cleared to make way for new farms, where pineapple, pepper, cashew and banana grow. The clearance is especially noticeable here, and chunchiet villagers who have been moved out of the forest now live in roadside settlements. Further on there is still plenty of jungle, with tiny tracks leading away from the road. Here you'll often see families on their way to the fields.

On the outskirts of **Voen Sai** the **Virachey National Park** has an office, where there's a small photographic display about the park and its wildlife. From here it's a couple of kilometres to the river and the centre of the village, where food and drink stalls and a couple of shops cluster together around the ferry to the far bank (500 riel one way), on which there are some Chinese and Lao villages, notably different in appearance to others in the area. The Chinese village a couple of kilometres to the west has a tidy school and a general store; the main street is flanked by neat bright-blue houses planted firmly on the ground rather than on stilts. **Boats** can be hired at the river bank in Voen Sai for the trip east upstream to Kreung and Kraval villages (30min–1hr) and further on to a chunchiet cemetery (1hr 30min); the trip all the way to the cemetery costs around $15–20.

The waterfalls

There are a few modest but picturesque **waterfalls** within easy reach of Banlung. The falls at **Chha Ong** (2000 riel) are the largest, the river flowing through lush jungle before plunging 30m into a gorge. The pool at the base is deep enough to swim in, and daring souls can climb onto a ledge behind the curtain of water. To reach the falls, head 2km west on National Route 78 to the signposted junction, then turn right (northwest) and continue 6km to the falls.

If you turn left (south) at the junction, the road runs through rubber plantations and past a rubber factory before heading downhill to a small bridge just
beyond a line of food stalls and karaoke joints about 4km from the main road.
Just before the bridge, a small path to the right leads into a bamboo-clad
valley and down to the **Ka Chhang** falls, just 10m high, with a pool for
taking a dip.

To get to **Katieng** falls, head back towards town and take the first narrow
road on the left leading up a slope, then continue for about 4km until you
reach a small river. Follow the path to the right on the opposite side of the
river to reach the falls. Some locals offer **elephant rides** for about $10–15

▲ Chha Ong waterfall

per hour around here, but it's easier to make arrangements through your hotel or guesthouse. However, for a more authentic elephant-back excursion you're better off in Mondulkiri.

Lumphat

LUMPHAT is around 35km from Banlung, reached by heading west on the road to Stung Treng and, after about 8km, taking a southbound turning (the first after the English signpost for the waterfalls). It's a scenic journey, the landscape varying from rice fields to scrubby forest until you arrive at the town and the Srepok River. Lumphat was the provincial capital during the Sihanouk era, and many maps still show the airport here, although it ceased to be the provincial capital in 1975 when the Khmer Rouge moved it to Voen Sai. Today, Lumphat is a scattered village, and a few ruined concrete buildings are all that remains of its days as provincial capital. Patches of cratered wasteland bear the scars of B-52 bombing runs and rusty metal lies around in the undergrowth; if you want to see bomb craters, the best spot is on the edge of the village near the water tower. Though there are no land mines here, **unexploded ordnance** may still be a risk.

Mondulkiri province

Mountainous, sparsely populated **Mondulkiri** province sees fewer travellers in a year than Rattanakiri does in a month. Despite heavy logging, Mondulkiri still has impenetrable jungle and is home to rare and endangered wildlife, including water buffalo, Asian dogs, elephants and green peafowl. Besides its jungle scenery and cool climate (conducive to hiking), Mondulkiri's attraction lies in its isolation, although the only sights accessible to visitors are the compact provincial capital, **Sen Monorom**, and several gushing **waterfalls**, among them the mighty **Bou Sraa**. It's also the place to come for an authentic elephant trek, and possibly even the chance to help out with an elephant care programme.

Nearly eighty percent of the inhabitants of this impoverished province are chunchiet from the Phnong tribe. In the 1990s they were joined by an influx of Khmer, who returned from the refugee camps in Thailand and could not

Getting to Mondulkiri

The great majority of travellers reach Mondulkiri from **Phnom Penh**, a gruelling journey that takes at least eight hours. A few shared taxis and pick-up trucks make the long haul from the capital to Sen Monorom on a more or less daily basis, subject to breakdowns and demand. Vehicles also run from **Kompong Cham** and **Snoul,** although getting a lift anywhere in between is difficult as it's hard to find a spare seat. From Snoul, vehicles head east through Snoul Wildlife Reserve after which the road climbs steadily until it reaches the 900-metre-high plateau around 40km from Sen Monorom. Close to town, the landscape changes to rolling grass-covered hills – more reminiscent of England than Cambodia, and possibly the result of years of slash-and-burn cultivation – dotted with copses of pine, planted in the late 1960s at the king's behest.

Experienced off-road bikers sometimes brave the atrocious tracks and countless streams that separate **Banlung** in Rattanakiri province from Sen Monorom, but this is possible in the dry season only (Nov–May).

afford to live in Cambodia's towns. Furthermore, since 2001, Vietnamese hill tribes (*montagnards*) have fled here to avoid persecution at home. Initially they were put in refugee camps set up by the UN, but most have now either been repatriated or have emigrated to the US, although there are still lingering tensions in the border areas.

Unfortunately, Mondulkiri's unique, grassy rolling hillsides are under threat; bauxite has been discovered and the Australian giant BHP Billiton is in Sen Monorom undertaking exploration, something that the Cambodian government fully supports. If open-cast mining is allowed the face of the landscape will change for ever.

Sen Monorom and around

SEN MONOROM is little more than a large village with houses spread sparsely over a couple of kilometres, culminating in a cluster of buildings around the market in the centre of town. You can set off on foot in any direction and soon be in unspoilt and isolated countryside, though there are only a limited number of tracks. The two lakes close to town are pleasant for an early morning or late afternoon stroll, while 2km from town is Phnom Dosh Kramom (known as Youk Srosh Phlom to the Phnong, for whom the mountain is sacred) a small mountain with a meditation pagoda, from which there are splendid views.

Transport arrives and leaves from the north of town, just uphill from the market; arriving, the driver will usually drop you off at a guesthouse of your choice on the way into town. At some point you're going to want to get out of town; regular and off-road motorbikes are available to rent at the guesthouses ($6–15 per day, plus fuel), but road conditions vary dramatically so it's best to check before you commit yourself; you'll also need to be proficient at finding your own way (or speak some Khmer), as there are no road signs. If you're at all nervous it's best to hire a moto driver (around $20 per day). Note that the chances of getting an English-speaking guide are slim.

Although there's an Acleda Bank, it doesn't change traveller's cheques or advance money on cards, so make sure you have sufficient cash for your stay. You can change dollars into riel at the market.

Accommodation

Considering its inaccessibility, Sen Monorom has a startling range of decent accommodation, none of it expensive, so your main consideration is probably going to be whether you want stay in town (close to restaurants and the market), on the outskirts of town or out in the country.

Arun Reah II ☎012/856667 or 012/999191, ✉richardcambodia@yahoo .com). On the Phnom Penh road, about 2km from town, Arun Reah's huts and bungalows are spread out over the hillside. At their most basic the huts have a cold shower, balcony and fantastic views, while deluxe bungalows come with hot water and TV. There's a restaurant, Internet access and free motorbike loan for trips to town. ❶–❸

Holiday ☎012/936606. A good budget option, this newish guesthouse has clean, tidy rooms in the centre of town, just down from the traffic circle. ❶–❷

Mondulkiri ☎073/390139, ⓦwww .mondulkiri-hotel.com. The plushest place around, this hotel is on the back road between the hospital and the wat. It has smart rooms, all with hot water, air conditioning, TV and mini-bar; there's also a restaurant. ❸

Nature Lodge ☎012/230272. Accommodation in basic huts on the hillside about 4km from town down a narrow track, only open in the dry season (roughly Nov–Apr). ❶

Oeun Sakona ☎012/950680. On the main road into town, just down from the market, this sparkling new hotel takes some beating; its plush

Elephant treks

Any of the guesthouse or bar owners in Sen Monorom can help you arrange an elephant trek through the jungle, starting either from the village of Phulung, about 8km north of town, or from Potang, 8km to the south. A half- or full day rolling around on the back of an elephant costs $15/30, including transport to the village, a Phnong-speaking guide and lunch if you are out for the full day. Overnight camping treks are also possible, but for many the novelty wears off after a few hours of bumping about.

ELIE (Elephants Livelihood Initiative Environment) is an NGO working in Mondulkiri with the Phnong and their domestic elephants. At the time of writing ELIE was working on an eco-tourism project 10km from Sen Monorom where it will be possible to stay in a Phnong-style dwelling, take jungle treks and both learn about and help to care for the elephants. Contact ELIE at ☏012/1613833, ⓦwww.elie-cambodia.com.

rooms have hot water and TV. A restaurant is due to open, but you're so close to town that you have plenty of choice for eating anyway. ②–③

Pich Kiri ☏012/932102. Sen Monorom's longest-running guesthouse is just east of the market, on the uphill stretch on the way into town. With a range of slightly musty rooms (some with hot water), restaurant and leafy garden with plenty of seating it's run by a friendly family. At the time of writing, they were putting the final touches on a classy new hotel behind the current guesthouse. ②–③

Eating, drinking and nightlife

In general, food is less varied and slightly more expensive in Mondulkiri than elsewhere in Cambodia. On the plus side, Mondulkiri is the one place in the country where avocados grow, and in season (April–June) you can buy enough for a feast at a giveaway price. In addition to the hotels and guesthouses, you'll find several restaurants on the main road near the market. The *Sok Leap* has an extensive Khmer menu, with a limited English translation, but they can rustle up acceptable Cambodian cuisine in a trice. At the top of the hill, near the traffic circle, the *Sen Monorom* does all the standard Cambodian dishes and has the advantage that you can sit and watch the world go by from its terrace. 🏃 *Chom Nor Themei* is a popular place with a good (translated) menu and a few Western choices; their chicken or beef with Cambodian spices goes down well after a hard day on the hills. Basic rice dishes and noodle soup can be had for breakfast at the market.

Sen Monorom goes to bed early, so the nights can seem quite long, but the town now has a couple of options for whiling away a few hours. 🏃 *The Green House*, on the main road near the market, opens in the late afternoon serving beer, cocktails and shakes; it's a good place to pick up local news and arrange trips, it has Internet ($2/hr) although the spasmodic power cuts don't help reliability of the connections. Newly opened, *Bananas* is about 500m down the road beside the *Oeun Sakona* hotel. This bar/restaurant/travellers' hang out organizes events on an *ad hoc* basis, ranging from kite flying to a jungle picnic or a DVD documentary night. The garden is work-in-progress and green-fingered visitors are welcome to help.

Waterfalls around Sen Monorom

Immortalized in a song by the late, great Cambodian singer Sin Sisamot, **Bou Sraa** waterfall is a fabulous two-tiered cascade 35km from Sen Monorom, towards the Vietnamese border. The setting alone makes the falls worth visiting, the river dropping over 30m into a jungle gorge, though the track to the falls is tortuous in the dry season and impassable with the onset of the rains – making

▲ Banlung morning market

it easy to see why the locals get around by elephant. The road has now been improved by a private concern and you have to pay a toll of around $2. The bonus is that the falls are now just an hour and a half away.

Not nearly as dramatic as Bou Sraa, but easier to get to and reasonably pretty, are the three-tier **Romanea falls**: take the main road back towards Snoul for about 10km, crossing over three bridges and then fork left and left again (no signs). To get to either Bou Sraa or Romanea you'll need either to rent a motorbike from a guesthouse (around $6–15 a day) or hire a moto (about $20 a day); note though that the road is unsurfaced and at the time of writing was in an atrocious state – with no plans for it to be improved.

It's possible to take a moto or walk 5km northwest of town to the ten-metre-high **Monorom waterfall** (also known as the Sihanouk falls). Along the way you'll pass the ruins of the (rarely used) royal residence, after which you should follow the left fork to the falls. You can swim in the pool at the base of the falls, even in the dry season.

Travel details

Shared taxis and **pick-up trucks** leave to no set schedule from roughly 6am until 2pm (to and from Rattanakiri and Mondulkiri you'll need to be on the road by 8am) and they usually wait to fill up before they leave. Note that the frequencies given below are only approximate, and the earlier in the day you get to the transport stop, the easier it is to find transport.

Buses

Banlung to: Phnom Penh (daily; 10–12hr); Voen Sai (daily; 2hr 30min).
Kompong Cham to: Kratie (3 daily; 3hr); Phnom Penh (11 daily; 2hr 30min); Poipet (daily; 7–8hr); Siem Reap (twice daily; 5hr); Stung Treng (daily; 5 hr).
Kratie to: Kompong Cham (3 daily; 5hr); Phnom Penh (3 daily; 7hr).
Stung Treng to: Kompong Cham (daily; 5hr); Phnom Penh (daily; 8hr).
Voen Sai to: Banlung (daily; 2hr 30min).

Shared taxis, minibuses and pick-up trucks

Banlung to: Kompong Cham (several daily; 8hr); Kratie (3 daily; 6hr); Phnom Penh (several daily; 10hr); Stung Treng (4 daily; 4hr).

Kompong Cham to: Banlung (several daily; 8hr); Kompong Thom (6 daily; 2hr 30min); Kratie (6 daily; 3hr); Phnom Penh (20 daily; 2hr); Poipet (several daily; 7hr); Prey Veng (4 daily; 2hr); Sen Monorom (1–2 daily; 6hr at least); Siem Reap (6 daily; 4–5hr); Skone (20 daily; 30min).
Kratie to: Banlung (3 daily; 6hr); Kompong Cham (6 daily; 3hr); Stung Treng (6 daily; 3hr).
Sen Monorom to: Kompong Cham (daily; 6hr); Phnom Penh (2–3 daily; at least 8hr); Snoul (1–2 daily; 5hr).
Stung Treng to: Banlung (4 daily; 4hr); Kratie (6 daily; 3hr); Phnom Penh (4 daily; 8hr).

Sihanoukville
and the south

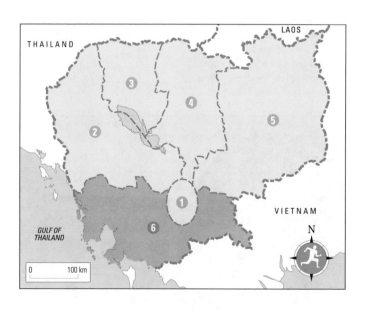

THAILAND

LAOS

THAILAND

③

④

②

⑤

①

VIETNAM

GULF OF
THAILAND

⑥

N

0   100 km

CHAPTER 6 # Highlights

✴ **Kirirom National Park**
Cool, pine-forested hills with
walking trails, waterfalls, lakes
and colourful vegetation.
See p.264

✴ **Sihanoukville** Laze on white-
sand beaches, eat succulent
seafood and party in the
vibrant bars and clubs at this
relaxing seaside town.
See p.267

✴ **Ream National Park**
Stunning coastal scenery,
beautiful white-sand beaches
and the chance to take a
boat trip down the mangrove-
fringed Prek Toeuk Sap River.
See p.280

✴ **Bokor National Park** Rising
from sea level up to the
cool heights of the Elephant
Mountains, Bokor has lush
jungle, cool waterfalls, walking
tracks and commanding
views of the coast, plus an
eerily deserted former hill
station. See p.291

✴ **Kep** Enjoy crab feasts at
the beachside market or sip
a sundowner in sumptuous
luxury at this 1960s seaside
resort now being restored
to its former elegance.
See p.294

▲ Bokor National Park

Sihanoukville
and the south

ambodia's southern provinces divide into three distinct regions. Blessed with over 440km of palm-fringed coastline, much of the **southwest** of the country remains relatively inaccessible, thanks to heavy forest cover, the presence of the Cardamom Mountains and the lack of roads. The central part of southern Cambodia – roughly comprising **Kampot** and **Takeo provinces** – is vastly different. Dotted with craggy karst formations which project starkly from the plains, this is one of the country's most productive agricultural regions: parts of Kampot province are like one vast market garden, producing durian, watermelon and coconuts, while in Takeo province rice paddies dominate. Salt and pepper are also key products here. The former is extracted from the saltpans of the coast and plays an important part in the manufacture of the country's *prohok* (salted fermented fish paste); the latter is cultivated almost like hops, with regimented vines clinging to cords. In stark contrast again, the heavily populated provinces of **Svay Rieng** and **Prey Veng** east of the Mekong are among the poorest in Cambodia, with most people living in meagre wattle-and-daub houses; the rice crop here is badly affected by flood in the rainy season, quickly followed by drought in the dry.

Most visitors come to the south to hit the beach at **Sihanoukville**, its pristine white sands washed by balmy seas. The town sits on a peninsula jutting into the Gulf of Thailand; its coastline is scalloped with gently shelving, tree-fringed white-sand beaches, while, out to sea, misty islands loom enticingly. But don't expect atoll-like isolation: the increasing number of visitors means that beach bars and grass-roofed umbrellas have sprung up along most stretches of sand, and food vendors ply their wares even in quite remote spots. That said, you can still find places to chill, and have a decent stretch of beach to yourself, particularly during the week.

En route to Sihanoukville, just two hours' drive south from the capital, you could stop off at **Kirirom National Park** to enjoy mountain scenery and explore a deserted hill station. Sihanoukville itself is the jumping-off point for another area of outstanding natural beauty, **Ream National Park**, with mangrove forest and fine sandy beaches. East of Sihanoukville, **Bokor National Park** has an abandoned hill station amid its jungle-clad slopes, and is most easily reached from the charming riverside town of **Kampot**, as is **Kep**, an increasingly popular seaside destination.

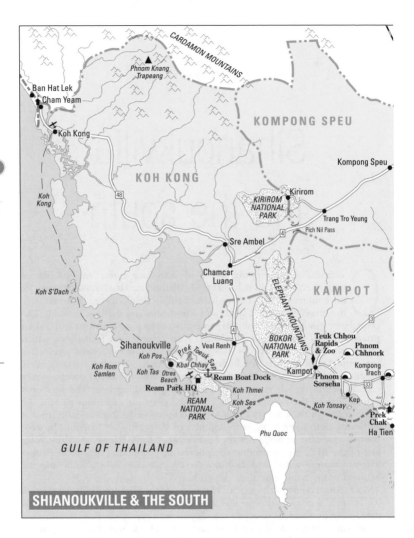

East of here, there are relatively slim pickings for visitors. The down-at-heel remains of the Funan-era city of **Angkor Borei** is home to a fascinating museum of early statuary and interesting records of archeological digs of the ancient city, sites of which are scattered around the town; close by, the hilltop temple of **Phnom Da** is most easily visited by boat from the shabby little town of **Takeo**. Best known for its ferry across the Mekong, **Neak Leung** is a transit stop for a downriver boat to the Vietnamese border. Continuing east here, you'll pass through the country's poorest provinces and the sprawling town of **Svay Rieng** before reaching the border town of **Bavet**, Cambodia's principal land crossing into Vietnam.

Communications in most parts of the south are pretty good by Cambodian standards. Travelling along **National Route 4**, one of the country's busiest

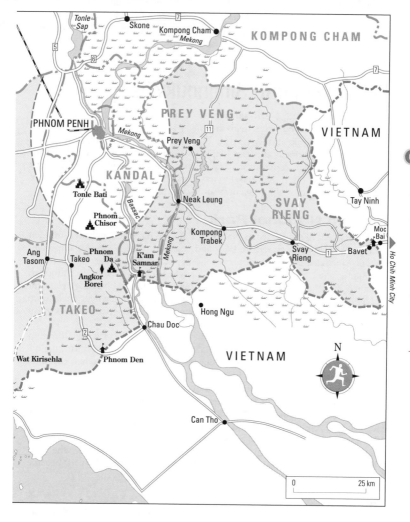

roads, you can get from Phnom Penh to Sihanoukville in just a few hours. From Phnom Penh, two other major roads lead south. **National Route 3** to Kampot is in pretty decent condition for most of its length, although if you're heading through to Vietnam the road beyond Kep is quite atrocious in parts. While **National Route 2** is adequate as far as Takeo, further on towards to Phnom Den, for the crossing to Vietnam, it also gets a bit rough. If you're arriving in this part of Cambodia **from Thailand**, it's possible to reach the capital using **National Route 48**, which links up with National Route 4, or to get to Sihanoukville by express boat. The area stretching from Takeo to Neak Leung, is flooded from roughly August to March every year when both the Mekong and Bassac rivers overflow their banks, and travel here is most commonly undertaken by **boat**, even in the dry season, when the network of canals that criss-crosses the area is exposed. It's no surprise, therefore, that you can't travel by road from the southeastern provinces of Prey Veng and Svay Rieng to the rest of the south, without going via Phnom Penh.

Phnom Penh to Sihanoukville

Leaving Phnom Penh, **National Route 4** makes its way through a typical Cambodian landscape of rice fields and sugar palms. South of Kompong Speu the views alter dramatically as the distant blue peaks of the Cardamom Mountains to the north and the Elephant Mountains to the south begin to loom on the horizon. A detour here takes you to the pine-clad hills of **Kirirom National Park**, often ignored by travellers, but well worth the effort of reaching for its almost alpine scenery and crisp mountain air.

Kirirom National Park

The rolling hills of the **Kirirom National Park** are zigzagged with well-trodden trails and dotted with waterfalls, lakes and abundant wild plants. An important wildlife sanctuary, the park's slopes are home, despite illegal logging, to forests of *Pinus merkusii*, a pine tree not found anywhere else in Cambodia. Although poaching has taken its toll, species of deer, wild ox (gaur and banteng), elephant and leopard still inhabit the depths of the park. In a 1995 survey, tiger tracks were found, but the lack of subsequent sightings gives little hope that tigers survive here today.

In the 1940s a road was cut through the forest, and in 1944 King Norodom Sihanouk made his first visit naming the area Kirirom, "Happiness Mountain". Development of a hill station began, but had to be abandoned when the anti-royalist guerrilla group Khmer Issarak overran the area in 1947. Consequently it wasn't until 1962 that the hills could be visited again. The cool climate and proximity to Phnom Penh encouraged its development as a resort, with not only summer and weekend villas but its own pagoda and two royal residences. However, the hills were abandoned again as civil war divided the country in the 1970s and the Khmer Rouge took control. Although a 350-square-kilometre area was designated a national park in 1993, it was only in 1996, when the Khmer Rouge in the area went over to the government, that the park became accessible again.

The park

From the entrance, the road climbs steadily for 16km to a rolling forested **plateau**, where you'll find the majority of the park's attractions and its few facilities. About halfway up the hill, a signpost points down a narrow path to **Outasek waterfall**, a series of cascades just a short hike off the main road. There's always some water for splashing about in here, except during the very driest part of the year.

One of the first things you'll see when you arrive on the plateau is the *Kirirom Guesthouse*; a side road beyond here leads to a cluster of derelict buildings, including the newer of the two **royal residences**, a fairly well-preserved white-ish building with a red roof. A bit further on, the other, older royal residence, is also derelict, and you can scramble through the overgrown garden for views over the forest and out to a magical lake, **Sras Srorng**, which can be reached by heading downhill along a rough track from the palace. About 1km beyond the guesthouse is the **park office**; unsurprisingly, it has

Cambodia's conservation muddle

With proper, sustainable management, Cambodia's **forests** could represent a valuable source of income for the country, not just in terms of providing timber, but also as a focus for eco-tourism. Regrettably, the last few decades have seen forest cover in Cambodia decline dramatically, with the most recent survey by the UN Food and Agriculture Organization (FAO) suggesting it has decreased by nearly a third over a five-year period. Initially the forests were logged, mainly illegally for timber, but more recently they have been cleared in vast swathes to make way for plantations, such as rubber in Kompong Cham province. Needless to say, the timber has been sold (see p.149). In 2001, the Cambodian government (forced by the **World Bank**) began to take action to reduce some of the most glaring environmental abuses. However, the government soon fell out with **Global Witness** (Ⓦwww.globalwitness .org), the environmental watchdog appointed by the Bank to monitor Cambodia's forests, when its findings were not to its liking. Their most recent spat is a result of a damning report issued in June 2007 by Global Witness in which it named a number of high-ranking government officials as using the country's resources for personal gain; the government responded by calling for heads to roll at Global Witness. In the meantime, the fact remains that nearly a decade after a cessation in logging was announced, little has really happened and the country's natural resources continue to diminish at an alarming rate.

At present, the Ministry of the Environment administers 23 designated **protected areas** (seven national parks, ten wildlife sanctuaries or reserves, three "multi-use zones" and three "scenic zones"), but none of these is fenced off and few are even marked by signs. The more popular ones – Kirirom, Bokor and Virachey, for example – are policed, though by a woefully inadequate (if dedicated) number of rangers. A case in point are the stalls which line the main roads in various places around the country and continue to sell cut **logs** obtained from the forest, either chopped up into bundles of sticks or converted into charcoal in makeshift kilns. These are eagerly bought by visitors, many from Phnom Penh. Even in the capital, many people still believe that traditional wood- or charcoal-fired stoves produce the tastiest food.

Cambodia's forests are home to a vast, diverse **wildlife** population, including globally threatened species, like the tiger. Ironically, the improvements in infrastructure that followed the establishment of the country's national parks have sometimes made it easier for poachers to capture wild animals, which are either sold in local markets for the pot or used to produce medicines and even charms. Until a government clampdown in 2001 it was possible to buy **game** taken from the park, particularly venison, along National Route 4 near Kirirom, while **restaurants** specializing in rare meats such as pangolin were easy to find in Phnom Penh. Nowadays, most of this appears to have stopped and you'll see anti-hunting posters along National Route 4 instead, though the message certainly isn't being directed at the poachers themselves, who continue to see the profits from hunting as too enticing to relinquish.

So, while Cambodia initially has made some of the right gestures, banning logging and outlawing trafficking in wildlife under the international CITES convention, it lacks the will to implement sound conservation policies. Most recently, concessions have been granted to international companies to explore for oil and gas (offshore), and – after a nifty change in the law – for bauxite, gold and copper in a protected area of Mondulkiri.

Though it's easy to think that the government simply may not recognize the long-term implications of the present shambles, it's hard not to agree with the ecological organizations that exploiting the country's natural resources offers just too many tempting opportunities for personal profit. For the foreseeable future, wildlife organizations working in Cambodia will continue to face a severe uphill struggle, producing useful surveys while generally being unable to affect government policy.

no information for visitors, although a nearby notice board has a useful map and shots of various park locations, as well as displaying photos of dead animals illegally caught here.

After another 500m or so you reach the only major road **junction** in the park, from where signs point towards various sights. The most appealing option is the track north to a series of three **waterfalls**, I, II and III, numbered according to increasing size, and located roughly every 2km. In the dry season, they decline to a mere trickle; it's only during the rainy season that they flow impressively – although this, of course, is when the dirt road is most difficult to negotiate.

Practicalities

The park is just over 100km southwest of Phnom Penh; it can be reached by public transport, though with some difficulty, as it's a 26-kilometre trip from the turn-off from National Route 4 to the upland plateau. **From Phnom Penh**, take a bus from Psar Thmei to Trang Tro Yeung (8000 riel) and then hire one of the moto drivers who are inevitably hanging around the market here to take you to the park (about $10 return). **From Sihanoukville**, you can take a minibus or shared taxi to Trang Tro Yeung (10,000 riel), and then pick up a moto. Alternatively, it's easy to visit the park as a day-trip from either Phnom Penh or Sihanoukville by hiring a motorbike or a car and driver (around $60). The road to the top is sealed (if potholed), so access is possible all year round. It is, however, well worth staying a few days if you can. Kirirom just begs to be explored on foot, and you need have no worries about land mines, as the area has been cleared. The temperature up on the plateau averages 25°C by day, dropping by 5–10°C at night, making long trousers and warm clothing essential after dark. **Staying overnight**, especially on weekdays, allows you to fully appreciate the tranquil surroundings and pine-scented air. At weekends it tends to get overrun with trippers from the city, though few of these stay overnight.

To enter the park (daily 8am–5pm), you'll need to pay an **admission fee** ($5 per person for foreigners) at the small shack at the park entrance opposite the *Kirirom Hillside Resort*, which is 10km from the main road. If you're staying at the top for the night, you can arrange for your driver to return the next day to take you back to Trang Tro Yeung; otherwise you'll need to beg a lift with the accommodation's supply truck.

Accommodation and eating

Just opposite the park entrance at the foot of the hill is the fancy new *Kirirom Hillside Resort* (T016/590999, W www.kiriromresort.com; ⑤), which attracts day-trippers from the capital as well as affluent tourists who stay in the luxurious bungalows scattered around the landscaped gardens. Not everyone will find the dinosaur sculptures and piped birdsong in the restaurant to their taste, but the resort (admission $3) offers an impressive range of activities, including canoeing, horse-riding, fishing, tennis, swimming and biking, as well as a small zoo. The **restaurant** also comes as a surprise compared to most in Cambodia, with attentive, smartly dressed waiters and a menu featuring dishes like lamb chops and fillet of salmon, as well as well-prepared Khmer food.

The only other place to stay is the government-run *Kirirom Guesthouse and Restaurant* (T012/363459; ③), which has a much nicer location on top of the plateau, but only basic facilities. Its five rooms are overpriced, though they have en-suite bathrooms (albeit with icy-cold water) while an in-house generator provides electricity from dusk until about 10pm. The restaurant serves steak and chips as well as tasty Khmer food, and there are wonderful views over the surrounding hills from the rooftop terrace. The only other places to get food in the park are the **stalls** beyond the park office, which are open at lunchtime only.

Kirirom to Sihanoukville

South of Kirirom, there are regular traffic jams on National Route 4 at the **Pich Nil** pass, where most Cambodian motorists break their journey to make offerings at the **shrine of Yeah Mao**, "Black Grandmother", who is believed to protect travellers and fishermen along the coast. Legends of Yeah Mao vary with the telling; one version of the tale relates that her husband went to sea to fight in a war and that Yeah Mao missed him so much that she went to find him – only to perish in a storm. Her shrine is easily picked out: look for the one with an eye-watering haze of burning incense and a smoke-dimmed image of Yeah Mao. The rows of spirit houses are recent additions and are a bit of a scam by local stallholders to induce vehicles to linger and thus increase their income, but Khmer are often superstitious and so most would prefer to make an offering rather than risk offending the spirits.

Beyond **Pich Nil**, and some 10km off National Route 4, the riverside town of **SRE AMBEL** has lost its purpose since the suspension of the boat route to Koh Kong. The only half-decent sight here is **Wat Angkor**, with a quirky new pagoda built on top of the laterite remains of an ancient temple, Prasat Chas. The twelve decayed towers of the original temple, dating from the Angkor period, have been ingeniously refurbished as shrines. A stairway down to the river is protected by 118 concrete soldiers wielding guns, along with abundant concrete mushrooms and a crocodile fountain.

Back on National Route 4, the agricultural landscape gives way to massive palm-oil plantations, until about 20km from the coast the road forks, with a side road leading to Sihanoukville's newly refurbished airport and Ream National Park (see p.280). Continuing along National Route 4, you get your first glimpse of the sea from the crest of a steep hill, closely followed by the modern, industrial buildings of Cambrew, Cambodia's national brewery, source of the ubiquitous Angkor beer. From here, it's just a few kilometres to the centre of Sihanoukville.

Sihanoukville and around

Cambodia's prime beach resort, **SIHANOUKVILLE** occupies a hilly headland rising above island-specked waters and six gently shelving white-sand beaches. At the height of the hot season (March–May), cooling breezes waft in from the sea; in the cool season (Nov–Feb), the town is bathed in warming winds; and during the rainy season (June–Oct) it's still warm and dry enough to spend the morning on the beach, although in the afternoons rain whips in from the sea.

Although Sihanoukville is the town's official name, honouring the king who secured the country's independence, it continues to be known as **Kompong Som**, after the tiny fishing village that was established here before the deep-sea port was built in 1956. The town centre is a little way inland, and although the sprawling layout and architecture are workaday – plain concrete blocks connected by wide, undulating streets – the relaxed atmosphere is still what you'd expect of a seaside resort, as are the predictable numbers of vendors working the beaches.

Should you weary of the beaches, there are inland **waterfalls** to visit north of town, and the **Ream National Park**, 18 kilometres to the east, which includes a protected marine area enclosing a diverse landscape of rivers, mangrove forest, islands and farmland.

Arrival, information and city transport

All **express buses** from Phnom Penh stop at the **transport depot** on Street 109, within a couple of hundred metres of town-centre accommodation. **Shared taxis**, **minibuses** and **pick-ups** from everywhere other than Kampot, come in at the same depot, while arrivals from Kampot stop on the street in front of the market. The **daily boat** from Koh Kong docks on Hun Sen Beach Drive, a kilometre north of the port. The principal guesthouses send transport to meet buses and boats, though there are always motos on hand, too. Sihanoukville's **airport** (off National Route 4, 23km from town) has recently been refurbished with a view to enticing tourists from Siem Reap to stay longer in the country. However, a fatal plane crash near Kampot in 2007 resulted in flights to Sihanoukville being suspended, so you'll need to check with a travel agent if you're thinking of using this route.

Two booklets, *The Sihanoukville Visitors Guide* and *The Sihanoukville Advertiser*, keep abreast of new places to sleep, eat and drink. Both are available free in bars, restaurants and guesthouses; the latter has a "Volunteer" section with information on opportunities to help out in town. The **tourist office** (Mon–Fri 8–11am & 2–5pm), at the corner of Street 109 and Sopheakmongkol West, is friendly enough, but, as ever, has no real information. The compact town centre is home to the town's **banks**, a Camintel office for overseas **phone** calls, places for **Internet** access (for details see p.279) and the town's market and supermarkets.

Moving on from Sihanoukville

Travelling from Sihanoukville to other parts of the south and the capital is straightforward, though to reach the southeastern provinces of Prey Veng and Svay Rieng you'll need to travel via Phnom Penh.

By bus

Bus operators, Phnom Penh Sorya Transport, Mekong Express, GST and others have offices at the transport depot (Phnom Penh Sorya also has an office on Ekareach Street) from where they run efficient express buses to **Phnom Penh** (12,000 riel), with departures from early morning to early afternoon. You'll seldom have a problem getting a seat except on public holidays, when it's best to book in advance. Phnom Penh Sorya in theory operates a daily bus to Kampot (16,000 riel), although if there aren't enough people it sometimes doesn't run. **Capitol Guesthouse** (Capitol Tours and Transport, Ekareach Street, ☎034/934042) runs its own coaches three times a day between Sihanoukville and Phnom Penh (12,000 riel); *G'day Mate* runs a minibus (daily at 11am; $6.50) to Kampot.

By shared taxi and minibus

From the transport stop, shared taxis and minibuses depart throughout the day for **Phnom Penh** and destinations en route (12,000 riel by shared taxi, 10,000 riel by minibus); for **Koh Kong**, there are intermittent shared taxis and pick-ups (40,000 riel for both, or 30,000 in the back of a pick-up). Taxis and minibuses for Kampot leave from the street in front of Psar Leu (12,000 riel in a shared taxi, 10,000 riel by minibus).

By boat

An express boat leaves at noon for Koh Kong ($20), stopping briefly at Koh S'Dach. It is best avoided during stormy weather if you're at all prone to seasickness.

Be aware

As Sihanoukville begins to flourish, so has petty crime. It is rarely serious, and mostly opportunistic, and certainly not something that should put you off visiting, but the days when you could leave stuff unattended on the beach have gone. Most hotel rooms have safety boxes and most guesthouses will arrange safe-storage for your passport, money and other valuables.

Personal safety is another issue altogether; there have been several incidents of assault at **Weather Station Hill** at night, and drunken brawls are not uncommon. On a couple of occasions recently motorbikes deliberately rammed motos with foreign passengers on Ekareach Street towards Weather Station Hill, a rather lonely dark stretch of road at night.

Although none of this is anything to be paranoid about, it's as well to ask your guesthouse when you arrive if there have been any recent incidents. It is probably wise for single travellers to let someone know where they are going and when they expect to return.

The main areas of interest are quite spread out, and as Sihanoukville is hilly, getting around on foot can be hard work. **Motos** and tuk-tuks are readily available around the centre and at Ochheuteal Beach, and motos hang around most other tourist spots. Expect to pay 3000–4000 riel from the market to the beaches or port by moto, more by tuk-tuk. Due to a clamp down by the police (allegedly for safety reasons) it's currently hard for tourists to rent motorbikes; this may change, but be prepared to have to take motos and tuk-tuks, or to cycle or walk. A few enterprising places rent out electric bicycles for $3–4 a day.

Accommodation

Sihanoukville has plenty of places to stay in all categories, from $200 and more for luxury suites to $2 for a dorm bed. Hotels and guesthouses can get incredibly busy during public holidays and festivals, when it's as well to **book** if you want to stay at a particular place, though you're unlikely to be completely stuck for anywhere to sleep. Note that during peak season (Nov–March) and major holidays (particularly Khmer New Year), hotels hike their prices up by 25–30 percent. It's worth trying to negotiate a discount if you plan to stay for a week or more, or if you arrive during the week, even during the peak season.

Weather Station Hill

Once the backpackers' area, Weather Station Hill, aka Victory Hill, has given way to late-night girlie bars, and has been the recent scene of moto-muggings. Many of the guesthouses have closed down, leaving just a stalwart few to carry on; those that remain are pretty pleasant and do their best to minimize the effect of late-night bars on their visitors.

Chez Mari-yan Towards Victory Beach ☏ 034/933709. Set on a steep, boulder-strewn hillside facing the sea, accommodation here is in wooden bungalows with terraces surrounded by leafy gardens. All bungalows have their own verandahs – though the cheaper ones have only cold water and fan – and are decorated with traditional Khmer materials. The terrace restaurant serves Khmer and French food. ❷–❹

Green Gecko ☏ 012/560944, ✉ greengecko_guesthouse@yahoo.com. Just off the main drag, the genial *Green Gecko* has a great view to the sea, with clean, tidy rooms and its own restaurant. ❶

Mealy Chenda ☏ 034/933472. A massive guesthouse occupying three buildings and dominating the hill. Rooms in the newest block are the best – bright and cheerful, with pleasant en-suite bathrooms and a sea view from the balcony. There

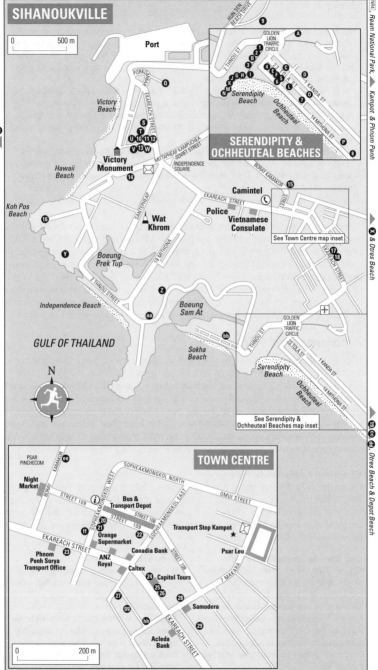

SIHANOUKVILLE

0 — 500 m

Port

Victory
Beach

Hawaii
Beach

Koh Pos
Beach

Victory
Monument

Wat
Khrom

Boeung
Prek Tup

Independence Beach

GULF OF THAILAND

N

Camintel

Police

Vietnamese
Consulate

See Town Centre map inset

Boeung
Sam At

Sokha
Beach

See Serendipity &
Ochheuteal Beaches map inset

SERENDIPITY &
OCHHEUTEAL BEACHES

GOLDEN
LION
TRAFFIC
CIRCLE

Serendipity
Beach

Ochheuteal
Beach

GOLDEN
LION
TRAFFIC
CIRCLE

Serendipity
Beach

Ochheuteal
Beach

TOWN CENTRE

0 — 200 m

PSAR
PINCHECOM

Night
Market

Bus &
Transport Depot

Orange
Supermarket

Transport Stop Kampot

Phnom
Penh Sorya
Transport Office

ANZ
Royal

Canadia Bank

Psar Leu

Caltex

Capitol Tours

Samudera

Acleda
Bank

ACCOMMODATION				RESTAURANTS & CAFÉS		BARS & CLUBS	
Angkor Inn	ff	Ochheuteal Beachside		Angkor Beach	6	Angkor Beer	15
Chez Claude	Z	Bungalows	F	Apsara	22	Biba Night Club	9
Chez Mari-yan	V	Orchidee	O	Chez Claude	Z	Blue Storm	23
Chne Chulasa	A	Queen Hill Resort	cc	Corner Bar	10	Chiva's Shack	8
Cloud 9	N	Reef Resort	B	Espresso Kampuchea	21	Fishermans Den	27
Coasters	J	Ramada	Q	Gelato Italiano	28	Freedom	20
Don Bosco	X	Romny Family		Happa	3	G'Day Mate	26
Eden	H	Bungalows	D	Happy Herb Pizza	18	Oasis	25
Golden Sand		Seaside	L	Holy Cow	17	Rainy Season	12
Hotel	C	Serenity	M	K2	5	Snake Pit	14
Green Gecko	T	Sokha Beach Resort	bb	Indian Curry Pot	11	Star	19
GST Guesthouse	E	Star Bar Bungalows	dd	Le Vivier de la Paillote	13	utopia	4
House of Malibu	G	Sunset Garden Inn	U	Marlin Bar & Grill	24		
Independence	Y	Tespheap Poykompenh	aa	Mick and Craig's	1		
King Gold	ee	The Cove Beach		Monkey Republic	2		
Long Meng Beach		Bungalows	K	Sea Dragon	7		
Bungalows	I	The Small Hotel	gg	Snake House	15		
Makara	P	The Small Green Hotel	hh	Starfish Bakery	29		
Mealy Chenda	S	The White House	W	Treasure Island			
Mirax Resort	R			Seafood	16		

are also cheaper, somewhat scruffy rooms, with shared bathrooms, and a number of dorm beds for $2. The restaurant has cheap Asian and Western food, though service can be slow; the rooftop bar is a great place for a sunset beer. ❶–❸

Remada Port Hill ☎034/393916. Freshly refurbished to international standards this hotel and resort has a terrific location on the hill above the port. The international restaurant serves a mix of cuisines, and there is a garden bar,

swimming pool, tennis courts, gym, running track and Wi-Fi. ❽

Sunset Garden Inn ☎012/761340. Lovely family house in charming gardens overlooking the bay with simple, but spacious, spotless rooms. ❶

The White House ☎012/913714. Black, white and red predominate in this stylish wooden guesthouse; rooms come with hot water, TV and fan or a/c. ❷

Town centre

The town centre has a mix of budget and mid-range accommodation, some of it excellent value. Several of the area's sports bars (many of doubtful repute) also have rooms, though these are obviously best avoided by single women travellers or anyone who wants peace and quiet.

Angkor Inn Sopheakmongkol West, round the corner from the transport stop ☎016/896204. This long-established budget guesthouse gets plenty of repeat custom and is run by one of the kindest families in town. Though plain, the rooms are clean, cool and tidy; the quietest rooms are at the back. The inexpensive restaurant serves freshly prepared Asian food, with some Western options. ❶

Don Bosco 3km from town heading east from Psar Leu ☎034/933765, ⓦwww .donboscosihanoukville.org, ⓔdonboscoadmin @camshin.net. This hotel doubles as a hotel school giving its students, all from poor backgrounds, training in the tourist industry. Rooms are large, smart, bright and slightly more luxurious than you'd expect of the price range. Though the restaurant and bar are functional rather than opulent, it's more than compensated for by the garden, swimming pool and attentive service from the students and teaching staff.

Profits from the hotel are ploughed back into student training. Booking essential. ❹

King Gold Boray Kamkor St ☎012/815708, ⓕ034/933829. A well-equipped, modern hotel offering mid-range comforts at budget prices, with a loyal expat following. Rooms all have hot water, as well as TV, a/c and fridge. There's also a swimming pool, fitness room and sauna. ❸

The Small Green Hotel 7 Makara, south of Ekareach ☎034/399052. Centrally located and painted a virulent green outside, the dozen rooms here are large and bright though slightly dated; the terrace restaurant has a range of vegetarian specialities based on the day's fresh produce. ❸

The Small Hotel One block southeast of Caltex off Ekareach St ☎012/716385, ⓔthesmallhotel @yahoo.com. As the name suggests, a small establishment with a mix of fan and a/c rooms and enthusiastic staff who can help arrange tours and transport. The small restaurant has Swedish dishes and is especially noted for the meatballs. ❸

The beaches

In general you'll pay a little more to stay near one of Sihanoukville's beaches, though there are a few budget alternatives tucked between the big hotels. The nearest beaches to town are the tiny Serendipity and the two-kilometre-long Ochheuteal, both about 4km to the southeast; over the hill and about the same distance to the southwest, is the immaculate Sokha Beach, while a couple of kilometres further southwest is the as yet fairly undeveloped Independence Beach.

There's a range of places to stay just south of the distinctive Golden Lions roundabout, about a kilometre from Serendipity and Ochheuteal beaches; although it's about a kilometre to the beaches there's quite a lot going on here with plenty of places to stay, eat and drink. Further on, down the hill at voguish **Serendipity Beach**, mid-range bungalow accommodation is the norm; rooms here fill up quickly, and the cheapest are almost impossible to get hold of. There are both budget guesthouses and mid-range hotels at **Ochheuteal Beach**, the most popular area in town, while **Sokha Beach** has been virtually hijacked for the exclusive use of residents at the *Sokha Beach Hotel*, the town's first five-star establishment. If you're looking for simple accommodation on the sand, the three-kilometre **Otres Beach** as yet remains mainly undeveloped with just some beach bars, a couple of which have basic accommodation in bamboo shacks.

Near the Golden Lions roundabout

Chne Chulasa (aka CCS) Ekareach St ☎034/933720, ✉hotelccs@yahoo.com. Modern hotel complex with well-appointed a/c rooms with hot water – the more expensive with bathtubs. For $30 you can rent a whole bungalow comprising two double bedrooms, bathrooms and lounge with TV and minibar. ❹

Reef Resort Serendipity Beach Rd ☎034/934281 or 012/315338, ⓦreefresort.com.kh, ✉rooms@reefresort.com.kh. This classy boutique hotel has fashionable rooms with plenty of white linen, and rattan furniture set in blocks around the swimming pool. Breakfast included. The restaurant serves Western food with an Asian slant, and there's a cocktail bar and pool table. ❺

Serendipity Beach

Cloud 9 ☎012/479365. Wooden bungalows on the hill, and a stylish beach restaurant-bar shaded by palm trees. ❸

Coasters ☎034/933776, ⓦwww.cambodia-beach.com, ✉coasters@camintel.com. Idyllic bungalows, some with hot water, climbing the hillside overlooking the bay. Seaside restaurant-bar serves both Western and Asian food. Tours arranged, including overnight stays on Koh Russei (Bamboo Island) see p.281. ❸

Eden ☎034/933585, ✉serendipityeden@yahoo.com. This popular beachside bar has just five rooms, all with a/c and hot water, though they're often full. Night-time party scene. ❸

House of Malibu ☎034/933844. Attractive complex on the hill running down to the bar-restaurant on the beach. The a/c rooms are very smart, but smallish, and the en-suite bathrooms have hot water. ❺

Leng Meng Beach Bungalows ☎034/934237. Smart concrete bungalows in a garden, just a step from the beach with bar and restaurant overlooking the sea. ❹

Serenity Towards Sokha ☎011/696009, ✉chhengsopeake@yahoo.com. Charming beachside guesthouse with accommodation either in the longhouse, or in bungalows on the hill; restaurant and bar. ❷

The Cove Beach Bungalows Towards Sokha ☎011/410446, ✉thecovebeachbungalows@yahoo.com. Simple wooden bungalows on the hill, restaurant-bar on the beach. ❶–❷

Ochheuteal Beach

Golden Sand 23 Tola St ☎034/933607, ⓦwww.hotelgoldensand.com. Located a block back from the beach, this business-oriented hotel has sumptuous rooms with all amenities. Big off-season discounts are available, and breakfast is included. ❺

GST Guesthouse 14 Mithona St ☎016/210222. Run by the GST bus company, this popular place has a choice of fan or a/c rooms at some of the cheapest prices on (or at least very close to) this beach. ❶–❷

Makara 14 Mithona St ☎034/933448 ✉makarashv@camintel.com. At the south end of the beach, this sprawling guesthouse has a range of rooms and is always busy; travellers' bar and restaurant with all the services. ❶–❸

Ochheuteal Beachside Bungalows
☎016/953896. Lovely thatched a/c rooms with verandah and attached bathrooms (some have hot water) and an excellent restaurant. It's not exactly "beachside", but only 70m away. ❸

Orchidee 23 Tola St ☎034/933639 or 012/380300, Ⓦwww.orchideeguesthouse.com. Colourful orchids hang everywhere in the shady courtyard of this hotel. Rooms are light and airy, with TV, a/c; bathrooms have hot water. There's a swimming pool, plus a quiet balcony sitting area. Popular with expats escaping from Phnom Penh, so worth booking at weekends and holidays. ❸

Romny Family Bungalows 1 Kanda St ☎016/861459, Ⓔromnytour@yahoo.com. Families are actively encouraged here. Accommodation is in tidy bungalows, and there is a simple bar and restaurant. Staff are friendly and caring, and tours and onward travel can be arranged. If you want to cook for yourself they'll let you use the kitchen. 100m from the beach. ❷

Seaside ☎034/933662 or 015/340711, Ⓕ034/933640. Looking more like a temple than a hotel, this distinctive place has a terrific location opposite the beach and attracts NGO workers from Phnom Penh for its friendliness. Rooms have en-suite bathroom TV and a/c, although the cheaper ones have no windows. Breakfast included. ❹

Independence and Sokha beaches

Chez Claude On the hill between Independence and Sokha beaches ☎012/824870, Ⓔ012824870 @mobitel.com.kh. En-suite accommodation in individually designed wooden bungalows on the hill overlooking the bay, with private balconies looking out to sea. The hotel also has a French restaurant, and can arrange diving trips. ❹

Independence ☎034/934300, Ⓦwww .independencehotel.net. Sympathetically restored to its former glory, this hotel has an aura of romance in its new guise as a resort and spa. Many of the sumptuous rooms and suites on its gleaming seven floors have fantastic views over

the bay and islands. Cocktails can be taken in the *History Bar* and the restaurant offers fine dining. Facilities include swimming pool, spa, gardens and access to the private beach. ❽–❾

Sokha Beach Resort Sokha Beach ☎034/935999, Ⓦwww.sokhahotels.com. This luxurious hotel has nearly two hundred rooms in a huge complex occupying almost the whole of Sokha Beach. Rooms have all the amenities you'd expect and some have great views; there's also a beautiful swimming pool, a spa, fitness centre, tennis courts, water-sports equipment and a choice of restaurants and bars. Free shuttle to town and other beaches. ❽

Tespheap Poykompenh Independence Beach ☎016/622230. Away from the crowds, this basic guesthouse has clean rooms just across from the beach. ❶

Otres Beach

Queen Hill Resort ☎012/482418, Ⓦwww .queenhillresortbungalows.com. Well-appointed bungalows, most with terrific views of the bays, perched on the headland at Otres Beach. Some have hot water and a/c. ❷

Star Bar Bungalows Otres Beach. A few basic bamboo and grass huts just two steps from the beach. ❶

The islands

Until late 2007 opportunities for staying on the islands were limited to a few beach enterprises such as *Jonty's Jungle Camp* (☎092/502374, Ⓦwww.jontysjunglecamp.com; ❸) on Koh Ta Kiev, with a few land-based guesthouses also offering overnight stays on off shore islands, especially Koh Russei (contact *Coasters* or *Romny Family Bungalows*). Recently, a luxurious new off shore resort opened and more are sure to follow.

Mirax Resort Koh Dek Koule, off Sihanoukville beyond Koh Pos ☎012/763805, Ⓔinfo @miraxresort.com, Ⓦwww.miraxresort.com. Idyllic tropical island retreat, with deluxe accommodation, restaurant, bar, infinity pool and spa. Activities include diving and power-snorkelling, and there's an electronic telescope for viewing the stunning night sky. ❾

The Town

The **town centre** has little of interest: by day, it's moderately busy with shoppers; in the evening, restaurants and bars attract the foreign party-crowd – some staying open till dawn if the custom is there. Sadly, the best thing in town – the rambling market, **Psar Leu** – was decimated by a fire in January 2008. This used to be a fabulous place: its fish section selling sea urchins, octopus, huge crabs in various colours – indeed, just about anything from itsy-bitsy tiddlers to mighty

Paradise lost?

Cambodia's coastal waters are peppered by hundreds of tropical islands lapped by clear, balmy seas, many graced with white-sand beaches. But this island idyll is at risk. Since 2006 the government has leased at least seven islands (with suggestions that this may actually be as many as 22) to international companies for the development of luxury hotels and golf courses. So far, fourteen five-star resorts and, a staggering **eighteen golf courses** have been mooted, and a Russian company, which has leased both Hawaii Beach and its off-island, Koh Pos, is even proposing to build a bridge between the two.

Koh Pos was originally leased for the first time in 1995 – although no development took place, this time the government has stipulated a time clause in the leases to ensure work actually starts. So it's pretty certain that a **rash of resorts** will appear in the next few years. On the upside, these will provide much-needed **employment** for Cambodians, but it would seem that the downsides are greater, with the money spent by tourists going directly to the overseas corporations, and the resorts adding a further drain on resources such as water, which is already severely limited (in the summer months it's not unknown for Sihanoukville to run out of water for several weeks).

Resorts are not the only developments off Cambodia coast. In 2002 the multinational petrochemicals company **Chevron**, was granted a licence to explore for off shore oil and gas and it is already probing the seabed off Sihanoukville. While this could be good news for Cambodia, bringing in valuable revenue that could be used to improve the country's infrastructure, the terms of the leases have not been divulged, even to the World Bank, which provides funds for Cambodia's development. In November 2007 the *Phnom Penh Post* reported that a new licence for offshore exploration had been granted to an Indonesian company in exchange for a payment of $4.5 million to a "social development project fund" – but just what that is the paper has not been able to establish.

sea creatures with fierce eyes and bristling whiskers. It was also the place to stock up on everything from fishing lines to fruit and vegetables before heading out on a trip to the islands. At the time of writing, the stallholders are planning to carry on, selling from make-shift stalls nearby, while the government has pledged money for replacing the market's roof. Whether Psar Leu will be rebuilt or the sellers forced to move to the rather unlovely, and currently deserted, Sihanoukville Trade Centre around the corner remains to be seen.

Sihanoukville's modest sights are scattered around town and best visited by moto (or a rented motorbike if the ban on tourists hiring them is lifted). Furthest out, **Phnom Sihanoukville**, accessed by a track behind the Cambrew Brewery, is the highest point around, although at 132m it's hardly a mountain. The town also has a couple of pagodas: Wat Leu, on the summit of Phnom Sihanoukville, and **Wat Krom**, set on a boulder-strewn hillside off Santepheap Street, where a sanctuary commemorates **Yeah Mao**, of Pich Nil fame.

One landmark that you won't miss towering above the north end of Independence Beach is the **Independence Hotel** (see p.273), which after years of neglect has been refurbished. Known locally as *bprahm-bpel jawn* ("seven storeys"), the hotel was once a glamorous venue attracting celebrities such as Catherine Deneuve. It was abandoned in the early 1970s at the onset of war, and from 1975 to 1979 housed high-ranking Khmer Rouge officials, during which period it's said that the swimming pool was roofed over and used as a prison. Post-1979 it became a hideout for crooks and smugglers until it was appropriated by UNTAC troops in the early 1990s. Reputedly haunted, it's now a luxurious hotel and spa.

Sihanoukville has some of the nicest **sunsets** in the country, and you're never far from a good vantage point. To catch the sun sinking below the horizon, head to Independence or Hawaii beaches, or to one of the guesthouse restaurants up on Weather Station Hill. At the fishing harbour on Hun Sen Beach Drive, you might get a classic photo of the small flotilla of fishing boats heading out to sea against the setting sun.

The beaches

There's a great choice of beaches in and around Sihanoukville; indeed at a stretch you could visit a different beach every day for a week. Ochheuteal and Serendipity are incredibly popular and have toilets and showers, beach umbrellas and restaurants, while others, like Sokha and Hawaii, have been leased off to private developers. However, midweek at least on Independence and Otres, you can still find a little seclusion. On the downside, most of the beaches are pretty narrow, with barely enough space to lie stretched out at high tide.

For Khmer, a visit to Sihanoukville is an excuse for an eating and drinking binge, with a dip in the briny as a fringe benefit. Their conservative nature, coupled with a concern – verging on paranoia for the women – about maintaining whiteness, means that shade is everything. Accordingly, the most popular beaches have a plethora of beach parasols and deckchairs for rent at a nominal sum, and men, women and even the young take to the sea fully clothed. Consequently, they stare in amazement at foreigners stripped off and baking in the blazing sun; don't be surprised if people start taking pictures of you, or even ask to have their photo taken with you. For women, bikinis are just about acceptable, but going topless is a definite no-no. Hawkers everywhere peddle **coral** and brightly coloured seashell ornaments; be warned that this coral has been gathered through the destructive dynamiting of the offshore reefs.

Victory Beach to Independence Beach

West of the town, and the closest beach to Weather Station Hill, the dark-golden sands of **Victory Beach** make a good place for an early morning or evening stroll, but, with the busy port just to the north, it is hardly the city's most attractive beach. A strip of public garden divides beach from road, but it's still the least secluded of the town's beaches and not particularly conducive to stripping off for the day. This may be about to change, however, as the beach has just been leased to developers. A row of beach bars is under construction to the north, while a full-sized Antonov plane has been installed on plinths at the south, apparently to house a restaurant and bar. More restaurants and bars are sure to follow suit, along with showers and toilets.

Offshore from here lies the island **Koh Pos** which presents a rocky face towards Sihanoukville. There are still deserted beaches on the far side, though for how long is anyone's guess: the island has just been leased to developers (see box, p.274), and for the time being there seems to be no access.

Ten to fifteen minutes' walk to the south is **Hawaii Beach**, named after a now-defunct restaurant. At the time of writing, the northern end was a massive construction site (possibly for yet another new hotel). Until work is completed, its probably better to skip its wide, tree-fringed sands and continue around the headland to a tiny beach nestling in a cove, accessible from the *Treasure Island Seafood Restaurant*; it's a perfect place to laze until sunset, supping beers from the restaurant.

You'll need to rejoin the road to reach **Independence Beach**, less popular than its southern neighbours, Sokha and Ochheuteal, despite plenty of rustic beach huts and a few food stalls. The beach, over a kilometre long, is rather narrow, and so best visited at low tide. At the northern end, and around the rocky headland, the beach is reserved for guests of the *Independence Hotel*.

Sokha Beach

Perhaps the most attractive of Sihanoukville's beaches, **Sokha Beach** is a kilometre-long stretch of curving white sand, fringed by trees and edged by scrub grass. However, only a 200m stretch at the south (you can walk here over the headland from Serendipity) is fully accessible to the public as most of it is reserved for residents of the *Sokha Beach Resort*. It is OK for foreigners (but not Cambodians) to walk along the full length of the beach, but if you want to crash out here you'll have to pay ($4 per day Mon–Fri, $6 per day Sat–Sun and public holidays – which, incidentally, also gives you use of the hotel swimming pool). Rocky headlands at both ends of the beach draw small fish and make for great snorkelling, and it's a wonderful place at sunset when the islands of Koh Tre and Koh Dah Ghiel are thrown into silhouette.

Ochheuteal Beach and Serendipity Beach

Ochheuteal, the town's longest and most popular beach, is a three-kilometre stretch of fine sand lined with casuarina trees, which you can just see poking out between the bars and restaurants that crowd the beach. The roads behind the beach have a great selection of hotels and guesthouses, though none is right on the sand. There are beach umbrellas, deck chairs and tables, tubes, freshwater showers and toilets, but this is a beach best avoided if you want peace and quiet as there's activity pretty much 24 hours a day. During the day it's packed with Cambodian families and sun-soaking tourists; by dusk tourist couples are strolling along the water's edge, stopping for food and drinks; then at around 10pm the parties start up and go through till dawn.

At the north end of the beach, the area known as **Serendipity** has plenty more restaurants and bungalows on the hill. While the sand here is soft and inviting, the beach is very narrow and is scattered with large rocks, so it's not as safe for swimming as Ochheuteal Beach.

The government has recently announced plans to upgrade Ochheuteal, creating a new boulevard between the road and the beach and providing public toilets and showers. Whether or not this has anything to do with Prime Minister Hun Sen's villa nearing completion next to the *Seaside Hotel* must remain a matter for speculation. In the meantime, owners of the beach's bars and restaurants seem unconcerned, no doubt figuring that their ramshackle shacks are reasonably transportable and that they can move them temporarily to other beach sites. It is thought that Serendipity, where the restaurants and bars are permanent structures, will be unaffected, though of course there is bound to be quite a bit of noise from the construction plant.

Otres Beach and Depot Beach

A six-kilometre moto ride southeast from the town centre will bring you to **Otres Beach**, the best bet if you want to escape the constant hassling of vendors at the beaches closer to town. The land here was sold off years ago and plots are possessively ring-fenced, but for now there are no hotels, just a guesthouse on the hill near the small fishing village and a few bars, with an occasional beach bungalow along 3km of golden sands.

Some 3km north of town, beyond the express-boat dock and around the headland, **Depot Beach** is an untouched expanse of sand separated from the road by grass and scrub, and edged by trees conveniently spaced for slinging your hammock. En route to the beach you'll pass a long, sprawling **fishing village** where stilt-houses are built out over the water and a small fleet of boats puts to sea in the late afternoon. The only people you are likely to see here are fishermen, though as the water is very shallow it's not much good for swimming.

Eating

Don't leave town without savouring the local **seafood**, priced by the kilogram and cheaper than anywhere else in the country. If you prefer something informal, you can flop in a deck chair on the beach and order what you fancy from passing hawkers or one of the ubiquitous food stalls, which offer a fantastic range of fish and seafood dishes. For a more formal meal, head for somewhere like *Sea Dragon* or *Treasure Island Seafood*.

For cheap eats in the centre, various nameless Khmer restaurants around town can whip up tasty plates of fried rice and fried noodles, and it's worth checking around Psar Leu where it's probable some food stalls will have opened up again. In the late afternoon, the **night market** opens up along Ekareach Street between Sopheakmongkol West and East. Inexpensive **Western-oriented** places serve up burgers, pasta and similar fare in the town centre and on Ochheuteal Beach, where you'll find some great barbecues too; if you want to splash out, there are several restaurants serving delicious **French cuisine**.

▲ Fresh crab at a beachfront restaurant

Weather Station Hill

Corner Bar Popular bar-restaurant serving sandwiches, great pizzas and other Western dishes. Daily noon until late.

Indian Curry Pot Generous portions of Indian food with a big selection of vegetarian dishes; their *thali*s ($4.50) with a curry, vegetable dish, popadom, rice and chapatis are particularly tasty; rooftop bar. Also runs *K2* on Ochheuteal Beach.

Le Vivier de la Paillote Classy restaurant and bar (with its own swimming pool) serving superb French cuisine in a lovely garden. Good-value set menus ($8 for lunch, $12 for dinner) and an excellent à la carte menu including a wide selection of fish and meat dishes and range of salads.

Snake House Off Soviet St. International and Russian food is served up at this unique location, where you'll find rare and exotic snakes in glass cases around the shady garden and occasionally under the glass-topped tables (but not, fortunately, on the menu). For $2 you can visit its crocodile farm, while late at night the place morphs into a girlie bar with much reptilian cavortings. Daily 11am–11pm.

Town centre

Apsara Corner of Sopheakmongkol East and Street 109. Khmer and Chinese dishes, with a particular accent on seafood; busy from early morning until mid-evening. Though foreigners get charged more than Cambodians ($5 a dish), the food is worth it. English-language menu available.

Espresso Kampuchea Sopheakmongkol West. Small coffee shop serving all styles of coffee, along with beer, cocktails and a small range of desserts and cakes. Daily 10am–9.30pm.

Gelato Italiano Sopheakmongkol East. Ice-cream parlour serving delicious Italian-style ices (2000 riel) made by the *Don Bosco Hotel* School; seasonal flavours, such as mango or jackfruit, are exceptional. Also has an outlet on Ochheuteal Beach.

Happy Herb Pizza Ekareach St. Reliable pizzas, pasta dishes and salads in a branch of the popular Phnom Penh pizzeria.

Holy Cow Ekareach St. Inexpensive Khmer and Western food ($2–$3) served in a traditional wooden house; laid-back atmosphere, eclectic music and *Cambodia Daily* on hand. 9.30am–8pm.

Marlin Bar & Grill *Marlin Guest House*, Ekareach St. Popular sports bar-restaurant on the town's main street with Western breakfasts, imported steaks and some Asian dishes. Daily 6.30am until late.

Starfish Bakery Off Sopheakmongkol East, behind the Samudera Supermarket. Run by disabled Khmer women who bake delicious Western breads, cakes, scones and other goodies to eat at tables in the garden or take away. Part of the Starfish Project (⊛www.starfishcambodia .org), with profits going to help needy people. Daily 7am–6pm.

The beaches

Angkor Beach Ochheuteal Beach. By day this beach bar and restaurant looks like all the rest on the strip, but come sundown the barbecue is fired up and the place is packed; the seafood barbecue ($3) is superb value, washed down with cocktails or a chilled beer.

Chez Claude *Chez Claude* hotel, on the hill between Independence and Sokha beaches. Excellent, moderately priced French cuisine – the grills, succulent steaks and pork chops are particularly recommended, though there's not much for vegetarians. The terrace is an excellent place for a sunset drink, overlooking the peninsula, with views to the islands beyond.

Happa Serendipity Beach Rd. Cosy place where you grill your own food on a tepanyaki hot-plate, and eat with a choice of tasty and tangy sauces. Tapas-size portions of fresh fish, meat and tofu at $2.50–$3.50 per plate.

K2 10m inland from Ochheuteal Beach. Thatched restaurant with a terrific inexpensive Indian and Bengali menu from the same owners as the *Indian Curry Pot*.

Mick and Craig's Between Golden Lions Roundabout and Serendipity Beach. Look out for the special nights at this popular bar-restaurant; their $4 barbecues are legendary. Also has burgers, wood-fired pizza and pasta dishes and moderate prices. Daily 8am–2am.

Monkey Republic Between Golden Lions Roundabout and Serendipity Beach. Welcoming restaurant and bar serving inexpensive burgers, fish and pasta.

Sea Dragon Ochheuteal Beach. Reliable Khmer restaurant, short on atmosphere but long on taste (it also has a beach shack), serving crabs the size of dinner plates and enormous prawns at moderate prices and cooked to order, to be eaten with various dips.

Treasure Island Seafood Independence headland. Head down the steps behind the decrepit *Koh Pos Hotel* to reach this idyllic, moderately priced, beachside Chinese restaurant, specializing in fish and seafood – the crab and shrimp dishes are delicious, and there's a lovely little beach to laze on while you digest your lunch. English-language menu available. Daily 10am–10pm.

Drinking and nightlife

Sihanoukville has plenty of night-time buzz, with lots of Western-oriented **bars**, as well as discos and karaoke bars aimed at locals.

Angkor Beer Boray Kamakor St. Compact disco popular with young Khmer, the music a mix of Thai, Filipino and Indonesian, plus a few European numbers played extra loud. Nightly 8pm–2am.

Biba Night Club Hun Sen Beach Drive, 2km from town near the port. Long-standing Khmer disco playing Asian pop, though it's not the place for unescorted females as it's located on the edge of the town's red-light area. Nightly 8pm–12.30am.

Blue Storm Ekareach St. Expensive nightclub for *really* loud Khmer, Thai and other Asian music, popular with rich kids from Phnom Penh.

Chiva's Shack South end of Ochheuteal Beach. Legendary and happening beach bar with parties every Tue & Fri.

Fisherman's Den Sopheakmongkol East, off Ekareach St near Caltex. Bustling Western-oriented rooftop beer garden, with satellite TV usually showing sports. Closes when the last customer leaves.

Freedom *Freedom Hotel*, Sopheakmongkol West. One of the town's biggest bars, with two pool tables and cheap beers and eats. 8am until late.

G'day Mate Ekareach St. 24/7 expat bar and restaurant, with the usual Western and Asian dishes, plus pool table.

Oasis *Oasis Hotel*, Ekareach St. Bloke-ish bar with live sports screen, free pool, cheap draught beer and Thai and Western food such as burgers and pizzas.

Rainy Season Weather Station Hill. With draught beer at 50c a glass you can't go far wrong at this busy roof top and garden bar with a pool table and DVD room.

Snake Pit *Snake House,* southwest of Independence Monument. Exotic bar with two-metre screen and plenty of female (and reptilian) company. 8pm until late.

Star Otres Beach. Beach bar in the true sense. Chill out or party till the small hours with fine sand between your toes.

utopia Ochheuteal Beach Rd. Possibly the busiest Western bar in town, with draught beer promotions from noon till 7pm, and parties starting up most nights from 10pm onwards. Restaurant and bunk room (free).

Listings

Airlines Contact a local travel agent for up-to-date information, At the time of writing, flights had been suspended.

Banks ANZ Royal, Canadia and Union Commercial banks all have branches on Ekareach St, where you can change traveller's cheques and get cash advances on cards. ANZ Royal also has ATMs at: Ocean Mart, next to the *CCS* hotel on Ekareach near the Golden Lions; *Golden Sand* hotel on Ochheuteal Beach; and at the *Holiday Palace Hotel* on Victory Beach. You can change dollars to riel at Acleda Bank, also on Ekareach St, or at the exchange booths and telephone shops in or around the market. For Western Union money transfers, head to Acleda Bank, or Western Union at the Golden Lions traffic circle.

Books and newspapers Mr Heinz and Q & A, both on Ekareach St, and Casablanca Books, near the Golden Lions roundabout, have second-hand books to buy, sell or swap and a selection of new (well, photocopied) titles. *Cambodia Daily* and the *Phnom Penh Post* can be bought at stands in front of Psar Leu.

Car hire Hotels, guesthouses and tour operators can help you hire a car and driver for the day. Alternatively, head to the transport stop and negotiate with the drivers directly.

Cookery courses Traditional Khmer Cookery Classes (335 Ekareach St towards the Independence Monument ☎092/738615; $25 per day). It has individual wok stations so you actually get to cook not just watch, and runs one-, two- and three-day courses on its airy rooftop. Cost includes drinks throughout the day, beer or wine with lunch and laminated recipe cards.

Consulate The Vietnamese consulate is on Ekareach St, towards Independence Square ☎034/933724. Vietnamese visas issued on the same day for $35.

Hospital Sihanoukville Referral Hospital is on Ekareach St, towards the Golden Lions roundabout ☎034/933111, and has limited facilities. International Peace Hospital on Ekareach St towards the Independence Monument ☎012/794269 has a 24hr emergency service. Alternatively call International SOS Medical Clinic (Phnom Penh) ☎023/216911.

Internet access Getting online is easy and costs between $1 and $1.50 per hour, with places all over town and even on Ochheuteal Beach.

Massage and spas Seeing Hands 3 on Ekareach near the *Holy Cow* restaurant (☎012/799016; $4/hr) gives massage by the blind and sight-impaired.

More exclusive is the Jasmine Spa (*Sokha Beach Resort* ☎034/935999, from $30) where you can choose from a range of pampering massages and treatments.

Motorbike rental At the time of writing, the police had banned foreign tourists from renting motorbikes; it is not yet known if this will be permanent, so check locally.

Music Boom Boom Room on Serendipity Beach have a massive selection of tracks ($0.75 each) for iPOD and MP3; their catalogues are in many of the bars and restaurants.

Phones You can make international calls from Camintel on Ekareach St or, more cheaply, via the Internet at most of the Internet shops. Domestic calls can be made from phone booths around the market and dotted about town.

Photography Ana on Ekareach St near Orange Supermarket can transfer digital shots to CD.

Police The main police station is on Ekareach St, 1km west of town towards Independence Square; there are tourist police (☎012/882071) stationed at Serendipity Beach and towards the middle of Ochheuteal Beach. To report child abuse call the police on ☎012/181 7281 or use the nationwide hotline ☎023/997919.

Post office The main post office is on Ekareach St near the Independence Monument and has all the usual services, including poste restante. You can buy stamps and post letters in the town centre at the small branch office opposite Psar Leu.

Shopping Western groceries, toiletries and wines can be bought at a number of supermarkets and minimarts around town. These include Samudera, 7 Makara, just north of Ekareach St; Orange, corner Ekareach St and Sopheakmongkol West; Caltex, Ekareach St; and at Ocean Mart, Ekareach St near the Golden Lions. M'Lop Tapang (ⓦwww .mloptapang.org), a local NGO working with street children in Sihanoukville, has an outlet on the hill near Serendipity Beach selling crafts, clothes and souvenirs made by local street children, who get paid directly for their work. On Ekareach, Khmer Artisans has a good selection of products including silk scarves, bags and clothes. Zoco Clothes (near Golden Lions) is the place to pick up something trendy for party night.

Swimming pools You can pay to use the swimming pool and other facilities as a day visitor at the *Sokha Beach Resort* ($4 per day Mon–Fri, $6 per day Sat–Sun and public holidays).

Tennis There are floodlit tennis courts ($5 per hour) at *Sokha Beach Resort*.

Travel agents and tour operators The following can all arrange visas/extensions, boat tickets, bus tickets, car hire and local tours. Ana Internet and Travel (Ekareach St next to Orange Supermarket, ☎034/933929); Romny Family Travel & Tour Service (at *Romny Family Bungalows*, 1 Kanda St, ☎016/861459). In addition to the above services, Sokun Travel & Tours, Serendipity Beach Rd, ☎034/933791, can also arrange international and domestic flights.

Around Sihanoukville

The top attraction outside town is the coastal **Ream National Park**, which covers a range of habitats and boasts fine scenery and plentiful wildlife. If you still haven't had your fill of beaches, then an outing to one of the **offshore islands** (a couple of which lie within Ream) could be just the thing, especially if you're planning on staying a couple of days.

Closer to hand are the **Kbal Chhay waterfalls**, a series of cascades fed by the Prek Toeuk Sap; these are fairly impressive in the rainy season, though there's not much to see in the dry. To reach them, head out of Sihanoukville on National Route 4, turning left after about 10km at a sign for the falls, then continuing another 7km. A moto there and back costs around $5.

Ream National Park

Unique in Cambodia, **Ream National Park** (also known as the Preah Sihanouk National Park) covers 210 square kilometres of both terrestrial and marine habitat, including stunning coastal scenery, mangrove swamps, lowland evergreen forest and the islands of Koh Thmei and Koh Ses. At least 155 species of **bird** have been recorded in the park, and for resident and visiting waders, the mangrove-lined **Prek Toeuk Sap** River is an important habitat. Besides supporting a large population of fishing eagles, the river is also home to milky and adjutant storks and kingfishers, which are regularly spotted on the river trips.

The list of **mammals** includes deer, wild pig and fishing cats, though these are all elusive and you're more likely to see monkeys.

Most visitors to the park go on an all-day **trip** arranged through guesthouses and cafés, such as *Romny Family Bungalows,* or *Q & A* (about $15 per person, depending on numbers) in Sihanoukville; these include a boat trip down the Prek Toeuk Sap, a walk through the jungle either from or to Thmor Tom, a small village in the park, and swimming and picnicking at the stunningly beautiful white-sand **beach** of Koh Sam Pouch, followed by the return boat journey.

Alternatively, staff at the **park headquarters** also run boat trips on the river (about $35 for up to five people, plus $6 for each additional person), as well as organizing **guided walks** ($6 per person; around 2hr) along nearby nature trails. The headquarters (daily 7.30–11am & 2–5pm; ℡012/875096) are in a green wooden building just beyond the entrance to Kang Keng Airport, 23km from Sihanoukville – turn up early or phone the day before to book a boat and guide. A moto from Sihanoukville will cost about $5; ask your moto driver to drop you at the bridge over the Prek Toeuk Sap, on National Route 4, 25km towards Phnom Penh, which is where the boats leave from. You'll need to take food, water and sun protection.

Islands near Sihanoukville

The coast is sprinkled with hundreds, if not thousands, of islands. Although some have been leased to private investors and are off-limits (see p.274), it is still possible to visit others, either making your own arrangements with a local fisherman or taking one of the organized excursions (about $10) with a Sihanoukville guesthouse such as *Coasters* or *Romny Family Bungalows*. **Koh Russei** is a common destination, although, with a couple of beach bars, it is not precisely a Robinson Crusoe experience; Koh Tas (an hour away by boat) has sandy, gently shelving beaches, great snorkelling and a good chance, if you take fishing tackle (check when you book if it's provided and if not buy it cheaply in the market), of hooking a fish for the barbecue.

Diving

Much underrated, diving Cambodia's uncharted waters is a colourful experience, all the better for the lack of other divers. In places **visibility** reaches a staggering 30m, and, with a wealth of islands to choose from, operators can offer itineraries ranging from reefs encased in coral to an almost over-abundance of marine life, including barracuda, puffer fish, moray eels, giant mussels and parrot fish. Closest to Sihanoukville, Koh Rong Samloem is the most popular day excursion; it is two hours out, allowing time for a couple of dives, a lazy lunch and a bit of beach-combing on its uninhabited sands between dives. Further afield, more experienced divers might prefer Koh Tang and Koh Prins (a 6–8hr boat ride away) which are dived on over-night trips, with reefs, a wreck or two and good visibility in their deep waters.

The enthusiastic **Scuba Nation** (Serendipity Hill, ℡012/604680, ⓦwww.scubanation .com) is fully insured and the only five-star PADI centre in Cambodia; it offers a four-day Open Water course, day trips ($75) and overnighters ($195) – including night dives – on their tailor-made boat. **Chez Claude** (between Sokha and Independence beaches, ℡012/840870) pioneered diving in Sihanoukville and runs superior trips for experienced divers. **Eco Dive** between Golden Lions and Serendipity Hill, (℡012/654104, ⓦwww.ecoseadive.com) runs PADI courses, fun dives, day- and overnight-trips, plus a three-day exploration of the waters around Koh Rong Samloem and Koh Tang.

Koh Rong Samloem, two and a half hours beyond **Koh Tas**, has eight beaches and a rocky reef with good diving (see p.281); to the south, just off the coast, **Koh Khteah**, **Koh Chraloh** and **Koh Ta Kiev** offer reasonable **snorkelling**, with giant mussels to look out for in the waters north of Koh Ta Kiev. If you've got more time, you can get out to deeper waters, such as those around **Koh Tang** and **Koh Prins** five to eight hours from shore, see box, p.281). Koh Tang's claim to fame is as the site of a major battle to free the *Mayaguez*, an American-owned container ship captured by the Khmer Rouge on May 13, 1975, in the early days of their regime. The US navy and air force launched a mission to liberate the ship but met heavy resistance, and Ream naval base and the industrial areas of Sihanoukville were bombed during the battle. Divers can try to check out two shipwrecks 40m down, northwest of Koh Prins.

Koh S'dach

Lying in clear blue waters roughly halfway between Sihanoukville and Koh Kong, just off the coast of Koh Kong province, the small rocky island of **Koh S'dach** (King's Island) gets its name from the legend surrounding the **royal spring** behind the port, which is said to have gushed forth miraculously when the king and his army were desperate for drinking water as they battled invaders here. Supporting a population of a couple of thousand, the island may not look too exciting at first glance, but offers wonderful snorkelling and fishing (even quite close to shore, though you'll need your own equipment) and a base from which to explore outlying islands, which for the time being at least are completely undeveloped. It's also, by fishing village standards anyway, quite a prosperous little community due to the ice factory, which supports the fishing fleet.

The island is just a couple of kilometres long, and a kilometre wide. There's a rocky **beach** on its seaward side, reached by a path through the compound of the island's simple pagoda, **Wat Koy Koh**. The beach isn't brilliant, but it's compensated for by the vivid coral and shoals of fish found close to shore. The island is a pleasant spot to mess about in boats and visit nearby islands, the closest of which is **Koh K'Maoit**, just 1km away, home to a small fishing community and with some sandy beaches. Alternatively, you can hop in one of the small, fibreglass boats that go across to the mainland (5min; $1), where there are also some fine, deserted beaches.

Practicalities

Express boats between Koh Kong and Sihanoukville make a brief stop at Koh S'dach's jetty, giving just enough time to hop on or off. Boats to Koh S'dach leave Sihanoukville daily at noon, and Koh Kong at 8am; the journey from both places takes about two hours and costs $10. **Leaving Koh S'dach**, boats depart daily at 10am for Sihanoukville and at 2pm for Koh Kong ($10). You'll need to **hire a boat** to get to neighbouring islands or go fishing; agree a programme with the boatman beforehand and expect to pay upwards of $20 per day.

The *Koh S'Dach Guesthouse* (☎011/983806; ❶–❷), signposted when you get off the boat, has small, clean rooms in a wooden family house, as well as bungalows and a restaurant, which is fortunate as the only other places to **eat** are near the pier, where to be sure of getting a meal in the evening you'll need to order early in the day so they can get supplies in for you. Additionally, a couple of breakfast spots open up near the market, and in the evening, a few stalls set up selling *borbor* (rice porridge) and drinks. The grocery shop is well stocked with water, drinks, biscuits and general products, but expect to pay slightly more than you would on the mainland.

Koh Kong and around

Until 2001, **KOH KONG**, tucked away in the southwest corner of Cambodia, was accessible only by sea (and three flights weekly from Phnom Penh). Years of neglect, coupled with safety concerns first of the Khmer Rouge and then of banditry, had reduced the road through the impenetrable, jungle-clad Cardamom Mountains to a cart track. Now though, a massive new road, cut through the mountains by the military, links the town to National Route 4, and hence the rest of Cambodia. The reason most people come here is for the **border crossing**, 12km from town over the two-kilometre bridge across the Kaw Bpow River, at Cham Yeam. With improved onward transportation few people hang around to enjoy the simple pleasures of the area – stunning virgin forests, pristine beaches and white-water rapids. At present limited access means that you're somewhat restricted in the amount of exploration you can do, though there's some indication that this may change, as a couple of Western-run establishments are now offering treks into the mountains.

The town and around

Koh Kong used to be a prosperous little logging town, though it's now lapsed into a quiet backwater, with an easy familiarity. Laid out on a simple grid on the east bank of the river, the town consists mostly of wooden houses whose style owes more to neighbouring Thailand – only a few are built on stilts in Cambodian style, and there's no colonial architecture at all.

The sights within town, such as they are, are all low-key. Locals will point you to the unexciting **Red House**, built for Norodom Sihanouk, who never visited it; it's a pleasant enough walk 1km north from the centre, along the river. A pleasant jaunt can be made across the river to **Beach 2000**, a weekend haunt for locals, where there are thatched huts, refreshment stalls and jet skis for hire. To get there, hire a motorbike or moto (about 30 baht) and look for a dirt road

---

Moving on from Koh Kong

Shared taxis (50,000 riel) and minibuses (30,000 riel) leave from the transport stop at the market to Sihanoukville and Phnom Penh. National Route 48 is in great shape and it's a scenic trip as it winds through the foothills of the Cardamom Mountains – though it's a shame so much jungle has had to be cleared in the process. However, it is still a long journey, taking from six to eight hours to Phnom Penh, with four **ferry crossings** to be negotiated before the road joins National Route 4 at Chamcar Luang. This will hopefully improve in early 2008 when two of the missing bridges are completed, leaving just two ferry crossings; but from the look of things these bridges are going to be a few more years in the making – one of them doesn't even have piers in place yet. Taxis for the border at Cham Yeam leave from the transport stop 2km west of town beyond the disused airport, so it's easier to get a moto for the 20-minute trip.

The **boat** for Sihanoukville leaves Koh Kong at 8am, so if you're arriving from Thailand, you'll be hard pushed to catch it even if you manage to enter Cambodia, as the border only opens at 7am. You'll either have to stay the night and catch the boat the next day, or travel by road.

Border scams

Watch out for the latest scam at Cham Yeam border. This is the attempt to charge 1000 baht (around $30) or more for a Cambodian visa, with the excuse that "this is a land crossing, it's different". No it isn't! A Cambodian visa is $20 regardless of where or how you enter the country. If this happens to you demand a receipt; record the time, date and the name of the border official and report it, as soon as you get the opportunity, to the Ministry of Tourism (☎023/212837, @info@mot.gov.kh) and the Immigration Department (☎012/581558, visa_online.com.kh.

branching left about 1.5km beyond the bridge, from where it's another 2km to the beach.

A short distance downriver from the express-boat jetty, you can hire a boat to explore **waterfalls** upstream or the **beaches** on nearby Koh Kong island. If you bargain hard, you should be able to hire a boat for $20 a day, though the price can vary depending on the number of passengers. **Koh Kong island** is a surprisingly large and attractive place, with pristine stretches of sand on its seaward side. The boat ride there takes about an hour.

Upriver from Koh Kong, it takes five minutes to reach a **pagoda** overlooking the river on the west bank, where rock paintings portray scenes of torture in hell, mixed up with what appear to be scenes of Khmer Rouge atrocities – the latter presumably painted quite recently, as this was Khmer Rouge territory until around 1997. As you journey further upstream, the imposing backdrop of the Cardamom Mountains comes into view. After about fifty minutes you'll reach a stretch of river between towering cliffs, where you can stop to take in a pounding waterfall and a stretch of rapids.

Right by the Thai border the Disney-like **Koh Kong Safari World** (daily 9am–5pm; $12, children $8; ☎016/800811) can make a fun day out, especially for kids, with shows featuring dolphins, orang-utans, crocodiles, sea lions and parrots at various times through the day. (Call before you go, as there were plans at the time of writing for the park to move to Phnom Penh in 2008.)

Practicalities

Arriving by **road**, you'll be dropped at the transport stop beside the market in the southeast of town, 500m from the river. **Express boats** from Sihanoukville ($20) leave at 12 noon and arrive at 4pm, allowing time to get a moto or a shared taxi (about 50 baht or 5000 riel) to the **border crossing** at Cham Yeam (daily 7am–8pm), 12km from town, before it closes. From Sihanoukville, the boat is still quicker (though more expensive) than going by road; if the sea's calm it's a pleasant way to travel, though it can be unpleasant in stormy weather. Minibuses (30,000 riel) and shared taxis (50,000 riel) run to Koh Kong direct **from Phnom Penh**, bypassing Sihanoukville. Shared taxis and minibuses to Sihanoukville run from the market (50,000 riel and 30,000 riel respectively).

Baht, riel and dollars are all accepted in town, though baht is the favoured **currency**. Dollars can be exchanged at stalls in and around the market, or at the Acleda Bank just north of the market. The **hospital** is 500m north of the market, but you may be better off going across the border to the one at Trat. The **post office** is further north along the same road. International **phone calls** can be made from some shops near the market; they are routed through Thailand, and so are usually cheaper than calling from Sihanoukville. There's **Internet** access at the *Asean Hotel* (60 baht/hr).

Accommodation

Most accommodation is within walking distance of the jetty, though there are plenty of motos around if you need one.

Asean Just across the street from the boat dock ☎035/936667. This smart, modern hotel is often full as it's used by visiting NGOs; the rooms are spotlessly clean, bright and reasonably equipped. ❷

Koh Kong City On the riverfront, just north of the boat dock ☎035/936777, ✉kkcthotel@netkhmer .com. Posh, new hotel with business-class rooms and a riverside restaurant-bar. ❸

Koh Kong Guesthouse Just south of the boat dock ☎099/800200. Rooms in this friendly, cheerful, family-run establishment are small, but kept scrupulously clean and fresh. The upstairs restaurant and bar serves up economical and tasty Asian and Western food, including an unforgettable pad Thai. ❶

Koh Kong International Resort Club 12 km from town at Cham Yeam ☎016/700970. Massive, luxurious hotel and casino complex at the border, with a choice of deluxe rooms and bungalow suites, in tropical gardens running down to an attractive beach. ❺

Koh Kong Riverside 500m south of the boat dock ☎016/823221, ✉viraksour@yahoo.com. The cheapest rooms at this guesthouse are with fan and shared bathrooms, but even if your budget doesn't run to a/c, for just a little more you can get

hot water. Travellers' restaurant, transport and tours. ❶–❷

Oasis 2km north of town ☎092/228342, ⓦoasisresort.netkhmer.com. The resort has five simple, but roomy, family bungalows with adequate amenities in a garden. There is also a swimming pool, restaurant and great views to the mountains, along with eco-tours to the nearby mountains. ❸

Otto's Signposted 50m down a small road from the boat dock ☎012/924249. Located in a traditional stilt-house, this was the first of the town's backpacker guesthouses and seems to trade on that reputation; rooms are small and rather dingy with shared bathrooms, but none the less it still attracts plenty of trade. Inexpensive restaurant and bar. ❶

The Rainbow Lodge Tatai Koh Kong, 25km towards Sre Ambel ✉therainbowlodge@netkhmer.com, ⓦgreenescape.netkhmer.com. Newly opened eco-lodge of seven stilted bungalows set in verdant scrubland with river views; eco-initiatives include solar power and rainwater collection. Prices are fully inclusive of breakfast, lunch and three-course dinners (menu choices available). Can organize treks to the Cardamom Mountains and boat trip to the waterfalls. Book by email as there's no phone. ❺

Eating

The *Koh Kong City* hotel has a good Khmer **restaurant**, especially attractive in the early evening when the sun sets over the river; east along the river road, *Champa Inn* has a busy restaurant that's open from breakfast to dinner serving the usual Cambodian staples. All the guesthouses listed above also have restaurants and turn out reasonable Asian – especially Thai – food, and most have some Western dishes. Three blocks to the north of the market, the *Baan Peakmai* has a covered terrace around a garden and serves good Khmer, Thai and Western food, including many vegetarian dishes, all at reasonable prices. From time to time Western-run establishments open up, only to close quite quickly, presumably when they can't make a profit. Ask locally to see if there's anything new to try.

Kampot and around

Charming, compact **KAMPOT TOWN** enjoys one of the nicest settings in Cambodia, situated on the north bank of the Teuk Chhou River, with a panoramic view of the forested Bokor hill slopes. Once a bustling trading port, Kampot still boasts a large Chinese population, their single-storey houses, built without stilts, contrasting with the Khmer stilt-houses and colonial shophouses that grace the town's streets.

Kampot has become a popular destination for weekending Khmer and expats from Phnom Penh, as well as for foreign tourists: the surrounding province is one of Cambodia's most picturesque, the landscape ranging from the cloud-topped mountains of the **Bokor National Park** to salt-flats and misty, uninhabited offshore islands. Kampot is ideally located for visiting both Bokor and the tiny seaside resort of **Kep**, and there are other attractions close to town, including white-water rapids, lush fruit plantations and cave-riddled hills, plus an opportunity to see tigers at the Teuk Chhou Zoo.

Arrival, transport and information

Built on a grid system, the town is bordered on the west by the Teuk Chhou River (aka Kampong Bay River), spanned in the south by a rustic old bridge for local traffic, while to the north a modern concrete bridge carries National Route 3. The town centre is a roundabout at which roads converge from all directions. Arriving by **road** from Phnom Penh, you can either get dropped by the market, north of the centre on the main road or 700m further on at the **transport stop**, which is also where taxis, pick-ups and the bus from Sihanoukville arrive.

Kampot can be easily explored on foot; the lack of traffic and the pleasant climate make it a relaxing place to wander around. The owners of all the main guesthouses can arrange sight-seeing trips, including visits to Bokor and boat trips upriver or to the islands. For Bokor, expect to pay around $10 (plus your park entrance) per person for a day-trip, which usually includes a picnic lunch and white-water trip down the Teuk Chhou River. A boat trip out to the islands (normally Koh Tonsay), visiting Kampot's caves and pepper plantations en route, costs around $10–15. If you'd rather go it alone, there are plenty of English-speaking moto drivers – most

The Chinese in Cambodia

There has been a **Chinese presence** in Cambodia since the very earliest times – indeed accounts written by Chinese traders and envoys from the third century onwards have played a major part in chronicling the country's history – but it was only after the fifteenth century that the Chinese began to settle in significant numbers. Marrying into rich Khmer families and assuming positions as tax collectors, bankers, gold dealers and restaurateurs, ethnic Chinese soon established themselves as arguably the most influential minority in the country.

A flood of new immigrants arrived as a result of China's economic crisis in the 1930s. In the main, the Chinese community continued to prosper until the 1970s, when they were **persecuted** first by the Lon Nol government – which resented their success – and then by the Khmer Rouge – who wanted them eliminated by virtue of both their race and their wealth. Things became more complicated in 1979 when the Vietnamese liberation of Cambodia was followed by a short-lived Chinese invasion of Vietnam. This resulted in many Cambodian Chinese fleeing to Thailand; those Chinese who remained were subsequently permitted to resume limited business activities, but it wasn't until after the 1993 elections that they were properly able to reassert their influence on business – which they did wholeheartedly, capitalizing on their access to investment capital through their extensive overseas networks. Nowadays, the number of Chinese-owned businesses is clear to see from the Chinese signage on streets in any Cambodian town.

Cambodia's Chinese have managed to retain their own culture and language (most are **bilingual**) while at the same time integrating very well into the Cambodian population. It is not easy to pick them out, though in towns such as Voen Sai and Kampot they are more visible by virtue of maintaining their own Chinese-language **schools**. Indeed, although Chinese New Year is not an official holiday, it assumes a festive importance in Phnom Penh akin to the Khmer New Year, with energetic dragon dances performed in the streets.

▲ Kampot

of them a good source of local **information**. Hiring a moto for the day to visit Bokor or Kompong Trach costs around $10–12, while a day-trip by moto to Kep is around $8–$10, including waiting time. The **tourist office** is 1km from the main roundabout on the Kep road.

Accommodation

There's a pleasant selection of **places to stay** in Kampot, so you shouldn't have a problem finding a decent room.

Blissful On a quiet side street about 1km south of the roundabout ☎012/513024, ✉blissfulguesthouse@yahoo.com. Western-run place with very competitive rates. Rooms are well kept and all beds have mosquito nets. There's a nice garden with plenty of seating, a balcony lounge area and a travellers' restaurant (closed Tues). Unfortunately, standards tend to go down when the owner's away. ❶

bodhi villa 1.5km out of town across the river towards Teuk Chou ☎012/728884, ✉bodhivilla @mac.com. Unique, chilled-out guesthouse set in a veritable jungle of garden on the river. It looks more like a deserted temple from the outside with aged stone and laterite walls; room options are either the basic ones in the main house, or floating bamboo bungalows on the river – at night the paths are lit by fairy lights. Dorm beds (dry season only) $1.50. It also has a restaurant, a bar for party

nights, a recording studio and a movie screen. Tuk-tuk available for trips to town. ❶–❷

Bokor Mountain Lodge South of the town bridge, on the riverfront ☎033/932314, ⊛www.bokorlodge .com. If it's location you want, this terrific colonial-era building will fit the bill, though the rooms are looking a little tired, and in spite of all its natural advantages, the place lacks atmosphere. ❹

Borey Bokor One block north of the main road to the bridge ☎016/960700. Reliable, if unexciting, pleasant modern hotel with decent, roomy accommodation with hot showers, TV, fridge and a/c. ❸

Little Garden North of the bridge on the riverfront ☎012/256901, ⊛www.littlegardenbar.com. A few smart rooms above a congenial restaurant and bar, some with nice river views; booking essential. ❹

Long Villa Southwest of the market towards the new bridge ☎012/210820. Clean and simple rooms with their own bathrooms start at just $2 in this family-run guesthouse. In a cheerful courtyard, it provides all travellers' services, plus there's a blackboard of Cambodian phrases in the restaurant to help you with your language skills. 1–3

Orchid Across the road from the Acleda Bank ⓣ033/932634, ⓔorchidguesthousekampot@yahoo.com. Charming bungalows with their own tiny balconies in a garden. Prices depend on the amenities you choose. Restaurant, tours and pleasant owners combine to make this a good choice. 2–3

Rikitikitavi On the riverfront south of the old bridge ⓣ012/235102, ⓦwww.rikitikitavi-kampot.com. Booking is recommended here to secure one of the four comfortable and stylish rooms. 4

Sen Monorom Guest House Just off the north side of the roundabout ⓣ012/650330. Looking more like a hotel than a guesthouse, this place has good-value en-suite rooms, big and bright, with a choice of fan or a/c. 2

Ta Eng 36 Street 726 ⓣ012/330058. This long-established guesthouse is a little way out of the centre, but it gets a lot of repeat custom for the kindness of the family who run it. Rooms are large and clean, and there's a dorm ($2/person), plus a small outside restaurant and sitting area. 1

Utopia 8km from Kampot ⓣ012/1724681. Surrounded by orchards and with tiger roars drifting through the air, this out-of-the way guesthouse is perched on the river bank opposite Teuk Chou Zoo. With just a few well-appointed rooms, booking is essential, especially at weekends when it fills up with expats from Phnom Penh. Restaurant, bar and water sports – the owner will teach you to row standing up Khmer-style, if you're interested. 2–4

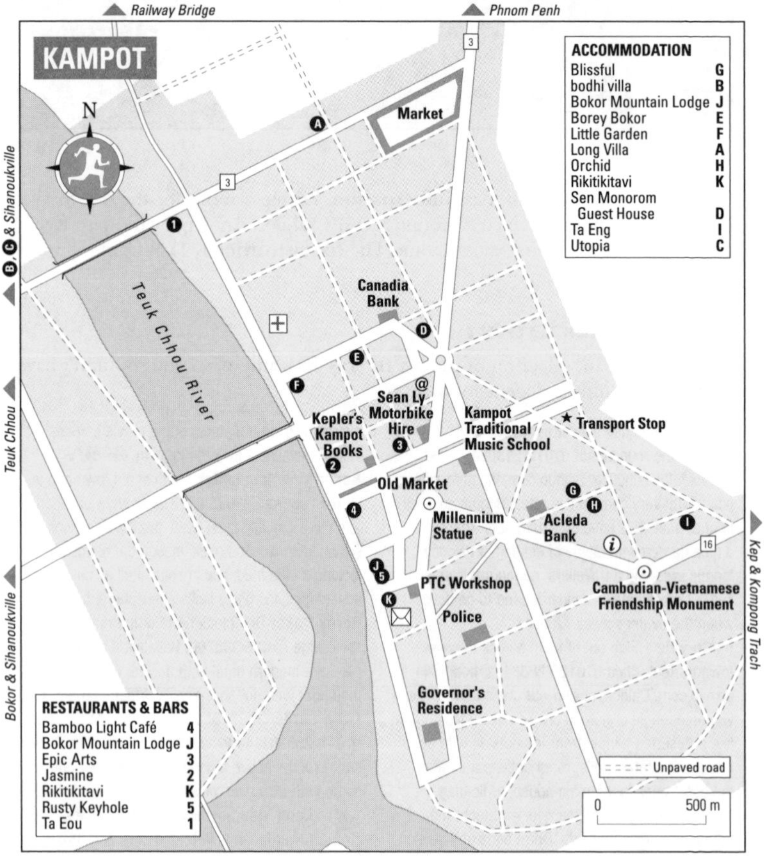
Railway Bridge
Phnom Penh
KAMPOT
N
ACCOMMODATION
Blissful G
bodhi villa B
Bokor Mountain Lodge J
Borey Bokor E
Little Garden F
Long Villa A
Orchid H
Rikitikitavi K
Sen Monorom Guest House D
Ta Eng I
Utopia C
Market
Teuk Chhou River
Canadia Bank
Sean Ly Motorbike Hire
Kepler's Kampot Books
Kampot Traditional Music School
Transport Stop
Old Market
Millennium Statue
Acleda Bank
PTC Workshop
Police
Cambodian-Vietnamese Friendship Monument
Governor's Residence
B, C & Sihanoukville
Teuk Chhou
Bokor & Sihanoukville
Kep & Kompong Trach
RESTAURANTS & BARS
Bamboo Light Café 4
Bokor Mountain Lodge J
Epic Arts 3
Jasmine 2
Rikitikitavi K
Rusty Keyhole 5
Ta Eou 1
Unpaved road
0 500 m

The Town

Most people use Kampot just for a couple of overnight stays between visits to Bokor and Kep, which is a shame, as it's a pleasant little town to wander around, even though there are no sights as such. To the southwest of the central roundabout is the colourful **French quarter**, where shophouses line the streets through to the river and flowers planted in cans, pots and just about any other available container, give the place a Mediterranean atmosphere. A grassy tree-lined walkway south of the road bridge along the riverfront lends an air of indolence, and there are a plenty of places where you can settle in and soak up the ambience. Although the old market here is abandoned – it was closed some years ago when a new market building was constructed and stallholders forced to move – it still looks in better condition than its successor. Further along are the government offices, post office and, at the end of the road, the Governor's Residence, which has been restored to its original opulent grandeur.

Another pleasant stroll is to follow the river from the old road bridge to the south to the disused railway bridge in the north. At the railway bridge you can cross the river on the rusty, pockmarked walkway, and return to town along the other bank.

While in town you could drop in at **Kampot Traditional Music School**, (see p.290), where you can see students practising traditional dance and music. Alternatively, visit the Provincial Training Centre Kampot (PTC Kampot), located in a compound behind the post office, which trains women from the province in weaving. The theory is that they can learn a trade, which will give them a sustainable income, but in practice once they leave, there simply isn't enough demand for their products, you can help by buying a silk length, a cotton scarf or *kramar* at the workshop, which comes complete with a label bearing the weaver's name and photograph.

Eating, drinking and nightlife

Kampot has plenty of **eating** options. In addition to the restaurants listed below, there are the usual rice and noodle shops around the market, by the transport stop and along the road from the roundabout to the old bridge. In the evening, stalls selling fruit shakes and desserts set up west of the roundabout on the road to the old bridge. **Nightlife** in Kampot is low-key, with a couple of Western bars along with the ubiquitous karaoke places, the most popular of which are across the river near the old road bridge.

Bamboo Light Café South of the old bridge on the riverfront. Sri Lankan/Indian restaurant with plenty of choices at very reasonable prices, and vegetarian options too.

Bokor Mountain Lodge Terrific riverfront location for a pre-dinner cocktail or post-dinner brandy, though the food is not recommended.

Epic Arts Just northeast of the old market ⓦwww.epicarts.org.uk. Run by a group of deaf people, this tiny café serves home-made cakes, teas and coffee. Instructions in the menu help you sign your order.

Jasmine On the riverfront, one block north of the old market. A foodie's heaven, where you can dine on excellent Asian-French dishes such as crab with Kampot pepper, for around $5 a dish. Specials change daily depending on market availability. If you only eat at one "posh" place in Cambodia make it here.

Little Garden Bar North of the bridge on the riverfront. Pleasant welcoming place in a quiet garden. Drinks and snacks are better than the full meals.

Rikitikitavi On the riverfront south of the old market. Famous for its tasty Saraman curry, made to an old Cambodian recipe with fresh herbs and peanuts, followed, if you have room, by hot apple pie. The polished wood balcony restaurant is just the kind of place to linger long after you've eaten, so it's a shame that the staff hurry you away.

Rusty Keyhole On the riverfront south of the old market. This welcoming bar and restaurant is the busiest place in town. There's a great atmosphere and it's a good spot to relax over a beer or two while your spare ribs are barbecued; one portion will fill two.

Ta Eou East bank of the river ☎012/820832. This breezy restaurant protrudes over the river on stilts, with fine views up to Bokor and inexpensive, tasty Khmer and Chinese dishes, including superb grilled shrimps and steamed crabs, and excellent fried fish with coconut cream. English-language menu.

Listings

Banks and exchange To change traveller's cheques and get cash advances on Visa and Mastercard, go to the Canadia Bank a block northwest of the traffic circle. There are money changers in the market and in shops round the traffic circle; there's an Acleda Bank near the *Blissful* guesthouse.

Books Kepler's Kampot Books near the old market has a great selection of second-hand and photo-copied books, with a good range on Cambodia; the *Blissful* guesthouse has a book exchange and sells some second-hand books too.

Buses Phnom Penh Sorya Transport and Hua Lian have adjacent booking desks at the restaurant opposite the transport stop; both run buses (16,000 riel; 5hr) to Phnom Penh via Kep. The former also runs a supposedly daily bus (2.30pm, 3hr; $3) to Sihanoukville via Kep, but if there aren't enough people it doesn't always go. A private fourteen-seater minibus leaves *Bokor Mountain Lodge* daily at 2.00pm (1.5hrs; $6.5) for Sihanoukville. It is run by the bar, *G'Day Mate*, in Sihanoukville, but you're under no obligation to take one of their rooms.

Car and motorbike rental Cars with driver can be hired through hotels and guesthouses for around $50 per day. Motorbikes are available for rent at Sean Ly, on the street that runs to the west of the *Phnom Khieu Hotel*; a 100cc runabout costs $3 per day, a smart 250cc off-road bike is $10.

Cultural performances Kampot Traditional Music School, on the edge of the park southeast of the old market, gives lessons in traditional and folk music and dance to orphaned and disabled children. Visitors are welcome (free, but a donation is appreciated) and a timetable is displayed outside.

Hospital On the riverfront, between the new and old bridges.

Internet For Internet access check out the streets west and south of the roundabout, where you'll usually find a place or two, but note that these change frequently; expect to pay around $1.50/hr.

Massage Seeing Hands Massage, near *Bokor Mountain Lodge* on the riverfront ($4/hr).

Phones There are booths around the market for domestic calls; international calls can be made from the Internet shops.

Post office On the riverfront, south of the old bridge.

Shopping The nearest thing to a convenience store is Heng Dy on the roundabout, which sells toiletries, snacks and a few Western goods.

Volunteering If you're interested in volunteering around Kampot, contact Angela at the *Blissful* guesthouse, or Barbara or Norman at *Little Garden Bar. Little Garden Bar* runs Tin Lid Kids, which provides treats such as trips to the zoo for the street children who collect cans.

Around Kampot

The biggest tourist draw in these parts is **Bokor National Park**, accessible from National Route 3 towards Sihanoukville. At the southern end of the Elephant Mountains, the park has a lot to offer – lush jungle, cool waterfalls, walking tracks and commanding views of the coast and surrounding area, though the highlight is a ghost town complete with abandoned casino, church and hotel. The park is also an important area for **wildlife**, home to over three hundred species of animals and birds.

The other reason most visitors come to Kampot, is to make the side-trip to **Kep** to spend a day or two chilling out by the sea. Closer to Kampot, some wild **rapids**, a well-maintained **zoo** and a smattering of **temple caves** can all be explored in a day.

Bokor National Park

Bokor National Park was originally developed by the French as an elegant hill station in the early twentieth century, and during the 1920s visitors flocked to the mountain to enjoy the cool climate and luxurious amenities. It's since been abandoned twice, first in the 1940s – when the Japanese invaded Cambodia during World War II – and again in the 1970s, when the Khmer Rouge engulfed the country. In 1979, Bokor was the scene of an extended battle between the Vietnamese and the Khmer Rouge, who holed up 500m apart in the hotel and the Catholic church respectively; today both structures bear the scars of the fighting. Designated a national park in 1993, Bokor remained inaccessible to the public until 1998, when it was finally secured against bandits. Even now, the lack of infrastructure means that few people get beyond the main hill.

Rising from just above sea level, the park's densely forested lower slopes gradually give way with altitude to boggy scrub, ferns and moss, and grassland. Near the highest point is a plateau which drops away sharply in steep cliffs that stop just short of the coast; cloud permitting, there are fabulous views over the countryside from here. Though it's unlikely you'll spot any rare wildlife, a recent environmental survey has confirmed that several globally threatened species inhabit the park, including tigers, Asian elephants and green peafowl, and the park **rangers** may be able to point you to some good birdwatching sites. With an annual rainfall of over 5000mm, the mountain has its share of waterfalls and is a watershed for several rivers, including the Teuk Chhou, which flows through Kampot town.

It may be that Bokor won't be deserted for much longer. Rumours are that the casino has been leased to a private enterprise, which plans to improve the road and develop a "resort". There's even talk of a new road being cut to drop down to the river just north of Teuk Chhou rapids. In fact Teuk Chhou rapids themselves may be at risk, as a massive, new hydroelectric power station is being built by the Chinese 3km upstream and locals are concerned that this will change the water flow.

Practicalities

Bokor is easily visited from Kampot by moto or four-wheel drive, the trip taking around two hours or so up a poor, winding road to the ranger station on the plateau. Most people go on a **day-trip**, which gives time to have a quick look around the derelict buildings of the abandoned hill station and take a detour to the Popokvil waterfall. **Staying overnight** gives you the chance to drink in the full atmosphere of the mountains, making a more leisurely exploration of the ruins and exploring trails across the plateau.

The **turning** for the park is 10km west of Kampot on National Route 3; the ticket booth (daily 6am–6pm; 20,000 riel per person) is about 1km along the road.

From here, the road climbs a further 30km or so up to the plateau, meandering up to a prominent signposted junction; to the right here is the Popokvil waterfall, while to the left is the **ranger station** and the former hill station.

If you're staying the night it's best to head straight to the ranger station to secure a bunk bed ($5 per night). You may also need to pay for your driver to sleep here (although some prefer to sleep on the floor or in their vehicle). There's a rudimentary kitchen, but you'll need to bring your own food and water (as well as torches and warm clothes – particularly in December and January, when temperatures are at their lowest and strong winds sweep the hill). Also be prepared for an icy-cold shower.

The park

The narrow and bumpy road from the park entrance winds steeply up into the jungle through a magical landscape of huge trees, massive ferns, lichen-covered boulders and small waterfalls. About halfway up, a massive rock, eroded into the profile of a face, overhangs the road; it's known locally as *kbal barang* (French head), and offerings are often made here for a safe journey.

The main attractions on the plateau are the ghostly shells of the buildings of the former hill station. Before you reach the main hill station, you pass a few once-beautiful villas which enjoy sweeping views of the coast.

The hill station and pagoda

A few kilometres across the plateau, the road comes to a junction. Taking a left here brings you to the abandoned **hill station**. The **Catholic church**, containing a small altar and plenty of graffiti, is unmistakable, but as cloud often obscures the view you may not see it until you're practically there. From the knoll here you can look across to the hotel, on top of the ridge, and get a panoramic view of the deserted town. The buildings are rendered all the more surreal by being encrusted with orange lichen, particularly during the rainy season, when the colour becomes preternaturally vivid and the plateau is smothered with ground orchids and other delicate wild flowers.

The **casino** is now a mere skeleton, while up the hill is the **hotel**, an eerie relic, its windowpanes smashed and its walls covered in graffiti. As mist wafts through the empty windows, sounds are deadened and the air temperature drops uncannily. Behind the building, the **terrace** is a fabulous spot to take in the atmosphere while listening to birdsong drifting up from the trees below – though don't go too close to the cliff edge, as it's not fenced off and there's a sheer drop of hundreds of metres to the jungle floor.

Heading back towards the junction, about 500m past the church a minor signposted turning brings you to **Wat Sumbpo Bpram** (Five Boats Pagoda), recently restored with funds from a Japanese NGO, but still with a patina of orange lichen. Perched on the edge of a precipice, it's said to take its name from the large boulders outside, which resemble boats; a mural within has been painted with a scene of the boats. A few monks eke out an existence here, though how they manage to beg their daily rice is a mystery.

Popokvil waterfall

Back at the junction, it's 4km to the two-tiered **Popokvil waterfall**, Popokvil rather appropriately translating as "swirling clouds". You have to walk the last kilometre from the end of the track, crisscrossing over a winding stream which leads to the top of the falls. The upper falls, plunging 15m into a pool, are connected by a steep, slippery path to the slightly taller, lower falls, though the pool into which the latter plunge is quite difficult to reach. It's not worth visiting in the dry season, however, because the falls dry up altogether.

Teuk Chhou Zoo and rapids

Set among gardens and fruit plantations at the foot of the Elephant Mountains on the west bank of the Teuk Chhou River, 12km northeast of Kampot, the **Teuk Chhou Zoo** (daily 7am–5.30pm; $4) is home to a wide range of fauna, including tigers, a pair of playful young elephants, lemurs and gibbons. The zoo is privately managed and spreads over a wide area, permeated by incongruous piped music. As in most zoos, the animals look none too happy, belying the almost unintelligible praises of the zoo's founders on a board at the entrance.

Just a couple of hundred metres further upstream from the zoo, the river becomes particularly scenic, racing down the valley and bubbling over the rocks in a series of gurgling **rapids**. There's a fee ($1 per day) to go further, which gives you access to the rapids and car park, where you'll find plenty of food stalls and places to hire inflated inner tubes. Paths lead down to the river, where you can paddle or, if you're a good swimmer and the water isn't in full spate, plunge in for a swim – but be careful at all times, as the current is deceptively strong and the water incredibly cold. The north bank of the river gets really busy at weekends and it's worth paying 500 riel to cross the chain link bridge to the other side where you'll find plenty of quieter bathing spots. You can reach the zoo and rapids in twenty minutes from Kampot by hiring a moto for a half-day ($4).

Caves around Kampot

East of Kampot, looming up from flat rice paddies, the rugged limestone outcrops of **Phnom Chhnork** and **Phnom Sorseha** have some caves to scramble through. Although you could visit both these sites in a morning, to give yourself time to walk between them and explore properly, you'd do as well to allow a couple of hours each. Note that there are no facilities in the caves and it is a good idea to wear stout shoes and take a torch.

Phnom Chhnork (foreigners' fee of 4000 riel) is closest to Kampot; turn left off the road to Kep about 5km from town and then head out along a well-made but unsurfaced road to the hill (about 14km in total). The entrance to the hill is through a wat, where you can leave your motorbike with one of the shop holders for a few hundred riels. From here it's a kilometre-or-so's walk through fields of well-tended vegetable plots to the foot of the hill. Intrepid explorers can explore a couple of pokey holes at the foot of the hill before venturing up the rickety steps, passing a collection of pagoda buildings, to the main caves. If you look carefully, through the gloom you will see a brick-built **pre-Angkor prasat**; the rock seems to be trying to claim the ruin, which is slowly being coated with limestone as water drips from the roof. Many of the formations in the cave have names; look out for the **elephant** at the entrance and a **tortoise** just beyond it. A couple more caves on the hill can be explored if you're keen.

Back at the main road, the dirt-track turning for **Phnom Sorseha** is further on towards Kep, on the left about 14km out of Kampot; the track stops after 1km at the foot of the hill; steps within the grounds of the pagoda here lead up to the caves. From the top it has a great view over the province to the Vietnamese island of Phu Quoc, and more caves to explore.

Turn left at the top of the steps and follow the rocky path for 50m to reach **Ruhng Dhumrey Saw** (White Elephant Cave). Just inside the entrance is a seated Buddha statue, from where rickety steps head down into the cave proper; here you can see the large cream and grey rock formation, vaguely resembling an elephant's head, which gives the cave its name. Back at the main steps, take the path to the right which leads after about 150m to the far side of the hill and **Leahng Bpodjioh** (Bat Cave), filled with the ear-splitting sound of squeaking bats. The stench of ammonia is overpowering, and watch you don't get guano in the eye if you look up. The cave is smaller and darker than Ruhng Dhumrey Saw, although a few shafts of light penetrate the gloom, highlighting the tree roots that poke down spookily from the roof of the chamber. Back outside, you may be lucky enough to see the monkeys that live in the woods on the hillside, while from the top of the hill there's a good view over the rice paddies along the coast.

Kep and around

KEP was already an affluent seaside resort back in the 1960s, when Sihanoukville was just a fishing village, though subsequent events were unkind to the town. Despite being eclipsed by Sihanoukville, Kep is now making a spirited comeback as a day-trip destination from Phnom Penh, though not for its beach, which is narrow, black and pebbly. Instead, Cambodians come for its food – particularly the crab. Foreigners too are arriving in ever-increasing numbers, attracted by its mellow atmosphere and increasingly attractive accommodation. Currently, apart from just kicking back and relaxing, the main attraction here are the trips to offshore islands, which can be organized through any of the guesthouses or hotels.

Traces of the town's sombre past remain, however. As at Bokor, the region is dotted with the gutted shells of colonial villas – tragic evidence of the Khmer Rouge's wanton lust for destruction. Until recently, most of these were smothered by the prolific tropical vegetation and home to squatters; now some have been restored and it's likely that more will follow, although the difficulty of establishing ownership means this'll be a relatively slow process.

East of Kep, the coast runs to the **Vietnamese border**, and the newly opened crossing at Prek Chak (for Ha Tien and Phu Quoc).

The town and around

Kep is a sprawling sort of place. The road for Kep branches away from National Route 33 at the prominent White Horse Monument, from where it's about five or six kilometres to the right turn to **Psar K'Dam**, the crab market; from here the road runs along the seafront for a kilometre or so, to the beach at Kep Thmei. Narrow and pebbly, the beach broadens out only fractionally at Kep Thmei. You'll know when you've arrived at Kep Thmei, as there are places to park, food stalls, showers and toilets. The beach gets crowded at weekends with day-trippers from the capital, so plan your visit for a weekday if you're looking for peace and quiet. If you carry on along the seafront, at the end of Kep Thmei you'll come to a massive white statue of a naked woman, **Yeah Mao**, of Pich Nil fame (see p.267), looking out to sea for her husband. Between here and Psar Chas, the tiny market at the east end of town, you can still see villas which were deliberately wrecked by the Khmer Rouge and left to be swallowed up by the jungle. You'll also see plenty of ostentatious government buildings and a vast mansion on the hill belonging to a government minister.

Trips to the offshore islands are well worth making. Closest is **Koh Tonsay** (Rabbit Island), with three good beaches. Further out, **Koh Poh** (Coral Island) has clean white-sand beaches, turquoise water, coral reefs and great snorkelling. The huge island that dominates the horizon is **Phu Quoc**, in Vietnamese waters; some Cambodians still call it Koh Kut, from the times when it belonged to Cambodia. **Boats** can be arranged to Koh Tonsay and Koh Poh through the town's guesthouses, or you can charter long-tailed boats on the beach – ask at the food stalls or at the new pier towards Psar Chas. To reach Koh Tonsay takes about forty minutes and costs about $10 for the return trip, while the two-hour trip to Koh Poh costs $40, though it shouldn't be considered in stormy weather.

On the hill behind Kep, you can get quite away from it all and enjoy fantastic views over the province and bay, by following a track through the jungle (access is behind *Veranda Natural Resort*); the hike to the mountain top will take about an hour and a half or you can go around the mountain in two to three hours.

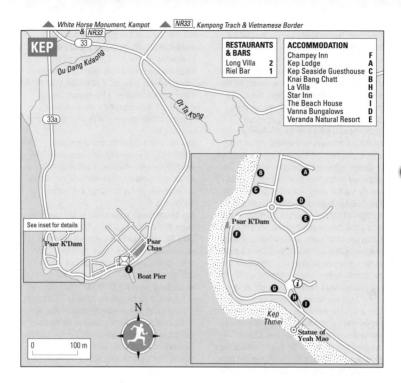

KEP

RESTAURANTS & BARS	
Long Villa	2
Riel Bar	1

ACCOMMODATION	
Champey Inn	F
Kep Lodge	A
Kep Seaside Guesthouse	C
Knai Bang Chatt	B
La Villa	H
Star Inn	G
The Beach House	I
Vanna Bungalows	D
Veranda Natural Resort	E

Practicalities

Kep is 25km from Kampot (10,000 riel by moto). There's a **tourist office** on the beachfront near the showers, though it has little to offer. There are no banks, but you can change dollars to riel at the market; the post office is on the way to Psar Chas opposite the new pier. Most of the guesthouses have their own **restaurants** serving Khmer and Western food; the one at the *Veranda* is particularly recommended. It's also worth checking out the food stalls along the seafront and at the crab market. These major on seafood, of course, but can also rustle up some standard Cambodian dishes. They open for breakfast and lunch, but close around dusk, when day-tripping Khmer make their way back to the capital. *Long Villa Restaurant*, on the way to Psar Chas near the new pier, has Khmer and Western dishes with the emphasis on fish, crab (check out the crab fried rice) and seafood. Outside of the hotels and guesthouses the only bar is *The Riel Bar* (6pm until late), on the main road near the turning to the hillside resorts. It has regular live music and dancing, plus a discount if you pay in riel.

Accommodation

Accommodation in Kep ranges from stunning converted villas to rustic guesthouses; the very best are sumptuous and stylish. While the cheaper places are clean, they may have electricity for only part of the day.

Champey Inn West of the beach on the one-way system ☎012/501742, ⊛ www.nicimex.com. Secluded bungalows with fancy decor and decent

bathrooms in a tranquil garden around a swimming pool; it has a French/Khmer restaurant and a beachside bar (across the road) for taking in the sunset. Non-residents can use the pool for $5/day. ⑥

Kep Lodge Pepper St, 2–3km from the centre of Kep ☎092/435330, ⓦwww.keplodge.com. Leave from the White Horse Monument, turning left after a couple of kilometres. If you reach the Aspeca orphanage, you've gone too far; the turning is 500m back. These hillside bungalows are decorated with a personal touch – there are original watercolours on the walls and each is named after the plant that grows in its own patch of garden; bathrooms have cold water only. The restaurant serves fresh produce from the garden, and the bar has great views at sunset views. ③

Kep Seaside Guesthouse Down a side road on the right off the main road into town, just before the start of the one-way system ☎012/684241. Comfy and clean rooms with cold-water showers and fans right on the beach; there's also a small restaurant serving Western and Khmer food, and the friendly owners speak a little English. ①–②

🏃 **Knai Bang Chatt** On the coast down a track just before the one-way system, ☎012/349742, ⓦwww.knaibangchatt.com. This exclusive resort comprises eleven contemporary rooms in three different villas, one of them designed by a student of the Khmer architect Vann Molyvann in 1962. With cool linen, polished stone floors and the copious use of driftwood and other beach finds, it feels more like a country house than a hotel. The grounds stretch down to the sea where an impromptu beach has been created – complete with muslin tents for relaxing out of the glare of the midday sun. Meals are served at a vast, single-plank table (8m long) at the water's edge. There's a swimming pool, sailing, bar and sunset views. Booking essential. ⑨

La Villa In the centre of Kep across from the beach ☎012/1702648, ⓦwww.thomasvilla-kep.com.

With tree trunks still clinging to the walls this restored French villa dating from 1908 retains its deserted look; the bar and restaurant are in the ceiling-less ground-floor rooms of the house. Accommodation, however, is up to date, in spacious modern bungalows around the grounds; rooms are cool with terracotta floors, and each has a secluded outdoor shower and all amenities. Internet available. ⑤

Star Inn Beach end of the one-way system ☎012/765777, ⓦwww.starinnkepcity.com. This pink birthday cake of a hotel is just across from the beach. Rooms are clean and large, but slightly old-fashioned; all-day restaurant with karaoke in the evening. ⑤

The Beach House In the centre of Kep near the beach ☎012/240090, ⓦwww.TheBeachHouseKep.com. Smart modern rooms with sea views and all amenities at a new hotel on the hillside in the centre of Kep; swimming pool, spa and terrace café. ⑤

Vanna Bungalows Kep Mountain Hillside Rd, 500m up the road to the hill opposite the Aspeca orphanage ☎012/755038, ⓦwww.vannabungalows.com. An ex pat favourite, this friendly resort on the hill has cheerful, simple bungalows with their own verandahs and fabulous sunset views out to sea. There are also cheaper rooms in a terraced block. Own restaurant and bar. ②–③

Veranda Natural Resort Kep Mountain Hillside Rd, 1 km up the road to the hill opposite the Aspeca orphanage, ☎012/888619, ⓦwww.veranda-resort.com. For spectacular views and nature at your fingertips, this takes some beating. Located on the hill behind the town, this funky and well-run complex of thatched bungalows offers a range of rooms from simple to sophisticated, including a few suites, as well as a good restaurant and the atmospheric *Jungle Bar*. ④–⑥

Kompong Trach and Wat Kirisehla

East of Kep, amid stunning karst landscapes, lies the friendly town of **KOMPONG TRACH**. The main reason to head out here is to visit **Wat Kirisehla**, 5km outside town, which is home to a reclining Buddha set in a substantial natural cavity in the limestone hills. To reach the wat, take the turning north off the main road, about 100m east of the market; the road passes the hospital before leaving town and heading off into the rice fields, where you'll soon see a large craggy hill ahead. Once you reach the temple, one of the nuns or lay helpers will show you the way to the passage leading into the heart of the hill. Though it's only 100m long, the tunnel is rather dark, and a torch is helpful. You end up right in the centre of the hill, in an almost circular cavity around 50m in diameter, ringed by high cliffs whose walls are eroded into caves. The large **reclining Buddha** here is a recent replacement for one destroyed by the Khmer Rouge, who holed up here for years without being rumbled.

Kompong Trach is on National Route 33, 30km east of Kampot and 15km from Kep. The road has recently been upgraded, making the journey relatively painless. You can get **food and drink** at the market and a couple of restaurants, all of which are opposite the main pagoda in the middle of town.

Takeo and around

Pancake-flat, much of **Takeo province** disappears in an annual inundation by the waters of the Mekong and Bassac rivers, leaving **Takeo town** isolated on the shore of a vast inland sea, and outlying villages transformed into islands. As the waters recede, an ancient network of canals, which once linked the area to the trading port of Oc Eo (now a ruined site across the border in Vietnam), is revealed. These continue to be vital to local communication and trade, and getting around the area is still easiest by boat – indeed, for much of the year there is no alternative.

The only reason to come to Takeo is to use it as a base to visit the only **Funanese** sites so far identified in Cambodia, **Angkor Borei** and the nearby **Phnom Da**, which can be combined on a boat trip from Takeo; an informative museum at Angkor Borei displays artefacts and statues unearthed at both sites. Since Takeo is little more than an hour's journey from Phnom Penh, it's possible to visit these sights on a day-trip.

Takeo

A key port on the trading route with Vietnam, **TAKEO** (pronounced *ta-kow*) consists of two separate hives of activity: to the south, a dusty (or muddy, depending on the season) market and transport stop on National Route 2 – which has little to recommend it unless you want to visit one of the karaoke parlours – and to the north, a more interesting area around the lake, canal and port. The **lakeside**, southwest of the canal, has been given a face-lift and there is now a park with views over the marshy, lily-covered lake, which makes a pleasant spot for an early-morning or sunset stroll. You can while away a little time at the port watching large wooden boats arriving from Vietnam laden with cheap terracotta tiles destined for Phnom Penh; the vessels are easily identified by the protective all-seeing eye painted on their bows. A crumbling square behind the waterfront is evidence of Takeo's colonial past, and there's a small market here, **Psar Nat**, which is busy in the early morning and late afternoon with local farmers and fisher-folk. The town's shophouses are sadly neglected, but still retain a discernible sense of French style.

Practicalities

Takeo is straightforward to reach by bus or shared taxi on National Route 2 from Phnom Penh (8000 riel); if you're arriving from the south you can get a shared taxi from Kampot (10,000 riel). Wherever you're arriving from, you'll enter the town on National Route 2. Shortly afterwards, the road forks; the left branch takes you past the lake and out to the port, while the right fork (National Route 2) continues 1km to the Independence Monument traffic roundabout and then a further 1km to the market and nearby **transport stop**. Here you'll be able to get onward transport for the 30km trip to Phnom Den (for Tinh Bien in Vietnam border open daily 7am–8pm, Vietnamese visas not available). **Boats** to Angkor Borei and Phnom Da can be hired at the waterfront. Set back a couple of blocks from the boat jetty is the **tourist office** (Mon–Fri 7–11am & 2.30–5pm; ☎032/931323). **Money changers** can be found at the market, and there's an Acleda Bank by the Independence Monument, though there's nowhere in town to cash traveller's cheques. **Internet access** (5000 riel/hr) is available at the *Mittapheap Guesthouse*, next to the Acleda Bank.

There's no outstanding **accommodation** in Takeo, but the friendly *Mittapheap Guesthouse* (☎032/931205; ❷–❸), set back from the road off the Independence Monument roundabout, has acceptable rooms, some with a/c and hot water, and it's the place of choice for NGOs and business visitors to town; although there's no restaurant, it's close to inexpensive food stalls. Near the lakeside *Boeng Takeo Guesthouse* (☎032/931306; ❷) has reasonable en-suite rooms with cable TV, fan or a/c and balcony. On the canal near the boat dock the newly opened *Phnom Da* has good rooms (no phone; ❶); you'll probably get invited to join in a game of dominoes or cards. They also have a boat for rent ($25 for one person, $27 for two or more people). A block back from the canal, overlooking Psar Nat, the *Angkor Borei Guesthouse* (☎032/931340; ❶) has basic en-suite fan rooms with TV.

Eating options in Takeo are severely limited. The road from the market to the Independence Monument has a number of restaurants, but none has a name or menu in English. On stilts over the canal just south of the boat jetty, the *Thmor Sor Restaurant* has a menu in English and a wide range of Khmer dishes, including some tasty preparations of fish and specializes in freshwater lobster – though it's expensive at $10 per kilo. There are also the usual food and drink stalls around the market.

Angkor Borei and Phnom Da

Twenty-five kilometres from Takeo lies the pre-Angkorian site of **Angkor Borei**. The site can be reached year-round by boat, an interesting journey through wetlands which are home to a variety of water birds, with all types of boats coming and going. The fine local **museum** is the main reason to come here, but you may well want to explore the excavated Funan-era archeological sites here and at **Phnom Da** (though be warned that these are closed in the rainy season).

The easiest way to get to Angkor Borei and Phnom Da is by **hiring a boat** in Takeo (about $20–$25). These have powerful outboard motors and seat six to eight people, making the trip to Angkor Borei in forty minutes (the onward leg to Phnom Da takes fifteen minutes), either across open water between June and January (approximately), or by canal and river the rest of the year. There are also occasional **boat taxis** to Angkor Borei (3000 riel per person one way), but you'll probably face a long wait both to go and to come back. You should allow a full day if you want to do justice to both sites, though a half-day excursion is sufficient to get a feel for them.

Angkor Borei

The pleasantly leafy town of **ANGKOR BOREI** sits on the banks of the Prek Angkor, a tributary of the Bassac. The town is well known to scholars as the site where the earliest-known example of written Khmer was discovered, and archeological excavations here have identified many features of the town that once stood on the site, including a moat 22m wide, a section of high brick wall and numerous extensive water tanks. Unfortunately, there is now little to see apart from the finds in the museum.

Boats pull up on the riverside near the bridge, just downstream from which, on the same side of the river, a white colonial building surrounded by a large garden houses Angkor Borei's well-managed **museum** (daily 7–11am & 2–4.30pm; $1), with a diverse collection of ceramics, beads, stone statues, carved pediments from the Funanese era and a photographic exhibition of the excavations. Some stylish sculptures of Vishnu and Shiva line the walls, but the eight-armed Vishnu surrounded by an arc is a reproduction. One of the highlights is a pediment removed from Phnom Da showing Vishnu reclining on a dragon. Aerial photos show clearly the extent of the old settlement and identify many of the features being excavated.

Phnom Da

Ironically for a site that has given its name to a style of sculpture, the remains of the temple of **Phnom Da** are now rather bare, as everything of value has been removed to the museums in Phnom Penh and Angkor Borei for safekeeping. The ruins remain pretty imposing, however, constructed on top of two forty-metre-high mounds built to protect the temple from rising waters. Experts differ on the temple's vintage, some believing that it was built in the early sixth century by Rudravarman, others that it dates from a later period, perhaps the seventh century.

Boats moor at the small village at the foot of Phnom Da, where local children will offer to show you up meandering paths to the top of the hill, passing at least three of the site's five caves on the way. On the higher of the two mounds the ancient **Prasat Phnom Da** ($2) comprises a single laterite tower, visible from way off and dominating the landscape. The tower's four doorways boast ornate sandstone columns and pediments of carved naga heads, though all but the eastern entrance are false.

On the lower hill, to the west, is a unique Hindu temple, **Ashram Maha Russei**, dedicated to Vishnu and built of grey laterite. Dating from the seventh century, the structure is a temple in miniature, the enclosing walls so close together that there's barely room to squeeze between them. On the outside, a spout can still be seen poking through the wall, through which water that had been blessed by flowing over the temple's linga would once have poured.

Prey Veng and Svay Rieng

The desperately poor southeastern provinces of **Prey Veng** and **Svay Rieng** are little visited by Khmer from other parts of the country, let alone foreign tourists, other than to make the journey along National Route 1 to the **Vietnamese border** crossings at Bavet and Chau Doc. The inhabitants here eke out an existence which is often below subsistence level: their rice crops are frequently washed away when the Mekong floods in the rainy season, and in the dry season the land bakes as hard as stone.

Neak Leung is the jumping-off point to both gateways into Vietnam: its ferries form a crucial link between Phnom Penh and the border at **Bavet**, while boats set off down the Mekong for the alternative crossing at **Chau Doc**. If you need somewhere to stay en route to the border, the pleasant provincial town of **Svay Rieng** has guesthouses and restaurants, while Bavet has really improved its image and even has a decent guesthouse and restaurant, a useful place to stay if you want to cross to Vietnam first thing in the morning.

Neak Leung

Divided by the Mekong, the dusty transit town of **NEAK LEUNG** still lacks a bridge, and is consequently inevitably congested with vehicles revving up in semi-orderly queues to board the ferries that crisscross the Mekong. Arriving from Phnom Penh, you'll be dropped on the west bank of the river. The town's restaurants and market are all on the east bank. Ferry tickets can be bought at the ticket office by the traffic barrier at the end of the road (500 riel per person). Neak Leung is known for its great river lobster (*bong kong*), which is served up in the **restaurants** close by the east-bank ferry terminal. The town's other culinary speciality is sparrow; you'll see plucked birds strung up and ready for cooking.

Most people heading for **Chau Doc** in Vietnam go on organized trips from Phnom Penh (about $8), in which case your guide will arrange transfers between the various different forms of transport. If you're travelling alone, when you alight on the west bank of the Mekong River at Neak Leung, walk a short way south along the riverfront and ask for a boat to **K'am Samnar** (10,000 riel; 1hr 30min). The various immigration and customs buildings at the border post (open daily 7am–8pm) are quite scattered, so you'll need to hire a moto (about 3000 riel). After entering Vietnam at Vinh Xuong, you need to take a *xe om* (moto in Vietnamese; about $4) to get to Chau Doc, a journey of around an hour.

If you're heading for **Kompong Cham** (see p.230) via the rural town of **Prey Veng**, north of Neak Leung, where there are pleasant views out over rice paddies and a couple of decent guesthouses, then get the ferry across the river and catch onward transport from the roundabout on the east bank.

Svay Rieng

The spread-out town of **SVAY RIENG** lies just off National Route 1, and chances are you'll see very little of it if you're rushing between the Vietnamese border and Phnom Penh. Other than the riverfront area near the landmark *Tonle Waikor Hotel*, named after the river which flows behind it, the nearest that the town gets to a "sight" is **Preah Bassac**, a tree-clad mound of rubble about 8km from town reached by moto in the dry season and by boat in the rainy. All that can be seen of the prasat is a single brick wall, which the locals will make sure that you find, but it has a delightful shady setting by the river, overlooking rice fields in the dry season and ringed by tiny hidden hamlets.

Transport to and from Phnom Penh and Bavet arrives and departs from the **market**, 1km or so from the centre, where you can get a moto to the guesthouses on the main street near the river. Arriving from the border, you can ask to be let off near the *Tonle Waikor Hotel*, from where it's just 300m west to the guesthouses.

Refurbished in 1999, the massive *Tonle Waikor Hotel* is undoubtedly the best place to **stay** (℡044/945718; ❷–❸), featuring spacious – though rather plain – en-suite rooms with TV, fridge and a/c. There are several guesthouses clustered on the main road with similar, slightly worn rooms. The pick of these – as much for the friendliness of the management as the rooms themselves – is the *Santapheap* (no phone; ❶), with windowless rooms downstairs and airier ones above.

There's decent Khmer **food** at the *Thunthean Sathea Restaurant*, 100m east of the guesthouses; their *sumlar ngam ngouw* (lemon chicken soup) is very tasty. About 200m beyond the *Tonle Waikor*, on the road towards Bavet, the *Boueng Meas Restaurant* serves up acceptable Khmer fare.

Other than enjoying a *tuk kralok* on the riverfront, the only other thing to do in the evening is enjoy a Khmer film in the smart new cinema just west of the *Tonle Waikor Hotel*.

Bavet

The town of **BAVET** is usually referred to not by name but as *viut-nahm*, thanks to its border location, or even as **Moc Bai** – the name of the adjacent town on the Vietnamese side. The formerly atrocious National Route 1 here was slowly disintegrating, until in early 2001 Prime Minister Hun Sen loaded his ministers onto a coach and took them along the road to the border, then left them to return the same way (he flew back by helicopter); work commenced on upgrading the road soon after, and is now complete. It's a pretty dull ride as the province was heavily bombed by the US during the Vietnam War, and has never quite recovered.

Practicalities

With a smart new border crossing (daily, 7am – 8pm) and its decent road Bavet has improved out of all recognition. All transport to and from the border turns round at the border itself. If you're arriving in Cambodia here, you can get a **shared taxi** to **Phnom Penh** (20,000 riel). Heading to **Ho Chi Minh City** (HCMC) on a **guesthouse bus** from Phnom Penh, you'll have to walk across the border with your luggage, picking up their associate transport on the other side. If you haven't booked through-transport to HCMC, then one of the moto drivers will wheel your bags across for free (they get a commission from the driver on the Vietnamese side), while you walk across 300m or so of no-man's-land. Once across in **Moc Bai**, you can get a motorbike taxi or minibus for the ten-kilometre ride to **Go Dau**, where you can get direct onward transport to HCMC – the whole trip takes under two hours.

If you cross to Cambodia late at night, or want to get over to Vietnam first thing in the morning, *Nouveau Pho de Paris* (☎044/946055; ②–③) is a classy new guesthouse and restaurant about 100m from the border. In the evening you could visit one of the town's seven casinos, maybe not to gamble, but to have a meal and take in a show (check the hoardings for what's on). Internet access is available next door to *Nouveau Pho de Paris* (8000 dong/hr).

Travel details

Shared taxis and **pick-up trucks** leave to no set schedule from early morning until early afternoon (roughly 6am–2pm); you may have to wait for them to fill up before they leave. Note that the frequencies given below are only approximate, and the earlier in the day you get to the transport stop, the easier it is to find transport.

Buses
Kampot to: Sihanoukville (daily; 2hr 30min).
Neak Leung to: Phnom Penh (10 daily; 2hr).
Sihanoukville to: Kampot (daily; 2hr 30min); Phnom Penh (6 daily; 3hr 30min).
Takeo to: Phnom Penh (10 daily; 2hr).
Tonle Bati to: Phnom Penh (10 daily; 1hr).

Shared taxis, minibuses and pick-up trucks
Bavet to: Neak Leung (12 daily; 1hr 20min); Phnom Penh (20 daily; 3hr); Svay Rieng (6 daily; 30min).
Kampot to: Phnom Penh (12 daily; 3hr); Sihanoukville (10 daily; 1hr 30min); Takeo (4 daily; 2hr).

Koh Kong to: Phnom Penh (several daily; 6hr); Sihanoukville (6 daily; 4–6hr).

Neak Leung to: Bavet (12 daily; 1hr 20min); Phnom Penh (20 daily; 1hr 30min); Prey Veng (4 daily; 2hr); Svay Rieng (4 daily; 1hr).

Prey Veng to: Kompong Cham (4 daily; 2hr); Neak Leung (4 daily; 2hr).

Sihanoukville to: Kampot (10 daily; 1hr 30min); Koh Kong (6 daily; 4–6hr); Phnom Penh (20 daily; 3hr 30min).

Svay Rieng to: Bavet (6 daily; 30min); Neak Leung (6 daily; 1hr); Phnom Penh (10 daily; 2hr 30min).

Takeo to: Kampot (6 daily; 2hr); Phnom Penh (12 daily; 2hr).

Boats

Koh Kong to: Koh S'dach (daily; 2hr); Sihanoukville (daily; 4hr).

Koh S'dach to: Koh Kong (daily; 2hr); Sihanoukville (daily; 2hr).

Neak Leung to: Chau Doc, Vietnam (6 daily; 3hr).

Sihanoukville to: Koh Kong (daily; 4hr); Koh S'dach (daily; 2hr).

Contexts

Contexts

The historical framework

The study of Cambodia's history is hampered by a lack of records. During the time of Angkor, the texts that filled temple libraries were written on **tanned skins** or **palm leaves**, but unfortunately these were not copied by successive generations and none has survived; inscribed stone steles at temple sites often recorded only aspects of temple life, and even this information ceased to be compiled with the demise of Angkor. But the steles, coupled with accounts by Chinese traders and envoys, have at least allowed historians to piece together something of Cambodia's story up until the late thirteenth century. Though foreign traders and Western missionaries in Cambodia wrote various accounts after the sixteenth century, these leave substantial periods unaccounted for; more recently, the French documented their protectorate in some detail, but these records were largely destroyed by the Khmer Rouge. What is known of Cambodia's history is thus something of a hotchpotch, and though much has been deduced from known reference points, even more remains obscure and will probably continue to be unknown.

Beginnings

The **earliest settlements** so far uncovered in Cambodia, dating from 6800 BC, were situated along the coast, where the risk of annual flooding was reduced and there was a ready supply of food. Hunter-gatherers were living in the caves at Leang Spean, northwest of Battambang, by 4300 BC, where they cultivated dry-season rice and produced ceramics, which are uncannily similar in shape and decoration to those used today. **Neolithic** settlements uncovered at **Samrong Sen**, in central Cambodia, indicate that by 2000 BC animals had been domesticated and slash-and-burn agriculture developed. Five hundred years later, Cambodia entered the **Bronze Age** when the art of smelting copper and tin was mastered, the ores probably originating from present-day Thailand. By 500 BC, a prosperous **Iron Age** civilization was in full swing; farming implements and weapons were produced, and skills for working with ceramics, metal and glass were being refined. The population slowly divided: highland dwellers continued growing only rainy-season rice, while lowland settlers farmed the river valleys and coastal strips, where they made best use of the floods, conserving water for dry-season irrigation and prospering from the fertile soils deposited.

Funan

Around the first century AD warring tribes forced traders to seek alternatives to the established overland trading routes between China and India. Sailing along the coast, these traders landed at Oc Eo, in the state of **Funan**, on the Gulf of Thailand (in what is now Vietnam) – an area populated by the **Khmer**, a dark-skinned, curly-haired tribe who had migrated from the north along the Mekong, and from whom Cambodians today trace their origins.

Funan is first mentioned in Chinese chronicles of the third century, and scholars believe the name may have originated from the Chinese transliteration of the word *bnam*, an old Khmer word for "mountain". It's known from Chinese accounts that the Funanese were an affluent, Indian-influenced society, living in wooden, stilted houses thatched with palm, speaking Khmer but writing in Sanskrit. They were able to dig canals, using engineering skills learnt from Indian traders, and developed an inland port, Angkor Borei; drainage and irrigation channels were cut to allow wet-rice cultivation and, importantly, provide fresh water. The Funanese ruthlessly exploited their advantageous situation: shipping had to pay dues to travel up the canals to the wharf, to berth and to take on fresh water. Huge warehouses were built to store the high-value cargoes – animal hides, rhinoceros horn, spices and gold.

Accompanying the Indian traders were Brahmans, Hindu priests, who converted many Funanese to Hinduism. Rich Funanese gained merit by financing temples, while the poor earned theirs by contributing the labour to build them. By the fifth century, shrines had been built on Funan hilltops and the king had begun to add the suffix – *varman* to his name, meaning "protector".

Funan was partly the architect of its own downfall when, in the late fifth or early sixth century, it increased already steep shipping tariffs, assuming its position to be unassailable. New ports along the coast began to compete, feuds sprang up, and the state fragmented and declined during the sixth century. One of the last mentions of Funan is in the Chinese chronicles of 539, when it is reported that King Rudravarman I sent the Chinese emperor a live rhinoceros.

Chenla

During the late sixth century, **Chenla**, previously a northern dependency of Funan, was able to gain its independence. Details of the Chenla period are particularly sparse, and such information as there is comes from Chinese sources; some scholars suggest that the word "Chenla" may have been the name by which the Chinese referred to parts of present-day Cambodia, though there is no clear picture of the extent to which Chenla and Cambodia might have overlapped. Early Chenla temples, constructed of wood and brick, were on a modest scale and few have survived – **Sambor Prei Kuk** is one of the best-preserved.

All references to Funan ceased by the seventh century. Around this time **Bhavavarman I** founded a capital at Sambor Prei Kuk, in Kompong Thom province. He was succeeded by **Ishanavarman I** (reigned 610–625), who founded Ishanapura (named in accordance with the Indian-derived custom of naming a capital by suffixing the king's name with *pura* – the Sanskrit word for town), whose state-temple (the southern group of Sambor Prei Kuk) was the largest in Southeast Asia. Although already elderly when he became king, Ishanavarman seems to have succeeded in annexing many smaller states. He was succeeded by his son, **Bhavavarman II**, about whom nothing is known.

Jayavarman I (great-grandson of Ishanavarman; reigned 635–681) ruled over an area extending at least from Battambang to Prey Veng. Although many sanctuaries were consecrated during his reign, none can specifically be attributed to him, and his capital has so far not been identified (the capital tended to change location with each new king). Inscriptions indicate that he was an able soldier who succeeded in extending his territory, though he was ultimately killed by invaders, probably from Java, after which the succession passed first to his son-in-law and then to his daughter, **Jayadevi** (one of only a handful of queens in the whole of Cambodian history, in spite of the fact that women were regarded as equals and inheritance of property, slaves and lands passed through the female line).

By the eighth century, Chenla had **divided** into two states, Land (or Upper) Chenla and Water (Lower) Chenla. Little is known about the split or of subsequent history until, in the late eighth century, **Jayavarman II** mysteriously appeared on the scene, supposedly arriving from Java; an inscription dating from the eleventh century, now in the National Museum in Bangkok, records that "he spent time at court in Java". In 795, he declared himself ruler of a kingdom called Kambujadesa and, after moving his court no less than five times, in 802 he settled at **Phnom Kulen**, northeast of Siem Reap.

The Khmer Empire

Jayavarman II's arrival at Phnom Kulen marked a northward shift of power to the region that would later be known as **Angkor** and become the capital of the **Khmer Empire**. It is from this date, therefore, that the **Angkorian period** is deemed to have begun, although it was some years before temples that are now considered Angkorian were built.

Until the eleventh century Khmer kings followed the **Hindu** religion, and temple-building was considered one of their most important duties. Temples were considered akin to a palace for the god to whom they were dedicated (most were consecrated to Shiva), and with whom the king was believed to merge on his death. Accordingly, temples built by one king were seldom used by a succeeding monarch; instead the next king would begin his own building programme in a new location – which accounts for the constantly shifting capitals of the Angkorian period. These enormous building works invariably absorbed vast resources, both in terms of labour and materials. Some temples were not completed before the death of the king – in which case a later king would finish the construction for his own use.

The little that is known about the reign of Jayavarman II (ruled at Angkor 802–850) derives from inscriptions made two centuries later, when he was held in high regard, though no records have been uncovered to substantiate this reputation. Arguably the most notable thing about his reign is that Jayavarman II founded the **devaraja** cult (see Religion and beliefs p.325), which would persist for over five hundred years. Jayavarman II subsequently moved his court from Phnom Kulen to Hariharalaya, present-day Roluos, where he died. He was succeeded by his son **Jayavarman III** (850–877).

The empire in the ascendant

Indravarman I (877–889) established a pattern of three-fold building work which most subsequent Angkorian kings would emulate. First, he honoured the water gods (by creating the Indratataka baray at Roluos); secondly, he built a temple to his ancestors (Preah Ko); thirdly, he erected a temple-mountain which was also his state-temple (the Bakong), and which housed his devaraja deity.

Indravarman was succeeded by his son, **Yasovarman I** (889–900), who had to fight his brothers to assume the throne, and his reign seems to have carried on in a similarly military vein. After completing the temple of Lolei at Roluos he moved northwest, where he followed his father's example, constructing the first state-temple in the Angkor area proper, on the hill of Phnom Bakheng. He followed this up by excavating the massive East Baray, over 7km long and almost 2km wide. Yasovarman was succeeded by his two sons, **Harshavarman I** (900–922), who built only the small temple of Baksei Chamkrong, and **Ishanavarman II** (922–927), in whose reign the only notable events were the consecrations of Prasat Kravan, at Angkor, and Prasat Neing Kmau, near Takeo. Their uncle, **Jayavarman IV** (928–941), became the only Angkorian king to rule from a distance, as he ascended the Angkorian throne when he was already ruling his own state, with a substantial capital at Koh Ker, some 150km east of Angkor.

After the death of Jayavarman IV, his son **Harshavarman II** (941–944) gained the throne, though he lasted just a short time before he was ousted by his cousin, **Rajendravarman I** (944–968), who had been waiting on the sidelines at Sambor Prei Kuk. To appease the gods of his ancestors, he had the temple of Baksei Chamkrong decorated and rededicated, and went on to build two massive temple-mountains, the East Mebon in the middle of the East Baray, and his state-temple, Pre Rup. He also granted land to his guru, Yajnavaraha, to build a temple, the beautiful citadel of Banteay Srei. He waged war against the Cham, who populated the state of **Champa** on the coast of Vietnam, and annexed neighbouring states, making them provinces of the Khmer Empire.

When Rajendravarman I died, his son **Jayavarman V** (968–1001) was just 10, and officials had to rule on his behalf. At some time he was successful in extending his territory into what is now northeast Thailand. Many inscriptions relating to the period survive, some of which are decrees about the temples, while many others concern land disputes over which the king had to adjudicate – gruesome punishments were meted out to those he deemed guilty, including having their nose, lips or ears cut off; one unfortunate woman was sentenced to have her head crushed with a rock.

In 1002, two rivals, Jayaviravarman (1002–10) and Suryavarman I were both proclaimed king. **Jayaviravarman** resumed work on Ta Keo, the state-temple begun by Jayavarman V, though it was never completed as it was hit by lightning and the evil omens this signified could not be expunged. Jayaviravarman also built the North Kleang and a fortifying wall to the northeast of Angkor Thom before he was overthrown by **Suryavarman I** (1011–50), during whose long reign further territory was added to the kingdom, with provinces as far away as Lopburi in present-day Thailand paying allegiance to him. Suryavarman I left a substantial legacy: at Angkor, his palace was the first to be surrounded with defensive walls; a number of religious settlements, including Phnom Chisor and Preah Vihear, were founded; and he built a massive reservoir, the West Baray, still impressive today.

His successor, **Udayadityavarman II** (1050–66), had his work cut out warding off rival claimants to the throne, but he still found time to build the Baphuon, which lay at the heart of his capital, in the vicinity of Angkor Thom. The only thing known of his brother, **Harshavarman III** (1066–80), is that in 1076, according to Chinese annals, he was ordered by the Chinese emperor (who considered the Cambodians and Cham to be under his rule) to join with the Cham to fight against the Vietnamese; he disappears from the records in 1080. His successor, **Jayavarman VI** (1080–1107), was not the natural heir, coming from a remote line of the royal family, but enjoyed a peaceful reign, and was content to make additions to existing temples rather than build new ones, although he may have had a hand in the construction of the impressive temple of Phimai, near Nakhon Ratchasima in Thailand.

Angkor at its height

Dharanindravarman I (1107–13), the brother of Jayavarman VI, was soon overthrown by his nephew, **Suryavarman II** (1113–50), who became possibly the best-known of Angkor's kings, thanks to his state-temple, Angkor Wat. A few minor ups and downs apart, his reign marked the beginning of a golden period for Angkor; the empire was at its height, stretching from Champa in the east to Pagan (in present-day Burma) in the west, and from the north of Thailand south into the Malay peninsula. Both diplomat and warrior, he restored relationships with China (with whom trade had ceased in the eighth century) and fought a great battle against the Vietnamese. In forcing the Cham to join in on his side, he succeeded in alienating them, before completely destroying the relationship by installing a king of his own choosing on their throne.

Uncertainty surrounds his supposed successor, **Dharanindravarman II** (1150–60); some scholars doubt that he actually ascended the throne, suggesting that he merely ruled over an independent kingdom in the area. He was the **first Buddhist king** of the Khmer, but did not attempt to convert his subjects. He is credited with building Preah Palilay and (with less certainty) the addition of Buddhist carvings to Banteay Samre and Beng Mealea. After him came **Yashovarman II** (1160–65), who built no new monuments, but continued work on those of his predecessors, including restoration at Roluos. He was overthrown in 1165 by **Tribhuvanadityvarman** (1165–77), who was killed during the Cham invasion of 1177, during which Angkor Thom was sacked and a Cham prince, Jaya-Indravarman IV, briefly put on the Khmer throne.

It was **Jayavarman VII**, son of Dharanindravarman II, who restored the status quo, leading his troops to war with the Cham and winning a huge naval battle against them on the Tonle Sap; his success is commemorated in the bas-reliefs of the Bayon. Once Angkor was regained from the Cham and Champa annexed, he set about re-establishing the kingdom's institutions; by 1181 he had rebuilt Angkor Thom and reunited the country sufficiently to have himself consecrated devaraja. As well as managing his vast empire, which rivalled that of Suryavarman II, the king was a prolific temple-builder, completing Ta Som, Preah Khan, Banteay Chhmar and Neak Pean, among others, as well as a state-temple, the Bayon, consecrated to Mahayana Buddhism (Jayavarman VII was, like his father, a devout Buddhist). Under his direction, Angkor Thom gained not only its fortifying wall but also extravagant causeways edged with gods and demons; furthermore, Banteay Kdei and Srah Srang were restored, and the irrigation system was improved. The enormous Terrace of Elephants and the Terrace of the Leper King also owe their existence to his reign. An inscription made in 1186 at the newly consecrated Ta Prohm records some of his good works, noting that 102 hospitals and 121 "houses of fire" – resthouses for travellers – had been built across the country.

The decline of Angkor

After Jayavarman VII's death the Khmer Empire began to fragment; it's likely that Jayavarman VII's massive building programme was partly responsible for the decline, as it had heavily depleted the kingdom's resources. Little is known about the following two kings, **Indravarman II** (1219–43) and **Jayavarman VIII** (1243–95); the Mongols arrived in Southeast Asia during the latter's reign, and he seems to have been prudent enough to send tribute to Kublai Khan. A zealous Hindu, Jayavarman VIII was also responsible for destroying many of Cambodia's Buddhist images.

Legend tells that Jayavarman's daughter, whom he loved very much, took the sacred sword, Preah Khan, and gave it to her husband, in whose favour Jayavarman VIII abdicated. The tale was mentioned in the writings of the Chinese envoy Chou Ta-Kuan, who spent a year at Angkor in 1296 and left a colourful account of the court, its buildings and ceremonial pomp. But in spite of Chou's glowing account, Angkor was weakening. The kingdom was dramatically reduced in size by the middle of the thirteenth century, by which time the Thais had ousted the Khmer from Sukhothai, and Lopburi had claimed independence. By the early fourteenth century, the Cham had also reclaimed their independence, leaving what was left of the Khmer kingdom exposed and unable to summon much resistance to Thai invasions.

When the Thais sacked Angkor again in 1432, **King Ponhea Yat** left Angkor, taking his court with him, and set up a new capital in **Phnom Penh**, where he created a number of Buddhist monasteries which still exist today.

Lovek and Oudong

Some evidence exists in Thai records that the capital may have returned briefly to Angkor around 1467, but by the early sixteenth century, **Ang Chan** (1505 or 1516–56) had set up court at **Lovek**. While the Thais were busy fending off advances from invading Burmese, Ang Chan gathered an army and made a successful attack on the Thais, managing to regain control of towns such as Pursat and Battambang, which had been lost when Angkor was abandoned.

The sixteenth century saw the arrival of the first **Western** missionaries and explorers in Cambodia; though the former were utterly unsuccessful in gaining converts, some of the latter became influential within the Khmer establishment, such as the Spanish adventurers Blas Ruiz and Diego Veloso, whose knowledge of firearms would eventually earn them marriages with Cambodian princesses and provincial governorships under **King Satha** (1575–94). Accounts of the time, by Spanish and Portuguese colonials from the Philippines and Malacca respectively, report multicultural trading settlements at Lovek and Phnom Penh, with quarters for the Chinese, Arabs, Japanese, Spanish and Portuguese; the area around these two towns was the most prosperous in the country, trading in gold, animal skins and ivory, silk and precious stones.

The Khmer court continued to face threats from the **Thais**, however, forcing King Satha to seek help from the Spanish in the Philippines. This aid never materialized, though, and Satha fled to Laos where he subsequently died, while Lovek was sacked by the Thais in 1594. The succession subsequently passed rapidly to a number of kings, including **Chey Chettha**, who took the throne and established his capital at **Oudong**, between Lovek and Phnom Penh, where it would remain for some two hundred years.

Towards the end of the seventeenth century, the **Vietnamese** began to move south into Champa and, before long, the Mekong Delta. Cambodia was now squeezed between two powerful neighbours, and over the next century the royal family aggravated matters by splitting into pro-Vietnamese and pro-Thai factions, the crown changing hands frequently as each incumbent was deposed by the opposing faction and their supporting power. The populace, without a strong king to look to, paid scant regard to what was said in Oudong, which further aggravated the king's inability to resist invasions.

Events took a turn for the worse in 1767 when a Thai prince sought refuge in Cambodia, intending to set up a government in exile. This incensed the Thai general, Taksin, who, launching an invasion, destroyed Phnom Penh and assumed control of Cambodia for several decades. The Thais put a 7-year-old prince, **Ang Eng** (1779–97), on the throne, under a Thai regent, and reinforced their influence by taking Ang Eng to Bangkok, where he resided for four years. On his return, Ang Eng installed himself at Oudong, where he died in 1797, leaving four sons and a lineage that lasts to this day.

The run-up to the French protectorate

Worsening to-ing and fro-ing between the Thais and Vietnamese would ultimately lead to the Cambodians appealing to France for protection. Ang Eng's eldest son and heir, **Chan**, was only 6 at the time of his father's death and didn't assume the throne for nine years. Meanwhile, the Thais annexed the province of Battambang, which then stretched as far as Siem Reap, and which was to remain under Thai rule until 1907. By the time he was crowned, Chan (1806–34) had become fervently anti-Thai and soon asked the Vietnamese for help; the Vietnamese promptly annexed the whole of the Mekong Delta and also took control of Cambodia. In 1812, Chan relocated the court to Phnom Penh, from where he proceeded to send secret emissaries to Bangkok, trying to keep them sweet by assuring them of his continued allegiance.

The Thai king, Rama III, decided in the early 1830s to re-exert his influence on Cambodia and, seizing upon the opportunity provided by the death of the Vietnamese viceroy in 1832, sent in an army to oust the Vietnamese – who had already left, taking Chan with them, by the time Thai troops arrived. The Thais sought to install as king one of Chan's two brothers who had been living in exile in Bangkok, but later abandoned the idea, unable to gain any popular support for either. The Vietnamese, with Chan under close supervision, returned to Phnom Penh a couple of years later, where he died shortly afterwards, leaving no male heir. They duly installed as queen Chan's second daughter **Mei** (1835–41), who they thought would be malleable, and set about imposing Vietnamese culture and customs on the Cambodians. Their disregard for Theravada Buddhism and their attempts to enforce the use of the Vietnamese language sowed deep resentment, and anti-Vietnamese riots flared repeatedly from 1836. Losing their patience, the Vietnamese blamed Queen Mei for their own failure to install a disciplined Vietnamese-style administration, and arrested her in 1840; though the Cambodians had not much liked being forced to accept a Vietnamese-appointed queen, they now resented her detention and rioted again. Thai troops poised on the border marched in and forced out the Vietnamese, and despite sporadic skirmishes over several years the Vietnamese never re-established control, withdrawing totally from Cambodia in 1847. The following year, **Duang** (1848–59), Chan's brother, was crowned king at Oudong with full Buddhist ceremony, the reinstatement of which, after years of Vietnamese disapproval, contributed to the Khmer's sense of national identity.

Meanwhile, the **French** had arrived in Southeast Asia, but were rebuffed in their attempt to establish trading arrangements with Vietnam. On the pretext that French missionaries were being persecuted, they eventually invaded the Mekong Delta and annexed the southern provinces of Vietnam. In Cambodia, Duang feared another Vietnamese invasion and asked the French for help, but when they eventually sent a diplomatic mission it was turned back before it could reach him at Oudong. Duang died before any discussions could be held, leaving it to his successor, **Norodom** (1859–1904), to agree a treaty with the French in 1863.

The French protectorate

Norodom's **treaty** with France afforded Cambodia French protection in exchange for wide-ranging mineral and timber rights, along with freedom for the French to preach Christianity and to move around the country. Having signed the treaty, however, Norodom continued the double-dealing of his predecessors and was secretly reassuring the Thais of his loyalty to Bangkok. On discovering this, the French lost their trust in Norodom and, in due course, their confidence in his ability to govern at all. With riots flaring in the provinces against Norodom and his allegiance to France, the French decided it was time to exert more control themselves, and began to press for a new treaty that would allow them to install administrative **residents** in all provincial centres and take over day-to-day running of the country. Rebellion sprang up across the nation, which the French, even with the assistance of Vietnamese troops, had difficulty in quelling. By the time the treaty was signed in 1886, the French had eroded much of Norodom's power and were collecting all taxes; two years later they had residents installed in ten provincial towns.

When Norodom, already an **opium addict** (this habit fed by the French) became ill towards the end of the century, the French *résident supérieur* was granted permission from Paris to assume executive authority, and before Norodom died in 1904, France was ruling Cambodia. His compliant half-brother **Sisowath** was installed on the throne in Phnom Penh (1904–27), the French having passed over Monivong, Norodom's son and natural heir; a mere figurehead, Sisowath had little impact on affairs during his reign.

By the early part of the twentieth century, the French were thoroughly disillusioned with the Cambodians, whom they regarded as indolent and corrupt. Consequently, the French did little to develop Cambodia's human resources (the most tangible legacy of their ninety-year rule is arguably the country's communications network, including over 5000km of roads and the railway line from Phnom Penh and Battambang to the Thai border). Instead, the French filled key clerical positions with Vietnamese, who also ran many of the small businesses and took jobs as labourers; meanwhile, the ethnic Chinese, who had been established in Cambodia for centuries, continued their lucrative trades as bankers and merchants.

This neglect of the Khmer, and the crippling taxes which the French levied on Cambodia, bred resentment to which the French, in their complacency, remained oblivious. They were shocked when revolts against taxation broke out in 1916, and doubly horrified when Felix Bardez – the French resident in Kompong Chhnang – was **beaten to death** by locals in 1925 while investigating resistance to tax payments in a provincial village.

World War II

The **Japanese invasion** of Southeast Asia in 1941–42 brought little change to the status quo in Indochina, where the Japanese allowed the (now Vichy) French to continue administering the day-to-day running of the country. The Thais, who were allies of the Japanese and who sensed a degree of vulnerability in the French position, took the opportunity to launch attacks across the border into Cambodia, with the aim of recovering the provinces of Battambang and Siem Reap which they had reluctantly given up to Cambodia earlier in the century. The French roundly defeated the Thai navy, however, forcing the Japanese to save Thai face by compelling the French administration to hand over the provinces for a nominal sum. **King Sisowath Monivong** blamed the French for this loss of territory and refused to treat with them ever again; in fact he died shortly afterwards. The Japanese actually allowed the next king to be chosen by the French who, seeking a compliant successor, passed over Monivong's son in favour of his youthful and inexperienced grandson, **Norodom Sihanouk**, who was duly crowned in September 1941.

Despite their hands-off approach in Indochina, the Japanese were supportive of anti-colonial feeling, partly to gain support for their own presence. The effect of these sentiments would become manifest after the Japanese surrender in August 1945, by which time they had actually dissolved the French administration.

Towards independence

Though the French had reinstated their officials by the end of 1945, the prewar status quo was never quite restored. In 1944, the Thai government began to fund anti-Japanese and anti-French causes, and anti-royalist Cambodian groups in exile began to gather along the Thai border. A year later these factions had banded together to form the essentially left-wing **Khmer Issarak**, a band of fledgling idealists which grew into a powerful armed guerrilla movement that waged something approaching a war of independence against the French over the next few years; between 1947 and 1950, the Khmer Issarak actually controlled fifty percent of the country.

In fact, the seeds of the movement had been sown back in the 1930s with the opening of Cambodia's first high school, the **Lycée Sisowath** in Phnom Penh, whose students soon began to question the standing of educated Khmer in a country where Vietnamese dominated the middle levels of the administration. When the first Khmer-language **newspaper**, *Nagara Vatta*, was launched (Khmer had only been used for the publication of religious texts hitherto), it was aimed at these newly educated Cambodians, propounding Khmer nationalist views and objecting to the influence of the Vietnamese and Chinese on Cambodian society. The editors were allied to the *sangka* (the Buddhist clergy), led by Phnom Penh's **Institut Bouddhique**, the backbone of Buddhism in Cambodia, which had taken responsibility for most education until the opening of the *lycée*.

When Sihanouk requested Cambodia's independence late in 1945, the French (afraid of losing their grip on Indochina) reluctantly agreed to allow elections and the formation of a National Assembly, but refused to contemplate granting complete independence. Thus, for the first time in Cambodian history, political parties were formed, **elections** held (in 1946) and a new government formed. The election was resoundingly won by the democratic (and anti-royalist) party, Krom Pracheathipodei, which adopted a constitution along the lines of that of republican France; Sihanouk, although he retained his throne, was left virtually powerless. Late in 1949, Cambodia was granted **partial independence**, though the French chose to retain control over the judiciary, customs and excise and foreign policy, and the right to maintain military bases in the country.

Frustrated by his lack of political power and the residual French grip on the country, in June 1952 Sihanouk staged a **coup**, dismissing the cabinet, suspending the constitution and appointing himself prime minister; in the early months of 1953 he declared martial law and dissolved the National Assembly. Sihanouk then took the first of what was to become a habitual series of trips abroad "for his health" – in reality to lobby the French in Paris to withdraw and grant Cambodia full independence, unsuccessfully at first. But with France running into trouble in Vietnam, where they were fighting a losing battle against the communist Viet Minh forces, the French government did an about-face; on **November 9, 1953**, Cambodia duly celebrated full independence.

The Sihanouk era

Cambodians were ecstatic at achieving full independence, and Sihanouk was feted as a national hero. The following year, accords were signed in Geneva laying down the terms of French withdrawal from Indochina, including among its key points the disbanding of the Khmer Issarak, **neutrality** on the part of Cambodia and the **partition of Vietnam** at the seventeenth parallel into what would become communist North Vietnam and the non-communist South Vietnam.

Early on, it was clear that Sihanouk, though politically adept, could change sides at the drop of a hat to achieve his ends, driven by an unassailable belief that, having won independence for Cambodia, he should be the one to run it. He needed the adulation of his public and took to making trips to the countryside, where he made lengthy orations and attracted polite attention thanks to an ingrained respect for the monarchy going back generations. These outings stoked his huge ego and made him believe that his "children", as he referred to the people, supported his policies. However, for subsistence farmers, who formed the majority of the population, independence had brought no benefits; they still had to work overlong hours in the rice fields and suffer the effects of flood and drought.

When Sihanouk's efforts to manipulate the constitution to gain power for the monarchy failed, he surprised everyone by **abdicating** in 1955 in favour of his father Norodom Suramarit, taking once again the title of prince. Gambling on the continuation of massive popular support for himself in the wake of the independence struggle, he set up his own political party, **Sangkum Reastr Niyum**, the Popular Socialist Community (Sangkum for short). The party managed to win all the seats in the National Assembly in the heavily rigged 1955 elections, during which opposition candidates and electors were intimidated by the military (on the king's orders), ballot papers tampered with and ballot boxes lost. Sihanouk's tactics ensured that Sangkum remained unchallenged at the next elections two years later. The monarchy was effectively dissolved in 1960 when King Suramarit died, whereupon Sihanouk became head of state.

Sihanouk was both hard-working and creative – he even found time to produce a number of films which drew upon traditional Cambodian cultures and values, a subject close to his heart – but his conceited attitude and bullying approach made him difficult to work with. Many right-wing intellectuals, whom the prince perceived as competition, mysteriously disappeared; meanwhile he toyed with socialism and often favoured the left. At the same time, in the schools and colleges left-wing teachers such as **Saloth Sar** (later known as Pol Pot) and **Ieng Sary** (so-called Brother Number Three in the Khmer Rouge hierarchy) had become senior communist party figures by the early 1960s and were recruiting members; another future senior figure in the Khmer Rouge, Khieu Samphan, meanwhile hid his communist leanings and joined Sangkum.

In 1963, in yet another of Sihanouk's policy shifts, a government purge of known communists saw Saloth Sar flee Phnom Penh to take up the life of a full-time revolutionary. Along with many others in the Cambodian communist movement, he spent time in Vietnam and China, where he was trained and groomed by communist forces to carry on the struggle.

The slide towards war

In the late 1950s, with the knowledge of the United States, plots had been hatched against Sihanouk by a paramilitary right-wing group, the **Khmer Serei** (led by a former editor of *Nagara Vatta*), who were recruited and supported by the Thai and South Vietnamese governments. Although these events compounded his distrust of the pro-American Thais and South Vietnamese, the prince continued to court the US and accept American military aid – while at the same time forming an alliance with China, who wanted to prevent US dominance in the area. But in another abrupt change of direction, in mid-1963 Sihanouk accused the US of supplying arms to the Khmer Serei, and later that year ordered all US aid stopped. That same year, Sihanouk nationalized banking, insurance and all import-export trade.

The economy was soon destabilized by the combination of Sihanouk's policies and the spillover into Cambodia of the conflict between North and South Vietnam. Sihanouk had to perform a delicate **balancing act** to preserve some semblance of neutrality and avoid Cambodia being drawn into the Vietnamese conflict. In 1963, he broke off relations with South Vietnam, which was receiving financial and military support from the US, though US planes were not prevented from overflying Cambodia in the mid-1960s, en route to bombing raids in North Vietnam. Meanwhile Sihanouk had been unable to prevent North Vietnam sending men and arms via Cambodian territory to the communist **Viet Cong** guerrillas in South Vietnam, leaving him little option but to sign a secret agreement with the North Vietnamese in 1966, allowing them safe passage.

The prince made a serious political error, though, when in 1966 he was involved with arrangements for a prestigious visit from Charles de Gaulle and neglected to pay sufficient attention to preparations for the elections; as a result, the National Assembly for the first time included members not handpicked by the prince, who were to prove a focal point for opposition to him a few years later. Meanwhile, in the northeast of the country, the CPK (Communist Party of Kampuchea) – or the **Khmer Rouge**, as Sihanouk dubbed them – comprising Cambodian communists who had been sheltering in North Vietnam, began a campaign of insurgency. Ironically, the Khmer Rouge probably owe their eventual victory to the United States, who launched a vast covert bombing programme, code-named **Operation Menu**, over supposedly neutral Cambodia, aimed at destroying communist bases and supply lines in the southern provinces of Cambodia along the border with Vietnam. All in all, over half a million tonnes of ordnance were dropped on the country in three thousand raids between March 1969 and January 1973, which had the effect of forcing communist Vietnamese deeper into Cambodian territory and alienating provincial Cambodians, causing them to side with the CPK.

Lon Nol takes charge

Elected prime minister in 1966, **General Lon Nol** had been regarded as Sihanouk's man, but began to shift his position in response to unrest among the military, upset by a lack of equipment and supplies, and among the middle class, dissatisfied with the prince's economic policies. Plots continued to be hatched against Sihanouk, some of the protagonists being anti-Sihanouk MPs elected three years before, and in 1970, while he was out of the country, **Lon Nol** headed a coup, removing the prince as chief of state, abolishing the monarchy and renaming the country the **Khmer Republic**. Sihanouk broadcast an impassioned plea from Beijing, begging his supporters to fight Lon Nol, but the Chinese persuaded him to join with the communists whom he had forced into exile in 1963 to form an alternative government.

At home, details of Sihanouk's secret treaty with the North Vietnamese had already surfaced, and the elimination of their supply trail from Cambodian soil became a national preoccupation. Thousands of Cambodians joined the army to help, but they were poorly trained and ill-equipped (despite renewed US financial support, which served only to feed widespread corruption). In the event, the Cambodians were no match for the battle-hardened Vietnamese, and after tens of thousands of Cambodians died in fighting, Lon Nol called a halt to the offensive in 1971.

The **Khmer Rouge** meanwhile were battling towards Phnom Penh. In 1970 they already controlled an estimated twenty percent of Cambodia, primarily in the northeast and northwest; by the end of 1972, all but Phnom Penh and a few provincial capitals were under their control. Although heavy American bombing brought a momentary halt to their advance in 1973, they pushed steadily forward; refugees fled to Phnom Penh ahead of their advance, bringing with them tales of whole villages being slaughtered. These stories were dismissed by the capital's inhabitants as unfounded, and any blame to be attributed was laid at the door of the Vietnamese. By early 1975, Phnom Penh was surrounded, all access to the rest of Cambodia was cut off and the US was flying in supplies to the besieged city. The corruption of the Khmer Republic and constant war had taken their toll on the population, and when the communists walked into Phnom Penh on April 17, 1975 they were greeted with relief. Two weeks later, on April 30, the last Americans withdrew from Saigon, just ahead of North Vietnamese forces, and US military involvement in Indochina came to an end.

It's believed that over 300,000 Cambodians were killed as a result of the four years of fighting against the Vietnamese and the Khmer Rouge, coupled with indiscriminate bombing by the US. Sihanouk's worst fears had been realized, but this was nothing compared to what was to come.

The Khmer Rouge era

The Khmer Rouge had its roots in the Khmer People's Revolutionary Party (**KPRP**), formed in the early 1950s. As well as appealing to anti-monarchist elements, the KPRP attracted young Cambodians who had been exposed to communist ideals while studying in France. Three of these rose to powerful positions in the Khmer Rouge: Saloth Sar – later known as **Pol Pot** – who rose to the exalted rank of "Brother Number One" within the Khmer Rouge; his contemporary, Ieng Sary, who eventually became foreign minister; and Khieu Samphan, the future party chairman.

When the Khmer Rouge arrived in Phnom Penh, they set out to achieve their ideal: a nation of **peasants** working in an agrarian society where family, wealth and status were irrelevant. Family groups were broken up, money was abolished and everyday life – down to the smallest detail – was dictated by **Angkar**, the secretive revolutionary organization behind the Khmer Rouge. Within hours of their entering Phnom Penh, the Khmer Rouge had begun to clear the city; within a week the capital was deserted. In other towns around Cambodia (now renamed **Democratic Kampuchea**) the scenario was repeated, and practically the whole population of the country was displaced. **Forced labour** was deployed in the fields or on specific building projects

▲ Victims of the Pol Pot era at Toul Sleng Genocide Museum

supervised by party cadres. The regime under which people worked was harsh and nutrition inadequate; hundreds of thousands perished in the fields, dying of simple illnesses and starvation.

Almost immediately after seizing power, the Khmer Rouge began a programme of **mass execution**, though the twisted logic that lay behind this has never been made clear. Senior military commanders were among the first to die, and before long it was the turn of monks, the elite, the educated, those who spoke a foreign language, even those who wore glasses.

Prince Sihanouk, his wife and family had returned to Phnom Penh from exile in Beijing in mid-1975, living in the Royal Palace and welcoming the few diplomatic guests who came to the country, until April 1996, when he was replaced as head of state; they lived out the rest of the Khmer Rouge years under virtual house arrest.

As time went on, the regime became increasingly paranoid and began to look inward, murdering its own cadres. It's estimated that between one and two million people, around twenty percent of the population, died under the Khmer Rouge. Those who could escape fled to refugee camps in Thailand or across the border to Vietnam, but the majority had no option but to endure the three years, eight months and twenty days – as any older Cambodian will still say today – of Khmer Rouge rule, which they still refer to as *sa'mai a-pot*, the Pol Pot era.

The Khmer Rouge's eventual **downfall** was orchestrated by their original mentors, the Vietnamese. Frequent border skirmishes initiated by the Khmer Rouge annoyed the Vietnamese, who sent troops into Cambodia in 1977, though this incursion lasted just a few months. The final straw for the Vietnamese came when the Khmer Rouge massacred Vietnamese villages along the border in early 1978. This caused Vietnam to begin supporting anti-Khmer Rouge factions, a shift that led to the formation of the Khmer National United Front for National Salvation, or **KNUFNS**. On December 22, 1978, a Vietnamese invasion force of more than 100,000 entered Cambodia, and just seventeen days later they had taken Phnom Penh. The leaders of the Khmer Rouge made their escape just ahead of the invading forces, Pol Pot by helicopter to Thailand,

The contemptible Pot was a lovely child.

Loth Suong, Pol Pot's older brother

The factors which turned Pol Pot from a sweet-natured child into a paranoid mass-murderer will probably never be fully understood. He was born **Saloth Sar** in 1928 at Prek Sbaur, near Kompong Thom, where his father was a prosperous farmer. Sent to live with his brother, Loth Suong, in Phnom Penh, at the age of 6, he had a relatively privileged upbringing – the family was well connected through a cousin, who was a ballet dancer at the royal court. Educationally Saloth Sar was unremarkable, and it was probably thanks to the influence of his cousin rather than through innate aptitude that he was chosen to attend the newly opened Collège Norodom Sihanouk in Kompong Cham in 1942 – Sar subsequently left the college without passing a single exam. Going on to study at the Lycée Sisowath in Phnom Penh his academic performance must, at some point, have improved, since in 1949 he was amongst a hundred students chosen to study in France.

In Paris, Sar joined the French Communist Party (along with his friends Ieng Sary and Khieu Samphan) and was exposed to radical new ideas; he also met Khieu Ponnery, a highly educated Cambodian woman who was to become his first wife. Returning to Cambodia in 1952, Saloth Sar joined the Vietnamese-run Indochina Communist Party and set about campaigning for the socialist cause in Cambodia. Imperceptibly, he began veiling himself in secrecy, isolating himself from his family, keeping a low profile and beginning to use an alias, "Pol". An ardent member of the newly created **Cambodian Communist Party**, he appeared content to work in the lower ranks of the party, giving seminars and recruiting for the cause through his job as a teacher. Those who met him at this time remarked that he was a kind-hearted and mild-mannered – albeit enigmatic – figure. Without ever seeming to promote himself, he rose steadily through the party ranks, from lowly assistant to Party Secretary.

By 1963, Sihanouk's support for the socialists had turned to persecution, and Saloth Sar, along with other key party members, was forced to flee the capital and seek refuge on the border with Vietnam. Moving frequently, the Cambodian communists were supported first by their North Vietnamese comrades, and later by the Chinese – whom "Pol" visited on several occasions and held in great esteem for the "success" of their Cultural Revolution. Isolated in the northeast by the escalating Vietnam War, "Pol" had ample time to develop his own plan for a better state, run on Marxist–Leninist principles. Living simply in the jungle he developed great admiration for the peasant's life, and by the time the revolutionaries – now dubbed the **Khmer Rouge** – had gained control of Cambodia in 1975, he was probably reasonably certain of his formula for returning to a basic agrarian society and the implementation of his (ultimately disastrous) "Four Year Plan".

the rest crowded onto the train north to Battambang. Following their leaders, Khmer Rouge troops and villagers loyal to them retreated to the jungles along the northwest border.

The Vietnamese era

Although opinions about the **Vietnamese era** are divided between those who call them liberators and those who speak of their occupation, no one disputes that they were widely welcomed, their arrival saving countless Cambodian lives.

Ever secretive, the Khmer Rouge leaders, rather than expose themselves as individuals, now hid behind a collective name, the mysterious **"Angkar"** – the central committee of the "Organization", as the leaders now referred to the party. This committee comprised thirteen members (eleven men and two women), its unchallenged head being Pol Pot, as Saloth Sar was by now known, (it isn't known why he chose this pseudonym, which has no meaning in Cambodian), a.k.a. "Brother Pol" and, after his appointment as prime minister of Democratic Kampuchea (1976), **Brother Number One**. Other leading members of Angkar were Pol Pot's long-standing comrade and second in command, Nuon Chea (Brother Number Two); and Pol Pot's friends from his student days, Ieng Sary (Brother Number Three) and Khieu Samphan, the party frontman.

Increasingly suspicious, the cadre were convinced that they were surrounded by traitors; it was Pol Pot, though, who had direct responsibility for **purging** the party of "enemies", personally authorizing the torture and murder of around 20,000 comrades and their families at the Toul Sleng torture prison (interrogation at Toul Sleng was reserved for those who were close to the leadership – in fact most were loyal party members). Whilst it's not clear whether Pol Pot directly ordered the interrogations and killings, it is certain that he was fully aware of, and probably supported, them. Whether or not he ever felt any remorse isn't known, but he certainly refused to acknowledge any responsibility – instead, when the atrocities were exposed by liberating Vietnamese forces in 1979, he accused the Vietnamese of being the perpetrators. Choosing to flee rather than face the Vietnamese army, he escaped to Thailand. He never doubted that the path he had chosen for Cambodia was the right one, believing instead that he had been betrayed by those whom he had trusted.

Sentenced to death by a Cambodian tribunal in absentia, Pol Pot lay low and remained at liberty in Thailand. In the mid-1980s, Khieu Ponnery went insane; Pol Pot divorced her in 1987 and married again, fathering his only child, a daughter called Malee. At some point, probably around 1993, Pol Pot crossed back into northern Cambodia where, surrounded by loyal supporters in the relative security of a Khmer Rouge enclave in the vicinity of Anlong Veng, he organized guerrilla attacks against the newly elected Cambodian government. Meanwhile, Ieng Sary, who had been waging a disruptive guerrilla war against the government from Pailin, defected to them in 1996. This must have come as a blow to Pol Pot, and signalled the end of the Khmer Rouge. Just a year later, an increasingly paranoid Pol Pot ordered the murder of his long-standing friend, Sun Sen and his family; for this murder he was tried by his own people and sentenced to life imprisonment. Eleven months later he was dead – though whether he was murdered or died from natural causes remains unknown. Bizarrely, Pol Pot has something of a cult status among Cambodians, and the site of his cremation at Anlong Veng is now a tourist attraction.

The Vietnamese found the country starving and devastated, the infrastructure shattered. Cambodia now became the **People's Republic of Kampuchea** (PRK), as the Vietnamese formed an interim government in Phnom Penh made up of members of the KNUFNS; the president was Heng Samrin, an ex-Khmer Rouge divisional commander, and its foreign minister another ex-Khmer Rouge member, **Hun Sen**, who had fled to Vietnam in 1977.

Under the PRK, markets, schools, freedom of movement and private farming were re-established immediately, and by the following year, the use of money and religious practice on a limited scale were reintroduced. Nevertheless, the formation of the PRK caused many educated Cambodians, who had no intention of suffering more communist rule, to flee to Thailand, where they swelled the already bursting refugee camps; by 1981, 630,000 refugees had descended on Thailand (many of them Khmer Rouge) and a further 150,000 were living in Vietnam.

Although coverage of Cambodia's plight brought limited aid from the West, the havoc wrought by the Khmer Rouge was in general disregarded by the major powers, who deemed Cambodia to be occupied under the Vietnamese and consequently **ostracized** the PRK (the USSR and India were notable exceptions). Safely in Thailand, Pol Pot was supported by the Thai, Chinese and US governments, all ardently anti-Vietnamese, as the prime minister of the legitimate government. As news of the atrocities committed by the Khmer Rouge surfaced, his supporters preferred to continue to punish Vietnam; bizarrely, the Thais and Chinese fed, clothed, trained and even rearmed Khmer Rouge soldiers, while UN agencies were allowed to look after Khmer Rouge in their camps, but were prevented from helping the decimated population of Cambodia.

As a counterweight to the PRK, the **Coalition Government of Democratic Kampuchea** (CGDK) was created as a government-in-exile in Thailand in 1982. It comprised Prince Sihanouk, persuaded to join by the Chinese, and his FUNCINPEC party; Son Sann, a previous prime minister of Cambodia and leader of the Khmer People's National Liberation Front (KPNLF); and members of the Khmer Rouge. Although the CGDK shared a common aim to rid Cambodia of the Vietnamese, they had no mechanism for achieving it. The Khmer Rouge had the superior military forces and sent frequent sorties across the border into Cambodia where they were repelled by the Vietnamese and PRK. After particularly harsh fighting in 1983–85, the PRK went on a mine-laying spree along the border with Thailand in an attempt to prevent these forays – the start of the land-mine scourge which still plagues Cambodia today.

The Vietnamese withdrawal and its aftermath

Vietnam had never considered the occupation of Cambodia to be a long-term goal, and while in charge had trained the Cambodian army in preparation for its own withdrawal. With the crisis in Eastern Europe building up, the USSR drastically reduced aid to the PRK government, making the occupation too expensive for the Vietnamese to sustain, and by the end of September 1989 they had withdrawn completely; shortly afterwards, the PRK government renamed the country the **State of Cambodia (SOC)**. Meanwhile, the government had altered the constitution to institute Buddhism as the state religion and allowed people the right to own, trade and inherit property. This was all very well, but the country was virtually bankrupt; practically no aid was being received, electricity and fuel were in short supply, and even basic needs such as health care couldn't be provided. Corruption, although not on the scale of earlier regimes, was still rife: the nouveaux riches built spacious villas, drove smart cars and ate out in restaurants, while the majority of Cambodians could barely afford rice. On the borders, a black economy thrived, with gems and timber flowing out, and consumer goods – which commanded a premium price on the home market – coming in.

Meanwhile, the Khmer Rouge was stepping up guerrilla activities, capturing Pailin in 1989. During 1990 they consolidated their position along the Thai border and regularly encroached further into Cambodia, destroying bridges, mining roads and raiding villages; by the end of that year they controlled the jungle areas to the northwest and southwest, going so far as to threaten Sihanoukville and Kampot. In the middle of that year, however, first the US, then China, changed their stance and **withdrew support** from the Khmer Rouge, which was to prove something of a turning point: a ceasefire was declared in

July 1991, and in October a conference was held in **Paris** to discuss the future of the country.

To the millennium

Thirteen years of war should have come to an end with the Paris conference, at which a number of agreements were reached. The central idea was to establish an interim coalition government for Cambodia, the **Supreme National Council**, to be made up of representatives of the three factions of the CGDK and the SOC, pending United Nations-supervised elections; to this end, factional groups would disarm and 300,000 refugees be repatriated from Thailand. But the Khmer Rouge had other ideas and, still supported by Thailand, continued to create insurgency around the country, unsettling an already shaky peace.

UNTAC

The United Nations Transitional Authority in Cambodia, **UNTAC**, was created to stabilize the country and supervise the promised elections, though its forces didn't arrive in Cambodia until March 1992, and even then they were deployed slowly, allowing the Khmer Rouge to expand the area under its control. Refusing to lay down arms or be monitored, the Khmer Rouge continued with disruptive attacks, mining roads and railways, intimidating villagers and murdering over one hundred ethnic Vietnamese over two years; they also refused to stand in the elections. The return of refugees proceeded relatively peacefully, at least.

Costing $2 billion, the UNTAC mission (numbering 22,000 military and civilian staff) was, at the time, the most expensive operation ever launched by the UN, though it's debatable just how successful it really was. The international forces (from around a dozen countries, including Indonesia, India, Ghana, Uruguay, Pakistan and Bangladesh) were ill-prepared for their role as peacekeepers – many were only trained for combat – and had little concept of what was required of them or what to expect of Cambodia. Often criticized for insensitivity, many of the UNTAC forces – unaccustomed to the high salaries they were being paid – led high-rolling lifestyles, paying well over the odds for even basic services. At the time, business boomed, only to collapse when UNTAC withdrew; a fledgling tourist industry started up (albeit limited by the guerrilla tactics of the Khmer Rouge); and prostitution mushroomed – UNTAC did not test staff for HIV and, rightly or wrongly, is widely blamed for the AIDS epidemic now affecting Cambodia. Today, Cambodians' feelings about UNTAC remain decidedly ambivalent. The naysayers argue that it failed to restore peace and indeed created more problems than it solved, and that the subsequent elections were far from fair. The alternative view, just as widespread, is that without UNTAC the country might well have fallen again to the extremism of the Khmer Rouge.

The return of constitutional monarchy

The elections of July 1993, although marred by intimidation and political killings, were a resounding success with the electorate, with a turnout of nearly ninety percent. However, even though the **FUNCINPEC** party – headed by

Sihanouk's son **Prince Ranariddh** – emerged with a majority, the interim government, led by Hun Sen, refused to cede the authority they had held since 1979. In the event, a government was formed which had two prime ministers, Prince Ranariddh and Hun Sen. A **constitutional monarchy** was reinstated, and Prince Sihanouk persuaded to resume the throne that he had abdicated in 1955, without being given any direct say in government.

Political infighting soon led to the government being dominated by the Cambodian People's Party (**CPP**) of Hun Sen, which had retained control of police, defence and provincial governments, and Prince Ranariddh became little more than a figurehead. The tensions between the two prime ministers grew until July 1997, when fighting broke out on the streets of Phnom Penh, resulting in many deaths, and Prince Ranariddh, who had just left the country, was ousted by Hun Sen. Foreseeing a bloody struggle, many foreign workers fled the country and investors hurriedly pulled out, leaving projects half completed, bills unpaid and thousands out of work; the Asian financial crisis of the time only exacerbated matters.

The **1998 elections** were the first to be self-administered post-Khmer Rouge. In addition to the CPP and FUNCINPEC, the elections were contested by **Sam Rainsy Party**, a breakaway association of ex-FUNCINPEC members (for all the proliferation of parties, there remains little real ideological difference between them, although FUNCINPEC is generally regarded as royalist, the CPP as "communist", and Sam Rainsy as "democratic"). Even though the run-up to the polls was tense, with widespread intimidation of candidates and voters, the election itself was peaceful; scrutineers pronounced it "not perfect", but sufficiently free and fair, in spite of allegations of ballot rigging. The CPP won the majority of the seats in the Assembly, but failed to achieve the required two-thirds of the vote to form a government, and a tense few months ensued until another coalition was formed, with Hun Sen as prime minister and Prince Ranariddh as speaker of parliament.

The end of the Khmer Rouge

Outlawed in 1994, the Khmer Rouge started to suffer **defections** to the government almost immediately. Nevertheless, they retained control of the north and northwest of the country, where their leaders remained in hiding, amassing immense wealth from the proceeds of illegal logging and gem-mining, primarily through trade across the border with Thailand. Their guerrillas continued to stage random attacks, kidnapping and murdering foreigners and Cambodians, while their presence prevented access to many parts of Cambodia and deterred tourists and investors alike.

The ultimate demise of the Khmer Rouge came a step closer in 1996, when after striking a deal of immunity from prosecution, **Ieng Sary**, erstwhile Brother Number Three, and two thousand of his troops defected to the government side, leaving a last rebel enclave, led by Ta Mok and Pol Pot, isolated in the north around Anlong Veng and Preah Vihear. An internal feud led to Pol Pot being tried by a court of his comrades in July 1997 for the apparent attempted murder of a cadre. Some nine months later he was dead, though it remains unclear if this was due to natural causes or whether he was murdered; whatever the truth, he was hastily cremated in Anlong Veng. Late in 1998, **Khieu Samphan**, who had been the public face of the Khmer Rouge and president of Democratic Kampuchea, and **Nuon Chea**, Brother Number Two, gave themselves up to the authorities. Anlong Veng was effectively returned to Cambodian jurisdiction the following year. **Ta Mok**, "The Butcher", was arrested attempting to cross to Thailand in March 1999, and finally, in May the same year, Kang Kek Leu, alias **Duch**, the notorious commandant of Toul Sleng torture prison, was tracked down and arrested.

The new millennium

Modern Cambodia faces many challenges, and progress is slow at best. In spite of being supported by hundreds of millions of dollars of aid per annum, the country's infrastructure is slow to improve, in no small part due to entrenched corruption. While some city-folk may have seen a modest improvement in their standard of living, for the majority of Cambodians, whose homes lack fresh water and electricity, there has been no change; health care remains inadequate and land mines and unexploded ordnance continue to be a problem. Aid donors, fed up with deep-rooted corruption, repeatedly try to get tough, but their warnings are consistently ignored and things carry on pretty much as before.

Essentially an agricultural nation, Cambodia has never had much of a manufacturing base, although investors tempted by a plentiful supply of cheap labour have set up garment and shoe factories in Phnom Penh, Sihanoukville and Bavet. It was thought Cambodia's prospects for trade would improve with its entry to **ASEAN** (the Association of Southeast Asian Nations) in 1999, but so far the benefits don't seem to cover the $5m annual membership fee.

The country's first-ever **local elections** were held in February 2002, against a background of political intimidation and the murder of several candidates, and the result was a landslide victory for the CPP. The fact that the polls were

The Khmer Rouge on trial

After considerable procrastination, in 2001, the government finally, if reluctantly, put in place the laws for a tribunal against the Khmer Rouge to go ahead. In 2003 a budget of $56.3 million for the UN-supported trials was finally agreed, and thanks to considerable donor aid, the "Extraordinary Chambers of the Courts of Cambodia for the Prosecution of Crimes Committed during the Period of Democratic Kampuchea" was instituted in late 2004. Judges – both Cambodian and international – are now being recruited and trained, and Khmer Rouge leaders are being rounded up. It is expected that the trials proper will commence in 2008.

Of the Khmer Rouge leaders arrested so far, **Ta Mok** (see p.322) died in 2006; in July 2007 born-again-Christian **Duch** was charged with crimes against humanity and his appeal for bail has since been refused. Now just 63 years old, he seems the most likely to serve a long prison sentence if convicted. Nuon Chea, **Brother Number Two**, was arrested in September 2007 and continues to protest his ignorance of Khmer Rouge atrocities; Pol Pot's brother-in-law, **Ieng Sary** – who lived in considerable comfort in Phnom Penh for the last ten years – was arrested in November 2007, along with his wife, **Ieng Thirith**, the minister of social affairs for Democratic Kampuchea; **Khieu Samphan**, the public face of the Khmer Rouge, was likewise arrested in late 2007 shortly after having been hospitalized for a suspected heart attack.

Whether the Cambodians want a tribunal, however, remains a matter of debate. For many it offers a chance to ask "Why?" and to effect closure on tragic events, and recently there were pro-tribunal marches on the streets of Phnom Penh. However, others, in spite of having lost family and friends to the Khmer Rouge, fear that the trials will just resurrect bad memories and leave even more questions unanswered.

held at all, however, was an achievement, as was the fact that fewer people died than during any previous election. **National elections**, held the following year, were acknowledged as having been the most successful to date. Although they were won, unsurprisingly, by the CPP, opposition parties were well represented, with Sam Rainsy Party (SRP) – the nearest the country has to a liberal party – and FUNCINPEC polling enough votes between them to stop the CPP forming a government. The resulting stalemate lasted the best part of a year, and it wasn't until June 2004 that Hun Sen and Prince Ranariddh agreed to form a coalition.

The new king

In October 2004, just days before his eighty-second birthday, Cambodia's long-reigning king, Norodom Sihanouk, surprised the country by abdicating, something he had threatened to do on many occasions previously. Writing to Prince Ranariddh (who had announced several years before that he did not want to be considered as an heir) from Beijing, the former king cited ill-health and advancing age as the reasons for stepping down, and left it to his son to break the news to the government and media. Royal succession is not hereditary in Cambodia: the constitution merely states that a new monarch must be over 30 years old, a member of the royal family and descended from one of three previous kings, but gives no clear method for making a choice, which was left to the hurriedly assembled Throne Council – comprising six members of the government and two Buddhist leaders. Selecting the sole surviving son (four others had died during the Khmer Rouge era) of Norodom Sihanouk and his wife, Monineath, **Norodom Sihamoni** (who had earlier been "suggested" by Sihanouk himself), seems to have been uncontroversial. A former ballet dancer, the 51-year-old Sihamoni has been a UNESCO ambassador and has lived mostly in France; he returned to Cambodia in mid-October 2004 just days ahead of the coronation, pledging to do all he could for the country.

In the three years since his coronation King Sihamoni has kept a low profile. That said, he has regular, and reportedly outspoken, meetings with the government, and though it's not reported often in the press, he pays regular visits to towns and villages around the country and seems to be held generally in kind regard. Meanwhile, the self-named King Father, Norodom Sihanouk, continues to be in ill-health, although this isn't bad enough to stop him writing regular bulletins on his website and issuing letters to the media when he disagrees with something.

Parties and politics

National elections are due again in July 2008, and the electorate now has four key political parties, along with a host of minor ones, to choose from. In 2006 FUNCINPEC replaced Norodom Ranariddh as its leader, soon after it accused him of "breach of trust" – for which he was sentenced to eighteen months in prison; he's now out of the country and risks jail if he returns, which leaves a bit of a problem for his recently formed political party – the Norodom Ranariddh Party (NRP), the formation of which effectively splits the royalist vote (FUNCINPEC are also royalist). While few are under any illusions over the outcome of the 2008 elections, which is unlikely to leave Hun Sen retiring to Sihanoukville just yet, on recent performance it may be that Sam Rainsy and his SRP may scoop up enough votes to have some say in the government.

Religion and beliefs

Buddhism influences practically every aspect of Cambodian life, as is evident from the daily gifts of food made to barefoot, saffron-robed monks, and the almost obsessive dedication to preparing for offering days and major festivals, when pagodas take on a carnival air. However, it was **Hinduism** which predominated among the Khmer from the first century until the decline of the Khmer Empire in the early fourteenth century; consequently, much temple art and architecture is influenced by the Hindu cosmology.

Islam is the most widespread of Cambodia's minority faiths, being practised by the Cham community. **Christianity**, introduced by various missionary groups, has failed to make much impact.

Buddhism in Cambodia is noticeably less dogmatic and formal than in Thailand or Burma, and the age-old traditions of paying respects to **spirits** and deceased **ancestors** survive, so woven into the fabric of Cambodian life that at times there is no clear line between them and local Buddhist practice.

Hinduism's historical role

Hinduism was introduced to the area by the Brahman priests who accompanied Indian traders to Funan around the first century, and was adopted by the majority of the pre-Angkorian and Angkorian kings. Even today, **Hindu influences** play an important cultural role in Cambodia: two Hindu epics, the *Ramayana* and (to a lesser extent) the *Mahabharata*, form the basis for classical dance and shadow-puppet performances and a subject for contemporary artists.

The Hindu creed is particularly diverse, encompassing a belief in **reincarnation**, the notion of **karma** (the idea that deeds in one life can influence a person's status in subsequent reincarnations), a colourful **cosmology** – including a vast pantheon of gods – and the building of temples. The three principal deities are **Brahma**, the creator and lord of all gods; **Vishnu**, the benevolent preserver who regulates fate and has ten avatars (incarnations); and **Shiva**, the destroyer, who is responsible for both death and rebirth. Shiva was especially worshipped in the form of a **linga**, a phallic-shaped stone pillar. Frequently these linga were carved in three sections, the square base representing Brahma, the octagonal middle corresponding to Vishnu, and the circular top symbolizing Shiva. Just as the linga were frequently a melding of the triad of gods, so the **Harihara**, a popular deity of the pre-Angkorian era, melded the characteristics of both Shiva (on the right-hand side of Harihara images) and Vishnu (on the left).

In the ninth century, Cambodian Hinduism was pervaded by the **devaraja cult** introduced by King Jayavarman II. The idea was that, on ascending the throne, the king created an image (consecrated to Shiva or Vishnu) which was installed in the main sanctuary of the king's state-temple. On his death the king was believed to become one with the god and to be able to protect his kingdom from beyond the grave.

Buddhism

Buddhism has its origins in India, developing out of Hinduism around the sixth century BC, when the teachings of prince-turned-ascetic, **Siddhartha Gautama**, became popular. Born to a royal family in Lumbini, in present-day Nepal, around 560 BC, Gautama was protected from the sufferings of the outside world and knew nothing other than the comfortable life of the court, where he married and fathered a son. When he reached the age of 29, however, curiosity caused him to venture out of the palace, where he variously encountered an old man, a sick person, a funeral procession and a monk begging for alms. Horrified by what he had seen, Gautama undertook to give up his life as a prince, leaving the palace and taking up the simple life to see if he could discover a way to end suffering. Having sought out different religious instructors to no avail, he eventually adopted a programme of self-denial, fasting almost to the point of death, until he finally understood that this austerity only perpetuated the suffering he was trying to resolve. On three successive nights, while meditating under a bodhi tree, he received revelations leading to his **enlightenment**: on the first night he saw his former lives pass before him; on the second night he understood the cycle of life, death and rebirth; on the third night the four holy truths of suffering were shown to him. Rather than passing straight to **nirvana** – a state free of suffering – as was his right as one who had attained Buddhahood, he remained on earth to spread the **dharma**, the doctrine of the **middle way**, encompassing the four noble truths (see below) and avoiding both the extremes of self-indulgence and self-denial. He preached his first sermon at Sarnath, near Varanasi in northern India; his converts were sent out to pass on the teachings; and for the rest of his life, the Buddha travelled India, teaching and begging for food.

Schools

Soon after the Buddha's death at the age of 80, his followers met to agree a consensus on his teachings, which were passed on by word of mouth. By the time another meeting of this type was called a hundred years later, variations had crept in (indeed Buddhist teachings weren't to be written down until around 100 BC), leading to a schism: two schools of Buddhism developed, Theravada and Mahasanghika, the latter giving rise to **Mahayana Buddhism**. Mahayana Buddhism propounds that some individuals who have attained enlightenment remain on earth in order to help others; known as **Bodhisattvas**, "beings of wisdom", they are worshipped in their own right as compassionate deities. An example is Lokesvara, whose image appears at Angkor in the four-faced gateways of the Bayon. Crucial to Mahayana Buddhism is the notion that nirvana is accessible to everyone, not confined to just a few ascetics.

In contrast, **Theravada Buddhism** does not encompass the notion of the Bodhisattva, and has it that enlightenment can only be attained by following a lengthy path of meditation, making nirvana practically unattainable even for monks, let alone lay people. Ancient Theravada Buddhist texts tell that seven Buddhas have already been to earth, the most important of whom was Gautama, with one left to come, though later texts say that nearly thirty Buddhas would appear. Among Buddhist countries, it is only in Burma, Cambodia, Laos, Sri Lanka and Thailand that Theravada Buddhism dominates.

Doctrine

The objective of Buddhist teachings is to release the individual from the cycle of birth, death and rebirth. Each life is affected by the actions of the previous life, and it is possible to be reborn at a higher or lower status depending on earlier actions. By right thoughts and deeds, individuals accrue **karma**, or merit, in this life towards the next world and the next reincarnation.

At the heart of Buddhist teachings are the **Four Noble Truths**, revealed to the Buddha under the bodhi tree. The first is that all of human life is suffering;. The second deems that suffering results from desire – the need for possessions, company, food, even for rebirth – or is born of ignorance – doing the right things, but in the wrong way. The third reveals that suffering can cease, and that once it is removed, the cycle of reincarnation is broken and the ultimate goal of nirvana nearly achieved.

The fourth truth is the path to the removal of suffering, namely the **Eightfold Path** (also called the Middle Way), comprising right knowledge – an understanding of the Four Noble Truths; right attitude (a quiet mind free from desire, envy and greed); right speech (truthful, thoughtful and wise words); right action (good moral conduct); right occupation (one's way of life must not harm others); right effort (good actions develop good thoughts and deeds); right mindfulness (carefully considered actions, speech and mental attitude); and right composure (concentration and focus). The Eightfold Path fosters morality, spirituality and insight without either austerity or indulgence; much store is set by meditation, putting away the ups and downs of everyday life to achieve a calm, level mind, relinquishing the desire for status and wealth and ultimately achieving peace.

Buddhism in Cambodia

In Cambodia, Mahayana Buddhism survived side by side with Hinduism from the days of Funan, both creeds having been brought by Indian traders, but was not widely adopted until the twelfth century when, under Jayavarman VII, it briefly replaced Hinduism as the state religion. With the passing of Jayavarman VII, Hinduism experienced a brief resurgence in the early thirteenth century, but thereafter it was Theravada Buddhism that gripped the population, though the reasons for the change are unclear. This decisive switch to Buddhism resulted in the cessation of temple construction, in whose stead **monasteries** were founded; the pagodas founded by King Ponhea Yat in Phnom Penh in the middle of the fifteenth century are the oldest surviving Buddhist places of worship in Cambodia today. Monasteries provided schooling, housed collections of texts and acted as guardians of the national religion, language and moral code; it also fell to them to provide other social services such as care for the elderly and sick.

In 1975, the Khmer Rouge banned all religion, destroying or desecrating pagodas, texts and statues, and persecuting Buddhist monks; fewer than 3000 out of an estimated 65,000 monks survived the regime. Buddhism was tolerated, if not encouraged, during the Vietnamese occupation, and reinstated as the national religion in 1989, when the reconstruction of pagodas commenced. Today, Buddhism is practised by some 95 percent of the country's population.

Wats

The typical rendering of **wat** into English as "pagoda" can be confusing, as a wat is essentially a monastery. Cambodians are under no pressure to go to the wat, but will pop in on offering days and as and when they feel the need; in fact they also visit as something of a leisure activity, even picnicking within the grounds.

The wat is enclosed by walls with entrances on each side; at its heart is the **vihara**, the main sanctuary, which contains the most important Buddha images. The walls of the vihara are generally painted with colourful scenes from the life of the Buddha, many of which will have been donated by rich Cambodians to earn merit for the next life; many are personalized to reflect the donor or the times. The vihara is used solely by the monks for their religious ceremonies, and is often kept locked. A separate hall is the main centre of the pagoda's activity; here meals and religious classes are taken and ceremonies for the laity performed. Scenes from the *Jataka*, a collection of tales of the previous lives of the Buddha, are frequently to be found painted on the walls; most commonly depicted are those tales dealing with the Buddhist perfections – generosity, virtue, renunciation, wisdom, energy, patience, truthfulness, resolution, kindness and even temper.

Also commonly found within pagodas are **crematoria**, reflecting the prevalence of cremation rather than burial, and **chedi** containing the ashes of the deceased. The small huts which are often dotted around the pagoda compound may be used as places for meditation, though more often they are quarters for nuns and for elderly folk.

At the **altar**, Buddhists pay their respects to (rather than worship) the Buddha: palms are placed together in front of the chin and either they are raised to the forehead while bowing slightly, or the forehead is touched to the floor; either action is carried three times. It's also usual to light three sticks of incense and place them in a holder near the altar or by the main door; if asking for divine assistance, lotus buds are placed in vases near the altar. It's customary for worshippers to leave a donation of around 1000 riel.

For information on suitable dress and other points of **etiquette** when visiting a temple, see p.52.

The Sangha

Monks play an important role in Cambodian life, and it's still commonplace for Cambodian men to enter the **Sangha**, or monkhood, for a period in their lives, often between the ages of 13 and 15 or upon the death of a parent. Their ordination can be for quite short periods, perhaps a couple of months. Novices are ordained in the rainy season, when their heads are shaved and they receive their saffron robes, comprising the *sampot ngout*, the undergarment; a *sbang*, covering the lower body; a *hang sac*, a garment with many pockets worn over one shoulder; and the *chipor*, a shawl that covers the upper body and is thrown across the shoulders (inside the pagoda, the right shoulder is left uncovered). Women are never ordained but can become lay nuns, undertaking various tasks around the pagoda, including looking after the senior monks and maintaining the altar; often this is a way for older women and widows with no family to be looked after in their twilight years.

Besides practising meditation and chanting, monks have to follow 227 precepts, and undertake daily study of Buddhist scriptures and philosophy. Life in the pagoda is governed by ten basic injunctions, including not eating after noon, abstaining from alcohol and sexual relations, not partaking of entertainment (television is thus not permitted), not wearing personal adornments or sleeping on a luxurious bed.

The most evident aspect of the monkhood in Cambodia is the daily need to go out into the community to ask for **alms**. Begging monks go barefoot, signifying the simplicity of their lives (the donor should also be barefoot when giving alms). Donations of money go to support the pagoda or to pay for transport, while food is collected in the monks' bowls or bags, to be shared among all the monks at the pagoda. In return, the donors receive a simple blessing from the monk, helping them to gain merit for the next life.

Though monks themselves are not allowed to marry, they are often asked to bless couples who are to be married, and they also officiate at funerals, presiding over the cremation of the body and storage of the ashes at the pagoda. Monks also play a major role in the private religious ceremonies which many Cambodians undertake, for reasons ranging from alleviation of bad luck to acquiring merit for the next life. These events can involve anything from a blessing at the pagoda, with elaborate offerings and chanting monks, to making a small offering of fruit or the purchase and release of a small bird from a cage.

Islam and Christianity

Islam arrived with the **Cham**, who fled to Cambodia from Vietnam around the beginning of the eighteenth century; today, the Cham (for more on whom see p.236) account for some three percent of the population. The most striking thing about Islam in Cambodia is the mixing of the precepts of the faith (the monotheistic worship of Allah, the requirement to pray five times a day and make the pilgrimage to Mecca, and so on) with elements of traditional animist worship – some Cambodian Muslims will use charms to ward off evil spirits or consult sorcerers for magical cures.

The Cham suffered badly at the hands of the Khmer Rouge; mosques were destroyed or desecrated, and forty thousand Muslims murdered in Kompong Cham alone. After the Khmer Rouge, the Cham were able to resume their religious practices, rebuilding their own mosques, each with its own *hakim* or leader, and imam, responsible for communal prayers; the number of followers now exceeds that pre-1975. The country's **main mosque**, built with Saudi money in 1994, is located on the bank of Boeung Kak in Phnom Penh and has room for five hundred worshippers.

In spite of the efforts of missionaries and a lengthy period under the Catholic influence of the French, **Christianity** is followed by less than one percent of the population. Phnom Penh once had a Catholic cathedral but it was razed to the ground by the Khmer Rouge and not a stone remains. Over a hundred Christian NGO and missionary groups operate freely in Cambodia today, providing valuable services in the fields of education (in particular English-language lessons), health care and rural development, though they still fail to attract many followers.

Animism, ancestor worship and superstitions

According to **animist** belief, all things in nature have an associated spirit; trees, rocks, streams and so forth may be deemed sacred for either their beauty or their supposed magical or medicinal properties. To keep these spirits happy, and to request good luck or give thanks, particularly before the rice harvest, offerings of incense, fruit, flowers and water are made at **spirit houses**, found all over Cambodia; trees and boulders, private houses and businesses sport anything from a simple wooden tray with a tin can for the burning of incense, to an elaborate, gaudily painted concrete affair resembling a doll's-house version of a pagoda.

Respect for the **ancestors** is important to most Cambodians. In **chunchiet** culture small wooden funerary figurines are placed on graves to protect the dead. **Buddhists** celebrate their ancestors in the three-day festival of **Bonn Pchum Ben**, in September or October, when offerings are taken to as many as seven pagodas and picnics are shared by the family around the chedi. The homes of ethnic **Chinese** often have two spirit houses, one dedicated to the house spirit, the other to the ancestors; incense should be burnt daily to assure good fortune.

Cambodians are highly **superstitious**, regularly consulting fortune-tellers, astrologists and psychics, and even making use of sacred **tattoos** for self-protection. Fortune-tellers are often found at the pagoda, where they give readings from numbered sticks drawn at random or a book of fortunes. Astrologers are key to arranging a marriage and are normally consulted early on to ensure that couples are compatible and to determine the best day for a wedding. The Cambodians also practise a form of *feng shui*, and practitioners are consulted particularly to assess land before purchase and advise on the removal of trees and construction of property.

Books

U
ntil recently the majority of books about Cambodia fell into two categories: dry, factual tomes about the temples of Angkor, and harrowing Khmer Rouge-era autobiographies. Coverage of culture and the rest of Cambodia's history was relatively sparse, and novels hardly existed. Now, however there's an ample choice of contemporary books, but it's still worth seeking out older titles if you are interested in its pre- Khmer Rouge history. Out-of-print titles or those with overseas publishers can most easily be tracked down over the Internet – ⓦwww.AbeBooks.com and ⓦwww.amazon .com are good starting places. Note that if you are buying books in Cambodia, apart from in reputable bookshops and hotels, most will be photocopies, albeit tidily bound and sometimes even in colour.

In the reviews below, if a book's **publisher** is the same worldwide, the publisher is simply stated after the title; otherwise the publishers in the UK and the US are given in that order, or indicated by "UK" or "US" if the book is published in only one of the two countries. For books published outside these two countries, we also give the city of publication. Titles marked ⚞ are particularly recommended.

Travel and general

Liz Anderson *Red Lights and Green Lizards* (Green Print reprint due 2008). Moving account of Cambodia in the early 1990s as seen through the eyes of a British doctor who volunteered to work in the riverside brothels of Phnom Penh, setting up the city's first-ever clinic for prostitutes.

Ghillie Basan *The Food and Cooking of Cambodia* (Southwater). Illustrated cookery book with more than sixty authentic Cambodian recipes. Although many of the dishes aren't what people eat at home, or even things you'll find on typical restaurant menus, it has a good selection of easy-to-follow recipes and plenty of mouth-watering photographs.

⚞ **François Bizot** *The Gate* (Vintage). Gripping first-person account of being kidnapped by the Khmer Rouge for three months in 1971 – the author's release was attributable to the rapport he built up with Duch, the man who would later be responsible for the notorious Toul Sleng torture prison.

Ian Brown *Cambodia: An Oxfam Country Profile* (Oxfam, UK). Slightly dated overview of the economic, social and environmental issues affecting aid work in Cambodia, illustrated with touching accounts of how the lives of individuals are blighted by poverty, ill health and disability.

⚞ **Robert Casey** *Four Faces of Siva* (Simon Publications). Eminently readable 1920s travelogue, in which the author weaves fact and fantasy into his personal discovery of Cambodia's hidden cities. Includes a compelling description of the author's foolhardy trek to explore the then remote Preah Khan in Kompong Thom province.

⚞ **Karen J Coates** *Cambodia Now: Life in the Wake of War* (McFarland & Company Inc, US). Smashing, recently published collection of insightful, anecdotal tales from the time the author spent in

Cambodia as a journalist on the *Cambodia Daily*. She sensitively portrays the lives of the ordinary people of Cambodia, probes the events that affect them and depicts how they survive in often harrowing circumstances.

Adam Fifield *A Blessing Over Ashes* (HarperCollins, US). The author's candid account of growing up in 1980s America with Soeuth, his adopted Cambodian brother, seen from both sides of the cultural gap. Especially touching is the visit to Cambodia, where Soeuth discovers that his Khmer family is still alive.

Amit Gilboa *Off the Rails in Phnom Penh* (Graham Brash (Pte) Ltd, Singapore). Self-styled, voyeuristic "guns, girls and ganja" foray into the seedy side of Phnom Penh in the mid-1990s.

Geoffrey Gorer *Bali and Angkor: A 1930s Pleasure Trip Looking at Life and Death* (o/p). The acidic, condescending comments on everything from transport to temples make it hard to see why Gorer bothered to visit Angkor at all, but his off-the-wall interpretations of the rationale behind Khmer art certainly make for an alternative view to the accepted texts.

Gillian Green *Traditional Textiles of Cambodia: Cultural Threads and Material Heritage* (River Books, Thailand). Full-colour study of Cambodian textiles; comprehensively researched and containing a wealth of information on how and why textiles are produced.

Christopher J. Koch *Highways to a War* (Vintage). This novel embraces the war in both Cambodia and Vietnam; the conflict is given a human touch through the experiences of its hero, an intrepid war photographer.

Bree Lafreniere *Music through the Dark* (University of Hawaii Press,

US). The true story of musician Daran Kravanh, who survived imprisonment by the Khmer Rouge because the cadre took a liking to his music, and often called him in to play his accordion after a day toiling in the fields.

Norman Lewis *A Dragon Apparent: Travels in Cambodia, Laos and Vietnam* (Eland Publishing). Though light on Cambodia content, what there is gives a fascinating, all-too-rare glimpse of the country around the time of independence; at its best in its observations of local people and everyday events.

Carol Livingstone *Gecko Tails* (Weidenfeld & Nicolson; o/p). A lighthearted account of the life of a would-be foreign correspondent during Cambodia's free-rolling UNTAC era; a bit of politics, some history and a lot of human interest wrapped up in a sensitively told yarn.

Jeff Long *The Reckoning* (Simon & Schuster). Novel with a supernatural bent: a missing-in-action team search the Cambodian countryside for lost comrades; while deep in the jungle a deserted temple gradually gives up the secrets of a disappeared GI patrol, but not without wreaking revenge on those who dare to venture inside its walls.

Chris Moon *One Step Beyond* (Pan Books). The author, himself a land-mine victim, is a noted campaigner for the mine-disabled in Asia and Africa, and here he tells his story with humour and without self-pity. More than half the book is concerned with his time in Cambodia, including the kidnap by the Khmer Rouge of himself and two Cambodian colleagues, while they were de-mining in the jungles.

Longteine De Monteiro and Katherine Neustadt *The Elephant Walk Cookbook: Cambodian Cuisine*

from the Nationally Acclaimed Restaurant (Houghton Mifflin, US). Many of the recipes in this vast cookbook were lost to Cambodians when the Khmer Rouge decimated the population. The author, owner of the *Elephant Walk* restaurant in Boston, fled Cambodia in the 1970s and has written them down here to preserve them. Also contains detailed instructions on where to source ingredients and how to prepare the dishes.

Henri Mouhot *Travels in Siam, Cambodia, Laos and Annam* (White Lotus Co). The first Cambodian travelogue, Mouhot's dairy, containing a fascinating account of the "discovery" of Angkor Wat in 1856, was responsible for sparking off Cambodia-fever in nineteenth-century Europe.

Haing S. Ngor and Roger Warner *Survival in the Killing Fields* (James Bennett Pty Ltd, US). Harrowing account by a doctor who survived torture by the Khmer Rouge, but was unable to help his wife, who died in childbirth. Fleeing to Thailand, the author eventually reached America, where he won an Oscar for his role in the film *The Killing Fields*.

Toni Samantha Phim and Ashley Thompson *Dance in Cambodia* (Oxford University Press). A great introduction to its subject, this compact guide crams in information on the history and styles of Cambodian dance, as well as a pictorial glossary of traditional musical instruments.

Geoff Ryman *The King's Last Song* (HarperCollins) Page-turner of a novel centred around the discovery of an ancient diary etched in gold. The story cleverly interweaves the intrigue of the twelfth-century Angkorian court with the lives of its present-day heroes, an ex-Khmer Rouge soldier and a young moto driver.

Lucretia Stewart *Tiger Balm: Travels in Laos, Vietnam and Cambodia* (Chatto & Windus; o/p). A sizeable chunk of this book is taken up with a visit to the poverty-stricken and oppressed Cambodia of 1989, when only the bravest of travellers ventured there; a good read, not so much for the historical details as for the characters the author meets along the way.

Jon Swain *River of Time* (Vintage). Part love affair with Indochina, part eyewitness account of the fall of Phnom Penh, written by a respected war correspondent.

Loung Ung *First They Killed My Father* (HarperCollins, US). The author pulls no punches in this heart-rending personal narrative of the destruction of her family under the Khmer Rouge regime.

History and politics

David Chandler *A History of Cambodia* (Westview, US). Now in its fourth edition, this is a readable, concise history of Cambodia from prehistoric times to the early 1990s by a pre-eminent author on Cambodia.

David Chandler *Voices from S-21* (University of California Press, US).

Using archive material from the interrogation and torture centre at Toul Sleng, this thought-provoking book attempts to figure out why the atrocities committed there were able to happen, especially as sometimes neither captive nor interrogator knew exactly what crime was supposed to have been committed.

Chou Ta-Kuan *The Customs of Cambodia* (Siam Book Society, Bangkok). The sole surviving record of thirteenth-century Cambodia, written by a visiting Chinese envoy, with graphic accounts of the customs of the time and ceremonies at court.

Charles Higham *The Civilization of Angkor* (Weidenfeld & Nicolson). Dry but extremely detailed account of Cambodia's history, from pre-history to the closing days of the Khmer Empire.

Roland Leveu *Cambodia: The Years of Turmoil* (Asia Horizons Books). Subtitled *Witness to War, Misery and Turmoil*, this *expensive* coffee-table record of the years 1973–99 contains a large amount of photographic material, the best of which was shot by the author in Phnom Penh as it fell to the Khmer Rouge.

John Martson and Elizabeth Guthrie *History, Buddhism and New Religious Movements in Cambodia* (University of Hawaii, US). A rare book in English on Cambodian religion, this collection of contemporary essays looks at how Cambodian religious beliefs are linked to individual and national identity and at their effect on social and gender issues.

Eva Mysliwiec *Punishing the Poor: The International Isolation of Kampuchea* (Oxfam; o/p). Chronicle of the isolation of Cambodia after the Vietnamese invasion and how the West turned its back on the country.

Vann Nath *A Cambodian Prison Portrait: One Year in the Khmer Rouge's S-21* (White Lotus, Bangkok). A first-person account of Toul Sleng by one of its few survivors, a trained artist; his paintings documenting the appalling practices once visited on inmates can now be seen in the Toul Sleng Genocide Museum.

William Shawcross *Sideshow: Kissinger, Nixon and the Destruction of Cambodia* (Simon & Schuster, US). The story of the horrendous clandestine bombing of Cambodia by the United States. Starting with a single mission to destroy a North Vietnamese command base believed to be located in Cambodia, the book traces the unfolding of the campaign and its subsequent cover-up – compulsive reading.

Tauch Chhuong *Battambang During the Time of the Lord Governor* (Cedoreck, Phnom Penh). Valuable insight into the culture and customs of Battambang under Thai rule.

Angkor

George Cœdes *Angkor, An Introduction* (o/p). This old faithful offers useful background to the temples in a slightly rambling vein.

Bruno Dagens *Angkor, Heart of an Asian Empire* (Thames & Hudson; o/p). The story of the rediscovery of Angkor Wat and the explorers who brought the magnificent temple to the attention of the Western world, illustrated with old photographs and detailed sketches.

Michael Freeman and Claude Jacques *Ancient Angkor* (River Book Guides). Superb photographically illustrated guide to the monuments of Angkor. Ideal for those who don't want to spent every moment at the temples gazing though their own camera lens or to tempt arm-chair traveller to venture there.

Maurice Glaize *The Monuments of the Angkor Group* (o/p). Classic guide to the temples, originally published in 1944, with detailed maps and photographs; read it online or download in full from ⓦwww.theangkorguide.com.

Claude Jacques *Angkor: Cultural Studies* (Konemann UK Ltd). Stimulating English translation of a coffee-table volume featuring fabulous photographs, plans and descriptions of the temples.

Eleanor Mannikka *Angkor Wat, Time, Space and Kingship* (University of Hawaii Press). This painstaking analysis attempts to establish relationships between solar and lunar alignments and the dimensions of Angkor Wat – hard going, though interesting if you like metaphysical theories.

Steve McCurry *Sanctuary: The Temples of Angkor* (Phaidon Press). Magical images of the temples from this renowned photographer; paperback edition available.

Henri Parmentier *Guide to Angkor* (EKLIP, Phnom Penh). Classic 1940s

pocket-sized temple guide by an acknowledged expert on Khmer architecture; still useful today.

Christopher Pym *The Ancient Civilization of Angkor* (o/p). Fascinating wander through the life and times of the ancient Khmer, exploring everything from how kingfishers were caught to the techniques used to move massive stone blocks for the building of temples.

🏃 **Dawn Rooney and Peter Danford** *Angkor: Cambodia's Wondrous Khmer Temples* (Odyssey). Easy-to-use guide, with good background information and plans for each of the principal temples; now in its fifth edition.

Vittorio Roveda *Sacred Angkor: The Carved Reliefs of Angkor Wat* (River Books Press). Perfect for temple buffs, this is a detailed study of the reliefs, offering alternative suggestions for their interpretation.

Biography

David Chandler *Brother No 1: A Political Biography of Pol Pot* (Westview Press, US). The original work on Pol Pot, this meticulously researched book reconstructs the life of this reclusive subject. The rather scant actual information about him is bolstered by juicy details about other Khmer Rouge leaders.

Nic Dunlop *The Lost Execu-tioner: A Story of the Khmer Rouge* (Bloomsbury Publishing). Discovered living in a remote area of Cambodia near the Thai border, Duch was the infamous commandant of the Khmer Rouge torture prison S-21. Details of his life are revealed in this easy-to-read book which ponders the rise of the Khmer Rouge, comparing

their philosophy to those of Stalin and the French Revolution.

Harish C. Mehta and Julie B. Mehta *Hun Sen, Strongman of Cambodia* (Graham Brash (Pte) Ltd, Singapore). Based on interviews with Hun Sen himself, as well as his family and colleagues, this provides a frank and accurate portrait of the man, though the authors have undoubt-edly chosen their words carefully.

Milton Osborne *Sihanouk, Prince of Light, Prince of Darkness* (University of Hawaii Press). No-nonsense behind-the-scenes look at the King-Father who, unable to accept the role of figurehead, abdicated to rule the country as an elected politician. The contradictory aspects of Sihanouk's nature are accurately picked out, and he comes across as an all-too-human character, likeable, though often petulant and egotistical.

Philip Short *Pol Pot: The History of a Nightmare* (John Murray).

Although rather lengthy, the author draws on such first-hand accounts as there are for this in-depth analysis of Pol Pot and the circumstances that allowed the Khmer Rouge to come to power.

Language

Language

Khmer

Belonging to the Austro-Asiatic family of languages, **Khmer** is the national language of Cambodia, and is also spoken in the Mekong Delta and pockets of northeast Thailand, as well as forming the basis of the language used at the Thai royal court. Many Khmer words have their origins in two old Indian languages – Sanskrit (which was introduced along with Hinduism during the Funan era) and Pali – while Malay, Chinese, Vietnamese, Thai, French and English have all added to the language's development.

Although an increasing number of people can speak some English in the major towns and tourist centres, learning even a few words of Khmer will go a long way to endearing you to Cambodians, and off the beaten track you'll find it especially helpful to know some basic Khmer phrases. Fortunately, Khmer is a relatively easy language to get to grips with, being **non-tonal** and relatively simple in its grammar. Sentences follow the subject–verb–object pattern of English, although adjectives are added after the noun as in French. Khmer verbs don't conjugate, and tenses are indicated by the addition before the verb of a word indicating the timeframe; *nung,* for instance, indicates an action taking place in the future. Articles – "a", "an" and "the" in English – and plurals aren't used in Khmer (quantity is indicated by stating the number or using general terms for "some" or "many").

If you are trying out your skills, the Cambodians will do their best to understand you and will patiently repeat words for you to copy. Understanding what is being said to you is another issue; **regional dialects** present a challenge, as many words are quite different from the formally correct words in Phnom Penh. Another problem is that Cambodians often abbreviate their sentences, missing out many words, chopping them short and changing words and phrases around.

Khmer **script** is an artistic mix of loops and swirls, comprising 33 **consonants** and 23 **vowels**; the vowels are written above and below the consonants and to either side. Capital forms of the letters exist, but are seldom used. In writing, words run left to right with no spaces in between; sentences end with a little symbol that looks a bit like the numeral "7", playing the role of a full stop or period.

A variety of self-study Khmer **courses** are available. Multilingual Books (ⓦ www.multilingualbooks.com) produces basic courses on CD-ROM and cassette aimed at travellers, and an intensive course for those wishing to delve deeper; both are good, if pricey. Also available is David Smyth's *Colloquial Cambodian* (Routledge), with an optional accompanying cassette. The best for those who want more than tourist Khmer is the Masterlanguage course comprising sixteen CDs and supporting book; developed for American foreign service personnel, it is comprehensive, if slightly dated (1996) and formal. In Phnom Penh, at Psar Thmei and Psar Toul Tom Poung, you can purchase the excellent *Seam & Blake's English–Khmer* pocket dictionary ($3–4), which lists words in Khmer script and in Roman transliteration. At the same outlets, you can also pick up the useful *United Nations English–Khmer Phrase Book*, though the phonetics leave something to be desired.

Pronunciation

Some sounds in Khmer have no English equivalent and require a little time and practice to master, the best way being to listen to and imitate native speakers. Cambodians use intonation for emphasis, but while you're learning Khmer it's best to keep your speech somewhat monotonous in order to avoid causing misunderstanding.

Transliteration of Khmer into the Roman alphabet is not straightforward, and differences in approach account for many of the variations on maps and restaurant menus. The rudiments of a system were developed during the French protectorate, though this is rarely employed nowadays.

Consonants

Most consonants in our transliteration scheme are pronounced as they would be in English, though note that consecutive consonants are to be pronounced individually. The following combinations should also be noted:

bp sharp sound, between the English "b" and "p".

dt sharp sound between the English "d" and "t".

gk guttural sound between the English "g" and "k".

ng as in sing; often found at the beginning of words.

ny as in canyon.

Vowels

a as in ago.
aa as in bar.

ai as in tie.
ao or **ou** as in cow.
ay as in pay.
e as in let.
ea as in ear.
ee as in see.
eu is similar to the French fleur.
i as in fin.
o as in long.
oa as in moan.
ohs as in pot (the hs is practically silent).
oo as in shoot.
OO as in look.
ow as in toe.
oy as in toy.
u as in fun.

Useful words and phrases

The polite **form of address** for men is "*loak*", for women "*loak srei*"; in a formal situation Cambodians will often introduce themselves with the appropriate one of these two terms, then give their full name with the family name first. Although you will be asked your name a lot as you travel around, Cambodians do not really use names in everyday situations, preferring to use a range of respectful forms of address. These terms can be either polite or familiar depending on the situation, and are used even when meeting someone for the first time. The choice of term depends not only on whether the person being spoken to is male or female, but also on whether they are older or younger than the speaker. An older person is often (both politely and familiarly) addressed as either *yeah* or *dah* (grandmother or grandfather), or *ming* or *boh* (auntie or uncle), depending on just how much older they are than the speaker. When speaking to someone younger, *kmoouy bprohs* or *kmoouy srei* (nephew or niece) can be used, or more familiarly, *bpohn bprohs* or *bpohn srei* (younger brother or sister). Take your lead from the Cambodians and listen to how they address you or other people.

Greetings and civilities

chum ree-eu-bp soo-a/soo-a s'day	hello (formal/informal)
swah-ghOOm	welcome
nee'ak sok sa bai gee-ar dtey?	how are you?
k'nyom sok sa bai	I'm well/fine
chum ree-eu-bp lear/lear haowee	goodbye (formal/informal)
chewubp kynear t'ngai keraowee	see you later
som	please
unchurn	if you please
or-kOOn	thank you
som dtohs	excuse me/sorry

Basic terms and phrases

baht/jahs	yes (spoken by a male/female)
dtay	no
tom	large or big
toight	little or small
mow/dhow	come/go
mee-un	to have (also used for "there is/are")
gayn	sleep
daea	take
nee'ak … ai?	what is your … ?
ch-moo-ah	name
jon-jee-ut	nationality
nee'ak mau bpe pro-teh nar?	where do you come from?
k'nyom mau bpe pro-teh …	I am from …
onglais	Britain
ear-lond	Ireland
amei-rik	US
kana-daa	Canada
orstra-lee	Australia
nyew seelend	New Zealand
nee'ak riep-ghar hauwee roo now?	are you married?
nee'ak mee-un gk'cone bpon maan nee'ak?	how many children do you have?
k'nyom ot towan mee-un	I don't have any children

k'nyom mee-un gk'cone moi/bpee	I have one child/two children
nee'ak s'nak now ai nar?	where are you staying?
nee'ak jehs nit-yaiy pia-sar onglai/ k'mair roo dtay?	can you speak English/ Cambodian?
k'nyom jehs tick-tick	I know (can speak) a little
k'nyom s'dabp men baan/k'nyom ot yull	I don't understand
a'yup bpon-maan chnam?	how old are you?
ot toe-un	not yet
k'nyom ot dung	I don't know
ot mee-un …	there aren't … /we don't have …
ohs haowee	none left/finished
ot baarn	it can't be done
ot banyaha	no problem
som jam bon tick	just a minute/please wait a minute

Getting around

dtow nar?	where are you going? (also used as a general greeting)
k'nyom dtow …	I am going to a/an/the …
k'nyom chong dtow …	I want to go to a/an/ the …
… now ai nar?	where is the … ?
jom nort yoo-un hohs/drang yoo-unhohs	airport
seta-nee laan kerong	bus station
seta-nee laan dtak-see	taxi stand
seta-nee roteh pleung	train station
gkumpong bpai	jetty
t'nee-a-geer	bank
sa-tarn-toot (tai/lao/vietnam)	(Thai/Lao/ Vietnamese) embassy
pteah sumnat	guesthouse
sontdakee-a/owhtel	hotel

psar	market
gonlaing dt'loi	money changer
sarat montee	museum
farmasee	pharmacy
bpohs bpoli	police station
bprey-sa-nee	post office
porjarnee-a tarn/restoran	restaurant
harng	shop
dtow dtrong	go straight
som choap tee neeh	please stop here
(bot) ch'wayng/ s'dam	(turn) left/right
dteu khang jeung	north
dteu khang kea-et	east
dteu khang tb'ohng	south
dteu khang leh'j	west
laan tom	bus
see-klo	cyclo
laan dubp-bpee gonlaing	minibus
motodubp/moto	motorbike taxi
laan nee-san/laan ch'noo-ul laan gk'bah	pick-up
dtak-see	taxi
karnowt lou-en	express boat
karnowt	slow boat
dtook	small boat
k'nyom trouw ting sambort now ai nar?	where do I buy a ticket?
dtow ... bpon maan?	how much to go to ... ?
dtow ... baan tday?	will you go for ... ?
... moi nee'ak	... per person
laan neeh mee-an dtow... dtay?	does this ... go to?
... neeh je-ny dtow maung bpon maan?	when does the ... depart?
doll ... o'h bpon maan maung?	how long does it take to get to ... ?
... che-ngai dtay?	is the ... far away?
(ot) che-ngai	it's (not) a long way
ch'noo-el teeyeng oughs ... nee'ak yor bpon maan?	how much to hire ... outright?

kgom to-tooel nee'ak dhum-now tee-et dtoh	don't pick up any other passengers
dumlai neeh baan dtay?	do you agree to the price?
gonlaing neeh dohs dtey roo dtay?	is this seat vacant?
dohs dtey	it's vacant
mee-un nee'ak	it's taken
laan neeh koit dtay?	what's wrong with the vehicle?
k'nyom som choap bot cheung	I need to stop to go to the toilet

Accommodation

nee'ak mee-un bontobp roo dtay?	do you have any rooms?
bontobp sum-rab moi nee-ak	single room
bontobp graiy bpee	room with two beds
mee-un ...	with ...
maa-sin dtro-chey-at	air conditioning
bontobp dtuek	bathroom
dong harl	fan
dtuek g'daow	hot water
bong-kgun	toilet
bong-ooit	window
moi yoobp bpon-maan?	how much is it per night?
som merl baan dtay?	can I see the room?
johs bon-tick baan dtay?	can you discount the price?
k'nyom som ... ?	can I have ... ?
bphooey	a blanket
moohng	a mosquito net
toora-saap	a telephone
souw bontobp leik	the room key
gro-dahs	toilet paper
gkon-saing	a towel
nee'ak s'nak now tee neeh bpon maan yoobp?	how many nights will you stay?
som sum-art bontobp neeh baan dtay?	can you clean the room?
k'nyom som doa bon-tobp?	can I move to another room?

bontobp neeh ...	this room is ...
mee-un moohs che-raan	full of mosquitos
telong payk	too noisy
mee-un bauk cao-aow?	do you have a laundry service?
mee-un kong/moto sum-rabp ch'ooel?	do you have a bicycle/ motorbike for rent?

Shopping and changing money

gay mee-un loo-uk ... now ai nar?	where do they sell ... ?
nee'ak mee-un ... ?	do you have ... ?
dtien	candles
baar-rai	cigarettes
cao-aow	clothes
t'nam	medicine
took dot	mosquito coils
soort	silk
saa-boo	soap
kgar-dow/ soo-ven-neer	souvenirs
t'nam doh t'meny	toothpaste
saa-bo bowk cao-aow	washing powder
neeh how awaiy?	what do you call this?
telai bpon maan?	how much does it cost?
telai nahs	very expensive!
dait bpon maan?	what is your best price?
johs bon tick baan dtay?	can you go down a bit?
k'nyom mee-un dtai riel/dol-lar	I only have riel/dollars
k'nyom chong dow loi	I want to change money

Emergencies and health matters

choo-ee	help!
jowl	thief
brum-dain/pa'hport rebohs k'nyom gai lou'it	my passport has been stolen
k'nyom bat lik-khet ch'long ...	I have lost my ...
gkar-borb/val-lee trauv bat	my pack/suitcase is missing
mee-un kroo-ah t'nak	there's been an accident
som june k'nyom dtow mon-tee pey-et	please take me to hospital
som hao laan pay-et	please call an ambulance
k'nyom men se-rooel kloo-un dtay	I am not well
k'nyom trauv ghar gkroo pay-et	I need a doctor
k'nyom mee-un ...	I have ...
gkrun	a fever
rey'ak	diarrhoea
choohs	pain
mee-un bong-khun now ai nar?	where is the toilet?
gon-laing neeh mee-un min dtay?	are there any land mines here?
k'nyom vung-veing plaow	I'm lost

Numbers

sohn	zero
moi	one
bpee	two
bpai	three
bpoun	four
bphrahm	five
bphrahm-moi	six
bphrahm-bpee/bpel	seven
bphrahm-bpai	eight
bphrahm-bpoun	nine
dhop	ten
dhop-moi, dhop-bpee	eleven, twelve, etc
m'pay	twenty
m'pay-moi, m'pay-bpee	twenty-one, twenty-two, etc
sam-sep	thirty
si-sep	forty
hahs-sep	fifty
hohk-sep	sixty
jet-sep	seventy
bpaet-sep	eighty
cow-sep	ninety
moi-roi, bpee-roi ...	one hundred, two hundred, etc

moi-roi moi	one hundred and one
moi-bpouhn, bpee-bpouhn …	one thousand, two thousand, etc
moi-meun	ten thousand
dhop-meun	one hundred thousand
moi-leuhn	one million
dte-moi, dte-bpee	first, second, etc

Times and dates

The time is generally expressed by stating the word for hour, then the hour itself, then the number of minutes past the hour and the word minute; thus 5.05 is rendered *maung bprahm, bprahm nee-ar tee*. Morning, afternoon or night are added to confirm the right time. In business the 24-hour clock is usually used, and months are referred to by number – thus October is *kai dhop*.

maung bpon maan?	what's the time?
maung	hour
nee-ar tee	minute
bpel p'ruk	morning
t'ngai terong	noon
bpel rohsiel	afternoon
bpel l'ngeit	evening
bpel yob	night
t'ngai	day
t'ngai neeh	today
t'ngai sa-ait	tomorrow
m'sell-mine	yesterday
t'ngai jarn	Monday
t'ngai ong-keeya	Tuesday
t'ngai bot	Wednesday
t'ngai brou-hohs	Thursday
t'ngai sok	Friday
t'ngai sou	Saturday
t'ngai ah-tet	Sunday
… mun/k'raowee /neeh	last/next/this …
ah tet	week
kai	month
chnam	year
ailouw neeh	now
bpel k'raowee	later
ot t'w-an	not yet
a-bany mainy	just now
hauwee	already

A food and drink glossary

As most Khmer dishes are ordered simply by stating what type of food you want to eat and how you'd like it prepared (thus stir-fried pork with ginger is *sait jerook cha khyay*), we've listed Khmer terms for various ingredients and standard cooking methods; a few specific dishes are also listed by name. To specify that a particular ingredient should *not* be added to your food, prefix the item in question with *ot dak* (without) – thus if you don't want sugar in your drink, say *ot dak skar*.

Cooking methods and general terms

… cha	stir-fried …
… cha knyay	stir-fried … with ginger
… jew aim	sweet-and-sour …
… ang	grilled …
… dot	roasted …
ma-horb	food (prepared)
n00m-bpang	bread
pong mowan (hen's)/pong dteer (duck's)	egg
be jaing/msow sobp	monosodium glutamate (MSG)
m'rik	pepper
um-beul	salt
skar	sugar
bong ai'm	dessert
k'nyom poo ahs	I'm vegetarian
k'nyom nyam bai t'ngai neih l'ngeit	I'd like to eat in the evening (to order meals in advance where restaurants would normally be shut by late afternoon)

ot bpah'aim	not sweet (useful when ordering drinks)

Meat, poultry and fish

sait gow	beef
sait mowan	chicken
g'dam	crab
sait dteer	duck
trei	fish
kongaib	frog
ot yoh kroeng knong	offal, intestine or gizzard
sait jerook	pork
trei muk	squid

Vegetables (bon lai)

sun dike	beans
sun dike bon dohs	bean sprouts
spei	cabbage
mteahs plouwk	capsicum
karot	carrot
pgar katnar	cauliflower
mteahs	chilli
draw sok	cucumber
tro-ab	aubergine/eggplant
k'tum	garlic
gee	herbs
sal-lat	lettuce
trokooen	morning glory
pset	mushroom
k'tum barang	onion
sundike day	peanuts
dumlong barang	potato
bpowrt sngaow	sweet corn
bpenh pohs	tomato

Soups (sumlar/sop), stews (kor) and curries (ka-ree)

amok trei	mild fish curry cooked in banana leaves
kaar	stew made with pig's trotters
sop chhnang day	fondue-like dish, cooked in a clay pot at the table
sumlar mjew gruoeng	slightly spicy soup made with beef, deer or chicken, along

	with lemon grass, turmeric and galangal
sumlar mjew vietnam	Vietnamese sour soup, usually based on fish (it can be made with chicken), complemented by pineapple, tomato and lotus flower stems, sometimes with added egg
sumlar ngam ngouw	lemon chicken soup
sumlar sngaow jerooet	clear chicken or fish soup
sumlar troyoung jayk sait mowan	chicken with banana-flower soup (variations use fish or duck in place of chicken)

Noodles (mee) and rice (bai) dishes

bai sait mowan/ sait jeruk	rice topped with fried chicken/pork
borbor	rice porridge
borbor sawr	unseasoned rice porridge
geautieuv	rice noodles
geautieuv sop (sait ...)	rice noodle in soup (with ... meat)
loat chat	fried macaroni-like noodle
mee ganychop	instant noodles made up from a packet
mee kilo	yellow noodles
nom bany jowk	flat white noodle served cold with a curry sauce

Some common meat and vegetable dishes

cha bon lai cropmok	fried mixed vegetables
cha katnar chia moi pset	fried pak choy with mushrooms
chhnang phnom pleung	thin slices of beef barbecued at the table over a charcoal burner
dumlong barang gee-yan	French fries

jay yior	spring rolls
mowan dort	baked chicken

Fruit (pelai cher)

pelai bporm	apples
pelai burr	avocado
jayk	banana
tee-ab swut	custard apple
pelai sroegar ne-yak	dragon fruit
tooren	durian
dum pay-yang bai jew	grape
troubike	guava
kroit chhmar	lime
meeyan	longan
koulen	lychee
svai	mango
morkgoot	mangosteen
kroit pursat	orange
lehong	papaya
pelai seyree	pear
manoahs	pineapple
kroit telong	pomelo
sow maow	rambutan
le-mot	sapodilla
tee-ab barang	soursop
umpbel	tamarind
ohluck	watermelon

Snacks (jum neigh arehar) and cakes (noam)

banh chhaev	savoury pancake stuffed with bean sprouts, pork and shrimp
bok lehong/som tam	papaya salad
chook	lotus seed
grolan	sticky rice in bamboo
jayk ang	grilled bananas
jeruik	pickles
nam bpaow	dumplings
noam downg dot	coconut cake
noam eclair	éclair

noam ensaum jayk	sticky rice cakes with banana
noam gachiey	chive burger
noam gdam	croissant (literally, crab cake)
noam pang patey	sandwich made with pâté
noam pong teeya/ noam barang	cup cake
noam srooey	cookie
pong dteer braiy	"thousand-year egg", a duck's egg preserved in salt
pong dteer gowne	duck's egg containing unhatched duckling
prohok	fermented fish paste
sait kreyuam	dried meat slices

Drinks (pay-sejeyat)

tuk kork	ice
dtai	tea
dtai tuk kork kroit chhmar	iced tea with lemon
dtai gdouw kroit chhmar	hot lemon tea
dtai grolab	strong local tea
ka-fei	coffee
kafei kmaow (tuk kork)	black (iced) coffee
kafei tuk duh gow (tuk kork)	white (iced) coffee
tuk duh	milk
tuk sun dike	soya milk
siro	syrup
tuk umpow	sugar-cane juice
tuk dhowng	juice of green coconut
coca	Coca-Cola
sraa bier	beer
tuk tnaowt jew	sugar-palm beer
tuk krolok	fruit shake
tuk krolok dak kropmok	mixed fruit shake
dorbp	bottle
kumpong	can

Glossary

Abacus Upper, flat part of the capital of a column.

Achar Learned lay-person at a pagoda.

APSARA Authority for the Protection and Management of Angkor and the Region of Siem Reap.

Apsara Celestial dancer of Hindu mythology, born of the Churning of the Ocean of Milk.

ASEAN Association of Southeast Asian Nations.

Asura Demon (from Hindu mythology).

Avatar Incarnation of a Hindu deity.

Banteay Citadel or fortified enclosure.

Barang Slang term meaning French, and often applied to foreigners in general.

Baray Reservoir.

Bodhisattva One who has attained enlightenment but forgoes nirvana to remain on earth and help others.

Brahma Hindu god, often referred to as the Creator.

Brahman Hindu priest.

Buddha One who has achieved enlightenment.

Chedi Structure in which cremated ashes are interred; also called a stupa.

Chunchiet Generic term for the minority hill-tribe groups.

CITES Convention on International Trade in Endangered Species of Wild Fauna and Flora.

CPP Cambodian People's Party.

Cyclo Three-wheeled bicycle rickshaw.

Deva God.

Devaraja Literally "god who would be king"; the Khmer king, according to the devaraja cult, would fuse with a deity upon his death.

FUNCINPEC Front Uni National pour un Cambodge Indépendant, Neutre, Pacifique et Coopératif – the royalist political party.

Garuda Mythical creature associated with Vishnu, having the body of a man with the head and feet of a bird.

Gopura Entry pavilion, gatehouse to the sacred area of a temple.

Harihara God created from the union of Shiva and Vishnu.

Heng Cambodian mythical bird.

Hol Method of weaving and a pattern of silk fabric.

Indochina Cambodia, Laos and Vietnam.

Jataka Tales recounting the past lives of the Buddha.

Kala Mythical creature with bulbous eyes, claws and no lower jaw.

Khapa Chunchiet basket with shoulder straps, worn on the back.

Khmer The principal indigenous people of Cambodia – the term is often used interchangeably with Cambodian – and also the name of their language.

Koh Island.

Kompong Village on a river or lake.

Kramar Cambodian checked scarf.

Krishna The eighth incarnation of Vishnu.

Lakshmi Wife of Vishnu, and the goddess of good fortune and beauty.

Laterite Soft, porous rock that hardens in the sun to a hard, resilient stone.

Leahng Cave.

Linga Phallic-shaped stone representing Shiva.

Lokesvara One of the Bodhisattvas, often called "the compassionate".

Mahabharata Hindu epic dealing with the rivalry between the Kaurava and Pandava families.

Makara Mythical sea monster with the body of a crocodile and the trunk of an elephant.

Mount Meru Mountain home of the gods, at the centre of the universe in Hindu cosmology.

Mudra Traditional Buddhist poses, widely depicted in Buddhist art, and also in Cambodian classical dancing.

Naga Sacred multi-headed snake, seen as a protector and often depicted along staircases or across causeways.

Nandin Sacred bull, and mount of Shiva.

NGO Non-governmental organization engaged in relief or campaigning work.

Nirvana A state in which desire ends and the cycle of birth, death and rebirth is broken.

NRP Norodom Ranariddh Party.

Pagoda Cambodian wat.

Pediment Section above the lintel of a doorway.

Phnom Mountain or hill.

Phum Village.

Pilaster Shallow rectangular column attached to a wall.

Prasat Sanctuary tower.

Preah A title of spiritual respect, used for gods and holy men; also means "sacred".

Psar Market.

Quincunx Arrangement of five objects with one at the centre and the others at each corner of a rectangle – like the five dots on the face of a dice. Used to describe the placing of sanctuary towers in Cambodian architecture.

Rahu Demon with a monster's head and no body, usually depicted swallowing the sun and moon.

Rama Seventh avatar of Vishnu, hero of the *Ramayana*.

Ramayana Hindu epic tale describing the battle between Rama (an incarnation of Vishnu) and the demon Ravana.

Reamker Cambodian version of the *Ramayana*.

Sampot Wraparound skirt; by extension, a length of fabric sufficient to make a skirt.

Shiva One of the three principal Hindu gods, often referred to as the Destroyer.

Sita Wife of Rama, who was kidnapped in the *Ramayana*.

Spean Bridge.

SRP Sam Rainsy Party.

State-temple Principal temple built to house the god with whom the devaraja king was associated; a temple-mountain.

Stele Upright stone block inscribed with writing.

Stucco A type of plaster made with lime, and used for decoration, particularly of brick buildings.

Stung Medium-sized river, smaller than a *tonle*.

Stupa See *chedi*.

Temple In the context of Cambodia, an ancient building or collection of buildings, built by kings to honour ancestors, or to house the devaraja god.

Temple-mountain Temple constructed as a representation of Mount Meru.

Tonle Major river.

Toul Low mound.

Tuk-tuk Motorbike-drawn passenger carriage.

Tympanum Recessed section of a pediment, bound by the cornices.

UNESCO United Nations Educational, Scientific and Cultural Organization.

UNTAC United Nations Transitional Authority for Cambodia.

UXO Unexploded ordnance.

Vihara Main sanctuary of a wat.

Vishnu One of three principal Hindu gods, the Preserver.

Wat Buddhist monastery and associated religious buildings; often translated into English as "pagoda".

Yaksha Male spirit, depicted with bulging eyes, fangs and a leer; serves as a temple guardian.

Yama God of the Underworld.

Yeak Giant.

Travel store

www.roughguides.com

Information on over 25,000 destinations around the world

- **Read** Rough Guides' trusted travel info
- **Access** exclusive articles from Rough Guides authors
- **Update** yourself on new books, maps, CDs and other products
- **Enter** our competitions and win travel prizes
- **Share** ideas, journals, photos & travel advice with other users
- **Earn** points every time you contribute to the Rough Guide community and get rewards

ROUGH GUIDES Complete Listing

UK & Ireland
Britain
Devon & Cornwall
Dublin **D**
Edinburgh **D**
England
Ireland
The Lake District
London
London **D**
London Mini Guide
Scotland
Scottish Highlands & Islands
Wales

Europe
Algarve **D**
Amsterdam
Amsterdam **D**
Andalucía
Athens **D**
Austria
Baltic States
Barcelona
Barcelona **D**
Belgium & Luxembourg
Berlin
Brittany & Normandy
Bruges **D**
Brussels
Budapest
Bulgaria
Copenhagen
Corfu
Corsica
Costa Brava **D**
Crete
Croatia
Cyprus
Czech & Slovak Republics
Denmark
Dodecanese & East Aegean Islands
Dordogne & The Lot
Europe
Florence & Siena
Florence **D**
France
Germany
Gran Canaria **D**
Greece
Greek Islands
Hungary
Ibiza & Formentera **D**
Iceland
Ionian Islands
Italy
The Italian Lakes
Languedoc & Roussillon
Lanzarote & Fuerteventura **D**
Lisbon **D**
The Loire Valley
Madeira **D**
Madrid **D**
Mallorca **D**
Mallorca & Menorca
Malta & Gozo **D**
Menorca
Moscow
The Netherlands
Norway
Paris
Paris **D**
Paris Mini Guide
Poland
Portugal
Prague
Prague **D**
Provence & the Côte D'Azur
Pyrenees
Romania
Rome
Rome **D**
Sardinia
Scandinavia
Sicily
Slovenia
Spain
St Petersburg
Sweden
Switzerland
Tenerife & La Gomera **D**
Turkey
Tuscany & Umbria
Venice & The Veneto
Venice **D**
Vienna

Asia
Bali & Lombok
Bangkok
Beijing
Cambodia
China
Goa
Hong Kong & Macau
Hong Kong & Macau **D**
India
Indonesia
Japan
Kerala
Laos
Malaysia, Singapore & Brunei
Nepal
The Philippines
Rajasthan, Dehli & Agra
Singapore
Singapore **D**
South India
Southeast Asia
Sri Lanka
Taiwan
Thailand
Thailand's Beaches & Islands
Tokyo
Vietnam

Australasia
Australia
Melbourne
New Zealand
Sydney

North America
Alaska
Baja California
Boston
California
Canada
Chicago
Colorado
Florida
The Grand Canyon
Hawaii
Honolulu **D**
Las Vegas **D**
Los Angeles
Maui **D**
Miami & South Florida
Montréal
New England
New Orleans **D**
New York City
New York City **D**
New York City Mini Guide
Orlando & Walt Disney World® **D**
Pacific Northwest
San Francisco
San Francisco **D**
Seattle
Southwest USA
Toronto
USA
Vancouver
Washington DC
Washington DC **D**
Yellowstone & The Grand Tetons
Yosemite

Caribbean & Latin America
Antigua & Barbuda **D**
Argentina
Bahamas
Barbados **D**
Belize
Bolivia
Brazil
Cancùn & Cozumel **D**
Caribbean
Central America
Chile
Costa Rica
Cuba
Dominican Republic
Dominican Republic **D**
Ecuador
Guatemala
Jamaica
Mexico
Peru
St Lucia **D**
South America
Trinidad & Tobago
Yúcatan

Africa & Middle East
Cape Town & the Garden Route
Dubai **D**
Egypt
Gambia
Jordan

D: Rough Guide **DIRECTIONS** for short breaks

Available from all good bookstores

NOTES

NOTES

Small print and

Index

A Rough Guide to Rough Guides

Published in 1982, the first Rough Guide – to Greece – was a student scheme that became a publishing phenomenon. Mark Ellingham, a recent graduate in English from Bristol University, had been travelling in Greece the previous summer and couldn't find the right guidebook. With a small group of friends he wrote his own guide, combining a highly contemporary, journalistic style with a thoroughly practical approach to travellers' needs.

The immediate success of the book spawned a series that rapidly covered dozens of destinations. And, in addition to impecunious backpackers, Rough Guides soon acquired a much broader and older readership that relished the guides' wit and inquisitiveness as much as their enthusiastic, critical approach and value-for-money ethos.

These days, Rough Guides include recommendations from shoestring to luxury and cover more than 200 destinations around the globe, including almost every country in the Americas and Europe, more than half of Africa and most of Asia and Australasia. Our ever-growing team of authors and photographers is spread all over the world, particularly in Europe, the USA and Australia.

In the early 1990s, Rough Guides branched out of travel, with the publication of Rough Guides to World Music, Classical Music and the Internet. All three have become benchmark titles in their fields, spearheading the publication of a wide range of books under the Rough Guide name.

Including the travel series, Rough Guides now number more than 350 titles, covering: phrasebooks, waterproof maps, music guides from Opera to Heavy Metal, reference works as diverse as Conspiracy Theories and Shakespeare, and popular culture books from iPods to Poker. Rough Guides also produce a series of more than 120 World Music CDs in partnership with World Music Network.

Visit www.roughguides.com to see our latest publications.

Rough Guide travel images are available for commercial licensing at www.roughguidespictures.com

Rough Guide credits

Text editor: Ros Belford
Layout: Nikhil Agarwal
Cartography: Jasbir Sandhu
Picture editor: Nicole Newman
Production: Rebecca Short
Proofreader: Jennifer Speake
Cover design: Chloë Roberts
Photographer: Tim Draper
Editorial: **London** Ruth Blackmore, Alison Murchie, Karoline Thomas, Andy Turner, Keith Drew, Edward Aves, Alice Park, Lucy White, Jo Kirby, James Smart, Natasha Foges, Róisín Cameron, Emma Traynor, Emma Gibbs, James Rice, Kathryn Lane, Christina Valhouli, Monica Woods, Mani Ramaswamy, Joe Staines, Peter Buckley, Matthew Milton, Tracy Hopkins, Ruth Tidball; **New York** Andrew Rosenberg, Steven Horak, AnneLise Sorensen, April Isaacs, Ella Steim, Anna Owens, Sean Mahoney, Paula Neudorf, Courtney Miller; **Delhi** Madhavi Singh, Karen D'Souza
Design & Pictures: **London** Scott Stickland, Dan May, Diana Jarvis, Mark Thomas, Sarah Cummins, Emily Taylor; **Delhi** Umesh Aggarwal, Ajay Verma,

Jessica Subramanian, Ankur Guha, Pradeep Thapliyal, Sachin Tanwar, Anita Singh
Production: Vicky Baldwin
Cartography: **London** Maxine Repath, Ed Wright, Katie Lloyd-Jones; **Delhi** Jai Prakash Mishra, Rajesh Chhibber, Ashutosh Bharti, Rajesh Mishra, Animesh Pathak, Karobi Gogoi, Amod Singh, Alakananda Bhattacharya, Swati Handoo
Online: Narender Kumar, Rakesh Kumar, Amit Verma, Rahul Kumar, Ganesh Sharma, Debojit Borah, Saurabh Sati, Ravi Yadav
Marketing & Publicity: **London** Liz Statham, Niki Hanmer, Louise Maher, Jess Carter, Vanessa Godden, Vivienne Watton, Anna Paynton, Rachel Sprackett, Libby Jellie, Jayne McPherson, Holly Dudley; **New York** Geoff Colquitt, Katy Ball; **Delhi** Ragini Govind
Manager India: Punita Singh
Reference Director: Andrew Lockett
Operations Manager: Helen Phillips
PA to Publishing Director: Nicola Henderson
Publishing Director: Martin Dunford
Commercial Manager: Gino Magnotta
Managing Director: John Duhigg

Publishing information

This third edition published August 2008 by
Rough Guides Ltd,
80 Strand, London WC2R 0RL
345 Hudson St, 4th Floor,
New York, NY 10014, USA
14 Local Shopping Centre, Panchsheel Park,
New Delhi 110017, India
Distributed by the Penguin Group
Penguin Books Ltd,
80 Strand, London WC2R 0RL
Penguin Group (USA)
375 Hudson Street, NY 10014, USA
Penguin Group (Australia)
250 Camberwell Road, Camberwell,
Victoria 3124, Australia
Penguin Books Canada Ltd,
10 Alcorn Avenue, Toronto, Ontario,
Canada M4V 1E4
Penguin Group (NZ)
67 Apollo Drive, Mairangi Bay, Auckland 1310,
New Zealand

Cover concept by Peter Dyer.

Typeset in Bembo and Helvetica to an original design by Henry Iles.

Printed and bound in China

© Rough Guides, 2008

368pp includes index

A catalogue record for this book is available from the British Library

ISBN: 978-1-85828-677-8

The publishers and authors have done their best to ensure the accuracy and currency of all the information in **The Rough Guide to Cambodia**, however, they can accept no responsibility for any loss, injury, or inconvenience sustained by any traveller as a result of information or advice contained in the guide.

1   3   5   7   9   8   6   4   2

Help us update

We've gone to a lot of effort to ensure that the third edition of **The Rough Guide to Cambodia** is accurate and up to date. However, things change – places get "discovered", opening hours are notoriously fickle, restaurants and rooms raise prices or lower standards. If you feel we've got it wrong or left something out, we'd like to know, and if you can remember the address, the price, the hours, the phone number, so much the better.

Please send your comments with the subject line "**Rough Guide Cambodia Update**" to ✉ mail@roughguides.com. We'll credit all contributions and send a copy of the next edition (or any other Rough Guide if you prefer) for the very best emails.

Have your questions answered and tell others about your trip at
🌐 community.roughguides.com

SMALL PRINT

Acknowledgements

Steven Martin A warm thank you to Benjamin Sirirat for all his support, as well as to John and Narisa Murray for their hospitality in Siem Reap. Also, a special thanks to Ros Serey Sothea and all those involved in the making of the soundtrack for the film *City of Ghosts*. The inspiration these tracks gave me throughout this project cannot be overstated.

Beverley Palmer Thanks to my dear friends, Paula Brinkley for her patient translating and insight into Cambodian culture, Ray Warner for answering all my emailed queries and Mr Leng in Banlung for his ongoing friendship; Andy Brouwer for his superb web pages; to the moto drivers who got me safely around the country, and especially to Kim Sea in Sihanoukville and Kheang in Kampot for their diligence when researching more obscure places; to the people of Cambodia for their friendliness and enduring cheerfulness; Ros Belford, my editor, for her cheerful inspiration.

Readers' letters

Thanks to all the readers who have taken the time to write in with comments and suggestions (and apologies if we've inadvertently omitted or misspelt anyone's name):

SMALL PRINT

Birte Autzen, Jeremy Baldock, Judith Barrow, Paul Beach, Bernd Bieder, Klaus Bormuth, Nick Butler, Jeannette Croft, John and Gill Farrington, Gerhard Faul, Friedhelm Fischer, Sophy Fisher, Mark French, Felix Frenzel, Kevin Friel, Dave Gartside, Jesse Goodman, Chris Goward, David Granger, Joan Gregoire, Bernd Greiner, Richard Grindle, Simon Hardy, Sylvia Heimes, Stephanie Hennig, J.O. Hoffmann, Ethan Holtzman, Tobias Jackson, Sarah Jhirad, Jennifer Jordan, Lars Kroon, Julien Lake, Earnpin Lee, Frank Leinz, Monica Mackaness, Bill and Sandra Martin, Andreas Massow, Annie McCann, Ombretta Melli, Silke Menne and Jochen Wild, Josie Mercer, Olaf Meyer, Ian Morgan, Natalie Neumann, Stefan Nöst, Ian Parson, Ann and Darren Petersen, Timothy Pike, Helen Quaggin, Kathrin Reinhardt, Sarah Riches, Allan Rickmann, Elke and Klaus Rieger, Christine Ross, Eng Saloth, Dietmar Sauermann, Joerg Scherrer and Mirjam Bekavac, Marc Schneider, Ann and Tony Stockle, Nick Trautmann, Peter Tudor and Paul Meadows, Filip Vandamme, Emma van Hoof, Trudy Walpole, Thomas Wiser, Martin York.

Photo credits

All photos © Rough Guides except the following:

Introduction
Underwater Carvings at Kbal Spean © Mike
  Kemp/Corbis

Things not to miss
08 An Irrawaddy dolphin © Ho New/Reuters
11 Phnom Penh Wat Phnom © Henry Westheim
  Photography/Alamy

Colour section: Festivals and ceremonies
Khmer Buddhist ritual offerings, Phnom Penh
  © Christophe Boisvieux/Corbis
Khmer New Year celebration © Tang Chhin
  Sothy/AFP/Getty Images
Offering © Robert Harding Library/Alamy
Ancient royal ploughing ceremony in Phnom Penh
  © Reuters/Corbis
Ankgor Wat Nun © Nicole Newman

Colour section: Temple architecture
Angelina Jolie in the role of Lara Croft in the film
  Tomb Raider © Corbis Sygma
Angkor Wat © Nicole Newman
Western Gallery at Angkor Wat depicts a royal
  procession from the Ramayana © Craig
  Lovell/Corbis
Angkor Wat and surrounding moat
  © Luca Tettoni/Corbis
Traditional costumes of Cambodian culture
  © Serdar Yagci/iStock

Black and whites
p.124 Killing fields © Andrew McConnell/Alamy

SMALL PRINT

Index

Map entries are in colour.

Map symbols

maps are listed in the full index using coloured text

-------	International boundary	◉	Accommodation
—— ···	Provincial boundary	■	Restaurant/bar
— — —	Chapter division boundary	@	Internet access
———	Road	∴	Ruins
======	Unpaved road	⊠	Gate/gopura
- - - - -	Path	⊙	Statue
—■—	Railway	🏛	Monument
— — —	Ferry route	ⓘ	Information office
———	Waterway	ℂ	Telephone
⊢⊣	Bridge	⊞	Hospital
▲	Peak	⊠	Post office
⌃⌃	Mountains	🛕	Pagoda
◠	Cave	⛩	Khmer temple
⋀⋁	Spring	🏯	Chinese pagoda
🍃	Waterfall	▨	Building
✈	International airport	⊞	Church
✗	Domestic airport	▢	Market
★	Transport stop	▦	Park
♦	Point of interest	▦	Beach
♁	Border crossing	⩙	Swamp/seasonally flooded area